KJ3

Literal
Translation
New Testament

D1602952

KJ3

Literal
Translation
New Testament

**An English
Word For Word
Translation
From The
Greek Textus Receptus Text
(Received Text)**

Translated By
Jay P. Green, Sr.,
(Translator of the Interlinear Hebrew-Greek-English Bible)

**AUTHORS FOR CHRIST, INC.
P.O. BOX 4998
LAFAYETTE, IN 47903
(765) 429-4122**

The KJ3 LITERAL TRANSLATION NEW TESTAMENT
Copyright © 2006
by Jay P. Green, Sr.
Lafayette, Indiana 47903, U. S. A.

I.S.B.N.: 1-58960-472-5 - Paperback Edition
I.S.B.N: 1-58960-475-X - Hardback Edition

Published by Authors For Christ, Inc.
P.O. Box 4998
Lafayette, Indiana 47903
United States of America

Printed in the United States of America

THE BOOKS OF
The New Testament

PREFACE

This is a special Edition of the newest English version of the Bible. It is named **KJ3 - Literal Translation Bible**

This is so named *because* it is the literal, word-for-word translation of the Hebrew text (Masoretic) and the Greek Text (Received Text, *Textus Receptus)* that was used by the translators of the *Authorisec/King James Version.*

The King James Version (1611, latest revision in 1769) was the predominant Bible in the English-speaking world for over 360 years. However, it was not a perfect literal translation of the Hebrew and Greek words before them. Therefore it does not report to the reader all the very words that God wrote *(breathed out - see 2 Timothy 3:16)*. Because of this, the reader of that version, and all other Bible Versions until this day, cannot know precisely from the previous and present versions what God has written for the guidance of all peoples. This is because those knowing Hebrew and Greek have not consistently translated literally and word-for-word the original words God has written. This has left all of us in ignorance of the complete instructions and warnings that God has written for us to believe and obey. For if we do not know precisely what God has said, It is impossible to please Him. Faith is a gift of God (Ephesians 2:8), and faith is based on the very words God has written. It is written,

"But without faith, it is impossible to please God" *(Hebrews 11:6)*
"So faith is from hearing, and hearing through the Word of God" *(Romans 10:17).*

When men change God's words by putting in their own words, it cheats the reader. For having faith in men's words instead of in God's words will lead astray.

This Edition of the *KJ3 - Literal Translation Bible*

The words you will read are the very words that God has written. There is no attempt to make the words easier for younger people to read. Why? It is because God did not write two Bibles, one for the very young and one for the more mature persons. It is because they are God's words that they are so very important. For first readers it is useful for someone to sit beside them and help them with words they do not know. A Pennsylvania church proved the truth of this by having six and seven year old children read the Bible for one and a half hours without stopping. Young children are quick to learn, and eager too. Grown people do not recognize this, so they discourage them.

There are two examples in the Bible of two young boys who began to read and study the Scriptures early in their lives.

1. Samuel was only two years of age when he was given to the Lord by his mother Hannah. He lived in the Tabernacle with the High Priest, Eli. Samuel early on was spoken to by God Himself. And as he grew up toward manhood, he was recognized as one who was specially loved by God, and that he was to be much involved in teaching the Holy Scriptures. When Eli died, his sons were killed the same day. Then Samuel became a Prophet, and the leader of Israel by God's appointment. For 40 years he was both judge and Prophet in Israel..

2. The Apostle Paul spoke of young Timothy in this way: Remembering "the unpretended faith of you, which firstly was in your grandmother Lois, and in your mother Eunice, and I am assured that *it is* also in you"; "but you keep on in what you learned and were assured of, knowing from whom you learned, and that from a babe you know the Holy Scriptures, those being able to make you wise to salvation through belief in Christ Jesus" (2 Timothy 1:5 and 3:14, 15).. Timothy was but a young teen-ager when Paul took him as his traveling companion. He became loved and trusted by the apostle Paul, so much so that when Paul was in prison in Rome, he left Timothy in charge of the assembly in Ephesus.

As for girls, note that both Deborah (Judges 4:4) and Huldah (2 Chronicles 34:22) became Prophetesses.

By these examples you can see the value of learning the Holy Scriptures early.

From the age of eight years both boys and girls should be able to read the Bible without help at hand. Both the glossary in the back and the dictionary can be used to gradually learn words not yet known. Here is God's description of the importance of His words:

"For the Word of God is living, and working effectively, and sharper than every two-edged sword, and piercing as far as the division of both soul and spirit, of both joints and marrow, and able to judge of the thoughts and intentions of the heart" (Hebrews 4:12).

God never slumbers nor sleeps. You, and everyone else, are constantly in His sight.

Why Homeschooler's need this edition of the Bible now?

You are the hope of the nation and of the world. Why? It is because in the public schools, from kindergarten to graduate universities, all students are being deceived by being told there is no God. Special creation by God cannot be taught in any public school. The claim that it is a violation of the doctrine of "the separation of church and state." is false. Thomas Jefferson, our third president, wrote these words in The Declaration of Independence That he never intended to ban God and the Bible from public schools is proven by the fact that when he was governor he required all the schools in Virginia to teach the Bible. To deny the teaching of the Bible, or even the mention of God, is a violation of the First Amendment which guarantees the right of free speech. Education is by definition the exchange of ideas, Anything else is nothing more than state propaganda. It is the foundation for oppressive dictatorship.

Because the home schooled are free from such deceptive practices, they alone will be the truly educated persons of the world if their curriculum includes the teaching of the Bible. A president of Yale University once told the student body that regardless of how much they had learned, or how many degrees they had earned, if they have not read the Bible through they were still ignorant. There is no higher education, no more productive and useful knowledge, than the knowledge of what God has written for our learning.

What about all the new versions that have appeared in recent years?
You may say, "Are there not many other new versions that have appeared in the past several years?" Yes, but every English version in the past and present add words to God's words, and take away many of His words
God expressly forbids this disobedience to His clear commands:
KJ3: *"You shall not add onto <u>the word</u> I command you, neither shall you take away from it . . . "* (Deuteronomy 4:2*).*
In fact, when a translator mistranslates the words God has written, and thus deceives the reader by telling him or her that God said what He never said, God calls that lying: This is also true when he substitutes his own words for God's words.
.KJ3: *"Every word of God [is] refined . . . . Do not add to His words; that He not reprove you, and you be proven a liar"* (Proverbs 30:5, 6).

For the first time you have a Bible that has no words but God's own words*
This is the first time ever a translator has produced a Bible with God's words, all of them. He has commanded this many times in the

Scriptures Thus, for the first time, the reader of this **KJ3 BIBLE** will be among the first to know precisely what God has written in the original words of both the Old and New Testaments in the way God formulated the Holy Scriptures in eternity?

*Words supplied intended to help the reader understand the sense are carefully written in another type style (italic).— these are <u>not</u> God's words, and they may be safely ignored.

This entire **KJ3 Bible** is translated using today's words from the same Hebrew and Greek texts used by the translators of the Authorized/ King James Version (only in this Bible God's very words are translated word-for-word with the literal meanings given of each of the Hebrew and Greek words used in writing the Bible (every word gives the meaning that appears in the Hebrew and Greek lexicons/dictionaries)

God's words are eternal; they were breathed out in eternity.

"The heaven and the earth will pass away, <u>but My words will not</u> <u>pass away,</u>, not *ever!* (Matthew 24:35.)

God's words are eternal words. This is because He, God the Spirit, was present in the eternal counsels when the eternal words of the Scriptures were formulated. He wasalso given the important duty to bear along the ones who wrote out the eternal Scriptures for the children of God through the centuries when they were decreed to be written (2 Peter 1:21). And this spiritual certainty remains until today because the Holy Spirit indwells the child of God when he or she reads the true, original words in the Bible This is true whether the Hebrew and Greek words themselves, or a careful, honest translation of those words is made in another language, such as English. But where is such a Bible to be found, one in which these words are translated in the very words God breathed out, and in the very form that He used?. One may say that such exactitude can be found only in the Hebrew, Aramaic and Greek words which the *"holy men of God spoke"* as they were *"being borne along by the Holy Spirit"* (2 Peter 1:21). Those of us whose native language is not Hebrew or Greek must rely on a translation which faithfully reports the holy words in the same precise words that God used in writing them, <u>and in the very grammatical form</u> <u>which He chose in writing them.</u>

The only way truth can be expressed is by the use of words.

Therefore, in the case of the Holy Scriptures, it is the very words of God alone that can express the *truth*. In the words of our God and Savior, He says to the Father, *"Your Word is Truth"* (John 17:17).

Since the Scriptures are made up of God's words, and no other, He strictly commands that no words may be added to His Word, and that not a single word may be omitted of the words He has written in Hebrew, Aramaic, and Greek. And it is God Himself who says that anyone adding to, or casting out a word of His, is lying to the reader:

"Do not add to His words, that He not reprove you, and you be proven to be a liar" (Proverbs 30:6).

"You shall not add to the Word that I command you, nor take from it, to keep the commandments of Jehovah your God which I command you." (Deuteronomy 4:2).

The meaning is in the words, therefore God's meaning is in His own words, and no other. Let not anyone use other words to express God's truth than an exact translation of His original words. God forbids it, for any adding to, or deleting from, His precise words is to change God's meaning., because in doing so they are lying to the reader.

That is why it can be said that only a strictly literal, word-for-word translation is acceptable to God.

"The following translation of the New Testament is based upon the belief that every word of the original is "God-breathed," The Apostle Paul was being borne along by God the Spirit when he says this in 2 Timothy 3:16.."

This is explained by B. B. Warfield"

". . . This inspiration extends only to the original text as it came *from the pens of the writers,* not to any translation ever made by man, however aged, venerable, or good, and only in so far as any of these adhere to the original – neither adding to nor omitting from it one particle — are they of any *real value,* for, to the extent that they vary from the original, the doctrine of verbal inspiration is lost, so far as that version is concerned." (B. B. Warfield, *Inspiration and Authority of the Bible,* p. 135)

To answer any charge that this is merely a personal opinion, note this quotation from the Preface to Young's *Literal Translation of the Holy Bible*:

"If a translation gives *a present tense* when the original gives a *past,* or *a past* when it has *a present tense; a perfect* for *a future,* or *a future* for *a perfect,* or an *a* for a *the;* or a *the* for an *a; an imperative* for a *subjunctive,* or a *subjunctive* for an *imperative; a verb* for a *noun, or a noun* for *a verb,* it is clear that verbal inspiration is so much overlooked as if it had no existence. THE WORD OF GOD IS MADE VOID BY THE TRADITION OF MEN."

"a *strictly literal* rendering may not be so pleasant to the ear as one where the *apparent sense* is chiefly aimed at, yet it is not *euphony* but *truth* that ought to be sought, and where in such a version as the one commonly in use in this country there are scarcely *two consecutive verses* where is some departure from the original . . . and where these variations may be counted by *tens of thousands*, as admitted on all hands, it is difficult to see how verbal inspiration can be of the least practical use to those who depend on that version alone."

"Modern scholarship is beginning to be alive to the inconsistency of thus gratuitously obscuring, and really changing, the meaning of the sacred writers by subjective notions of what they *ought* to have written, rather than what they *did* write . . .if we do so in one passage, to bring out what may appear to us might, could, would or should, be the Scriptural meaning, we cannot deny the same privilege to others who may twist passages in the same manner." – Robert Young

As anyone may see, the same words could and should be applied to the new non-literal translations which completely ignore the original languages, and by doing so they are ignoring God's many warnings not to add to, or omit from, what God has written. The readers of this version should remember that it is what God actually *said* that is vital to your spiritual interests, rather than what other men *say* that God said.. It is today as Robert Young said in the last century, mere men are adding tens of thousands of words in their "new" versions, such deceit is forbidden by God. Also, they do not dare to italicize these added words, nor will they tell the reader just how many of the words are merely words out of their own minds and prejudices.

Now, at last, all can read in English the very words that God wrote in Hebrew and Greek.

For in this KJ3 Bible the reader has every word that God breathed out and had written for our instruction.. Nothing has been added, and no word has been taken away. There are no substitute words (such as synonyms), no paraphrases, no ignoring of the frequent double negatives in the Scriptures, and no interpretations (for God is His own interpreter; we can know His meanings only by His very words, and no other way).

Jesus shows the importance of only reading or speaking God's words only:

John 12:49

"For I did not speak from Myself, but He who sent Me, *the* Father, He has given Me command, what I should say, and what I should speak."

If the Lord Jesus did not have permission to add or take away from

God's words, how can sinful men dare to change a word when God commands them not to do it?

What are some of the differences in this Bible?

It is important to recognize that God wrote in grammatical forms when He breathed out the words of the Scriptures (see 2 Timothy 3:16). In the 160+ versions in English in the past it was not recognized just how many times the translators were commanded by God not to add any word to what God actually wrote, nor to take away words He wrote. The words of the Scriptures were *"breathed out"* in eternity (this is the true meaning of the Greek word):

"All Scripture is God-breathed and profitable for doctrine, for reproof, for correction, for instruction in righteousness, so that the man of God may be perfected, being fully equipped for every good work." (2 Timothy 3:16).The Greek word is qeopneustol, which translated into English is *"God-breathed."*

KJII/LIT: *"I know that whatever God does it shall be <u>forever;</u> nothing is to be added to it, and nothing is to diminish from it. And God does [it] so that they fear before Him."* (Ecclesiastes. 3:14)

God's grammar and English grammar are very closely related.

For the first time, a much closer watch for the grammar God used has been carefully studied out and translated accordingly. God commands the translator to carefully and accurately report to the reader just what He wrote, and how He wrote it. Yet a study of previous English translations of the Bible <u>before</u> this *KJ3 - Literal Translation Bible* will show that they have ignored or mistranslated God's use of the grammatical forms.

The difference to the reader will become quickly apparent as this edition is being read. There is obviously a stronger impact, and a clearer understanding, that comes from using God's very words in the very form that He wrote them. How could we ever have been so foolish as to think that God would overlook the giving of an incorrect, and thus untrue, translation of His words? Now, at last, we have recognized the importance of such obvious differences in the way God formulated the Holy Scriptures in eternity?

Verbs, nouns, adjectives, adverbs, conjunctions, etc. have not been distinguished. in other versions This practice of confusing the grammatical forms have deceived the reader. Especially, all the other translations erred in translating verbs as nouns. For instance, many dozens of times verbs in the Psalms are translated as nouns. Many hundreds of times "inhabitants of" is a mistranslation of the word "to live." For instance most of the time

such should be honestly translated like this: "the inhabitants of Jerusalem" should be translated as, "*the ones* living *in* Jerusalem." In such cases
hardly any indication was given that a verb was used, not a noun

Translating exactly the words God wrote
and how He wrote them often shocks:

Difference 1. The most serious mistranslation, and one that God abhors is this: Translating God's own chosen name appears more than 6,000 times in the Holy Scriptures. His name is Jehovah, not LORD, and not Yahveh or Yahweh. Lord is a title, not a name. Yahveh and Yahweh cannot be right, and all other names in the Bible, cannot be translated in English beginning with the letter "y." The Hebrew gives only the letters YHWH in the 6,000+ mentions of God's name begins with the Hebrew letter ""yodh." All the names in the Bible beginning with the letter "y" (:yodh") in English are translated with the letter "j" (Jacob, Jehoshaphat, and all the others). There is no name in the Strong's or Young's concordances beginning with a "y". No and not in the NIV concordance either. An interesting question: Why do all the new versions (beginning in the eighteenth century") insist that God's name is "Yahveh" or "Yahweh"? Yet they begin all the other names beginning with the Hebrew letter "yodh" with the letter "j"! Should they not be consistent and spell all these names with a "y", such as "Jacob," "Jehoshaphat"?

"I am *Jehovah,* that is my *name.* and I will not give my glory t.p. another, . . ;" (Isaiah 42:8). The only other name God chose to have Himself called is :I AM" He said to Moses, "*You shall say this to the sons of Israel, I AM has sent me to you"* (Exodus 3:14).

Difference 2: Among the great many changes that are startling to readers when only the words God wrote are translated into English are these:
There is a change from "church" to "assembly" (for there is no word in either Greek or Hebrew for "church." In the New Testament it is always "assembly." In the Hebrew there are three words which may fairly translate the meeting of groups to worship: "assembly," "congregation," or, "the gathering".

Difference 3. Another change: The word ordinarily translated as "Gentiles." is not a word God used in either Testament; no such group or parties are recognized in either Greek or Hebrew. To the Jews, they were "the people," all other countries were referred to as "the nations." The Greek word so wrongly translated as "Gentiles" also means simply, "the nations."
Other examples: the adjective "oppressing *one*" was translated as "oppres-

xiv

sor;"

In the Hebrew "the saints" is an adjective that literally means "godly *ones.*" As an adjective,"Poor *one*" shows that it is singular; the plural would be "poor *ones*", God thought it important to show the plural and singular of the adjective.

God often literally says, "stretch out your ear"instead of "incline your ear," or "bow your ear".In another place the Lord Jesus said, "You lay these words into your ears"; (Luke 9:44) It is forbidden to change these divine words to merely say, "Listen".

The word "to see" is often also used to say, "cause us to see".

"Behold" appears in the Bible some 2,000 times. It is used to call attention to an important statement of God, and many times should be emphasized as Behold! It is not proper to use "behold" as a meaning of "to see".

"Miracle" is not a Scriptures word, but the word "sign" is used throughout; often in this edition we have indicated this as "*miraculous* sign" so that the miracles God performed are not discounted;

"Therefore," and often, "For" can be properly translated as "On account of this".

One change we have not made in a bow to the well-known words which mean "the tent of meeting" we have left it as, "The tabernacle of the congregation."

Frequent changes that result from a literal word-for-word translation.
It must be recognized that God, being all-wise, knew what He meant to say, and He used the right grammatical form to say it. For instance, the verb for "to hate" many times has been wrongly translated as "hater" by others.

Again, "put to death" are words God did not write, but rather, "cause to die." The difference to the reader will become quickly apparent as this Bible is being read. There is obviously a stronger impact, and a clearer understanding, that comes from using God's very words in the very form that He wrote them.

"The word translated "Trespass" is most often "transgression, but very often it should be translated as "deviations," because the word means literally "to slip aside." Adam slipped aside, deviated, from God's Law. See Romans 5.

"Trumpet is sometimes correct, but most often it refers to a "rams' horn."

"regenerate"is the English word often translated "beget." It means to create new life. "spirit-knowers" is a correct translation for "soothsayers, fortune-tellers, wizards." "justice" is very often "judgment." "Dowry" in the Bible should be "bride-price." The "new versions" get rid of the doctrine of election by calling it "the chosen." When God cleared the land for Israel, it is properly translated that He "dispossessed." the people of Canaan.

In the New Testament "to betray" is properly "to give over."

There is never a word for "nor" in the Hebrew, but always "and not."

When the Israelites "traveled, "journeyed, or "broke camp" the Hebrew word is, "pulled up," to which we have added *"stakes,"* because they then pulled up their tent pegs and took the tents with them.

Bowing before a dignitary is called "bowed with his nose to the ground."

In the New Testament "Bride" is the correct translation, not "daughter-in-law" (Matt. 10:35; Luke 12:53),

A very important mistranslation is putting :I am *he*" when the Lord Jesus is saying "I AM" identifying Himself as the "I AM" of Exodus 3:14. At His mock trial, they called it blasphemy when He said "I AM," for they knew He was calling Himself God. Three times in John 18 He used these words "I AM" (verses 5, 6, 8). In verse 6, He said "I AM" to those arresting Him, and they " fell away backward.". Sixteen times He identified Himself as God, saying, "I AM." (Matt. 14:27; Mark 6:5; 13:6; 14:16; Luke 21:8; 22:70; John 4:26; 6:20; 8:24, 28; 58, 13:13, 19; 18:5, 6, 8 (**See Acts 7:35).**

Some of the most serious mistranslations of our day:

Putting "gentle" for "meek," indicating that those who so translate are ignorant of the meaning of the English word "meek."

Deceiving the reader by putting "donkey" for the animal "ass. The kings and princes, also the Lord Jesus, rode on "asses." not "donkeys." Would the crowd have been shouting "Hosanna, Hosanna" to Jesus if He had ridden into Jerusalem riding on a "donkey"? (Matthew 21:9), This is deliberate mistranslation, for there is no word meaning "donkey" in the Bible.

The Word in Hebrew or in Greek most certainly means "an ass," an animal totally different from a "donkey."Those who go to the zoo know the cast difference.

The doctrine of the deity of Jesus Christ is badly treated in the new versions

The deity and integrity of the Lord Jesus is taken away from Him dozens of times in today's "translations". They also dare to charge Him with sinning:

References from the NIV, NASB, NRSV, REB, NAB, GNB, ESV

1. Christ causes men to stumble and fall, so it is <u>His</u> fault if they sin (Isa. 8:14; Romans. 8:33; 1 Pet. 2:8 — All but ESV)

2. As Wisdom He is said to be the first of God's <u>works</u>, so a creature Prov. 8:22-31 are About Christ! (Prov. 8:22 — All seven)

3. He is made to be subject to the Judgment, a sinner (Matt.5:22 — All seven)

7. His omnipresence is denied Him in the only place where it is personally ascribed to Him in the Bible (John 3:13 — NIV, NASB, NRSV, NAB, ESV)

8. Christ's knowledge of God is equated to the knowledge of God that men have of God (A Manichean error, John 10:14, 15 — All seven)

9. He is denied the right to affirm that He is God when He says I AM!

15 times:(Matt. 14:27; Mark 6:5; 13:6; 14:16; Luke 21:8; 22:70; John 4:26; 6:20; 8:24, 28; 13:13, 19; 18:5, 6, 8 **(See Acts 7:35)** — All except NAB)

10: His propitiation is consistently denied to be sufficient in various ways (Romans. 3:25, 26; Heb. 1:3; 1 John 2:2 — All seven)

12. Christ was sacrificed, but it was not specifically for His sheep alone (1 Cor. 5:7 — All seven)

13. He was made sin, but not for "us," His elect (2 Cor. 5:21 — All seven)

14. The prophecy that He would be the promised Seed is nullified in the Old Testament because the new versions persist in translating the singular word "seed" as a plural there (Gen. 3:15; 21:12; 22:18; Gal. 3:16 — All seven)

16. In Phil. 2:5, it is said He made Himself "nothing" (Philippians 2:5 — NIV, REB, ESV)

17. They all deny that He is "*God manifest in the flesh*" (1 Tim. 3:16 — All seven)

18. In Hebrews 1:3 He is a "copy,", a "representation,"a replica, an imprint of God, but not what the Greek says: "*the express image of His essence*" (Hebrews 1:3 — All seven)

19. He is made to taste death for "everyone," rather than for His elect only, His sheep – thus nullifying the efficacy of His Substitutionary sacrifice for His elect (Heb. 2:9, John 10:11— All seven)

20. He is said to have suffered, but not for us, His beloved. If His suffering is universal, then of no unique value (1 Pet. 2:21; 4:1 — All seven)

21. He is not allowed to specifically take away **"our"** sins alone;

same reasoning as in #19 and #20. (1 John 3:5 — All seven)

22. He is allowed to be our Master, but not our God (Jude 4 — All seven)

23. He is made to violate His own vow not to drink the fruit of the vine until He would drink it new in "the kingdom of God." As God He could not violate His vow. (Mark 14:25; John 19:29 — All seven)

24. God says that Christ as the "*Antitype*" of the Ark now saves us, but in these new versions by changing the position of the Greek words they make God say instead that "baptism now saves you." Thus they say that the blood of Christ alone is insufficient to save, but must be augmented by baptism by the hands of men (1 Peter 3:20, 21 — All seven)

25. They say that His origins are in this world; so it is denied that He is eternal, thus destroying the prophecy of Christ in Micah 5:2 (Micah 5:2, Matt. 2:6 — All seven)

28. All six deny that Christ is "*the Son of the living God*," saying instead, "You are the Holy One of God." (John 6:69 — NIV, NRSV, NASB, REB, NAB, ASV, CEV, ERV, RV, ESV)

28. They deny Christ the title of Son of God, instead having Jesus say, "Do you believe in the Son of man?" ["the Son of Man" is never connected with "believe", or "believing" in the true Scriptures]. (John 9:35 — All seven)

29. All seven say that Jesus lied to His brothers (John 7:8 — All seven)

God's message to us must be given to us in God's very words. He will not recognize any other words but His own, and all will be judged by those very words than those. that He wrote for our understanding. All the mistranslations in today's versions may be quickly seen and checked for accuracy in *The Interlinear Hebrew-Greek-English Bible.* There you will find not only the true meanings, but also for your convenience a number is placed over each original word. We have put these numbers into the Hebrew and Greek lexicons and concordance. It is not necessary to know the original Hebrew ad Greek languages to find the original words, their place, and the history and the explanation of the word. The lexicon often explains why the word sometime is translated in different ways

God has chosen to use double negatives in the same sentence

This, of course, is not proper in English. The way to express these has always been to use an adverb for one of the negatives. For instance: in the English Standard Version in Isaiah 24:19, 20a: "The earth is utterly broken, the earth is split apart, the earth is <u>violently</u> shaken:, The earth staggers like a drunken man;"

Here you see, in the underlined words, a serious mistranslation. God did not use those adverbs. Instead here is the true literal translation of those words:

"The earth is breaking, breaking! The earth is crashing, crashing! The earth is tottering, tottering! Like a drunken man, the earth is staggering, staggering! (KJ3).

In this case there are four double words, not negatives, but easily translated into a correct translation into English. And note that it is so much clearer. No adverbs were used here by God, but you will find all the other versions failing to translate the four double words. that God used.

Now for one of the many verses where God uses a double negative (not not):

"The heaven and the earth will pass away, <u>but My words will not pass away,</u>, not *ever!* (Matthew 24:35.)

Note that both the negatives in this sentence have been translated without doing wrong to English rules. The other versions will substitute "not at all," or, "by no means." God did not write that. So He will count that as adding to His words.

There are a great many verses when God uses two negatives; He does it for emphasis In Revelation 18:21-23 there are seven sentences in succession with double negatives: Two examples:

"Babylon the great city will be thrown down, and it will not still be found, not ever!

"And every craftsman of every craft will not be found in you, not ever.

The translation of words transliterated allows
the reader to know what is said

In many places we have translated the Hebrew words instead of transliterating them. You can see the difference plainly in Hosea, chapter 1, where the Hebrew words "lo-ruhamah" means "No Mercy," and "Lo-ammi" means "Not My People." This proper translation is noted in Romans 9:25: *"As also He says in Hosea, I will call those Not My People, My People! And those not beloved, Beloved!* (Hosea 2:23).

The Hebrews gave descriptive names to places and events. Instead of transliterating these words, in this version you will find them translated into English: Hor-hagideed" is "The Hole in the Cleft." Kibroth-hattavah" means "Graves of lust", etc.

In Isaiah 8:3 when the prophetess bore a son, the Lord told Isaiah to "Call his name, "Make Haste to Plunder! Hurry to the Spoil!" which is the English translation of the Hebrew words *"maher-shalal-hash-baz."*

In the Psalms the titles have been translated for the reader. "Altaschith" means "Do not destroy;" Jonath-elem-rechokim"means "Concerning the Silent Dove," "Michtam" means "treasure;"etc.

THINGS TO REMEMBER

In the many new versions there are many words they have omitted or substituted from the original words that God *did* write. There is neither authenticity nor authority in any of them. Those trusting the word of men, rather than the words of God, are of all persons most pitiable.

You, my young friends, are the hope of the world. A world without the true infallible, omniscient God is a place ruled by Satan, who is described as *"the spirit now working in the sons of disobedience"*. All who choose to deny God's rulership over all persons or things are being disobedient to Him, *"among whom we also conducted ourselves in times past in the lusts of our flesh, acting out all things, the wills of our flesh and of the understandings, and were by nature the children of wrath even as the rest." (Ephesians 2:1)*

The generations before you have left you in a world that is plunging downward , now under the wrath of God more than ever. That is why you are the hope of the world. Yes. you can change the world. Take the words of this Bible into your heart and follow God. Then nothing will be impossible to you. There was a man named Martin Luther who challenged the evils of the world around him. The ruling powers tried to kill Him. But he survived to lead a great reformation of the world, leading them into the Light, who is the Lord Jesus Christ. He is *the Way, the Truth and the Life"* (John 14:6). Through Him alone you may have everlasting life. Believe into Him and you will live forever.

Carry that message to the world. You could do nothing greater, whatever occupation or calling you will choose under His leading.

"Grace and peace be to you from God our Father and the Lord Jesus Christ" (Romans 1:7)

Jay P. Green, Sr., Translator

The Gospel According to
MATTHEW

Matthew 1

1 The genealogy of Christ from Abraham to Joseph. 18 He was conceived by the Holy Ghost, and born of the virgin Mary. 19 The angel interprets the names of Christ.

1 ¶ The Book of the genealogy of Jesus Christ *the* Son of David, *the* son of Abraham:

2 Abraham fathered Isaac, and Isaac fathered Jacob, and Jacob fathered Judah and his brothers.

3 And Judah fathered Pharez and Zarah out of Tamar, and Pharez fathered Hezron, and Hezron fathered Aram,

4 and Aram fathered Amminadab, and Amminadab fathered Nahshon, and Nahshon fathered Salmon,

5 and Salmon fathered Boaz out of Rahab, and Boaz fathered Obed out of Ruth, and Obed fathered Jesse,

6 and Jesse fathered David the king. And David the king fathered Solomon out of *her who had been* the *wife* of Uriah,

7 and Solomon fathered Rehoboam, and Rehoboam fathered Abijah, and Abijah fathered Asa,

8 and Asa fathered Jehoshaphat, and Jehoshaphat fathered Jehoram, and Jehoram fathered Uzziah,

9 and Uzziah fathered Jotham, and Jotham fathered Ahaz, and Ahaz fathered Hezekiah,

10 and Hezekiah fathered Manasseh, and Manasseh fathered Amon, and Amon fathered Josiah,

11 and Josiah fathered Jehoiachin and his brothers, at the deportation of Babylon.

12 And after the deportation of Babylon, Jehoiachin fathered Shealtiel, and Shealtiel fathered Zerubbabel,

13 and Zerubbabel fathered Abiud, and Abiud fathered Eliakim, and Eliakim fathered Azor,

14 and Azor fathered Sadoc, and Sadoc fathered Achim, and Achim fathered Eliud,

15 and Eliud fathered Eleazar, and Eleazar fathered Matthan, and Matthan fathered Jacob,

16 and Jacob fathered Joseph, the husband of Mariam (*Mary*), out of whom Jesus was born, *the One* called Christ.

17 So all the generations from Abraham to David *were* fourteen generations, and from David to the deportation to Babylon, fourteen generations, and from the deportation to Babylon until the Christ, fourteen generations.

18 ¶ Now the birth of Jesus Christ was this way (for His mother Mariam (*Mary*) had been betrothed to Joseph) before the coming together of them, she was found having *babe* in womb of *the* Holy Spirit.

19 But her husband, Joseph, being just, and not willing to make her a public example, he purposed to put her away secretly.

20 And *as* he *was* thinking about these things, behold, an angel of *the* Lord was seen by him in a dream, saying, Joseph, son of David, do not be afraid to take Mariam (*Mary*) *as* your wife. For that in her is generated of *the* Holy Spirit.

21 And she will bear a son, and you shall call His name Jesus, for He shall save His people from their sins.

22 And all this happened so that might be fulfilled that *which was* spoken by the Lord through the prophet, saying,

23 "Behold, The virgin will have *a babe* in *her* womb and will bear a son, and they will call His name Emmanuel" (which translated is, God with us). *Isa. 7:14*

24 And being aroused from sleep, Joseph did as the angel of *the* Lord commanded him, and took *as* his wife,

25 and did not know her until she bore her son, the First-born. And he called His name Jesus.

Matthew 2

1 Jesus born in Bethlehem, 3 Herod troubled, 7 Herods sends wise men to inquire about Christ, 11 Wise men present gifts, 13 Angel orders flight into Egypt, 16 Herod kills all boys two years and under in Bethlehem, 22 travel to Galilee

1 ¶ And when Jesus had been born in Bethlehem of Judea in *the* days of Herod the king, behold, wise men arrived from *the* east to Jerusalem,

2 saying, Where is He born King of the Jews? For we saw His star in the east and have come to worship Him.

3 But Herod the king having heard *this, he* was troubled and all Jerusalem with him.

4 And having gathered all the chief priests and scribes of the people, he asked of them where the Christ was to be born.

5 And they said to him, In Bethlehem of Judea, for so it has been written by the prophet,

6 "And you, Bethlehem, *in* the land of Judah, by no means are you least among the rulers of Judah, for out of you shall come out *One* ruling, who shall shepherd My people Israel." *Mic. 5:2*

7 Then secretly calling the wise men, Herod asked of them exactly the time of the star appearing.

8 And sending them to Bethlehem, he said, Having gone, exactly inquire about the child. And when you find *Him,* bring me word again so that coming I may also worship Him.

9 ¶ And having heard the king, they departed. And, behold, The star which they saw in the east went before them until it had come and stood over where the child was.

10 And seeing the star, they rejoiced exceedingly *with* a great joy.

11 And having come into the house, they saw the child with His mother Mary. And falling down, they worshiped Him. And opening their treasures, they presented gifts to Him: gold and frankincense and myrrh.

12 And having been warned by a dream not to return to Herod, they went back into their own country by another way.

13 ¶ And they having departed, behold, an angel of *the* Lord appeared to Joseph by a dream, saying, Rise up! Take the child and His mother with you, and flee into Egypt. And be there until I shall tell you. For Herod is about to look for the child in order to destroy Him.

14 And rising up, he took along the child and His mother by night and withdrew into Egypt.

15 And he was there until the end of Herod, that might be fulfilled that spoken by the Lord through the prophet, saying, "Out of Egypt I have called My Son." *Hosea 11:1*

16 ¶ Then seeing that he was mocked by the wise men, Herod was greatly enraged, and having sent, he killed all the boys in Bethlehem and in all its districts, from two years old and under, according to the time which he exactly asked from the wise men.

17 Then was fulfilled that spoken by Jeremiah the prophet, saying:

18 "A voice was heard in Ramah, lamenting and bitter wailing, and great mourning, Rachel weeping *for* her children and would not be comforted, because they were not." *Jer. 31:15*

19 ¶ But Herod having died, behold, an angel of *the* Lord appears to Joseph by a dream in Egypt,

20 saying, Rising up, take along the child and His mother and pass over into *the* land of Israel; for those seeking the soul of the child have died.

21 And rising up, he took along the child and His mother and came into *the* land of Israel.

22 But hearing that Archelaus reigned over Judea in place of his father Herod, he feared to go there. And being warned by a dream, he departed into the parts of Galilee.

23 And coming, he dwelt in a city called Nazareth, so as to fulfill that spoken by the prophets, He shall be called a Nazarene.

Matthew 3

1 John preaches: his office: life, and baptism, 7 He reprehends the Pharisees, 13 and baptizes Christ in Jordan.

1 ¶ And in those days John the Baptist arrives preaching in the deserted *places* of Judea,

2 and saying, Repent! For the kingdom of Heaven has drawn near.

3 For this is he spoken of by Isaiah the prophet, saying: "The voice of *one* crying in

the deserted *place*: Prepare the way of *the* Lord! Make His paths straight!" *Isa. 40:3*

4 And John himself had his clothing from hairs of a camel, and a belt of leather about his loin. And his food was locusts and wild honey.

5 Then Jerusalem and all Judea went out to him, and all the surrounding region of the Jordan,

6 and were baptized by him in the Jordan, having confessed their sins.

7 ¶ But seeing many of the Pharisees and Sadducees coming to his baptism, he said to them, Offspring of vipers! Who warned you to flee from the wrath to come?

8 Therefore, bring forth fruits worthy of repentance.

9 And do not think to say within yourselves, We have a father, Abraham. For I say to you that God is able to raise up children to Abraham from these stones.

10 But already the axe is even laid at the root of the trees. Therefore any tree not bringing forth good fruit is cut off and is thrown into fire.

11 I indeed baptize you in water to repentance; but He who is coming after me is stronger than me, whose sandals I am not able to lift. He will baptize you in *the* Holy Spirit and fire,

12 whose fan *is* in His hand, and He will cleanse His threshing-floor and will gather His wheat into the storehouse. But He will burn up the chaff with unquenchable fire.

13 ¶ Then Jesus arrives from Galilee to the Jordan, to John, to be baptized by him.

14 But John restrained Him, saying, I have need to be baptized by You, and do You come to me?

15 But answering, Jesus said to him, Allow *it* now, for it is becoming to us this way to fulfill all righteousness. Then he allows Him.

16 And having been baptized, Jesus went up immediately from the water. And, behold! The heavens were opened to Him, and He saw the Spirit of God coming down as a dove, and coming upon Him.

17 And behold! A voice out of the heavens saying, This is My Son, the Beloved, in whom I have been well-pleased. *Psa. 2:7; Gen. 22:2; Isa. 42:1*

Matthew 4

1 Christ fasts, and is tested. 11 The angels minister to him. 18 He calls Peter, and Andrew, 21 James and John, 23 and heals all the diseased.

1 ¶ Then Jesus was led up into the deserted *place* by the Spirit, to be tempted by the devil.

2 And having fasted forty days and forty nights, afterwards He hungered.

3 And coming near to Him, the Tempter said, If You are *the* Son of God, speak that these stones may become loaves.

4 But answering, He said, It has been written: "Man shall not live on bread alone, but on every Word going out of *the* mouth of God." *Deut. 8:3*

5 Then the devil takes Him to the holy city, and he sets Him on the wing of the temple.

6 And *he* said to Him, If You are the Son of God, throw Yourself down; for it has been written: "He shall give His angels charge concerning You, and they shall bear You on *their* hands, lest You strike Your foot against a stone." *LXX-Psa. 90:11, 12; MT-Psa. 91:11, 12*

7 Jesus said to him, Again it has been written: "You shall not tempt *the* Lord your God." *Deut. 6:16*

8 Again the devil takes Him to a very high mountain, and shows to Him all the kingdoms of the world and their glory.

9 And *he* said to Him. I will give all these things to You if, falling down, You will worship me.

10 Then Jesus said to him, Go, Satan! For it has been written: "You shall worship *the* Lord your God, and you shall serve Him only." *Deut. 6:13*

11 Then the Devil leaves Him. And behold! Angels came near and ministered to Him.

12 ¶ But Jesus hearing that John was given over, He withdrew into Galilee.

13 And having left Nazareth, having come He lived at Capernaum, beside the sea in *the* districts of Zebulun and Naphtali,

14 so that might be fulfilled that spoken by Isaiah the prophet, saying:

15 "Land of Zebulun and land of Naphtali, way of *the* sea, beyond the Jordan, Galilee of the nations:

16 the people sitting in darkness saw a great Light; and to those sitting in *the* region and shadow of death, Light arose to them." *Isa. 9:1, 2*

17 From that time Jesus began to preach and to say, Repent! For the kingdom of Heaven has drawn near.

18 ¶ And walking beside the sea of Galilee, Jesus saw two brothers, Simon being called Peter and his brother Andrew, casting a net into the sea; for they were fishers.

19 And He says to them, Come after Me, and I will make you fishers of men.

20 And leaving the nets, they immediately followed Him.

21 And going on from there, He saw two other brothers, James the *son* of Zebedee and his brother John in the boat with their father Zebedee, mending their nets. And He called them.

22 And at once leaving the boat and their father, they followed Him.

23 ¶ And Jesus went about all Galilee teaching in their synagogues and proclaiming the gospel of the kingdom, and healing every disease and every sickness among the people.

24 And the report of Him went out into all Syria. And they brought to Him all *the ones* badly having *illness*, suffering various diseases and torments, also *those* being demon-possessed, and *those* being moonstruck, and paralytics; and He healed them.

25 And large crowds followed Him from Galilee and Decapolis, and Jerusalem, and Judea, and beyond the Jordan.

Matthew 5

1 Christ begins his sermon on the mount: 3 declaring who are blessed: 38 exhorts to suffer wrong, 44 to love our enemies, 48 to labor after perfection.

1 ¶ But seeing the crowds, He went up into the mountain, and He having sat down, His disciples came near to Him.

2 And opening His mouth, He taught them, saying:

3 ¶ Blessed *are* the poor in spirit! For theirs is the kingdom of Heaven.

4 Blessed *are* the *ones* mourning! For they shall be comforted.

5 Blessed *are* the meek! For they shall inherit the earth. *Psa. 37:11*

6 Blessed *are* they who hunger and thirst after righteousness! For they shall be filled.

7 Blessed *are* the merciful! For they shall obtain mercy.

8 Blessed *are* the pure in heart! For they shall see God.

9 Blessed *are* the peacemakers! For they shall be called sons of God.

10 Blessed *are the ones* who have been persecuted for righteousness' sake! For theirs is the kingdom of Heaven.

11 Blessed are you when they shall reproach you, and persecute *you*, and shall say every evil word against you, lying, on account of Me.

12 Rejoice and be exceeding joyful, for your reward *is* great in Heaven; for in this way they persecuted the prophets, the *ones* before you.

13 ¶ You are the salt of the earth, but if the salt becomes tasteless, with what shall it be salted? For it has strength for nothing any more but to be thrown out and to be trampled under by men.

14 You are the light of the world. A city situated on a mountain cannot be hidden.

15 Nor do they light a lamp and put it under the grain measure, but on the lampstand; and it shines for all those in the house.

16 So let your light shine before men, so that they may see your good works, and may glorify your Father in Heaven.

17 ¶ Do not think that I came to annul the Law or the Prophets; I did not come to annul, but to fulfill.

18 For truly I say to you, Until the heaven and the earth should pass away, not one iota or one point shall pass away from the Law, not until all things should occur.

19 Therefore, whoever looses one of these commandments, the least, and shall teach men so, he shall be called least in the kingdom of Heaven. But whoever does and teaches *them*, this one shall be called great in the kingdom of Heaven.

20 For I say to you, If your righteousness shall not exceed *that* of the scribes and Pharisees, you shall not enter into the kingdom of God, not *ever*!

21 ¶ You have heard that it was said to the ancients: "Do not commit murder!" And,

Whoever commits murder shall be liable to the Judgment. *Ex. 20:13; Deut. 5:17*

22 But I say to you, Everyone who is angry with his brother without cause shall be liable to the Judgment. And whoever says to his brother, Raca, shall be liable to the sanhedrin; but whoever says, Fool! shall be liable *to be thrown* into the fire of Hell.

23 Therefore if you offer your gift on the altar, and remember there that your brother has something against you,

24 leave your gift there before the altar, and go. First, be reconciled to your brother, and then, coming, offer your gift.

25 Be well-disposed toward your opponent quickly, while you are in the way with him, that the opponent not give you over to the judge, and the judge give you over to the officer, and you be thrown into prison.

26 Truly, I say to you, you shall not come out from there, not until you pay the last kodrantes.

27 ¶ You have heard that it was said to the ancients: "Do not commit adultery." *Ex. 20:14; Deut. 5:18*

28 But I say to you, Everyone looking at a woman to lust after her has already committed adultery with her in his heart.

29 But if your right eye causes you to stumble, take it out and throw *it* from you, for it is profitable to you that one of your members should be destroyed and all your body not be thrown into Hell.

30 And if your right hand causes you to stumble, cut it off and throw *it* from you, for it is profitable to you that one of your members should be destroyed and all your body not be thrown into Hell.

31 It was also said, Whoever puts away his wife, "let him give her a bill of divorce." *Deut. 24:1*

32 But I say to you, Whoever puts away his wife, apart from a matter of fornication, causes her to commit adultery. And whoever shall marry the one put away commits adultery.

33 ¶ Again, you have heard that it was said to the ancients: "You shall not swear falsely, but shall give your oaths to the Lord." *Lev. 19:12; Num. 30:2*

34 But I say to you, Do not swear at all, neither by Heaven, because it is God's throne; *Isa. 66:1*

35 nor by the earth, because it is the footstool of His feet; nor by Jerusalem, because it is *the* city of the great King. *Isa. 66:1; Psa. 48:2*

36 Nor shall you swear by your head, because you are not able to make one hair white or black.

37 But let your word be Yes, yes; No, no. For the excess of these is from the evil.

38 ¶ You have heard that it was said: "An eye for an eye, and a tooth for a tooth;" *Ex. 21:24; Lev. 24:20; Deut. 19:21*

39 but I say to you, Do not resist the evil; but whoever strikes you on the right cheek, turn the other to him also.

40 And to him desiring to sue you, and to take your tunic, allow him also *to have* the coat.

41 And whoever shall compel you to go one mile, go with him two;

42 to the *one* asking you, Give, and to the *one* wishing to borrow from you, do not turn away.

43 ¶ You have heard that it was said, "You shall love your neighbor" and hate your enemy; *Lev. 19:18*

44 but I say to you, Love your enemies; bless those cursing you, do well to those hating you; and pray for those abusing and persecuting you,

45 so that you may become sons of your Father in Heaven. Because He causes His sun to rise on *the* evil and *the* good, and sends rain on *the* just and unjust.

46 For if you love those loving you, what reward do you have? Do not even the tax-collectors do the same?

47 And if you only greet your brothers, what exceptional *thing* do you do? Do not the tax-collectors do so?

48 Therefore, you be perfect even as your Father in Heaven is perfect.

Matthew 6

1 Christ speaks of kindness, 5 prayer, 14 forgiving our brethren, 16 fasting, 19 our treasure, 24 of serving God, and mammon: 25 care for worldly things: 33 but to seek God's kingdom.

1 ¶ Take care not to do your merciful deeds before men in order to be seen by them.

But if not, you have no reward from your Father in Heaven.

2 Therefore, when you do merciful deeds, do not trumpet before you as the hypocrites do in the synagogues and in the streets, so that they may be glorified by men. Truly I say to you, They have their reward.

3 But you doing merciful deeds, do not let your left know what your right *hand* does,

4 so that your merciful deeds may be in secret. And your Father, the *One* seeing in secret, Himself will repay you in the open.

5 ¶ And when you pray, you shall not be as the hypocrites, for they love to pray standing in the synagogues and in the corners of the open streets so that they may appear *to be seen* of men. Truly I say to you, They have their reward.

6 But you, when you pray, enter into your inner room and shutting your door, pray to your Father in secret. And your Father, the *One* seeing in secret, will repay you in the open.

7 But when you pray, do not be babbling vain words, as the nations; for they think that they shall be heard in their much speaking.

8 Therefore do not be like them, for your Father knows what things you have need of before you ask Him.

9 ¶ Therefore, you *should* pray: Our Father, the *One* in Heaven, Hallowed be Your name.

10 Your kingdom come; Your will be done, as *it is* in Heaven, also on the earth.

11 Give us today our daily bread,

12 and forgive us our debts as we also forgive our debtors.

13 And do not lead us into temptation, but deliver us from the evil, for Yours is the kingdom and the power and the glory, to the ages. Amen.

14 For if you forgive men their deviations, your heavenly Father will also forgive you.

15 But if you will not forgive men their deviations, neither will your Father forgive your deviations.

16 ¶ And when you fast, do not be as the hypocrites, *with* sullen face, for they disfigure their faces so that they may appear to men to be fasting. Truly I say to you that they have their reward.

17 But you *in* fasting, anoint your head and wash your face,

18 so as not to appear to men to be fasting, but to your Father in secret. And your Father, the *One* seeing in secret, will repay you in the open.

19 ¶ Do not treasure up for you treasures on the earth, where moth and rust consume, and where thieves dig through and steal.

20 But treasure up for you treasures in Heaven, where neither moth nor rust consume, and where thieves do not dig through and steal.

21 For where your treasure is, there your heart will be also.

22 The lamp of the body is the eye. Then if your eye is sound, all your body is bright.

23 But if your eye is evil, all your body is dark. If, therefore, the light in you is darkness, how great is the darkness!

24 No one is able to serve two lords; for either he will hate the one, and he will love the other; or he will cleave to the one, and he will despise the other. You are not able to serve God and wealth.

25 ¶ Because of this, I say to you, Do not be anxious for your soul, what you eat and what you drink, nor for your body, what you put on. Is not the soul more than the food and the body than the clothing?

26 Observe the birds of the heaven, that they do not sow, nor do they reap, nor do *they* gather into granaries, yet your heavenly Father feeds them. Do you not rather excel them?

27 But who of you *by* being anxious is able to add one cubit onto his stature?

28 And why are you anxious about clothing? Consider the lilies of the field, how they grow. They do not labor nor do they spin,

29 but I say to you that not even Solomon in all his glory was clothed as one of these.

30 If God so enrobes the grass of the field (which is today, and is thrown into a furnace tomorrow) *will He* not much rather you, little-faiths?

31 Therefore do not be anxious, saying, What may we eat? Or, what may we drink? Or, what may clothe us?

32 For after all these things the nations seek. For your heavenly Father knows that you have need of all these things.

33 But seek first the kingdom of God and His righteousness, and all these things will be added to you.

34 Therefore do not be anxious into the morrow. For the morrow will be anxious of itself. Sufficient to *each* day is its *own* badness.

Matthew 7

1 Christ ends his sermon on the mount, warns of rash judgment, 7 exhorts to prayer, 13 to enter in at the narrow gate, 15 and to beware of false prophets.

1 ¶ Do not judge, that you may not be judged;

2 for with whatever judgment you judge, you will be judged; and with whatever measure you measure, it will be measured again to you.

3 But why do you look on the chip that *is* in the eye of your brother, but do not see the beam in your eye?

4 Or how will you say to your brother, Allow me to take out the chip from your eye; and behold, the beam *is* in your eye!

5 Hypocrite, first take the beam out of your eye, and then you will see clearly to take the chip out of the eye of your brother.

6 Do not give that which *is* holy to the dogs, nor throw your pearls before the pigs, that they should not trample them with their feet, and turning, they charge you.

7 ¶ Ask, and it will be given to you; seek, and you will find; knock, and it will be opened to you.

8 For each one that asks receives, and the *one* that seeks finds; and to the *one* knocking, it will be opened.

9 Or what man of you is there, if his son should ask a loaf of him, not a stone will he give him, *will he*?

10 And if he should ask a fish, not a snake will he give him, *will he*?

11 Therefore, if you, being evil, know to give good gifts to your children, how much more will your Father, the *One* in Heaven give good things to those that ask Him?

12 ¶ Therefore, all things, as many *things* as you ever desire that men should do to you, so also you should do to them; for this is the Law and the Prophets.

13 Go in through the narrow gate; for wide *is* the gate and broad *is* the way that leads away to destruction, and many are the ones entering in through it.

14 For narrow *is* the gate, and constricted *is* the way that leads away into life, and few are the ones finding it.

15 ¶ But beware of the false prophets who come to you in sheep's clothing, but inside they are plundering wolves.

16 From their fruits you shall know them. Do they gather grapes from thorns, or figs from thistles?

17 So every good tree produces good fruits, but the corrupt tree produces evil fruits.

18 A good tree cannot produce evil fruits, nor a corrupt tree produce good fruits.

19 Every tree not producing good fruit is cut down and is thrown into fire.

20 Surely from their fruits you shall know them.

21 ¶ Not everyone who says to Me, Lord, Lord, will enter into the kingdom of Heaven, but the *ones* who do the will of My Father in Heaven.

22 Many will say to Me in that day, Lord, Lord, did we not prophesy in Your name, and in Your name cast out demons, and in Your name do many works of power?

23 And then I will declare to them, I never knew you; "depart from Me, *the ones* working lawlessness!" *Psa. 6:8*

24 Therefore everyone who hears these Words from Me, and does them, I will compare him to a wise man who built his house on the rock;

25 and the rain came down, and the rivers came up, and the winds blew, and fell against that house; but it did not fall, for it had been founded on the rock.

26 And everyone who hears these words of Mine, and who does not do them, *he* shall be compared to a foolish man who built his house on the sand;

27 and the rain came down, and the rivers came up, and the winds blew and beat against that house; and it fell, and great was the fall of it.

28 And it happened, when Jesus had finished these words, the crowds were astonished at His doctrine.

29 For He was teaching them as having authority, and not as the scribes.

Matthew 8

2 Christ cleanses the leper, 5 heals the centurion's servant, 14 Peter's mother-in-law, 16 and many diseased: 18 shows how He is to be followed: 23 stills the tempest, 28 drives the demons from two men possessed, 31 and allows them to go into pigs.

1 ¶ And He having come down from the mount, great crowds followed Him.

2 And behold, coming up, a leper worshiped Him, saying, Lord, If You will, You are able to cleanse me.

3 And stretching out His hand, Jesus touched him, saying, I will! Be cleansed! And instantly his leprosy was cleansed.

4 And Jesus said to him, See that you tell no one, but go, show yourself to the priest and offer the gift which Moses commanded, for a testimony to them.

5 ¶ And Jesus, entering into Capernaum, a centurion came near to Him, begging Him,

6 and saying, Lord, my child has been laid in the house, a paralytic, being grievously tormented.

7 And Jesus said to him, I will come and heal him.

8 And answering, the centurion said, Lord, I am not worthy that You should enter under my roof, but only speak *by* a word and my child will be healed.

9 For I am also a man under authority, having soldiers under myself. And I say to this one, Go; and he goes; and to another, Come; and he comes; and to my slave, Do this; and he does *it*.

10 And hearing, Jesus marveled, and said to those following, Truly I say to you, Not even in Israel did I find so much faith.

11 But I say to you that many will come from east and west, and will recline with Abraham and Isaac and Jacob in the kingdom of Heaven,

12 but the sons of the kingdom shall be cast out into the outer darkness. There shall be weeping and gnashing of the teeth.

13 And Jesus said to the centurion, Go, and as you have believed, *so* let it be to you. And his child was healed in that hour.

14 ¶ And coming into the house of Peter, Jesus saw his mother-in-law laid *out* and burning with fever.

15 And He touched her hand, and her fever left her. And she rose up and served Him.

16 And evening becoming, they brought to Him many having been possessed by demons. And He cast out the spirits by a word, and He healed all those badly having *illness*,

17 so that it might be fulfilled that spoken through Isaiah the prophet, saying, "He took *upon Himself* our weaknesses, and bore *our* diseases." *Isa. 53:4*

18 ¶ And seeing great crowds around Him, Jesus gave orders to go away to the other side.

19 And one scribe, coming near, said to Him, Teacher, I will follow You wherever you go.

20 And Jesus said to him, The foxes have holes, and the birds of the heaven *have* nests, but the Son of Man has nowhere He may lay *His* head.

21 And another of His disciples said to Him, Lord, allow me first to go away and bury my father.

22 But Jesus said to him, Follow Me, and allow the dead *ones* to bury their own dead *ones*.

23 ¶ And He entering into the boat, His disciples followed Him.

24 And, behold, a great shaking occurred in the sea, so that the boat was covered by the waves; but He was sleeping.

25 And coming near, His disciples awakened Him, saying, Lord, save us! We are perishing.

26 And He said to them, Why are you afraid, little-faiths? Then rising up, He rebuked the winds and the sea. And a great calm occurred.

27 And the men marveled, saying, What kind *of man* is this, that even the winds and the sea obey Him?

28 ¶ And He coming to the other side, into the country of the Gergesenes, two men being demon-possessed met Him coming out of the tombs, very violent, so that no one was able to pass through that way.

29 And, behold! They cried out, saying, What *is* to us and to You, Jesus, Son of

God? Have You come here beforetime to torment us?

30 And far off from them there was a herd of many pigs feeding.

31 And the demons begged Him, saying, If You cast us out, allow us to go away into the herd of pigs.

32 And He said to them, Go! And coming out, these went away into the herd of pigs. And, behold, all the herd of pigs rushed violently down the precipice into the sea, and died in the waters.

33 But the *ones* who fed *them* fled, and going into the city, *they* told all the things of the ones who had been demon-possessed.

34 And, behold, all the city went out to meet with Jesus. And seeing Him, they begged that He move away from their borders.

Matthew 9

2 Christ cures a paralytic, 9 calls Matthew the tax collector, 10 eats with tax collectors and sinners, 14 defends his disciples for not fasting, 20 cures the bloody issue, 23 raises Jairus' daughter from the dead, 27 gives sight to two blind men, 32 heals a dumb man possessed.

1 ¶ And entering into the boat, He passed over and came to *His* own city.

2 And, behold! They were bringing a paralytic lying on a pallet to Him. And seeing their faith, Jesus said to the paralyzed *one*, Have courage, child. Your sins have been remitted.

3 And, behold, some of the scribes said within themselves, This one blasphemes.

4 And seeing their thoughts, Jesus said, Why do you think evil in your hearts?

5 For what is easier, to say, Your sins have been remitted, or to say, Rise up and walk?

6 But that you may know that the Son of Man has authority on earth to remit sins, then He said to the paralytic, Rising up, lift up your pallet and go to your house.

7 And rising up, he went away to his house.

8 And seeing, the crowds marveled, and *they* glorified God, the *One* giving such authority to men.

9 ¶ And passing from there, Jesus saw a man named Matthew sitting at the tax office. And *He* said to him, Follow Me. And rising up, he followed Him.

10 And it happened as He reclined in the house, behold, many tax collectors and sinners having come, *these* were reclining with Jesus and His disciples.

11 And seeing, the Pharisees said to His disciples, Why does your teacher eat with tax collectors and sinners?

12 But Jesus hearing, He said to them, The ones being strong have no need of a healer, but the ones badly having *illness*.

13 But going, learn what *this is*, "I desire mercy and not sacrifice." For I did not come to call righteous *ones*, but sinners to repentance. *Hos. 6:6*

14 ¶ Then the disciples of John came to Him, saying, Why do we and the Pharisees fast much, and Your disciples do not fast?

15 And Jesus said to them, Can the sons of the bridechamber mourn as long as the bridegroom is with them? But the days will come when the bridegroom will have been taken from them, and then they will fast.

16 But no one puts a piece of new cloth onto an old garment. For its filling up takes away from the garment, and a worse tear takes *its* place.

17 Nor do they put new wine into old wineskins; otherwise, the wineskins are burst, and the wine pours out, and the wineskins will be ruined. But they put new wine into fresh wineskins, and both are preserved together.

18 ¶ *As He was* speaking these things to them, behold, one ruler coming worshiped before Him, saying, My daughter has just now died; but coming lay Your hand on her, and she will live.

19 And rising up, Jesus and His disciples followed him.

20 And behold, a woman who had a flow of blood for twelve years came near behind *Him, and she* grasped the fringe of His garment.

21 For she said within herself, If only I shall grasp His garment, I will be cured.

22 But turning and seeing her, Jesus said, Take courage, daughter; your faith has cured you. And the woman was cured from that hour.

23 And Jesus coming into the house of the ruler, and seeing the flute-players and the crowd causing a tumult,

24 *He* says to them, Go back, for the little girl has not died, but she sleeps. And they ridiculed Him.

25 But when the crowd had been put out, entering He took hold of her hand, and the little girl rose up.

26 And this report went out into all that land.

27 ¶ And Jesus passing on from there, two blind *ones* followed Him, crying and saying, Have mercy on us, Son of David.

28 And coming into the house, the blind *ones* came near to Him. And Jesus says to them, Do you believe that I am able to do this? And they said to Him, Yes, Lord.

29 Then He touched their eyes, saying, According to your faith let it be to you.

30 And their eyes were opened. And Jesus strictly ordered them, saying, See, let no one know.

31 But going out, they spread news about Him in all that land.

32 And as they were going out, behold, they brought to Him a mute man having been possessed by a demon.

33 And the demon being cast out, the mute *one* spoke. And the crowds marveled, saying, Never it appeared thus in Israel.

34 But the Pharisees said, He casts out the demons by the ruler of the demons.

35 ¶ And Jesus went about all the cities and the villages teaching in their synagogues, and proclaiming the gospel of the kingdom, and healing every disease and every infirmity of body among the people.

36 And seeing the crowds, He was moved with pity concerning them, because they were weary and scattered, like sheep having no shepherd.

37 Then He said to His disciples, The harvest truly *is* much, but the workers few.

38 Pray, therefore, *to* the Lord of the harvest that He send out workers into His harvest.

Matthew 10

1 Christ sends his twelve apostles, enabling them with power to do cures, 5 gives them their charge, teaches them, 16 comforts them against persecutions: 40 and promises a blessing to those that receive them.

1 ¶ And having called His twelve disciples, He gave them authority *over* unclean spirits, so as to cast them out, and to heal every disease and every infirmity *of body*.

2 And the names of the twelve apostles are these: First, Simon who is called Peter and his brother Andrew, James the *son* of Zebedee and his brother John,

3 Philip, and Bartholomew, Thomas, and Matthew the tax-collector, James *the son* of Alpheus, and Lebbaeus, whose last name was Thaddaeus,

4 Simon the Canaanite, and Judas Iscariot, the *one* also giving Him over.

5 ¶ Jesus sent these twelve out, charging them, saying: Do not go into the way of the nations, and do not go into a Samaritan city.

6 But rather go to the lost sheep of *the* house of Israel.

7 And going on, proclaim, saying, The kingdom of Heaven has drawn near.

8 Heal feeble *ones*, cleanse lepers, raise dead *ones*, cast out demons. You freely received, freely give.

9 Do not acquire gold, nor silver, nor copper in your belts,

10 nor provision bag for *the* road, nor two tunics, nor sandals, nor staves. For the worker is worthy of his food.

11 And into whatever city or village you enter, search out who in it is worthy; and remain there until you go out.

12 But entering into the house, greet it;

13 and if the house truly is worthy, let your peace come upon it. But if it is not worthy, let your peace return to you.

14 And whoever will not receive you, nor will hear your words, having gone out of that house or city, shake off the dust from your feet.

15 Truly I say to you, It will be more bearable to the land of Sodom and Gomorrah in *the* day of judgment than *for* that city.

16 ¶ Behold, I send you forth as sheep in *the* midst of wolves. Therefore, be wise as serpents and harmless as doves.

17 But beware of men. For they will give you over to councils, and they will scourge you in their synagogues.

18 And also you will be brought before governors and kings for My sake, for a testimony to them and to the nations.

19 But when they give you over, do not be anxious how or what you should say, for it is given to you in that hour what you should say.

20 For you are not the ones speaking, but the Spirit of your Father who speaks in you.

21 But brother will give over brother to death, and *the* father *his* child. And children will rise up against parents and will put them to death.

22 And you will be hated by all on account of My name, but the *one* enduring to *the* end shall be kept safe.

23 But when they persecute you in this city, flee to another. For truly I say to you, not will you have finished the cities of Israel, not *at all* until the Son of Man comes.

24 A disciple is not above the teacher, nor a slave above his lord.

25 *It is* enough for the disciple *to* become as his teacher, and the slave as his lord. If they called the master of the house Beelzebub, how much more they of his household?

26 Therefore, you should not fear them, for nothing is covered which will not be uncovered; and hidden, which will not be made known.

27 What I say to you in the darkness, speak in the light. And what you hear in the ear, proclaim on the housetops.

28 And you should not fear the *ones* killing the body, but not being able to kill the soul. But rather fear Him, the *One* being able to destroy both soul and body in Hell.

29 Are not two sparrows sold for an assarion? Yet not one of them shall fall to the ground without your Father.

30 But even the hairs of your head are all numbered.

31 Therefore do not fear; you are better than many sparrows.

32 Therefore everyone who shall confess Me before men, I will also confess him before My Father, the *One* in Heaven.

33 But whoever denies Me before men, I also will deny him before My Father, the *One* in Heaven.

34 Do not think that I came to send peace on earth. I did not come to send peace, but a sword.

35 I came to divide a man against his father, and a daughter against her mother, and a bride against her mother-in-law.

36 "Hostile ones of the man *shall be* those of his house." *Mic. 7:6*

37 The *one* loving father or mother more than Me is not worthy of Me. And the *one* loving son or daughter more than Me is not worthy of Me.

38 And who does not take up his cross and follow after Me is not worthy of Me.

39 The *one* finding his life shall lose it. And the *one* losing his life on account of Me shall find it.

40 The *one* receiving you receives Me, and the *one* receiving Me receives Him, the *One* sending Me.

41 The *one* receiving a prophet in *the* name of a prophet will receive a prophet's reward, and the *one* receiving a just *one* in the name of a just *one* will receive a just *one's* reward.

42 And whoever gives only a cup of cold *water to* drink to one of these little ones in *the* name of a disciple, truly I say to you, he will not lose his reward, not *ever*!

Matthew 11

2 John sends His disciples to Christ. 7 Christ's testimony concerning John. 18 The opinion of the people concerning John and Christ. 20 Christ upbraids the unthankfulness and unrepentance of Chorazin, Bethsaida, and Capernaum: 28 and calls to Him all such as feel the burden of their sins.

1 ¶ And it happened when Jesus finished commanding His twelve disciples, He left there to teach and to proclaim in their cities.

2 But hearing in the prison of the works of Christ, sending two of his disciples,

3 John said to Him, Are You the *One* coming, or are we to look for another?

4 And answering, Jesus said to them, Going, relate to John what you hear and see:

5 The blind *ones* receive sight, and the lame *ones* walk; lepers are cleansed, and the deaf *ones* hear; the dead *ones* are raised, and the poor *ones* are given the gospel. *Isa. 61:1*

6 And blessed is the *one*, whoever *is* not caused to stumble in Me.

7 ¶ But as these were going, Jesus began to say to the crowds about John, What did you go out into the wilderness to behold? A reed being shaken with the wind?

8 But what did you go out to see? A man being clothed in soft garments? Behold, those wearing soft things are in the houses of kings.

9 But what did you go out to see? A prophet? Yes, I say to you, and *one* more excellent than a prophet.

10 For this is *the one* about whom it has been written: "Behold, I send out My messenger before Your face, who shall prepare Your way before You." *Mal. 3:1*

11 Truly I say to you, *There* has not arisen among *those* born of a woman *any* greater than John the Baptist. But the least in the kingdom of Heaven is greater than he is.

12 But from the days of John the Baptist until now, the kingdom of Heaven suffers violence, and *the* violent seize it.

13 For all the Prophets and the Law prophesied until John.

14 And if you are willing to receive, he is Elijah, the *one* going to come.

15 The *one* having ears to hear, let him hear.

16 ¶ But to what shall I compare this generation? It is like little children sitting in *the* markets, and calling to their companions,

17 and saying, We piped to you, and you did not dance; we mourned to you, and you did not wail.

18 For John came neither eating nor drinking, and they say, He has a demon.

19 The Son of Man came eating and drinking, and they say, Behold, a gluttonous man and a wine drinker, and a friend of tax collectors, and of sinners. And wisdom was justified of her children.

20 Then He began to reproach the cities in which most of His powerful acts had occurred, for they did not repent.

21 Woe to you, Chorazin! Woe to you, Bethsaida! For if the powerful acts which had happened in you had happened in Tyre and Sidon, they would have repented long ago in sackcloth and ashes.

22 But I say to you, It shall be more bearable for Tyre and Sidon in *the* day of judgment than for you.

23 And you, Capernaum, who "have been exalted to the heaven, *you* will be thrown down to Hades." For if the powerful acts happening in you had taken place in Sodom, it would remain until today. *Isa. 14:13, 15*

24 But I say to you, It will be more bearable for the land of Sodom in *the* day of judgment than for you.

25 ¶ Answering at that time, Jesus said, I praise You, Father, Lord of Heaven and of earth, because You hid these things from *the* sophisticated and learned *ones* and revealed them to babes.

26 Yes, Father, for so it was pleasing before You.

27 All things were given over to Me by My Father; and no one knows the Son except the Father; nor does anyone know the Father, except the Son, and to whomever the Son purposes to reveal *Him*.

28 Come to Me, all those laboring and being burdened, and I will give you rest.

29 Take My yoke upon you and learn from Me, because I am a meek and lowly *one* in heart, "and you will find rest to your souls." *Jer. 6:16*

30 For My yoke *is* easy, and My burden is light.

Matthew 12

1 Christ reproves the blindness of the Pharisees concerning the breach of the sabbath. 22 He heals the blind and dumb one. 31 Blasphemy against the Holy Ghost shall never be forgiven. 38 He rebukes the unfaithful, who seek a sign:

1 ¶ At that time on the sabbath, Jesus went through the grain fields. And His disciples were hungry, and began to pluck heads *of grain* and to eat.

2 But seeing, the Pharisees said to Him, Behold, your disciples are doing what it is not lawful to do on a sabbath.

3 But He said to them, Have you not read what David did, when he and the *ones* with him hungered?

4 How he entered into the house of God, and he ate the Loaves of the Presentation, which it was not lawful for him to eat, nor for *the ones* with him, but for the priests only?

5 Or have you not read in the Law that on the sabbaths the priests in the temple profane the sabbath and are guiltless?

6 But I say to you, *One* greater than the temple is here.

7 But if you had known what *this* is, "I desire mercy and not sacrifice," you would not have condemned the guiltless. *Hos. 6:6*

8 For the Son of Man is also Lord of the sabbath.

9 And moving from there, He came into their synagogue.

10 And, behold, a man having *a* withered hand was there. And they asked Him, saying, Is it lawful to heal on the sabbaths? (that they might accuse Him).

11 But He said to them, What man of you will be who will have one sheep, and if this one fall into a pit on the sabbaths, will he not lay hold of it and raise *it* up?

12 How much more, then, does a man excel a sheep! So that it is lawful to do well on the sabbath.

13 Then He said to the man, Stretch out your hand! And he stretched out. And it was restored sound as the other.

14 ¶ But as they were leaving, the Pharisees took up a council against Him, how they might destroy Him.

15 But knowing, Jesus withdrew from there. And great crowds followed Him, and He healed them all

16 and warned them that they should not make Him manifest.

17 So that might be fulfilled that spoken through Isaiah the prophet, saying,

18 "Behold My Child whom I chose, My Beloved, in whom My soul has delighted! I will put My Spirit on Him, and He will declare judgment to the nations.

19 He will not strive nor cry out, nor will anyone hear His voice in the streets.

20 A bruised reed He will not break, and smoking flax He will not quench, until He bring forth judgment to victory." *Isa. 42:1-3*

21 "And the nations will hope in His name." *Isa. 42:1-4*

22 ¶ Then a blind and mute *one* having been demon-possessed was brought to Him, And He healed him, so that the blind and mute *one could* both speak and see.

23 And all the crowds were amazed, and said, Is this not the Son of David?

24 But hearing, the Pharisees said, This *One* does not cast out demons except by Beelzebub, ruler of the demons.

25 But Jesus, knowing their thoughts, He said to them, Every kingdom divided against itself is brought to desolation. And every city or house divided against itself will not stand.

26 And if Satan throws out Satan, he was divided against himself. How then will his kingdom stand?

27 And if I cast out the demons by Beelzebub, by whom do your sons cast *them* out? Because of this, they shall be your judges.

28 But if I cast out the demons by the Spirit of God, then the kingdom of God has come on you.

29 Or how is anyone able to enter the house of the strong one and plunder his goods, if he does not first bind the strong one; and then he will plunder his house?

30 The *one* who is not with Me is against Me, and the *one* who does not gather with Me scatters.

31 Because of this, I say to you, Every sin and blasphemy shall be forgiven to men, but the blasphemy concerning the Spirit shall not be forgiven to men.

32 And whoever speaks a word against the Son of Man, it shall be forgiven him. But whoever speaks against the Holy Spirit, it shall not be forgiven him, not in this age nor in the coming *one*.

33 Either make the tree good and its fruit good, or make the tree corrupt and its fruit corrupt; for the tree is known by the fruit.

34 Offspring of vipers! How can you, being evil, speak good things? For out of the abundance of the heart the mouth speaks.

35 The good man out of the good treasure of the heart puts forth good things. And the evil man out of the evil treasure puts forth evil *things*.

36 But I say to you, that every idle word, whatever men may speak, they shall give an account of it in *the* day of judgment

37 For by your words you will be justified, and by your words you will be condemned.

38 ¶ Then some of the scribes and Pharisees answered, saying, Teacher, we desire to see a sign from You.

39 But answering, He said to them, An evil and adulterous generation seeks a sign, and a sign shall not be given to it, except the sign of Jonah the prophet.

40 And even as "Jonah was in the belly of the huge fish three days and three nights," so shall the Son of Man be in the heart of the earth three days and three nights. *Jon. 1:17*

41 Men, Ninevites, will stand up in the Judgment with this generation and will condemn it. For they repented at the preaching of Jonah, and, behold, a Greater-than-Jonah *is* here.

42 *The* queen of *the* south will be raised in the Judgment with this generation and will condemn it. For she came from the ends of the earth to hear the wisdom of Solomon, and, behold, a Greater-than-Solomon *is* here.

43 But when the unclean spirit goes from a man, he goes through dry places seeking rest and does not find *it*.

44 Then he says, I will return to my house from which I came out. And coming, he finds *it* standing empty, swept and decorated.

45 Then he goes and takes with him seven other spirits more evil than himself, and entering dwells there. And the last things of that man become worse than the first. So it will be also to this evil generation.

46 ¶ But while He was yet speaking to the crowds, behold, *His* mother and brothers were standing outside, seeking to speak to Him.

47 Then one said to Him, Behold, Your mother and Your brothers are standing outside, seeking to speak to You.

48 But answering, He said to the *one* speaking to Him, Who is My mother? And who are My brothers?

49 And stretching out His hand to His disciples, He said, Behold, My mother and My brothers.

50 For whoever does the will of My Father in Heaven, that one is My brother and sister and mother.

Matthew 13

3 The parable of the sower and the seed. 24 The parable of the tares, 31 of the mustard seed, 33 of the leaven, 44 of the hidden treasure, 45 of the pearl, 47 of the dragnet cast into the sea.

1 ¶ And going out from the house in that day, Jesus sat down by the sea.

2 And great crowds were gathered to Him, so that having entered the boat, He sat down. And all the crowd stood on the shore.

3 And He spoke to them many things in parables, saying: Behold, the sower went out to sow.

4 And in his sowing, some fell by the roadside, and the birds came and ate them.

5 And other fell on the stony places where they did not have much earth, and it immediately sprang up because *it* had no depth of earth.

6 And *the* sun rising, it was scorched; even because of having no root, it was dried up.

7 And other fell on the thorn-bushes, and the thorn-bushes grew up and choked them.

8 And other fell on the good ground and yielded fruit; indeed, one a hundredfold, and one sixty, and one thirty.

9 The *one* having ears to hear, let him hear.

10 And coming near, the disciples said to Him, Why do You speak to them in parables?

11 And answering, He said to them, To you it has been given to know the mysteries of the kingdom of Heaven, but it has not been given to those.

12 For whoever has, to him will be given, and he will have overabundance. But whoever does not have, even what he has will be taken from him.

13 Because of this, I speak to them in parables, because seeing they do not see, and hearing they do not hear, nor do they understand.

14 And the prophecy of Isaiah is fulfilled on them, which says, "In hearing you will hear and not understand, not *ever;* and seeing you will see and not perceive, not *ever*.

15 For the heart of this people has grown fat, and they heard heavily with the ears, and they have closed their eyes, that they not see with the eyes, or hear with the ears,

and understand with the heart, and be converted, and I *shall* heal them." *Isa. 6:9, 10*

16 But your eyes *are* blessed because they see; and your ears because they hear.

17 For truly I tell you that many prophets and righteous ones longed to see what you see and did not see, and to hear what you hear and did not hear.

18 You, therefore, hear the parable of the sower:

19 Everyone hearing the Word of the kingdom, and not understanding, *then* the evil *one* comes and catches away that which was sown in his heart: this is that sown by the roadside.

20 And the *seed* sown on the rocky *places* is this: the *one* hearing the Word, and immediately receiving it with joy,

21 but has no root in himself, but is temporary, and tribulation, or persecution occurring because of the Word, he is at once stumbled.

22 And the *seed* sown into the thornbushes is this: the *one* hearing the Word, and the anxiety of this age, and the deceit of riches, choke the Word, and it becomes unfruitful.

23 But the *seed* sown on the good ground is this: the *one* hearing the Word, and understanding it, who indeed bears and produces fruit, one truly a hundredfold, and one sixty, and one thirty.

24 ¶ He put before them another parable, saying: The kingdom of Heaven is compared to a man sowing good seed in his field.

25 But while the men were sleeping, a hostile *one* came to him and sowed darnel in the midst of the wheat, and went away.

26 And when the blade sprouted and produced fruit, then the darnel also appeared.

27 And coming near, the slaves of the housemaster said to him, Lord, did you not sow good seed in your field? Then from where does it have the darnel?

28 And he said to them, A hostile man did this. And the slaves said to him, Do you desire, then, that going out we should gather them?

29 But he said, No, lest gathering the darnel you should uproot the wheat with them.

30 Allow both to grow together until the harvest. And in the time of the harvest I will say to the reapers, First gather the darnel, and bind them into bundles to burn them, but gather the wheat into my granary.

31 He put another parable before them, saying: The kingdom of Heaven is compared to a grain of mustard, which taking, a man sowed in his field;

32 which indeed is smaller than all the seeds, but when it is grown it is greater *than* the herbs, and becomes a tree, so that the birds of the heaven come and dwell in its branches.

33 He spoke another parable to them: The kingdom of Heaven is compared to leaven, which taking, a woman hid in three measures of meal until the whole was leavened.

34 Jesus spoke all these things in parables to the crowds, and He did not speak to them without a parable,

35 so that was fulfilled that spoken through the prophet, saying: "I will open My mouth in parables; I will speak out things hidden from *the* foundation of *the* world." *Psa. 78:2*

36 Then sending away the crowds, Jesus came into the house. And His disciples came to Him, saying, Explain to us the parable of the darnel of the field.

37 And answering, He said to them, The *One* sowing the good seed is the Son of Man.

38 And the field is the world; and the good seed, these are the sons of the kingdom; but the darnel are the sons of the evil *one*.

39 And the hostile *one* who sowed them is the devil, and the harvest is the end of the age, and the angels are the reapers.

40 Then as the darnel is gathered and is consumed in the fire, so it will be in the completion of this age.

41 The Son of Man will send forth His angels, and they will gather out of His kingdom all the stumbling blocks, and those who practice lawlessness.

42 And they will throw them into the furnace of fire; there will be weeping and gnashing of the teeth.

43 Then the righteous *ones* will shine out like the sun in the kingdom of their Father. The *one* having ears to hear, let him hear.

44 ¶ Again, the kingdom of Heaven is compared to treasure being hidden in the field, which finding, a man hid; and for the joy of it, he goes and sells all things, as many as he has, and buys that field.

45 Again, the kingdom of Heaven is compared to a man, a merchant seeking excellent pearls;

46 who finding one very precious pearl, going away has sold all things, as many as he had, and bought it.

47 Again, the kingdom of Heaven is compared to a drag net thrown into the sea, and gathering together of every kind;

48 which, when it was filled, drawing it up on the shore, and sitting down, *they* gathered the good into containers, and they threw out the rotten.

49 So it will be in the completion of the age: the angels will go out and will separate the evil *ones* from the midst of the righteous *ones*,

50 and will throw them into the furnace of fire; there will be weeping and gnashing of the teeth.

51 Jesus said to them, Have you understood all these things? They said to Him, Yes, Lord.

52 And He said to them, Because of this, every scribe schooled to the kingdom of Heaven is like a man, a master of a house, who puts forth out of his treasure new and old.

53 ¶ And it happened, when Jesus had finished these parables, He moved from there.

54 And coming into His own country, He taught them in their synagogue, so that they were astonished, and said, from where did this *One get* this wisdom, and the powerful works?

55 Is this not the carpenter's son? *Is* not His mother called Mary, and His brothers, James, and Joses, and Simon, and Judas?

56 And are not His sisters all with us? From where then did this *One* get all these things?

57 And they were stumbled in Him. But Jesus said to them, A prophet is not without honor, except in his own fatherland, and in his own house.

58 And He did not do many works of power there because of their unbelief.

Matthew 14

1 Herod's opinion of Christ. 3 Why John Baptist was beheaded. 13 Jesus departs to a desert place: 15 He feeds five thousand men with five loaves and two fish: 22 He walks on the sea: 34 and landing at Gennesaret, heals the sick.

1 ¶ At that time Herod the tetrarch heard the fame of Jesus.

2 And he said to his servants, This is John the Baptist. He has risen from the dead *ones*, and because of this, powerful works are at work in him.

3 For seizing John, Herod bound him and put *him* into prison, because of Herodias, the wife of his brother Philip.

4 For John said to him, It is not lawful for you to have her.

5 And desiring to kill him, he feared the multitude, because they held him as a prophet.

6 But a birthday *feast for* Herod being held, the daughter of Herodias danced in the midst and pleased Herod.

7 From which he assented with an oath to give her whatever she should ask.

8 But she being urged on by her mother, she says, Give me here on a platter the head of John the Baptist.

9 And the king was grieved, but because of the oaths, and those who reclined with *him*, he ordered *it* to be given.

10 And sending, he beheaded John in the prison.

11 And his head was brought on a platter and was given to the girl, and she brought *it* to her mother.

12 And having come, his disciples took the body and buried it; and coming, *they* told Jesus.

13 ¶ And having heard, Jesus withdrew privately from there in a boat, into a deserted place. And hearing, the crowds followed Him on foot out of the cities.

14 And going out, Jesus saw a great crowd and was filled with pity toward them. And He healed the *ones* of them being infirm.

15 And evening coming, His disciples came near to Him saying, The place is deserted, and the hour is already gone by. Dismiss the crowds, that going away into the villages they may buy foods for themselves.

16 But Jesus said to them, They have no need to go away. You give them *food* to eat.

17 But they said to Him, We have nothing here except five loaves and two fish.

18 And He said, Bring them here to Me.

19 And commanding the crowds to recline on the grass, and taking the five loaves and two fish, looking up to Heaven, He blessed. And breaking, He gave the loaves to the disciples, and the disciples *gave* to the crowds.

20 And they all ate and were satisfied. And they took up the left over pieces, twelve baskets full.

21 And the *ones* eating were about five thousand men, besides women and children.

22 ¶ And immediately Jesus constrained His disciples to enter into the boat and to go before Him to the other side until He should dismiss the crowds.

23 And having dismissed the crowds, He went up into the mountain alone to pray. And evening coming on, He was there alone.

24 But the boat was already in *the* middle of the sea, distressed by the waves, for the wind was contrary.

25 But in the fourth watch of the night, Jesus went out to them, walking on the sea.

26 And seeing Him walking on the sea, the disciples were troubled, saying, It is a phantom! And they cried out from the fear.

27 But immediately Jesus spoke to them, saying, Have courage, I AM! Do not fear.

28 And answering Him, Peter said, Lord, if it is You, command me to come to You on the waters.

29 And He said, Come! And going down from the boat, Peter walked on the waters to go to Jesus.

30 But seeing the wind strong, he was afraid, and beginning to sink, he cried out, saying, Lord, save me!

31 And immediately stretching out the hand, Jesus took hold of him, and said to him, Little-faith, at what did you doubt?

32 And coming into the boat, the wind ceased.

33 And those in the boat came and worshiped Him, saying, Truly, You are the Son of God.

34 ¶ And having passed over, they came to the land of Gennesaret.

35 And recognizing Him, the men of that place sent out to all that neighborhood, and brought to Him all those badly having *illness*.

36 And *they* begged Him that they might touch the fringe of His garment. And as many as touched were completely cured.

Matthew 15

3 Christ questions the scribes and Pharisees: 11 teaches how that which goes into the mouth does not defile a man. 21 He heals the daughter of the woman of Canaan, 32 and with seven loaves and a few small fish feeds four thousand people.

1 ¶ Then the scribes and Pharisees came to Jesus from Jerusalem, saying,

2 Why do Your disciples transgress the tradition of the elders? For they do not wash their hands when they eat bread.

3 But answering He said to them, And why do you transgress the command of God on account of your tradition?

4 For God commanded, saying, "Honor your father and mother," *Ex. 20:12; Deut. 5:16* also, "He speaking evil of father or mother, by death let him die." *Exodus 21:17*

5 But you say, Whoever says to the father or the mother, A gift, whatever you would gain from me;

6 and he does not honor his father or his mother, not *at all*. And you nullified the command of God on account of your tradition.

7 Hypocrites! Well did Isaiah prophesy concerning you, saying:

8 "This people draws near to Me with their mouth, and with the lips honor Me; but their heart holds away from Me.

9 But in vain they worship Me, teaching *as* doctrines *the* precepts of men." *Isa. 29:13*

10 ¶ And calling the crowd near, He said to them, Hear and understand:

11 *It is* not the *thing* entering into the mouth that defiles the man, but the *thing* coming forth out of the mouth, this defiles the man.

12 Then coming, the disciples said to Him, You know that hearing the Word, the Pharisees were stumbled?

13 But answering, He said, Every plant which My heavenly Father has not planted shall be rooted up.

14 Leave them alone. They are blind leaders of the blind; and if the blind lead the blind, both will fall into a pit.

15 And answering, Peter said to Him, Explain this parable to us.

16 But Jesus said, Are you also still not understanding?

17 Do you not yet perceive that everything entering into the mouth goes into the belly, and is expelled into *the* latrine?

18 But the things which come out of the mouth come forth from the heart, and these defile the man.

19 For out of the heart come forth evil reasonings, murders, adulteries, fornications, thefts, false witnessings, blasphemies.

20 These things are the *things* defiling the man. But eating with unwashed hands does not defile the man.

21 ¶ And going out from there, Jesus withdrew to the parts of Tyre and Sidon.

22 And, behold, a woman of Canaan coming forth from those borders cried out to Him, saying, Have mercy on me, Lord, Son of David! My daughter is badly being demon-possessed.

23 But He did not answer her a word. And coming near, His disciples asked Him, saying, Send her away, for she cries out behind us.

24 But answering, He said, I was not sent except to the lost sheep of *the* house of Israel.

25 But coming, she worshiped Him, saying, Lord, help me!

26 But answering, He said, It is not good to take the bread of the children to throw *it* to the little dogs.

27 But she said, Yes, Lord; for even the little dogs eat of the crumbs falling from the table of their lords.

28 Then answering, Jesus said to her, O woman, great is your faith; let it be to you as you desire. And her daughter was healed from that hour.

29 ¶ And moving from there, Jesus came beside the Sea of Galilee. And going up into the mountain, He sat there.

30 And great crowds came to Him, having with them lame *ones*, blind *ones*, mute *ones*, maimed *ones*, and many others. And they threw them down at the feet of Jesus. And He healed them;

31 so that the crowds marveled, seeing mute *ones* speaking, maimed *ones* sound, lame *ones* walking, and blind *ones* seeing. And they glorified the God of Israel.

32 But having called His disciples near, Jesus said, I am filled with pity on the crowd, because they already have remained with Me three days and have nothing they may eat. And I do not desire to send them away fasting, that they may not faint in the way.

33 And His disciples said to Him, From where in a deserted *place will come* to us so many loaves as to satisfy so great a crowd?

34 And Jesus said to them, How many loaves do you have? And they said, Seven, and a few small fish.

35 And He ordered the crowds to recline on the ground.

36 And taking the seven loaves and the fish, giving thanks, He broke and gave to His disciples, and the disciples to the crowd.

37 And all ate and were satisfied. And they took up the left over pieces, seven baskets full.

38 And the ones eating were four thousand men, apart from women and children.

39 And sending away the crowds He went into the boat and came to the borders of Magdala.

Matthew 16

1 The Pharisees require a sign. 6 Jesus warns His disciples of the leaven of the Pharisees and Sadducees. 16 Peter's confession of Him. 21 Jesus foretells His death, 23 reproving Peter for dissuading Him from His saying 24 and admonishes those that follow Him, to bear the cross.

1 ¶ And coming, the Pharisees and Sadducees asked *Him* to show them a sign out of the heaven, tempting *Him.*

2 But answering, He said to them, Evening coming on, you say, Clear sky, for the heaven is red.

3 And at morning, Today a winter storm, for the heaven is red, being overcast. Hypocrites! You indeed know how to discern the face of the heaven, but you cannot the signs of the times.

4 An evil and adulterous generation seeks a sign, and a sign will not be given to it,

except the sign of Jonah the prophet. And leaving them, He went away.

5 ¶ And His disciples coming to the other side, they forgot to take loaves.

6 And Jesus said to them, Watch and take heed from the leaven of the Pharisees and Sadducees.

7 And they reasoned among themselves, saying, We did not take loaves.

8 And knowing, Jesus said to them, Why do you reason among yourselves that you took no loaves, little-faiths?

9 Do you not perceive nor recall the five loaves of the five thousand, and how many baskets you took up?

10 Neither the seven loaves of the four thousand, and how many baskets you took up?

11 How do you not perceive that *it was* not about loaves that I said to you to take heed from the leaven of the Pharisees and Sadducees?

12 Then they knew that He did not say to take heed from the leaven of bread, but from the doctrine of the Pharisees and Sadducees.

13 ¶ And Jesus coming into the parts of Caesarea of Philip, He questioned His disciples, saying, Whom do men say Me the Son of Man to be?

14 And they said, Some *say* John the Baptist, and others Elijah, and others Jeremiah, or one of the prophets.

15 He said to them, But you, whom do you say Me to be?

16 And answering, Simon Peter said, You are the Christ, the Son of the living God.

17 And answering, Jesus said to him, Blessed are you, Simon, son of Jonah, for flesh and blood did not reveal *it* to you, but My Father in Heaven.

18 And I also say to you that you are Peter, and on this rock I will build My Assembly, and *the* gates of Hades will not prevail against her.

19 And I will give to you the keys of the kingdom of Heaven. And whatever you bind on earth shall be, having been bound in Heaven. And whatever you may loose on the earth shall be, having been loosed in Heaven.

20 Then He charged His disciples that they should tell no one that He is Jesus the Christ.

21 ¶ From then Jesus began to show to His disciples that it was necessary for Him to go away to Jerusalem, and to suffer many things from the elders and chief priests and scribes, and to be killed, and to be raised on the third day.

22 And having taken Him near, Peter began to rebuke Him, saying, *God be* gracious to You, Lord; this shall not be to You, not *ever*

23 But turning He said to Peter, Go behind Me, Satan! You are a stumbling block to Me, for you do not think of the things of God, but the things of men.

24 ¶ Then Jesus said to His disciples, If anyone desires to come after Me, let him deny himself, and let him take up his cross, and let him follow Me.

25 For whoever desires to save his life will lose it. But whoever loses his life for My sake will find it.

26 For what will a man be benefited if he should gain the whole world, but forfeits his soul? Or what will a man give *as* an exchange *for* his soul?

27 For the Son of Man is about to come with His angels in the glory of His Father. And then "He will give reward to each according to his practice." *LXX-Psa. 61:13; Pro. 24:12; MT-Psa. 62:12*

28 Truly I say to you, There are some standing here who will not taste of death, not until they see the Son of Man coming in His kingdom.

Matthew 17

1 The transfiguration of Christ. 14 He heals the boy from the demon's affliction on him, 22 foretells His own passion, 24 and pays tribute.

1 ¶ And after six days, Jesus takes along Peter and James, and his brother John, and leads them up into a high mountain privately.

2 And He was transfigured before them, and His face shone like the sun, and His clothing became white as the light.

3 And, behold! Moses and Elijah appeared to them, talking with Him.

4 And answering, Peter said to Jesus, Lord, it is good for us to be here. If You desire, let us make three tents here, one for You, one for Moses, and one for Elijah.

5 While he was yet speaking, behold, a radiant cloud overshadowed them. And, behold, a voice out of the cloud saying, This is My Son, the Beloved, in whom I am well-pleased; hear Him. *Psa. 2:7; Gen. 22:2; Isa. 42:1; Deut. 18:15*

6 And hearing, the disciples fell on their face and greatly feared.

7 And coming near, Jesus touched them and said, Rise up, and do not fear.

8 And lifting up their eyes, they did not see anyone except Jesus alone.

9 And as they were coming down from the mountain, Jesus enjoined them, saying, Tell the vision to no one until the Son of Man is raised from the dead *ones*.

10 And His disciples questioned Him, saying, Why then do the scribes say that Elijah must come first?

11 And answering, Jesus said to them, Elijah indeed comes first and shall restore all things.

12 But I say to you, Elijah already came, and they did not know him, but did to him as many *things* as they desired. So also the Son of Man is about to suffer by them.

13 Then the disciples understood that He spoke to them about John the Baptist.

14 ¶ And they having come toward the crowd, a man came near to Him, kneeling down to Him, and saying,

15 Lord, have mercy on my son. For he is moonstruck and suffers badly. For he often falls into the fire, and often into the water.

16 And I brought him to Your disciples, and they did not have power to heal him.

17 And answering, Jesus said, O faithless and perverted generation! Until when shall I be with you? Until when shall I bear with you? Bring him here to Me.

18 And Jesus rebuked it, and the demon came out from him; and the boy was healed from that hour.

19 Then coming up to Jesus privately, the disciples said, Why did we not have power to cast him out?

20 And Jesus said to them, Because of your unbelief. For truly I say to you, If you have faith as a grain of mustard, you will say to this mountain, Move from here to there! And it will move. And nothing shall be impossible to you.

21 But this kind does not go out except by prayer and fasting.

22 ¶ And they returning in Galilee, Jesus said to them, The Son of Man is about to be given over into the hands of men.

23 And they will kill Him, and on the third day He will be raised. And they grieved exceedingly.

24 ¶ And they having come into Capernaum, those receiving the didrachmas came to Peter and said, Does your teacher not pay the didrachmas?

25 He said, Yes. And when he entered into the house, Jesus anticipated him, saying, What do you think, Simon? From whom do the kings of the earth receive customs or tribute? From their sons or from strangers?

26 Peter said to Him, From strangers. Jesus said to him, Then truly the sons are free.

27 But that we may not stumble them, going to the sea, throw in a hook and take the first fish coming up. And opening its mouth, you will find a stater. Taking that, give to them for you and Me.

Matthew 18

1 Christ warns His disciples to be humble and harmless: 7 to avoid offenses, and not to despise the little ones: 15 how to deal with our brothers, when they offend us: 21 and how often to forgive them: 23 He sets forth by a parable of the king, that took account of his servants.

1 ¶ In that hour the disciples came to Jesus, saying, Who then is greater in the kingdom of Heaven?

2 And having called forward a little child, Jesus set him in their midst.

3 And *He* said, Truly I say to you, If not you be converted and become as the little children, you may not enter into the kingdom of Heaven, not *ever*!

4 Therefore whoever will humble himself as this little child, this *one* is the greater in the kingdom of Heaven.

5 And whoever will receive one such little child in My name receives Me.

6 But whoever causes one of these little *ones* believing in Me to stumble, it is profitable for him that a millstone turned by an ass be hung on his neck, and he be sunk in the depth of the sea.

7 ¶ Woe to the world from *its* stumbling blocks! It is *a* necessity for the stumbling blocks to come, yet woe to that man through whom the stumbling block comes!

8 And if your hand or your foot causes you to stumble, cut it off and throw them from you; it is good for you to enter into life lame or maimed, than having two hands or two feet to be thrown into the everlasting fire.

9 And if your eye causes you to stumble, pluck it out and throw *it* from you; for it is good for you to enter into life one-eyed, than having two eyes to be thrown into the Hell of fire.

10 See *that* you do not despise one of these little *ones*, for I tell you that their angels in Heaven continually look on the face of My Father in Heaven.

11 For the Son of Man has come to save that which was lost.

12 What does *it* seem to you? If there be to any man a hundred sheep, and one of them strays away, will he not leave the ninety nine on the mountains, *and* having gone he seeks the *one* having strayed?

13 And if he happens to find it, truly I say to you that he rejoices over it more than over the ninety nine not having gone astray.

14 So it is not *the* will before your Father in Heaven that one of these little *ones* should perish.

15 ¶ But if your brother sin against you, go and reprove him between you and him alone. If he hears you, you have gained your brother.

16 But if he does not hear, take one or two more with you, "so that on the mouth of two or three witnesses every word may stand". *Deut. 19:15*

17 But if he refuses to hear them, tell *it* to the assembly. And if he also refuses to hear the assembly, let him be to you as the pagan and the tax collector.

18 Truly I say to you, as many *things* as you bind on the earth will be, having been bound in Heaven. And as many *things* as you loose on the earth will be, having been loosed in Heaven.

19 Again I say to you, If two of you agree on earth as to anything, whatever they shall ask, it shall be to them from My Father in Heaven.

20 For where two or three are gathered together in My name, there am I in the midst of them.

21 Then coming near to Him, Peter said, Lord, how often shall my brother sin against me, and I forgive him? Up to seven times?

22 Jesus said to him, I do not say to you, Up to seven times, but, Up to seventy times seven.

23 Because of this the kingdom of Heaven has been compared to a man, a king, who desired to take account with his slaves.

24 And he having begun to take account, one debtor of ten thousand talents was brought near to him.

25 But he not having *any* to repay, the lord of him commanded him to be sold, also his wife and children, and all things, as much as he had, and to be repaid.

26 Therefore having fallen down, the slave bowed the knee to him, saying, Lord, have patience with me, and I will pay all to you.

27 And being filled with pity, the lord of that slave released him and forgave him the loan.

28 But having gone out, that slave found one of his fellow slaves who owed him a hundred denarii. And seizing him, he choked *him*, saying, Pay me whatever you owe.

29 Then having fallen down at his feet, his fellow slave begged him, saying, Have patience with me, and I will repay all to you.

30 But he would not, but having gone away he threw him into prison until he *should* pay back the *amount* owing.

31 But his fellow slaves, seeing the things happening, they were greatly grieved. And having come they reported to their lord all the things happening.

32 Then having called him near, his lord said to him, Wicked slave! I forgave you all that debt, since you begged me.

33 Ought you not also to have mercy on your fellow slave, as I also had mercy?

34 And being angry, his lord gave him over to the tormentors until he pay back all that debt to him.

35 So also My heavenly Father will do to you unless each of you from your hearts forgive his brother their deviations.

Matthew 19

2 Christ heals the sick: 3 answers the Pharisees about divorce:10 when marriage is necessary: 13 receives little children: 16 instructs the young man how to attain eternal life: 23 how hard it is for a rich man to enter into the kingdom of God.

1 ¶ And it happened when Jesus had finished these words, He moved from Galilee and came into the borders of Judea beyond the Jordan.

2 And great crowds followed Him, and He healed them there.

3 ¶ And the Pharisees came near to Him, tempting Him, and saying to Him, Is it lawful for a man to dismiss his wife for every reason?

4 But answering, He said to them, Have you not read that He who created *them* from the beginning "created them male and female"? *Gen. 1:27*

5 And He said, "On account of this a man shall leave father and mother, and shall be joined to his wife, and the two shall become one flesh." *Gen. 2:24*

6 So that they are no longer two, but one flesh. Therefore, what God has joined together, let not man separate.

7 They said to Him, Why then did Moses command to "give a bill of divorce," "and to dismiss her?" *Deut. 24:1*

8 He said to them, In view of your hardheartedness, Moses allowed you to dismiss your wives. But from the beginning it was not so.

9 And I say to you, Whoever shall dismiss his wife, if not for fornication, and shall marry another, *that one* commits adultery. And the *one* marrying her having been dismissed commits adultery.

10 His disciples said to Him, If the case of the man be so with *his* wife, it is not profitable to marry.

11 But He said to them, Not all make room for this Word, but *those* to whom it is given.

12 For there are eunuchs who were born thus from *their* mother's womb, and there are eunuchs who were made eunuchs by men, and there are eunuchs who made eunuchs *of* themselves for the sake of the kingdom of Heaven. He who is able to receive, let him receive it.

13 ¶ Then little children were brought to Him, that He might lay hands on them and might pray. But the disciples rebuked them.

14 But Jesus said, Allow the little children and do not prevent them to come to Me, for of such is the kingdom of Heaven.

15 And laying hands on them, He went away from there.

16 ¶ And, behold, coming near, one said to Him, Good Teacher, what good *thing* shall I do that I may have eternal life?

17 And He said to him, Why do you call Me good? No one *is* good except One, God! But if you desire to enter into life, keep the commandments.

18 He said to Him, Which? And Jesus said, "You shall not commit murder, nor commit adultery, nor steal, nor bear false witness,

19 honor your father and your mother," and, "You shall love your neighbor as yourself." *Ex. 20:12-16; Lev. 19:18; Deut. 5:16-20*

20 The young man said to Him, All these things I have kept from my youth. What do I still lack?

21 Jesus said to him, If you desire to be a perfect *one*, go sell the things belonging to you and give to *the* poor *ones*, and you will have treasure in Heaven; and come, follow Me.

22 But having heard the Word, being sorrowful, the young man went away, for he had many possessions.

23 ¶ And Jesus said to His disciples, Truly I say to you that a rich man will with great difficulty enter into the kingdom of Heaven.

24 And again I say to you, It is easier for a camel to pass through a needle's eye, than for a rich man to enter the kingdom of God.

25 And His disciples were exceedingly astonished when they heard this, saying, Who then can be saved?

26 But having looked at *them*, Jesus said

to them, With men this is impossible, but with God all things are possible.

27 Then answering, Peter said to Him, Behold, we left all things and followed You. What then shall be to us?

28 And Jesus said to them, Truly I say to you, You who have followed Me, in the regeneration when the Son of Man sits on the throne of His glory, you also will sit on twelve thrones, judging the twelve tribes of Israel.

29 And everyone who left houses, or brothers, or sisters, or father, or mother, or wife, or children, or lands, for the sake of My name, shall receive a hundredfold, and shall inherit everlasting life.

30 But many first *ones* shall be last, and last *ones* first.

Matthew 20

1 Christ shows that God is debtor to no man: 20 by answering the mother of Zebedee's children He teaches his disciples to be lowly.

1 ¶ For the kingdom of Heaven is like a man, a housemaster, who went out early in the morning to hire workers into his vineyard.

2 And agreeing with the workers for a denarius *for* the day, he sent them into his vineyard.

3 And going out about the third hour, he saw others standing idle in the market.

4 And he said to them, You also go into the vineyard, and I will give you whatever may be just. And they went.

5 Again, going out about *the* sixth and ninth hour, he did likewise.

6 And going out about the eleventh hour, he found others standing idle, and said to them, Why do you stand here idle all day?

7 They said to him, Because no one has hired us. He said to them, You also go into the vineyard, and you will receive whatever may be just.

8 But evening having come, the Lord of the vineyard said to his overseer, Call the workers and pay them the wage, beginning from the last *ones* to the first *ones*.

9 And the *ones* having come the eleventh hour each received a denarius.

10 And having come, the first supposed that they would receive more. And they also each received a denarius.

11 And having received *it*, they murmured against the housemaster,

12 saying, These last have performed one hour, and you have made them equal to us, the *ones* having borne the burden and the burning heat of the day.

13 But answering, he said to one of them, Friend, I do not wrong you. Did you not agree to a denarius with me?

14 Take yours and go. But I desire to give to this last as also to you.

15 Or is it not lawful for me to do what I desire with my things? Or is your eye evil because I am good?

16 So the last *ones* shall be first *ones*, and the first *ones* last *ones*; for many are called, but few elect *ones*.

17 ¶ And going up to Jerusalem, Jesus took the twelve disciples aside in the way, and said to them,

18 Behold, we are going up to Jerusalem, and the Son of Man will be given over to the chief priests and scribes. And they will condemn Him to death.

19 And they will give Him over to the nations to mock, and to scourge, and to crucify. And the third day He will rise again.

20 ¶ Then the mother of the sons of Zebedee came near to Him, along with her sons, worshiping, and asking something from Him.

21 And He said to her, What do you desire? She said to Him, Say that these two sons of mine may sit one at Your right, and one at *Your* left in Your kingdom.

22 But answering, Jesus said, You do not know what you ask. Are you able to drink the cup which I am about to drink, and to be baptized with the baptism with which I am to be baptized? They said to Him, We are able.

23 And He said to them, Indeed you shall drink My cup, and you shall be baptized with the baptism with which I am baptized; but to sit at My right and at My left *hand* is not Mine to give, but *to those* for whom it was prepared by My Father.

24 And hearing, the ten were indignant about the two brothers.

25 But having called them to *Himself*, Jesus said, You know that the rulers of

the nations exercise lordship over them, and the great *ones* exercise authority over them.

26 But it will not be so among you. But whoever desires to become a great *one* among you, let him be your servant.

27 And whoever desires to be first among you, let him be your servant;

28 Even as the Son of Man did not come to be served, but to serve, and to give His life a ransom for many.

29 ¶ And as they were going out from Jericho, a great crowd followed Him.

30 And, behold, two blind *ones* sitting beside the way, hearing that Jesus was passing by, *they* cried out, saying, Have mercy on us, Lord, Son of David!

31 But the crowd rebuked them, that they be quiet. But they cried out the more, saying, Have mercy on us, Lord, Son of David!

32 And stopping, Jesus called them, and said, What do you desire that I do to you?

33 They said to Him, Lord, that our eyes may be opened.

34 And being moved with compassion Jesus touched their eyes. And instantly their eyes saw again, and they followed Him.

Matthew 21

1 Christ rides to Jerusalem, 12 drives the buyers and sellers out of the temple, 23 silences the priests and elders, 28 and rebukes them by the similitude of the two sons.

1 ¶ And when they drew near to Jerusalem and came into Bethphage, toward the Mount of Olives, then Jesus sent two disciples,

2 saying to them, Go into the village opposite you, and immediately you will find an ass tied, and a young ass with her. Loosing, lead *them* to Me.

3 And if anyone says anything to you, you shall say, The Lord has need of them. And he will send them at once.

4 But all this happened that might be fulfilled that spoken by the prophet, saying:

5 "Tell the daughter of Zion, Behold, your King comes to you, meek and mounted on an ass, even a young ass, *the* son of a she-ass." *Isa. 62:11; Zech. 9:9*

6 And the disciples, having gone and having done as Jesus ordered them,

7 they led the ass and the young ass. And *they* put on them their garments, and set Him on them.

8 And the very great crowd strewed their garments in the road. And others were cutting branches from the trees and were spreading *them* in the way.

9 And the crowd, the *ones* going before and the *ones* following, were crying out, saying, Hosanna to the Son of David! "Blessed *is* He coming in *the* name of *the* Lord"! Hosanna in the highest! *Psa. 118:26*

10 And as He entered into Jerusalem, all the city was shaken, saying, Who is this?

11 And the crowds said, This is Jesus, the Prophet, the *One* from Nazareth of Galilee.

12 ¶ And Jesus entered into the temple of God and threw out all the *ones* selling and buying in the temple. And He overthrew the tables of the money changers and the seats of those selling the doves.

13 And He said to them, It is written, "My house shall be called a house of prayer," but you have "made it a den of plunderers." *Isa. 56:7; Jer. 7:11*

14 And blind *ones* and lame *ones* came to Him in the temple, and He healed them.

15 But the chief priests and the scribes, seeing the wonders which He did, and the children crying out in the temple, and saying, Hosanna to the Son of David, they were incensed.

16 And *they* said to Him, Do you hear what these say? And Jesus said to them, Yes. Did you never read, "Out of *the* mouth of babes and sucklings You have perfected praise?" *LXX-Psa. 8:3; MT-Psa. 8:2*

17 And leaving them, He went out of the city to Bethany, and lodged there.

18 ¶ And returning early in the morning to the city, He hungered.

19 And seeing one fig tree by the road, He went up *to* it, and found nothing on it except leaves only. And He said to it, Let there be no more fruit from you forever. And the fig tree immediately dried up.

20 And seeing, the disciples marveled, saying, How quickly the fig tree is dried up!

21 And answering, Jesus said to them, Truly I say to you, If you have faith and do not doubt, not only will you do *the*

miracle of the fig tree, but even if you should say to this mountain, Be taken up and thrown into the sea, it will be so.

22 And all things, as many *things* as you may ask in prayer, believing, you shall receive.

23 ¶ And He having come into the temple, the chief priests and elders of the people came near to Him *as He was* teaching, saying, By what authority do You do these things? And who gave this authority to You?

24 And answering, Jesus said to them, I also will ask you one thing, which if you tell Me, I also will tell you by what authority I do these things.

25 The baptism of John, from where was it? From Heaven, or from men? And they reasoned among themselves, saying, If we shall say, From Heaven, He will say to us, Why then did you not believe him?

26 But if we should say, From men, we fear the people. For all hold John to be a prophet.

27 And answering Jesus, they said, We do not know. And He said to them, Neither do I tell you by what authority I do these things.

28 ¶ But what do you think? A man had two children, and coming to the first he said, Child, go today; work in my vineyard.

29 And answering, he said, I will not. But caring afterward, he went.

30 And having come to the second, he said the same. And answering, he said, I *go*, sir; but *he* did not leave.

31 Which of the two did the will of the father? They said to Him, The first. Jesus said to them, Truly I say to you, The tax collectors and the harlots go before you into the kingdom of God.

32 For John came to you in *the* way of righteousness, and you did not believe him. But the tax-collectors and the harlots believed him. And seeing, you did not care afterwards to believe him.

33 ¶ Hear another parable: There was a certain man, a house manager, who planted a vineyard and placed a hedge around it; and *he* dug a winepress in it, and built a tower. And *he* rented it to vinedressers and went abroad *Isa. 5:1, 2*

34 And when the season of the fruits came, he sent his slaves to the vinedressers to receive his fruits.

35 And the vinedressers, taking his slaves, one indeed, they beat, and one they killed, and one they stoned.

36 Again he sent other slaves, more than the first. And they did the same to them.

37 But at last he sent his son to them, saying, They will respect my son.

38 But seeing the son, the vinedressers said among themselves, This is the heir. Come, let us kill him and possess his inheritance.

39 And taking him, they threw *him* out of the vineyard and killed *him*.

40 Therefore, when the lord of the vineyard comes, what will he do to those vinedressers?

41 They said to Him, Bad *men*! He will badly destroy them, and he will rent out the vineyard to other vinedressers who will give to him the fruits in their seasons.

42 Jesus said to them, Did you never read in the Scriptures, "A Stone which the builders rejected, this One became the Head of *the* Corner? This was from the Lord, and it is a wonder in our eyes?" *Psalm 118:22, 23*

43 Because of this I say to you, The kingdom of God will be taken from you, and it will be given to a nation producing the fruits of it.

44 And he who falls on this Stone will be broken; but on whomever It falls, It will pulverize him.

45 And hearing His parables, the chief priests and the Pharisees knew that He was speaking about them.

46 And seeking to lay hold of Him, they feared the crowds, because they had Him as a prophet.

Matthew 22

1 The parable of the marriage of the king's son. 12 The punishment of him that lacked the wedding garment. 15 Tribute ought to be paid to Caesar. 23 Christ proves to the Sadducees there is a resurrection: 34 and answers the lawyer, which is the first and great commandment.

1 ¶ And answering, Jesus again spoke to them in parables, saying:

2 The kingdom of Heaven is compared to a man, a king, who made a wedding feast for his son.

3 And he sent his slaves to call the *ones* being invited to the wedding feast, but they did not desire to come.

4 Again, he sent other slaves, saying, Tell the *ones* being called, Behold, I have prepared my supper; my oxen, and the fatlings *are* killed, and all things ready; come to the wedding feast.

5 But the *ones* not caring went off, the *one* indeed to *his* own field, and the *one* to *his* trading.

6 And the rest, seizing his slaves, *they* insolently mistreated and killed *them.*

7 And hearing, the king became angry. And sending his armies, *he* destroyed those murderers and burned up their city.

8 Then he said to his slaves, Indeed, the wedding feast is ready, but those invited were not worthy.

9 Therefore go onto the exits of the highways and call to the wedding feast as many as you may find.

10 And going out into the highways, those slaves gathered all, as many as they found, both evil and good. And the wedding feast was filled with reclining guests.

11 And the king coming in to look over the *ones* reclining, he saw a man there not having been clothed *in* a wedding garment.

12 And he said to him, Friend, how did you come in here, not having a wedding garment? But he was speechless.

13 Then the king said to the servants, Binding his feet and hands, take him away and throw *him* out into the outer darkness. There shall be weeping and gnashing of the teeth.

14 For many are called, but few elect *ones.*

15 ¶ Then going, the Pharisees took counsel so as they might trap Him in discourse.

16 And they sent to Him their disciples with the Herodians, saying, Teacher, we know that You are true, and teach the way of God in truth, and it does not concern You about anyone, for You do not look to *the* face of men.

17 Then tell us, what do You think? Is it lawful to give tribute to Caesar, or not?

18 But knowing their wickedness, Jesus said, Why do you test Me, hypocrites?

19 Show Me the tribute coin. And they brought a denarius to Him.

20 And He said to them, Whose image and inscription is this?

21 They said to Him, Caesar's. Then He said to them, Then give back to Caesar the things of Caesar, and to God the things of God.

22 And hearing, they marveled. And leaving Him, they went away.

23 ¶ On that day, Sadducees, who say there is no resurrection, came to Him. And they questioned Him,

24 saying, Teacher, Moses said, If any should die not having children, his brother shall marry his wife, and shall raise up seed to his brother. *Deut. 25:5*

25 And seven brothers were with us. And having married, the first *one* died, and not having seed left his wife to his brother.

26 In the same way also the second *one*, and the third *one*, until the seven.

27 And last of all, the woman also died.

28 Then in the resurrection, of which of the seven will she be wife? For all had her.

29 And answering, Jesus said to them, You err, not knowing the Scriptures nor the power of God.

30 For in the resurrection they neither marry nor are given in marriage, but they are as the angels of God in Heaven.

31 But concerning the resurrection of the dead *ones*, have you not read that spoken to you by God, saying:

32 "I am the God of Abraham, and the God of Isaac, and the God of Jacob?" God is not God of the dead *ones*, but of the living. *Ex. 3:6*

33 And hearing, the crowds were astonished at His doctrine.

34 ¶ But hearing that He had silenced the Sadducees, the Pharisees were gathered together.

35 And one of them, a lawyer, questioned *Him*, testing Him, and saying,

36 Teacher, which *is the* great commandment in the Law?

37 And Jesus said to him, "You shall love the Lord your God with all your heart, and

with all your soul, and with all your mind."
Deut. 6:5

38 This is the first and great commandment.

39 And the second *one is* like it: "You shall love your neighbor as yourself." *Lev. 19:18*

40 On these two commandments all the Law and the Prophets hang.

41 ¶ But the Pharisees having been gathered, Jesus questioned them,

42 saying, What does it seem to you concerning the Christ? Whose son is He? They say to Him, David's.

43 He said to them, Then how does David in Spirit call Him Lord, saying,

44 "The Lord said to my Lord, Sit at My right until I should put Your hostile *ones as* a footstool for Your feet?" *LXX-Psa. 109:1; MT-Psa. 110:1*

45 Then if David calls Him Lord, how is He his son?

46 And no one was able to answer Him a word, nor did anyone dare from that day to question Him any more.

Matthew 23

1 Christ admonishes the people not to follow the evil examples of the scribes and Pharisees.

5 His disciples must beware of their ambition.

1 ¶ Then Jesus spoke to the crowds and to His disciples,

2 saying, The scribes and the Pharisees have sat down on Moses' seat.

3 Therefore all things, as many things as they tell you to keep, keep and do. But do not do according to their works, for they say, and do not do.

4 For they bind heavy and hard to bear burdens, and lay *them* on the shoulders of men, but they do not desire to move them with *their* finger.

5 But they do all their works to be seen by men. And they make their phylacteries broad and enlarge the borders of their robes.

6 And they love the first couch in the suppers, and the first seats in the synagogues,

7 and the greetings in the markets, and to be called by men, Rabbi, Rabbi.

8 But do not you be called Rabbi, for One is your Leader, the Christ, and you are all brothers.

9 And call no one your father on earth, for One is your Father, the *One* in Heaven.

10 Neither be called leaders, for One is your Leader, the Christ.

11 But the greater of you shall be your servant.

12 And whoever will exalt himself shall be humbled, and whoever will humble himself shall be exalted.

13 ¶ But woe to you, scribes and Pharisees, hypocrites! For you shut up the kingdom of Heaven before men; for you do not enter, nor do you allow the *ones* entering to go in.

14 Woe to you, scribes and Pharisees, hypocrites! For you devour the houses of widows, and pray at length as a pretext. Because of this you will receive more abundant judgment.

15 Woe to you, scribes and Pharisees, hypocrites! For you go about the sea and the dry *land* to make one proselyte; and when he has become so, you make him twofold more a son of Hell than yourselves.

16 Woe to you, blind guides, who say, Whoever swears by the Holy Place, it is nothing; but whoever swears by the gold of the Holy Place owes a debt.

17 Fools and blind! For which is greater, the gold, or the Holy Place that sanctifies the gold?

18 And *you say*, Whoever swears by the altar, it is nothing; but whoever swears by the gift on it owes a debt.

19 Fools and blind! For which *is* greater, the gift, or the altar that sanctifies the gift?

20 Therefore the *one* swearing by the altar swears by it, and by all things on it.

21 And the *one* swearing by the Holy Place swears by it, and by the *One* dwelling in it.

22 And the *one* swearing by Heaven swears by the throne of God, and by the *One* sitting on it.

23 Woe to you, scribes and Pharisees, hypocrites! For you pay tithes of mint and dill and cummin, and you have left the weightier *matters* of the Law: judgment, and mercy, and faith. It was right to do these, and not to have left those.

24 Blind guides, straining out the gnat, but swallowing the camel!

25 Woe to you, scribes and Pharisees, hypocrites! For you cleanse the outside of the cup and of the dish, but within they are full of plunder and intemperance

26 Blind Pharisee! First cleanse the inside of the cup and of the dish, that the outside of them may become clean also.

27 Woe to you, scribes and Pharisees, hypocrites! For you are like whitewashed tombs which outwardly indeed appear beautiful, but within are full of bones of *the* dead *ones*, and of all uncleanness.

28 So you also indeed outwardly appear righteous *ones* to men, but within are full of hypocrisy and lawlessness.

29 Woe to you, scribes and Pharisees, hypocrites! For you build the tombs of the prophets, and adorn the monuments of the righteous *ones*.

30 And you say, If we were in the days of our fathers, we would not have been partakers with them in the blood of the prophets.

31 So you witness to yourselves that you are the sons of those who murdered the prophets.

32 And you fill up the measure of your fathers.

33 Serpents! Offspring of vipers! How shall you escape the judgment of Hell?

34 ¶ Because of this, behold, I send to you prophets and wise *ones* and scribes. And *some* of them you will kill and crucify, and some of them you will scourge in your synagogues and will persecute from city to city;

35 so that should come on you all *the* righteous blood poured out on the earth, from the blood of righteous Abel to the blood of Zechariah the son of Berechiah whom you murdered between the Holy Place and the altar.

36 Truly I say to you, All these things will come on this generation.

37 Jerusalem, Jerusalem, the *one* killing the prophets and stoning those sent to her. How often I desired to gather your children in the way a bird gathers her chicks under *her* wings! And you did not desire it.

38 Behold, "your house is left to you desolate." *Jer. 22:5*

39 For I say to you, You shall not see Me from now on; not until you say, "Blessed is the *One* coming in *the* name of *the* Lord." *Psa. 118:26*

Matthew 24

1 Christ foretells the destruction of the temple:
3 what calamities shall be before it.

1 ¶ And going out, Jesus left the temple. And His disciples came near to show Him the buildings of the temple.

2 But Jesus said to them, Do you not see all these things? Truly I say to you, Not will be left one stone on a stone which not will be thrown down, not *one*!

3 And as He was sitting on the Mount of Olives, the disciples came to Him privately, saying, Tell us, when will these things be? And, What *is* the sign of Your coming and of the completion of the age?

4 ¶ And answering, Jesus said to them, See that you do not lead anyone astray.

5 For many will come in My name, saying, I am the Christ. And *they* will cause many to be led astray.

6 But you are going to hear of wars and rumors of wars. See, do not be terrified. For all things must take place, but the end is not yet.

7 For nation will be raised up against nation, and kingdom against kingdom; and there will be famines and plagues and earthquakes against *many* places.

8 But all these *are* a beginning of birth pangs

9 Then they will give you over to affliction, and will kill you, and you will be hated by all nations because of My name.

10 And then many will be ensnared, and they will give over one another and will hate one another.

11 And many false prophets will be raised up and will cause many to err.

12 And because lawlessness shall have been multiplied, the love of the many will grow cold.

13 But the *one* who endures to *the* end, this *one* will be kept safe.

14 And this gospel of the Kingdom shall be preached in all the inhabited earth for a testimony to all the nations, and then will come the end.

15 Therefore when you see the abomination of desolation, which was spoken of

by Daniel the prophet, standing in *the* holy place (the *one* reading, let him understand), *Dan. 11:31; 12:11*

16 then let those in Judea flee into the mountains;

17 the *one* on the housetop, let him not go down to take anything out of his house;

18 and the *one* in the field, let him not turn back to take his clothes.

19 But woe to the *ones* having *a babe* in womb, and to those suckling in those days!

20 And pray that your flight will not occur *in* winter nor in a sabbath.

21 For there will be great affliction, such as has not happened from *the* beginning of *the* world until now, nor will be, not *ever*!

22 And except those days were cut short, not any flesh would be saved. But on account of the elect, those days will be cut short.

23 Then if anyone says to you, Behold, here *is* the Christ! Or, Here! Do not believe.

24 For false christs and false prophets will rise up. And *they* will give great signs and wonders, so as to lead astray, if possible, even the elect.

25 Behold, I have told you in advance.

26 Then if they say to you, Behold, he is in the deserted *place*; do not go out. Behold, *he is* in the private rooms, not do believe.

27 For as the lightning comes forth from *the* east and shines as far as *the* west, so also will be the coming of the Son of Man.

28 For wherever the carcass may be, there the eagles will be gathered.

29 And immediately after the affliction of those days the sun will be darkened and the moon will not give its light, and the stars will fall from the heaven, and the powers of the heavens will be shaken.

30 And then the sign of the Son of Man will appear in the heavens. And then all the tribes of the land will wail. And they will see the Son of Man coming on the clouds of heaven with power and much glory. *Dan. 7:13*

31 And He will send His angels with a great sound of a trumpet, and they will gather His elect from the four winds, from *the* extreme *limits* of *the* heavens to *the* extreme *limits* of them.

32 ¶ But learn the parable of the fig tree: When its branch already becomes tender and it puts out leaves, you know that the summer *is* near;

33 so also you, when you see all these things, know that it is near at *the* doors.

34 Truly I say to you, This generation will not pass away, not *at all*, not until all these things have occurred.

35 The heaven and the earth will pass away, but My words will not pass away, not *ever*!

36 But about that day and that hour, no one has known, neither the angels of Heaven, except My Father only.

37 But as the days of Noah, so also will be the coming of the Son of Man.

38 For as they were in the days before the flood: eating, and drinking, marrying, and giving in marriage, until *the* day *when* Noah went into the ark.

39 And they did not know until the flood came and took all away. So also will be the coming of the Son of Man.

40 At that time two will be out in the field; the one is taken and the one is left;

41 two grinding at the mill; one is taken, and one is left.

42 Be awake, therefore, for you do not know in what hour your Lord comes.

43 But know this, that if the housemaster had known in what watch the thief comes, he would have kept awake and not have allowed his house to be dug through.

44 Because of this, you also be ready, for in that hour you think not, the Son of Man comes.

45 Who then is the faithful and wise slave whom his master has appointed over his servants, to give to them the food in season?

46 Blessed *is* that slave whom his master shall find so doing when He comes.

47 Truly I say to you, He will set him over all belonging *to* him.

48 But if that wicked slave says in his heart, My Lord delays to come,

49 and begins to beat *his* fellow slaves, and to eat and to drink with the *ones* being drunk.

50 the Lord of that slave comes in a day in which he does not expect and in an hour which he does not know,

51 and will cut him in two, and will appoint his portion with the hypocrites. There will be weeping and gnashing of the teeth.

Matthew 25

1 The parable of the ten virgins, 14 and of the talents. 31 Also the description of the last judgment.

1 ¶ Then the kingdom of Heaven shall be compared to ten virgins who taking their lamps, went out to a meeting of the bridegroom.
2 And five of them were prudent *ones* and five foolish *ones.*
3 *The ones* who *were* foolish *ones* having taking their lamps did not take oil with them.
4 But the prudent *ones* took oil in their vessels with their lamps.
5 But the bridegroom delaying, all nodded and slept.
6 And *in the* middle of night a cry occurred: Behold, the bridegroom comes! Go out to meet him.
7 Then all those virgins were aroused and prepared their lamps.
8 And the foolish *ones* said to the prudent *ones*, Give us *some* of your oil, for our lamps are going out.
9 But the prudent *ones* answered, saying, *No*, lest there not be enough for us and you. But rather, go to the *ones* who sell and buy for yourselves.
10 But they going away to buy, the bridegroom came. And the *ones* ready went in with him to the wedding feast, and the door was shut.
11 And afterwards, the rest of the virgins also came, saying, Lord, lord, open to us.
12 But answering, he said, Truly I say to you, I do not know you.
13 Therefore, be awake, for you do not know the day nor the hour in which the Son of Man comes.
14 ¶ For *it is* as if a man going abroad called *his* own slaves and gave over his belongings to them.
15 And to one indeed he gave five talents, and to another, two, and to another, one, to each according to his ability. And *he* went abroad at once.

16 And going, the *one* who received the five talents worked with them and made another five talents.
17 In the same way, the *one with* the two also *did*; he also gained another two.
18 But going away, the *one* who received the one dug in the earth and hid his lord's silver.
19 And after much time, the lord of those slaves came and took account with them.
20 And coming up, the *one* receiving the five talents brought another five talents near, saying, Lord, you gave over five talents to me. Behold, I gained another five talents over them.
21 And his lord said to him, Well *done*, good and faithful slave. You were faithful over a few things; I will set you over many. Enter into the joy of your lord.
22 And coming up, the *one* receiving two talents also said, Lord, you gave over two talents to me. Behold, I have gained two other talents above them.
23 His lord said to him, Well *done*, good and faithful slave. You were faithful over a few things, I will set you over many. Enter into the joy of your lord.
24 And also the *one* having received the one talent coming up, said, Lord, I knew you, that you are a hard man, reaping where you did not sow, and gathering where you did not scatter;
25 and being afraid, going away, I hid your talent in the earth. Behold, you have yours.
26 And answering, his lord said to him, Evil and slothful slave! You knew that I reap where I did not sow, and I gather where I did not scatter.
27 Therefore you ought to have put my silver to the money exchangers, and coming I would have received mine with interest.
28 Therefore, take the talent from him and give *it* to him who has the ten talents.
29 For to everyone having, *more* will be given, and he will abound. But from him not having, even that which he has will be taken from him.
30 And throw the worthless slave out into the outer darkness. There will be weeping and gnashing of the teeth.

31 ¶ But when the Son of Man comes in His glory, and all the holy angels with Him, then He will sit on the throne of His glory.

32 And before Him shall be gathered all the nations; and He will separate them from one another, as the shepherd separates the sheep from the goats.

33 And indeed *He* will set the sheep at His right, but the goats at *the* left *hand*.

34 Then the King will say to those at His right, Come, the *ones* blessed of My Father, inherit the kingdom prepared for you from *the* foundation of *the* world.

35 For I hungered, and you gave Me food to eat; I thirsted, and you gave Me drink; I was a stranger, and you gathered Me in;

36 naked, and you clothed Me; I was sick, and you came to see Me; I was in prison, and you came to Me.

37 Then the righteous *ones* will answer, saying, Lord, when did we see You hungering, and we fed *You*; or thirsting, and we gave *You* drink?

38 And when did we see You a stranger, and gathered *You* in; or naked, and clothed *You*?

39 And when did we see You sick, or in prison, and came to You?

40 And answering, the King will say to them, Truly I say to you, In so far as you did *it* to one of these, the least of My brothers, you did *it* to Me.

41 Then He will also say to the *ones* at *the* left, Go away from Me, the *ones* cursed, into the everlasting fire having been prepared for the devil and his angels.

42 For I hungered, and you did not give Me *a thing* to eat. I thirsted and you did not give Me *a thing* to drink;

43 I was a stranger, and you did not gather Me in; naked, and you did not clothe Me; sick, and in prison, and you did not come to see Me.

44 Then they also will answer Him, saying, Lord, when did we see You hungering, or thirsting, or a stranger, or naked, or sick, or in prison, and did not minister to You?

45 Then He will answer them, saying, Truly I say to you, In as much as you did not do *it* to one of these, the least, neither did you do *it* to Me.

46 And these shall go away into everlasting punishment, but the righteous *ones* into everlasting life.

Matthew 26

1 The rulers conspire against Christ. 14 Judas sells him. 47 Christ, being given over with a kiss, 57 is carried to Caiaphas, 69 and denied by Peter.

1 ¶ And it happened, when Jesus finished all these sayings, He said to His disciples,

2 You know that the Passover will be after two days, and the Son of Man is given over to be crucified.

3 Then the chief priests and the scribes and the elders of the people were assembled to the court of the high priest, the *one* named Caiaphas.

4 And *they* plotted together in order that they might seize Jesus by deceit and kill *Him*.

5 But they said, Not in the Feast, that there be no turmoil among the people.

6 ¶ And Jesus being in Bethany, in Simon the leper's house,

7 a woman came near to Him having an alabaster vial of ointment *of* great value. and poured *it* down on His head, *He* reclining.

8 But seeing, His disciples were indignant, saying, For what *is* this waste?

9 For this ointment could have been sold for much and be given to *the* poor *ones*.

10 But knowing, Jesus said to them, Why do you cause troubles to the woman? For she worked a good work toward Me.

11 For you always have the poor *ones* with you, but you do not always have Me.

12 For in putting this ointment on My body, she did *it* in order to bury Me.

13 Truly I say to you, Wherever this gospel is proclaimed in all the world, also what she did will be spoken of for a memorial of her.

14 ¶ Then one of the twelve going to the chief priests, the *one* called Judas Iscariot,

15 said, What will you give to me, and I will give Him over to you? "And they weighed to him thirty silver pieces." *Zech. 11:12*

16 And from then he sought opportunity that he might give Him over.

17 ¶ And on the first *day* of the *Feast of Unleavened Bread*, the disciples came to

Jesus, saying to Him, Where do you desire we should prepare for You to eat the Passover?

18 And He said, Go into the city to a certain one and say to him, The Teacher says, My time is near; with you I am making the Passover with My disciples.

19 And the disciples did as Jesus ordered them, and prepared the Passover.

20 And *it* becoming evening, He reclined with the Twelve.

21 And as they were eating, He said, Truly I say to you that one of you will give Me over.

22 And grieving exceedingly, they began to say to Him, each of them, not I am *the one*. Lord?

23 But answering, He said, The *one* dipping the hand with Me in the dish will give Me over.

24 Indeed, the Son of Man goes, as it is written about Him. But woe to that man by whom the Son of Man is given over. It were good for him if that man was never born.

25 And answering, the *one* giving Him over, Judas, said, Not I am *he*, Rabbi? He said to him, You have said *it*.

26 ¶ And as they ate, taking the bread and blessing *it*, Jesus broke and gave to the disciples, and said, Take, eat; this is My body.

27 And taking the cup, and giving thanks, He gave to them, saying, Drink of it. all *of* you.

28 For this is My blood of the New Covenant which concerning many is being poured out for remission of sins.

29 But I say to you, I will not drink of this fruit of the vine after this, not until that day when I drink it new with you in the kingdom of My Father.

30 And singing a hymn, they went to the Mount of Olives.

31 ¶ Then Jesus said to them, You all will be caused to stumble in Me in this night. For it is written, "I will smite the Shepherd, and the sheep of the flock will be scattered." *Zech. 13:7*

32 But after My resurrection I will go before you into Galilee.

33 And answering, Peter said to Him, Even if all will be caused to stumble in You, I will never be caused to stumble

34 Jesus said to him, Truly I say to you, In this night, before a cock sounds, you will deny Me three times.

35 Peter said to Him, Even if I must die with You, I will not deny You, not *I*! And all the disciples said the same.

36 ¶ Then Jesus came with them to a place called Gethsemane. And He said to the disciples, Sit here, until going away, I shall pray there.

37 And taking along Peter and the two sons of Zebedee, He began to grieve and to be deeply troubled.

38 Then He said to them, My soul is deeply grieved, even unto death. Stay here with Me, and keep awake.

39 And going forward a little, He fell on His face, praying, and saying, My Father, if it is possible, let this cup pass from Me; yet not as I will, but as You *will*.

40 And He comes to the disciples and finds them sleeping. And *He* said to Peter, So! Did you not have strength to keep awake one hour with Me?

41 Keep awake and pray that you do not enter into temptation. The spirit indeed *is* willing, but the flesh *is* weak.

42 Again, going away a second *time*, He prayed, saying, My Father, if *it is* not possible for this cup to pass away from Me except I drink it, let Your will be done.

43 And coming, He again finds them sleeping, for their eyes were weighed down.

44 And leaving them, going away again, He prayed a third time, saying the same word.

45 Then He came to His disciples and said to them, Sleep on, and rest *for* what *time* remains. Behold, the hour draws near, and the Son of Man is given over into *the* hands of sinners.

46 Rise up, let us go. Behold, the *one* giving Me over draws near.

47 ¶ And *as* He was yet speaking, behold, Judas came, one of the twelve. And with him was a numerous crowd with swords and clubs, from the chief priests and elders of the people.

48 And the *one* giving Him over gave them a sign, saying, Whomever I may kiss, it is He; seize Him.

49 And coming up at once to Jesus, he said, Hail, Rabbi. And *he* ardently kissed Him.

50 But Jesus said to him, Friend, why are you here? Then coming up, they laid hands on Jesus and seized Him.

51 And, behold, one of those with Jesus, stretching out the hand, drew his sword and struck the slave of the high priest *and* took off the ear of him.

52 Then Jesus said to him, Put your sword back into its place. For all who take *the* sword shall perish by a sword.

53 Or do you think that I am not able now to call on My Father, and He will stand beside Me more than twelve legions of angels?

54 How then should the Scriptures be fulfilled, that it must happen this way?

55 In that hour, Jesus said to the crowds, Did you come out to take Me with swords and clubs, as against a plunderer? I sat with you according to a day teaching in the temple, and you did not lay hands on Me.

56 But all this is happening that the Scriptures of the prophets may be fulfilled. Then all the disciples ran away, forsaking Him.

57 ¶ And the *ones* who had seized Jesus led *Him* away to Caiaphas the high priest, where the scribes and the elders were assembled.

58 And Peter followed Him from a distance, even to the court of the high priest. And going inside, *he* sat with the under-officers to see the end.

59 And the chief priests and the elders and the whole sanhedrin looked for false testimony against Jesus, so that they might put Him to death,

60 and they did not find *any*, even *though* many false witnesses *were* coming forward, they did not find *any*. But at last, coming up two false witnesses

61 said, This *One* said, I am able to destroy the temple of God, and through three days to build it.

62 And standing up, the high priest said to Him, Do You answer nothing? What do these witness against You?

63 But Jesus kept silent. And answering, the high priest said to Him, I put You on oath by the living God that You tell us if You are the Christ, the Son of God.

64 Jesus said to him, You said *it*. I tell you more. From this time you shall see the Son of Man sitting at *the* right *hand* of power, and coming on the clouds of the heaven. *Psa. 110:1; Dan. 7:13*

65 Then the high priest tore his garments, saying, He blasphemed! What need do we have any more of witnesses? Behold, now you have heard His blasphemy.

66 What does it seem to you? And answering, they said, He is liable to death.

67 Then they spat in His face, and beat Him with the fist, and *some* slapped *Him*,

68 saying, Prophesy to us, Christ. Who is the *one* striking You?

69 ¶ And Peter sat outside in the courtyard. And one slave-girl came near to him, saying, And you were with Jesus the Galilean.

70 But he denied before all, saying, I do not know what you say.

71 And he, going out into the porch, another saw him and says to the *ones* there, And this *one* was with Jesus the Nazarene.

72 And again he denied with an oath, I do not know the man.

73 And after a little, coming near, those standing by said to Peter, Truly you also are of them, for even your speech makes you evident.

74 Then he began to curse and to swear, I do not know the man. And immediately a cock sounded.

75 And Peter recalled the word of Jesus, saying to him, Before a cock sounds you will deny Me three times. And going out, he wept bitterly.

Matthew 27

1 Christ is bound and given over to Pilate. 3 Judas hangs himself. 19 Pilate, admonished by his wife, 24 washes his hands. 29 Christ is crowned with thorns, 34 crucified, 50 dies, and is buried.

1 ¶ And early morning occurring, all the chief priests and the elders of the people took counsel together against Jesus, so as to put Him to death.

2 And binding Him, they led *Him* away and gave Him over to Pontius Pilate the governor.

3 Then Judas, the *one* giving Him over, seeing that He was condemned, caring afterward, returned the thirty pieces of silver to the chief priests and the elders,

4 saying, I sinned, giving over innocent blood. But they said, What *is it* to us? You see *to it*.

5 And tossing the silver pieces into the temple, he left. And going away he hanged himself.

6 And taking the pieces of silver, the chief priests said, It is not lawful to put them into the treasury, since it is *the* price of blood.

7 And taking counsel, they bought of them the potter's field, for burial for the strangers.

8 So that field was called Field of Blood until today.

9 Then was fulfilled that spoken through Jeremiah the prophet, saying, And I took the thirty pieces of silver, the price of Him who had been priced, on whom they of the sons of Israel set a price,

10 and gave them for the potter's field, as the Lord directed me. *Zech. 11:12, 13*

11 ¶ And Jesus stood before the governor. And the governor questioned Him, saying, Are You the King of the Jews? And Jesus said to him, You say *it*.

12 And when He was accused by the chief priests and the elders, He answered nothing.

13 Then Pilate said to Him, Do You not hear how many things they testify against You?

14 And He did not answer him, not even to one word, so that the governor greatly marveled.

15 And at a feast, the governor was accustomed to release one prisoner to the crowd, whom they wished.

16 And they had then a notable prisoner being called Barabbas.

17 Therefore they, having been assembled, Pilate said to them, Whom do you wish I may release to you, Barabbas, or Jesus being called Christ?

18 For he knew they gave Him over through envy.

19 But as he was sitting on the judgment seat, his wife sent to him, saying, Let nothing *be* to you and that just *One*. For I have

suffered many things today by a dream because of Him.

20 But the chief priests and the elders persuaded the crowds, that they should ask *for* Barabbas, and to destroy Jesus.

21 And answering, the governor said to them, From the two, which do you wish that I release *to* you? And they said, Barabbas.

22 Pilate said to them, What then should I do to Jesus being called Christ? They all say to him, Crucify *Him*!

23 But the governor said, For what badness did He do? But they the more cried out, saying, Crucify!

24 And seeing that nothing is gained, but rather an uproar occurs, taking water, Pilate washed *his* hands before the crowd, saying, I am innocent of the blood of this just *One*; you will see.

25 And answering, all the people said, His blood *be* on us and on our children.

26 ¶ Then he released Barabbas to them. But having scourged Jesus, he gave *Him* over that He might be crucified.

27 Then taking Jesus into the praetorium, the soldiers of the governor gathered all the cohort against Him.

28 And stripping Him, they put a scarlet cloak around Him.

29 And plaiting a crown of thorns, they placed *it* on His head, and a reed on His right *hand*. And bowing the knee before Him, they mocked Him, saying, Hail, King of the Jews.

30 And spitting at Him, *they* took the reed and struck at His head.

31 And when they ridiculed Him, they stripped off His cloak, and they put His garments on Him and led Him away to crucify *Him*.

32 And going out, they found a man, a Cyrenean, named Simon. They compelled this one, that he bear His cross.

33 ¶ And coming to a place called Golgotha, which is called, Of a Skull Place,

34 they gave Him vinegar mingled with gall to drink. And having tasted, He would not drink.

35 And having crucified Him, they divided His clothing, casting a lot, that might be fulfilled that spoken by the prophet, "They di-

vided My clothing *to* themselves, and they cast a lot over My clothing." *Psa. 22:18*

36 And sitting down, they guarded Him there.

37 And they put up over His head His charge, *it* having been written: THIS IS JESUS, THE KING OF THE JEWS.

38 Then two plunderers were crucified with Him, one on *the* right, and one on *the* left *of Him.*

39 But those passing by blasphemed Him, shaking their heads,

40 and saying, *You* the *One* razing the temple and building *it* in three days, save Yourself. If You are the Son of God, come down from the cross.

41 And in the same way, the chief priests with the scribes and elders, mocking, said,

42 He saved others; He is not able to save Himself. If He is the King of Israel, let Him come down now from the cross, and we will believe Him.

43 He trusted on God. Let Him rescue Him now, if He desires Him. For He said, I am Son of God.

44 And also the plunderers crucified with Him defamed Him, *saying* the same.

45 And from *the* sixth hour occurred darkness over all the land until *the* ninth hour.

46 And about the ninth hour, Jesus cried out with a great voice, saying, Eli, Eli, lama sabachthani; that is, "My God, My God, why did You forsake Me?" *Psa. 22:1*

47 And hearing, some of those standing there said, This *One* calls Elijah.

48 And at once, one of them running and taking a sponge, and filling *it* with "vinegar," put *it* on a reed and "gave drink to Him." *Psa. 69:21*

49 But the rest said, Let be; let us see if Elijah is coming to save Him.

50 ¶ And crying again with a loud voice, Jesus released *His* spirit.

51 And, behold, the veil of the temple was torn into two from above as far as below. And the earth quaked, and the rocks were sheared!

52 And the tombs were opened, and many bodies of the saints who had fallen asleep were raised.

53 And coming forth out of the tombs af-ter His resurrection, *they* entered into the holy city and were revealed to many.

54 But the centurion and those with him guarding Jesus, seeing the earthquake and the things taking place, *they* feared exceedingly, saying, Truly this *One* was Son of God.

55 And many women were there, watching from afar off, *those* who followed Jesus from Galilee, ministering to Him;

56 among whom was Mary Magdalene, and Mary the mother of James and Joses, and the mother of the sons of Zebedee.

57 ¶ And evening having come, a rich man from Arimathea (Joseph by name) who also himself was discipled to Jesus,

58 coming up to Pilate, this *one* asked *for* the body of Jesus. Then Pilate commanded the body to be given.

59 And taking the body, Joseph wrapped it up in *a* clean linen *sheet,*

60 and laid it in his new tomb, which he had cut out in the rock. And having rolled a great stone *to* the door of the tomb, *he* departed.

61 And there was Mary Magdalene and the other Mary, sitting across from the grave.

62 And on the next day, which is after the Preparation, the chief priests and the Pharisees were assembled to Pilate,

63 saying, Sir, we have recalled that that deceiver while living said, After three days I will rise.

64 Therefore, command that the grave be secured until the third day, that His disciples may not come by night and steal Him away, and may say to the people, He is raised from the dead. And the last deception will be worse than the first.

65 And Pilate said to them, You have a guard, go away, make *it as* secure as you know *how.*

66 And going along with the guard, they made the grave secure, sealing the stone.

Matthew 28

1 Christ's resurrection is declared by an angel to the women. 9 He himself appears to them, 19 and sends His disciples to baptize and teach all nations.

1 ¶ But late in *the* sabbaths, at the dawning into *the* first of *the* sabbaths, Mary the

Magdalene and the other Mary came to gaze upon the grave.

2 And, behold! A great earthquake occurred! For descending from Heaven and coming near, an angel of *the* Lord rolled away the stone from the door and *was* sitting on it.

3 And the appearance of him was as lightning and his clothing white as snow.

4 And the *ones* keeping guard were shaken from the fear of him, and they became as dead *men*.

5 But answering, the angel said to the women, You must not fear, for I know that you seek Jesus who has been crucified.

6 He is not here, for He was raised, as He said. Come, see the place where the Lord was lying.

7 And going quickly say to His disciples that He was raised from the dead *ones*. And behold! He goes before you into Galilee. You will see Him there. Behold! I told you.

8 And going away from the tomb quickly, with fear and great joy, they ran to report to His disciples.

9 But as they were going to report to His disciples, behold, Jesus also met them, saying, Rejoice! And coming near, they lay hold of His feet and worshiped Him.

10 Then Jesus said to them, Do not fear. Go tell your brothers that they may go into Galilee, and there they will see Me.

11 ¶ And they, having gone, behold, some of the guard coming into the city reported to the chief priests all things that occurred.

12 And being assembled with the elders, and taking counsel, *they* gave enough silver to the soldiers,

13 saying, Say that the disciples of Him came *and* stole Him by night, we being asleep.

14 And if this is heard by the governor, we will persuade him and will make you free from anxiety.

15 And taking the silver, they did as they were taught. And this report was spread by the Jews until today.

16 ¶ But the eleven disciples went into Galilee, to the mount where Jesus appointed them.

17 And seeing Him, they worshiped Him but the *ones* doubted.

18 And coming up, Jesus spoke with them, saying, All authority in Heaven and on earth was given to Me.

19 Therefore going, disciple all the nations, baptizing them into the name of the Father and of the Son and of the Holy Spirit,

20 teaching them to observe all things, as many *things* as I commanded you. And, behold, I am with you all the days until the completion of the age. Amen.

The Gospel According to
MARK

Mark 1

1 Office of John the Baptist. 9 Jesus is baptized, 12 tempted, 14 He preaches: 16 calls Peter, Andrew, James, and John: 32 heals many diseased persons.

1 ¶ The beginning of the gospel of Jesus Christ, *the* Son of God,

2 as it has been written in the Prophets, "Behold, I send forth My messenger before Your face, who will prepare Your way before You;

3 *the* voice *of one* crying in the wilderness. Prepare the way of *the* Lord, make His paths straight." *Mal. 3:1; Isa. 40:3*

4 John came baptizing in the wilderness and proclaiming a baptism of repentance for remission of sins.

5 And all the Judean country and *those of* Jerusalem went out to him, and were all baptized by him in the Jordan River, confessing their sins.

6 And John was clothed in camel's hair, and a leather girdle about his loin, and eating locusts and wild honey.

7 And he proclaimed, saying, He who comes after me is mightier than I, of whom bending down I am not fit to loose the thong of His sandals.

8 I indeed baptized you in water, but He will baptize you in *the* Holy Spirit.

9 ¶ And it happened in those days, Jesus came from Nazareth of Galilee and was baptized by John in the Jordan.

10 And going up from the water, immediately He saw the heavens splitting, and the Spirit coming down as a dove upon Him.

11 And there was a voice out of the heavens, You are My Son, the Beloved, in whom I am well-pleased. *Psa. 2:7; Gen. 22:2; Isa. 42:1*

12 And the Spirit at once thrusts Him out into the deserted *place*.

13 And He was there in the deserted *place* forty days, being tempted by Satan, and was with the wild beasts. And the angels ministered to Him.

14 ¶ And after John was given over, Jesus came into Galilee proclaiming the gospel of the kingdom of God,

15 and saying, The time has been fulfilled, and the kingdom of God draws near. Repent and believe in the gospel.

16 And walking along beside the Sea of Galilee, He saw Simon and his brother Andrew casting a small net in the sea; for they were fishers.

17 And Jesus said to them, Come after Me, and I will make you to become fishers of men.

18 And at once, having left their nets, they followed Him.

19 And going forward from there a little, He saw James the *son* of Zebedee, and his brother John. And they were in the boat mending the nets.

20 And at once He called them. And leaving their father Zebedee in the boat with the hired servants, they went after Him.

21 And they are going into Capernaum. And entering into the synagogue, at once He taught on the sabbaths.

22 And they were astounded at His doctrine, for He was teaching them as having authority, and not as the scribes.

23 ¶ And a man with an unclean spirit was in their synagogue. And he cried out,

24 saying, What *is* to us and to You, Jesus, Nazarene? Have You come to destroy us? I know You, who You are, the Holy *One* of God.

25 And Jesus rebuked him, saying, Be muzzled, and come out of him.

26 And the unclean spirit convulsing him, and crying out with a loud voice, he came out of him.

27 And all were astonished, so as to be questioning to themselves, saying, What is this? What new teaching *is* this, that He

commands even the unclean spirits with authority, and they obey Him?

28 And His fame went out at once into all the Galilean region around.

29 ¶ And at once going out of the synagogue, they came into the house of Simon and Andrew, with James and John.

30 And the mother-in-law of Simon was laid down, fever-stricken. And at once they spoke to Him about her.

31 And coming near, He raised her up, holding her hand. And the fever left her instantly, and she served them.

32 And evening coming, when the sun set, they brought to Him all those badly having *illness* and those having been demon-possessed.

33 And the whole city was gathered at the door.

34 And He healed many of various diseases, badly having *illness*. And he cast out many demons, and *He* did not allow the demons to speak, because they knew Him.

35 And rising up quite early in *the* night, He went out and went away into a deserted place. And *He* was praying there.

36 And Simon and those with him searched for Him.

37 And finding Him, they said to Him, All are seeking You.

38 And He said to them, Let us go into the neighboring towns, that I may proclaim there also. For it was for this I came forth.

39 And He was proclaiming in their synagogues in all Galilee, and casting out the demons.

40 ¶ And a leper came to Him, begging Him, and falling on *his* knees to Him, and saying to Him, If You will, You are able to make me clean.

41 And being moved with compassion, reaching out the hand, Jesus touched him, and said to him, I will! Be made clean!

42 And *He* having spoken, instantly the leprosy departed from him, and he was made clean.

43 And strictly warning him, He at once put him out,

44 and said to him, See, tell no one a thing, but go show yourself to the priest, and offer what Moses directed concerning your cleansing, for a testimony to them.

45 But going out he began to proclaim much, and to spread about the matter, so that He no longer could openly enter into a city. But He was outside in deserted places. And they came to Him from every quarter.

Mark 2

1 Christ heals a paralytic, 14 calls Matthew from the receipt of custom, 18 and excuses His disciples for not fasting.

1 ¶ And again He entered into Capernaum after *some* days. And it was heard that He was in *a* house.

2 And at once many were gathered, so as no longer to have room, not even to the door. And He spoke the Word to them.

3 And they came to Him carrying a paralyzed *one*, being borne by four.

4 And not being able to draw near to Him, due to the crowd, they unroofed the roof where He was. And having dug through, they lowered the cot on which the paralyzed *one* was lying.

5 And seeing their faith, Jesus said to the paralyzed *one*, Child, your sins are remitted to you.

6 But some of the scribes were sitting there and reasoning in their hearts,

7 Why does this one speak blasphemies this way? Who is able to remit sins, except One, God?

8 And instantly knowing in His spirit that they reasoned this way within themselves, Jesus said to them, Why do you reason these things in your hearts?

9 Which is easier? To say to the paralyzed *one*, *Your* sins are remitted to you, or to say, Rise up and take your pallet and walk?

10 But that you may know that the Son of Man has authority to remit sins on the earth, He said to the paralyzed *one*,

11 I say to you, Rise up and take up your pallet and go to your house.

12 And he rose up at once. And taking his pallet, he went out before all, so as all to be astonished and glorified God, saying, Never did we see *it* this way.

13 ¶ And He went out by the sea again. And all the crowd came to Him, and He taught them.

14 And passing on, He saw Levi the *son* of Alpheus sitting at the tax office. And *He* said to him, Follow Me. And rising up, he followed Him.

15 And it happened as He reclined in his house, even many tax collectors and sinners reclined with Jesus and His disciples, for they were many. And they followed Him.

16 And the scribes and Pharisees seeing Him eating with tax collectors and sinners, *they* said to His disciples, Why *is it* that He eats and drinks with the tax collectors and sinners?

17 And hearing, Jesus says to them, Those who are strong have no need of a physician, but those badly having *illness*. I did not come to call the righteous *ones* to repentance, but sinners.

18 ¶ And John's disciples, and those of the Pharisees, were fasting. And they came and said to Him, Why do John's disciples and those of the Pharisees fast, but Your disciples do not fast?

19 And Jesus said to them, Are the sons of the bridechamber able to fast in which the groom is with them? As much time they have the groom with them, they cannot fast.

20 But the days will come when the groom will be taken away from them, and then they will fast in those days.

21 And no one sews a patch of unmilled cloth on an old garment, else *it* takes away its fullness, the new *from* the old, and a worse tear occurs.

22 And no one puts new wine into old wineskins, else the new wine bursts the wineskins, and the wine pours out, and the wineskins will be destroyed. But new wine is put into fresh wineskins.

23 And it happened, He went along through the grain fields in the sabbaths. And His disciples began to make way, plucking the heads *of grain*.

24 And the Pharisees said to Him, Behold, why do they do that which is not lawful on the sabbaths?

25 And He said to them, Did you never read what David did when he had need and hungered, he and the *ones* with him,

26 how he entered the house of God *in the days of* Abiathar the high priest, and ate the Loaves of the Presentation, which it is not lawful to eat, except for the priests, and *he* even gave to the *ones* being with him?

27 And He said to them, The sabbath came into being for man's sake, not man for the sabbath's sake.

28 So then the Son of Man is Lord of the sabbath also.

Mark 3

1 Christ heals the withered hand: 13 He chooses His twelve apostles.

1 ¶ And again He entered into the synagogue. And there was a man having the hand withered.

2 And they watched Him, whether He will heal him on the sabbath, that they might accuse Him.

3 And He said to the man having a withering of the hand, Rise up into the middle.

4 And He said to them, *Is it* lawful to do good on the sabbath, or to do evil? To save a soul, or to kill? But they were silent.

5 And having looked around on them with anger, being greatly grieved over the hardness of their heart, He said to the man, Stretch out your hand! And he stretched out, and his hand was restored sound as the other.

6 And going out, the Pharisees at once took counsel with the Herodians against Him, how they might destroy Him.

7 And Jesus withdrew to the sea with His disciples; and a great multitude from Galilee and from Judea followed Him,

8 also from Jerusalem, and from Idumea, and beyond the Jordan, also those around Tyre and Sidon. A great multitude, hearing how much He was doing, came to Him.

9 And He spoke to His disciples that a small boat should stay near to Him because of the crowd, that they might not press upon Him.

10 For He healed many, so that they fell on Him, that they might touch Him, as many as had plagues.

11 And when the unclean spirits saw Him, *they* fell down before Him, and cried out, saying, You are the Son of God!

12 And He warned them very much that they should not make Him known.

13 ¶ And He went up into the mountain, and He called near whom He desired. And they went to Him.

14 And He made *disciples of* twelve, that they might be with Him; and that He might send them to proclaim,

15 and to have authority to heal diseases, and to cast out the demons.

16 And He put on Simon *the* name Peter.

17 And on James the *son* of Zebedee, and John the brother of James, He put on them *the* names Boanerges, which is, Sons of Thunder.

18 Also *He appointed* Andrew, and Philip, and Bartholomew, and Matthew, and Thomas, and James the *son* of Alpheus, and Thaddaeus, and Simon the Canaanite,

19 and Judas Iscariot, who also gave Him over. And He came into a house.

20 And again a crowd came together, so as they *were* not able even to eat bread.

21 And hearing, those with Him went out to take hold *of* Him; for they said, He is out of *His* mind.

22 ¶ And coming down from Jerusalem, the scribes said, He has Beelzebub; and He casts out demons by the ruler of the demons.

23 And calling them near, He spoke to them in parables, *saying*, How can Satan cast out Satan?

24 And if a kingdom is divided against itself, that kingdom cannot stand.

25 And if a house is divided against itself, that house is not able to stand.

26 And if Satan rises upon himself, and has been divided, he is not able to stand, but he has an end.

27 No one, not *any*, having entered into his house, is able to plunder the vessels of the strong *one*, unless he first tie up the strong *one;* and then he will plunder his house.

28 Truly I say to you, All the sins will be forgiven to the sons of men, also blasphemies, as many as they may blaspheme, but whoever blasphemes against the Holy Spirit has no remission unto the age, but is liable to eternal judgment

30 (because they said, He has an unclean spirit).

31 ¶ Then His mother and brothers came. And standing outside, *they* sent to Him, calling Him.

32 And a crowd sat around Him. And they said to Him, Behold, Your mother and Your brothers seek You outside.

33 And He answered them, saying, Who is My mother *or* My brothers?

34 And having looked around on those sitting around Him in a circle, He said, Behold, My mother and My brothers!

35 For whoever does the will of God, this one is My brother, and My sister, and My mother.

Mark 4

1 The parable of the sower, 14 and the meaning.
26 The parable of the seed growing secretly.
35 Christ calms the storm at sea.

1 ¶ And again He began to teach beside the sea. And a large crowd was gathered to Him, so that He stepped into the boat in order to sit in the sea. And all the crowd were on the land toward the sea.

2 And He taught them many things in parables, and said to them in His teaching:

3 Listen! Behold, the *one* sowing went out to sow.

4 And as he sowed, it happened that one indeed fell beside the road; and the birds of the heaven came and devoured it.

5 And another fell on the rocky *place* where it did not have much earth. And it sprang up at once, due to not having depth of earth.

6 And *the* sun rising, it was scorched. And through not having root, it was dried out.

7 And another fell into the thorn-bushes, and the thorn bushes grew up and choked it; and it did not yield fruit.

8 And another fell into the good ground, and yielded fruit, going up and increasing; and one bore thirty, and one sixty, and one a hundredfold.

9 And He said to them, The *one* having ears to hear, let him hear.

10 And when He was alone, the *ones* around Him, with the Twelve, asked Him *as to* the parable.

11 And He said to them, To you *it* has been given to know the mystery of the kingdom of God. But to these, the *ones* outside, all things are being *given* in parables,

12 that seeing they may see and not perceive; and hearing they may hear, and not understand, that not they should convert, and the sins be remitted to them.
Isa. 6:9, 10

13 And He said to them, Do you not know this parable? And how will you know all the parables?

14 The sower sows the Word.

15 And these are the *ones* beside the road where the Word is sown. And when they hear, Satan comes at once and takes away the Word being sown in their hearts.

16 And likewise, these are the *ones* being sown on the rocky *places*, who, when they hear the Word, *they* immediately receive it with joy,

17 yet they have no root in themselves, but are temporary. Then trouble or persecution occurring through the Word, immediately they are stumbled.

18 These are the *ones* being sown into the thorn-bushes, the *ones* hearing the Word,

19 and the anxieties of this age, and the deceitfulness of riches, and the lusts about other things entering in, *they* choke the Word, and it becomes unfruitful.

20 And these are the *ones* being sown on the good ground, who hear and welcome the Word and bring forth fruit, one thirty, and one sixty, and one a hundredfold.

21 ¶ And He said to them, Does the lamp come that it may be put under the grain measure, or under the bed? *Is it* not also that it may be put on the lampstand?

22 For not anything is hidden but that it will be revealed, nor *anything* become covered but that it will come to light.

23 If anyone has ears to hear, let him hear.

24 And He said to them, Watch what you hear. With what measure you measure, it will be measured to you; and more will be given to you, the *ones* hearing.

25 For whoever may have, it will be given to him; and who does not have, even what he has will be taken away from him.

26 And He said, So is the kingdom of God, as if a man should cast seed on the earth,

27 and should sleep, and rise night and day; and the seed should sprout and lengthen of itself, while he does not know.

28 For of itself the earth bears fruit: first greenery, then an ear, then full grain in the ear.

29 And whenever the fruit gives over, immediately he "sends forth the sickle, for the harvest has come." *Joel 3:13*

30 And He said, To what shall we compare the kingdom of God? Or with what parable shall we compare it?

31 *It is* like a grain of mustard, which, when it is sown on the earth, it is smallest than all the seeds of the *ones* on the earth.

32 And when it is sown, *it* comes up and becomes greater than all the plants, and produces great branches, so as to enable the birds of the heaven to dwell.

33 And many such parables He spoke the Word to them, even as they were able to hear.

34 But He did not speak to them without a parable. And He explained all things to His disciples privately.

35 ¶ And evening having come, He said to them on that day, let us pass over to the other side.

36 And leaving the crowd they took Him along in the boat as He was. And other small boats also were with Him.

37 And a great windstorm occurred, and the waves beat into the boat so that it was filled already.

38 And He was on the stern, sleeping on the headrest. And they awakened Him, and said to Him, Teacher, does it not matter to You that we are perishing?

39 And being awakened, He rebuked the wind, and said to the sea, Silence! Be muzzled! And the wind ceased, and there was a great calm.

40 And He said to them, Why are you so fearful? How do you not have faith?

41 And they feared a great fear and said to one another, Who then is this, that even the wind and the sea obey Him?

Mark 5

1 Christ delivers the possessed of the legion of devils. 25 He heals the bleeding woman, 35 and raises Jairus' daughter from the dead.

1 ¶ And they came to the other side of the sea, to the country of the Gadarenes.

2 And He coming out from the boat, immediately out of the tombs a man with an unclean spirit met Him,

3 who had *his* abode among the tombs; and no one was able to bind him, not even with chains.

4 Because he had often been bound with fetters and chains, and the chains had been torn by him, and the fetters had been shattered. And no one was able to subdue him.

5 And continually night and day in the hills, and in the tombs, he was crying and cutting himself with stones.

6 And seeing Jesus from afar, he ran and prostrated himself before Him.

7 And crying with a loud voice, he said, What *is* to me and to You, Jesus, Son of the most high God? I adjure You by God, do not torment me.

8 For He said to him, Unclean spirit, come out of the man!

9 And He asked him, What *is* your name? And he answered, saying, My name *is* Legion, because we are many.

10 And he was imploring Him much that He would not send them outside the country.

11 And a great herd of pigs was feeding there near the hills.

12 And all the demons implored Him, saying, Send us into the pigs, that we may enter into them.

13 And Jesus immediately allowed them. And coming out, the unclean spirits entered into the pigs. And the herd rushed down the precipice into the sea (and they were about two thousand), and *they* were choked in the sea.

14 And The *ones* who fed the pigs fled, and *they* told *it* to the city, and to the fields. And they came out to see what is the thing having happened.

15 And they come to Jesus, and behold the *one* being demon-possessed, sitting and being clothed, and being of sound mind, the *one* having had the legion. And they feared.

16 And The *ones* seeing *it* related to them how it happened to the *one* being demon possessed, and about the pigs.

17 And they began to implore Him to go away from their borders.

18 And He stepping into the boat, the *former* demoniac was imploring Him, that he be with Him.

19 But Jesus did not allow him, but says to him, Go to your house, to your *own*, and report to them as many things as the Lord has done to you and had mercy on you.

20 And he went and began to proclaim in Decapolis as many things as Jesus did to him. And all marveled.

21 ¶ And Jesus crossing over in the boat again to the other side, a large crowd was gathered upon Him; and He was beside the sea.

22 And, behold, one of the synagogue rulers, Jairus by name, comes; and seeing Him, *he* falls at His feet.

23 And *he* much implores Him, saying, My little daughter has finally *come to the* end. *I pray* that coming You may lay hands on her, that she may be cured and live.

24 And He went with him. And a large crowd was following and was pressing on Him.

25 And a certain woman being with a flow of blood twelve years,

26 and who had suffered many things by many physicians, and had spent all things that she had, and having gained nothing, but rather coming to worse,

27 hearing about Jesus, coming in the crowd behind *Him*, she touched His garment.

28 For she said, If I may but touch His garments, I will be cured.

29 And instantly the fountain of her blood was dried up, and she knew in *her* body that she is healed from the plague.

30 And knowing instantly within Himself that power had gone forth out of Him, turning in the crowd, Jesus said, Who touched My garments?

31 And His disciples said to Him, You see the crowd pressing on You, and do You say, Who touched Me?

32 And He looked around to see the *one* having done this.

33 And the woman, being afraid and trembling, knowing what had happened on her, she came and fell down before Him and told Him all the truth.

34 And He said to her, Daughter, your faith has healed you. Go in peace and be well from your plague.

35 ¶ As He was speaking, they came from the synagogue ruler saying, Your daughter

has died. Why do you still trouble the Teacher?

36 But hearing the word spoken, Jesus said to the synagogue ruler at once, Do not fear, only believe.

37 And He did not allow any*one* to accompany Him except Peter and James and John, the brother of James.

38 And He comes into the synagogue ruler's house. And He saw a tumult, and weeping and much wailing.

39 And going in, He said to them, Why do you make a tumult and weep? The child has not died, but is sleeping.

40 And they ridiculed Him. But having put all out, He took along the father and the mother of the child, and the *ones* with Him, and passed on into where the child was lying.

41 And taking hold of the child's hand, He said to her, Talitha koumi; which is, being translated, Little girl, I say to you, Rise up!

42 And immediately the little girl rose up and walked. For she was twelve years *old*. And they were amazed with great amazement.

43 And very much He charged them that no one should know this. And He said to give her something to eat.

Mark 6

1 Christ's countrymen amaze Him. 27 John Baptist is beheaded, 29 and buried. 34 The miracle of the loaves and fish.

1 ¶ And He went out from there and came to His fatherland. And His disciples follow Him.

2 And a sabbath having come, He began to teach in the synagogue. And hearing, many were astonished, saying, From where *came* these things to this One? And what *is* the wisdom given to Him, that even such works of power are occurring through His hands?

3 Is this One not the carpenter, the son of Mary, and brother of James and Joses and Judas and Simon? And are not His sisters here with us? And they were stumbled in Him.

4 And Jesus said to them, A prophet is not without honor, except in his fatherland, and among the relatives, and in his own house.

5 And He could do no work of power there, except He performed healing on a few sick *ones*, laying on *His* hands.

6 And He marveled because of their unbelief. And He went about the villages in a circuit, teaching.

7 ¶ And He called the Twelve to Him and began to send them out two by two. And He gave them authority over the unclean spirits,

8 and charged them that they take nothing in *the* way, except only a staff; no bag, no bread, no copper in the belt;

9 but having tied on sandals, and not putting on two tunics.

10 And He said to them, Wherever you enter into a house, remain there until you go out from there.

11 And as many as will not receive you, nor hear you, going out from there, shake off the dust under your feet for a testimony to them. Truly I say to you, It will be more bearable for Sodom or Gomorrah in Judgment Day than for that city.

12 And going out, they proclaimed that *men* should repent.

13 And they cast out many demons, and anointed with oil many sick *ones* and healed *them*.

14 ¶ And Herod the king heard, for His name became well known. And he said, John the baptizing *one* was raised from the dead *ones*, and because of this the works of power operate in Him.

15 Others said, He is Elijah; and others said, He is a prophet or as one of the prophets.

16 But hearing, Herod said, This one is John whom I beheaded. He has risen from the dead *ones*.

17 For having sent, Herod himself had seized John and bound him in the prison, because of Herodias the wife of his brother Philip, because he had married her.

18 For John had said to Herod, It is not lawful for you to have the wife of your brother.

19 And Herodias held it against him, and desired to kill him, but was not able.

20 For Herod feared John, knowing him *to be* a holy and just man, and kept him

safe. And hearing him, he did many things, and gladly heard from him.

21 And a well-timed day having come, when Herod made a dinner for his chief men on his birthday, also the chiliarchs, and the chief ones of Galilee.

22 And the daughter of Herodias herself entering, and having danced, she also pleased Herod and the *ones* reclining with *him*. The king said to the girl, Ask me whatever you will, and I will give *it* to you.

23 And he swore to her, Whatever you ask me, I will give to you, up to half of my kingdom.

24 And going out, she said to her mother, What shall I ask? And she said, The head of John the Baptist.

25 And immediately going in with haste to the king, she asked, saying, I desire that at once you give to me the head of John the Baptist on a platter.

26 And having become deeply grieved, *but* because of the oaths and those reclining together, the king did not wish to reject her.

27 And the king sending an executioner at once, he commanded his head to be brought. And going, he beheaded him in the prison,

28 and *he* brought his head on a platter and gave it to the girl. And the girl gave it to her mother.

29 And having heard, his disciples went and took his corpse and placed it in a tomb.

30 ¶ And the apostles gathered to Jesus. And *they* told Him all things, even as many *things* as they did and as many *things* they taught.

31 And He said to them, *You* yourselves come apart into a deserted place, and rest a little. For the *ones* coming and the *ones* going were many, and they did not even have opportunity to eat.

32 And they departed by boat into a deserted place privately.

33 And the crowds saw them going, and many recognized Him. And *they* ran together on foot there, from all the cities, and came before them, and came together to Him.

34 And going out, Jesus saw a large crowd, and had compassion on them, be-cause "they were as sheep having no shepherd." And He began to teach them many things. *Num. 27:17; Eze. 34:5*

35 And now a much *later* hour having come, drawing near to Him, His disciples said, The place is deserted, and *it is* now a much *later* hour.

36 Send them away, that going away to the surrounding farms and villages they may buy bread for themselves. For they do not have what they may eat.

37 And answering, He said to them, You give them *food* to eat. And they said to Him, Going, should we buy two hundred denarii of bread and give them to eat?

38 And He said to them, How many loaves do you have? Go and see. And knowing, they said, Five, and two fish.

39 And He ordered them all to recline, group *by* group on the green grass.

40 And they sat, ranks *by* ranks each hundred, and each fifty.

41 And taking the five loaves and the two fish, looking up to Heaven, He blessed, and broke the loaves, and giving out to His disciples, that they might set before them. And He divided the two fish to all.

42 And all ate, and were satisfied.

43 And they took up twelve baskets full *of* fragments, also from the fish.

44 And the *ones* eating the loaves were about five thousand men.

45 ¶ And at once He constrained His disciples to enter into the boat, and to go before to the other side, to Bethsaida, until He should send away the crowd.

46 And taking leave *of* them, He went away to the mountain to pray.

47 And evening having come, the boat was in *the* middle of the sea, and He alone on the land.

48 And He saw them being distressed in the rowing, for the wind was against them. And *it was* about the fourth watch of the night *when* He came toward them, walking on the sea. And *He* willed to go by them.

49 But seeing Him walking on the sea, they thought *it* to be a phantom. And *they* cried out.

50 For all saw Him, and were troubled. And immediately He spoke to them and

said to them, Have courage. I AM! Do not fear.

51 And He went up to them into the boat, and the wind ceased. And they were amazed, exceedingly out of measure within themselves, and marveled.

52 For they did not understand about *the miracle of* the loaves, for their heart was hardened.

53 And crossing over, they came into the land of Gennesaret and drew to shore.

54 And they, coming out of the boat, at once having recognized Him,

55 they ran around all that surrounding region. And they began to carry about those badly having *illness* on cots to wherever they heard that there He is.

56 And wherever He went into villages or cities or fields, they laid the feeble *ones* in the markets and begged Him if only they may grasp the fringe of His garment. And as many as grasped Him were healed.

Mark 7

1 The Pharisees find fault with the disciples for eating with unwashed hands. 14 Food does not defile one. 24 He heals the daughter of a woman from Syria of an unclean spirit.

1 ¶ And the Pharisees were assembled to Him, also some of the scribes, coming from Jerusalem.

2 And seeing some of His disciples eating bread with unclean, that is unwashed hands, they found fault.

3 For the Pharisees and all the Jews do not eat unless they wash the hands with *the* fist, holding the tradition of the elders.

4 And *coming* from the market, if they *do* not dip themselves, they do not eat. And there are many other things which they received to hold: immersings of cups, and of utensils, and of copper vessels, and couches.

5 Then the Pharisees and scribes questioned Him, Why do Your disciples not walk according to the tradition of the elders, but eat bread with unwashed hands?

6 And answering, He said to them, Well did Isaiah prophesy concerning you, hypocrites; as it has been written: "This people honors Me with the lips, but their heart is far away from Me;

7 and in vain they worship Me, teaching *as* doctrines the commandments of men." *Isa. 29:13*

8 For, forsaking the commandment of God, you hold the tradition of men: immersings of utensils and cups, and many other such like things you do.

9 And He said to them, Do you do well to set aside the commandment of God so that you may keep your tradition?

10 For Moses said, "Honor your father and your mother," *Ex. 20:12; Deut. 5:16* and, "The one speaking evil of father or mother, let him end by death." *Ex. 21:17*

11 But you say, If a man says to his father or mother, Corban, (which is, A gift!) whatever you may profit by me.

12 And you no longer allow him to do anything for *his* father or mother,

13 making void the Word of God by your tradition which you gave over. And many such like things you do.

14 And calling all the crowd near, He said to them, Hear Me, all *of you* and understand.

15 There is nothing from outside the man, entering into him, which is able to defile *him*. But the things going out from him, those are the things defiling the man.

16 If anyone has ears to hear, let him hear.

17 And when He entered into a house from the crowd, His disciples questioned Him about the parable.

18 And He said to them, Are you also so without understanding? Do you not perceive that everything entering from the outside into the man is not able to defile him?

19 *This is* because it does not enter into his heart, but into the belly, and goes out into the latrine, purging all the foods.

20 And He said, That out of the man coming out, *it is* the *thing* that defiles the man.

21 For from within, out of the heart of men go out the depraved reasonings, adulteries, fornications, murders,

22 thefts, greedy desires, depravities, deceit, unbridled lusts, an evil eye, blasphemy, pride, recklessness.

23 All these evil things come out from within and defile the man.

24 ¶ And rising up from there, he went away into the borders of Tyre and Sidon. And entering into the house, He desired no one to know, but He could not be hidden.

25 For hearing about Him, a woman came up, *one* whose little daughter had an unclean spirit, coming *she* fell down at His feet.

26 And the woman was a Greek, a Syrophoenician by race. And she asked Him, that He would cast out the demon from her daughter.

27 And Jesus said to her, First, allow the children to be satisfied, for it is not good to take the children's bread and to throw to the little dogs.

28 But she answered and said to Him, Yes, Lord; for even the little dogs under the table eat from the crumbs of the children.

29 And He said to her, Because of this word, go. The demon has gone out from your daughter.

30 And going away to her house, she found the demon had gone out, and her little daughter being laid on the bed.

31 ¶ And again going out from the borders of Tyre and Sidon, He came to the Sea of Galilee, in the midst of the borders of Decapolis.

32 And they brought a deaf *one* to Him, hardly speaking. And they begged Him, that He put *His* hand on him.

33 And taking him away from the crowd privately, He put His fingers into his ears; and spitting, He touched his tongue;

34 and looking up into Heaven, He groaned and said to him, Ephphatha! (which is, Be completely opened!)

35 And instantly his ears were opened completely, and the bond of his tongue was loosed, and he spoke correctly.

36 And He charged them that they should tell no one. But as much as He charged them, much even more, they proclaimed.

37 And they were most exceedingly amazed, saying, He has done all things well. He makes even the deaf *one* to hear, and the mute *one* to speak.

Mark 8

1 Christ miraculously feeds the people: 22 gives a blind man his sight: 27 and acknowledges that He is the Christ, who should suffer and rise again.

1 ¶ The crowd being very great in those days, and not having anything they may eat, Jesus, calling His disciples near, said to them,

2 I have compassion on the crowd because now three days they remain with Me, and they do not have what they may eat.

3 And if I send them away fasting to their house, they will faint in the way, for some of them come from afar.

4 And His disciples answered Him, From where will anyone here be able to satisfy these *with* loaves on a place of solitude?

5 And He asked them, How many loaves do you have? And they said, Seven.

6 And He ordered the crowd to recline on the ground. And taking the seven loaves, having giving thanks, He broke and gave to His disciples, that they may set before *them*. And they set before the crowd.

7 And they had a few fish. And blessing, He said for these also to be set before *them*.

8 And they ate, and were satisfied. And they took up *the* surplus, seven baskets of fragments.

9 And the *ones* eating were about four thousand. And He sent them away.

10 ¶ And at once stepping into the boat with His disciples, He came into the parts of Dalmanutha.

11 And the Pharisees went out and began to question Him, seeking from Him a sign from Heaven, tempting Him.

12 And sighing in His spirit, He said, Why does this generation seek after a sign? Truly I say to you, *As if* this generation will be given a sign!

13 And leaving them, again stepping into the boat, He went away to the other side.

14 And *the disciples* forgot to take loaves. And they did not have *any* with them, except one loaf in the boat.

15 And He charged them, saying, See! Look out *for* the leaven of the Pharisees, and *of* the leaven of Herod.

16 And they reasoned with one another, saying, We have no loaves.

17 And knowing, Jesus said to them, Why do you reason that you have no loaves? Do you not yet perceive nor understand? Have you still hardened your heart?

18 "Having eyes, do you not see? And having ears, do you not hear?" And do you not remember? *Jer. 5:21*

19 When I broke the five loaves to the five thousand, how many baskets full of fragments did you take up? They said to Him, Twelve.

20 And when the seven to the four thousand, how many baskets did you take up *with the* fillings of fragments? And they said, Seven.

21 And He said to them, How do you not understand?

22 ¶ And He came to Bethsaida. And they bring a blind *one* to Him, and begged Him that He would touch him.

23 And having taken hold of the blind *one's* hand, He led him forth outside the village. And having spit into his eyes, having laid *His* hands on him, He asked him if he saw anything.

24 And having looked up, he said, I see men as trees walking around.

25 Then again He placed *His* hands on his eyes, and made him look up. And he was restored and saw all clearly.

26 And He sent him to his house, saying, You may not go into the village, nor may tell anyone in the village.

27 ¶ And Jesus and His disciples went out to the villages of Caesarea of Philip. And in the way, He questioned His disciples, saying to them, Whom do men say Me to be?

28 And they answered, John the Baptist, and others *say* Elijah; but others, one of the prophets.

29 And He said to them, And you, whom do you say Me to be? And answering, Peter said to Him, You are the Christ.

30 And He warned them that they may tell no one about Him.

31 And He began to teach them that it is necessary for the Son of Man to suffer many things and to be rejected of the elders and chief priests and scribes, and to be killed, and after three days to rise again.

32 And He spoke the Word plainly. And taking Him aside, Peter began to rebuke Him.

33 But turning around and seeing His disciples, He rebuked Peter, saying, Go behind Me, Satan, because you do not think the things of God, but the things of men.

34 And calling near the crowd with His disciples, He said to them, Whoever desires to come after Me, let him deny himself and take up his cross, and let him follow Me.

35 For whoever desires to save his life, *he* shall lose it. But whoever may lose his life for My sake and the gospel, this one shall save it.

36 For what shall it profit a man if he gain the whole world, yet forfeit his soul?

37 Or what shall a man give *as* an exchange *for* his soul?

38 For whoever may be ashamed of Me and My Word in this adulterous and sinful generation, the Son of Man will also be ashamed of him when He comes in the glory of His Father with the holy angels.

Mark 9

2 Jesus is transfigured. 11 He instructs his disciples concerning Elijah: 14 casts forth a dumb and deaf spirit: 30 and foretells his death.

1 ¶ And He said to them, Truly I say to you, There are some of the *ones* standing here who not shall taste of death, not until they see the kingdom of God coming in power.

2 And after six days Jesus takes along Peter and James and John, and leads them into a high mountain apart, alone. And He was transfigured before them.

3 And His garments became shining, very white like snow, such as a fuller on earth is not able to whiten.

4 And Elijah with Moses was seen by them, and they were speaking with Jesus.

5 And answering, Peter said to Jesus, Rabbi, it is good *for* us to be here; and, Let us make three tents, one for You, and one for Moses, and one for Elijah.

6 For he did not know what to say, for they were terrified.

7 And came to be a cloud overshadowing them, and a voice came out of the cloud, saying, "This is My Son," the Beloved; hear Him. *Psa. 2:7; Gen. 22:2; Deut. 18:15*

8 And suddenly, having looked around, they saw no one any longer, but Jesus alone with themselves.

9 And as they were coming down from the mountain, He charged them that they should tell no one what they saw, except when the Son of Man should rise from *the* dead *ones*.

10 And they held the word to themselves, debating what *it* is to rise from *the* dead *ones*.

11 And they asked Him, saying, Do the scribes say that Elijah must come first?

12 And answering, He said to them, Indeed, Elijah coming first restores all things. And how it is written concerning the Son of Man that He should suffer many things and be utterly despised?

13 But I say to you, Elijah also has come and they did to him as many *things* as they desired, even as it is written about him.

14 ¶ And coming to the disciples, He saw a great crowd around them, and scribes disputing with them.

15 And at once all the crowd seeing Him were greatly amazed. And running to *Him*, they greeted Him.

16 And He questioned the scribes, What are you arguing with them?

17 And one answered out of the crowd, saying, Teacher, I brought my son to You, having a mute spirit.

18 And wherever it seizes him, it convulses him; and he foams and gnashes his teeth. And he wastes away. And I told Your disciples, that they might expel it. And they were not able.

19 And answering them, He said, O unbelieving generation! How long will I be with you? How long shall I endure you? Bring him to Me.

20 And they brought him to Him. And seeing Him, the spirit immediately convulsed him. And falling on the ground, he wallowed, foaming.

21 And He questioned his father, How long a time is it while this has happened to him? And he said, From childhood.

22 And often it threw him both into fire and into water, that it might destroy him. But if You are able to do anything, help us, having compassion on us.

23 And Jesus said to him, If you are able to believe, all things *are* possible to the *ones* believing.

24 And immediately crying out, the father of the child said with tears, Lord, I believe! Help my unbelief!

25 And seeing that a crowd is running together, Jesus rebuked the unclean spirit, saying to it, Mute and deaf spirit, I command you, Come out from him, and you may no more go into him!

26 And crying out, and convulsing him very much, it came out. And he became as if dead, so as *for* many to say that he died.

27 But taking hold of his hand, Jesus raised him up, and he stood up.

28 And He entering into a house, His disciples questioned Him apart, *Why* were we not able to cast it out?

29 And He said to them, This kind can go out by nothing except by prayer and fasting.

30 ¶ And going forth from there, they passed by through Galilee. And He desired that no one know.

31 For He was teaching His disciples, and said to them, The Son of Man is given over into *the* hands of men, and they will kill Him. And being killed, He will rise up the third day.

32 But they did not know the Word, and feared to question Him.

33 And they came to Capernaum. And being in the house, He questioned them, What were you disputing among yourselves in the way?

34 But they were silent, for they disputed with one another in the way *as to* who *was* greater.

35 And sitting, He called the Twelve and said to them, If anyone desires to be first, he shall be last of all and servant of all.

36 And taking a little child, He set it in their midst, and having embraced it, He said to them,

37 Whoever receives one of such little children on My name receives Me. And whoever receives Me does not receive Me, but the One having sent Me.

38 And John answered Him, saying, Teacher, we saw someone casting out demons in Your name, who does not follow

us. And we forbade him, because he does not follow us.

39 But Jesus said, Do not forbid him. For there is no one who shall do a work of power in My name, yet be able to speak evil of Me quickly.

40 For who is not against us is for us.

41 ¶ For whoever gives you a cup of cold water to drink in My name, because you are of Christ, truly I say to you, not he will lose his reward, not *ever*.

42 And whoever causes one of *these* little ones that believe into Me to stumble, it is good for him if rather a millstone be laid about his neck, and he be thrown into the sea.

43 And if your hand causes you to stumble, cut it off. For it is profitable for you to enter into life maimed, than having two hands to go away into Hell, into the un-quenchable fire,

44 where their worm does not die, and the fire is not quenched. Isa. 66:24

45 And if your foot causes you to stumble, cut it off, for it is profitable for you to enter into life lame, than having two feet to be thrown into Hell, into the unquench-able fire,

46 where their worm does not die, and the fire is not quenched. *Isa. 66:24*

47 And if your eye causes you to stumble, cast it out. For it is profitable for you to enter into the kingdom of God one-eyed, than having two eyes to be thrown into the Hell of fire,

48 "where their worm does not die and the fire is not quenched." *Isa. 66:24*

49 For everyone will be salted with fire, and every sacrifice will be salted with salt.

50 Salt *is* good, but if the salt becomes saltless, by what will you season it? Have salt in yourselves and be at peace with one another.

Mark 10

2 Christ disputes with the Pharisees concerning divorce: 13 blesses the children: 46 and causes Bartimaeus to see again.

1 ¶ And rising up from there, He came into the borders of Judea by the other side of the Jordan. And again crowds came to-

gether to Him, and as He usually did, He again was teaching them.

2 And coming near, the Pharisees asked Him if it is lawful for a man to dismiss a wife, testing Him.

3 But answering, He said to them, What did Moses command you?

4 And they said, Moses allowed "to write a bill of divorce, and to dismiss." *Deut. 24:1*

5 And answering, Jesus said to them, With respect to your hardheartedness he wrote this command to you.

6 But from *the* beginning of creation "God made them male and female." *Gen. 1:27*

7 "Because of this, a man shall leave his father and mother and shall be joined to his wife,

8 and the two shall be one flesh;" so that they no longer are two, but one flesh. *Gen. 2:24*

9 Therefore, what God yoked together, let not man put apart.

10 And again, in the house His disciples asked Him about the same.

11 And He said to them, Whoever shall dismiss his wife and marry another commits adultery against her.

12 And if a woman shall dismiss her husband and marries another, she commits adultery.

13 ¶ And they brought children to Him, that He might touch them. But the disciples were rebuking the *ones* carrying *them*.

14 But seeing, Jesus was indignant. And He said to them, Allow the children to come to Me, and do not hinder them. For of such is the kingdom of God.

15 Truly I say to you, Whoever does not receive the kingdom of God as a child may not enter into it, not *ever*.

16 And having taken them in *His* arms, laying hands on them, He blessed them.

17 ¶ And He having gone out into *the* highway, running up and kneeling down to Him, one questioned Him, Good Teacher, what shall I do that I may inherit eternal life?

18 But Jesus said to him, Why do you call Me good? No one is good except One, God.

19 You know the commandments: Do not commit adultery, do not commit murder, do not steal, do not bear false witness, do

not defraud, honor your father and mother. *Ex. 20:12-16*

20 And answering, he said to Him, Teacher, I observed all these from my youth.

21 And looking at him, Jesus loved him, and said to him, One *thing* is lacking to you. Go, sell as many things as you have, and give to the poor. And you will have treasure in Heaven. And come, follow Me, taking up the cross.

22 But being sad at the Word, he went away grieving; for he had many possessions.

23 And having looked around, Jesus said to His disciples, How hardly those having riches will enter into the kingdom of God!

24 And the disciples were astonished at His Words. And answering again, Jesus said to them, Children, how hard it is for The *ones* trusting on riches to enter into the kingdom of God!

25 It is easier *for* a camel to pass through the eye of the needle, than *for* a rich *one* to enter into the kingdom of God.

26 And they were exceedingly astonished, saying to themselves, And who is able to be saved?

27 But looking at them, Jesus said, From men *it is* impossible, but not from God. For all things are possible from God.

28 And Peter began to say to Him, Behold, we left all and followed You.

29 But answering, Jesus said, Truly I say to you, There is no one who forsook house, or brothers, or sisters, or father, or mother, or wife, or children, or fields, for My sake and the gospel,

30 that will not receive a hundredfold now in this time, houses and brothers and sisters and mothers and children, and lands, with persecutions; and in the coming age, eternal life.

31 But many first shall be last, and the last *shall be* first.

32 ¶ And they were in the highway, going up to Jerusalem. And Jesus was going before them, and following they were astonished and were afraid. And taking the Twelve again, He began to tell them the things about to happen to Him:

33 Behold, we are going up to Jerusalem. And the Son of Man will be given over to the chief priests and to the scribes. And they will condemn Him to death and will give Him over to the nations.

34 And they will mock Him and will scourge Him and will spit at Him, and will kill Him. And on the third day He will rise again.

35 And coming up to Him, James and John, the sons of Zebedee, said, Teacher, we desire that whatever we may ask You would do for us.

36 And *He* said to them, What do you desire for Me to do for you?

37 And they said to Him, Give us that we may sit one on *the* right of You and one on *the* left of You in Your glory.

38 But Jesus said to them, You do not know what you ask. Are you able to drink the cup which I drink, and to be baptized *with* the baptism I am baptized *with*?

39 And they said to Him, We are able. But Jesus said to them, Indeed you will drink the cup which I drink, and you will be baptized *with* the baptism *with* which I am baptized.

40 But to sit on My right and on My left is not Mine to give, but for whom it has been prepared.

41 And hearing, the ten began to be indignant about James and John.

42 But having called them near, Jesus said to them, You know that The *ones* seeming to rule the nations lord it over them, and The *ones* great among them exercise authority over them.

43 But it shall not be so among you, but whoever desires to become great among you shall be your servant.

44 And whoever of you desires to become first, *he* shall be servant of all.

45 For even the Son of Man did not come to be served, but to serve, and to give His life *as* a ransom instead of many.

46 ¶ And they come into Jericho. And He and His disciples and a considerable crowd having gone out from Jericho, a son of Timaeus, Bartimaeus the blind, sat beside the highway begging.

47 And hearing that it was Jesus the Nazarene, he began to cry out and to say, Son of David, Jesus, have mercy on me!

48 And many warned him that he be quiet. But he much more cried out, Son of David have mercy on me!

49 And standing still, Jesus said for him to be called. And they called the blind *one*, saying to him, Have courage, rise up, He calls you.

50 And throwing away his garment, rising up, he came to Jesus.

51 And answering, Jesus said to him, What do you desire I should do to you? And the blind *one* said to Him, My Lord, that I may see again.

52 And Jesus said to him, Go, your faith has healed you. And instantly he saw again, and followed Jesus in the highway.

Mark 11

1 Christ rides into Jerusalem: 12 curses the fruitless tree: 20 and exhorts His disciples to steadfastness of faith.

1 ¶ And when they drew near to Jerusalem, to Bethphage and Bethany, toward the Mount of Olives, He sent two of His disciples,

2 and said to them, Go into the village opposite you. And going into it, at once you will find a young ass tied, on which no one of men has sat. Loosing it, bring *it*.

3 And if anyone says to you, Why do you do this? say, The Lord has need of it. And he will at once send it here.

4 And they departed and found the young ass tied at the door outside, by the crossway; and they loosed it.

5 And some of those standing there said to them, What are you doing, loosing the young ass?

6 And they said to them as Jesus commanded, and they let them go.

7 And they led the young ass to Jesus. And they threw their garments on it, and He sat on it.

8 And many spread their garments on the road, and others were cutting branches from the trees and were spreading *them* into the road.

9 And those going before, and those following after, were crying out, saying, Hosanna! "Blessed *is* the *One* coming in *the* name of *the* Lord!" *Psa. 118:26*

10 Blessed *is* the coming kingdom of our father David in *the* name of *the* Lord! Hosanna in the highest!

11 And Jesus entered into Jerusalem, and into the temple. And having looked around at all things, the hour already being late, He went out to Bethany with the Twelve.

12 ¶ And on the morrow, they going out from Bethany, He hungered.

13 And seeing afar off a fig tree having leaves, He went *toward it*, if perhaps He would find anything on it. And coming on it, He found nothing except leaves, for it was not *the* season of figs.

14 And answering, Jesus said to it, Let no one eat fruit of you any more to the age. And His disciples heard.

15 And they came to Jerusalem. And entering into the temple, Jesus began to throw out those selling and buying in the temple; also He overturned the tables of the money changers and the seats of those selling the doves.

16 And *He* did not allow any to carry a vessel through the temple.

17 And *He* taught, saying to them, Is it not written, "My house shall be called a house of prayer for all the nations." "But you have made it a den of plunderers."? *Isa. 56:7; Jer. 7:11*

18 And the scribes and the chief priests heard. And they sought how they might destroy Him, for they feared Him, because all the crowd was astonished at His doctrine.

19 And when evening came, He went outside the city.

20 And passing along early, they saw the fig tree withered from *the* roots.

21 And remembering, Peter said to Him, Rabbi, behold, the fig tree which You cursed has withered.

22 And answering, Jesus said to them, Have faith of God.

23 For truly I say to you, Whoever says to this mountain, Be taken up and be thrown into the sea, and does not doubt in his heart, but believes that what he says will happen, it will be to him, whatever he says.

24 Therefore I say to you, All things, as many *things* as you ask, praying, believe that you *will* receive, and it will be to you.

25 And when you stand praying, if you have anything against anyone, forgive *it*, so that your Father in Heaven may also forgive your deviations.

26 But if you do not forgive, neither will your Father in Heaven forgive your deviations.

27 ¶ And they come again to Jerusalem. And as He was walking in the temple, the chief priests and the scribes and the elders came to Him.

28 And they said to Him, By what authority do You do these things? And who gave You this authority that You do these things?

29 And answering, Jesus said to them, I will also ask you one thing, and answer Me, and I will tell you by what authority I do these things:

30 The baptism of John, was *it* from Heaven, or from men? Answer Me.

31 And they were reasoning to themselves, saying, If we say, From Heaven, He will say, Why then did you not believe him?

32 But if we say, From men, they feared the people. For all held that John truly was a prophet.

33 And answering, they said to Jesus, We do not know. And answering, Jesus said to them, Neither do I tell you by what authority I do these things.

Mark 12

1 The parable of the vineyard. 13 Christ avoids snare of the Pharisees about paying tribute: 41 and commends the poor widow for her two coins.

1 ¶ And He began to speak to them in parables: "A man planted a vineyard," and set a fence around *it* and dug a winevat, "and built a tower." And *he* rented it to vinedressers and went abroad. *Isa. 5:1, 2*

2 And at the season, he sent a slave to the vinedressers, that he might receive from the vinedressers the fruit of the vineyard.

3 But taking him, they beat *him*, and sent *him* away empty.

4 And again he sent to them another slave; stoning that one, they struck *him* in the head and sent *him* away, dishonoring him.

5 And again, he sent another, and they killed that one; also many others, indeed beating these, and killing these.

6 Yet having one son, his own beloved, therefore he sent him to them also, last *of all*, saying, They will respect my son.

7 But those vinedressers said to themselves, This is the heir; come, let us kill him and the inheritance will be ours.

8 And taking *him*, they killed him and threw *him* outside the vineyard.

9 What, therefore, will the lord of the vineyard do? He will come and will destroy the vinedressers and will give the vineyard to others.

10 Have you not even read this Scripture: *The* "Stone which the builders rejected, this One came to be Head of *the* Corner;

11 this came about from *the* Lord, and it is marvelous in our eyes"? *Psalm 118:22, 23; Acts 4:11*

12 And they sought to seize Him, and feared the crowd. For they knew that He spoke the parable against them. And leaving Him, they went away.

13 ¶ And they sent some of the Pharisees and of the Herodians to Him, that they might catch Him in a word.

14 And coming, they said to Him, Teacher, we know that You are true, and there is not a care to You about anyone, for You do not look to *the* face of men, but teach the way of God *in* truth: Is it lawful to give tribute to Caesar, or not?

15 Should we give, or should we not give? But knowing their hypocrisy, He said to them, Why do you tempt Me? Bring Me a denarius that I may see.

16 And they brought *one*. And He said to them, Whose image and inscription is this? And they said to Him, Caesar's.

17 And answering, Jesus said to them, Give back the things of Caesar to Caesar, and the things of God to God. And they marveled at Him.

18 ¶ And Sadducees came to Him, who say there is no resurrection. And they questioned Him, saying,

19 Teacher, Moses wrote for us that if a brother of anyone should die and leave behind a wife, and leave no children, that his brother should take his wife and raise up seed to his brother. *Deut. 25:5*

20 Then there were seven brothers. And the first took a wife, and dying, *he* left no seed.

21 And the second took her, and died, and neither did he leave seed; and the third likewise.

22 And the seven took her and left no seed. Last of all the woman also died.

23 Therefore in the resurrection, when they rise again, of which of them will she be the wife? For the seven had her as wife.

24 And answering, Jesus said to them, Do you not err because of this, not knowing the Scriptures nor the power of God?

25 For when they rise again from *the* dead *ones*, they neither marry nor are given in marriage, but are as angels in Heaven.

26 But concerning the dead *ones*, that they are raised, have you not read in the book of Moses, as God spoke to him at the Bush, saying, "I am the God of Abraham, and the God of Isaac, and the God of Jacob"? *Ex. 3:6*

27 He is not the God of *the* dead *ones*, but God of *the* living *ones*. Therefore, you greatly err.

28 ¶ And coming near, one of the scribes, hearing them arguing, knowing that He answered them well, he questioned Him, What is *the* first commandment of all?

29 And Jesus answered him, The first of all the commandments *is*: "Hear, Israel. *The* Lord our God is one Lord,

30 and you shall love *the* Lord your God out of all your heart, and out of all your soul" and out of all your mind, "and out of all your strength." This is the first commandment. *Deut. 6:4, 5*

31 And *the* second *is* like this, "You shall love your neighbor as yourself." There is not another commandment greater than these. *Lev. 19:18*

32 And the scribe said to Him, You say well, Teacher. You have spoken according to truth, "that God is one," and "there is no other except Him;" *Deut. 4:35; 6:4, 5*

33 "and to love Him from all the heart," and from all the understanding, "and from all the soul, and from all the strength;" and "to love one's neighbor as oneself" is more than all the burnt offerings and the sacrifices. *Lev. 19:18; Deut. 6:4, 5*

34 And seeing that he answered wisely, Jesus said to him, You are not far from the kingdom of God. And no one dared to question Him any more.

35 ¶ And teaching in the temple, answering, Jesus said, How do the scribes say that Christ is the son of David?

36 For David himself said by the Holy Spirit, "The Lord said to my Lord, Sit on My right until I place Your enemies as a footstool for Your feet." *LXX-Psa. 109:1; MT-Psa. 110:1*

37 Then David himself calls Him Lord. And from where is He his son? And the large crowd heard Him gladly.

38 And He said to them in His teaching, Watch out from the scribes, the *ones* desiring to walk about in long robes, and *desiring* greetings in the marketplaces,

39 and chief seats in the synagogues, and chief couches in the dinners,

40 those devouring the houses of widows, and for a pretense praying at length. These will receive more abundant judgment.

41 ¶ And sitting down opposite the treasury, Jesus was watching how the crowd is throwing copper *coins* into the treasury. And many rich ones threw in much.

42 And coming, one poor widow threw in two lepta (which is a kodrantes).

43 And having called His disciples near, He said to them, Truly I say to you that this poor widow has thrown *in* more than all of those casting into the treasury.

44 For all threw *in* out of that abounding to them, but she out of her poverty threw *in* all, as much as she had, her whole livelihood.

Mark 13

1 Christ foretells the destruction of the temple: 10 that the gospel must be preached to all nations: 14 and that great calamities shall happen to the Jews.

1 ¶ And as He was going out of the temple, one of His disciples said to Him, Teacher, Behold! What kind of stones and what kind of buildings!

2 And answering, Jesus said to him, Do you see these great buildings? Not a stone shall be left, not a stone on a stone which will not be thrown down, not *one*.

3 And *as* He *was* sitting in the Mount of Olives opposite the temple, Peter and James and John and Andrew questioned Him privately:

4 Tell us when these things shall be? And what *is* the sign when all these things are about to be done?

5 ¶ And Jesus answering to them began to say, Watch out not anyone you lead astray.

6 For many will come in My name, saying, I AM! And they will lead many astray.

7 But when you hear *of* wars and rumors of wars, do not be disturbed, for it must occur; but the end *is* not yet.

8 For nation will be raised against nation, and kingdom against kingdom. And there shall be earthquakes in *many* places. And there shall be famines and tumults. These things *are* the beginnings of birth-pangs.

9 But you watch yourselves, for they will give you over to sanhedrins and to synagogues. You will be beaten, and you will stand before governors and kings for My sake, for a testimony to them.

10 And the gospel must first be proclaimed to all the nations.

11 But whenever they lead you away, giving you over, do not be anxious beforehand, what you should say, nor ponder. But whatever is given to you in that hour, speak that. For you are not the *ones* speaking, but the Holy Spirit.

12 And a brother will give over a brother to death, and a father the child. And children will rise up on parents and will put them to death.

13 And you will be hated by all on account of My name. But the *one* enduring to the end, this *one* will be kept safe.

14 ¶ But when you see "the abomination of desolation," the *one* spoken of by Daniel the prophet, standing where it ought not (he reading, let him understand), then let those in Judea flee into the mountains. *Dan. 11:31; 12:11*

15 And the *ones* on the housetop, let him not go down into the house, *and* not go in to take a thing out of his house.

16 And the *one* in the field, let him not return to the things behind to take his garment.

17 But woe to *those* holding *a babe* in womb, and to the *ones* giving suck in those days!

18 And pray that your flight will not be in winter;

19 for there will be affliction *in* those days such as has not been the like, not from *the* beginning of creation which God created until now, and not will be.

20 And if *the* Lord had not cut short the days, not any flesh would be saved; but because of the elect whom He elected, He has cut short the days.

21 And then if anyone says to you, Behold, here *is* the Christ! Or, Behold, there! You shall not believe.

22 For false christs and false prophets will be raised, and they will give *miraculous* signs and wonders in order to lead astray, if possible, even the elect.

23 But you watch out. Behold, I have foretold you all things.

24 ¶ But in those days, after that affliction, the sun will be darkened, and the moon will not give her light;

25 and the stars of the heaven will be falling, and the powers in the heavens will be shaken.

26 And then they will see the Son of Man coming in clouds with much power and glory. *Dan. 7:13*

27 And then He will send His angels and will gather together His elect from the four winds, from *the* end of earth to *the* end of *the* heaven.

28 ¶ And from the fig tree learn the parable: When its shoot already becomes tender and puts out leaves, you know the summer is near.

29 So you also, when you see these things happening, know that it is near, at *the* doors.

30 Truly I say to you, This generation will not pass away, not *ever*, not until all these things occur.

31 The heaven and the earth will pass away, but My words will not pass away, not *ever*!

32 But concerning that day and the hour, no one has known, not the angels in Heaven, nor the Son, except the Father.

33 Watch! Be wakeful, and pray. For you do not know when the time is.

34 As a man going away, having left his house, and giving his slaves authority, and to each his work (and he commanded the doorkeeper, that he watch),

35 Therefore be wakeful, for you do not know when the lord of the house is coming, *at* evening, or at midnight, or at cockcrowing, or early;

36 so that, coming suddenly, he not find you sleeping.

37 And what I say to you, I say to all. Be wakeful!

Mark 14

1 A conspiracy against Christ. 3 Precious ointment is poured on His head by a woman. 10 Judas sells his Master for silver. 22 Christ institutes His supper. 26 Peter's denial. 43 Judas gives Him over to the Jews 46 He is taken, falsely accused, and condemned by the Jews' council.

1 ¶ And it was the Passover, and *the Feast* of Unleavened *Bread* after two days. And the chief priests and the scribes sought how, having seized Him by guile, they might kill *Him.*

2 But they said, Not during the Feast, lest there will be a tumult of the people.

3 And He being in Bethany in the house of Simon the leper, *He* reclining, a woman came, having an alabaster vial of pure, costly ointment of nard. And breaking the alabaster vial, she poured *it* down on His head.

4 And some were being indignant within themselves, and saying, For what has this waste of the ointment occurred?

5 For this could be sold *for* over three hundred denarii, and to be given to the poor. And they were very angry *with* her.

6 But Jesus said, Let her alone. Why do you cause her troubles? She worked a good work toward Me.

7 For you have the poor with you always, and when you wish, you can do well *toward* them. But you do not have Me always.

8 What this one had, she did. She took beforehand to anoint My body for the burial.

9 Truly I say to you, Wherever this gospel is proclaimed in all the world, what this *one* did will also be spoken of for a memorial of her.

10 And Judas Iscariot, one of the Twelve, went away to the chief priests, that he might give Him over to them.

11 And hearing, they rejoiced and promised to give him silver. And he sought how he might opportunely give Him over.

12 ¶ And on the first day of the Unleavened *Bread*, when they killed the Passover, His disciples said to Him, Where do You desire *that* going we may prepare that You may eat the Passover?

13 And He sent two of His disciples, and said to them, Go into the city. And you will meet a man carrying a pitcher of water. Follow him.

14 And wherever he goes in, say to the housemaster, The Teacher says, Where is the guest room where I may eat the Passover with My disciples?

15 And he will show you a large upper room, having been spread *and* made ready. Prepare for us there.

16 And His disciples went out and came into the city and found *it* as He told them. And they prepared the Passover.

17 And evening having come, He comes with the Twelve.

18 And as they were reclining and eating, Jesus said, Truly I say to you, One of you will give Me over, the *one* eating with Me.

19 And they began to be grieved, and to say to Him one by one, No, not I, *is it*? And another, No, not I, *is it*?

20 But answering, He said to them, *It is* one from the Twelve, the *one* dipping in the dish with Me.

21 Truly the Son of Man goes as it is written concerning Him, but woe to that man through whom the Son of Man is given over! It were good for him if that man had not been born.

22 And *as* they *were* eating, Jesus taking a loaf, blessing, He broke and gave to them. And He said, Take, eat, this is My body.

23 And taking the cup, giving thanks, He gave to them. And they all drank out of it.

24 And He said to them, This is My blood, that of the New Covenant, which is poured out concerning many.

25 Truly I say to you, No more, I may not drink from the produce of the vine, not until that day when I drink it new in the kingdom of God!

26 And singing a hymn, they went out to the Mount of Olives.

27 And Jesus said to them, All of you will be stumbled in Me in this night, because it has been written: "I will strike the Shepherd, and the sheep will be scattered." *Zech. 13:7*

28 But after the raising up of Me, I will go before you into Galilee.

29 But Peter said to Him, Even if all are being stumbled, yet not I.

30 And Jesus said to him, Truly I say to you that today, in this night, before a cock sounds twice, you will deny Me three times.

31 But rather he said more fervently, If I must die with You, I will not deny You, not *ever*! And likewise also they all said.

32 ¶ And they came to a place which *was* named Gethsemane. And He said to His disciples, Sit here while I pray.

33 And He took along Peter and James and John with Him. And He began to be much amazed and to be deeply distressed

34 And *He* said to them, My soul is deeply grieved, unto death. Remain here and stay awake.

35 And going forward a little, He fell on the ground and prayed that if it were possible, the hour might pass from Him.

36 And He said, Abba, Father, all things *are* possible to You; take this cup from Me. Yet not what I will, but what You *will*.

37 And He comes and finds them sleeping. And *He* says to Peter, Simon, do you sleep? Were you not strong enough to keep awake one hour?

38 Keep awake and pray, that you may not enter into temptation. The spirit truly *is* ready, but the flesh *is* weak.

39 And going away again, He prayed, saying the same thing.

40 And returning, He found them sleeping again, for their eyes were heavy. And they did not know what to answer Him.

41 And He came a third time, and said to them, Sleep on now, and rest. It is enough. The hour has come. Behold, the Son of Man is given over into the hands of sinners.

42 Rise up, let us go. Behold, the *one* giving Me over has drawn near.

43 ¶ And at once, He yet speaking, Judas arrives, being one of the Twelve. And with him *was* a great crowd with swords and clubs, from the chief priests and the scribes and the elders.

44 And the *one* giving Him over had given them a signal, saying, Whomever I kiss, *it* is He; seize Him and lead *Him* away safely.

45 And coming, at once drawing near to Him, he said, Rabbi, Rabbi! And *he* ardently kissed Him.

46 And they laid their hands on Him and seized Him.

47 But a certain one of those standing by, drawing a sword, struck the slave of the high priest and took off his ear.

48 And answering, Jesus said to them, Did you come out with swords and clubs to take Me, as against a plunderer?

49 According to a day I was with you teaching in the temple, and you did not seize Me. But *it is* that the Scriptures may be fulfilled.

50 And leaving Him, all fled.

51 And one, a certain young man, was following Him, having thrown a linen cloth about *his* naked *body*. And the young men seized him.

52 But leaving behind the linen cloth, he fled from them naked.

53 ¶ And they led Jesus away to the high priest. And all the chief priests and the elders and the scribes came together to him.

54 And Peter followed Him from a distance, to the inside of the courtyard of the high priest. And he was sitting with the under-officers, also warming himself toward the light.

55 And the chief priests and the whole sanhedrin sought testimony against Jesus, to put Him to death, and *were* not finding.

56 For many falsely testified against Him, but the testimonies were not identical.

57 And standing up, some falsely testified against Him, saying,

58 We heard Him saying, I will throw down this temple made with hands, and through three days I will build another not made with hands.

59 And neither in this was their testimony identical.

60 And standing in the middle, the high priest questioned Jesus, saying, Do you not answer? Nothing? What *do* these testify against you?

61 But He was silent and answered nothing. Again the high priest questioned Him, and said to Him, Are you the Christ, the Son of the Blessed?

62 And Jesus said, I AM! And you will see the Son of Man sitting at *the* right *hand* of power, and coming with the clouds of the heaven. *Psa. 110:1; Dan. 7:13*

63 And tearing his garments, the high priest said, What need do we still have of witnesses?

64 You heard the blasphemy. What does it appear to you? And they all adjudged Him liable of death.

65 And some began to spit at Him, and to cover His face, and to beat Him with a fist, and to say to Him, Prophesy! And the under-officers struck Him with slaps.

66 ¶ And Peter being in the courtyard below, one of the high priest's slave-girls comes.

67 And seeing Peter warming himself, looking at him, she said, You also were with Jesus the Nazarene.

68 But he denied, saying, I do not know nor understand what you say. And he went out into the forecourt. And a cock sounded.

69 And seeing him again, the female slave began to say to those standing by, This *one* is of them.

70 And again he denied. And after a little, those standing by again said to Peter, Truly you are from them, for you are both a Galilean and your speech is like *theirs.*

71 But he began to curse and to swear, I do not know this man of whom you speak.

72 And a second time a cock sounded. And Peter remembered the word Jesus said to him, Before a cock sounds twice, you will deny Me three times. And thinking on *it,* he wept.

Mark 15

1 Jesus accused before Pilate. 15 The murderer Barabbas is freed, and Jesus given over to be crucified. 17 He is crowned with thorns, 19 and mocked, 27 and is crucified 43 and is buried.

1 ¶ And immediately in the early *morning,* the chief priests with the elders and scribes and all the sanhedrin having made a council, having bound Jesus, *they* led *Him* away and gave *Him* over to Pilate.

2 And Pilate questioned Him, Are you the king of the Jews? And answering, He said to him, You say *it.*

3 And the chief priests accused Him *of* many things. But He answered nothing.

4 But Pilate again questioned Him, saying, Do You not answer? Nothing? Behold, how many things they testify against You.

5 But Jesus answered no more, nothing, so as *for* Pilate to marvel.

6 And at a feast, he released to them one prisoner, whomever they asked.

7 And there was *one* called Barabbas, having been bound with the fellow-insurrectionists, who *all* in the insurrection had committed murder.

8 And crying aloud, the crowd began to beg *him to do* as he always did for them.

9 But Pilate answered them, saying, Do you desire I should release to you the king of the Jews?

10 For he knew that the chief priests had given Him over through envy.

11 But the chief priests stirred up the crowd, that rather he should release Barabbas to them.

12 But answering again, Pilate said to them, What then do you desire I do to *him* whom you call king of the Jews?

13 And again they cried out, Crucify Him!

14 But Pilate said to them, For what bad *thing* did He do? But they much more cried out, Crucify Him!

15 ¶ And having decided to do the easiest *to* the crowd, Pilate released Barabbas to them. And having scourged *Him,* he gave over Jesus, that He might be crucified.

16 And the soldiers led Him away inside the courtyard, which is *the* praetorium. And they called together all the cohort.

17 And they clothed Him *with* purple, and having plaited a crown of thorns, they put *it* around Him.

18 And they began to salute Him, Hail, king of the Jews!

19 And they struck His head with a reed, and spat at Him. And placing the knees, *they* did homage to Him.

20 And when they had mocked Him, they took the purple off Him, and put His own garments on Him. And they led Him out, that they might crucify Him.

21 And they compelled one passing by, Simon, a Cyrenian, coming from a field, the father of Alexander and Rufus, that he might bear His cross.

22 ¶ And they brought Him to Golgotha Place, which translated is, Of a Skull Place.

23 And they gave Him wine spiced with myrrh to drink. But He did not take *it*.

24 And having crucified Him, they divided His garments, casting a lot on them, who should take what. *Psa. 22:18*

25 And it was *the* third hour, and they crucified Him.

26 And the inscription of His accusation was written over *Him*, THE KING OF THE JEWS.

27 And they crucified two plunderers with Him, one at *the* right, and one at *the* left of Him.

28 And the Scripture was fulfilled which says, "And He was numbered with *the* lawless." *Isa. 53:12*

29 And those passing by blasphemed Him, shaking their heads, and saying, Aha! *You* razing the temple, and in three days building *it*,

30 save Yourself and come down from the cross.

31 And also the chief priests and the scribes mocking to one another said likewise, He saved others; He is not able to save Himself.

32 The Christ, the king of Israel, let Him now come down from the cross, that we may see and believe Him. And the *ones* crucified with Him were reviling Him.

33 ¶ And *it* being *the* sixth hour, darkness came over all the land until the ninth hour.

34 And at the ninth hour Jesus cried with a loud voice, saying, Eloi, Eloi, lama sabachthani? (Which being translated is, "My God, My God, why did You forsake Me?") *Psa. 22:1*

35 And hearing, some of those standing by said, Behold, He calls Elijah.

36 And one running up, and filling a sponge with vinegar, and putting *it* on a reed, was giving Him to drink, saying, Leave alone, let us see if Elijah comes to take Him down. *Psa. 69:21*

37 And letting out a cry, Jesus breathed out *His* spirit.

38 And the veil of the temple was torn into two, from top to bottom.

39 And the centurion standing near across from Him, seeing that crying out so He breathed out *His* spirit, *he* said, Truly, this Man was Son of God.

40 And also women were watching from afar, among whom also was Mary Magdalene; also Mary the mother of James the younger, and of Joses, and Salome,

41 who also followed Him and ministered to Him when He was in Galilee; and many other *women* who came up to Jerusalem with Him.

42 ¶ And it becoming evening already, since it was *the* preparation, that is, *the* day before sabbath,

43 Joseph from Arimathea came, an honorable councillor, who himself was also waiting for the kingdom of God. *And* taking courage, he went in to Pilate and begged the body of Jesus.

44 And Pilate marveled if He had already died. And calling the centurion he asked him if He died long ago.

45 And knowing from the centurion, he granted the body to Joseph.

46 And having bought a linen cloth, and having taken Him down, he wrapped *Him* in the linen, and laid Him in a tomb which was cut out of rock. And *he* rolled a stone against the mouth of the tomb.

47 And Mary Magdalene, and Mary of Joses, beheld where He was laid.

Mark 16

1 An angel declares the resurrection of Christ to three women 9 Christ appears to Mary Magdalene: 12 to two going to the country: 14 then to the apostles, 15 whom He sends forth to preach the gospel.

1 ¶ And the sabbath passing, Mary Magdalene and Mary the *mother* of James and Salome, bought spices, so that coming they might anoint Him.

2 And very early on the first of the sabbaths, the sun having risen, they came upon the tomb.

3 And they said to themselves, Who will roll away the stone from the door of the tomb for us?

4 And looking up, they saw that the stone had been rolled back; for it was very great.

5 And having entered into the tomb, they saw a young man sitting on the right, having been clothed *in* a white robe. And they were much amazed.

6 But he says to them, Do not be much-amazed. You seek Jesus the Nazarene who has been crucified. He was raised. He is not here. Behold! The place where they put Him.

7 But go, say to the disciples and to Peter, He goes before you into Galilee. You will see Him there, even as He told you.

8 And going out quickly, they fled from the tomb. And trembling and ecstasy took hold of them. And they told no one, not a thing, for they were afraid.

9 ¶ And having risen early on the first of the sabbath, He first appeared to Mary Magdalene, from whom He had cast out seven demons.

10 Going, that *one* reported to thoe *ones* having been with Him, mourning and weeping.

11 And they having heard that He lives, and was seen by her, they did not believe.

12 And after these things, He was revealed in a different form to two of them walking *and* going into the country.

13 And going, they reported to the rest; not even did they believe those.

14 ¶ Afterward, as they reclined, He was revealed to the Eleven. And *He* reproached their unbelief and hardness of heart, because they did not believe the *ones* who had seen Him, having been raised.

15 And He said to them, Going into all the world, proclaim the gospel to all the creation.

16 The *one* believing and being baptized will be saved; but the *one* not believing will be condemned.

17 And *miraculous* signs will follow to those believing these things: they will cast out demons in My name; they will speak new languages;

18 they will take up snakes; and if they drink anything deadly, it will not hurt them, not *any;* they will lay hands on *ones* being infirm, and they will be well.

19 ¶ Then indeed, after speaking to them, the Lord was taken up into Heaven, and sat at *the* right of God. *Psa. 110:1*

20 And going out, they preached everywhere, the Lord working with *them* and confirming the Word through the *miraculous* signs following after.

Amen

The Gospel According to
LUKE

Luke 1

1 ¶ Since many have undertaken to draw up in order an account concerning the matters having been borne out among us,

2 even as the *ones* from *the* beginning gave over to us, becoming eye-witnesses and ministers of the Word,

3 it seemed good also to me, having traced out all things accurately from the first, to write in order to you, most excellent Theophilus,

4 that you may know the certainty concerning the words which you were taught.

5 ¶ In the days of Herod the king of Judea, there was a certain priest named Zacharias, of *the* daily course of Abijah. And his wife *was* of the daughters of Aaron, and her name *was* Elizabeth.

6 And they were both righteous *ones* before God, walking in all the commandments and ordinances of the Lord, blameless *ones*.

7 And no child was *born* to them, because Elizabeth was barren. And both were advanced in age in their days.

8 And it happened in his serving as priest in the order of his course before God,

9 according to the custom of the priests, entering into the Holy Place of the Lord, *it was Zacharias'* lot to burn incense.

10 And all the multitude of the people was praying outside at the hour of incense.

11 And an angel *of the* Lord appeared to him, standing on *the* right of the altar of incense.

12 And seeing *this*, Zacharias was troubled, and fear fell on him.

13 But the angel said to him, Do not fear, Zacharias, because your prayer was heard, and your wife Elizabeth will bear a son to you, and you shall call his name John.

14 And he will be joy and exultation to you, and many will rejoice over his birth.

15 For he shall be great in the eyes of the Lord, and he shall not drink wine or intoxicating drink. And he will be filled of *the* Holy Spirit, even from his mother's womb.

16 And he will turn many of the sons of Israel to *the* Lord their God.

17 And he will go ahead before Him in *the* spirit and power of Elijah "to turn *the* hearts of fathers to *their* children," and disobedient ones to *the* wisdom of just *ones*, to make ready a people having been prepared for *the* Lord. *Mal. 4:5, 6*

18 And Zacharias said to the angel, By what shall I know this? For I am an old man and my wife is advanced in her days.

19 And answering, the angel said to him, I am Gabriel, who stands before God, and I was sent to speak to you and to announce to you *the* good news of these things.

20 And behold, you shall be keeping silent and not able to speak until the day these things take place, because you did not believe my words which shall be fulfilled in their season.

21 And the people were expecting Zacharias, and they wondered at his delay in the temple.

22 But coming out, he was not able to speak to them, and they recognized that he had seen a vision in the temple. And he was making signs to them and remained mute.

23 And it happened when the days of his service were fulfilled, he went away to his house.

24 And after these days his wife Elizabeth conceived. And she hid herself five months, saying,

25 So has the Lord done to me in *the* days in which He looked on *me* to take away my reproach among men.

26 ¶ And in the sixth month, the angel Gabriel was sent by God to a city of Galilee named Nazareth,

27 to a virgin who had been betrothed to a man to whom *was* a name Joseph, of *the* house of David; and the virgin's name *was* Mariam *(Mary)*.

28 And entering, the angel said to her, Rejoice *Mary, one* having received grace! The Lord *is* with you. You *are* blessed among women!

29 And seeing *this*, she was disturbed at his word, and considered what kind of greeting this might be.

30 And the angel said to her, Fear nor, Mariam *(Mary)*, for you have found grace from God.

31 And behold! You will conceive in *your* womb and bear a Son, and you will call His name Jesus.

32 This One will be great and will be called Son of *the* Most High. And the Lord God will give Him the throne of His father David.

33 And He will reign over the house of Jacob to the ages, and of His kingdom there will be no end.

34 But Mariam *(Mary)* said to the angel, How will this be since I do not know a man?

35 And answering, the angel said to her, The Holy Spirit will come upon you, and *the* power of *the* Most High will overshadow you, and on account of this the Holy *One* being born of you will be called Son of God.

36 And behold, your kinswoman Elizabeth! She also conceived a son in her old age, and this *is* the sixth month to her who *was* called barren;

37 for not will be impossible with God every thing.

38 And Mariam *(Mary)* said, Behold, the slave woman of *the* Lord! May it be to me according to your word. And the angel departed from her.

39 ¶ And rising up in these days, Mariam *(Mary)* went into the hill country with haste to a city of Judah.

40 And *she* entered into the house of Zacharias and greeted Elizabeth.

41 And it happened, as Elizabeth heard Mariam's *(Mary's)* greeting, the babe in her womb leaped, and Elizabeth was filled of the Holy Spirit.

42 And *she* cried out with a loud voice and said, Blessed *are* you among women and blessed *is* the fruit of your womb!

43 And why *is* this to me that the mother of my Lord comes to me?

44 For behold, as the sound of your greeting came to my ears, the babe in my womb leaped in exultation.

45 And blessed *is* the *one* believing, because there will be a completion to the things spoken to her from *the* Lord.

46 And Mariam *(Mary)* said, My soul magnifies the Lord,

47 and my spirit exulted in God my Savior.

48 For He looked upon the lowliness of His slave woman. For, behold, from now on all generations will count me blessed. *ISam. 1:11*

49 For the Mighty One did great things to me, and holy *is* His name.

50 And His mercy *is* to generations of generations to the *ones* fearing Him. *Psa. 103:17*

51 He performed mightily with His arm; He scattered proud *ones* in *the* thought of their heart.

52 He put down potentates from thrones, and lifted up lowly *ones*.

53 He filled *the* hungry with good things, and He sent *the* rich away empty.

54 He helped His servant Israel in order to remember mercy,

55 even as He spoke to our fathers, to Abraham, and to his seed to the age.

56 And Mariam *(Mary)* remained with her about three months, and returned to her house.

57 ¶ And the time was fulfilled to Elizabeth *for* her to bear, and she bore a son.

58 And the neighbors and her relatives heard that *the* Lord magnified His mercy with her, and they rejoiced with her.

59 And it happened on the eighth day, they came to circumcise the child and were calling it by his father's name, Zacharias.

60 And his mother answered, saying, Not so, but he shall be called John.

61 And they said to her, No one is among your kindred who is called by this name.

62 And they signaled to his father, what he might desire him to be called.

63 And asking for a writing tablet, he wrote, saying, John is his name. And all marveled.

64 And instantly his mouth was opened and his tongue *loosed*, and he spoke, blessing God.

65 And fear came on all those living around them. And in all the hill country of Judea all these things were talked about.

66 And all who heard laid *them* up in their hearts, saying, What then will this child be? And the hand of *the* Lord was with him.

67 ¶ And his father Zacharias was filled of *the* Holy Spirit and prophesied, saying,

68 Blessed be *the* Lord, the God of Israel, because He visited and worked redemption for His people.

69 And *He* raised up a Horn of salvation for us in the house of His servant David;

70 even as He spoke through the mouth of His holy prophets from the age *before*:

71 Salvation from the hostile *ones* of us, and from *the* hand of all the *ones* hating us,

72 to execute mercy with our fathers, and to remember His holy covenant,

73 *the* oath which He swore to our father Abraham, to give to us,

74 *that we* being delivered out of the hand of hostile *ones* of us, in order to serve Him without fear,

75 in consecration and righteousness before Him all the days of our life.

76 And you, child, will be called Prophet of *the* Most High, for you will go before *the* face of *the* Lord to prepare His ways, *Mal. 3:1*

77 to give a knowledge of salvation to His people by remission of their sins,

78 through *the* tender bowels of mercy of our God, in which *the* Dayspring from on high will visit us,

79 to shine on the *ones* sitting in darkness and *in* shadow of death, to direct our feet into *the* way of peace. *Isa. 9:2*

80 And the child grew, and became strong in spirit. And he was in deserted *places* until *the* day of his showing to Israel.

Luke 2

1 Augustus registers the Roman empire. 6 The nativity of Christ. 8 An angel relates it to the shepherds. 21 Christ is circumcised.

1 ¶ And it happened in those days, a decree went out from Caesar Augustus *for* all the habitable world to be registered.

2 This registration first occurred *under* the governing of Syria *by* Cyrenius.

3 And all went to be registered, each to *his* own city.

4 And Joseph also went from Galilee, out of *the* city of Nazareth to Judea, to *the* city of David which is called Bethlehem, because of his being of *the* house and family of David,

5 to be registered with Mariam (*Mary*), the *one* having been betrothed to him as wife, *she* being pregnant.

6 And it happened as they were there, the days were fulfilled *for* her to bear.

7 And she bore her son, the First-born. And she wrapped Him and laid Him in the manger, because there was no place for them in the inn.

8 ¶ And shepherds were in the same country living in the fields and keeping guard over their flock *by* night.

9 And, behold, an angel of *the* Lord came on them. And *the* glory of *the* Lord shone around them. And they feared a great fear.

10 And the angel said to them, Do not fear. For, behold, I proclaim good news to you, a great joy, which will be to all people,

11 because today a Savior, who is Christ *the* Lord, was born to you in *the* city of David.

12 And this *is* the sign to you: You will find a babe having been wrapped, lying in the manger.

13 And suddenly there was with the angel a multitude of *the* heavenly host, praising God and saying,

14 Glory to God in the highest, and peace on earth, good will among men.

15 And it happened as the angels departed from them into the heaven, even the men, the shepherds, said to one another, Indeed, let us go over to Bethlehem, and let us see this thing occurring, which the Lord made known to us.

16 And hurrying, they came and sought out both Mariam (*Mary*) and Joseph, and the Babe lying in the manger.

17 And seeing, they publicly told about the Word spoken to them about this Child.

18 And all the *ones* hearing marveled about the things spoken to them by the shepherds.

19 And Mariam (*Mary*) kept all these words, meditating in her heart.

20 And the shepherds returned, glorifying and praising God for all things which they heard and saw, even as was spoken to them.

21 ¶ And when eight days were fulfilled to circumcise the child His name was called Jesus, *the name* called by the angel before He was conceived in the womb.

22 And when were fulfilled the days of her cleansing according to the Law of Moses they took Him up to Jerusalem to present *Him* to the Lord,

23 as it has been written in *the* Law of the Lord: Every male opening a womb shall be called holy to the Lord; *Ex. 13:2*

24 and to offer a sacrifice according to that said in the Law of *the* Lord, a pair of turtledoves, or two nestlings of doves. *Lev. 12:8*

25 ¶ And behold, there was a man in Jerusalem whose name *was* Simeon. And this man *was* righteous and devout, eagerly expecting *the* Consolation of Israel. And *the* Holy Spirit was upon him.

26 And *it* was *said* to him, having been alerted by the Holy Spirit, *that he was* not to see death before he would see *the* Christ of *the* Lord.

27 And by the Spirit he came into the temple. And *as* the parents *were* bringing in the child Jesus *for* them to do according to the custom of the Law concerning Him,

28 even *Simeon* received Him into his arms. And *he* blessed God and said,

29 Now, Master, You will let Your slave go in peace according to Your Word;

30 because my eyes saw Your Salvation,

31 which You prepared before *the* face of all the peoples;

32 a Light for revelation *to the* nations, and *the* Glory of Your people Israel.

33 And Joseph was marveling, also His mother, at the things being said concerning Him.

34 And Simeon blessed them and said to His mother Mariam (*Mary*), Behold, this One is set for *the* fall and rising up of many in Israel, and for a sign spoken against;

35 yea, a sword also will go through the soul of you, *yourself*, so that *the* thoughts of many hearts may be revealed.

36 And there was Anna, a prophetess, a daughter of Phanuel, of *the* tribe of Asher. She was advanced in many days, having lived seven years with a husband from her virginity;

37 and she *was* a widow *of* eighty four years, who did not depart from the temple, serving night and day with fastings and prayers.

38 And coming on at the very hour, she gave thanks to the Lord, and spoke concerning Him to all those in Jerusalem eagerly expecting redemption.

39 And as they finished all things according to *the* Law of *the* Lord, they returned to Galilee, to Nazareth their city.

40 And the Child grew, and became strong in spirit, being filled with wisdom. And the grace of God was upon Him.

41 ¶ And His parents went into Jerusalem year by year at the Feast of the Passover.

42 And when He was twelve years *old*, they, going up to Jerusalem according to the custom of the Feast,

43 and fulfilling the days, in their returning, the boy Jesus stayed in Jerusalem. And Joseph and His mother did not know.

44 But supposing Him to be in the company, they went a day on the way. And they looked for Him among the relatives and friends.

45 And not finding Him, they returned to Jerusalem, looking for Him.

46 And it happened after three days they found Him in the temple sitting in the midst of the teachers, even hearing them and questioning them.

47 And all the *ones* hearing Him were amazed at His intelligence and His answers.

48 And seeing Him, they were astounded. And His mother said to Him, Child, why did You do so to us? Behold, Your father and I were looking for You, greatly distressed.

49 And He said to them, Why did you look for Me? Did you not know that I must be *busy* in the *affairs* of My Father?

50 And they did not understand the Word which He spoke to them.

51 And He went with them and came to Nazareth and was being subject to them. And His mother carefully kept all these words in her heart.

52 And Jesus progressed *in* wisdom and stature and favor before God and men.

Luke 3

1 The preaching and baptism of John. 20 Herod imprisons John. 21 Christ baptized, receives testimony from Heaven. 23 The genealogy of Christ.

1 ¶ And in *the* fifteenth year of the government of Tiberius Caesar, Pontius Pilate governing Judea, and Herod ruling as tetrarch of Galilee, and his brother Philip ruling as tetrarch of Iturea and *the* Trachonitis country, and Lysanias ruling as tetrarch of Abilene,

2 upon *the* high priesthood of Annas and Caiaphas, a word of God came on John the son of Zacharias in the deserted *place.*

3 And he came into the region around the Jordan proclaiming a baptism of repentance for remission of sins,

4 as it is written in *the* scroll of the words of Isaiah the prophet, saying: "*the* voice of one crying in the wilderness, Prepare the way of *the* Lord, make His paths straight.

5 Every valley shall be filled up, and every mountain and hill shall be made low; and the crooked places shall be made into straight, and the rough into smooth ways;"

6 "and all flesh shall see the salvation of God." *Isaiah 40:3-5*

7 Then he said to the crowds going out to be baptized by him, Offspring of vipers! Who warned you to flee from the coming wrath?

8 Then bring forth fruits worthy of repentance, and do not begin to say within yourselves, We have Abraham as father. For I say to you that God is able to raise up children to Abraham out of these stones.

9 And also the axe is already laid to the root of the trees; therefore, every tree not producing good fruit is being cut down and being thrown into the fire.

10 And the crowd asked him, saying, What then shall we do?

11 And answering, he says to them, The *one* having two tunics, let him share with him that has not. And the *one* having foods, let him do the same.

12 And tax collectors also came to be baptized. And they said to him, Teacher, what shall we do?

13 And he said to them, Exact nothing more than that commanded to you.

14 And also ones serving as soldiers asked him, saying, And we, what shall we do? And he said to them, Do not forcibly extort anyone nor accuse falsely, and be satisfied with your wages.

15 ¶ But the people were expecting, and all reasoning in their hearts about John, lest perhaps he is the Christ,

16 John answered all, saying, I indeed baptize you with water; but the *One* stronger than I comes, of whom I am not fit to loose the thong of His sandals. He will baptize you in *the* Holy Spirit and fire,

17 whose sifting fan *is* in His hand; and He will fully purge His threshing-floor, and will gather the wheat into His storehouse, but the chaff He will burn up with fire that cannot be put out.

18 And then indeed exhorting many different things, he preached the gospel to the people.

19 But Herod the tetrarch, being reproved by him concerning Herodias, the wife of his brother, Philip, and concerning all *the* evil things Herod did,

20 he also added this above all, he even shut up John in the prison.

21 ¶ And it happened, in the baptizing of all the people, Jesus also being baptized, and praying, the heaven was opened;

22 and the Holy Spirit came down in a bodily form as a dove upon Him. And there was a voice out of Heaven, saying, You are My Son, the Beloved; in You I am well-pleased. *Psa. 2:7; Gen 22:2; Isa. 42:1*

23 And Jesus Himself *was* beginning *to be* about thirty years *of age,* being, as was supposed, the son of Joseph, the *son* of Heli,

24 the *son* of Matthat, the *son* of Levi, the *son* of Melchi, the *son* of Janna, the *son* of Joseph,

25 the *son* of Mattathias, the *son* of Amos, the *son* of Nahum, the *son* of Esli, the *son* of Naggai,

26 the *son* of Maath, the *son* of Mattathias, the *son* of Semei, the *son* of Joseph, the *son* of Judah,

27 the *son* of Joannas, the *son* of Rhesa, the *son* of Zerubbabel, the *son* of Shealtiel, the *son* of Neri,

28 the *son* of Melchi, the *son* of Addi, the *son* of Cosam, the *son* of Elmodam, the *son* of Er,

29 the *son* of Joses, the *son* of Eliezer, the *son* of Jorim, the *son* of Matthat, the *son* of Levi,

30 the *son* of Simeon, the *son* of Judah, the *son* of Joseph, the *son* of Jonan, the *son* of Eliakim,

31 the *son* of Melea, the *son* of Menan, the *son* of Mattatha, the *son* of Nathan, the *son* of David,

32 the *son* of Jesse, the *son* of Obed, the *son* of Boaz, the *son* of Salmon, the *son* of Nahshon,

33 the *son* of Amminadab, the *son* of Aram, the *son* of Hezron, the *son* of Pharez, the *son* of Judah,

34 the *son* of Jacob, the *son* of Isaac, the *son* of Abraham, the *son* of Terah, the *son* of Nahor,

35 the *son* of Serug, the *son* of Reu, the *son* of Peleg, the *son* of Eber, the *son* of Salah,

36 the *son* of Cainan, the *son* of Arphaxad, the *son* of Shem, the *son* of Noah, the *son* of Lamech,

37 the *son* of Methuselah, the *son* of Enoch, the *son* of Jared, the *son* of Mahalaleel, the *son* of Cainan;

38 the *son* of Enos, the *son* of Seth, the *son* of Adam, the *son* of God.

Luke 4

1 The trial and fasting of Christ. 13 He overcomes the devil: 14 begins to preach. 33 He cures one possessed of a devil, 38 Peter's mother-in-law, 40 and other sick persons.

1 ¶ And full of the Holy Spirit, Jesus returned from the Jordan, and was led by the Spirit into the deserted *place*, forty days, being tried by the devil. And He ate nothing in those days, and they being ended, He afterwards hungered.

3 And the devil said to Him, If You are Son of God, speak to this stone that it become a loaf.

4 And Jesus answered to him, saying, It is written: "Man shall not live on bread alone, but on every Word of God." *Deut. 8:3*

5 And leading Him up into a high mountain, the devil showed Him all the kingdoms of the world in a moment of time.

6 And the devil said to Him, I will give all this authority and their glory to You, because it has been given over to me, and I give it to whomever I wish.

7 Therefore if You worship before me, all will be Yours.

8 And answering, to him, Jesus said, Go behind Me, Satan! For it has been written: "You shall worship *the* Lord your God, and Him only you shall serve." *Deut. 6:13*

9 And he led Him to Jerusalem, and stood Him on the wing of the temple, and said to Him, If You are the Son of God, throw Yourself down from here;

10 for it is written: "He will command His angels about You, even to protect You,"

11 and, "that on *their* hands they shall lift You up, that you not strike Your foot against a stone." *LXX-Psa. 90:11, 12; MT-Psa. 91:11, 12*

12 And answering, Jesus said to him, It has been said: "You shall not tempt *the* Lord your God." *Deut. 6:16*

13 And having finished every temptation, the devil departed from Him until a time.

14 ¶ And Jesus returned in the power of the Spirit to Galilee. And a report went out through all the surrounding region about Him.

15 And He taught in their synagogues, being glorified by all.

16 And He came to Nazareth where He was brought up. And as was His custom, He went in on the day of the sabbaths, into the synagogue, and *He* stood up to read.

17 And *the* scroll of Isaiah the prophet was handed to Him. And unrolling the scroll, He found the place where it was written:

18 "*The* Spirit of *the* Lord *is* upon Me. Because of this He anointed Me to proclaim the gospel to *the* poor *ones*; He has sent Me" to heal the *ones* being broken *in* heart, "to proclaim freedom to captives, and to the blind *ones* to see again," to send away in freedom *the ones* being crushed,

19 "to preach an acceptable year of *the* Lord." *Isa. 61:1, 2*

20 And rolling up the scroll, returning to the attendant, He sat down. And the eyes of all in the synagogue were looking intently on Him.

21 And He began to say to them, Today this Scripture has been fulfilled in your ears.

22 And all bore witness to Him, and marveled at the gracious words coming out of His mouth. And they said, Is this not the son of Joseph?

23 And He said to them, All you will speak this parable to Me, Physician, heal yourself. As many things as *we* heard *were* happening in Capernaum, do also here in your fatherland.

24 But He said, Truly I say to you that no prophet is acceptable in his fatherland.

25 But on a truth I say to you, Many widows were in Israel in the days of Elijah when the heaven was shut up over three years and six months, when a great famine came on all the land;

26 and yet Elijah was sent to none of them except to Zarephath of Sidon, to a woman, a widow.

27 And many lepers were in Israel during the *time* of Elisha the prophet, and none of them was made clean except Naaman the Syrian.

28 And all were filled *with* anger, hearing these things in the synagogue.

29 And rising up, they threw Him outside the city, and *they* brought Him up to the brink of the hill on which their city was built, in order to throw Him down.

30 But He went away, passing through their midst.

31 ¶ And He went down to Capernaum, a city of Galilee. And He was teaching them *on* the sabbaths.

32 And they were astonished at His doctrine, because His Word was with authority.

33 And in the synagogue was a man who had a spirit of an unclean demon. And he cried out with a loud voice,

34 saying, Ah! What is to us and to You, Jesus, Nazarene? Did You come to destroy us? I know You, who You are, the Holy One of God.

35 And Jesus rebuked him, saying, Be silent, and come out from him! And throwing him into the midst, the demon came out from him, not harming him.

36 And astonishment came on all. And they spoke with one another, saying, What Word *is* this, that He commands the unclean spirits with authority and power, and they come out?

37 And a report about Him went out into every place of the surrounding region.

38 And rising up from the synagogue, He went into the house of Simon. And the mother-in-law of Simon was being seized with a great fever. And they asked Him concerning her.

39 And standing over her, He rebuked the fever; and it left her. And rising up instantly, she served them.

40 And the sun setting, all, as many as had *ones* being sick with various diseases, brought them to Him. And laying hands on each one of them, He healed them.

41 And also demons came out from many, crying out and saying, You are the Christ, the Son of God! And rebuking *them*, He did not allow them to speak, for they knew Him to be the Christ.

42 And day having come, going out, He went into a deserted place. And the crowds looked for Him, and came up to Him, and held Him fast, not to pass on from them.

43 But the *One* said to them, Also to the other cities it is necessary *for* Me to proclaim the gospel *of* the kingdom of God, because to this I was sent.

44 And He was proclaiming in the synagogues of Galilee.

Luke 5

1 Christ teaches the people from Peter's boat. 4 A miraculous taking of fish. 12 Christ cleanses the leper: 27 calls Matthew the tax collector: 29 eats with sinners:

1 ¶ And it happened that the crowd was pressing on Him to hear the Word of God. And He was standing by Lake Gennesaret.

2 And He saw two boats standing by the lake, but the fishermen had left them and were washing the nets.

3 And entering into one of the boats, which was Simon's, He asked him to put out a

little from the land. And sitting down, He taught the crowds from the boat.

4 And as He stopped speaking, He said to Simon, Put out into the deep and let down your nets for a haul.

5 And answering, Simon said to Him, Master, laboring all through the night we took nothing. But at Your word I will let down the net.

6 And doing this, they enclosed a great multitude of fish; and their net was being torn.

7 And they signaled the partners, those in the other boat, to come help them. And they came and filled both the boats, so that they were sinking.

8 And seeing, Simon Peter fell at the knees of Jesus, saying, Depart from me, for I am a sinful man, Lord.

9 For astonishment took hold of him, and all the *ones* with him, at the haul of fish which they took;

10 and in the same way also, James and John, *the* sons of Zebedee, who were partners with Simon. And Jesus said to Simon, Do not fear. From now on you will be taking men alive.

11 And bringing the boats down onto the land, forsaking all things, they followed Him.

12 ¶ And it happened, in His being in one of the cities, and behold, a man full of leprosy! And seeing Jesus, falling on *his* face, he begged Him, saying, Lord, if You be willing, You are able to cleanse me.

13 And stretching out the hand, He touched him, saying, I will! Be cleansed! And instantly the leprosy departed from him.

14 And He charged him to tell no one. But going away, show yourself to the priest and offer concerning your cleansing, as Moses commanded, for a testimony to them.

15 But the word about Him spread even more. And large crowds were coming to hear and to be healed from their infirmities by Him.

16 But He was drawing back in the deserted *places*, and praying.

17 ¶ And it happened on one of the days, even He was teaching. And Pharisees and teachers of *the* Law were sitting by, who were coming out of every village of Galilee and Judea, and Jerusalem. And *the* power of *the* Lord was there, for the curing *of* them.

18 And, behold, men carrying on a cot a man who was paralyzed. And they sought to bring him in, and to lay *him* before Him.

19 And not finding a way through *which* they might bring him in through the crowd, going up on the housetop, they let him down through the tiles with the cot, into the midst, in front of Jesus.

20 And seeing their faith, He said to him, Man, your sins have been remitted to you.

21 And the scribes and Pharisees began to reason, saying, Who is this who speaks blasphemies? Who is able to remit sins except God alone?

22 But knowing their thoughts, answering Jesus said to them, Why do you reason in your hearts?

23 Which is easier, to say, Your sins have been remitted to you, or to say, Rise up and walk?

24 But that you may know that the Son of Man has authority on the earth to remit sins, He said to the *one* having been paralyzed, I say to you, Rise up, and take your cot *and* go to your house.

25 And rising up at once before them, taking up *that* on which he was lying, he went to his house glorifying God.

26 And amazement seized all, and they glorified God, and were filled *with* fear, saying, We saw wonderful things today.

27 ¶ And after these things, He went out and saw a tax collector named Levi, sitting at the tax office. And *He* said to him, Follow Me!

28 And leaving all, rising up he followed Him.

29 And Levi made a great feast for Him in his house. And there was a crowd of many tax collectors reclining, and of others who were with them.

30 And the scribes and the Pharisees murmured at His disciples, saying, Why do you eat and drink with tax collectors and sinners?

31 And answering, Jesus said to them, The *ones* who are sound have no need of a healer, but the *ones* badly having *illness*.

32 I did not come to call the righteous *ones*, but sinners to repentance.

33 But they said to Him, Why do John's disciples fast often, and make prayers, and likewise the *ones* of the Pharisees, but the *ones close* to You eat and drink?

34 But He said to them, You are not able to make the sons of the bridechamber fast while the bridegroom is with them.

35 But days will come, even when the bridegroom is taken away from them, then in those days they will fast.

36 And He also told a parable to them: No one puts a piece of a new garment on an old garment; otherwise both the new will tear, and *the* old will not agree *with the* piece from the new.

37 And no one puts new wine into old wineskins; otherwise, the new wine will burst the wineskins, and it will be poured out, and the wineskins will perish.

38 But new wine is to be put into new wineskins, and both are preserved together.

39 And no one drinking old *wine* immediately desires new; for he says, The old is better.

Luke 6

1 Christ reproves the Pharisees' blindness about the observation of the sabbath: 13 chooses twelve apostles. 27 How we must love our enemies.

1 ¶ And it happened on the second chief sabbath, He passed along through the sown fields. And His disciples plucked the heads and were eating, rubbing with the hands.

2 But some of the Pharisees said to them, Why do you do that which is not lawful to do on the sabbaths?

3 And answering, Jesus said to them, Have you never read this, what David did when he hungered, and the *ones* being with him?

4 How he went into the house of God, and he took the Loaves of Presentation, and ate, and even gave to the *ones* with him, which it is not lawful to eat, except only the priests?

5 And He said to them, The Son of Man is Lord of the sabbath also.

6 And it also happened on another sabbath, He going into the synagogue and teaching. And a man was there, and his right hand was withered.

7 And the scribes and the Pharisees kept close by Him, *to see* if He would heal on the sabbath, so that they might find a charge against Him.

8 But He knew their reasonings. And *He* said to the man having the withered hand, Rise up and stand in the middle! And rising up, he stood.

9 Then Jesus said to them, I will ask you something, Is it lawful to do good on the sabbaths, or to do evil, to save a life, or to destroy *it*?

10 And having looked around at them all, He said to the man, Stretch out your hand! And he did so. And his hand was restored sound as the other.

11 But they were filled *with* madness and talked to one another *as to* what they might do to Jesus.

12 ¶ And it happened in these days, He went out into the mountain to pray. And He was in prayer of God through the night.

13 And when it became day, He called His disciples, also choosing out twelve from them, whom He also named apostles:

14 Simon, whom He also named Peter; and his brother Andrew; James and John; Philip and Bartholomew;

15 Matthew and Thomas; James the *son* of Alpheus, and Simon, the one being called Zealot;

16 Judas *brother* of James; and Judas Iscariot, who also came to be *the* betrayer.

17 And coming down with them, He stood on a level place. And a crowd of His disciples, and a great multitude of the people were there from all Judea and Jerusalem, and *from* the coast country of Tyre and Sidon. These came to hear Him, and to be healed from their diseases,

18 and the *ones* being troubled by unclean spirits; and they were healed.

19 And all the crowd sought to touch Him, because power went out from Him and healed all.

20 ¶ And lifting up His eyes to His disciples, He said: Blessed *are* the poor *ones*, for the kingdom of God is yours.

21 Blessed *are* the *ones* hungering now,

for you will be filled. Blessed *are* the *ones* weeping now, for you will laugh.

22 Blessed *are* you when men hate you, and when they cut you off, and will reproach *you*, and will cast out your name as evil, on account of the Son of Man;

23 rejoice in that day, and leap for joy; for, behold, your reward *is* much in Heaven! For their fathers did according to these things to the prophets.

24 But woe to you, rich *ones*, for you have your comfort!

25 Woe to you, The *ones* having been filled, for you will hunger! Woe to you, The *one* laughing now, for you will mourn and lament!

26 Woe to you when all men speak well *of* you, for their fathers did according to these things to the false prophets!

27 ¶ But I say to you, the *ones* hearing: Love the hostile *ones* of you, do well to the *ones* hating you.,

28 bless the *ones* cursing you and pray for the *ones* hating you.

29 *To* him striking you on the cheek, turn the other also. And from him taking your garment, do not keep back the tunic also. And to everyone asking you, give. And from the *one* taking your things, do not ask back.

31 And according as you desire that men should do to you, you also do the same to them.

32 And if you love the *ones* who love you, what thanks is there to you? For even sinners love the *ones* who love them.

33 And if you do good to the *ones* who do good to you, what thanks is there to you? For even the sinners do the same.

34 And if you lend *to those* from whom you hope to receive, what thanks is there to you? For the sinners lend to sinners so that they may receive the equal *things*.

35 But love the *ones* hostile *to* you, and do good, and lend, causing no one to despair, and your reward will be much; and you will be sons of the Most High, for He is kind to the unthankful and evil *ones*.

36 Therefore, be merciful, even as your Father also is merciful.

37 ¶ Judge not, and not be judged, not *ever*. Do not condemn, and not you will

be condemned, not *ever*. Forgive, and you will be forgiven.

38 Give, and *it* will be given to you; good measure, pressed down and shaken together, and running over, they will give into your bosom. For the same measure which you measure, it will be measured back to you.

39 And He spoke a parable to them: A blind *one* is not able to guide a blind *one*. Will they not both fall into a pit?

40 A disciple is not above his teacher, but everyone who has been perfected will be like his teacher.

41 But why do you look on the chip in your brother's eye, but do not consider the beam in *your* own eye?

42 Or how can you say to your brother, Brother, allow me to take out the chip in your eye, yourself not seeing the beam in your eye? Hypocrite! First take the beam out of your eye, and then you will see clearly to take out the chip in your brother's eye.

43 For there is not a good tree that produces corrupt fruit, nor a corrupt tree that produces good fruit.

44 For each tree is known from *its* own fruit. For they do not gather figs from thorns, nor do they gather grapes from a bramble bush.

45 The good man brings forth the good *thing* out of the good treasure of his heart. And the evil man brings forth the evil *thing* out of the evil treasure of his heart, for his mouth speaks out of the abundance of his heart.

46 And why do you call Me Lord, Lord, and do not do what I say?

47 Everyone coming to Me and hearing My words, and doing them, I will show you to whom he is like:

48 He is like a man building a house, who dug and deepened, and laid a foundation on the rock. And a flood occurring, the river burst against that house and had not strength to shake it, for it had been founded on the rock.

49 But he hearing and not doing, *he* is like a man having built *his* house on the earth without a foundation, on which the river burst, and it immediately fell; and the ruin of that house was great.

Luke 7

1 Christ finds a greater faith in the centurion than in any of the Jews: 10 heals his servant being absent: 11 raises from death the widow's son at Nain: 36 and shows, through a woman of sin, how he is a friend to believing sinners.

1 ¶ And when He had completed all His words in the ears of the people, He went into Capernaum.

2 And a certain slave of a centurion, *one* dear to him, badly having *illness*, was about to die.

3 And having heard about Jesus, he sent elders of the Jews to Him, asking Him that He might come *to* restore his slave.

4 And coming to Jesus, they earnestly begged Him, saying, He to whom You give this is worthy.

5 For he loves our nation, and he built the synagogue for us.

6 And Jesus went with them. But He being yet not far away from the house, the centurion sent friends to Him, saying to Him, Lord, do not trouble, for I am not worthy that You come under my roof.

7 For this reason I did not count myself worthy to come to You. But say a word, and let my servant be healed.

8 For I also am a man having been set under authority, having soldiers under myself. And I say to this one, Go! And he goes. And to another, Come! And he comes. And to my slave, Do this! And he does *it*.

9 And hearing these things, Jesus marveled at him. And turning to the crowd following Him, He said, I say to you, I did not find such faith in Israel.

10 And the *ones* being sent, returning to the house, found the slave well, *the one* being sick.

11 ¶ And it happened on the next day, He went into a city being called Nain. And many of His disciples went with Him; also a great crowd.

12 And as He drew near to the gate of the city, even behold, one having died was being borne, an only son born to his mother; and she was a widow. And a considerable crowd of the city was with her.

13 And seeing her, the Lord had compassion on her and said to her, Do not weep.

14 And coming up, He touched the bier ; and those carrying *it* stood still. And He said, Young man, I say to you, Arise!

15 And the dead *one* sat up and began to speak. And He gave him to his mother.

16 And fear took hold of all; and they glorified God, saying, A great prophet has risen up among us; and, God has visited His people.

17 And this word about Him went out in all Judea, and in all the region around.

18 And his disciples reported to John about all these things.

19 ¶ And having called near a certain two of his disciples, John sent to Jesus, saying, Are You the *One* coming? Or should we expect another?

20 And having come to Him, the men said, John the Baptist sent us to You, saying, Are You the *One* coming, or should we expect another?

21 And in the same hour He healed many from diseases and plagues and evil spirits. And He gave to many blind *ones ability* to see.

22 And answering, Jesus said to them, Going, report to John what you saw and heard; that blind *ones* seeing again, lame *ones* walking about, leprous *ones* being cleansed, deaf *ones* hearing, dead *ones* being raised, poor *ones* being preached the Gospel. *Isa. 35:5, 6; 61:1*

23 and blessed is *he*, whoever is not stumbled in Me.

24 And John's messengers going away, He began to speak to the crowds about John: What did you go out to the deserted *place* to see? A reed being shaken by the wind?

25 But what did you go out to see? A man being dressed in soft clothing? Behold, those in splendid clothing and being in luxury are in royal *palaces*.

26 But what did you go out to see? A prophet? Yes, I say to you, Even more than a prophet.

27 This is he about whom it has been written: "Behold, I send My messenger" before Your face, who "will prepare Your way before You." *Mal. 3:1*

28 For I say to you, Among *those* born of a woman, no prophet is greater than John the Baptist. But the least *one* in the kingdom of God is greater than he is.

29 And all the people and the tax collectors hearing, *they* justified God, having been baptized *with* the baptism of John.

30 But the Pharisees and the lawyers set aside God's counsel as to themselves, not being baptized by him.

31 And the Lord said, Then to what shall I compare the men of this generation? And to what are they like?

32 They are like children, the *ones* sitting in a marketplace and calling to one another, and saying, We piped to you, and you did not dance; we mourned to you, and you did not weep.

33 For John the Baptist has come neither eating bread nor drinking wine, and you say, He has a demon.

34 The Son of Man has come eating and drinking, and you say, Behold, a man, a glutton and a winedrinker, a friend of tax collectors and sinners.

35 But wisdom was justified from all of her children.

36 ¶ And a certain one of the Pharisees asked Him that He eat with him. And going into the Pharisee's house, He reclined.

37 And, behold, a woman in the city, who was a sinner, knowing that He reclined in the Pharisee's house, taking an alabaster vial of ointment,

38 and standing by His feet, weeping behind *Him*, she began to wash His feet with tears. And she was wiping with the hairs of her head. And *she* ardently kissed His feet and was anointing *them* with the ointment.

39 But seeing, the Pharisee who invited Him spoke within himself, saying, This One, if he were a prophet, would have known who and what the woman who touches Him *is*; for she is a sinner.

40 And answering, Jesus said to the man, Simon, I have a thing to say to you. And he said, Teacher, speak.

41 There were two debtors to a certain creditor: the one owed five hundred denarii and *the* other fifty.

42 But they not having *a thing* to pay, he freely forgave both. Therefore which of them do *you* say will love him most?

43 And answering, Simon said, I suppose *the one* to whom he freely forgave the most. And He said to him, You have judged rightly.

44 And turning to the woman, He said to Simon, Do you see this woman? I came into your house. You did not give water for My feet, but she washed My feet with tears and wiped *them* off with the hairs of her head.

45 You gave Me no kiss, but she from *when* I entered did not stop fervently kissing My feet.

46 You did not anoint My head with oil, but she anointed My feet with ointment.

47 For this reason I say to you, Her many sins are remitted, for she loved much. But to whom little is forgiven, he loves little.

48 And He said to her, Your sins are remitted.

49 And those reclining with *Him* began to say within themselves, Who is this who even remits sins?

50 But He said to the woman, Your faith has saved you. Go in peace.

Luke 8

3 Women minister to Christ. 4 The parable of the sower, 16 and of the candle. 22 Christ rebukes the winds: 37 is rejected of the Gadarenes: 49 and raises Jairus' daughter.

1 ¶ And it happened afterwards, and He traveled in every city and village, preaching and announcing the gospel of the kingdom of God. And the Twelve *were* with Him;

2 also certain women who were healed from evil spirits and infirmities: Mary, having been called Magdalene, from whom seven demons had gone out,

3 and Joanna, wife of Chuza, Herod's steward, and Susanna, and many others, who were ministering to Him of their possessions.

4 ¶ And a great crowd coming together, and the *ones* in each city coming to Him, He spoke through a parable:

5 The *one* sowing went out to sow his seed. And in his sowing, some indeed fell beside the way, and was trampled; and the birds of the heaven ate it.

6 And other fell on the rock; and growing, it dried up because of not having moisture.

7 And other fell in the middle of the thornbushes, and growing up with it, the thornbushes choked it.

8 And other fell on the good earth, and growing it produced fruit a hundredfold. Saying these things, He cried out, The *one* having ears to hear, let him hear.

9 And His disciples questioned Him, saying, What might this parable be?

10 And He said, To you it has been given to know the mysteries of the kingdom of God, but to the rest in parables, that seeing they might not see, and hearing, they might not understand. *Isa. 6:9*

11 And this is the parable: The seed is the Word of God.

12 And the *ones* by the roadside are the *ones* who hear, then the devil comes and takes away the Word from their heart, lest believing they may be saved.

13 And the *ones* on the rock *are* the *ones* who, when they hear, receive the Word with joy; and these have no root, who believe for a time, and in time of trial draw back.

14 And the *one* falling in the thornbushes, these are the *ones* hearing, but under cares and riches and pleasures of life, moving along, they are choked, and do not bear to maturity.

15 And the *one* in the good earth, these are *the ones* who in a right and good heart, hearing the Word, they hold *it* and bear fruit in patience.

16 But no one lighting a lamp covers it with a vessel, or puts *it* underneath a bed, but sets *it* on a lampstand, that the *ones* coming in may see the light.

17 For nothing is hidden which will not be visible, nor secret which will not *be* known and come to *be* visible.

18 Then observe how you hear; for whoever has, it will be given to him; and whoever does not have, even what he seems to have will be taken from him.

19 And His mother and *His* brothers came to Him, and were not able to come up with Him through the crowd.

20 And it was told to Him, saying Your mother and Your brothers are standing outside wishing to see You.

21 And answering, He said to them, My mother and My brothers are these: the *ones* hearing the Word of God, and doing it.

22 ¶ And it happened on one of the days that He and His disciples entered into a boat. And He said to them, Let us go over to the other side of the lake. And they set sail.

23 And they sailing, He fell asleep. And a storm of wind came onto the lake, and they were being filled and were in danger.

24 And coming up they awakened Him, saying, Master! Master! We are perishing! And being awakened, He rebuked the wind and the roughness of the water; and they ceased, and there was a calm.

25 And He said to them, Where is your faith? And being afraid, they marveled, saying to one another, Who then is this One, that He commands even the wind and the water, and they obey Him?

26 And they sailed down to the country of the Gadarenes, which is across from Galilee.

27 And He going out onto the land, a certain man out of the city met Him, who had demons from a long time. (And he put no garment on; and he did not stay in a house, but among the tombs).

28 And seeing Jesus, and crying out, he fell down before Him, and with a loud voice said, What to me and to You, Jesus, Son of God the Most High? I beg You, do not torment me.

29 For He charged the unclean spirit to come out of the man. For many times it had seized him, and he was bound with chains and fetters, being guarded. And tearing apart the bonds, he was driven by the demons into the deserted *places*.

30 And Jesus asked him, saying, What is your name? And he said, Legion (because many demons entered into him).

31 And they implored Him that He not order them to go away into the abyss.

32 And there was a herd of many pigs feeding there in the mountain. And they implored Him that He would allow them to enter into those. And He allowed them.

33 And coming out from the man, the demons entered into the pigs; and the herd rushed down the precipice into the lake and was choked.

34 And seeing the thing having been done, the *ones* feeding *the pigs* fled. And leaving, *they* reported to the city and to the farms.

35 And they went out to see the thing happening, and came to Jesus. And *they* found the man from whom the demons had gone out, sitting at the feet of Jesus, clothed and of sound mind. And they were afraid.

36 And also the *ones* who had seen related to them how the *one* having been demon-possessed was healed.

37 And all the multitude of the surrounding region of the Gadarenes were seized with a great fear, and asked Him to depart from them. And entering into the boat, He returned.

38 And the man from whom the demons had gone out begged Him, *desiring* to be with Him. But Jesus sent him away, saying,

39 Go back to your house and tell what God did to you. And he went away proclaiming through all the city as many *things* as Jesus did to him.

40 ¶ And it happened *as* Jesus returned, the crowd gladly received Him, for they were all waiting for Him.

41 And, behold, a man named Jairus came, and this one was a synagogue ruler. And falling at the feet of Jesus, he begged Him to come into his house,

42 because an only daughter was born to him, about twelve years *of age*; and she was dying. And in His going, the crowds pressed on Him.

43 And a woman being in a flow of blood from twelve years, who had spent her whole living on physicians, *and* could not be cured by anyone,

44 coming up behind she touched the fringe of His garment. And instantly the flow of her blood stopped.

45 And Jesus said, Who *was* touching Me? And all denying *it*, Peter and the *ones* with Him said, Master, the crowds are pressing You together and are pressing hard. And do You say, Who *was* touching Me?

46 But Jesus said, Someone touched Me, for I knew power *was* going from Me.

47 And seeing that she was not hidden, the woman came trembling and falling down before Him she declared to Him before all the people for what reason she touched Him, and how she was instantly cured.

48 And He said to her, Daughter, be comforted. Your faith has healed you. Go in peace.

49 As He was yet speaking, someone came from the synagogue ruler's, saying to him, Your daughter has died. Do not trouble the Teacher.

50 But hearing, Jesus answered him, saying, Do not fear; only believe and she will be healed.

51 And coming into the house, He did not allow anyone to enter, except Peter and James and John, and the father and mother of the girl.

52 And all were weeping and bewailing her. But He said, Do not weep. She has not died, but is sleeping.

53 And they ridiculed Him, knowing that she died.

54 But putting all outside, and taking hold of her hand, He called out, saying, girl, rise up!

55 And her spirit returned, and she rose up immediately. And He ordered that she be given *something* to eat .

56 And her parents were amazed. But He charged them to tell no one of that which occurred.

Luke 9

1 Christ sends His apostles to preach: 17 feeds five thousand: 22 foretells His passion. 28 The transfiguration. 37 He casts out a demon.

1 ¶ And having called together His twelve disciples, He gave them power and authority over all the demons, and to heal diseases.

2 And *He* sent them to proclaim the kingdom of God, and to heal the *ones* being sick.

3 And He said to them, Take nothing for the way, neither staffs, nor moneybags, nor bread, nor silver, nor each to have two tunics.

4 And into whatever house you enter, remain there, and go out from there.

5 And as many as may not receive you, going out from that city even shake off the dust from your feet, for a testimony against them.

6 And going out, they passed through the villages, having announced the gospel, and healing everywhere.

7 And Herod the tetrarch heard all the things happening by Him, and was perplexed, because of the saying by some that John had been raised from *the* dead *ones*,

8 and by some that Elijah had appeared. And others *said*, A prophet, one of the ancients rose again.

9 And Herod said, I beheaded John, but who is this about whom I hear such things? And he sought to see Him.

10 ¶ And having returned, the apostles told Him as many *things* as they did. And taking them, He went out privately to a deserted place of a city called Bethsaida.

11 But knowing *this*, the crowds followed Him. And having received them, He spoke to them about the kingdom of God. And He cured the *ones* having need of healing.

12 But the day began to decline. And coming up, the Twelve said to Him, Send away the crowd that going to the surrounding villages and farms they may lodge and find food, because here we are in a deserted place.

13 But He said to them, You give them to eat. But they said, *there* is not to us more than five loaves and two fish, unless going we buy food for all this people.

14 For they were about five thousand men. And He said to His disciples, Cause them to recline in groups, by fifties.

15 And they did so, and made all recline.

16 And taking the five loaves and the two fish, looking up to Heaven, He blessed them, and broke, and gave to the disciples to set before the crowd.

17 And they ate and were all filled. And twelve baskets of fragments of that left over to them were taken up.

18 ¶ And it happened *as* He was praying alone, the disciples were with Him. And He questioned them, saying, Whom do the crowds say Me to be?

19 And answering, they said, John the Baptist; and others, Elijah; and others that some prophet of the ancients has risen again.

20 And He said to them, But whom do you say Me to be? And answering, Peter said, The Christ of God.

21 And strictly warning them, He ordered no one to tell this,

22 saying, The Son of Man must suffer many things and be rejected by the elders and chief priests and scribes, and be killed, and be raised the third day.

23 And He said to all, If anyone desires to come after Me, let him deny himself and take up his cross daily. And let him follow Me.

24 For whoever desires to save his life, he will lose it. But whoever loses his life for My sake, this one will save it.

25 For what is a man profited gaining the whole world but destroying himself or suffering loss?

26 For whoever is ashamed of Me and My words, the Son of Man will be ashamed of that one when He comes in His glory, and *that* of the Father, and of the holy angels.

27 But truly I say to you, There are some of the *ones* standing here who shall not taste of death until they see the kingdom of God, not *at all*.

28 ¶ And it was about eight days after these sayings, also taking Peter and John and James, He went up into the mountain to pray.

29 And in His praying, the appearance of His face *became* different, and His clothing *was* dazzling white.

30 And, behold, two men talked with Him, who were Moses and Elijah,

31 who, appearing in glory, spoke of His exodus, which He was about to fulfill in Jerusalem.

32 But Peter and the *ones* with him were weighed down with sleep. But fully awakening, they saw His glory, and the two men standing with Him.

33 And it happened in their parting from Him, Peter said to Jesus, Master, it is good for *us* to be here. And, Let us make three tents, one for You, and one for Moses, and one for Elijah, not knowing what he said.

34 And he saying these things, a cloud came and overshadowed them. And they feared *as* they entered into the cloud.

35 And a voice came out of the cloud, saying, This is My Son, the Beloved; hear Him! *Psa. 2:7; Isa. 42:1; Deut. 18:15*

36 And as the voice occurred, Jesus was found alone. And they were quiet. And *they* reported to no one in those days, nothing which they had seen.

37 ¶ And it happened on the next day, they coming down from the mountain, a large crowd met Him.

38 And, behold, a man called aloud from the crowd, saying, Teacher, I beg You, look upon my son, because he is my only born.

39 And, behold, a spirit takes him, and *he* suddenly cries out, and *it* throws him into convulsions, with foaming. And *it* departs from him with pain, bruising him.

40 And I begged Your disciples, that they cast it out. And they were not able.

41 And answering, Jesus said, O unbelieving generation, and being perverted, until when shall I be with you and endure you? Bring your son here.

42 But as *he* was yet coming near, the demon tore him and violently convulsed *him*. But Jesus rebuked the unclean spirit and healed the child, and gave him back to his father.

43 ¶ And all were astonished at the majesty of God. And as all were marveling at all things which He did, Jesus said to His disciples,

44 You lay into your ears these sayings, for the Son of Man is about to be given over into *the* hands of men.

45 But they did not understand this saying, and it was hidden from them so that they might not perceive it. And they feared to ask Him about this word.

46 But there arose among them a reasoning, who might be *the* greater of them.

47 And seeing the reasoning of their heart, taking a child, Jesus stood it beside Himself,

48 and said to them, Whoever receives this child on My name receives Me. And whoever receives Me receives the *one* having sent Me. For the *one* being least among you all, this *one* shall be great.

49 And answering, John said, Master, we saw someone casting out demons on Your name, and we forbade him because he does not follow with us.

50 And Jesus said to them, Do not forbid *them*, for whoever is not against us is for us.

51 ¶ And it happened in the fulfilling *of* the days of His taking up, even He set His face to go to Jerusalem.

52 And *He* sent messengers before His face. And going they went into a village of Samaritans, so as to make ready for Him.

53 And they did not receive Him, because His face was going toward Jerusalem.

54 And seeing, His disciples, James and John, said Lord, do You desire *that* we tell fire to come down from Heaven, and to consume them even as Elijah did? *2 K. 1:10-12*

55 But turning He rebuked them. And He said, You do not know of what spirit you are.

56 For the Son of Man did not come to destroy men's souls, but to save. And they went to another village.

57 ¶ And it happened as they were going in the way, one said to Him, I will follow You wherever You may go, Lord.

58 And Jesus said to him, The foxes have holes, and the birds of the heaven nests, but the Son of Man has nowhere He may lay *His* head.

59 And He said to another, Follow Me. But he said, Lord, allow me to go first to bury my father.

60 But Jesus said to him, Leave the dead to bury their dead, but going out, you announce the kingdom of God.

61 And also another said, I will follow You, Lord, but first allow me to take leave of the *ones* in my house.

62 But Jesus said to him, No one putting his hand on the plow, and looking at the things behind, is fit for the kingdom of God.

Luke 10

1 Christ sends out at once seventy disciples: 17 admonishes them to be humble: 25 teaches the lawyer how to attain eternal life: 41 disappoints Martha, and commends Mary her sister.

1 ¶ And after these things, the Lord also appointed seventy others, and sent them each by two before His face into every city and place, even *to* where He was about to come.

2 Therefore He said to them, Indeed, the harvest *is* much, but the laborers *are* few. Therefore, pray *to* the Lord of the harvest, that He send out workers into His harvest.

3 Go! Behold, I send you out as lambs in *the* midst of wolves.

4 Do not carry a money bag, nor a provision bag, nor sandals; and greet no one by the way.

5 And into whatever house you may enter, first say, Peace to this house.

6 And if the son of peace is truly there, your peace shall rest on it; but if not so, it shall return to you.

7 And remain in the same house, eating and drinking the things *shared* by them; for the laborer is worthy of his wage. Do not move from house to house.

8 And into whatever city you enter, and they receive you, eat the things set before you.

9 And heal the sick in it, and say to them, The kingdom of God has drawn near to you.

10 But into whatever city you enter, and they do not receive you, going out into its streets, say,

11 Even the dust clinging to us out of your city, we shake off against you! Yet know this, that the kingdom of God has drawn near to you!

12 And I say to you that it shall be more bearable for Sodom in that day than for that city!

13 Woe to you, Chorazin! Woe to you, Bethsaida! For if the works of power which had been done in you had been done in Tyre and Sidon, they would have repented long ago sitting in sackcloth and ashes!

14 But it will be more bearable *for* Tyre and Sidon in the Judgment than *for* you.

15 And you, Capernaum, the *one* exalted to the heaven? "To Hades you will be thrust down!" *Isa. 14:13, 15*

16 The *one* hearing you hears Me, and the *one* rejecting you also rejects Me, and the *one* rejecting Me *also* rejects the *One* having sent Me.

17 ¶ And the seventy returned with joy, saying, Lord, even the demons are subject to us through Your Name.

18 And He said to them, I saw Satan falling out of Heaven as lightning!

19 Behold, I have given you the authority to tread on snakes and scorpions, and on all the power of the hostile *one*, and nothing shall hurt you, not *ever*!

20 But do not rejoice in this, that the *evil* spirits are subject to you but, rather rejoice that your names are written in Heaven.

21 In the same hour Jesus rejoiced in the Spirit, and said, I praise You, Father, Lord of Heaven and of earth, that You hid these things from *the* sophisticated and learned and revealed them to babes; yes, Father, because so it was pleasing before You.

22 All things were given over to Me by My Father, and no one knows who the Son is if not the Father; and who is the Father, if not the Son, and he to whom the Son may desire to reveal *Him*.

23 And having turned to the disciples alone, He said, Blessed *are* the eyes seeing what you see.

24 For I say to you that many prophets and kings desired to see what you see, and did not see, and to hear what you hear, and did not hear.

25 ¶ And behold, a certain lawyer stood up, testing Him and saying, Teacher, what *by* doing shall I inherit eternal life?

26 And the *One* said to him, What is written in the Law? How do you read *it*?

27 And answering, he said, "You shall love *the* Lord your God out of all your heart, and out of all your soul, and out of all your strength," and out of all your mind, and "your neighbor as yourself." *Deut. 6:5; Lev. 19:18*

28 And He said to him, You have answered rightly; do this, and you shall live.

29 But desiring to justify himself, he said to Jesus, And who is my neighbor?

30 And taking *it* up, Jesus said, A certain man was going down from Jerusalem to Jericho, and fell among plunderers, who both stripping him and laying on blows, went away, leaving *him* being half dead.

31 And by a coincidence, a certain priest was going on that road; and seeing him, he passed on the opposite *side*.

32 And in the same way, a Levite, also being at the place, coming and seeing *him*, he passed on the opposite *side*.

33 But a certain traveling Samaritan came upon him, and seeing him, he was filled with pity.

34 And coming near, *he* bound up his wounds, pouring on oil and putting him on his beast, *he* brought him to an inn and cared for him.

35 And going forth on the morrow, taking out two denarii, he gave *them* to the

innkeeper, and said to him, Care for him, and whatever more you spend, on my return I will repay you.

36 Which, therefore, of these three seems to you to have become a neighbor to the *one* having fallen among the plunderers?

37 And he said, The *one* doing the *deed of* mercy with him. Then Jesus said to him, Go, and you do likewise.

38 And it happened.in their entering in, He also entered into a certain village. And a certain woman, Martha by name, received Him into her house.

39 And to this *one* was a sister being called Mary, who also was sitting alongside, at the feet of Jesus, *and* heard His Word.

40 But Martha was distracted about much serving. And coming up she said, Lord, *is it* not a care to You that my sister left me alone to serve? Therefore tell her that she should help me.

41 But answering Jesus said to her, Martha, Martha, you are anxious and troubled about many things,

42 But there is need of *only* one; and Mary chose the good part, which shall not be taken from her.

Luke 11

1 Christ teaches to pray. 14 He, casting out a dumb demon, rebukes the blasphemous Pharisees: 29 and preaches to the people.

1 ¶ And it happened *as* He was praying in a certain place, when He ceased, one of His disciples said to Him, Lord teach us to pray, as John also taught his disciples.

2 And He said to them: When you pray, say, Our Father who *is* in Heaven, hallowed be Your name, let Your kingdom come, let Your will be done on earth as *it* also *is* in Heaven.

3 Give us our needful bread according to a day;

4 and forgive us our sins, for we ourselves also forgive everyone indebted to us. And bring us not into temptation, but deliver us from the evil.

5 And He said to them, Who out of you shall have a friend, and will come to him at midnight and say to him, Friend, lend me three loaves.

6 *For* a friend of mine arrived to me from a journey, and I do not have what I may set before him.

7 And answering from within that one may say, Do not cause me troubles. The door has already been shut, and my children are in bed with me. I cannot rise up to give to you.

8 I say to you, Even if rising up he will not give to him because he is a friend, yet because of his shameless insisting, rising up he will give him as many as he needs.

9 And I say to you, Ask, and it will be given to you; seek, and you will find; knock, and it will be opened to you.

10 For everyone asking receives, and the *one* seeking finds, and to the one knocking, it will be opened.

11 And what father of you, *if* the son asks *for* bread, will he give him a stone? And if a fish, will he give him a snake instead of a fish?

12 And if he should ask an egg, will he give him a scorpion?

13 Then if you being evil know to give good gifts to your children, how much more the Father out of Heaven will give *the* Holy Spirit to the *ones* asking Him.

14 ¶ And He was casting out a demon, and it was a mute *one*. And it happened as the demon *was* going out, the mute *one* spoke. And the crowds marveled.

15 But some of them said, He casts out the demons by Beelzebul the chief of the demons.

16 And tempting *Him*, others were seeking a *miraculous* sign from Heaven from Him.

17 But knowing their thoughts, He said to them, Every kingdom divided against itself is made a desolate *one*, and a house against a house falls.

18 And also if Satan is divided against himself, how shall his kingdom stand? Because you say I cast out the demons by Beelzebul.

19 And if I cast out the demons by Beelzebul, by whom do your sons cast out? Because of this they shall be your judges.

20 But if I cast out the demons by *the* finger of God, then the kingdom of God has come upon you.

21 When the strong *one*, having been armed, guards the dwelling of himself, in peace are the *things* belonging to him.

22 But as soon as the Stronger than he having come, *He* overcomes him; He takes away all his armor on which he trusted, and gives over his arms.

23 The *one* not being with Me is against Me. And the *one* not gathering with Me scatters.

24 When the unclean spirit goes out from the man, he goes through waterless places seeking rest. And not finding, *he* says, I will return to my house from where I came out.

25 And coming, he finds *it* having been swept and having been adorned.

26 Then he goes and takes along seven other spirits more wicked than himself, and entering he dwells there. And the last things of that man become worse than the first.

27 ¶ And it happened in His saying these things, lifting up *her* voice out of the crowd a certain woman said to Him, Blessed *is* the womb having borne You and *the* breasts which You sucked.

28 But He said, No; rather, blessed *are* the *ones* hearing the Word of God, and keeping it.

29 ¶ But the crowds pressing on *Him*, He began to say, This generation is evil. It seeks a *miraculous* sign, and a sign will not be given to it, except the sign of Jonah the prophet.

30 For even as Jonah became a *miraculous* sign to the Ninevites, so also the Son of Man will be to this generation.

31 *The* queen of *the* south will be raised in the Judgment with the men of this generation and will condemn them because she came from the ends of the earth to hear the wisdom of Solomon. And, behold, a Greater-than-Solomon *is* here.

32 Men, Ninevites will rise up in the Judgment with this generation, and will condemn it, because they repented at the preaching of Jonah. And, behold, a Greater-than-Jonah *is* here.

33 But no one having lit a lamp places *it* in secret, nor under the peck-measure, but on the lampstand, that the *ones* entering may see the light.

34 The lamp of the body is the eye. Therefore when your eye is sound, also all your body is light. But when it is evil, also your body *is* dark.

35 Mark, therefore, that the light in you is not darkness.

36 If, then, your whole body *is* light, not having any part dark, all will be light, as when the lamp enlightens you with *its* shining.

37 ¶ And *as He* was speaking, a certain Pharisee asked Him that He would dine with him. And going in, He reclined.

38 But seeing, the Pharisee marveled that He did not first wash before dinner.

39 But the Lord said to him, Now you Pharisees cleanse the outside of the cup and of the dish, but your inside is full of robbery and evil.

40 Fools! Did not He who made the outside also make the inside?

41 But give merciful *gifts of* the things which are within, and see all things *are* clean to you.

42 But woe to you, Pharisees, for you pay tithes of the mint, and the rue, and every plant, and pass by the judgment and the love of God. It was right to do these things, but not to leave aside those.

43 Woe to you, Pharisees! For you love the chief seat in the synagogues and the greetings in the marketplaces.

44 Woe to you, scribes and Pharisees! Hypocrites! For you are as the unseen tombs, and the men walking over *them* do not know.

45 And answering, one of the lawyers said to Him, Teacher, saying these things You also insult us.

46 And He said, Woe to you also, lawyers! Because you burden men with burdens hard to bear, and *you* yourselves do not touch the burdens with one of your fingers.

47 Woe to you! Because you build the tombs of the prophets, and your fathers killed them.

48 So you bear witness and consent to the works of your fathers; for they indeed killed them, and you build their tombs.

49 And because of this, the wisdom of God said, I will send prophets and apostles

to them, and they will kill and drive out *some* of them,

50 that the blood of all the prophets which has been shed from *the* foundation of the world may be required from this generation,

51 from the blood of Abel until the blood of Zechariah *who* perished between the altar and the House. Yea, I say to you, It will be required from this generation.

52 Woe to you, lawyers! Because you took the key of knowledge; you yourselves did not enter in, and you hindered the *ones* entering in.

53 And as He was saying these things to them, the scribes and the Pharisees began to be terribly angry, and to draw *Him* out concerning many things,

54 lying in ambush for Him, and seeking to catch something out of His mouth that they might accuse Him.

Luke 12

1 Christ preaches to his disciples to avoid hypocrisy: 13 warns the people to beware of covetousness. 36 We must be ready at a knock to open to our Lord.

1 ¶ At which time the myriads of the crowd being gathered together, so as to trample on one another, He began to say to His disciples first, Take heed to yourselves of the leaven of the Pharisees, which is hypocrisy.

2 But there is nothing which has been completely concealed which will not be uncovered, nor hidden which will not be known.

3 Therefore, as many *things* as you said in the darkness will be heard in the light; and whatever you spoke in the ear in the secret rooms will be proclaimed on the housetops.

4 But I say to you, My friends, stop being afraid of the ones killing the body, and after these things not having anything more *they can* do.

5 But I will warn you whom you should fear; fear the *One* who after killing has authority to cast into hell ; yea, I say to you, Fear that One!

6 Are not five sparrows sold for two assaria? And not one of them has been forgotten before God.

7 But even the hairs of your head have all been numbered. Therefore stop being afraid; you differ from many sparrows.

8 But I say to you, Everyone who may confess Me before men, the Son of Man will also confess him before the angels of God.

9 But the *one* denying Me before men shall be denied before the angels of God.

10 And everyone who shall say a word against the Son of Man, it shall be forgiven him; but the *one* blaspheming against the Holy Spirit, *it* will not be forgiven.

11 But when they bring you in before synagogues and rulers and the authorities, do not be anxious how or what you shall reply, or what you should say;

12 for the Holy Spirit will teach you in the same hour what you must say.

13 ¶ And one from the crowd said to Him, Teacher, tell my brother to divide the inheritance with me.

14 But He said to him, Man, who appointed Me a judge or a divider over you?

15 And He said to them, Beware, and be on guard from covetousness; for one's life is not in the abundance of the things belonging of him.

16 And He spoke a parable to them, saying of a man, The land of a certain rich man produced well.

17 And he reasoned within himself, saying, What should I do, for I have nowhere I may gather my fruits?

18 And he said, I will do this; I will tear down my storehouses and I will build larger; and I will gather there all my produce and my goods.

19 And I will say to my soul, Soul, you have many goods laid *up* for many years; take rest, eat, drink, *and* be glad.

20 But God said to him, Fool! This night they demand your soul from you; and that which you prepared, to whom will it be?

21 So *is* he treasuring up for himself, and not being rich toward God.

22 ¶ And He said to His disciples, Because of this I say to you, Do not be anxious as to your life, what you should eat; nor as to the body, what you should put on.

23 The life is more than food and the body than clothing.

24 Consider the ravens, for they do not sow, nor do they reap; to which there is no storeroom nor storehouse, and God feeds them. How much rather you differ from the birds!

25 And who of you *by* being anxious is able to add one cubit to his stature?

26 Then if you are not able *to do* even *the* least, why are you anxious about the rest?

27 Consider the lilies, how they grow: they do not labor, nor do they spin, but I say to you, Not even Solomon in all his glory was clothed as one of these.

28 But if God so dresses the grass, which today being in the field and tomorrow is thrown into the oven, how much more you, little-faiths?

29 And you, do not seek what you shall eat, or what you shall drink, and stop being in anxiety.

30 For all the nations of the world seek after these things, and your Father knows that you need these things.

31 But seek the kingdom of God and all these things will be added to you.

32 Do not fear, little flock, because your Father was pleased to give you the kingdom.

33 Sell the *things* belonging of you and give merciful *gifts*. Make for yourselves purses that do not grow old, an unfailing treasure in Heaven, where a thief cannot come near, nor moth can ruin.

34 For where your treasure is, there your heart will be also.

35 Let your loins be girded about, and the lamps burning,

36 and you *be* like men awaiting their lord when he returns from the wedding feast, so that *he* coming and knocking, they will at once open to him.

37 Blessed *are* those slaves whom the lord will find awake when *he* comes. Truly I say to you that he will gird himself and will make them recline, and coming near *he* will serve them.

38 And if he comes in the second watch, or he comes in the third watch, and finds *it* so, blessed are those slaves.

39 But know this, that if the housemanager had known *in* what hour the thief is coming, he would have watched and would not have allowed his house to be dug through.

40 And therefore you be ready, for *in* which hour you think not the Son of man comes.

41 ¶ And Peter said to Him, Lord, do You speak this parable to us, or also to all?

42 And the Lord said, Who then is the faithful and wise steward whom the lord will appoint over his service, to give the portion of food in season?

43 Blessed *is* that slave *when* his lord comes *and* will find *him* so doing.

44 Truly I say to you, He will set him over all the *things* belonging of him.

45 But if that slave should say in his heart, My lord delays to come, and should begin to beat the men servants and the female servants, and to eat and to drink and be drunk,

46 the lord of that slave will come in the day in which he does not expect, and in an hour which he does not know. And He will cut him in two and will put his portion with the unbelievers.

47 But that slave knowing the will of his lord, and not preparing, nor doing according to his will, will be beaten with many *stripes*.

48 But he not knowing, and doing *things* worthy of stripes, will be beaten with few. And everyone given much, much will be demanded from him. And to whom much was committed, more exceedingly they will ask *of* him.

49 I came to hurl fire into the earth, and what will I if it already was kindled?

50 But I have an immersion to be immersed in, and how am I pressed until it is finished!

51 Think *you* that I came to give peace in the earth? No, I say to you, But rather division.

52 For from now on five in one house will have been divided, three against two, and two against three.

53 Father will be divided against son, and son against father; mother against the daughter, and daughter against mother; mother-in-law against the bride, "and *the* bride against her mother-in-law." *Mic. 7:6*

54 ¶ And He also said to the crowd, When you see the cloud rising up from the west, you immediately say, A storm is coming; and it happens so.

55 And when a south wind *is* blowing, you say, There will be heat; and it occurs.
56 Hypocrites! You know to discern the face of the earth and of the heaven, but how *is it* you do not discern this time?
57 And why do you not judge the right even of yourselves?
58 For as you go with your adversary to a magistrate, give pains in the way to be freed from him, that he not drag you to the judge, and the judge deliver you to the officer, and the officer throw you into prison.
59 I say to you, Not you will go out from there, not until you pay back even the last lepton.

Luke 13

1 Christ preaches repentance on the punishment of the Galileans. 6 The fruitless fig tree. 11 He heals a woman who was unable to stand erect: 24 and exhorts to enter in at the narrow gate.

1 ¶ And some were present at the same time reporting to Him about the Galileans, whose blood Pilate mixed with their sacrifices.
2 And answering, Jesus said to them, Do you think that these Galileans were sinners beyond all the Galileans, because they suffered such things?
3 No, I say to you, But if you do not repent, you will all perish likewise.
4 Or those eighteen on whom the tower in Siloam fell, and killed them, do you think that these were sinners above all men living in Jerusalem?
5 No, I say to you, But if you do not repent, you will all likewise perish.
6 ¶ And He spoke this parable: A certain one had planted a fig tree in his vineyard. And he came looking for fruit on it and did not find *any*.
7 And he said to the vinedresser, Behold, three years I come looking for fruit on this fig tree, and do not find *any*. Cut it down; why does it even waste the ground?
8 And the vinedresser said to him, Sir, leave it also this year until I shall dig around it and throw manure;
9 and *see* if it indeed makes fruit. But if not, in the coming *year* you may cut it down.

10 ¶ And He was teaching in one of the synagogues on *one of* the sabbaths.
11 And, behold, there was a woman having a spirit of infirmity eighteen years, and was bent together and was not able to be erect to the complete *straightness*.
12 And seeing her, Jesus called *her* near and said to her, Woman, you have been loosed from your infirmity.
13 And He laid hands on her. And instantly she was made erect and glorified God.
14 But answering, being angry that Jesus healed on the sabbath, the synagogue ruler said to the crowd, There are six days in which it is right to work. Therefore, coming in these, be healed, and not on the sabbath day.
15 Then the Lord answered him and said, Hypocrite! Each *one* of you on the sabbath, does he not loose his ox or ass from the manger, and leading *it* away, give *it* drink?
16 And this one being a daughter of Abraham, whom Satan has bound, behold, eighteen years, ought *she* not to be loosed from this bond on the sabbath day?
17 And on His saying these things, all the *ones* opposing Him were ashamed. And all the crowd rejoiced over all the glorious things being done by Him.
18 ¶ And He said, To what is the kingdom of God like? And to what shall I liken it?
19 It is like a grain of mustard which a man having taken threw into his garden. And it grew and became a great tree, and the birds of the heaven dwelt in its branches.
20 And again He said, To what shall I liken the kingdom of God?
21 It is like leaven, which taking, a woman hid in three measures of meal until all was leavened.
22 And He went through cities and villages, teaching and making progress toward Jerusalem.
23 ¶ And one said to Him, Lord, *are* the ones being saved few? But He said to them,
24 Strive to enter in through the narrow gate, for I say to you that many will seek to enter in and will not have strength.
25 From the time the Master of the house shall have risen up, and He shuts the door,

and you begin to stand outside and to knock at the door, saying, Lord, Lord, open to us. And answering, He will say to you, I do not know you, from where you are.

26 Then you will begin to say, We ate and drank in Your presence, and You taught in our streets.

27 And He will say, I tell you I do not know you, from where you are. "Stand back from Me all workers of unrighteousness!" *Psa. 6:8*

28 There will be weeping and gnashing of the teeth when you see Abraham and Isaac and Jacob and all the prophets in the kingdom of God, but yourselves being thrown outside.

29 And they will come from east and west, and from north and south, and will recline in the kingdom of God.

30 And, behold, there are last *ones* who will be first, and there are first *ones* who will be last.

31 ¶ In the same day, certain Pharisees came, saying to Him, Go out and go on from here, for Herod desires to kill You.

32 And He said to them, Going, say to that fox, Behold, today and tomorrow I cast out demons and I complete cures, and the third *day* I will be finished.

33 But today and tomorrow and on the following *day* I must travel on. For it is not accepted *for* a prophet to perish outside Jerusalem.

34 Jerusalem! Jerusalem! The *one* killing the prophets, and stoning the *ones* having been sent to her, how often I desired to gather your children in the way a hen *gathers* her brood under the wings, and you did not desire *it*.

35 "Behold, your house is left to you desolate. And truly I say to you, You shall not at all see Me until it comes when you say, "Being blessed *is* the *One* coming in *the* name of *the* Lord."

Luke 14

2 Christ heals a man with dropsy on the sabbath.
15 The parable of the great supper.

1 ¶ And it occurred, on His going into a house of one of the Pharisee leaders on a sabbath to eat bread, and they were closely observing Him.

2 And behold, a certain man was dropsical before Him.

3 And answering, Jesus spoke to the lawyers and Pharisees, saying, Is it lawful to heal on the sabbath?

4 And they were silent. And taking *the man*, He healed him and sent him away.

5 And answering to them He said, Whose ass or ox of yours shall fall into a pit, and he will not at once pull it up on the sabbath day?

6 And they were not able to reply to Him against these things.

7 ¶ And He spoke a parable to the *ones* who had been invited, noting how they were choosing the chief seats, saying to them,

8 When you are invited by anyone to wedding feasts, do not recline at the chief seat lest *one* more honorable *than* you be invited by him,

9 and coming, he who invited you and him will say to you, Give this one place. And then you begin with shame to take the last place.

10 But when you are invited, going, recline at the last place, so that when the *one* who has invited you comes, he *may* say to you, Friend, go up higher. Then glory will be to you before the *ones* reclining with you.

11 For everyone exalting himself will be humbled, and the *one* humbling himself will be exalted.

12 And He also said to him having invited Him, When you make a dinner or supper, do not call your friends, nor your brothers, nor your relatives, nor rich neighbors, lest they also should invite you in return, and it become a repayment to you.

13 But when you make a banquet, call the poor *ones*, the crippled *ones*, the lame *ones*, the blind *ones*;

14 and you will be blessed, for they have nothing to repay you. For it will be repaid to you in the resurrection of the just *ones*.

15 ¶ And one of the *ones* reclining with *Him*, hearing these things, *he* said to Him, Blessed *is he* who eats bread in the kingdom of God.

16 But He said to him, A certain man made a great supper and invited many.

17 And he sent his slave at the supper hour to say to the *ones* who had been invited, Come, for now all is ready.

18 And all with one *mind* began to excuse themselves. The first said to him, I have bought a field, and I have need to go out and see it; I ask you, have me excused.

19 And another said, I bought five yoke of oxen and I am going to try them out; I ask you, have me excused.

20 And another said, I married a wife, and because of this I am not able to come.

21 And having come near that slave reported these things to his lord. Then being angry, the housemanager said to his slave, Go out quickly into the streets and lanes of the city, and bring in here the poor *ones* and crippled *ones*, and lame *ones* and blind *ones*.

22 And the slave said, Sir, *it* has been done as you ordered, and still there is room.

23 And the lord said to the slave, Go out into the highways and hedges and compel *them* to come in, so that my house may be filled.

24 For I say to you that not one of those men who had been invited shall taste of my supper.

25 ¶ And great crowds came together to Him. And turning, He said to them,

26 If anyone comes to Me and does not hate his father, and mother, and wife, and children, and brothers and sisters, and besides, even his *own* life, he cannot be My disciple.

27 And whoever does not bear his cross and come after Me, he cannot be My disciple.

28 For who of you desiring to build a tower does not first sit down *and* count the cost, whether he has the things to finish;

29 that having laid a foundation, and not having strength to finish, all those seeing begin to mock him,

30 saying, This man began to build, and did not have strength to finish.

31 Or what king going to encounter another king in war does not first sit down *and* take counsel whether he is able with ten thousand to meet those coming upon him with twenty thousand?

32 But if not, he being yet far off, sending a delegation, he asks the things for peace.

33 So then every one of you who does not separate from all his possessions is not able to be My disciple.

34 The salt *is* good, but if the salt becomes tasteless, with what will it be seasoned?

35 Neither for soil nor for manure is it fit; they throw it out. The *one* having ears to hear, let him hear.

Luke 15

1 The parable of the lost sheep: 8 of the piece of silver: 11 and of the prodigal son.

1 ¶ And all the tax collectors and sinners were coming near to Him, to hear Him.

2 And the Pharisees and the scribes murmured, saying, This one receives sinners and eats with them.

3 And He spoke to them this parable, saying,

4 What man of you having a hundred sheep, and losing one of them, does not leave the ninety-nine in the deserted *place* and go after the lost *one* until he finds it?

5 And finding *it*, he puts *it* on his shoulders, rejoicing.

6 And coming to the house, he calls together the friends and neighbors, saying to them, Rejoice with me, for I have found my sheep that had been lost.

7 I say to you that so is joy in Heaven over one sinner repenting, than over ninety nine righteous *ones* who have no need of repentance.

8 Or what woman having ten drachmas, if she loses one drachma does not light a lamp and sweep the house, and seek carefully until she finds it?

9 And finding *it*, she calls together the friends and neighbors, saying, Rejoice with me, for I have found the drachma which I lost.

10 I say to you, So there is joy before the angels of God over one sinner repenting.

11 ¶ And He said, A certain man had two sons.

12 And the younger of them said to the father, Father give me *that* part of the property falling *to* me. And he divided the living to them.

13 And not many days after, gathering up all things, the younger son went abroad to a distant country. And there he squandered his property, living dissolutely.

14 But having spent all his things, a severe famine occurred throughout that country, and he began to be in need.

15 And going, he was joined to one of the citizens of that country. And he sent him into his fields to feed pigs.

16 And he longed to fill his stomach from the husks which the pigs ate, and no one gave to him.

17 But coming to himself he said, How many servants of my father abound in bread, and I am perishing with famine.

18 Rising up, I will go to my father, and I will say to him, Father, I sinned against Heaven and before you,

19 and I am no longer worthy to be called your son. Make me as one of your hired servants.

20 And rising up, he came to his father. But he yet being far away, his father saw him and was moved with compassion. And running, *he* fell on his neck and fervently kissed him.

21 And the son said to him, Father, I have sinned against Heaven and before you, and no longer am I worthy to be called your son.

22 But the father said to his slaves, Bring out the best robe and clothe him, and give a ring to his hand and sandals to *his* feet.

23 And bring the fattened calf, slaughter and let us eat and be merry;

24 for this son of mine was a dead *one*, and lived again, and was lost, and was found. And they began to be merry.

25 But the son of him, the elder *one*, was in *the* field. And as coming, he drew near to the house, he heard music and dances.

26 And having called one of the servants, he inquired what these things may be.

27 And he said to him, Your brother came, and your father slaughtered the fattened calf, because he received him back in health.

28 But he was angry and not would go in. Therefore coming out, his father begged him.

29 But answering, he said to the father, Behold, so many years I serve you, and I have never transgressed a command of you. And you never gave a goat *to me*, so that I might be merry with my friends.

30 But when this son of yours came, the one devouring your living with harlots, you killed the fattened calf for him.

31 But he said to him, Child, you are always with me, and all of my things are yours.

32 But to be merry and it was right to rejoice, for this brother of yours was a dead *one*, and lived again; and being lost, also *he* was found.

Luke 16

1 The parable of the unjust steward. 14 Christ reproves the hypocrisy of the covetous Pharisees.

1 ¶ And He also said to His disciples, A certain man was rich; *and he* had a steward, and this one was accused to him as dissipating his goods.

2 And calling him, he said to him, What *is* this I hear about you? Give the account of your stewardship, for you can no longer be steward.

3 And the steward said within himself, What shall I do, for my lord is taking away the stewardship from me? I am not able to dig, and I am ashamed to beg.

4 I know what I will do, that when I am removed *from* the stewardship, they will receive me into their houses.

5 And having called to him each one of the debtors of his lord, he said to the first, How much do you owe my lord?

6 And he said, A hundred baths of oil. And he said to him, Take your statements and sitting quickly write fifty.

7 Then he said to another, And you, how much do you owe? And he said, a hundred cors of wheat. And he said to him, Take your statement and write eighty.

8 And the lord praised the unrighteous steward, because he acted prudently. For the sons of this age are more prudent than the sons of light themselves are in their generation.

9 And I say to you, Make to yourselves friends by the unrighteous wealth, that when it fails they may receive you into the eternal tabernacles.

10 He faithful in *the* least is also faithful in much. And he unrighteous in the least is also unrighteous in much.

11 Therefore if you were not faithful in the unrighteous wealth, who will entrust the true to you?

12 And if you were not faithful in that of another, who will give to you that *which is* yours?

13 No servant is able to serve two lords; for either he will hate the one, and he will love the other; or he will cling to one, and he will despise the other. You are unable to serve God and wealth.

14 And being lovers of money, the Pharisees also heard all these things; and they derided Him.

15 And He said to them, You are the *ones* justifying yourselves before men, but God knows your hearts; for the thing highly prized among men is an abomination before God.

16 The Law and the Prophets *were* until John; from then the kingdom of God is being preached, and everyone is entering into it by force.

17 But it is easier *for* the heaven and the earth to pass away than one point of the Law to fail.

18 Everyone putting away his wife, and marrying another, commits adultery. And everyone marrying her having been put away from a husband commits adultery.

19 ¶ And a certain man was a rich *one*; and dressed *in* a purple robe and fine linen, being merry *living* luxuriously according to a day.

20 And there was a certain poor *one*, Lazarus by name, who had been thrown at his doorway, being covered with sores,

21 and longing to be filled from the crumbs that were falling from the table of the rich *one*. But coming, even the dogs licked his sores.

22 And it came to be, the poor *one* died and was carried away by the angels into the bosom of Abraham. And the rich *one* also died and was buried.

23 And being in torments in hell, lifting up his eyes, he sees Abraham afar off and Lazarus in his bosom.

24 And calling he said, Father Abraham, have mercy on me and send Lazarus that he may dip the tip of his finger in water and cool my tongue, for I am tormented in this flame.

25 But Abraham said, Child, remember that you fully received your good things in your lifetime, and Lazarus likewise the bad things, and you are tormented.

26 And besides all these things, a great chasm has been fixed between us and you, so that the *ones* desiring to pass from here to you are not able, nor can they pass from there to us.

27 And he said, Therefore I ask you, father, that you send him to my father's house;

28 (for I have five brothers, so that he may witness to them, that they not also come to this place of torment).

29 Abraham said to him, They have Moses and the Prophets, let them hear them.

30 But he said, No, Father Abraham, but if one should go from dead *ones* to them, they will repent.

31 And he said to him, If they will not hear Moses and the Prophets, they will not be persuaded even if someone from dead *ones* should rise.

Luke 17

1 Christ teaches to avoid occasions of offense.
3 One to forgive another. 6 The power of faith.
7 How we are bound to God, and not He to us.

1 ¶ And He said to the disciples, It is impossible that the stumbling blocks should not come, but woe *to him* through whom they come!

2 It is profitable for him if a millstone turned by an ass is put around his neck, and he be thrown into the sea, than that he should stumble one of these little ones.

3 Take heed to yourselves. And if your brother sins against you, rebuke him; and if he repents, forgive him.

4 And if seven times in the day he sins against you, and seven times in the day returns to you saying, I repent, you shall forgive him.

5 And the apostles said to the Lord, Give more faith to us.

6 But the Lord said, If you had faith as a grain of mustard, you may say to this sy-

camine tree, Be rooted up and be planted in the sea! And it would obey you.

7 But which of you having a slave plowing or shepherding will say at once *to him* coming out of the field, Coming, recline?

8 But will he not say to him, Prepare something I may eat, and having girded yourself, serve me until I eat and drink, and after these things you shall eat and drink?

9 *Does* he have thanks to that slave because he did the things commanded him? I think not.

10 So also you,when you have done all things commanded you, say, We are useless slaves, what we ought to do we have done.

11 ¶ And it happened in His going to Jerusalem even He passed through the midst of Samaria and Galilee.

12 And He entering into a certain village, ten leprous men met Him, who stood afar off.

13 And they lifted *their* voice, saying, Jesus, Master, have mercy on us.

14 And seeing *them*, He said to them, Going, show yourselves to the priests. And it happened in their going they were cleansed.

15 And one of them, seeing that he was cured, returned glorifying God with a loud voice,

16 and fell on *his* face at His feet, thanking Him. And he was a Samaritan.

17 And answering, Jesus said, Were not the ten cleansed? But where *are* the nine?

18 Were not *any* found returning to give glory to God except this foreigner?

19 And He said to him, Rising up, go! Your faith has cured you.

20 ¶ And being questioned by the Pharisees *as to* when the kingdom of God comes, He answered them and said, The kingdom of God does not come with observation;

21 nor will they say,Behold, here! Or, Behold, there! For behold, the kingdom of God is within you.

22 And He said to the disciples, Days will come when you will long to see one of the days of the Son of Man, and will not see.

23 And they will say to you, Behold, here! Or, Behold, there! Do not go away, nor follow.

24 For as the lightning lighting up out of *one part* under heaven to *one part* under heaven shines, so also will the Son of Man be in His day.

25 But first He must suffer many things and be rejected from this generation.

26 And as it was in the days of Noah, so also it will be in the days of the Son of Man.

27 They were eating, drinking, marrying, giving in marriage, until *the* day Noah went into the ark. And the flood came and destroyed all.

28 And likewise, as it was in the days of Lot, they were eating, drinking, buying, selling, planting, building;

29 but on *the* day Lot went out from Sodom, it rained fire and brimstone from the heaven and destroyed all.

30 According to those things, it will be in the day the Son of Man is revealed.

31 In that day, *he* who will be on the housetop, let him not go down to take his goods *from* the house. And likewise, he in the field, let him not return to the things behind.

32 Remember Lot's wife.

33 Whoever seeks to save his life, *he* will lose it. And whoever will lose it, he will preserve it.

34 I say to you, In that night two will be on one bed; the one will be taken and the other will be left.

35 Two will be grinding at the same *thing*; one will be taken and the other will be left.

36 Two will be in the field, the one will be taken and the other will be left.

37 And answering, they said to Him, Where, Lord? And He said to them, Where the body *is*, there the eagles will be gathered together.

Luke 18

1 The importunate widow. 15 Children brought to Christ. 31 He foretells His death.

1 ¶ And He also spoke a parable to them to *teach that* it is always necessary to pray, and not to be wearied

2 saying, A certain judge was in a certain city, not fearing God and not respecting man.

3 And a widow was in that city, and she came to him, saying, Avenge me from my adversary.

4 And for a time he would not. But after these things he said to himself, Even if I do not fear God, and do not respect man,

5 yet because this widow causes me trouble, I will avenge her, that not coming to *the* end, she wear me down.

6 And the Lord said, Hear what the unrighteous judge says;

7 and will God not execute the avengement of His elect, not *any of* those crying to Him day and night, also being long-suffering over them, not *at all*?

8 I say to you that He will carry out the avengement of them speedily. But the Son of Man coming, really will He find faith on the earth?

9 ¶ And He also spoke this parable to some of those relying on themselves, that they are righteous *ones*, and despising the rest:

10 Two men went up into the temple to pray, the one a Pharisee, and the other a tax collector.

11 The Pharisee *was* standing, praying these things to himself: God, I thank You that I am not as the rest of men, rapacious *ones*, unrighteous *ones*, adulterers, or even as this tax collector.

12 I fast twice *on* the sabbath; I tithe all things, as many as I get.

13 And the tax collector, standing afar off, would not even lift up *his* eyes to Heaven, but smote on his breast, saying, God, be merciful to me, the sinner!

14 I say to you, This one went down to his house having been justified, *rather* than that one. For everyone exalting himself will be humbled. And the *one* humbling himself will be exalted.

15 ¶ And they brought infants to Him also, that He might touch them. But seeing, the disciples rebuked them.

16 But Jesus called them near, saying, Allow the children to come to Me, and do not stop them. For of such is the kingdom of God.

17 Truly I say to you, Whoever does not receive the kingdom of God like a child, will not enter into it, not *ever*.

18 ¶ And a certain ruler asked Him saying, Good Teacher, what may I do to inherit eternal life?

19 But Jesus said to him, Why do you say Me *to be* good? No one *is* good, except One: God.

20 You know the commandments: "Do not commit adultery," "do not murder," "do not steal," "do not bear false witness," "honor your father and your mother." *Ex. 20:12-16*

21 And he said, I have kept all these from my youth.

22 And hearing these things, Jesus said to him, Yet one *thing* is lacking to you: sell all, as much as you have, and distribute to the poor *ones* ; and you will have treasure in Heaven. And come, follow Me.

23 But hearing these things, he became very much grieved, for he was an extremely rich *one*.

24 And seeing him becoming very grieved, Jesus said, How hardly those having riches shall enter into the kingdom of God!

25 For it is easier *for* a camel to go in through a needle's eye than for a rich *one* to enter into the kingdom of God.

26 And the *ones* having heard said, And who is able to be saved?

27 But He said, The things impossible with men are possible with God.

28 And Peter said, Behold, we left all and followed You.

29 And He said to them, Truly I say to you, There is no one who has left house, or parents, or brothers, or wife, or children, for the sake of the kingdom of God,

30 who shall not receive many times more, not in this time, not *ever*, and in the age, the *one* coming, everlasting life.

31 ¶ And taking aside the Twelve, He said to them, Behold, we are going up to Jerusalem, and all things will be fulfilled which have been written through the prophets to the Son of Man.

32 For He will be delivered up to the nations, and will be mocked, and will be insulted, and will be spat upon.

33 And scourging *Him*, they will kill Him. And on the third day He will rise again.

34 And they understood none of these things! And this saying had been hidden

from them, and they did not know the things being said.

35 ¶ And it happened *as* He drew near to Jericho, a certain blind *one* sat by the highway, begging.

36 And hearing a crowd passing through, he asked what this might be.

37 And they reported to him that Jesus the Nazarene is passing by.

38 And he cried, saying, Jesus, Son of David, have mercy on me.

39 And those going before rebuked him, that he be quiet. But he much more cried out, Son of David, Have mercy on me!

40 And standing still, Jesus commanded him to be brought to Him. And he drawing near, He asked him,

41 saying, What do you desire I do to you? And he said, Lord, that I may see again.

42 And Jesus said to him, See again! Your faith has healed you.

43 And instantly he saw again. And *he* followed Him, glorifying God. And seeing, all the people gave praise to God.

Luke 19

1 Of Zacchaeus, a tax collector. 11 The ten pieces of money. 28 Christ rides into Jerusalem with triumph: 41 weeps over it: 45 drives the buyers and sellers out of the temple.

1 ¶ And going in, He passed through Jericho.

2 And, behold, a man called by name Zacchaeus; and he was a chief tax collector, and he was a rich *one*.

3 And he was seeking to see Jesus, who He is. And he was not able, because of the crowd, and because he was little in stature.

4 And running ahead, he went up onto a sycamore tree, so that he might see Him; for He was going to pass through that *way*.

5 And as He came to the place, looking up, Jesus saw him, and said to him, Zacchaeus, hurry, come down, for today I must stay in your house.

6 And hurrying, he came down and welcomed Him, rejoicing.

7 And having seen, all murmured, saying, He has gone in to lodge with a sinful man.

8 But standing, Zacchaeus said to the Lord, Behold, Lord, half of my possessions I give to the poor *ones*. And if *in*

anything I accused anyone falsely, I give *it* back fourfold.

9 And Jesus said to him, Today salvation has come to this house, for he also is a son of Abraham.

10 For the Son of Man came to seek and to save the thing having been lost.

11 ¶ But as they were hearing these things, adding, He spoke a parable, because He was near to Jerusalem, and they thought that the kingdom of God was immediately to be revealed.

12 Therefore He said: A certain wellborn man went to a distant country to receive a kingdom for himself, and to return.

13 And calling ten of his slaves, He gave to them ten minas and said to them, Trade until I come.

14 But his citizens hated him and sent a delegation after him, saying, We do not desire this one to reign over us.

15 And it happened as he returned, having received the kingdom, he even said *for* those slaves to be called to him, those to whom he gave the silver, that he might know what each *one* had gained by trading.

16 And the first came, saying, Lord, your mina has gained ten minas.

17 And he said to him, Well *done*, good slave! Because you were faithful in a least thing, have authority over ten cities.

18 And the second came, saying, Lord, your mina has made five minas.

19 And he said to this one also, And you be over five cities.

20 And another came, saying, Lord, behold your mina which I have stored up in a facecloth.

21 For I feared you, because you are an exacting man, taking what you did not lay down, and reaping what you did not sow.

22 But he said to him, I will judge you out of your own mouth, wicked slave. You knew that I am an exacting man, taking what I did not lay down, and reaping what I did not sow.

23 And why did you not give my silver on the *bank* table? And coming, I might have exacted it with interest.

24 And to those standing by, he said, Take the mina from him, and give *it* to him who has ten minas.

25 And they said to him, Lord, he has ten minas.

26 For I say to you, To everyone who has, it will be given. And from the *one* who does not have, even what he has will be taken from him.

27 But these hostile *ones* of me, the *ones* not desiring me to reign over them, bring them here and slaughter *them* before me.

28 ¶ And saying these things, He went in front, going up to Jerusalem.

29 And it happened as He drew near to Bethphage and Bethany toward the Mount being called Of Olives, He sent two of the disciples,

30 saying, Go into the opposite village in which having entered you will find a young ass being tied, on which no one of men ever yet sat. Loosing it, bring *it*.

31 And if anyone asks, Why do you loose *it*? you shall say to them, The Lord has need of it.

32 And going, the *ones* having been sent found as He told them.

33 And *as* they were loosing the young ass, its owners said to them, Why do you loose the young ass?

34 And the *ones* said, The Lord has need of it.

35 And they led it to Jesus. And throwing their garments on the young ass, they set Jesus on *it*.

36 And as He went, they were spreading their garments in the way.

37 And as He was already drawing near to the descent of the Mount of Olives, all the multitude of the disciples began rejoicing, to praise God with a loud voice concerning all *the* works of power which they saw,

38 saying, "Blessed *is* the coming King in the name of the Lord," Peace in Heaven, and glory in *the* highest! *(See Psa. 118:26)*

39 And some of the Pharisees from the crowd said to Him, Teacher, rebuke your disciples.

40 And answering, He said to them, I say to you, If these should be silent, the stones will cry out.

41 ¶ And as He drew near, seeing the city, He wept over it,

42 saying, If you had known, even you, even at least in this day of yours, the things for your peace! But now they were hidden from your eyes.

43 For the days will come on you, and hostile *ones to* you will raise up a rampart to you and will surround you and will keep you in on all sides,

44 and will tear you down, and your children in you, and will not leave in you a stone on a stone, because of which *things* you did not know the time of your visitation.

45 And entering into the temple, He began to throw out the *ones* selling and buying in it,

46 saying to them, It has been written, "My house is a house of prayer," but you made it "a den of plunderers." *Isa. 56:7; Jer. 7:11*

47 And He was teaching according to a day in the temple. But the chief priests and the scribes and the chief men of the people sought to kill Him.

48 And *they* were not finding what they might do; for all the people were hanging on Him, hearing.

Luke 20

1 Christ's authority. 9 The parable of the vineyard. 19 Of giving tribute to Caesar. 27 Christ convinces the Sadducees that denied the resurrection.

1 ¶ And it happened on one of those days, *with* Him teaching the people in the temple and proclaiming the gospel, the chief priests and the scribes came up with the elders,

2 and spoke to Him, saying, Tell us by what authority you do these things, or who is the *one* giving you this authority?

3 And answering, He said to them, I will also ask you one thing, and you tell me:

4 The baptism of John, was it from Heaven, or from men?

5 And they reasoned among themselves, saying, If we say, From Heaven, He will say, Why then did you not believe him?

6 But if we say, From men, all the people will stone us, for they are being convinced *that* John was a prophet.

7 And they answered *claiming* not to know from where.

8 And Jesus said to them, Neither do I tell you by what authority I do these things.

9 ¶ And He began to speak this parable to the people: A certain man planted a vineyard and gave it out to vinedressers.,and went abroad *for* considerable times. *Isa. 5:1, 2*

10 And in *harvest* time, he sent a slave to the vinedressers, that they might give him the fruit of the vineyard. But the vinedressers sent him away empty, beating *him*.

11 And he again sent another slave. But they also sent that one away empty, beating and dishonoring *him*.

12 And he added to send a third. But they also threw this one out, wounding *him*.

13 And the lord of the vineyard said, What shall I do? I will send my beloved son. Perhaps, having seen this one, they will respect *him*.

14 And seeing him, the vinedressers reasoned to themselves, saying, This is the heir. Come let us kill him so that the inheritance may become ours.

15 And throwing him out of the vineyard, they killed *him*. Therefore, what will the lord of the vineyard do to them?

16 He will come and will destroy these vinedressers and will give the vineyard to others. And hearing this, they said, Let it not be!

17 And looking at them He said, What then is this which has been written, "*The* Stone that the *ones* building rejected, this One came to be for *the* Head of *the* Corner"? *Psa. 118:22*

18 Everyone falling on that Stone will be crushed, but on whomever It falls, *It* will pulverize him.

19 And the chief priests and the scribes sought to lay hands on Him in the same hour. And *they* feared the people, for they knew that He told this parable against them.

20 ¶ And watching carefully, they sent spies, pretending themselves to be righteous *ones*, in order that they might seize upon a word of His, so as to give Him over to the power and to the authority of the governor.

21 And they questioned Him, saying, Teacher, we know that You say and teach rightly and do not receive a face, but You teach the way of God in truth.

22 Is it lawful for us to give tribute to Caesar or not?

23 But perceiving their slyness, He said to them, Why do you tempt Me?

24 Show Me a denarius. Whose image and superscription does it have? And answering, they said, Of Caesar.

25 And He said to them, Therefore give back the things of Caesar to Caesar, and the things of God to God.

26 And they were not able to lay hold of His speech before the people. And marveling at His answer, they were silent.

27 ¶ And some of the Sadducees coming up, those speaking against a resurrection, *that it was* not to be, they questioned Him,

28 saying, Teacher, Moses wrote to us, If anyone's brother dies having a wife, and this one should die childless, that his brother should take the wife and raise up seed to his brother. *Deut. 25:5*

29 So there were seven brothers. And the first having taken a wife died childless.

30 and the second took the wife, and this one died childless.

31 And the third took her, and likewise also the seven, and also did not leave children, and died.

32 And last of all the woman also died.

33 Therefore in the resurrection, of which of them does she become wife? For the seven had her *as* wife.

34 And answering, Jesus said to them, The sons of this age marry and are given in marriage.

35 But those counted worthy to obtain that age, and the resurrection from *the* dead *ones*, neither marry nor are given in marriage.

36 For they are not able to die *any* more; they are equal to angels, and are sons of God, being sons of the resurrection.

37 But that the dead *ones* are raised, even Moses pointed out at the Bush, when he calls *the* Lord "the God of Abraham, and the God of Isaac, and the God of Jacob." *Ex. 3:6*

38 But He is not God of *the* dead *ones*, but *of ones* being alive, for all live to Him.

39 ¶ And answering, some of the scribes said, Teacher, you speak well.

40 And they did not dare to question Him any more, not a thing.

41 And He said to them, How do they say the Christ is David's son?

42 Even David himself said in *the* Book of Psalms, "The Lord said to my Lord, Sit at My right *hand*

43 until I place the hostile *ones to* You *as* a footstool of Your feet." *LXX-Psa. 109:1; MT-Psa. 110:1*

44 David, then, calls Him Lord. And how is He his son?

45 And as all the people were hearing, He said to His disciples,

46 Be on guard from the scribes, the *ones* desiring to walk about in long robes, and loving greetings in the markets, and chief seats in the synagogues, and chief couches in the suppers,

47 who devour the houses of the widows, and under pretense pray long. These will receive a more abundant judgment.

Luke 21

1 Christ commends the poor widow. 5 He foretells the destruction of the temple, and of Jerusalem. 34 He warns them to be watchful.

1 ¶ And having looked up, He saw the rich *ones* putting their gifts into the treasury.

2 And He also saw a certain poor widow putting two lepta there.

3 And He said, Truly I say to you, This poor widow put *in* more than all.

4 For all these out of their abundance put into the gifts of God, but she out of her poverty put *in* all the living which she had.

5 ¶ And as some were speaking about the temple, that it had been adorned with beautiful stones and gifts, He said,

6 *As to* these things that you see, days will come in which a stone will not be left on a stone, which will not be thrown down.

7 And they asked Him, saying, Teacher, then when will these things be? And what *will be* the sign when these things are about to happen?

8 And He said, Watch that you not be led astray. For many will come on My name, saying, I Am! Also, The time has come! Do not then go after them.

9 And when you hear of wars and disturbances, do not be terrified. For these things must first occur, but the end *is* not at once.

10 Then He said to them, Nation will be lifted up against nation, and kingdom against kingdom.

11 Also there will be great earthquakes in *various* places, and famines, and plagues. And also there will be terrors and great signs from Heaven.

12 But before all these things, they will lay their hands on you, and will persecute *you*, giving *you* over into the synagogues and prisons, being led away before kings and governors on account of My name.

13 But it will turn out to you for a testimony.

14 Therefore put into your hearts not to premeditate to make a defense.

15 For I will give you a mouth and wisdom which all the *ones* opposing you will not be able to speak against nor withstand.

16 But you will be given over also by parents, and brothers, and relatives, and friends. And they will put *some* of you to death.

17 And you will be *as ones* being hated by all because of My name.

18 And a hair from your head shall not perish, not *ever*!

19 In your patience you will gain your souls.

20 ¶ And when you see Jerusalem being encircled by army camps, then recognize that its destruction has come near.

21 Then let the *ones* in Judea flee into the mountains; and the *ones* in its midst of her, let them go out. And the *ones* in the outer spaces, let them not go into her.

22 For these are days of vengeance *when* all things that have been written are to be fulfilled.

23 But woe to the *ones* having *a babe* in womb, and the ones suckling in those days; for great distress will be on the earth and wrath on this people.

24 And they will fall by *the* mouth of *the* sword and will be led captive into all the nations. And Jerusalem will be trodden down by nations, until *the* times of *the* nations are fulfilled.

25 And there will be signs in the sun and moon and stars. And on the earth *will be* anxiety of nations in perplexity, roaring of sea and of billows,

26 men fainting from fear, and expectation of the things coming on the earth. For the powers of the heavens will be shaken.

27 And then they will see the Son of Man coming in a cloud with power and great glory. *Dan. 7:13*

28 But these things beginning to happen, stand up and lift up your heads, because your redemption draws near.

29 ¶ And He spoke a parable to them: You see the fig tree and all the trees.

30 Now when they sprout leaves, seeing *it*, you will know from yourselves that now the summer is near.

31 So also when you see these things happening, you know that the kingdom of God is near.

32 Truly I say to you, this generation will not pass away until all *these* things occur, not *ever*.

33 The heaven and the earth will pass away, but My words will not pass away, not *ever*!

34 But take heed to yourselves that your hearts not be loaded down with headaches, and drinking, and anxieties of life, and that day come suddenly upon you.

35 For as a snare it will come in on all the *ones* sitting on *the* face of all the earth. *Isa. 24:17*

36 Therefore keep awake in every time, praying that you be counted worthy to escape all these things, the things being about to happen, and to stand before the Son of Man.

37 And *in* the days, He was teaching in the temple. And going out *in* the nights, He lodged in the mountain, the *one* being called *Mount* of Olives.

38 And all the people came early to Him in the temple, to hear Him.

Luke 22

1 The Jews conspire against Christ. 7 The apostles prepare the passover. 19 Christ institutes His holy supper. 39 He prays in the mount, and sweats blood, 47 is betrayed with a kiss: 50 He heals Malchus' ear, 54 Peter denies Christ thrice.

1 ¶ And the Feast of Unleavened *Bread* drew near, the *one* called Passover.

2 And the chief priests and the scribes sought how *they* might kill Him; for they feared the people.

3 And Satan entered into Judas, the *one* being called Iscariot, being of the number of the Twelve.

4 And going, he talked with the chief priests and the commanders *as to* how he might give Him over to them.

5 And they exulted, and they agreed to give him silver.

6 And he fully agreed and sought opportunity to give Him over to them, away from *the* crowd.

7 ¶ And the day of the Unleavened *Bread* came, on which the Passover must be killed.

8 And He sent Peter and John, saying, Having gone, prepare for us the Passover, that we may eat.

9 And they said to Him, Where do You desire that we prepare?

10 And He said to them, Behold, you going into the city, you will meet a man carrying a pitcher of water. Follow him into the house where he goes in.

11 And you will say to the housemanager of the house, The Teacher says to you, Where is the guest room where I may eat the Passover with My disciples?

12 And that one will show you a large upper room *which* has been spread. Prepare there.

13 And having gone, they found as He had told them, and they prepared the Passover.

14 And when the hour came, He reclined, and the twelve apostles with Him.

15 And He said to them, With desire I desired to eat this Passover with you before I suffer.

16 For I say to you that no more, I will not eat of it until when it is fulfilled in the kingdom of God, not *ever*!

17 And having received a cup, having given thanks, He said, Take this and divide *it* among yourselves.

18 For I say to you that I will not drink from the produce of the vine until the kingdom of God comes, not *ever*!

19 And having taken a loaf, having given thanks, He broke, and gave to them, saying, This is My body being given for you. This do in remembrance of Me.

20 And in like manner the cup, after having supped, saying, This cup *is* the New

Covenant in My blood, which is being poured out for you.

21 ¶ But, behold, the hand of the *one* giving Me over on the table with Me!

22 And, indeed, the Son of Man goes according as was determined, but woe to that man by whom He is given over!

23 And they began to discuss with themselves who then it may be of them, the *one* being about to do this.

24 And there came to be also a dispute among them, who of them should be accounted to be greater.

25 And He said to them, The kings of the nations lord it over them, and those exercising authority over them are called benefactors.

26 But you *be* not so, but the greater among you, let him be as the younger *one*; and the *one* governing as the *one* serving.

27 For who *is* greater, the *one* reclining, or the *one* serving? *Is it* not the *one* reclining? But I am in your midst as *One* serving.

28 But you are the *ones* having continued with Me in My trials

29 And I appoint to you, even as My Father appointed to Me, a kingdom,

30 that you may eat and drink at My table in My kingdom; and you will sit on thrones judging the twelve tribes of Israel.

31 And the Lord said, Simon, Simon, behold, Satan asked for you, to sift *you* as wheat;

32 but I prayed for you, that your faith not fail. And you, when turning back, make firm your brothers.

33 And he said to Him, Lord, I am ready to go both to prison and to death with You.

34 But He said, I say to you, Peter, A cock not will sound today, not before you will deny knowing Me three times.

35 And He said to them, When I sent you without a money-bag, and a wallet, and sandals, did you lack anything? And they said, Nothing.

36 Then He said to them, But now, the *one* having a money bag, let him take *it*; likewise also a wallet. And he not having, let him sell his garment, and let him buy a sword.

37 For I say to you that this that has been written must yet be fulfilled in Me: "And He was numbered with the lawless." *Isa. 53:12* For the thing concerning Me also has an end.

38 And they said, Lord, behold, here *are* two swords. And He said to them, It is enough.

39 ¶ And going out, He went, according to *His* custom, to the Mount of Olives; and His disciples also followed Him.

40 And having come on the place, He said to them, Pray *that* you *do* not enter into temptation.

41 And He was withdrawn from them, about a stone's throw. And having placed the knees, He prayed,

42 saying, Father, if You purpose *it*, take away this cup from Me; but let not be My will, but let be Your *will.*

43 And an angel from Heaven appeared to Him, strengthening Him.

44 And coming to be in agony, He prayed more intently. And His sweat came to be as drops of blood falling down onto the earth.

45 And rising up from the prayer, coming to His disciples, He found them sleeping from grief.

46 And *He* said to them, Why do you sleep? Rising up, pray, that you do not enter into temptation.

47 ¶ And *as* He *was* yet speaking, behold, a crowd! And the *one* called Judas, one of the Twelve, came in front of them and drew near to Jesus in order to kiss Him.

48. But Jesus said to hum, do you give over the Son of Man with a kiss?

49 And those around Him seeing that about to occur, said to Him, Lord, shall we strike with the sword?

50 And a certain one of them struck the slave of the high priest and cut off his right ear.

51 And answering, Jesus said, Allow *it* until this. And touching his ear, He healed him.

52 And Jesus said to the *ones* coming upon Him, chief priests, and commanders of the temple, and elders, As against a plunderer have you come out with swords and clubs?

53 According to a day, *I* being with you in the temple, you did not stretch forth your

hands on Me. But this is your hour and the authority of the darkness.

54 ¶ And having seized Him, they led *Him* away and brought Him into the house of the high priest. And Peter followed at a distance.

55 And lighting a fire in *the* midst of the courtyard, and they sitting down together, Peter sat in *the* midst of them.

56 And a certain slave-girl seeing him sitting near the light, and gazing at at him, *she* said, And this *one* was with Him.

57 But he denied Him, saying, Woman, I do not know Him.

58 Also after a short *while*, another seeing him said, You also are of them. But Peter said, Man, I am not.

59 And about an hour intervening, a certain other one firmly declared,

60 saying, On truth this *one* also was with Him, for he also is a Galilean.

60 And Peter said, Man, I do not know what you say. And immediately, while he yet spoke, the cock sounded.

61 And turning, the Lord looked at Peter. And Peter remembered the word of the Lord, how He told him, Before a cock would crow, you will deny Me three times.

62 And going outside, Peter wept bitterly.

63 ¶ And the men having Jesus in charge mocked Him, beating *Him*.

64 And covering over Him, *they were* striking His face and questioning Him, saying, Prophesy, who is the one striking You?

65 And many other things, blaspheming, they said to Him.

66 And as *it* came to be day, the body of elders of the people, both the chief priests and scribes, was assembled, and led Him away into their sanhedrin, saying,

67 If you are the Christ, tell us. And He said to them, If I tell you, you will not believe, not *at all*.

68 And also if I ask, you will not answer Me, nor release Me, not *at all*.

69 From now the Son of Man will be sitting at the right of the power of God. *Psa. 110:1*

70 And they all said, Are You, then, the Son of God? And He said to them, You say *it*, because I AM!

71 And they said, Why do we yet have need of witness? For we ourselves heard *it* from His mouth.

Luke 23

1 Jesus is accused before Pilate, and sent to Herod. 8 Herod mocks him. 13 Barabbas is desired of the people, and is freed by Pilate, and Jesus is given to be crucified. 34 He prays for his enemies. 46 His death. 50 His burial.

1 ¶ And rising up, all the multitude of them led Him to Pilate.

2 And they began to accuse Him, saying, we found this *man* perverting the nation, and forbidding to give tribute to Caesar, saying Himself to be Christ, a king.

3 And Pilate questioned Him, saying, Are You the king of the Jews? And He answering him, said, You say *it*.

4 And Pilate said to the chief priests and the crowds, I find no cause *of death* in this Man.

5 But they insisted, saying, He stirs up the people, teaching throughout all Judea, beginning from Galilee to here.

6 And Pilate, hearing Galilee, asked if the man is a Galilean.

7 And knowing that He is from Herod's jurisdiction, he sent Him up to Herod, *he* also being in Jerusalem in these days.

8 And Herod, seeing Jesus, greatly rejoiced, for he was wanting to see Him *for* a considerable *time*, because *he wished* to hear many things about Him, and he hoped to see some *miraculous* sign being done by Him.

9 And he questioned Him in many words. But He answered him not a thing.

10 And the chief priests and the scribes stood vehemently accusing Him.

11 And Herod having despised Him with his soldiery, and having mocked *Him* by putting around Him luxurious clothing, *he* sent Him back to Pilate.

12 And on that same day, both Pilate and Herod became friends with each other, for they before were at enmity *between* themselves.

13 ¶ And Pilate, having called together the chief priests and the leaders and the people,

14 said to them, You brought this Man to me as perverting the people. And, behold, examining Him before you, I found no cause *of death* in this Man *regarding that* which you bring charge against Him.

15 But neither did Herod, for I sent you up to him; and, behold, nothing worthy of death is done by Him.

16 Then scourging Him, I will release *Him.*

17 And he had to release to them one at the Feast.

18 And they all together cried out, saying, Take this *One,* and release to us Barabbas

19 (who was, due to some insurrection occurring in the city, and murder, thrown into prison.)

20 Therefore Pilate again called to *them,* desiring to release Jesus.

21 But they shouted, saying, Crucify! Crucify Him!

22 And a third *time* he said to them, For what evil *thing* did this *man* do? I found nothing *as* cause *of death* in Him; therefore scourging Him, I will release *Him.*

23 But *with* loud voices they were urgent, asking for Him to be crucified. And their voices, and *that* of the chief priests, prevailed.

24 And Pilate adjudged their request to be done.

25 And he released to them *the one* having been thrown into prison due to revolt and murder, *for* whom they asked. But he gave over Jesus to their will.

26 ¶ And as they led Him away, having laid hold on Simon, a certain Cyrenian, coming from a field, they put the cross on him, to bear *it* behind Jesus.

27 And a great multitude of people were following Him, and of women who also were bewailing and lamenting Him.

28 And turning to them, Jesus said, Daughters of Jerusalem, do not weep over Me, but weep over yourselves and over your children.

29 For behold, days will come in which they will say, Blessed *are* the barren, and *the* wombs that did not bear, and breasts that did not give suck.

30 "Then they will begin to say to the mountains, Fall on us! And to the hills, Cover us!" *Hosea 10:8*

31 For if they do these things in the green tree, what shall be done in the dry *tree*?

32 ¶ And also others, two criminals, were led with Him to be put to death.

33 And when they came on the place being called Skull, there they crucified Him and the criminals, one at *the* right, and one at *the* left.

34 And Jesus said, Father, forgive them, for they do not know what they are doing. And dividing His garments, they cast a lot. *Psa. 22:18*

35 And the people stood watching. And the rulers with them also scoffed, saying, He saved others; let Him save Himself, if this *One* is the Christ, the Elect of God.

36 And coming near, the soldiers also mocked Him and *were* offering vinegar to Him,

37 and saying, If You are the king of the Jews, save Yourself.

38 And also an inscription was written over Him, in letters, Greek and Latin and Hebrew: THIS IS THE KING OF THE JEWS.

39 And one of the hanged criminals blasphemed Him, saying, If You are the Christ, save Yourself and us.

40 But answering, the other rebuked him, saying, Do you not fear God, for *you* are in the same judgment?

41 And we indeed justly, for we receive things worthy of what we did. But this *One* did nothing amiss.

42 And he said to Jesus, Lord, remember me when You come in Your kingdom.

43 And Jesus said to him, Truly I say to you, Today you will be with Me in Paradise.

44 ¶ And it was about *the* sixth hour, and darkness came to be over all the land until *the* ninth hour.

45 And the sun was darkened, and the veil of the temple was torn apart in the middle.

46 And crying with a loud voice, Jesus said, Father, "into Your hands I commit My spirit." And saying this, He expired. *Psa. 31:5*

47 And the centurion, seeing the thing happening, glorified God, saying, Truly, this Man was righteous.

48 And all the crowd arriving together at this sight, watching the things happening, beating their breasts, *they* returned.

49 And all the *ones* known to Him stood at a distance, and *the* women, the *ones* having accompanied Him from Galilee, *were* seeing these things.

50 ¶ And, behold, a man, Joseph by name, being a councillor, a good and righteous man.

51 This one was not assenting to their counsel and action (*he was* from Arimathea, a city of the Jews), and who also himself was eagerly expecting the kingdom of God,

52 this *one*, coming near to Pilate, asked *for* the body of Jesus.

53 And taking it down, he wrapped it in linen, and placed it in a tomb hewn in stone, where no one was ever yet laid.

54 And it was Preparation Day, and a sabbath was coming on.

55 And having followed, also *the* women who were accompanying Him out of Galilee, watched the tomb, and how His body was placed.

56 And returning, *they* prepared spices and ointments. And indeed they rested *on* the sabbath, according to the commandment.

Luke 24

1 Christ's resurrection is declared by two angels. 13 He himself appears to the two disciples that went to Emmaus: 36 He appears to the apostles, and reproves their unbelief: 49 promises the Holy Spirit: 51 and so ascends into Heaven.

1 ¶ And the first of the sabbaths, *at* early dawn, they came on the tomb, carrying spices which they prepared; and some were with them.

2 And they found the stone having been rolled away from the tomb.

3 And going in, they did not find the body of the Lord Jesus.

4 And it happened, as they were perplexed about this, even behold, two men in shining clothing stood by them.

5 And they, becoming terrified, and bowing *the* face to the earth, they said to them, Why do you seek the living *One* with the dead *ones*?

6 He is not here, but was raised. Remember how He spoke to you, yet being in Galilee,

7 saying, The Son of Man must be given over into *the* hands of sinful men, and to be crucified, and the third day to rise again.

8 And they remembered His words.

9 And returning from the tomb, they reported all these things to the Eleven, and to all the rest.

10 And they were Mary Magdalene, and Joanna, and Mary *mother* of James, and the rest with them, who told these things to the apostles.

11 And their words seemed like nonsense before them, and they did not believe them.

12 But Peter, rising up, ran to the tomb, and bending down he *saw* the linen lying alone. And *he* went away wondering to himself *at what* had happened.

13 ¶ And, behold, two of them were going on the same day to a village being sixty stadia distant from Jerusalem, which was named Emmaus.

14 And they talked to each other about all these things taking place.

15 And it happened, in the *need of* them to converse and to discuss, Jesus Himself, coming near, also traveled with them.

16 But their eyes were held *so as* not to recognize Him.

17 And He said to them, What words *are* these which you exchange with each other *while* walking, and are sad of face?

18 And answering, one of them whose name was Cleopas, said to Him, Are You alone sojourning in Jerusalem, and do not know the things happening in it in these days?

19 And He said to them, What things? And they said to Him, The things concerning Jesus the Nazarene, who was a man, a prophet mighty in deed and word before God and all the people;

20 and how the chief priests and our rulers gave Him over to *the* judgment of death, and crucified Him.

21 But we were hoping that He is the *One* going to redeem Israel. But yet with all these *things*, this third day comes today since these things happened.

22 But also some of our women astounded us, having been early at the tomb,

23 and not finding His body, *they* came saying also to have seen a vision of angels, who were saying Him to live.

24 And some of those with us went to the tomb, and found *it* so, even as the women also said; but they did not see Him.

25 And He said to them, O foolish *ones*, and slow of heart to believe on all things which the prophets spoke!

26 Was it not necessary for the Christ to suffer these things, and to enter into His glory?

27 And beginning from Moses, and from all the prophets, He explained to them, in all the Scriptures, the things about Himself.

28 And they drew near to the village where they were going, and He seemed to be going further.

29 And they constrained Him, saying, Stay with us, for it is toward evening, and the day has declined. And He went in to stay with them.

30 And it happened *as* He reclined with them, having taken the bread, He blessed, and having broken He gave to them.

31 And their eyes were opened, and they knew Him. And He became invisible from them.

32 And they said to one another, Was not our heart burning within us as He spoke to us in the way, and as He opened up to us the Scriptures?

33 And rising up in the same hour, they went back to Jerusalem, and found, having been gathered together, the Eleven, and those with them,

34 saying, The Lord really was raised and appeared to Simon.

35 And they related the things in the way, and how He was known to them in the breaking of the loaf.

36 ¶ And as they were saying these things, Jesus Himself stood in the midst of them, and said to them, Peace to you!

37 But being terrified, and being filled with fear, they thought they beheld a spirit.

38 And He said to them, Why are you troubled? And why do reasonings come up in your hearts.

39 See My hands and My feet, that I am *My*self? Feel Me and see, because a spirit does not have flesh and bones, as you see Me having.

40 And saying this, He showed them *His* hands and feet.

41 But yet they not believing from the joy, and marveling, He said to them, Have you any*thing* edible here?

42 And they gave a part of a broiled fish to Him, and from a honeycomb.

43 And taking, He ate.before them.

44 And He said to them, These *are* the words which I spoke to you yet being with you, that all the things must be fulfilled having been written in the Law of Moses, and *the* Prophets, and *the* Psalms, concerning Me.

45 Then He opened up their mind to understand the Scriptures,

46 and said to them, Thus it is written, and so the Christ must suffer, and to rise from *the* dead the third day. *No OT passage*

47 And repentance and remission of sins *must* be preached on His name to all the nations, beginning from Jerusalem.

48 And you are witnesses of these things.

49 And, behold, I send forth the promise of My Father on you. But you sit in the city of Jerusalem until you are clothed with power from the height.

50 ¶ And He led them out as far as to Bethany. And lifting up His hands, He blessed them.

51 And it happened in *the way for* Him to bless them, He was parted from them and was carried into Heaven.

52 And they, worshiping Him, returned to Jerusalem with great joy,

53 and were through all in the temple, praising and blessing God. Amen.

The Gospel According to
the Apostle JOHN

John 1

1 The divinity, humanity, and office of Jesus Christ.
15 The testimony of John.

1 ¶ In *the* beginning was the Word, and the Word was with God, and the Word was God.

2 He was in *the* beginning with God.

3 All things came into being through Him, and without Him not even one *thing* came into being that has come into being.

4 In Him was life, and the life was the light of men;

5 ¶ and the light shines in the darkness, and the darkness did not overtake it.

6 There was a man having been sent from God; his name *was* John.

7 He came for a witness, that he might witness concerning the Light, that all might believe through Him.

8 He was not that Light, but that *he* might witness concerning the Light;

9 He was the true Light which, coming into the world, enlightens every man.

10 He was in the world, and the world came into being through Him, yet the world did not know Him.

11 He came to *His* own, and *His* own did not receive Him.

12 But as many as received Him, to them He gave authority to become children of God, to the *ones* believing into His name,

13 who were generated not of blood, nor of *the* will of *the* flesh, nor of *the* will of man, but were generated of God.

14 And the Word became flesh and tabernacled among us. And we beheld His glory, glory as of an only begotten *One* from *the* Father, full of grace and of truth.

15 ¶ John witnesses about Him, and has cried out, saying, This *One* was *He* of whom I said, The *One* coming after me has been before me, for He was first of me.

16 And out of His fullness we all received, and grace for grace.

17 For the Law was given through Moses, grace and truth came through Jesus Christ.

18 No one has seen God at any time; the only begotten Son, the *One* being into the bosom of the Father, that One declared Him.

19 ¶ And this is the witness of John, when the Jews sent priests and Levites from Jerusalem that they might ask him, Who are you?

20 And he confessed and did not deny; and *he* confessed, I am not the Christ.

21 And they asked him, What, then? Are you Elijah? And he said, I am not. Are you the Prophet? And he answered, No.

22 Then they said to him, Who are you, that we may give an answer to the *ones* sending us? What do you say about yourself?

23 He said, "I *am* a voice crying in the wilderness:" "Make straight" "the way of the Lord," as Isaiah the prophet said. *Isa. 40:3*

24 And the ones having been sent were of the Pharisees.

25 And they asked him and said to him, Why then do you baptize, if you are not the Christ, nor Elijah, nor the Prophet?

26 John answered them, saying, I baptize in water, but *One* has stood in your midst whom you do not know;

27 He it is the *One* coming after me, who has come to be before me, of whom I am not worthy that I should loose the thong of His sandal.

28 These things took place in Bethabara beyond the Jordan, where John was baptizing.

29 ¶ *On* the next day, John sees Jesus coming toward him and said, Behold! The Lamb of God, the *One* taking away the sin of the world!

30 This is the *One* about whom I said, After me comes a Man who has come to be before me, for He was first of me.

31 And I did not know Him; but that He might be revealed to Israel; on account of this I came baptizing in water.

32 And John witnessed, saying, I have seen the Spirit coming down as a dove out of Heaven, and He abode on Him.

33 And I did not know Him, but the *One* having sent me to baptize in water, that One said to me, On whomever you see the Spirit coming down and abiding on Him, this is the *One* baptizing in the Holy Spirit.

34 And I have seen and have witnessed that this *One* is the Son of God.

35 Again *on* the next day, John and two from his disciples stood.

36 And looking at Jesus walking, he says, Behold, the Lamb of God!

37 ¶ And the two disciples heard him speaking, and they followed Jesus.

38 But turning having seen them following, Jesus said to them, What do you seek? And they said to Him, Rabbi (which being translated is called Teacher), where do You stay?

39 He said to them, Come and see. They came and saw where He stays, and *they* stayed with Him that day. And *the* hour was about the tenth.

40 Andrew the brother of Simon Peter was one of the two, the *ones* hearing from John, and following Him.

41 This *one* first finds *his* own brother Simon and says to him, We have found the Messiah (which is, being translated, the Christ).

42 And he led him to Jesus. And looking at him, Jesus said, You are Simon the son of Jonah; you shall be called Cephas (which is translated Peter).

43 ¶ *On* the next day, Jesus desired to go out into Galilee. And He finds Philip, and says to him, Follow Me!

44 And Philip was from Bethsaida, of the city of Andrew and of Peter.

45 Philip finds Nathanael and said to him, We have found the *One of* whom Moses wrote in the Law and the Prophets, Jesus the son of Joseph, the *One* from Nazareth.

46 And Nathanael said to him, Can any good thing be out of Nazareth? Philip said to him, Come and see.

47 Jesus saw Nathanael coming toward Him and says concerning him, Behold, truly an Israelite in whom is no guile!

48 Nathanael said to Him, From where do You know me? Jesus answered and said to him, Before Philip called, you being under the fig tree, I saw you.

49 Nathanael answered and says to Him, Rabbi, You are the Son of God; You are the King of Israel.

50 Jesus answered and said to him, Because I said to you I saw you under the fig tree, do you believe? You will see greater *things* than these.

51 And He says to him, Truly, truly, I say to you, From now on you will see Heaven opened, and "the angels of God ascending and descending" on the Son of Man. *Gen. 28:12*

John 2

1 Christ turns water to wine, 12 departs to Capernaum, and to Jerusalem. 19 He foretells his death and resurrection.

1 ¶ And the third day a marriage took place in Cana of Galilee, and the mother of Jesus was there.

2 And Jesus and His disciples also were invited to the marriage.

3 And *they* lacking wine, the mother of Jesus says to Him, They have no wine.

4 Jesus says to her, What is that to Me and to you, woman? My hour has not yet come.

5 His mother said to the servants, Whatever He says to you, do.

6 And there were six waterpots of stone lying, according to the purification of the Jews, each containing two or three measures.

7 Jesus said to them, Fill the waterpots with water. And they filled them to *the* top.

8 And He says to them, Now draw out and carry to the master of the feast. And they carried it.

9 But when the master of the feast tasted the water that had become wine, and did not know from where it was (but the servants drawing the water knew), the master of the feast called the bridegroom,

10 and *he* says to him, Every man first sets on the good wine, and when they have drunk freely, then the inferior. You have kept the good wine until now.

11 This beginning of the *miraculous* signs Jesus did in Cana of Galilee and revealed His glory, and His disciples believed into Him.

12 ¶ After this He went down to Capernaum, He and His mother and His brothers and His disciples. And He remained there not many days.

13 And the Passover of the Jews was near. And Jesus went up to Jerusalem.

14 And He found the *ones* selling oxen and sheep and doves in the temple, and the money changers sitting.

15 And having made a whip out of ropes, He threw all out of the temple, both the sheep, and the oxen, and the money changers, poured out the coin and overturned the tables.

16 And to the ones selling the doves, He said, Take these things from here! Not do make My Father's house a market-house.

17 And His disciples remembered that it was written, "The zeal of Your house has consumed Me." *Psa. 69:9*

18 Then the Jews answered and said to Him, What sign do You show to us, since these things You do?

19 Jesus answered and said to them, Destroy this temple, and in three days I will raise it up.

20 Then the Jews said, This temple was forty-six years being built, and do You raise it up in three days?

21 But He spoke about the temple of His body.

22 Then when He was raised from the dead *ones*, His disciples remembered that He said this to them. And they believed the Scripture, even the Word that Jesus said.

23 ¶ And as He was in Jerusalem, at the Passover, at the Feast, many believed into His name, seeing the signs which He did.

24 But Jesus Himself did not commit Himself to them, because He knew all,

25 and because He had no need that anyone should witness concerning man, for He knew what was in man.

John 3

1 Christ teaches Nicodemus the necessity of regeneration. 14 Of faith in His death.

1 ¶ But there was a man from the Pharisees, Nicodemus his name, a ruler of the Jews.

2 This one came to Jesus by night and said to Him, Rabbi, we know that You have come *as* a teacher from God. For no one is able to do these *miraculous* signs which You do, except God be with Him.

3 Jesus answered and said to him, Truly, truly, I say to you, If one is not generated from above, he is not able to see the kingdom of God.

4 Nicodemus said to Him, How is a man able to be generated, being old? He is not able to enter into his mother's womb a second *time* and be generated.

5 Jesus answered, Truly, truly, I say to you, If one is not generated out of water and Spirit, he is not able to enter into the kingdom of God.

6 The *thing* having been generated out of the flesh is flesh, and that having been generated out of the Spirit is spirit.

7 Do not wonder because I said to you, You must be generated from above.

8 The Spirit breathes where He desires, and you hear His voice; but you do not know from where He comes, and where He goes; so is everyone having been generated from the Spirit.

9 Nicodemus answered and said to Him, How are these things able to occur?

10 Jesus answered and said to him, You are the teacher of Israel, and you do not know these things?

11 Truly, truly, I say to you, That what we know, we speak; and that which we have seen, we testify. And you do not receive our witness.

12 If I tell you earthly things, and you do not believe, how will you believe if I tell you heavenly things?

13 And no one has gone up into Heaven, except He having come down out of Heaven, the Son of Man who is in Heaven.

14 And even as Moses lifted up the serpent in the wilderness, so must the Son of Man be lifted up,

15 that everyone believing into Him should not perish, but may have everlasting life.

16 For God so loved the world that He gave His only begotten Son, that everyone believing into Him should not perish, but have everlasting life.

17 For God did not send His Son into the world that He might judge the world, but that the world might be saved through Him.

18 The *one* believing into Him is not condemned; but the *one* not believing has already been condemned, for he has not believed into the name of the only begotten Son of God.

19 And this is the judgment, that the Light has come into the world, and men loved the darkness more than the Light, for their works were evil.

20 For everyone practicing wickedness hates the Light, and does not come to the Light, that his works may not be exposed.

21 But the *one* doing the truth comes to the Light, that his works may be revealed, that they are being worked in God.

22 ¶ After these things Jesus and His disciples came into the land of Judea. And *He* stayed there with them and was baptizing.

23 And John was also baptizing in Aenon, near Salim, for many waters were there. And they were coming and were being baptized.

24 For John had not yet been thrown into the prison.

25 Then a questioning from John's disciples arose with the Jews about purification.

26 And they came to John and said to him, Teacher, *He* who was with you beyond the Jordan, to whom you have witnessed, behold, this *One* baptizes, and all are coming to Him.

27 John answered and said, A man is able to receive nothing if it is not given to him from Heaven.

28 You yourselves witness to me that I said, I am not the Christ, but that having been sent, I am before that One.

29 The *one* having the bride is *the* bridegroom. But the friend of the bridegroom, standing and hearing him, rejoices with joy because of the bridegroom's voice. Then this my joy has been fulfilled.

30 That One must increase, but me to decrease.

31 The *One* coming from above is above all. The *one* being of the earth is of the earth, and speaks of the earth. The *One* coming out of Heaven is above all.

32 And what He has seen and heard, this He testifies, and no one receives His testimony.

33 The *one* receiving His testimony has sealed that God is true.

34 For *the One* whom God sent speaks the words of God, for God does not give the Spirit by measure.

35 The Father loves the Son and has given all things into His hand.

36 The *one* believing into the Son has everlasting life; but the *one* disobeying the Son will not see life, but the wrath of God remains on him.

John 4

1 Christ talks with a woman of Samaria, and reveals Himself to her. 27 His disciples marvel. 39 Many Samaritans believe in Him. 43 He heals the ruler's son.

1 ¶ Therefore when the Lord knew that the Pharisees heard that Jesus is making more disciples and baptizing *more* than John

2 (though truly Jesus Himself did not baptize, but His disciples),

3 He left Judea and went away into Galilee again.

4 ¶ And it was needful for Him to pass through Samaria.

5 And He came to a Samaritan city called Sychar, near the piece of land which Jacob gave to his son Joseph.

6 And Jacob's well was there. Then being wearied by the journey, Jesus sat thus on the well. *The* hour was about *the* sixth.

7 A woman comes out of Samaria to draw water. Jesus said to her, Give Me to drink.

8 For His disciples had gone away into the city that they might buy foods.

9 Then woman said to Him the woman, the Samaritan, How *is it that* You, being a Jew, ask to drink from me, *I* being a Samaritan woman? For Jews do not use *things* together with Samaritans.

10 Jesus answered and said to her, If you knew the gift of God, and who is the *One* saying to you, Give Me to drink, you would have asked Him, and He would have given you living water.

11 The woman said to Him, Sir, You have no thing to draw with. From where, then, do You have living water?

12 Not You are greater *than* our father, Jacob, who gave us the well, and he drank

out of it, and his sons and his livestock *also*?

13 Jesus answered and said to her, Everyone drinking of this water will thirst again;

14 but whoever may drink of the water which I will give him will not thirst, not *ever*! But the water which I will give to him will become a fountain of water in him, springing up into everlasting life.

15 The woman said to Him, Sir, give me this water, that I may not thirst, nor come here to draw.

16 Jesus said to her, Go, call your husband and come here.

17 The woman answered and said, I have no husband. Jesus said to her, Well did you say, I have no husband.

18 For you have had five husbands, and now *he* whom you have is not your husband. This *thing* truly you have said.

19 The woman said to Him, Sir, I perceive that You are a prophet.

20 Our fathers worshiped in this mountain, and you say that in Jerusalem is the place where it is necessary to worship.

21 Jesus said to her, Woman, believe Me that an hour is coming when you will worship the Father neither in this mountain nor in Jerusalem.

22 You worship what you do not know; we worship what we know, because salvation is of the Jews.

23 But an hour is coming, and now is, when the true worshipers will worship the Father in spirit and in truth. For the Father also seeks such, the *ones* worshiping Him.

24 God *is* spirit, and the *ones* worshiping Him must worship in spirit and truth.

25 The woman said to Him, I know that Messiah is coming, the *One* being called Christ. When that One comes, He will announce to us all things.

26 Jesus said to her, I AM! the *One* speaking to you.

27 ¶ And upon this, His disciples came and marveled that He was speaking with a woman. However, no one said, What do You seek? Or, Why do You speak with her?

28 Then the woman left her waterpot and went away into the city and says to the men,

29 Come, see a Man who told me all things, as many as I did. Is not this the Christ?

30 Therefore they went out from the city and were coming to Him.

31 But in the meantime the disciples were asking Him, saying, Rabbi, eat.

32 But He said to them, I have food to eat which you do not know.

33 Then the disciples said to one another, Not did someone bring Him *food* to eat?

34 Jesus said to them, My food is that I should do the will of *Him* having sent Me, and *that* I may finish His work.

35 Do you not say, It is yet four months and the harvest comes? Behold, I say to you, Lift up your eyes and behold the fields, for they are already white to harvest.

36 And the *one* reaping receives wages, and gathers fruit to everlasting life, so that both the *one* sowing and the *one* reaping may rejoice together.

37 For in this the word is true, that another *is* the *one* sowing, and another the *one* reaping.

38 I sent you to reap what you have not labored over. Others have labored, and you have entered into their labor.

39 And many of the Samaritans out of that city believed into Him, because of the word of the woman testifying, He told me all things, as many as I did.

40 Then as the Samaritans came to Him, they asked Him to remain with them. And He remained there two days.

41 And many more believed through His Word.

42 And they were saying to the woman, We no longer believe because of your speech; for we ourselves have heard, and we know that this One is truly the Savior of the world, the Christ.

43 ¶ But after the two days, He went out from there, and *He* went into Galilee.

44 For Jesus Himself testified that a prophet has no honor in *his* own fatherland.

45 Then when He came into Galilee, the Galileans received Him, seeing all things which He did in Jerusalem at the Feast. For they also went to the Feast.

46 Then Jesus came again to Cana of Galilee where He made the water wine. And there was a certain royal *nobleman* whose son was sick in Capernaum.

47 This one, hearing that Jesus has come from Judea into Galilee, went out to Him and asked Him that He would come down and heal his son, for he was about to die.

48 Then Jesus said to him, Unless you see *miraculous* signs and wonders, you will not believe, not *ever*.

49 The royal *nobleman* said to Him, Sir, come down before my child dies.

50 Jesus said to him, Go! Your son lives. And the man believed the Word which Jesus said to him, and went away.

51 But already, as he was going down, his slaves met him and reported, saying, Your child lives.

52 He then asked from them the hour in which he had *become* better. And they said to him, Yesterday, *at the* seventh hour, the fever left him.

53 Then the father knew that *it was* at that hour in which Jesus said to him, Your son lives. And he himself, and his whole household, believed.

54 This, again, *is the* second *miraculous* sign Jesus did, coming from Judea into Galilee.

John 5

1 Jesus cures a man diseased thirty eight years on the sabbath. 10 The Jews persecute Him for it. 17 He answers for Himself by the testimony of His Father, 32 of John, 36 of His works, 39 of the scriptures, who He is.

1 ¶ After these things, there was a feast of the Jews, and Jesus went up to Jerusalem.

2 And in Jerusalem is a pool at the Sheep Gate, the *one* called in Hebrew, Bethesda, having five porches.

3 In these were lying a great multitude of the *ones* being infirm, blind *ones*, lame *ones*, withered *ones*, awaiting the stirring of the water.

4 For an angel at a *certain* time descended in the pool and agitated the water. Therefore the *one* first entering after the agitation of the water became well, whatever disease he was held by.

5 But a certain man was there, having *been* in infirmity thirty-eight years.

6 Jesus, seeing this *one* lying, and knowing that he had already *spent* much time,

He said to him, Do you desire to become well?

7 The *one* being infirm answered Him, Lord, I do not have a man, that when the water is agitated he may throw me into the pool; but while I am coming, another goes down before me.

8 Jesus said to him, Rise up, Take up your pallet and walk!

9 And instantly the man became well, and took up his pallet and walked. And it was a sabbath that day.

10 Therefore the Jews said to the *one* having been healed, It is sabbath. It is not lawful for you to lift up the pallet.

11 He answered them, The One making me well, that *One* said to me, Lift up your pallet and walk.

12 Then they asked him, Who is the man who told you, Lift up your pallet and walk?

13 But the *one* having been healed did not know who it is, for a crowd being in that place, Jesus had withdrawn.

14 After these things, Jesus found him in the temple and said to him, Behold, you have become well, sin no more that a worse thing not happen to you.

15 The man went away and told the Jews that Jesus is the *One* making him well.

16 And because of this the Jews were persecuting Jesus and were seeking to kill Him, because He did these things on a sabbath.

17 ¶ But Jesus answered them, My Father works until now, and I work.

18 Because of this, therefore, the Jews were seeking the more to kill Him, for not only did He break the sabbath, but also called God His own Father, making Himself equal to God.

19 Then Jesus answered and said to them, Truly, truly, I say to you, The Son is not able to do anything from Himself, except what He may see the Father doing; for whatever that One does, these things also the Son does likewise.

20 For the Father loves the Son and shows to Him all things which He does. And He will show Him greater works than these in order that you may wonder.

21 For even as the Father raises the dead, and makes alive, so also the Son makes alive whom He wills.

22 For the Father judges no one, but has given all judgment to the Son,

23 so that all may honor the Son, even as they honor the Father. The *one* not honoring the Son does not honor the Father who has sent Him.

24 Truly, truly, I say to you, The *one* who hears My Word, and believing the *One* having sent Me, has everlasting life, and does not come into judgment, but has passed out of death into life.

25 Truly, truly, I say to you that an hour is coming, and now is, when the dead *ones* will hear the voice of the Son of God, and the *ones* hearing will live.

26 For even as the Father has life in Himself, so He gave also to the Son to have life in Himself.

27 And He also gave authority to Him to execute judgment, for He is *the* Son of Man.

28 Marvel not *at* this, for an hour is coming in which all the *ones* in the tombs will hear His voice.

29 And will come out, the *ones* having done good *things*, into a resurrection of life; and the *ones* having practiced evil things into a resurrection of judgment.

30 I am not able to do *anything* of Myself, nothing! Just as I hear, I judge; and My judgment is just, because I do not seek My will, but the will of the Father having sent Me.

31 ¶ If I witness about Myself, My witness is not true;

32 it is Another that witnesses about Me, and I know that the witness which He witnesses about Me is true.

33 You have sent to John, and he has testified to the truth.

34 But I do not receive witness from man, but I say these things that you may be saved.

35 That one was the burning and shining lamp, and you were willing to exult in his light for an hour.

36 But I have the witness greater than the *one* of John, for the works which the Father has given Me, that I should finish them, the works which I do themselves witness concerning Me, that the Father has sent Me.

37 And the Father, the *One* having sent Me, has Himself borne witness about Me. You have neither heard His voice at any time, nor have you seen His form.

38 And you do not have His Word abiding in you, for *the One* whom that One sent, this *One* you do not believe.

39 You search the Scriptures, for you think in them you have everlasting life. And they are the *ones* witnessing concerning Me.

40 And you are not willing to come to Me that you may have life.

41 I do not receive glory from men;

42 but I have known you, that you do not have the love of God in yourselves.

43 I have come in the name of My Father, and you do not receive Me. If another comes in *his* own name, you will receive that one.

44 How are you able to believe, *you who* receive glory from one another, and the glory which *is* from the only God you do not seek?

45 Do not think that I will accuse you to the Father; there is *one* accusing you, Moses, in whom you have hoped.

46 For if you believed Moses, you would believe Me; for that one wrote about Me.

47 But if you do not believe his writings, how will you believe My words?

John 6

1 Christ feeds five thousand men with five loaves and two fish. 16 Withdrawing Himself, He walked on the sea to His disciples: 32 declares Himself to be the bread of life to believers.

1 ¶ After these things, Jesus went away over the Sea of Galilee, the Tiberian *Sea.*

2 And a great crowd followed Him, for they saw His *miraculous* signs which He did on the *ones* being sick.

3 And Jesus went up into the mountain and sat there with His disciples.

4 And the Passover was near, the feast of the Jews.

5 Then Jesus lifting up *His* eyes and seeing that a great crowd is coming to Him, He said to Philip, From where may we buy bread that these may eat?

6 But He said this to test him, for He knew what He was about to do.

7 Philip answered Him, Bread for two hundred denarii are not enough for them, that each of them may receive a little.

8 One of His disciples said to Him, Andrew the brother of Simon Peter,

9 There is one little boy here who has five barley loaves and two small fish; but what are these among so many?

10 And Jesus said, Make the men to recline. And much grass was in the place. Then the men reclined, the number was about five thousand.

11 And Jesus took the loaves of bread, and giving thanks distributed to the disciples, and the disciples likewise of the fish, as much as they wanted.

12 And when they were filled, He said to His disciples, Gather up the fragments left over, that not anything be lost.

13 Then they gathered and filled twelve baskets of fragments from the five barley loaves of bread which were left over to the *ones* having eaten.

14 Then the men, seeing what *miraculous* sign Jesus did, said, This is truly the Prophet, the *One* coming into the world.

15 ¶ Therefore knowing that they were about to come and seize Him, that they might make Him king, Jesus withdrew again to the mountain Himself alone.

16 And when it became evening, His disciples went down on the sea.

17 And entering into the boat, they were going across the sea to Capernaum. And darkness had already occurred, and Jesus had not come to them.

18 And the sea was aroused by a great wind blowing.

19 Then having rowed about twenty five or thirty stadia, they saw Jesus walking on the sea, and becoming near the boat, they were afraid.

20 But He said to them, I AM! Do not fear.

21 Then they desired to take Him into the boat. And the boat was instantly at the land to which they were going.

22 ¶ The next day, the crowd, the *one* standing across the sea had seen that no other little boat was there except one, that one into which His disciples entered, and that Jesus did not go in with His disciples into the small boat, but *that* the disciples went away alone.

23 But other small boats came from Tiberias near the place where they ate the bread, the Lord having given thanks.

24 Therefore, when the crowd saw that Jesus was not there nor His disciples, they themselves also stepped into the boats and came to Capernaum seeking Jesus.

25 And finding Him across the sea, they said to Him, Rabbi, when did you come here?

26 Jesus answered them and said, Truly, truly, I say to you, You seek Me not because you saw *miraculous* signs, but because you ate of the loaves of bread and were satisfied.

27 Do not work *for* the food, the *one* perishing, but for the food, the *one* enduring to everlasting life, which the Son of Man will give to you; for God the Father sealed Him.

28 ¶ Then they said to Him, What may we do that we may work the works of God?

29 Jesus answered and said to them, This is the work of God, that you believe into *Him* whom that One sent.

30 Therefore they said to Him, Then what *miraculous* sign do You do that we may see and may believe You? What do You work?

31 Our fathers ate the manna in the wilderness, even as it is written "He gave them bread out of the heaven to eat." *LXX-Psa. 77:24; MT-Psa. 78:24*

32 Then Jesus said to them, Truly, truly, I say to you, Moses has not given you the bread out of the heaven, but My Father gives you the true bread out of Heaven.

33 For the bread of God is the *One* coming down out of the heaven and giving life to the world.

34 Then they said to Him, Lord, always give us this bread.

35 And Jesus said to them, I am the Bread of life; the *one* coming to Me will not hunger, not *ever;* and the *one* believing into Me will not thirst, not *ever*

36 But I said to you that you also have seen Me and do not believe.

37 All who the Father gives to Me shall come to Me, and the *one* coming to Me I will not cast out, not *ever*,

38 for I have come down out of Heaven, not that I should do My will, but the will of Him who sent Me.

39 And this is the will of the Father sending Me, that of all that He has given Me, I shall not lose *any* of it, but shall raise it up in the last day.

40 And this is the will of the *One* having sent Me, that everyone seeing the Son and believing into Him should have everlasting life; and I will raise him up at the last day.

41 Therefore the Jews murmured about Him, because He said, I am the Bread coming down out of Heaven.

42 And they said, Is this not Jesus the son of Joseph, of whom we know the father and the mother? How, then, does this *One* now say, I have come down out of Heaven?

43 Therefore Jesus answered and said to them, Do not murmur with one another.

44 No one is able to come to Me if not the Father, the *One* having sent Me, draws him, and I will raise him up in the last day.

45 It is being written in the Prophets, They "shall" all "be taught of God." Therefore every *one* hearing and having learned from the Father comes to Me; *Isa. 54:13*

46 not that anyone has seen the Father, except He being from God, this One has seen the Father.

47 Truly, truly, I say to you, The *one* believing into Me has everlasting life.

48 I am the Bread of life.

49 Your fathers ate the manna in the wilderness and died.

50 This is the Bread, the *One* coming down out of Heaven, that anyone may eat of it and not die.

51 I am the Living Bread, the *One* having come down from Heaven. If anyone eats of this Bread, he will live to the age. And indeed the bread which I will give is My flesh, which I will give for the life of the world.

52 Therefore the Jews argued with one another, saying, How can this *One* give us *His* flesh to eat?

53 Then Jesus said to them, Truly, truly, I say to you, If you do not eat the flesh of the Son of Man, and drink His blood, you do not have life in yourselves.

54 The *one* eating My flesh and drinking My blood has everlasting life, and I will raise him up at the last day.

55 For My flesh is truly food, and My blood is truly drink.

56 The *one* eating My flesh and drinking My blood abides in Me, and I in him.

57 Even as the living Father sent Me, and I live through the Father; also the *one* eating Me, even that one will live through Me.

58 This is the Bread which came down out of Heaven, not as your fathers ate the manna and died; the *one* partaking of this Bread will live to the age.

59 He said these things teaching in a synagogue in Capernaum.

60 ¶ Then many of His disciples having heard, *they* said, This Word is hard; who is able to hear it?

61 But knowing in Himself that His disciples were murmuring about this, He said to them, Does this cause you to stumble?

62 Then *what* if you see the Son of Man going up where He was before?

63 It is the Spirit, the *One* making alive. The flesh does not profit, nothing! The words which I speak to you are spirit and are life.

64 But there are some of you who are not believing. For Jesus knew from *the* beginning who *they* are, the *ones* not believing, and who is the *one* giving Him over.

65 And He said, Because of this, I have told you that no one is able to come to Me if it is not given to him from My Father.

66 From this *time* many of His disciples went away into the things behind, and no longer walked with Him.

67 Therefore, Jesus said to the Twelve, Do you not also wish to go?

68 Then Simon Peter answered Him, Lord, to whom shall we go? You have *the* words of everlasting life.

69 And we have believed and have known that You are the Christ, the Son of the living God.

70 Jesus answered them, Did I not choose you, the Twelve? Yet one *of* you is a devil!

71 But He spoke *of* Judas Iscariot, Simon's son, for this *one* was going to give Him over, being one of the Twelve.

John 7

1 Jesus reproves the ambition and boldness of His kinsmen: 14 teaches in the temple. 40 Differing opinions of Him among the people.

1 ¶ And after these things Jesus was walking in Galilee; for He did not desire to walk in Judea, because the Jews were seeking to kill Him.

2 And the Feast of the Jews, The *Feast of* Tabernacles was near.

3 Therefore His brothers said to Him, Depart from here and go to Judea, that Your disciples will also see Your works which You are doing,

4 for no one does anything in secret and himself seeks to be in openness. If You do these things, reveal Yourself to the world.

5 For not even His brothers believed into Him.

6 Therefore Jesus said to them, My time is not yet present, but your time is always ready.

7 The world cannot hate you, but it hates Me because I witness about it, that its works are evil.

8 You go up to this feast. I am not yet going up to this feast, for My time has not yet been fulfilled.

9 And saying these things to them, He remained in Galilee.

10 But when His brothers went up, then He also went up to the feast, not openly, but as in secret.

11 Then the Jews sought Him in the feast, and said, Where is that One?

12 And much murmuring about Him was in the crowds. Some indeed said, He is a good *One*; but others said, No, but He deceives the crowd.

13 However, no one freely spoke about Him, because of the fear of the Jews.

14 ¶ But the feast now being in the middle, Jesus went up to the temple and taught.

15 And the Jews marveled, saying, How does this One know letters, not having learned?

16 Jesus answered them and said, My doctrine is not Mine, but of the *One* who sent Me.

17 If anyone desires to do His will, he will know concerning the doctrine, whether it is of God, or I speak from Myself.

18 The *one* speaking from himself seeks his own glory. But the *one* seeking the glory of the *One* who sent Him, this *One is* true, and unrighteousness is not in Him.

19 Has not Moses given you the Law, and not one of you does the Law? Why do you seek to kill Me?

20 The crowd answered and said, You have a demon. Who seeks to kill You?

21 Jesus answered and said to them, I did one work, and you all marvel.

22 Because of this Moses has given you circumcision; (not that it is of Moses, but of the fathers); and *on* a sabbath, you circumcise a man.

23 If a man receives circumcision *on* a sabbath, that the Law of Moses is not broken, are you angry with Me because I made a whole man healthy on a sabbath?

24 Do not judge according to sight, but judge righteous judgment.

25 Therefore some of the Jerusalemites said, Is it not this *One* whom they are seeking to kill?

26 And, behold, He speaks freely, and they say nothing to Him. Perhaps the rulers truly knew that this is truly the Christ?

27 But we know this *One*, from where He is. But when the Christ comes, no one knows from where He is.

28 Therefore teaching, Jesus cried out in the temple, and saying, You both know Me, and you know from where I am. And I have not come from Myself, but He is true, the *One* having sent Me, whom you do not know.

29 But I know Him, because I am from Him; and that *one* sent Me.

30 Therefore they sought to seize Him; yet no one laid *a* hand on Him, because His hour had not yet come.

31 But many of the crowd believed into Him, and said, The Christ, when He comes will He do more *miraculous* signs than these which this One did?

32 The Pharisees heard the crowd murmuring these things about Him, and the Pharisees and the chief priests sent officers, that they might seize Him.

33 Then Jesus said to them, Yet a little while I am with you, and I go to the *One* having sent Me.

34 You will seek Me, and you will not find *Me*; and where I am, you are not able to come.

35 Therefore the Jews said amongst themselves, Where is this *One* about to go that we will not find Him? Is He about to go to the Dispersion of the Greeks, and to teach the Greeks?

36 What is this word which He said, You will seek Me and will not find *Me*, and, Where I am, you are not able to come?

37 ¶ And in the last great *day* of the feast, Jesus stood and cried out, saying, If anyone thirsts, let him come to Me and drink.

38 The *one* believing into Me, as the Scripture said, Out of his belly will flow rivers of living water. *See John 4:14*

39 But He said this about the Spirit, whom the *ones* believing into Him were about to receive; for *the* Holy Spirit was not yet *given*, because Jesus was not yet glorified.

40 Then hearing the Word, many of the crowd said, This is truly the Prophet.

41 Others said, This is the Christ. But others said, For the Christ does not come out of Galilee, *does He*?

42 Has not the Scripture said that the Christ comes from the seed of David, and from Bethlehem, the village where David was? *Mic. 5:2*

43 Therefore a division occurred in the crowd because of Him.

44 And some of them desired to seize Him, but no one laid hands on Him.

45 ¶ Then the officers came to the chief priests and Pharisees. And those *men* said to them, Why did you not bring Him?

46 The officers answered, Never did a man so speak as does this man.

47 Therefore the Pharisees answered them, Have you also been deceived?

48 Not any from the rulers or from the Pharisees believed into Him?

49 But this crowd, not knowing the Law, is cursed.

50 Nicodemus said to them, the *one* coming by night to Him, being one of them.

51 Our Law does not judge the man if not it hear from him first, and know what he does?

52 They answered and said to him, Are you also from Galilee? Search and see that a prophet has not been raised out of Galilee.

53 And they each one went to his house.

John 8

1 Christ receives the woman taken in adultery.
12 He speaks, saying, He is the Light of the world,

1 ¶ But Jesus went to the Mount of Olives.

2 And at dawn, He again arrived into the temple; and all the people came to Him. And having sat down, He was teaching them.

3 And the scribes and the Pharisees bring to Him a woman having been taken in adultery. And standing her in *the* midst,

4 they said to Him, Teacher, this woman was taken in the very act, committing adultery.

5 And in the Law, Moses commanded that such should be stoned. You, therefore, what do You say?

6 But they said this, testing Him, that they may have *reason* to accuse Him. But bending down, Jesus was writing with the finger in the earth, not appearing *to hear*.

7 But as they continued questioning Him, bending back up, He said to them, The *one* among you without sin let him cast a stone at her first.

8 And bending down again, He wrote in the earth.

9 But they hearing, and being convicted by the conscience, went out one by one, beginning from the older *ones*, until the last. And Jesus was left alone, and the woman standing in *the* midst.

10 And Jesus bending back up, and having seen no one but the woman, He said to her, Woman, where are those, the accusers of you? Did not one give judgment against you?

11 And she said, No one, Lord. And Jesus said to her, Neither do I give judgment against you. Go, and sin no more.

12 ¶ Then Jesus again spoke to them, saying, I am the Light of the world. The *one* following Me will not walk in the darkness, not *ever*, but will have the light of life.

13 Therefore the Pharisees said to Him, You witness about Yourself; Your witness is not true.

14 Jesus answered and said to them, Even if I witness about Myself, My witness is true; for I know from where I came, and where I go. But you do not know from where I came, and where I go.

15 You judge according to the flesh. I judge no one.

16 But even if I judge, My judgment is true, because I am not alone, but I and *the* Father sending Me.

17 And in your Law it has been written that the witness of two men is true. *Deut. 19:15*

18 I am the One witnessing about Myself, and He sending Me, *the* Father, witnesses concerning Me.

19 Then they said to Him, Where is Your father? Jesus answered, You neither know Me, nor My Father. If you had known Me, then you also would have known My Father.

20 Jesus spoke these words in the treasury, teaching in the temple; and no one seized Him, for His hour had not yet come.

21 ¶ Then Jesus said to them again, I go, and you will seek Me. And you will die in your sin. Where I go, you are not able to come.

22 Therefore the Jews said, Will He not kill Himself, because He says, Where I go, you are not able to come?

23 And He said to them, You are from below; I am from above. You are from this world; I am not from this world.

24 Therefore, I said to you that you will die in your sins. For if you do not believe that I AM, you will die in your sins.

25 Then they said to Him, Who are You? And Jesus said to them, *At* the Beginning, what I also said to you.

26 I have many things to say and to judge concerning you; but the *One* sending Me is true, and what I heard from Him, these things I say to the world.

27 They did not know that He spoke to them *of* the Father.

28 Therefore Jesus said to them, When you lift up the Son of Man, then you will know that I AM; and from Myself I do nothing; but as My Father taught Me, these things I speak.

29 And the *One* having sent Me is with Me. The Father did not leave Me alone, for I do the things pleasing to Him always.

30 *As* He spoke these things, many believed into Him.

31 ¶ Then Jesus said to the Jews having believed into Him, If you continue in My Word, you are truly My disciples.

32 And you will know the truth, and the truth will set you free.

33 They answered Him, We are Abraham's seed, and we have been in slavery to no one, ever! How do You say, You will become free?

34 Jesus answered them, Truly, truly, I say to you, Everyone practicing sin is a slave of sin.

35 But the slave does not remain into the house to the age; the son remains to the age.

36 Therefore, if the Son sets you free, you are free indeed.

37 I know that you are Abraham's seed, but you seek to kill Me, because My Word is not given place in you.

38 ¶ I speak what I have seen with My Father. And you therefore do what you have seen with your father.

39 They answered and said to Him, Abraham is our father. Jesus said to them, If you were children of Abraham, you would do the works of Abraham.

40 But now you seek to kill Me, a man who has spoken the truth to you, which I heard alongside *of* God. Abraham did not do this.

41 You do the works of your father. Then they said to Him, We were not generated of fornication; we have one father, God.

42 Therefore Jesus said to them, If God were your Father, you would love Me, for I went forth and have come from God. For I have not come from Myself, but that One sent Me.

43 Why do you not know My speech? *It is* because you are not able to hear My Word.

44 You are of the devil as father, and the lusts of your father you desire to do. That one was a murderer from *the* beginning,

and he has not stood in the truth, because there is no truth in him. When he speaks *a* lie, he speaks from *his* own *things*, because he is a liar, and the father of it.

45 And because I speak the truth, you do not believe Me.

46 ¶ Who of you reproves Me concerning sin? But if I speak truth, why do you not believe Me?

47 The *one* who is of God hears the words of God; for this reason you do not hear, because you are not of God.

48 Then the Jews answered and said to Him, Do we not say well that You are a Samaritan and have a demon?

49 Jesus answered, I do not have a demon; but I honor My Father, and you dishonor Me.

50 But I do not seek My glory; *there* is One who seeks and judges.

51 ¶ Truly, truly, I say to you, If anyone keeps My Word, he will not see death, into the age, not *ever*!

52 Then the Jews said to Him, Now we know that You have a demon. Abraham died, and the prophets, and You say, If anyone keeps My Word, he will not taste of death into the age, not *ever*!

53 Are You greater than our father Abraham who died? And the prophets died! Whom do You make Yourself?

54 Jesus answered, If I glorify Myself, My glory is nothing; it is My Father who glorifies Me, whom you say is your God.

55 And you have not known Him; but I know Him, And if I say that I do not know Him, I shall be like you, a liar. But I know Him, and I keep His Word.

56 Your father Abraham leaped for joy that he should see My day, and he saw and was glad.

57 Then the Jews said to Him, You do not yet have fifty years, and have You seen Abraham?

58 Jesus said to them, Truly, truly, I say to you, Before Abraham came to be, I AM!

59 Because of this, they picked up stones that they might throw *them* on Him. But Jesus was hidden, and went forth out of the temple, going through *the* midst of them, and so passed by.

John 9

1 The man who was born blind is made to see.
13 The Pharisees excommunicate him: 35 But he is received by Jesus.

1 ¶ And passing by, He saw a man blind from birth.

2 And His disciples asked Him, saying, Teacher, who sinned, this *one*, or his parents, that he was born blind?

3 Jesus answered, Neither this *one* nor his parents sinned, but that the works of God might be revealed in him.

4 It is necessary *for* Me to work the works of the *One* having sent Me while it is day. Night comes when no one is able to work.

5 While I am in the world, I am *the* Light of the world.

6 Saying these things, He spat on the ground and made clay out of the spittle, and anointed clay on the eyes of the blind *one*.

7 And He said to him, Go wash in the pool of Siloam, which translated is Sent. Then he went and washed, and came seeing.

8 ¶ Therefore the neighbors and the *ones* formerly seeing him, that he was blind, said, Is this *one* not the *one* sitting and begging?

9 Others said, It is he; and others, He is like him. That one said, I am.

10 Therefore they said to him, How were your eyes opened?

11 That one answered and said, *A* man being called Jesus made clay and anointed my eyes, and told me, Go to the pool of Siloam and wash. And having gone and having washed I saw anew.

12 Then they said to him, Where is that One? He said, I do not know.

13 ¶ They lead him to the Pharisees, the *one* once blind.

14 And it was a sabbath when Jesus made the clay and opened his eyes.

15 Then also the Pharisees again asked him how he saw anew. And he said to them, He put clay on my eyes, and I washed, and I see.

16 Therefore some of the Pharisees said, This man is not from God, because He does not keep the sabbath. Others said, How can a man, a sinful *man*, do such *miraculous*

signs? And there was a division among them.

17 They said to the blind *one* again, What do you say about Him, because He opened your eyes? And he said, He is a prophet.

18 Therefore the Jews did not believe about him, that he was blind and saw anew, until they called the parents of him, the *one* seeing anew.

19 And they asked them, saying, Is this your son, whom you say that he was born blind? Then how does he now see?

20 His parents answered them and said, We know that this is our son, and that he was born blind.

21 But how he now sees, we do not know; or who opened his eyes, we do not know. He is of age, ask him. He will speak about himself.

22 His parents said these things because they feared the Jews; for the Jews had already agreed that if anyone should confess Him *as* Christ, he would be expelled from the synagogue.

23 Because of this, his parents said, He is of age, ask him.

24 Therefore a second time they called the man who was blind, and *they* said to him, Give glory to God. We know that this man is a sinner.

25 Therefore he answered and said, Whether He is a sinner, I do not know. One *thing* I do know; that being blind, now I see.

26 And they said to him again, What did He do to you? How did He open your eyes?

27 He answered them, I told you already, and you did not hear. Why do you want to hear again? Do you also want to become disciples of Him?

28 Then they reviled him and said, You are a disciple of that One, but we are disciples of Moses.

29 We know that God has spoken by Moses, but this One, we do not know from where He is.

30 The man answered and said to them, For this is a marvelous *thing*, that you do not know from where He is, and He opened my eyes.

31 But we know that God does not hear sinful *ones*, but if anyone is God-fearing, and does His will, He hears that *one*.

32 From *the beginning of* the age it was never heard that anyone opened the eyes *of one* having been born blind.

33 If this *One* was not from God, He could not do *a thing*, nothing

34 They answered and said to him, You were born wholly in sins, and do you teach us? And they threw him out outside.

35 ¶ Jesus heard that they threw him out outside, and finding him, He said to him, Do you believe into the Son of God?

36 And he answered and said, Who is He, Lord, that I may believe into Him?

37 And Jesus said to him, Even you have seen Him, and He speaking with you is that *One*.

38 And he said, I believe, Lord! And he worshiped Him.

39 ¶ And Jesus said, I came into this world for judgment, that the *ones* who do not see may see, and the *ones* seeing may become blind.

40 And *those* of the Pharisees who were with Him heard these things, and said to Him, Are we also blind?

41 Jesus said to them, If you were blind, you would have no sin. But now you say, We see; therefore, your sin remains.

John 10

1 Christ is the door, and the Good Shepherd.
  30 He tells them that He and the Father are one.

1 ¶ Truly, truly, I say to you, The *one* not entering through the door into the sheepfold, but going up by another way, that *one* is a thief and a plunderer.

2 But the *one* entering through the door is the shepherd of the sheep.

3 To this *one* the doorkeeper opens, and the sheep hear his voice, and he calls *his* own sheep by name, and leads them out.

4 And when he puts forth his own sheep, he goes on in front of them, and the sheep follow him because they know his voice.

5 But they will not follow a stranger, not *ever*! But *they* will flee from him, because they do not know the voice of a stranger.

6 Jesus spoke this allegory to them, but those *ones* did not know what it was which He spoke to them.

7 Then Jesus again said to them, Truly, truly, I say to you that I am the door of the sheep.

8 All who came before Me are thieves and plunderers, but the sheep did not hear them.

9 I am the door. If anyone enters through Me, he will be saved, and will go in, and will go out, and will find pasture.

10 The thief does not come except that he may steal, and kill, and destroy. I came that they may have life and may have *it* abundantly.

11 I am the Good Shepherd! The Good Shepherd lays down His life on behalf of the sheep.

12 But the hireling, not even being a shepherd, whose own the sheep are not, sees the wolf coming and forsakes the sheep and flees. And the wolf seizes them, and scatters the sheep.

13 But the hireling flees because he is a hireling, and there is not a care to him concerning the sheep.

14 I am the Good Shepherd, and I know the *ones* that *are* Mine, and I am known by the *ones that are* Mine.

15 Even as the Father knows Me, I also know the Father; and I lay down My life on behalf of the sheep.

16 And I have other sheep which are not of this fold. I must also lead those, and they will hear My voice; and there will be one flock, one Shepherd.

17 Because of this My Father loves Me, because I lay down My life, that I may take it again.

18 No one takes it from Me, but I lay it down of Myself. I have authority to lay it down, and I have authority to take it again. This command I received from My Father.

19 ¶ Therefore a division occurred again among the Jews, because of these words.

20 And many of them said, He has a demon and is raving. Why do you listen to Him?

21 Others said, These are not words of one having been possessed by a demon. Is a demon able to open *the* eyes of blind *ones*?

22 ¶ And *the Feast* of Dedications occurred in Jerusalem, and it was winter.

23 And Jesus was walking in the temple, in Solomon's Porch.

24 Then the Jews encircled Him, and said to Him, Until when do You lift up our soul? If You are the Christ, tell us plainly.

25 Jesus answered them, I told you, and you did not believe. The works which I do in the name of My Father, these bear witness about Me.

26 But you do not believe, for you are not of My sheep, even as I said to you.

27 My sheep hear My voice, and I know them, and they follow Me.

28 And I give eternal life to them, and they shall not perish to the age, not *ever*! And not anyone shall snatch them out of My hand.

29 My Father who has given *them* to Me is greater than all, and no one is able to snatch *them* out of My Father's hand.

30 I and the Father are One!

31 Then again the Jews took up stones, that they might stone Him.

32 Jesus answered them, I showed you many good works from My Father. On account of which work of them do you stone Me?

33 The Jews answered Him, saying, We do not stone You concerning a good work, but concerning blasphemy; and because You, being a man, make Yourself God.

34 Jesus answered them, Has it not been written in your Law, "I said, you are gods"? *Psa. 82:6*

35 If He said those *to be* gods to whom the Word of God was, and the Scripture cannot be broken,

36 do you say *of Him* whom the Father sanctified and sent into the world, You blaspheme, because I said, I am Son of God?

37 If I do not do the works of My Father, do not believe Me.

38 But if I do, even if you do not believe Me, believe the works, that you may perceive and may believe that the Father *is* in Me, and I in Him.

39 ¶ Then again they sought to seize Him. And He went forth from their hand.

40 And He went away again across the Jordan to the place where John was at first baptizing and remained there.

41 And many came to Him and said, John indeed did no *miraculous* sign, but as many things as John said concerning this *One* were true.

42 And many believed into Him there.

John 11

1 Christ raises Lazarus. 45 Many Jews believe.
49 Caiaphas prophesies.

1 ¶ And there was a certain sick *one*, Lazarus from Bethany, of the village of Mary and her sister Martha.

2 And it was Mary who anointed the Lord with ointment and wiped His feet with her hair, whose brother Lazarus was sick.

3 Then the sisters sent to Him, saying, Lord, behold, *the one* whom You love is sick.

4 And hearing, Jesus said, This is not sickness to death, but for the glory of God, that the Son of God be glorified by it.

5 And Jesus loved Martha and her sister and Lazarus.

6 Therefore, when He heard that he is sick, then, indeed, He remained in the place where He was two days.

7 Then after this He said to the disciples, Let us go to Judea again.

8 The disciples said to Him, Rabbi, just now the Jews were seeking to stone You, and are You going there again?

9 Jesus answered, Are there not twelve hours in the day? If anyone walks in the day, he does not stumble because he sees the light of this world.

10 But if anyone walks in the night, he stumbles because the light is not in him.

11 He said these things. And after this, He said to them, Our friend Lazarus has fallen asleep, but I am going that I may awaken him.

12 Then His disciples said, Lord, if he has fallen asleep, he will recover.

13 But Jesus had spoken about his death, but those thought that He spoke of the resting of sleep .

14 Therefore, then Jesus said to them plainly, Lazarus has died.

15 And I rejoice because of you, in order that you may believe, that I was not there. But let us go to him.

16 Then Thomas, the *one* having been called Twin, said to the fellow disciples, Let us also go, so that we may die with Him.

17 ¶ Therefore coming, Jesus found him already having *been* in the tomb four days.

18 And Bethany was near Jerusalem, *about* fifteen stadia from *it*.

19 And many of the Jews had come to the *ones* around Martha and Mary, that they might console them concerning their brother.

20 Then when Martha heard that Jesus is coming, she *went and* met Him; but Mary was sitting in the house.

21 Then Martha said to Jesus, Lord, if You were here, my brother would not have died.

22 But even now I know that as many things as You may ask God, God will give You.

23 Jesus said to her, Your brother will rise again.

24 Martha said to Him, I know that he will rise again in the resurrection in the last day.

25 Jesus said to her, I am the Resurrection and the Life. The *one* believing into Me, though he die, he shall live.

26 And everyone living and believing into Me shall not die to the age, not *ever*! Do you believe this?

27 She said to Him, Yes, Lord, I have believed that You are the Christ, the Son of God who comes into the world.

28 And saying these things, she went away and called her sister Mary secretly, saying, The Teacher is here and calls you.

29 That *one*, when she heard, rose up quickly and came to Him.

30 And Jesus had not yet come into the village, but was in the place where Martha met Him.

31 Then the Jews who were with her in the house, and consoling her, seeing that Mary quickly rose up and went out, *they* followed her, saying, She is going to the tomb so that she may weep there.

32 Then Mary, when she came where Jesus was, seeing Him, she fell at His feet, saying to Him, Lord, if You were here, my brother would not have died.

33 ¶ Therefore when He saw her weeping, and the Jews who came down with her weeping, Jesus groaned in the spirit and troubled Himself.

34 And *He* said, Where have you put him? They said to Him, Lord, come and see.

35 Jesus wept.

36 Therefore the Jews said, See how He loved him!

37 But some of them said, Was He, the *One* opening the eyes of the blind *one*, not able to have caused that this one should not die?

38 Then groaning again within Himself, Jesus came to the tomb. And it was a cave, and a stone was lying on it.

39 Jesus says, Lift the stone. Martha, the sister of the *one* having died, said to Him, Lord, he already smells, for it is *the* fourth *day*.

40 Jesus said to her, Not did I say to you that if you would believe you will see the glory of God?

41 Then they lifted the stone where was lying the *one* having died. And Jesus lifted *His* eyes upward and said, Father, I thank You that You heard Me.

42 And I know that You always hear Me, but because of the crowd standing around, I said *it*, that they might believe that You sent Me.

43 And saying these things, He cried out with a loud voice, Lazarus! Here! Outside!

44 And the *one* who had died came out, the feet and the hands having been bound with sheets, and his face being bound with a cloth. Jesus said to them, Loose him and allow *him* to go.

45 ¶ Therefore many of the Jews, the *ones* coming to Mary, and having seen what Jesus did, believed into Him.

46 But some of them went away to the Pharisees and told them what Jesus had done.

47 Then the chief priests and the Pharisees assembled a sanhedrin, and said, What are we doing? For this man does many *miraculous* signs?

48 If we leave Him *alone* thus, all will believe into Him, and the Romans will come and will take away from us both our place and the nation.

49 But a certain *one* of them, Caiaphas being high priest of that year, said to them, You know nothing,

50 nor do you consider that it is profitable for us that one man should die for the people, and not all the nation should perish.

51 But he did not say this from himself, but being high priest that year, he prophesied that Jesus was about to die on behalf of the nation,

52 and not only on behalf of the nation, but that He also might gather the children into one, the *ones* having been scattered.

53 Therefore from that day, they took counsel that they might kill Him.

54 Therefore Jesus no longer walked freely among the Jews, but went away from there into the country near *the* deserted *place*, into a city being called Ephraim, and stayed there with His disciples.

55 And the Passover of the Jews was near. And many went up to Jerusalem out of the country before the Passover, that they might purify themselves.

56 Then they were seeking Jesus, and were speaking with one another, standing in the temple, What does it seem to you? That He does not come to the Feast, not *at all*?

57 And all the chief priests and the Pharisees had given command that if anyone knew where He is, he should inform so that they might seize Him.

John 12

1 Jesus excuses Mary's anointing His feet. 10 The high priests consult to kill Lazarus. 12 Christ rides triumphantly into Jerusalem.

1 ¶ Therefore six days before the Passover, Jesus came to Bethany, where Lazarus was, the *one* having died, whom He raised from *the* dead.

2 Then they made Him a supper there, and Martha was serving. But Lazarus was one of the *ones* reclining with Him.

3 Then taking a pound of ointment of genuine, very costly spikenard, Mary anointed the feet of Jesus and wiped off His feet with her hair. And the house was filled with the fragrance of the ointment.

4 Then Simon's *son*, one of His disciples, Judas Iscariot, the *one* going to give Him over, said,

5 Why was this ointment not sold *for* three hundred denarii and given to poor *people*?

6 But he said this, not that he was caring for the poor *people*, but that he was a thief and held the money bag and carried away the things being put *in*.

7 Then Jesus said, Allow her, for she has kept it for the day of My burial.

8 For you always have the poor *people* with yourselves, but you do not always have Me.

9 Then a great crowd of the Jews knew that He is there. And they came, not because of Jesus only, but that they also might see Lazarus whom He raised from *the* dead *ones*.

10 But the chief priests took counsel that they might kill Lazarus also,

11 because through him many of the Jews went away and believed into Jesus.

12 ¶ On the next day a great crowd, the *one* coming to the Feast, hearing that Jesus is coming to Jerusalem,

13 took the branches of the palm trees and went out to a meeting with Him, and *they* were crying out, Hosanna! "Being blessed *is* the *One* coming in *the* name of *the* Lord, the King of Israel!" *Psa. 118:26*

14 And having found a little ass *colt*, Jesus sat on it, even as it is written,

15 "Do not fear," "daughter of Zion. Behold, your King comes" "sitting on" "*the* colt of an ass." *Isa. 40:9; Zech. 9:9*

16 But His disciples did not know these things at the first, but when Jesus was glorified, then they remembered that these things were written on Him, and *that* they did these things to Him.

17 Therefore the crowd was testifying, the *ones* being with Him when He called Lazarus out of the tomb and raised him out of dead *ones*.

18 On account of this also the crowd met Him, because it heard Him to have done this *miraculous* sign.

19 Therefore the Pharisees said to themselves, You see that you profit nothing. Behold, the world *has* gone after Him.

20 ¶ And there were some Greeks among the *ones* going up, that they might worship at the Feast.

21 Then these *people* came to Philip, the *one* from Bethsaida of Galilee, and they asked him, saying, Sir, we desire to see Jesus.

22 Philip comes and says to Andrew, and again Andrew and Philip told Jesus.

23 But Jesus answered them, saying, The hour has come that the Son of Man should be glorified.

24 Truly, truly, I say to you, If the grain of wheat falling into the earth does not die, *it* remains alone. But if it die, it bears much fruit.

25 The *one* loving his life will lose it, and the *one* hating his life in this world will keep it to everlasting life.

26 If anyone serves Me, let him follow Me; and where I am, there My servant will also be. And if anyone serves Me, the Father will honor him.

27 ¶ Now My soul is agitated, and what may I say? Father, save Me out of this hour? But on account of this I came to this hour.

28 Father, glorify Your name. Then a voice came out of the heaven: I both glorified *it*, and I will glorify *it* again.

29 Therefore the crowd, the *one* standing and hearing, said thunder to have occurred. Others said, An angel has spoken to Him.

30 Jesus answered and said, This voice has not happened on account of Me, but on account of you.

31 Now is *the* judgment of this world; now the ruler of this world shall be cast out.

32 And I, if I be lifted up from the earth, I will draw all to Myself.

33 But He said this, signifying by what kind *of* death He was about to die.

34 The crowd answered Him, We heard out of the Law that the Christ remains unto the age. And how do You say it is necessary that the Son of Man be lifted up? Who is this Son of Man?

35 Therefore Jesus said to them, Yet a little while the Light is with you. Walk while you have the Light, that darkness not overtake you. And the *one* walking in the darkness does not know where he is going.

36 While you have the Light, believe into the Light, that you may become sons of Light. Jesus spoke these things, and going away *He* was hidden from them.

37 ¶ But He having done so many *miraculous* signs before them, they did not believe into Him,

38 so that the word of Isaiah the prophet might be fulfilled, which he said, "Lord, who believed our report? And the arm of the Lord, to whom was it revealed?" *Isa. 53:1*

39 Because of this they could not believe, because Isaiah said again,

40 "He has blinded their eyes" and "has hardened their heart," "that they might not

see with the eyes" and "understand with the heart," "and turn back," "and I should heal them." *Isa. 6:10*

41 Isaiah said these things when he saw His glory, and spoke about Him.

42 ¶ Yet, however, even out of the rulers, many did believe into Him. But because of the Pharisees, they were not confessing, so that they not be put out of the synagogue.

43 For they loved the glory of men more than the glory of God.

44 ¶ But Jesus cried out and said, The *one* believing into Me does not believe into Me, but into the *One* having sent Me.

45 And the *one* seeing Me sees the *One* having sent Me.

46 I have come *as* a Light to the world, that every *one* who believes into Me may not remain in the darkness.

47 And if anyone hears My words and does not believe, I do not judge him; for I did not come that I might judge the world, but that I might save the world.

48 The *one* who rejects Me and does not receive My words has the *one* judging him: the Word which I spoke, that will judge him in the last Day.

49 For I did not speak from Myself, but He having sent Me, *the* Father, He has given Me command, what I should say, and what I should speak.

50 And I know that His command is everlasting life. Then what things I speak, as the Father has said to Me, so I speak.

John 13

1 Jesus washes the disciples' feet. 18 He foretells that Judas should give Him over to the priests : 36 and forewarns Peter of his denial.

1 ¶ And before the Feast of the Passover, Jesus knowing that His hour had come that He should pass from this world to the Father, having loved *His* own in the world, He loved them to *the* end.

2 And supper having occurred, the devil already having put into the heart of Judas, *the son* of Simon Iscariot, that he should give Him over,

3 Jesus knowing that the Father has given all things into *His* hands, and that He came out from God, and He goes to God,

4 He rises up from the supper and lays aside *His* garments. And taking a towel, He girded Himself.

5 Then He put water into the basin and began to wash the feet of the disciples, and to wipe off with the towel with which He was girded.

6 He then comes to Simon Peter. And that one said to Him, Lord, do You wash my feet?

7 Jesus answered and said to him, What I am doing, you do not yet know. But you will know after these things.

8 Peter said to Him, You may not wash my feet unto the age, not *ever*! Jesus answered him, If I do not wash you, you have no part with Me.

9 Simon Peter said to Him, Lord, not my feet only, but also the hands and the head.

10 Jesus said to him, The *one* having been bathed has no need *other* than to wash the feet, but is wholly clean. And you are clean, but not all *of you*.

11 For He knew the *one* giving Him over. On account of this He said, You are not all *of you* clean.

12 When, therefore, He washed their feet and took His garments, reclining again, He said to them, Do you know what I have done to you?

13 You call Me the Teacher, and, the Lord. And you say well, for I AM.

14 Therefore if I washed your feet, the Lord and the Teacher, you also ought to wash the feet of one another.

15 For I gave you an example, that as I did to you, you also should do.

16 Truly, truly, I say to you, A slave is not greater than his master, nor a messenger greater than the *one* having sent him.

17 If you know these things, blessed are you if you do them.

18 ¶ I do not speak concerning all of you; I know whom I chose out; but that the Scripture might be fulfilled, "The *one* eating the bread with Me lifted up his heel against Me." *Psa. 41:9*

19 From now I tell you before *it* happens, that when it happens you may believe that I AM.

20 Truly, truly, I say to you, if anyone I may send, the *one* who receives *that one*

receives Me; and the *one* receiving Me receives the *One* having sent Me.

21 Saying these things, Jesus was agitated in spirit and testified and said, truly, truly, I tell you that one of you will give Me over.

22 Therefore the disciples looked upon one another, being perplexed of whom He spoke.

23 But there was one of His disciples reclining at the bosom of Jesus, whom Jesus loved.

24 Therefore Simon Peter nods to this *one* to ask whom it might be of whom He spoke.

25 And that one lying on the breast of Jesus said to Him, Lord, who is it?

26 Jesus answers, It is that one to whom I, having dipped the morsel, shall give *it*. And dipping the morsel, He gave *it* to Judas Iscariot, *the son* of Simon.

27 And after the morsel, then Satan entered into that one. Then Jesus says to him, What you do, do quickly.

28 But no one of the *ones* reclining knew this, for what He spoke to him;

29 for some thought, since Judas held the money bag, that Jesus was saying to him, Buy what things we have need *of* for the feast; or that he should give something to the poor *ones*.

30 Then, having received the morsel, he immediately went out. And it was night.

31 ¶ Then when he went out, Jesus said, Now the Son of Man has been glorified, and God has been glorified in Him.

32 If God was glorified in Him, God also will glorify Him in Himself, and immediately will glorify Him.

33 Little children, yet a little while I am with you. You will seek Me; and, as I said to the Jews, Where I go, you are not able to come; I also say to you now.

34 I give a new commandment to you, that you should love one another; according as I loved you, you should also love one another.

35 By this all shall know that you are My disciples, if you have love among one another.

36 ¶ Simon Peter said to Him, Lord, where do You go? Jesus answered him, Where I go you are not able to follow Me now, but afterwards you shall follow Me.

37 Peter said to Him, Lord, why am I not able to follow You now? I will lay down my life for You!

38 Jesus answered him, Will you lay down your life for Me? Indeed, I tell you truly, not a cock will sound, until you deny Me three times, not *at all*.

John 14

1 Christ comforts His disciples: 6 professes Himself the Way, the Truth, and the Life, and one with the Father: 16 promises the Holy Spirit, the Advocate, 27 and leaves His peace with them.

1 ¶ Do not let your heart be troubled; you believe into God, believe also into Me.

2 In My Father's house are many dwelling places. But if not *so*, I would have told you, I am going to prepare a place for you!

3 And if I go and prepare a place for you, I am coming again and will receive you to Myself, that where I am you may be also.

4 ¶ And where I go you know, and the way you know.

5 Thomas says to Him, Lord, we do not know where You go, and how can we know the way?

6 Jesus says to him, I am the Way, and the Truth, and the Life. No one comes to the Father if not through Me.

7 If you had known Me, you know My Father also; and from now on you do know Him, and have seen Him.

8 And Philip says to Him, Lord, show us the Father, and it is enough for us.

9 Jesus says to him, Am I so long a time with you, and you have not known Me, Philip? The *one* having seen Me has seen the Father! And how do you say, Show us the Father?

10 Do you not believe that I *am* in the Father and the Father is in Me? The words which I speak to you I do not speak from Myself, but the Father, the *One* abiding in Me, He does the works.

11 Believe Me that I *am* in the Father, and the Father *is* in Me; but if not, believe Me because of the works themselves.

12 ¶ Truly, truly, I say to you the *one* believing into Me, the works which I do, that

one shall do also, and greater than these he will do, because I am going to My Father.

13 And whatever you may ask in My Name, this I will do, that the Father may be glorified in the Son.

14 If you ask anything in My Name, I will do *it*.

15 ¶ If you love Me, keep My commandments.

16 And I will ask the Father, and He will give you another Advocate, that He may remain with you to the age,

17 the Spirit of Truth, whom the world cannot receive because it does not see Him nor know Him; but you know Him, for He abides with you and shall be in you.

18 ¶ I will not leave you orphans; I am coming to you.

19 Yet a little *while* and the world no longer sees Me, but you see Me. Because I live, you also shall live.

20 In that day you shall know that I *am* in My Father, and you *are* in Me, and I *am* in you.

21 the *one* having My commandments and keeping them, that one is the *one* loving Me; and the *one* loving Me shall be loved by My Father, and I shall love him and will reveal Myself to him.

22 Judas says to Him, not the Iscariot, Lord, what has happened that You are about to reveal Yourself to us and not to the world?

23 Jesus answered and said to him, If anyone loves Me, he will keep My Word, and My Father shall love him. And We will come to him and will make an abode with him.

24 The *one* not loving Me does not keep My words. And the Word which you hear is not Mine but of the Father, the *One* having sent Me.

25 ¶ I have spoken these things to you, abiding with you;

26 but the Advocate, the Holy Spirit, whom the Father will send in My name, He shall teach you all things and shall remind you *of* all things that I said to you.

27 Peace I leave to you; My peace I give to you. Not as the world gives I give to you. Let not your heart be agitated, nor let *it* be fearful.

28 ¶ You heard that I said to you, I am going away, and I come *again* to you. If you loved Me, you would have rejoiced that I said I am going to the Father; for My Father is greater than I.

29 And now I have told you before *it is* to happen, that when *it is* to happen you may believe.

30 I shall no longer speak many things with you, for the ruler of this world is coming, and he has nothing in Me.

31 But that the world may know that I love the Father, even as the Father commanded Me, so I do. Rise up, let us go from here.

John 15

1 The mutual love between Christ and His members, under the parable of the vine. 26 The office of the Holy Spirit, and of the apostles.

1 ¶ I am the True Vine, and My Father is the Vinedresser.

2 Every branch in Me not bearing fruit, He takes it away; and every *branch* bearing fruit, He prunes, so that it may bear more fruit.

3 You are already pruned because of the Word which I have spoken to you.

4 Abide in Me, and I in you. As the branch is not able to bear fruit of itself, if not it abide in the vine, so neither *can* you if not you abide in Me.

5 I am the Vine; you *are* the branches. The *one* abiding in Me, and I in him, this one bears much fruit, because without Me you are not able to produce, nothing.

6 If not one abides in Me, he *is* cast out as the branch and is dried up; and they gather them, and they throw *them* into the fire, and they are burned.

7 If you abide in Me, and My words abide in you, whatever you desire you will ask, and it will be done to you.

8 In this My Father is glorified, that you should bear much fruit; and you will be disciples to Me.

9 ¶ As the Father loved Me, I also loved you; continue in My love.

10 If you keep My commandments you will continue in My love, as I have kept My Father's commandments and continue in His love.

11 I have spoken these things to you that My joy may abide in you, and your joy may be made full.

12 This is My commandment, that you love one another as I loved you.

13 Greater love *than* this has no one, that someone should lay down his soul for his friends.

14 You are My friends if you do whatever I command you.

15 I no longer call you slaves, for the slave does not know what his master does. But I called you friends, because all things which I heard from My Father I made known to you.

16 You have not chosen Me, but I chose you and appointed you, that you should go and should bear fruit, and your fruit remain, that whatever you may ask the Father in My name, He may give you.

17 These things I command you, that you love one another.

18 ¶ If the world hates you, you know that it has hated Me before you.

19 If you were of the world, the world would love its own. But because you are not of the world, but I chose you out of the world, because of this the world hates you.

20 Remember the Word which I said to you, A slave is not greater than his master. If they persecuted Me, they also will persecute you. If they kept My Word, they also will keep yours.

21 But all these things they will do to you on account of My name, because they do not know the *One* having sent Me.

22 If I had not come and had not spoken to them, they had no sin. But now they have no excuse as to their sin.

23 The *one* hating Me also hates My Father.

24 If I did not do the works among them which no other did, they had no sin. But now they both have seen and also have hated Me and My Father.

25 But that may be fulfilled the Word that has been written in their Law, "They hated Me undeservedly. *Psalms 69:4*

26 But when the Advocate comes, whom I will send to you from the Father, the Spirit of Truth who proceeds from the Father, that One will witness concerning Me.

27 And you also witness, because from *the* beginning you are with Me.

John 16

1 Christ comforts His disciples by the promise of the Holy Spirit: 23 assures prayers made in His name to be acceptable to His Father.

1 ¶ I have spoken these things to you so that you may not be made to stumble

2 They will make you *to be* expelled from *the* synagogue, but an hour is coming that every *one* killing you will think to he offers a divine service before God.

3 And they will do these things to you because they do not know the Father nor Me.

4 But I have spoken these things to you so that when the hour comes you may recall them, that I told you. But I did not say these things to you from *the* beginning because I was with you.

5 But now I am going to the *One* having sent Me. And not one of you asks Me, Where are You going?

6 But because I have said these things to you, grief has filled your heart.

7 But I speak the truth to you, *it is* profitable *for* you that I should go; for if I do not go away, the Advocate will not come to you. But if I go, I will send Him to you.

8 And having come, that One will convict the world concerning sin, and concerning righteousness, and concerning judgment;

9 concerning sin, truly, because they do not believe into Me;

10 and concerning righteousness, because I am going to the Father, and you no longer see Me;

11 and concerning judgment, because the ruler of this world has been judged.

12 I have yet many things to tell you, but you are not able to bear *them* now.

13 But when that One comes, the Spirit of Truth, He will guide you into all Truth, for He will not speak from Himself, but as many things as He hears, He will speak; and He will announce the coming things to you.

14 That One will glorify Me, for He will take from Mine and will announce to you.

15 All things, as many as the Father has are Mine. Because of this I said that He will take from Mine, and will announce to you.

16 ¶ A little *while* and you do not see Me. And again a little, and you will see Me, because I go away to the Father.

17 Then *some* of His disciples said to one another, What is this which He says to us, A little and you do not see me; and again, A little and you will see Me? And, Because I go away to the Father?

18 Therefore they said, What is this that He says, The little? Not we know what He says.

19 Therefore Jesus knew that they desired to ask Him. And *He* said to them, Are you inquiring with one another about this, because I said, A little *while*, and you do not see Me; and again a little and you will see Me?

20 Truly, truly, I say to you that you will weep and will lament, but the world will rejoice. And you will be grieved, but your grief will become joy.

21 The woman has grief when she bears, because her hour came, but when she bears the child, she no longer remembers the distress, because of the joy that a man was born into the world.

22 And you, therefore, truly have grief now; but I will see you again, and your heart will rejoice, and no one takes your joy from you.

23 ¶ And in that day you will ask Me nothing. Truly, truly, I say to you, As many things as you shall ask the Father in My name, He will give you.

24 Until now you asked nothing in My name; ask, and you will receive, so that your joy may be filled.

25 I have spoken these things to you in allegories. An hour comes when I will no longer speak to you in allegories, but concerning the Father I will plainly announce to you.

26 In that day you will ask in My name, and I do not say to you that I will ask the Father about you;

27 for the Father Himself loves you, because you have loved Me, and have believed that I came out from God.

28 ¶ I came out from the Father and have come into the world; Again, I leave the world and go to the Father.

29 His disciples said to Him, Behold, now You speak openly and You say not one allegory.

30 Now we know that You know all things and have no need that anyone ask You. By this we believe that You came out from God.

31 Jesus answered them, Do you believe now?

32 Behold, an hour is coming, and now has come, that you will be scattered, each *one* to his own things, and you will leave Me alone. Yet I am not alone, because the Father is with Me.

33 I have spoken these things to you that you may have peace in Me. You have distress in the world; but have courage, I have overcome the world.

John 17

1 Christ prays to his Father. 20 to give them glory, and all other believers with Him in heaven.

1 ¶ Jesus spoke these things and lifted up His eyes to Heaven, and said, Father, the hour has come. Glorify Your Son, that Your Son may also glorify You,

2 Even as You gave to Him authority *over* all flesh, so that to all which You gave to Him, He may give to them everlasting life.

3 And this is everlasting life, that they may know You, the only true God, and Jesus Christ, *the One* whom You sent.

4 I have glorified You on the earth. finishing the work that You have given to Me, that I should do.

5 And now Father, glorify Me with Yourself, with the glory which I had with You before the world *was* to be.

6 ¶ I revealed Your name to the men whom You have given to Me out of the world. They were Yours, and You have given them to Me; and they have kept Your Word.

7 Now they have known that all things, as many as You have given to Me, are from You.

8 For the words which You have given to Me, I have given to them. And they received and truly knew that I came out from beside You, and they believed that You sent Me.

9 I ask concerning them; I do not ask concerning the world, but concerning *the ones* whom You have given to Me, because they are Yours.

10 And all My things are Yours, and Yours *are* Mine; and I have been glorified in them.

11 ¶ And no longer am I in the world, yet these are in the world; and I come to You.

Holy Father, keep them in Your name, *the ones* whom You have given to Me, that *they* may be one even as We *are*.

12 While I was with them in the world, I was keeping them in Your name; I guarded the *ones* whom You have given to Me, and no one of them has been lost, if not the son of *eternal* destruction, that the Scripture might be fulfilled.

13 And now I am coming to You, and I speak these things in the world, that they may have My joy having been fulfilled in them.

14 I have given them Your Word, and the world hated them because they are not of the world, even as I am not of the world.

15 I do not ask that You take them out of the world, but that You keep them from the evil.

16 They are not of the world, even as I am not of the world.

17 ¶ Sanctify them in Your Truth; Your Word is Truth.

18 As You have sent Me into the world, I also have sent them into the world,

19 and I sanctify Myself on behalf of them, that they also may be sanctified in Truth.

20 ¶ And I do not ask concerning these only, but also concerning the *ones* who will believe into Me through their word;

21 that all may be one, as You *are* in Me, Father, and I in You, that they also may be one in Us, that the world may believe that You sent Me.

22 And I have given them the glory which You have given Me, that they may be one, as We are one:

23 I in them, and You in Me, that they may be perfected in one; and that the world may know that You sent Me and You loved them, just as You loved Me.

24 ¶ Father, I desire that *the ones* whom You have given Me, that where I am, those also may be with Me, that they may behold My glory which You gave Me, because You loved Me before *the* foundation of *the* world.

25 Righteous Father, indeed the world did not know You, but I have known You; and these have known that You sent Me.

26 And I made known to them Your name, and will make *it* known, that the love *with* which You loved Me may be in them, and I in them.

John 18

1 ¶ Having said these things, Jesus went out with His disciples across the torrent Kidron, where there was a garden into which He and His disciples entered.

2 And Judas, the *one* giving Him over, also knew the place, because Jesus many times assembled there with His disciples.

3 Therefore Judas, having taken the cohort and under-officers from among the chief priests and the Pharisees, comes there with lights and torches and weapons.

4 Therefore, knowing all the things coming upon Him, going forth, Jesus said to them, Whom do you seek?

5 They answered Him, Jesus the Nazarene. Jesus said to them, I AM! And Judas, the *one* giving Him over, also stood with them.

6 Therefore as He said to them, I AM, they went away into the rear and fell to the earth.

7 Therefore again He asked, Whom do you seek? And they said, Jesus the Nazarene.

8 Jesus answered, I told you that I AM; therefore if you seek Me, allow these to go,

9 (that the Word might be fulfilled which He said, "*Of* those whom You have given to Me, I lost not *one* of them, no one)."

10 Then having a sword, Simon Peter drew it and struck the slave of the high priest and cut off his right ear. And there was a name to the slave, Malchus.

11 Therefore Jesus said to Peter, Put your sword into the sheath: the cup which the Father has given Me, shall I not drink it, not *at all*?

12 Then the cohort, even the chiliarch and the under-officers of the Jews together, seized Jesus and bound Him.

13 ¶ And they led Him away first to Annas, for he was *the* father-in-law of Caiaphas, who was high priest of that year.

14 And Caiaphas was the *one* who *had* given counsel to the Jews that it was profitable *for* one man to perish on behalf of the people.

15 And Simon Peter and another disciple followed Jesus, and that disciple

was known to the high priest and entered together with Jesus into the courtyard of the high priest,

16 but Peter stood at the door outside. Therefore the other disciple who was known to the high priest went out and spoke to the portress, and brought Peter in.

17 Then the slave woman, the portress, said to Peter, Are you not also of the disciples of this man? That one said, I am not.

18 Now the slaves and the under-officers stood, and they were warming themselves, having made a fire of coals, for it was cold; and Peter was with them, standing and warming himself.

19 Then the high priest questioned Jesus about His disciples and about His doctrine.

20 Jesus answered him, I spoke openly to the world; I always taught in the synagogue and in the temple where the Jews always come together, and I spoke nothing in secret.

21 Why do you question Me? Question the *ones* hearing what I spoke to them: behold, these know what I said!

22 But *on* His having said these things, one of the under-officers standing by gave Jesus a slap, saying, Do You answer the high priest thus?

23 Jesus answered him, If I spoke badly, bear witness about the bad *thing*; but if well, why do you smite Me?

24 Then having bound *Him*, Annas sent Him forth to Caiaphas the high priest.

25 And Simon Peter was standing and warming himself. Therefore they said to him, Are you not also of His disciples? That one denied and said, I am not.

26 One of the slaves of the high priest, being a relative *of the one* whose ear Peter cut off, says, Did I not see you in the garden with Him?

27 Then again Peter denied, and immediately a cock sounded.

28 ¶ Then they led Jesus from Caiaphas into the praetorium, and it was early. And they did not enter into the praetorium that they might not be defiled, but that they might eat the Passover.

29 Then Pilate went out to them and said, What accusation do you bring against this man?

30 They answered and said to him, If this one were not an evildoer, then we would not have given Him over to you.

31 Then Pilate said to them, You take Him and judge Him according to your own Law. Then the Jews said to him, It is not lawful for us to kill, no one,

32 (that the Word of Jesus which He said might be fulfilled, signifying by what kind *of* death He was about to die).

33 Then Pilate again entered into the praetorium and called Jesus, and said to Him, Are You the King of the Jews?

34 Jesus answered him, Do you say this from yourself, or did others tell you about Me?

35 Pilate answered, Not, am I a Jew? Your nation, even the chief priests gave You over to me! What did You do?

36 Jesus answered, My kingdom is not of this world. If My kingdom was of this world, My servants would have fought that I might not be given over to the Jews. But now My kingdom is not from here.

37 Then Pilate said to Him, Therefore, then are you not a king? Jesus answered, You say that I am a king. For this *purpose* I have been born, and for this *purpose* I have come into the world, that I might witness to the Truth. Everyone being of the Truth hears My voice.

38 Pilate says to Him, What is truth? And saying this, he again went out to the Jews and said to them, I do not find not even *one* cause *of death* in Him!

39 But there is a common custom to you that I should release one *prisoner* to you at the Passover. Then do you will *that* I should release the King of the Jews to you?

40 Then all cried out again, saying, Not this *one*, but Barabbas! But Barabbas was a plunderer.

John 19

1 Christ is scourged, crowned with thorns, and beaten. 28 He dies. 38 He is buried by Joseph.

1 ¶ Therefore, then, Pilate took Jesus and scourged *Him*.

2 And having plaited a wreath out of thorns, the soldiers put *it* on His head. And they threw a purple garment around Him,

3 and said, Hail, King of the Jews! And they were giving Him slaps.

4 Then Pilate went outside again and said to them, Behold, I bring Him out to you that you may know that I find not even *one* cause *of death* in Him!

5 Then Jesus came outside, wearing the thorny wreath and the purple garment. And he says to them, Behold, the Man!

6 Therefore when the chief priests and the under-officers saw Him, they cried out, saying, Crucify! Crucify! Pilate says to them, You take Him and crucify *Him*, for I find not even *one* cause *of death* in Him!

7 Then the Jews answered him, We have a law, and according to our Law He ought to die because He made Himself Son of God!

8 Therefore when Pilate heard this word, he was more afraid.

9 And *he* entered into the praetorium again and said to Jesus, From where are You? But Jesus did not give him an answer.

10 Then Pilate says to Him, Do You not speak to me? Do You not know that I have authority to crucify You, and I have authority to release You?

11 Jesus answered, You would not have authority against Me, not even *any*, if it was not being given to you from above. Because of this the one giving Me over to you has a greater sin.

12 From this, Pilate sought to release Him. But the Jews were crying out, saying, If you release this *one*, you are not a friend of Caesar. Everyone making himself a king speaks against Caesar.

13 Then hearing this word, Pilate led Jesus out. And *he* sat down on the judgment seat, at a place called *The* Pavement, but in Hebrew, Gabbatha.

14 And it was *the* Preparation of the Passover, and about *the* sixth hour. And he says to the Jews, Behold, your King!

15 But they cried out, Away, Away! Crucify Him! Pilate said to them, Shall I crucify your King? The chief priests answered, We do not have a king except Caesar.

16 ¶ Therefore, then, he gave Him over to them, that He might be crucified. And they took Jesus and led *Him* away.

17 And He went out bearing His cross, to the place called Of a Skull (which is called in Hebrew, Golgotha),

18 where they crucified Him, and two oth-ers with Him, from here and from there, and Jesus in the middle.

19 ¶ And Pilate also wrote a title and put *it* on the cross. And having been written, it was: JESUS THE NAZARENE, THE KING OF THE JEWS.

20 Therefore, this title many of the Jews read, because the place where Jesus was crucified was near the city. And it was written in Hebrew, in Greek, in Latin.

21 Then the chief priests of the Jews said to Pilate, Do not write, The King of the Jews, but that One said, I am King of the Jews.

22 Pilate answered, What I have written, I have written.

23 Then when they crucified Jesus, the soldiers took His garments and made four parts, a part to each soldier, also the tunic. And the tunic was seamless, woven from the top through all.

24 Then they said to one another, Let us not tear it, but let us cast lots about it, whose it will be (that the Scripture might be fulfilled which said, "They divided My garments among them," and "they threw a lot *for* My garment"). Then indeed the soldiers did these things. *LXX-Psa. 21:19; MT-Psa. 22:18*)

25 And there stood His mother, and His mother's sister Mary, the *wife* of Clopas, and Mary Magdalene by the cross of Jesus.

26 Therefore Jesus, seeing *His* mother and the disciple whom He loved standing by, *He* says to His mother, Woman, behold your son!

27 Then He says to the disciple, Behold, your mother! And from that hour, the disciple took her into his own *home*.

28 After this, Jesus knowing that all things have now been finished that the Scripture be fulfilled, *He* says, I thirst.

29 Then a vessel full of vinegar was set, and having filled a sponge *with* vinegar, and putting hyssop around, they brought *it* to His mouth. *Psa. 69:21*

30 Therefore when Jesus took the vinegar, He said, It has been finished. And bowing *His* head, *He* gave over the spirit.

31 ¶ Therefore, since it was Preparation, that the bodies not remain on the cross on the sabbath, for great was the day of that sabbath, the Jews asked Pilate

that their legs might be broken and they be taken away.

32 Then the soldiers came and broke the legs of the first *man*, and of the other *one* crucified with Him.

33 But *on* coming to Jesus, when they saw Him having died already, they did not break His legs.

34 But one of the soldiers took a spear and pierced His side, and at once blood and water came out.

35 And the *one* having seen has borne witness and the witness of him is true; and that *one* knows that he says true *things*, that you may believe.

36 For these things happened that the Scripture might be fulfilled, "Not a bone of Him shall be broken." *Ex. 12:46; Psa. 34:20*

37 And again, a different Scripture says, "They shall look at *Him* whom they have pierced." *Zech. 12:10*

38 ¶ And after these things, Joseph, the *one* from Arimathea, being a disciple of Jesus, but having been hidden because of fear of the Jews, asked Pilate that he might take the body of Jesus. And Pilate gave permission. Then he came and took the body of Jesus.

39 And Nicodemus also came, the *one* coming at first to Jesus by night, bearing a mixture of myrrh and aloes, about a hundred *Roman* pounds.

40 Then they took the body of Jesus and bound it in linen strips, with the spices, just as is *the* custom with the Jews *in* burying.

41 And there was a garden in the place where He was crucified, and a new tomb in the garden, in which no one yet had been put, not one.

42 There, then, because of the Preparation of the Jews, because the tomb was near, they put Jesus.

John 20

1 Mary comes to the tomb. 11 Jesus appears to Mary Magdalene, 19 and to His disciples. 24 Thomas will not believe what the disciples say.

1 ¶ But on the first of the sabbaths, Mary Magdalene came early in the morning to the tomb, *it* yet being dark. And *she* sees the stone having been taken away from the tomb.

2 Therefore she runs and comes to Simon Peter, and to the other disciple whom Jesus loved, and said to them, They took away the Lord out of the tomb, and we do not know where they laid Him.

3 Then Peter and the other disciple went out and came to the tomb.

4 And the two were running together, and the other disciple ran in front more quickly *than* Peter and he came first to the tomb.

5 And stooping to look *in* he sees the linen strips lying; however, he did not go in.

6 Then Simon Peter comes following him, and went into the tomb and he sees the linen strips lying.

7 And the face cloth which was on His head *was* not lying with the linen strips, but was *lying* separately, having been wrapped up in one place.

8 Then, therefore, the other disciple also entered, the *one* having come first to the tomb, even he saw and believed.

9 For they did not yet know the Scripture, that it was necessary for Him to rise from *the* dead *ones*.

10 Then the disciples went away again to themselves.

11 ¶ But Mary stood outside at the tomb, weeping. Therefore as she wept she stooped to look into the tomb.

12 And *she* sees two angels in white, sitting one at the head, and one at the feet, where the body of Jesus had lain.

13 And those *ones* say to her, Woman, why do you weep? She says to them, Because they took away my Lord, and I do not know where they put Him.

14 And having said these things, she turned to the things behind and sees Jesus standing, and did not know that it is Jesus.

15 Jesus says to her, Woman, why do you weep? Whom do you seek? Thinking that it was the gardener, she says to Him, Sir, if You carried Him away, tell me where You put Him, and I will take Him away.

16 Jesus says to her, Mary! Turning around, she says to Him, Rabboni! (which is to say, Teacher).

17 Jesus says to her, Do not take hold *of Me*, for I have not yet ascended to My Father. But go to My brothers and say to them,

I am ascending to My Father and your Father, and My God, and your God.

18 Mary Magdalene comes reporting to the disciples that she had seen the Lord, and that He said to her these things.

19 ¶ Then it being evening on that day, the first of the sabbaths, and the doors having been locked where the disciples were gathered together because of fear of the Jews, Jesus came and stood in the midst and says to them, Peace to you.

20 And saying this, He showed them *His* hands and side. Then seeing the Lord, the disciples rejoiced.

21 Therefore Jesus said to them again, Peace to you. As the Father has sent Me, I also send you.

22 And saying this, He breathed on *them* and said to them, Receive *the* Holy Spirit.

23 Of whomever you may remit the sins, they are remitted to them. Of whomever you hold, they have been held.

24 But Thomas, one of the Twelve, the *one* called Twin, was not with them when Jesus came.

25 Therefore the other disciples said to him, We have seen the Lord. But he said to them, If I do not see the mark of the nails in His hands, and put my finger into the mark of the nails, and put my han*d* into His side, I will not believe, not *at all*!

26 ¶ And after eight days, His disciples were inside again, and Thomas was with them. The door having been locked, Jesus came and stood in the midst, and said, Peace to you.

27 Then He says to Thomas, Bring your finger here and see My hands, and bring your hand and put *it* into My side, and do not be unbelieving, but believing.

28 And Thomas answered and said to Him, My Lord and my God!

29 Jesus says to him, Because you have seen Me, Thomas, you have believed. Blessed *are* the *ones* not seeing, and believing.

30 Then truly Jesus also did many other *miraculous* signs in the sight of His disciples, which are not written in this book.

31 But these have been written that you may believe that Jesus is the Christ, the Son of God, and that believing you may have life in His name.

John 21

1 Christ appears again to his disciples, 15 earnestly commands Peter to feed His lambs and sheep: 18 and foretells the death of Peter.

1 ¶ After these things, Jesus revealed Himself again to the disciples at the Sea of Tiberias. And thus He revealed *Himself.*

2 *There* were together Simon Peter, and Thomas, the *one* being called Twin, and Nathanael from Cana of Galilee, and the *sons* of Zebedee, and two others of His disciples.

3 Simon Peter says to them, I am going away to fish. They say to him, We also are coming with you. They went out and went up into the boat at once. And in that night, they caught nothing.

4 But early morning now having become, Jesus stood onto the shore. However, the disciples did not know that it is Jesus.

5 Then Jesus says to them, Children, do you not have any thing for eating? They answered Him, No.

6 And He said to them, Cast the net into the right side of the boat and you will find. Therefore they cast, and they no longer had *the* strength to draw, from the multitude of the fish.

7 Therefore the disciple whom Jesus loved says to Peter, It is the Lord. Then Simon Peter hearing that it is the Lord, having girded on *his* outer garment (for he was unclad) and he threw himself into the sea.

8 And the other disciples came in the little boat, for they were not far from the land, from about two hundred cubits, dragging the net of the fish.

9 Then when they came down onto the land, they saw a coal fire lying, and a fish lying on *it*, and bread.

10 Jesus says to them, Bring from the little fish which you caught now.

11 Simon Peter went up and dragged the net onto the land, full of great fish, a hundred and fifty three. And *though* being so many, the net was not torn

12 Jesus says to them, Come, break fast. But no one of the disciples dared to ask Him, Who are You? knowing that it is the Lord.

13 Then Jesus comes and takes the bread, and gives to them, and the little fish likewise.

14 This *was* now a third *time* Jesus was revealed to His disciples, He having been raised from *the* dead *ones*.

15 ¶ Therefore when they broke fast, Jesus says to Simon Peter, Simon, *son* of Jonah, do you love Me more *than* these? He says to Him, Yes, Lord, You know that I love You. He says to him, Feed My lambs!

16 Again He says to him a second *time*, Simon, *son* of Jonah, do you love Me? He says to Him, Yes, Lord, You know that I love You. He says to him, Feed My sheep!

17 He says to him a third *time*, Simon *son* of Jonah, do you love Me? Peter was grieved that He said to him a third *time*, Do you love Me? And he said to him, Lord, You perceive all things, You know that I love You! Jesus said to him, Feed My sheep!

18 Truly, truly, I say to you, When you were younger, you girded yourself, and you walked where you desired. But when you grow old, you will stretch out your hands, and another will gird you, and will carry you where *you* do not desire.

19 But He said this signifying by what death he would glorify God. And having said this, He says to him, Follow Me.

20 ¶ But turning, Peter sees the disciple whom Jesus loved following *them*, who also leaned on His breast at the Supper, and said, Lord, who is the *one* giving You over?

21 Seeing this *one*, Peter said to Jesus, Lord, and what *of* this one?

22 Jesus says to him, If I desire him to remain until I come, what *is that* to you? You follow Me.

23 Therefore, this word went out to the brothers *that* that one, that disciple does not die. Yet Jesus did not say to him that he does not die, but, If I desire him to remain until I come, what *is that* to you?

24 This is the disciple, the *one* witnessing about these things, and having written these things. And we know that his witness is true.

25 And there are many other things, as many as Jesus did, which if they were written by *one* I suppose the world not even have room for the books being written. Amen.

THE ACTS
of the Apostles

Acts 1

1 Christ commands his apostles to expect the Holy Spirit. 9 After His ascension 12 they return, and choose Matthias apostle in the place of Judas.

1 ¶ Indeed, O Theophilus, I made the first report concerning all things which Jesus began both to do and to teach,

2 until the day He was taken up, having given directions to the apostles whom He had chosen, through *the* Holy Spirit,

3 to whom also He presented Himself living after His suffering, by many infallible proofs, being seen by them through forty days, and speaking the things concerning the kingdom of God.

4 And assembling together with *them*, He charged them not to leave Jerusalem, but to await the promise of the Father, "which you heard of Me;

5 for John indeed baptized in water, but you will be baptized in *the* Holy Spirit not many days after."

6 ¶ Then, indeed, having come together they questioned Him, saying, Lord, do You restore the kingdom to Israel at this time?

7 And He said to them, It is not yours to know times or seasons which the Father placed in His own authority;

8 but you will receive power, the Holy Spirit having come upon you, and you will be witnesses of Me both in Jerusalem, and in all Judea, and Samaria, and to *the* end of the earth.

9 And having said these things, they seeing, He was taken up, and a cloud received Him from their eyes.

10 And as they were intently looking into the heaven, He having gone, even behold, two men in white clothing stood by them,

11 who also said, Men, Galileans, why do you stand looking up to the heaven? This Jesus, the *One* being taken from you into the heaven, will come in the way you saw Him going into the heaven.

12 ¶ Then they returned to Jerusalem from *the* Mount, the *one* being called Of Olive Grove, which is near Jerusalem, having a journey of a sabbath.

13 And when they went in, they went up to the upper room where they were waiting: both Peter and James, and John and Andrew, Philip and Thomas, Bartholomew and Matthew, James *the son* of Alpheus and Simon the Zealot, and Judas *the brother* of James.

14 These all were continuing steadfastly in prayer and in supplication with one mind, with *the* women, and *with* Mary the mother of Jesus, and with His brothers.

15 ¶ And in these days, standing up in *the* midst of the disciples, (and *the* number of names together *being* about a hundred *and* twenty), Peter said,

16 Men, brothers, it was necessary *for* this Scripture to be fulfilled which the Holy Spirit spoke before through David's mouth concerning Judas, the *one* having become guide to the *ones* seizing Jesus;

17 for he was numbered with us, and obtained the portion of this ministry.

18 Indeed, then, this one bought a field out of the reward of unrighteousness; and falling headlong, he burst in the middle, and all his bowels poured out.

19 And it became known to all the *ones* living in Jerusalem, so as that field to be called in their own dialect, Akel Dama, this is, Field of Blood.

20 For it is written in *the* Book of Psalms, "Let his dwelling become deserted, and he not be living in it." And, "Let another take his office of overseer." *LXX-Psa. 68:26; Psa. 108:8; MT-Psa. 69:25; Psa. 109:8*

21 Therefore, it is necessary *that* of the men accompanying us all *the* time in which the Lord Jesus came in and went out among us,

22 beginning from the baptism of John until the day when He was taken up from us, for one of these to become a witness of His resurrection with us.

23 And they set two: Joseph, the *one* being called Barsabas, who was called Justus, and Matthias.

24 And having prayed, they said, You, Lord, knower of all hearts, show which one You chose from these two,

25 to take the share of this ministry and apostleship, from which Judas turned aside to go to *his* own place.

26 And they gave their lots. And the lot fell on Matthias; and he was counted with the eleven apostles.

Acts 2

1 The apostles, filled with the Holy Spirit, speak other languages. 14 Peter shows that they spoke by the power of the Holy Spirit. 43 They work many miracles.

1 ¶ And in the *day* to be fulfilled, the day of Pentecost, they were all with one mind upon the same *place and purpose*.

2 And suddenly a sound came out of the heaven, as being borne along by a violent wind! And it filled all the house where they were sitting.

3 And tongues as of fire appeared to them, being distributed, and it sat on each *one* of them.

4 And they were all filled of the Holy Spirit, and began to speak in other languages, as the Spirit gave to them to speak.

5 ¶ Now *there* were Jews dwelling in Jerusalem, devout men from every nation of the *ones* under the heaven.

6 But this sound occurring, the throng came together and were confounded, because they were each *one* hearing them speaking in *his* own dialect.

7 And all were amazed and marveled, saying to one another, Behold, *are* not all these, the *ones* speaking, Galileans?

8 And how do we hear each *one* in our own dialect in which we were born,

9 Parthians, and Medes, and Elamites, and those living in Mesopotamia, both Judea and Cappadocia, Pontus and Asia,

10 both Phrygia and Pamphylia, Egypt, and the regions of Libya over against Cyrene, and the sojourning Romans, both Jews and proselytes,

11 Cretans and Arabians; in our own languages we hear them speaking the great deeds of God?

12 And all were amazed and perplexed, saying to one another, What wishes this to be?

13 But ridiculing, others said, They are filled of sweet new wine.

14 ¶ But standing up with the Eleven, Peter lifted up his voice and spoke out to them, Men, Jews, and all the *ones* living in Jerusalem, let this be known to you, and give ear to my words:

15 For these are not drunk, as you assume, for it is *the* third hour of the day.

16 But this is that having been been spoken by the prophet Joel,

17 "And it shall be" in the last days, God says, "I will pour from My Spirit on all flesh, and your sons and your daughters shall prophesy;" "and your young men shall see visions," "and your old men shall dream dreams;"

18 "and also I will pour out My Spirit on My slaves and slave women in those days," and they shall prophesy.

19 "And I will give wonders in the heaven above," and *miraculous* signs "on the earth below, blood and fire and vapor of smoke.

20 The sun will be turned into darkness, and the moon into blood, before the" "coming of the great and glorious" "day of *the* Lord."

21 "And it shall be *that* everyone who shall call on *the* name of the Lord will be saved."
Joel 2:28-32

22 Men, Israelites, hear these words: Jesus the Nazarene, a Man from God, having been declared among you by works of power and wonders and *miraculous* signs, which God did through Him in your midst, as you yourselves also know,

23 this One given up by the pre-determined purpose and foreknowledge of God, *you* having taken by lawless hands, having crucified *Him*, you killed *Him*.

24 *But* God raised *Him* up, loosening the throes of death, because it was not possible for Him to be held by it.

25 For David said *as* to Him, "I foresaw the Lord before Me through all, because He is at My right *hand*, that I not be shaken.

26 Because of this My heart rejoiced, and My tongue exulted; and My flesh also will dwell on hope,

27 because You will not abandon My soul in Hades, nor will You give Your Holy One to see corruption.

28 You revealed to Me paths of life; You will fill Me with joy with Your face." *LXX-Psa. 15:8-11; MT-Psa. 16:8-11*

29 Men, brothers, it is permitted to say to you with boldness concerning the patriarch David, that he both died and was buried, and his tomb is among us until this day.

30 Being a prophet, therefore, and knowing that God swore with an oath to him that of *the* fruit of his loin, as concerning flesh, to raise the Christ to sit down on his throne, *see Psa. 132:11*

31 foreseeing, he spoke concerning the resurrection of the Christ, "that His soul was not left in Hades, nor did His flesh see corruption." *LXX-Psa. 15:10; MT-Psa. 16:10*

32 This Jesus, God raised up, of which we all are witnesses.

33 Therefore having been exalted to the right *hand* of God, and receiving the promise of the Holy Spirit from the Father, He poured out this which you now see and hear.

34 For David did not ascend into Heaven, but he says, "The Lord said to my Lord, Sit at My right *hand*

35 until I place *the* hostile *ones* to You as a footstool to Your feet." *LXX-Psa. 109:1; MT-Psa. 110:1*

36 Therefore assuredly, let all *the* house of Israel acknowledge that God made Him both Lord and Christ, this Jesus whom you crucified.

37 But hearing this, they were pierced in the heart, and said to Peter and the rest of the apostles, Men, brothers, what shall we do?

38 And Peter said to them, Repent and be baptized, each *one* of you on the name of Jesus Christ to remission of sins. And you will receive the gift of the Holy Spirit.

39 For the promise is to you and to your children, and to all the *ones* unto far off, as many as *the* Lord our God shall call.

40 And with many other words he earnestly testified and exhorted, saying, Be saved from this perverse generation.

41 Truly, then, the *ones* gladly welcoming his words were baptized. And about three thousand souls were added that day.

42 ¶ And they were continuing steadfastly in the doctrine of the apostles, and in fellowship, and in the breaking of bread, and in prayers.

43 And fear came to be to every soul, and many wonders and *miraculous* signs occurred through the apostles.

44 And all the believing *ones* were on the same *place* and had all things common.

45 And they sold possessions and belongings and divided them to all, according as anyone had need.

46 And according to a day continuing steadfastly with one mind in the temple, and breaking bread from house to house, they shared food in great joy and simplicity of heart,

47 praising God, and having favor with all the people. And the Lord was adding to the assembly the *ones* being saved according to a day.

Acts 3

1 Peter, preaching to the people that came to see a lame man restored, 19 tells them by repentance and faith to seek remission of their sins.

1 ¶ And on the same *day* Peter and John were going up into the temple at the hour of prayer, the ninth.

2 And a certain man, being lame from his mother's womb, was being carried, whom they put according to a day at the door of the temple, the *one* being called Beautiful, to ask merciful *gifts* from the *ones* going into the temple;

3 who seeing Peter and John being about to go into the temple, asked merciful *gifts*.

4 But Peter, together with John, gazing intently toward him, Peter said, Look toward us!

5 And he attended to them, expecting to receive something from them.

6 But Peter said, There is no silver and gold to me, but what I have, this I give to you: In the name of Jesus Christ the Nazarene, rise up and walk about!

7 And laying hold of the right hand of him, he raised *him* up. And immediately his feet and ankle-bones were made firm.

8 And leaping up, he stood and walked about, and went with them into the temple, walking about and leaping, and praising God.

9 And all the people saw him walking about and praising God.

10 And they recognized him, that it was the *one* who was sitting for merciful *gifts* at the Beautiful Gate of the temple. And they were filled *with* amazement and ecstasy at the *thing* having happened to him.

11 And the healed lame *one* was holding to Peter and John, *and* all the people ran together to them on the porch called Solomon's, greatly amazed.

12 ¶ And seeing *this*, Peter answered to the people, Men, Israelites, why do you marvel at this one? Or why do you stare *at* us, as *if* by our own power or piety we have made him to walk about?

13 The "God of Abraham and Isaac and Jacob," "the God of our fathers," *Ex. 3:15* glorified His Servant Jesus, whom you gave over, and denied Him to *the* face of Pilate, judging to set that One free.

14 But you denied the Holy and Just *One*, and asked for a man, a murderer, to be granted to you.

15 And the Author of Life you killed, whom God raised up from *the* dead, of which we are witnesses.

16 And on the faith of His name, this *one* whom you see and know was made firm *by* His name, and the faith which came through Him gave to him this complete soundness before you all.

17 And now, brothers, I know that you acted according to ignorance, as also *did* your rulers.

18 But what things God before proclaimed through the mouth of all His prophets, *that* the Christ should suffer, He fulfilled in this way.

19 Therefore, repent, and turn back, for the blotting out of your sins, so that times of refreshing may come from *the* face of the Lord,

20 and that He may send forth the *One* proclaimed to you before, Jesus Christ,

21 whom Heaven truly needs to receive until *the* times of restoration of all things, of which God spoke through *the* mouth of all His holy prophets from *the* age.

22 For Moses indeed said to the fathers, "*The* Lord your God will raise up to you a Prophet from among your brothers, *One*

like me; you shall hear Him according to all *things*," as many as He may speak to you. *Deut. 18:15-16*

23 And it shall be, every soul, whoever should not hear that Prophet shall be utterly destroyed from among the people.

24 And also all the prophets, from Samuel and the *ones* in order, as many as spoke, also before announced these days.

25 You are sons of the prophets and of the covenant which God made to our fathers, saying to Abraham, "And in your Seed all the families of the earth shall be blessed." *Gen. 22:18*

26 Having raised up His Servant Jesus, God sent Him first to you, blessing you in turning away each *one* from your iniquities.

Acts 4

1 The rulers of the Jews, offended with Peter's sermon, 4 imprison him and John. 18 They command him and John to preach no more in the name of Jesus.

1 ¶ And *as they* were speaking to the people, the priests, and the temple commander, and the Sadducees,

2 being distressed because of their teaching *of* the people, and *continuing* to proclaim in Jesus the resurrection from *the* dead *ones*.

3 *And they* laid hands on *them*, and put *them* into custody until the morrow, for it was already evening.

4 But many of the *ones* hearing the Word believed; and the number of the men came to be about five thousand.

5 ¶ And it happened on the next day that the rulers and elders and scribes gathered into Jerusalem;

6 also Annas the high priest, and Caiaphas, and John, and Alexander, and as many as were of *the* high priestly family.

7 And standing them in the midst, they were inquiring, By what sort of power, or by what kind of name did you do this?

8 Then being filled of *the* Holy Spirit, Peter said to them, Rulers of the people and elders of Israel,

9 if we are being examined today on a good work of an infirm man, by what this *one* has been healed,

10 let it be known to all of you, and to all the people of Israel, that in the name of

Jesus Christ the Nazarene, whom you crucified, whom God raised up from *the* dead *ones*, in this *name* this *one* stands before you whole.

11 "This One is the Stone" having been despised by you, the *ones* building, the *One* coming to be into *"the* Head of *the* Corner;" *Psa. 118:22*

12 and there is salvation in no other One, for neither is *there* another name under Heaven having been given among men by which it is necessary *for* us to be saved.

13 But beholding the boldness of Peter and John, and having perceived that they are uneducated and untrained men, they marveled. And they recognized them, that they were with Jesus.

14 But seeing the man standing with them, the *one* having been healed, they had nothing to speak against *him.*

15 ¶ But commanding them to go outside the sanhedrin, they conferred together with one another,

16 saying, What may we do to these men? For that a known *miraculous* sign indeed has occurred through them is evident to all the *ones* living in Jerusalem, and we are not able to deny *it.*

17 But that it may not be spread abroad further to the people, let us threaten them with a threat *that* they no longer speak on this name, to no one of men.

18 And calling them, they ordered them not at all to speak, nor to teach on the name of Jesus.

19 But answering them Peter and John said, Whether it is right before God to listen to you rather than God, you judge.

20 For we are not able not to speak what we saw and heard.

21 But having threatened them again, they released them, finding nothing how they might punish them, because of the people, because all glorified God on the thing happening.

22 For the man on whom this *miraculous* sign of healing had occurred was more than forty years of *age.*

23 ¶ And being set free, they came to *their* own and reported to them as many *things* as the chief priests and elders said.

24 And hearing *they* with one passion lifted voice to God and said, Master, You *are the* God, the *One* "making the heaven and the earth and the sea, and all things in them," *Ex. 20:11*

25 who through the mouth of Your servant David said, "Why did the nations rage, and the peoples meditate vain things?

26 The kings of the earth stood up, and the rulers were assembled on the same *day* against the Lord, and against His Anointed *One." Psa. 2:1, 2*

27 For on a truth both Herod and Pontius Pilate, with the nations and *the* peoples of Israel, were assembled against Your holy Servant, Jesus, whom You anointed,

28 to do as many *things* as Your hand and Your purpose pre-determined to occur.

29 And now, Lord, look upon their threatenings and give to Your slaves to speak Your Word with all boldness,

30 in Your hand to stretch out unto healing and *miraculous* signs and wonders to happen through the name of Your holy Servant, Jesus.

31 And they having petitioned, the place in which *they* were gathered was shaken, and they were all filled *with the* Holy Spirit and spoke the Word of God with boldness.

32 ¶ And of the multitude of the *ones* who believing, the heart and the soul were one. And no one said any of the possessions belonging *to* him to be *his* own, but all things were common to them.

33 And with great power the apostles gave testimony of the resurrection of the Lord Jesus, and great grace was upon them all.

34 For neither was anyone needy among them, for as many as were owners of lands or houses, selling *them,* they brought the value of the *things* being sold,

35 and laid *them* at the feet of the apostles. And it was distributed to each *one* according as any had need.

36 And Joses, the *one* being named Barnabas by the apostles, which being translated is, Son of Consolation, a Levite, a Cypriot by nation,

37 a field being his, having sold *it,* he brought the money and placed *it* by the feet of the apostles.

Acts 5

1 ¶ But a certain man named Ananias, with his wife Sapphira, sold a property,

2 and kept back for himself from the price, his wife also being aware *of it,* and bringing a certain part, *he* placed *it* at the feet of the apostles.

3 But Peter said, Ananias, why did Satan fill your heart *for* you to lie to the Holy Spirit and to keep back for yourself from the price of the land?

4 Remaining, did it not remain yours? And being sold, was it *not* in your authority? Why *is it* you put *this thing* into your heart? You did not lie to men, but to God!

5 And hearing these words, Ananias falling down, *he* expired. And great fear came on all the *ones* hearing these words.

6 And rising up the young *men* wrapped him, and carrying out, *they* buried *him.*

7 And it happened, about an interval of three hours, not knowing the *thing* having happened, his wife also came in.

8 And Peter answered her, Tell me if you gave over the land *for* so much? And she said, Yes, of so much.

9 And Peter said to her, Why *was it* that it was agreed with you to tempt the Spirit of *the* Lord? Behold, the feet of the *ones* burying your husband *are* at the door, and they will carry you out.

10 And she immediately fell by his feet and expired. And coming in, the young men found her dead, and carrying *her* out, *they* buried her beside her husband.

11 And great fear came on all the assembly and on all the *ones* hearing these things.

12 ¶ And through the hands of the apostles many *miraculous* signs and wonders among the people took place. And they were all with one mind in Solomon's Porch.

13 But of the rest, no one dared to be joined to them, but the people magnified them.

14 And more believing *ones* were added to *the* Lord, multitudes of both men and of women,

15 so as to bring out the sick *ones* along the streets, and to place *them* on pallets and mattresses, that *at the* coming of Peter, if even his shadow might overshadow some one of them.

16 And also the multitude came together *from* the round about cities, bringing sick *ones* into Jerusalem, and *ones* being disturbed by unclean spirits, who were all being healed.

17 ¶ And rising up, the high priest and all the *ones* with him, which is *the* sect of the Sadducees, were filled of jealousy,

18 and laid their hands on the apostles, and put them publicly in custody.

19 But an angel of *the* Lord opened the doors of the prison during the night, and leading them out, he said,

20 Go! And standing in the temple, speak to the people all the words of this Life.

21 And hearing, they went into the temple about daybreak and were teaching. But having come near, the high priest and the *ones* with him called together the sanhedrin and all the eldership of the sons of Israel. And *they* sent to the jail to have them brought.

22 But having come near, the officers did not find them in the prison. And returning, they reported,

23 saying, Indeed we found the jail having been shut in all security, and the guards outside standing before the doors. But opening *it,* we found no one inside.

24 And when they heard these words, both the priest and the temple commander and the chief priests were perplexed about them, what this might come to be.

25 But having come, someone reported to them, saying, Behold, the men whom you put in the prison are in the temple, standing and teaching the people.

26 ¶ Then the commander going with the officers, *they* brought them, not with force, for they feared the people, that they might not be stoned.

27 And bringing them, they stood *them* in the sanhedrin. And the high priest asked them,

28 saying, Did we not command you by a command *that* you not teach on this name? And, behold, you have filled Jerusalem with

your doctrine and intend to bring on us the blood of this man.

29 But answering Peter and the apostles said, It is right to obey God rather than men.

30 The God of our fathers raised up Jesus, whom you seized, hanging *Him* on a tree.

31 This One God *has* exalted *as* a Ruler and Savior to His right *hand*, to give to Israel repentance and remission of sins.

32 And we are His witnesses of these things, and also the Holy Spirit, whom God gave to the *ones* obeying Him.

33 But the *ones* hearing were cut through, and they took counsel to kill them.

34 But a certain *one* standing up in the sanhedrin, a Pharisee named Gamaliel, a teacher of the Law honored by all the people, commanded the apostles to be put outside a little while.

35 And he said to them, Men, Israelites, take heed to yourselves what you intend to do on these men.

36 For before these days Theudas rose up, claiming himself to be somebody, to whom was joined a number of men, about four hundred, who were killed, and all, as many as were persuaded by him, were dispersed and came to nothing.

37 After this, Judas the Galilean rose up in the days of the Registration. And *he* drew considerable people after him. Yet that one perished, and all were scattered, as many as were persuaded by him.

38 And now I say to you, stand off from these men and leave them alone; because if this counsel is of men, or this work, it will be destroyed.

39 But if it is from God, you will not be able to destroy it, lest even you will be found fighting against God.

40 And they were persuaded by him. And calling the apostles, *and* having scourged them, they charged *them* not to speak on the name of Jesus, and set them free.

41 Then they indeed departed from *the* face of the sanhedrin, rejoicing that they were deemed worthy to be dishonored on behalf of His name.

42 And every day they did not cease teaching and preaching the gospel *of* Jesus the Christ in the temple, and according to *each* house.

Acts 6

1 The apostles, desirous to have the poor regarded, 3 appoint the office of deaconship to seven chosen men.

1 ¶ But in those days, the disciples having multiplied, a murmuring of the Hellenists toward the Hebrews occurred, because their widows were being overlooked in the daily serving.

2 And having called near the multitude of the disciples, the Twelve said, It is not pleasing *to* us, having left the Word of God, to serve tables!

3 Then brothers, be looking for men among you receiving testimony, seven *men* full of *the* Holy Spirit and wisdom, whom we shall appoint over this need.

4 But we shall continue steadfastly in prayer and the service of the Word!

5 And the saying *was* pleasing before all the multitude. And they chose out Stephen, a man full of faith and *the* Holy Spirit, and Philip, and Prochorus, and Nicanor, and Timon, and Parmenas, and Nicolas, a proselyte from Antioch,

6 *each of* whom they made stand before the apostles. And having prayed, they placed *their* hands on them,

7 And the Word of God was growing, and the number of the disciples in Jerusalem was multiplying exceedingly. Even a great crowd of the priests were obeying the faith!

8 ¶ And Stephen, full of faith and power, was doing wonders and great signs among the people.

9 But some of the *ones* of the synagogue being called of *the* Libertines, rose up, also *some* Cyrenians and Alexandrians, and *some* of the *ones* from Cilicia and Asia Minor, disputing with Stephen.

10 And they had no strength to stand against the wisdom and the Spirit by which he spoke.

11 Then they suborned *some* men *to be* saying, We have heard him speaking blasphemous words against Moses and God!

12 And they stirred up the people and the elders and the scribes. And coming on, they together seized him and led him into the sanhedrin.

13 And they stood up false witnesses, *who were* saying, This man does not cease speaking blasphemous words against this holy place and the Law;

14 for we have heard him saying that this One, Jesus the Nazarene, will destroy this place and will change the customs which Moses gave over to us.

15 And having looked intently at him, all the *ones* having sat in the sanhedrin, saw his face as if *it were the* face of an angel.

Acts 7

1 Stephen shows that Abraham worshipped God rightly, and how God chose the fathers 20 before Moses was born: 37 that Moses himself witnessed of Christ. 54 He is stoned to death.

1 ¶ And the high priest said, *Tell me* then if you thus hold these things?

2 And he said, Men, brothers, and fathers, listen! The God of glory appeared to our father Abraham, being in Mesopotamia before he lived in Haran,

3 and said to him, "Go out from your land and from your kindred," "and come into a land which I will show to you." *Gen. 12:1*

4 Then going out from *the* land of the Chaldeans, he lived in Haran. And after his father died, *God* moved him from there into this land in which you now live.

5 And He did not give to him an inheritance in it, not even a step of a foot. And *He* promised to give it to him for a possession and to his seed after him, there being no child to him. *Gen. 17:8*

6 And God spoke thus, that his seed would be an alien in a strange land, and they would enslave it and mistreat *it* four hundred years. *Gen. 15:13*

7 And God said, I will judge the nation to which you will be in bondage." And, After these things they will come out and will serve Me in this place. *Gen. 15:14; Ex. 3:12*

8 And He gave to him a covenant of circumcision; and so he *fathered* Isaac and circumcised him on the eighth day. And Isaac *fathered* Jacob, and Jacob the twelve patriarchs.

9 And being jealous of Joseph, the patriarchs gave *him* over into Egypt; and God was with him,

10 and plucked him out from all his afflictions, and gave him favor and wisdom before Pharaoh *the* king of Egypt. And *Pharaoh* appointed him to be ruling over Egypt and all his household.

11 But a famine came over all the land of Egypt and Canaan, and great affliction. And our fathers did not find food.

12 But hearing grain was in Egypt, Jacob sent our fathers out first.

13 And at the second *time*, Joseph was made known to his brothers, and Joseph's family became known to Pharaoh.

14 And sending, Joseph called his father Jacob and all his kindred, seventy-five souls in *all. See Gen. 46:27*

15 And Jacob went down into Egypt and expired, he and our fathers.

16 And they were carried into Shechem, and were put in the tomb which Abraham bought *for* a price of silver from the sons of Hamor of Shechem.

17 ¶ But as the time of the promise drew near, which God swore to Abraham, the people increased and multiplied in Egypt,

18 until "another king rose up" "who did not know Joseph." *Ex. 1:8*

19 Dealing slyly with our family, this one mistreated our fathers, causing their infants *to be* exposed *so as* not to be kept alive.

20 In which time Moses was born and was truly fair to God; who was reared three months in his father's house.

21 And he being exposed, Pharaoh's daughter took him up and reared him for a son to her.

22 And Moses was instructed in all *the* wisdom of Egyptians and was powerful in words and in works.

23 And when a time of forty years was fulfilled to him, it arose in his heart to look upon his brothers, the sons of Israel.

24 And seeing one being wronged, he defended *him*, and he avenged the *one* being oppressed, striking the Egyptian.

25 And he thought his brothers *would* perceive that God would give them deliverance by his hand. But they did not perceive.

26 And on the following day he appeared to them *while* fighting. And he urged them to peace, saying, Men, you are brothers. Why do you wrong one another?

27 But the *one* wronging the neighbor thrust him away, saying, Who appointed you a ruler and a judge over us?

28 Do you not want to kill me *in* what way you killed the Egyptian yesterday? *Ex. 2:14*

29 "And Moses fled" at this word. "And he became an alien in *the* land of Midian," where he fathered two sons. *Exodus 2:15-22*

30 ¶ And forty years being fulfilled to him, *the* Angel of *the* Lord appeared to him in a flame of fire of a bush in the desert of Mount Sinai.

31 And seeing, Moses marveled at the sight. And he coming up to closely observe, a voice of *the* Lord came to him:

32 "I *am* the God of your fathers, the God of Abraham, and the God of Isaac, and the God of Jacob." *Ex. 3:6, 15* But becoming trembling, Moses did not dare to closely look.

33 And the Lord said to him, "Loose the sandal from your feet, for the place where you stand is holy ground."

34 "Seeing, I saw the mistreatment of My people in Egypt, and I have heard their groaning, and I came down to deliver them. And now, come, I will send you to Egypt. *"Ex. 3:5, 7, 10*

35 This Moses, whom they denied, saying, Who appointed you a ruler and a judge, this *one* God has sent as ruler and redeemer by *the* hand of *the* Angel who appeared to him in the Bush.

36 This *one* led them out, having worked wonders and *miraculous* signs in *the* land of Egypt and in *the* Red Sea, and forty years in the wilderness.

37 This is the Moses, the *one* who said to the sons of Israel, *"The* Lord your God will raise up a Prophet to you from your brothers, *One* like me." You shall hear Him. *Deut. 18:15*

38 This is the one who was in the assembly in the wilderness with the Angel who spoke to him in Mount Sinai, and *with* our fathers, who received living words to give to us,

39 to whom our fathers did not desire to give ear, but thrust *him* away, and turned their hearts back to Egypt,

40 saying to Aaron, "Make for us gods which will go before us; for this Moses who led us out of *the* land of Egypt, we do not know what has happened to him." *Ex. 32:1*

41 And they made a calf in those days, and brought up a sacrifice to the idol, and rejoiced in the works of their hands.

42 ¶ But God turned and gave them over to serve the host of the heaven, as it is written in *the* book of the Prophets: *"Did you* not bring victims and sacrifices to Me forty years in the wilderness, O house of Israel?

43 And you took up the tent of Moloch, and the star of your god Remphan, the figures which you made" "in order to worship them. And I will remove you beyond" Babylon. *Amos 5:25-27*

44 The tent of the testimony was among our fathers in the wilderness, even as the *One* commanded, speaking to Moses to make it according to the pattern which he had seen.

45 which also was brought in, our fathers having inherited with Joshua, in the taking of possession of the nations, whom God thrust out from the face of our fathers, until the days of David,

46 who found favor before God and asked to find a dwelling place for the God of Jacob;

47 but Solomon built Him a house.

48 But the Most High does not dwell in temples made by hand, as the prophet says,

49 "Heaven *is* My throne, and the earth a footstool of My feet; what sort of house will you build Me," "says *the* Lord," "or what the place of My rest?"

50 "Did not My hand make all these things?" *Isa. 66:1, 2*

51 ¶ *Oh* stiffnecked and uncircumcised *ones* in heart and in the ears! You always fall against the Holy Spirit. As your fathers *did*, you also *do*.

52 Which of the prophets did your fathers not persecute? And they killed the *ones* before proclaiming concerning the coming of the Just One, of whom you now have become betrayers and murderers,

53 who received the Law by the ordinances of angels, and did not keep *it*.

54 ¶ And hearing these things, they were cut to their hearts and gnashed the teeth on him.

55 But being full of *the* Holy Spirit, looking intently into the heaven, he saw the glory of God, and Jesus standing at the right of God.

56 And *he* said, Behold, I see the heavens having been opened, and the Son of man standing at the right of God!

57 And crying out with a loud voice, they held their ears and rushed on him with one mind.

58 And throwing *him* outside the city, they stoned *him*. And the witnesses put off their garments at the feet of a young man called Saul.

59 And they stoned Stephen, *he* calling on *God*, and saying, Lord Jesus, receive my spirit.

60 And placing the knees, he cried out with a loud voice, Lord, do not make this sin stand *against* them. And having said this, he fell asleep.

Acts 8

1 The Assembly being planted in Samaria by Philip, 14 Peter and John come to confirm and enlarge it. 26 The angel sends Philip to baptize the Ethiopian eunuch.

1 ¶ And Saul was consenting to the killing of him. And in that day a great persecution took place on the assembly, the *one* in Jerusalem; and all were scattered throughout the regions of Judea and Samaria, except the apostles.

2 But devout men together carried Stephen and made great lamentation over him.

3 But Saul ravaged the assembly, having entered, going in according to the houses; dragging away men and women, he gave *them* over into prison.

4 ¶ Then, indeed, the *ones* being scattered, *were* going about, preaching the gospel, the Word.

5 And going down to a city of Samaria, Philip proclaimed Christ to them.

6 And with one mind the crowds heeded that being said by Philip in their hearing, and seeing the many *miraculous* signs which he did.

7 For many of the *ones* having unclean spirits, crying with a great voice, *they* came out. And many who had been weakened and lame *ones* were healed.

8 And great joy was in that city.

9 But a certain man, Simon by name, had long been doing magic in the city and amazing the nation of Samaria, claiming himself to be someone great;

10 to whom all were paying attention to *him*, from small to great, saying, This *one* is the great power of God.

11 And they were paying attention to him because for a long time *he* had amazed them *with his* doing magic.

12 But when they believed Philip preaching the gospel, the things concerning the kingdom of God, and the name of Jesus Christ, they were baptized, both men and women.

13 And Simon himself also believed, and being baptized was continuing steadfastly with Philip. And seeing *miraculous* signs and mighty works happening, he was amazed.

14 ¶ And the apostles in Jerusalem, hearing that Samaria had received the Word of God, they sent Peter and John to them,

15 who going down prayed concerning them so that they may receive *the* Holy Spirit;

16 for He had not yet fallen on no one of them, but they were only being baptized into the name of the Lord Jesus.

17 Then they laid hands on them, and they received *the* Holy Spirit.

18 But Simon having seen that the Holy Spirit is given through the laying on of the hands of the apostles, he offered them money,

19 saying, Give to me also this authority that to whomever I may lay on the hands he may receive *the* Holy Spirit.

20 But Peter said to him, May your silver be with you into destruction, because you thought to get the gift of God through money.

21 There is neither part nor lot to you in this matter, for your heart is not upright before the face of God.

22 Repent, therefore, from this wickedness of you, and petition God if perhaps you will be forgiven the thought of your heart.

23 For I see you being into *the* gall of bitterness and the bond of unrighteousness.

24 And answering Simon said, You petition to the Lord for me, so that nothing of the *things* which you have spoken may come on me.

25 Then indeed having earnestly testified and having spoken the Word of the Lord,

they returned to Jerusalem, even having preached the gospel to many villages of the Samaritans.

26 ¶ But an angel of *the* Lord spoke to Philip, saying, Rise up and go along south on the way going down from Jerusalem to Gaza. This is *a* deserted *place*.

27 And rising up he went. And, behold, a man, an Ethiopian, a eunuch, a potentate *with* Candace, the queen of *the* Ethiopians, who was over all her treasure, who had come to Jerusalem to worship!

28 And *he* was returning. And sitting on his chariot he read the prophet Isaiah.

29 And the Spirit said to Philip, Go near and join yourself to this chariot.

30 And running near Philip heard him reading the prophet Isaiah, and said, Then, indeed, do you know what you are reading?

31 But he said, How should I be able except someone shall guide me? And he called Philip near, coming up, to sit with him.

32 And the content of the Scripture which he was reading was this: "He was led as a sheep to slaughter, and as a lamb is voiceless before the *one* shearing it, so He does not open His mouth.

33 In His humiliation His judgment was taken away. And who will recount His generation? For His life is taken away from the earth." *Isa. 53:7, 8*

34 And answering the eunuch said to Philip, I ask you, about whom does the prophet say this? About himself, or about some other *one*.

35 And opening his mouth, and beginning from this Scripture, Philip preached the gospel to him, Jesus.

36 And as they were going along the way they came on some water. And the eunuch said, Behold, water! What prevents me to be baptized?

37 And Philip said, If you believe from all the heart, it is lawful. And answering he said, I believe Jesus Christ to be the Son of God.

38 And he commanded the chariot to stand still. And both went down into the water, both Philip and the eunuch; and he baptized him.

39 And when they came up out of the water, *the* Spirit of *the* Lord caught away Philip. And the eunuch did not see him any more; for he went his way rejoicing.

40 And Philip was found at Azotus. And passing through he preached the gospel to all the cities until his coming to Caesarea.

Acts 9

1 Saul, going towards Damascus, 4 is stricken to the earth, 10 is called to the apostleship, 18 and is baptized by Ananias. 33 Peter heals Aeneas' paralysis, 36 and restores Tabitha to life.

1 ¶ But Saul, still breathing threat and murder toward the disciples of the Lord, coming to the high priest,

2 *he* asked from him letters to Damascus, to the synagogues, so that if he found any being of the Way, both men and women, *they* having been bound, he might bring *them* to Jerusalem.

3 But in the going it happened *for* him to draw near to Damascus, and suddenly a light from the heaven shone around him.

4 And falling on the earth he heard a voice saying to him, Saul, Saul! Why are you persecuting Me?

5 And he said, Sir, who are You? And the Lord said, I am Jesus, whom you are persecuting; *it is hard for you to kick against the goads.*

6 *Both trembling and being astonished he said, Lord, what do You desire me to do?* And the Lord *said* to him, Rise up and go into the city, and it will be told you what you must do.

7 But the men traveling with him had been standing speechless, indeed hearing the sound, but seeing no one.

8 And Saul was lifted up from the earth, but his eyes having been opened he saw no one. And leading him by the hand they brought *him* to Damascus.

9 And he was three days not seeing, and did not eat or drink.

10 ¶ And there was a certain disciple in Damascus, Ananias by name. And the Lord said to him in a vision, Ananias! And he said, Behold, Lord, I *am here.*

11 And the Lord *said* to him, Rising up go along on the street, the *one* being called Straight, and seek a Tarsian, Saul by name, in *the* house of Judas. For, behold, he is praying.

12 And *he* has seen in a vision a man, Ananias by name, coming in and putting a hand on him, so that he may see again.

13 And Ananias answered, Lord, I have heard from many about this man, how many bad things he did to Your saints in Jerusalem.

14 And here he has authority from the chief priests to bind all the *ones* calling on Your name.

15 And the Lord said to him, Go, for this one is a vessel of election to Me, to bear My name before nations and kings and *the* sons of Israel.

16 For I will show him how much he must suffer for the sake of My name.

17 And Ananias went away and entered into the house. And putting hands on him *he* said, Brother Saul, the Lord has sent me, Jesus, the *One* who appeared to you in the way which you came, that you may see again and be filled of *the* Holy Spirit.

18 And instantly fell away from his eyes as if *it were* scales. And rising up, *he* was baptized.

19 And taking food he was strengthened. And Saul was with the disciples in Damascus some days.

20 And at once in the synagogues he proclaimed the Christ, that this One is the Son of God.

21 And all the *ones* hearing were amazed and said, Not this one is the *one* destroying the *ones* calling on this Name in Jerusalem, and he had come here for this, that he might take *them,* having been bound, before the chief priests?

22 But Saul was more filled with power, and *he* confounded the Jews, the *ones* living in Damascus, proving that this One is the Christ.

23 ¶ And when many days were fulfilled, the Jews plotted together to kill him.

24 But their plot was known to Saul. And they carefully watched the gates both by day and by night so as to kill him.

25 But taking him by night, the disciples let him down through the wall, lowering in a basket.

26 And Saul arriving into Jerusalem, he tried to be joined to the disciples. And all feared him, not believing that he is a disciple.

27 But taking hold of him, Barnabas led *him* to the apostles and told them how he saw the Lord in the way, and that He spoke to him, and how in Damascus he spoke boldly in the name of Jesus.

28 And he was with them, entering in and going out in Jerusalem, and speaking boldly in the name of the Lord Jesus.

29 And he spoke and disputed with the Hellenists, and they took him in hand to kill him.

30 But knowing, the brothers led him down to Caesarea and sent him forth to Tarsus.

31 Then, indeed, the assemblies throughout all Judea, and Galilee, and Samaria, had peace, being built up and going on in the fear of the Lord, and in the comfort of the Holy Spirit, were multiplying.

32 ¶ And it happened, *that* Peter, passing through all *those parts,* also came down to the saints, the *ones* dwelling in Lydda.

33 And he found there a certain man, Aeneas by name, who had been lying on a pallet eight years, who was paralyzed.

34 And Peter said to him, Aeneas! Jesus the Christ heals you; rise up and spread for yourself. And instantly he rose up.

35 And all the *ones* dwelling in Lydda and the Sharon *Plain* saw him, who *then* turned to the Lord.

36 ¶ And in Joppa was a certain disciple Tabitha by name, which translated is called Dorcas *(Gazelle).* She was full of good works and of merciful deeds which she did.

37 And it happened in those days, being feeble, she died. And bathing her, they put *her* in an upper room.

38 And Lydda being near to Joppa, the disciples hearing that Peter is in it, they sent two men to him, entreating *him* not to delay to come to them.

39 And rising up Peter went with them, whom arriving they led *him* to the upper room. And all the widows stood by him, weeping and showing tunics and garments how many *things* Dorcas made *while* being with them.

40 And having put all out, placing the knees, Peter prayed. And turning to the body he said, Tabitha, Arise! And she opened her eyes; and seeing Peter she sat up.

41 And giving her a hand he raised her up. And calling the saints and the widows he presented her living.

42 And it became known throughout all Joppa. And many believed on the Lord.

43 And it was considerable days *that* he remained in Joppa with one Simon, a tanner.

Acts 10

1 Cornelius, a devout man, 5 being commanded by an angel, sends for Peter. 44 The Holy Ghost falls on the company, 48 and they are baptized.

1 ¶ But a certain man, Cornelius by name, was in Caesarea, a centurion of a cohort. the *one* being called Italian,

2 a devout *one* and fearing God, with all his household, both doing many merciful deeds to the people and praying to God through all.

3 About the ninth hour of the day, he saw clearly in a vision an angel of God coming to him, and saying to him, Cornelius!

4 And he was staring at him, and becoming terrified he said, What is it, Lord? And he said to him, Your prayers and your merciful deeds went up for a memorial before God.

5 And now send men to Joppa and call for Simon who is being called Peter.

6 This *one* is lodged with a certain Simon, a tanner, to whom is a house by *the* sea. This one will tell you what you must do.

7 And went away the angel, the *one* speaking to Cornelius, *who* calling two of his servants and a devout soldier of the *ones* continually waiting on him,

8 and explaining all things to them, he sent away them to Joppa.

9 ¶ And on the next day, those *ones* traveling on *the* road, and drawing near to the city, Peter went up on the housetop to pray about *the* sixth hour.

10 And he became hungry and wished to taste *food.* But *as* they *were* preparing, an ecstasy fell on him.

11 And he saw the heaven having been opened and a certain vessel like a great sheet coming down on him, being bound by four corners, and let down onto the earth;

12 in which were all the four-footed animals of the earth, and the wild beasts, and the reptiles, and the birds of the heaven.

13 And a voice came to him, Rise up, Peter, slay and eat.

14 But Peter said, Not at all, Lord, because I never did eat anything common or unclean.

15 And again a voice *came* to him a second *time*, What things God made clean, you do not make common.

16 And this happened three *times*, and the vessel was taken up into the heaven again.

17 And as Peter was perplexed within himself what the vision which he saw might be, even behold, the men, the *ones* having been sent from Cornelius, having inquired for the house of Simon, stood on the porch.

18 And calling out, they inquired if Simon being called Peter is lodged here.

19 ¶ And *as* Peter pondered concerning the vision, the Spirit said to him, Behold, three men are seeking you.

20 But rising up, go down and go with them, not discriminating, because I have sent them.

21 And going down to the men, the *ones* being sent from Cornelius to him, Peter said, Behold, I am *the one* whom you seek. What is the cause for which you are here?

22 And the *ones* said, Cornelius, a centurion, a just man and *one* fearing God, and being testified to by all the nation of the Jews, was divinely warned by a holy angel to call you to his house and to hear words from you.

23 Then calling them in, he lodged *them.* And on the next day Peter went out with them. And some of the brothers from Joppa accompanied him.

24 And on the next day they entered Caesarea. And Cornelius was awaiting them, having called together his relatives and *his* intimate friends.

25 And as Peter was coming in, meeting him, Cornelius fell at *his* feet *and* worshiped.

26 But Peter lifted him up, saying, Stand up! I myself am also a man.

27 And talking with him, he went in and found many having come together.

28 And he said to them, You know how unlawful it is *for* a man, a Jew, to unite with or to come near to a foreign *man.* And yet God showed to me not to call a man, not one, common or unclean.

29 Therefore, I also came without objecting, having been sent for. Therefore I ask for what reason did you send for me?

30 And Cornelius said, From *the* fourth day until this hour I was fasting, and the ninth hour

I was praying in my house. And, behold, a man stood before me in bright clothing.

31 And he said, Cornelius, your prayer was heard and your merciful deeds were remembered before God.

32 Therefore, send to Joppa and call for Simon who is called Peter; this *one* is lodged in *the* house of Simon, a tanner, by *the* sea; who coming, *he* will speak to you.

33 Therefore at once I sent to you, and you did well *to* come. Now then, we are all present before God to hear all the things having been commanded you by God.

34 ¶ And opening *his* mouth, Peter said, Truly I see that God is not a respecter of faces,

35 but in every nation the *one* fearing Him and working righteousness is acceptable to Him.

36 The Word which He sent to the sons of Israel, preaching the gospel of peace through Jesus Christ, this One is Lord of all.

37 You know the thing that happened throughout all Judea, beginning from Galilee after the baptism that John proclaimed,

38 Jesus the *One* from Nazareth, how God anointed Him with *the* Holy Spirit and with power, who went about doing good, and healing all the *ones* being oppressed by the devil, because God was with Him.

39 And we are witnesses of all things which He did, both in the country of the Jews, and in Jerusalem, whom they killed, hanging *Him* on a tree.

40 God raised up this *One* the third day and gave to Him to become visible;

41 not to all the people, but to witnesses, the *ones* having been before hand-picked by God, to us who ate and drank with Him after His rising again from *the* dead.

42 And He commanded us to proclaim to the people and to witness solemnly that it is *He* Himself who has been marked out by God *to be* Judge of *the* living and *the* dead.

43 To this *One* all the Prophets witness, *so that* through His name everyone believing into Him *will* receive remission of sins.

44 ¶ As Peter was yet speaking these words, the Holy Spirit fell on all the *ones* hearing the Word.

45 And were amazed the *ones* of faithful circumcision, as many as came with Peter, because the gift of the Holy Spirit was poured out on the nations also.

46 For they heard them speaking in languages and magnifying God. Then Peter answered,

47 Not is able anyone to forbid the water that these not be baptized, who the Holy Spirit received, even as we also?

48 And he commanded them to be baptized in the name of the Lord. Then they asked him to remain some days.

Acts 11

1 Peter, accused for going in to the nations, 5 makes his defense. 19 The gospel being spread into Phoenicia, and Cyprus, and Antioch, Barnabas is sent to confirm them.

1 ¶ And the apostles and the brothers, the *ones* who were throughout Judea, heard that the nations also received the Word of God.

2 And when Peter went up to Jerusalem, the *ones* of the circumcision disputed with him,

3 saying, You went in to uncircumcised men and ate with them.

4 But beginning, Peter set out to them in order, saying,

5 I was being in *the* city of Joppa, praying. And in an ecstasy, I saw a vision: a certain vessel was coming down, like a great sheet, being let down by four corners out of the heaven; and it came as far as me.

6 into which gazing, looking intently, even I saw the four-footed *animals* of the earth, and the wild beasts, and the reptiles, and the birds of the heaven.

7 And I heard a voice saying to me, Peter, rise up, slay and eat.

8 But I said, Not at all, Lord, because every *thing* common or unclean never entered into my mouth.

9 But a voice answered me the second *time* out of the heaven, What *things* God made clean, you must not make common.

10 And this took place three *times*, and all things were pulled up into the heaven again.

11 And, behold, at once three men stood at the house in which I was, having been sent from Caesarea to me.

12 And the Spirit said to me to go with them, not discriminating. And these six brothers also *were* with me, and we went into the man's house.

13 And he told us how he saw an angel in his house, standing and saying to him, Send men to Joppa and call for Simon, being called Peter,

14 who will speak words to you by which you and all your household will be saved.

15 And in my beginning to speak, the Holy Spirit fell on them, as also on us in *the* beginning.

16 And I recalled the Word of *the* Lord, how He said, John indeed baptized with water, but you shall be baptized in *the* Holy Spirit.

17 Then if God gave the same gift to them as also to us, believing on the Lord Jesus Christ, and I, who was I to be able to hinder God?

18 And hearing these things, they were silent and glorified God, saying, Then God also gave to the nations repentance unto life.

19 ¶ Then, indeed, the *ones* who were dispersed by the oppression, the *one* having occurred over Stephen, passed through to Phoenicia and Cyprus and Antioch, speaking the Word to no one, if not to Jews only.

20 But some of them were men, Cypriots and Cyrenians, who entering into Antioch, spoke to the Hellenists, preaching the gospel of the Lord Jesus.

21 And *the* hand of *the* Lord was with them, and a great number believing turned to the Lord.

22 And the Word about them was heard into the ears of the assembly in Jerusalem. And they sent out Barnabas to go through as far as Antioch;

23 who having come, and seeing the grace of God, rejoiced. And he exhorted all with purpose of heart to abide near the Lord.

24 For he was a good man, and full of *the* Holy Spirit and of faith. And a considerable crowd was added to the Lord.

25 And Barnabas went out to Tarsus to seek Saul.

26 And finding him, he brought him to Antioch. And it happened that *for* them to be assembled to them in the assembly a whole year. And they taught a considerable crowd. And the disciples were first called Christians at Antioch.

27 ¶ And in these days prophets came down from Jerusalem into Antioch.

28 And rising up one of them, Agabus by name, signified through the Spirit that a great famine was about to be over all the inhabited earth, which also happened on Claudius Caesar's *time*.

29 And according as any was prospered, the disciples, each of them, determined to send for ministry to the brothers living in Judea,

30 which they also did, sending to the elders through *the* hand of Barnabas and Saul.

Acts 12

1 King Herod persecutes the Christians, kills James, 6 and imprisons Peter. 20 In his pride, he is stricken by an angel, and dies miserably.

1 ¶ And at that time Herod the king put on the hands to mistreat some of the *ones* from the assembly.

2 And he killed James the brother of John with a sword.

3 And seeing that it was pleasing to the Jews, he added also to seize Peter (and they were *the* days of Unleavened *Bread*),

4 whom capturing *him* also, he put *him* into prison, giving *him over* to four sets of four soldiers to guard him, intending to bring him up to the people after the Passover.

5 ¶ Therefore Peter was indeed kept in the prison, but fervent prayer was made by the assembly to God on his behalf.

6 But when Herod was about to bring him out, in that night Peter was sleeping between two soldiers, having been bound with two chains, also guards were before the door keeping the prison.

7 And, behold! An angel of *the* Lord stood by, and a light shone in the building. And striking Peter's side, he aroused him, saying, Rise up in haste! And the chains fell off from *his* hands.

8 And the angel said to him, Gird yourself, and bind on your sandals. And he did so. And he said to him, Throw around your garment and follow me.

9 And going out, he followed him, and did not know that this happening through the angel was true, but he thought he saw a vision.

10 And going through a first and a second guard, they came on the iron gate leading into the city, which opened to them of itself. And going out, they went on one street; and instantly the angel withdrew from him.

11 And Peter coming to be within himself said, Now I know truly that *the* Lord

sent out His angel and delivered me out of Herod's hand, and *out* of all the expectation of the people of the Jews.

12 And comprehending, he came onto the house of Mary the mother of John, the *one* being called Mark, where many were gathered together, and praying.

13 And Peter knocking *at* the door of the porch, a slave-girl, Rhoda by name, came near to answer.

14 And recognizing Peter's voice, from joy she did not open the porch, but running in she reported Peter to stand before the porch.

15 But the *ones* said to her, You are raving. But she insisted, holding *it* to be so. And the *ones* said, It is his angel.

16 But Peter was continuing knocking. And opening, they saw him and were amazed.

17 And signaling to them with the hand to be silent, he told them how the Lord led him out of the prison. And he said, Report these things to James and the brothers. And going out, he went to another place.

18 And day having come, there was not a little disturbance among the soldiers, *saying*, What, then, became *of* Peter?

19 And searching for him, and not finding *him*, examining the guards, Herod commanded them to be led away. And going down from Judea to Caesarea, *he* spent time *there*.

20 ¶ And Herod *was* very angry with *the* Tyrians and Sidonians. But with one mind they came to him. And persuading Blastus, the *one* over the king's bedroom, they begged peace, because their country was fed from the royal *bounty*.

21 And on a set day, having put on regal clothing, and sitting on the tribunal, Herod made a speech to them.

22 And the people cried out, The voice of a god, and not of a man!

23 And instantly an angel of *the* Lord struck him, because he did not give the glory to God. And having been eaten of worms, he breathed out his soul.

24 But the Word of God grew and increased.

25 And Barnabas and Saul returned from Jerusalem, having fulfilled the ministry, and having taken with *them* the *one* being called Mark.

Acts 13

1 Paul and Barnabas go to the nations 7 Of Sergius Paulus, and Elymas the magician. 14 Paul preaches at Antioch, that Jesus is the Christ. 42 The nations believe; 45 but the Jews gainsay and blaspheme; 46 so they turn to the nations.

1 ¶ And in Antioch some among the existing assembly were prophets and teachers: both Barnabas and Simeon, the *one* being called Niger, and Lucius the Cyrenian, and Manaen, brought up with Herod the tetrarch, and Saul.

2 And *they* doing service to the Lord and fasting, the Holy Spirit said, Now separate both Barnabas and Saul to Me, for the work to which I have called them.

3 Then, having fasted and prayed, and placing hands on them, they let *them* go.

4 ¶ Then these indeed sent out by the Holy Spirit went down to Seleucia, and from there sailed away to Cyprus.

5 And coming unto Salamis, they preached the Word of God in the synagogues of the Jews. And they also had John as a helper.

6 And passing through the island as far as Paphos, they found a certain magician, a false prophet, a Jew named Bar-jesus,

7 who was with the proconsul, Sergius Paulus, an intelligent man. This *one* calling Barnabas and Saul to him, he sought to hear the Word of God.

8 But Elymas, the magician, withstood them (for so his name is translated) seeking to turn the proconsul away from the faith.

9 But Saul, the *one* also *is* Paul, being filled with *the* Holy Spirit, and looking intently on him,

10 said, O son of the devil, full of all deceit and of all villainy, hostile *to* all righteousness, will you not stop perverting the right ways of *the* Lord?

11 And now, behold, *the* hand of the Lord *is* on you, and you will be blind, not seeing the sun until a time. And instantly a mist and darkness fell on him, and going about he sought *some to* lead *him* by the hand.

12 Then the proconsul seeing the thing happening, he believed, being astounded at the doctrine of the Lord.

13 And setting sail from Paphos *with* those around *him*, Paul came to Perga of

Pamphylia. But John departing from them, returned to Jerusalem.

14 ¶ But going through from Perga, they came to Antioch-Pisidia, and going into the synagogue on the day of the sabbaths, they sat down.

15 And after the reading of the Law, and of the Prophets, the synagogue rulers sent to them, saying, Men, brothers, if there is a word of exhortation to the people, speak.

16 And rising up, and signaling with his hand, Paul said, Men, Israelites, and the *ones* fearing God, hear.

17 The God of this people Israel chose out our fathers, and lifted up the people in the sojourn in *the* land *of* Egypt. And with a high arm, He led them out of it.

18 And *for* about forty years time, He endured them in the wilderness. *Deut. 1:31*

19 And *He* pulled down seven nations in Canaan land, *and* gave their land to them as an inheritance. *Deut. 7:1*

20 And after these things, about four hundred and fifty years, He gave judges until Samuel the prophet.

21 And from there they asked *for* a king. And God gave Saul *the* son of Kish to them, a man of *the* tribe of Benjamin, *for* forty years.

22 And removing him, He raised up to them David for a king, to whom He also said, witnessing, I found David the *son* of Jesse *"to be* a man according to My *own* heart," who will do all My will. *1 Samuel 13:14; Psa. 89:20;*

23 From the seed of this one, according to promise, God raised up to Israel a Savior, Jesus;

24 John going before to proclaim before the face of His entrance a baptism of repentance to all the people of Israel.

25 And as John fulfilled the course, he said, Whom do you suppose me to be? Not I AM, but, behold, "He comes after me, *One* of whom I am not worthy to loose the sandal of *His* feet." *John 1:27*

26 Men, brothers, sons of *the* race of Abraham, and the *ones* among you fearing God, to you the Word of this salvation was sent.

27 For the *ones* dwelling in Jerusalem, and their rulers, not knowing this *One*, and

the voices of the prophets, the *ones* being read according to every sabbath, condemning *Him*, they fulfilled *the Scriptures*.

28 And finding no cause of death, they asked Pilate to kill Him.

29 And when they finished all the things having been written concerning Him, taking *Him* down from the tree, they laid *Him* in a tomb.

30 But God raised Him from *the* dead *ones*;

31 who appeared for many days to the *ones* coming up with Him from Galilee to Jerusalem, who are witnesses of Him to the people.

32 And we preach the gospel to you, the promise to the fathers having come into being,

33 that this God has fulfilled to us, their children, raising up Jesus; as also it is written in the second Psalm, "You are My Son, today I have begotten You." *Psa. 2:7*

34 And that He raised Him from *the* dead, no more being about to return to corruption, therefore He has said, "I will give You" "the faithful *and* holy things of David." *Isaiah 55:3*

35 Therefore He also said in another, "You will not give Your Holy One to see corruption." *LXX-Psa. 15:10; MT-Psa. 16:10*

36 For having served *his* own generation by the purpose of God, David truly fell asleep and was added to his fathers and saw corruption. *1 Kings. 2:10*

37 But *He* whom God raised up, *He* did not see corruption.

38 Therefore let it be known to you, men, brothers, that through this *One* is proclaimed to you remission of sins.

39 And from all the things from which you could not be justified in the Law of Moses, in this *One* every *one* believing is justified.

40 Therefore watch *that* the *things* spoken in the Prophets may not come on you:

41 "Behold, the despisers," "and marvel," "and perish, because I work a work in your days," a work which you will "not believe, not *even* if someone fully declares *it* to you," not *one*. *Hab. 1:5*

42 ¶ But the Jews going out of the synagogue, the nations begged that these words be spoken to them unto the next sabbath.

43 And the synagogue being broken up, many of the Jews and of the devout proselytes followed Paul and Barnabas, who

speaking *to them* persuaded them to continue in the grace of God.

44 But on the coming sabbath, almost all the city was gathered to hear the Word of God.

45 And the Jews seeing the crowds, they were filled with jealousy, and contradicted the things being spoken by Paul, contradicting and blaspheming.

46 But speaking boldly, Paul and Barnabas said, It was necessary *for* the Word of God to be spoken first to you; but since you indeed thrust it away and judge yourselves not worthy of eternal life, behold, we turn to the nations.

47 For so the Lord has commanded us, "I have set You for a Light of nations, that You be for salvation to *the* end of the earth." *Isa. 49:6*

48 And hearing, the nations rejoiced and glorified the Word of the Lord. And as many as were appointed to eternal life believed.

49 And the Word of the Lord was borne through all the country.

50 But the Jews incited the devout and honorable women, and the first *ones* of the city, and raised up a persecution against Paul and Barnabas, and threw them out from their borders.

51 But these shaking off the dust of their feet on them, they came into Iconium.

52 And the disciples were filled with joy and *the* Holy Spirit.

Acts 14

1 Paul and Barnabas are persecuted. 8 At Lystra Paul heals a cripple, 19 and is stoned. 26 At Antioch, the disciples report what God had done.

1 ¶ And it happened in Iconium, according to the same they entered into the synagogue of the Jews, and spoke thus, so that a large multitude of both Jews and Greeks *came* to believe.

2 But the unbelieving Jews excited and embittered the souls of the nations against the brothers.

3 Therefore, they stayed a considerable time, speaking boldly on the Lord, witnessing to the Word of His grace, and *He* giving *miraculous* signs and wonders to occur through their hands.

4 But the multitude of the city was divided; and the *ones* were with the Jews, but the *other ones* with the apostles.

5 And when a rush of the nations occurred, and both the Jews with their rulers *came* to shamefully treat and to stone them,

6 perceiving *it* all, they fled to the cities of Lycaonia, Lystra and Derbe, and the region around.

7 And there they were preaching the gospel.

8 And a certain man was sitting in Lystra, powerless in the feet, being lame from his mother's womb, who had never walked.

9 This *one* hearing Paul speaking, who, looking intently at him, and seeing that he had faith to be cured,

10 *he* said with a great voice, Stand up erect on your feet! And he leaped up and walked about.

11 And seeing what Paul did, the crowd lifted up their voice in Lycaonian, saying, The gods have come down to us, becoming like men.

12 And they called Barnabas, Zeus, and Paul, Hermes, because he was the *one* leading in the word.

13 And the priest of Zeus being before their city, bringing bulls and garlands to the gates, *he* wished to sacrifice along with the crowds.

14 But Paul and Barnabas, the apostles, hearing, tearing their garments, they leaped out into the crowd, crying out,

15 and saying, Men, why do you do these things? We also are men of like feelings to you, preaching the gospel to you to turn *you* from these vain *things* to the living God, who "made the heaven and the earth and the sea, and all the things in them," *Ex. 20:11*

16 who in the generations having passed allowed all the nations to go in their *own* ways.

17 And yet He did not leave Himself without witness, doing good, giving rain and fruitful seasons to us from heaven, filling our hearts with food and gladness.

18 And saying these things, they hardly settled down the crowds, *that they* not sacrifice to them.

19 ¶ But Jews came there from Antioch and Iconium, and having persuaded the

crowds, and having stoned Paul, they dragged *him* outside the city, supposing him to have died.

20 But the disciples surrounding him, arising he entered into the city. And on the next day he went out with Barnabas to Derbe.

21 And having preached the gospel to that city, and having made considerable disciples, they returned to Lystra and Iconium and Antioch,

22 confirming the souls of the disciples, exhorting to continue in the faith, and that through many afflictions we must enter into the kingdom of God.

23 And having hand-picked elders for them in every assembly, having prayed with fastings, they committed them to the Lord into whom they had believed.

24 And passing through Pisidia, they came to Pamphylia.

25 And speaking the Word in Perga, they came down to Attalia,

26 and from there they sailed away to Antioch, from where they were being given over to the grace of God for the work which they fulfilled.

27 And arriving, and gathering the assembly, they reported as many things God did with them and that He opened a door of faith to the nations.

28 And they remained there not a little time with the disciples.

Acts 15

1 Dissension arises touching circumcision. 39 Paul and Barnabas fall at strife, and depart asunder.

1 ¶ And some, coming down from Judea, were teaching the brothers, *saying,* If *you are* not circumcised *in* the custom of Moses, you are not able to be saved.

2 Therefore strife and not a little discussion with them occurring by Paul and Barnabas, they appointed Paul and Barnabas and some others of them to go up into Jerusalem to the apostles and elders concerning this question.

3 Therefore, indeed, being sent forward by the assembly they passed through Phoenicia and Samaria, relating in detail the conversion of the nations. And they caused great joy *among* all the brothers.

4 And arriving into Jerusalem, they were welcomed by the assembly and the apostles and the elders. And *they* reported as many things as God did with them.

5 But some of the *ones* rose up from the sect of the Pharisees, having believed, saying, It is necessary to circumcise them and to command *them* to keep the Law of Moses.

6 ¶ And the apostles and the elders were assembled to see about this matter.

7 And much discussion having occurred, rising up Peter said to them: Men, brothers, you recognize that from ancient days, God chose among us *that* through my mouth the nations *should* hear the Word of the gospel, and to believe.

8 And God, the knower of hearts, testified to them, giving them the Holy Spirit, even as also to us.

9 And He distinguished in nothing between both us and them, having purified their hearts by faith.

10 Now, therefore, why do you test God by putting a yoke on the neck of the disciples which neither our fathers nor we had strength to bear?

11 But through the grace of *the* Lord Jesus Christ, we believe to be saved, according to which manner those also *believed.*

12 And all the multitude was silent and were hearing Barnabas and Paul recounting as many things as God did through them among the nations, *even* the *miraculous* signs and wonders.

13 And after they were silent, James answered, saying, Men, brothers, hear me:

14 Simon recounted *how* even as *at* first God oversaw to take a people out from *among the* nations for His name.

15 And with this agree the words of the prophets, as it is written,

16 After these things "I" will return and "will build again the tabernacle of David, the *one* having fallen," "and I will build again the things " being destroyed of it, and I will set it up, *Amos 9:11, 12*

17 so that the remaining *ones* of men may seek the Lord, "even all the nations on whom My name has been called, says the Lord, the *One* doing all these things." *Amos 9:11, 12*

18 Known to God from eternity are all His works.

19 For this reason I judge not to cause trouble to the *ones* from the nations turning to God,

20 but to write to them to hold back from the pollutions of idols, and *from* fornication, and *from* the strangled *thing*, and blood.

21 For in according to a city from ancient generations Moses has the *ones* proclaiming him, being read in the synagogues according to every sabbath.

22 ¶ Then it seemed *good* to the apostles and the elders, with all the assembly, to send men being chosen from them to Antioch with Paul and Barnabas, Judas, the *one* being called Barsabas, and Silas, men leading among the the the brothers,

23 writing by their hand these things: The apostles and the elders and the brothers, to the brothers throughout Antioch, and Syria, and Cilicia, the *ones* from *the* nations: Greeting.

24 Since we heard that some of us going out have troubled you with words, unsettling your souls, saying, Be circumcised and keep the Law, to whom we gave no command;

25 it seemed *good* to us, having become of one mind, to send men being chosen out to you along with our beloved Barnabas and Paul,

26 men who have given over their souls on behalf of the name of our Lord, Jesus Christ.

27 Therefore, we have sent Judas and Silas, they by word also announcing the same things.

28 For it seemed *good* to the Holy Spirit and to us to put on you no more burden except these necessary *things*:

29 To hold back from idol sacrifices, and *from* blood, and *from* the strangled *thing*, and *from* fornication; from which carefully keeping yourselves, you will do well. Farewell.

30 Then they indeed being let go, they came to Antioch. And having assembled the multitude, *they* delivered the letter.

31 And reading *it*, they rejoiced at the comfort.

32 And Judas and Silas, themselves also being prophets, exhorted the brothers through much speech, and confirmed *them*.

33 And having made time, they were let go with peace from the brothers to the apostles.

34 But it seemed good to Silas to remain there.

35 And Paul and Barnabas spent time in Antioch, teaching and preaching the gospel, the Word of the Lord, with many others also.

36 ¶ And after some days Paul said to Barnabas, Indeed, Returning, let us look after our brothers throughout every city in which we proclaimed the Word of the Lord, how they have *fared*.

37 But Barnabas purposed to take John with *them*, the *one* being called Mark.

38 But Paul thought it fitting, *he* having withdrawn from them from Pamphylia, and not going with them to the work, not to take this *one* with *them*.

39 Therefore sharp contention happened, so as to be separated them from each other. And taking Mark, Barnabas sailed away to Cyprus.

40 But choosing Silas, Paul went out, being given over to the grace of God by the brothers,

41 and he went through Syria and Cilicia, making the assemblies strong.

Acts 16

1 Paul having circumcised Timothy, 14 Lydia believes. 16 He casts out a spirit of divination. 19 He and Silas are beaten and imprisoned.

1 ¶ And he arrived in Derbe and Lystra. And behold, a certain disciple by name Timothy was there, *the* son of a certain believing Jewish woman, but *his* father *was* a Greek.

2 who was testified to by the brothers in Lystra and Iconium.

3 Paul desired this *one* to go forth with him, and taking *him he* circumcised him, because of the Jews being in those places. For they all knew his father, that he was a Greek.

4 And as they went through the cities, they gave over to them to keep the decrees, the *ones* having been decided by the apostles and the elders in Jerusalem.

5 Therefore, indeed, the assemblies were being made stronger in the faith, and increased in number according to a day.

6 ¶ And passing through Phrygia and the Galatian region, being forbidden by the Holy Spirit to speak the Word in Asia,

7 coming against Mysia, they attempted to go alongside Bithynia, and the Spirit did not allow them.

8 And passing by Mysia, they came down into Troas.

9 And a vision appeared to Paul during the night: a certain man of Macedonia *was* standing, entreating him and saying, Passing over into Macedonia, help us!

10 And when he saw the vision, we immediately sought to go forth into Macedonia, concluding that the Lord had called us to preach the gospel *to* them.

11 Therefore setting sail from Troas, we ran a straight course into Samothrace, and on the next *day* into Neapolis,

12 and from there into Philippi, which is the first city of that part of Macedonia, a colony. And we were in this city, spending some days.

13 And on the day of the sabbaths, we went outside the city beside a river, where was supposed to be a place of prayer . And sitting down, we spoke to the women having come together *there*.

14 And a certain woman, Lydia by name, a seller of purple of *the* city of Thyatira, *one* worshiping God, heard *us*, whose heart the Lord opened thoroughly to pay attention to the things being spoken by Paul.

15 And as she and her household were baptized, she entreated *Paul*, saying, If you have judged me to be a believing *one* in the Lord, entering into my house, remain. And she strongly urged us.

16 ¶ And it happened, *as* we were going into *a place of* prayer, a certain slave girl having a Pythonic spirit met us, whose divining brought much profit to her masters.

17 Following after Paul and us, she cried out, saying, These men are slaves of the Most High God, who proclaim to us a way of salvation!

18 And she did this over many days. But becoming distressed, and turning around to the *demonic* spirit, Paul said, In the name of Jesus Christ I command you to come out from her! And it came out in the very hour.

19 And seeing that the hope of their profit went out, taking hold of Paul and Silas, her masters dragged *them* into the marketplace before the rulers.

20 And bringing them near to the magistrates, *they* said, These men are completely disturbing our city, being Jews,

21 and they are proclaiming customs which it is not lawful for us to receive, nor to do, being Romans.

22 And the crowd rose up against them. And tearing off their clothes, the magistrates ordered *men* to beat *them* with a rod.

23 And laying on them many strokes, they threw *them* into prison, charging the prison-keeper to keep them securely,

24 who, receiving such a charge, threw them into the inner prison, and locked their feet in the stocks.

25 ¶ And about midnight Paul and Silas were praying *and* singing praise to God, and the prisoners listened to them.

26 And suddenly there was a great earthquake, so that the foundations of the prison were shaken. And immediately all the doors were opened, and all of the bonds were loosed.

27 And becoming awake, and seeing the doors of the prison being opened, drawing a sword, the prison-keeper was about to kill himself, supposing the prisoners to have escaped.

28 But Paul called out with a great voice, saying, Do no harm *to* yourself! For we are all here.

29 And asking for lights, he rushed in. And becoming trembling, he fell before Paul and Silas.

30 And bringing them outside, he said, Sirs, what must I do that I may be saved?

31 And they said, Believe on the Lord Jesus Christ, and you will be saved, you and your household.

32 And they spoke the Word of the Lord to him, and *to* all the *ones* in his household.

33 And taking them in that hour of the night, he washed from *their* strokes. And he and all the *ones* of him were baptized at once.

34 And bringing them up to the house, he set a table before *them*, and exulted wholehousely, believing God.

35 ¶ And *it* becoming day, the magistrates sent the rod-carriers, saying, Set those men free.

36 And the prison-keeper announced these words to Paul, The magistrates have sent that you be set free. Now, therefore, going out, go in peace.

37 But Paul said to them, Having beaten us publicly, being Romans and uncondemned

men, they threw *us* into prison. And now do they throw us out secretly? No, indeed! But coming themselves, let them bring us out.

38 And the rod-carriers reported these words to the magistrates. And hearing that they were Romans, they were afraid.

39 And coming, they begged *them*. And bringing *them* out, *they* asked *them* to go out of the city.

40 And going out from the prison, *they* went into the *house of* Lydia. And seeing the brothers, they exhorted them, and went out.

Acts 17

1 Paul preaches at Thessalonica and Berea. 13 Being persecuted at Thessalonica, 15 he comes to Athens, and preaches, 34 whereby many are converted.

1 ¶ And traveling through Amphipolis and Apollonia, they came to Thessalonica, where there was a synagogue of the Jews.

2 And according to Paul's custom, he went in to them, and on three sabbaths *he* reasoned with them from the Scriptures,

3 opening and setting forth that the Christ must have suffered, and to have risen from *the* dead, and that this is the Christ, Jesus, whom I proclaim to you.

4 And some of them were persuaded and joined themselves to Paul and Silas, both a great multitude of the worshiping Greeks, and of the first *ones* of the women, not a few.

5 But becoming jealous, and taking some wicked men of the market loafers, and gathering a crowd, the disobeying Jews set the city into an uproar. And coming on the house of Jason, *they* sought to bring them on to the assembled people.

6 But not finding them, they dragged Jason and some brothers before the city judges, crying, The *ones* disturbing the inhabited earth have come here, too;

7 whom Jason has received. And these all act contrary to the decrees of Caesar, saying there is another king, Jesus.

8 And hearing these things, they agitated the crowd and the city judges.

9 And taking security from Jason and the rest, they let them go.

10 ¶ But the brothers at once sent away both Paul and Silas to Berea during the night; who having arrived went into the synagogue of the Jews.

11 And these were more noble than the *ones* in Thessalonica, who received the Word with all readiness, according to a day examining the Scriptures if these things might have *been* so.

12 Therefore truly many of them believed, and of the honorable Greek women and men, not a few.

13 But when the Jews from Thessalonica knew that the Word of God was also proclaimed in Berea by Paul, they came there also, shaking up the crowds.

14 And immediately, then, the brothers sent away Paul, to go as far as to the sea. But both Silas and Timothy remained there.

15 But the *ones* conducting Paul brought him as far as Athens. And receiving a command to Silas and Timothy that they come to him as quickly as possible, they went out.

16 ¶ But awaiting them in Athens, Paul's spirit was provoked within him, seeing the city utterly idolatrous.

17 Therefore, indeed, he addressed the Jews in the synagogue, and the *ones* worshiping, also in the marketplace according to every day, to the *ones* happening by.

18 And some of the Epicurean and of the Stoic philosophers encountered him. And some said, What may this seed-picker wish to say? And these *others*, He seems to be a proclaimer of foreign demons (because he proclaimed Jesus and the resurrection to them).

19 And taking hold of him, they led *him* to the Ares Hill, saying, Are we able to know what *is* this new doctrine being spoken by you?

20 For you bring some surprising things to our ears. We are minded, therefore, to know what these things wish to be.

21 And all Athenians and the strangers dwelling *there* have leisure for nothing else than to say and to hear newer *things*.

22 ¶ And standing in *the* midst of the Ares Hill, Paul said, Men, Athenians, I perceive how you in everything *are* gods-fearing *ones*;

23 for passing through and looking up at the objects of your worship, I also found an altar on which had been written, TO AN UNKNOWN GOD. Therefore, not

knowing *Him* whom you worship, I proclaim this *One* to you.

24 God, the *One* who made the world and all things in it, this One being Lord of Heaven and of earth, does not dwell in temples made by hand,

25 nor is served by hands of men, *as* having need of anything. *For* He is giving life and breath and all things to all.

26 And He made every nation of men of one blood, to live on all the face of the earth, having determined fore-appointed seasons and boundaries of their dwelling,

27 to seek the Lord, if perhaps they might feel after Him and might find *Him*, though indeed *He* not being far from each one of us.

28 For in Him we live and move and exist, as also some of the poets among you have said, For we are also His offspring.

29 Therefore being offspring of God, we ought not to suppose that the Deity is like gold or silver or stone, engraved by art and the imagination of man.

30 Indeed, therefore, God overlooking the times of ignorance, now strictly commands all men everywhere to repent,

31 because He set a day in which "He is going to judge the inhabited earth in righteousness," by a Man whom He appointed; having offered faith to all, having raised Him up from *the* dead *ones. Psa. 9:8*

32 ¶ And hearing *of* a resurrection of *the* dead, the *ones* indeed ridiculed, but said, We will hear you again concerning this.

33 And so Paul went out from their midst.

34 But some men believed, joining themselves to him, among whom also *were* both Dionysius the Areopagite and a woman named Damaris, and others with them.

Acts 18

3 Paul labors with his hands, and preaches at Corinth. 9 The Lord encourages him in a vision.

1 ¶ And after these things, departing from Athens, Paul came to Corinth.

2 And finding a certain Jew, Aquila by name, of Pontus by nationality, having recently come from Italy *with* his wife Priscilla, because Claudius had ordered all the Jews to leave Rome, he came to them.

3 And because *of his* being of the same trade, he lived and worked with them; for they were tentmakers by trade.

4 And he reasoned in the synagogue according to every sabbath, persuading both Jews and Greeks.

5 And when both Silas and Timothy came down from Macedonia, Paul was pressed by the Spirit, earnestly testifying to the Jews *that* Jesus *is* the Christ.

6 But *they* resisting, and blaspheming, having shaken *his* garments, he said to them, Your blood *be* on your head. I *am* pure *from it*; from now *on* I will go to the nations.

7 ¶ And having gone over from there, he went into *the* house of a certain one, Justus by name, *one* worshiping God, whose house was being next door to the synagogue.

8 And Crispus, the synagogue ruler, was believing the Lord along with all his household. And hearing, many of the Corinthians were believing and were being baptized.

9 And the Lord said to Paul through a vision in *the* night, Do not fear, but speak, and do not keep silence;

10 because I am with you, and no one shall set on you to oppress you; because there is much people to Me in this city.

11 And he remained a year and six months teaching the Word of God among them.

12 ¶ But Gallio *being* proconsul of Achaia, the Jews rushed against Paul with one mind and led him to the tribunal,

13 saying, This one persuades men to worship God contrary to the Law.

14 But Paul being about to open *his* mouth, Gallio said to the Jews, If, indeed, then, it was some wrong or wicked criminality, O Jews, according to reason I would endure you.

15 But if it is a question about a word, and names, and the law according to you, you will see to *it* yourselves; for I do not wish to be a judge of these things.

16 And he drove them from the tribunal.

17 And all the Greeks having seized Sosthenes the ruler of the synagogue, they beat *him* before the tribunal. And not one of these things mattered to Gallio.

18 ¶ And having remained considerable days more, bidding farewell to the brothers, Paul sailed to Syria, having shorn *his*

head in Cenchrea, for he had a vow. And Priscilla and Aquila *were* with him.

19 And he came to Ephesus, and he left those *two* there. But he having entered into the synagogue, he reasoned with the Jews.

20 And they asking *him* to remain over a longer time with them, he did not consent,

21 but bid farewell to them, saying, I must by all means to make the coming feast, the *one* at Jerusalem; but I will come again to you, God willing. And he set sail from Ephesus.

22 And landing at Caesarea, having gone up and greeted the assembly, he went down to Antioch.

23 And spending some time, he went out, in order passing through the Galatian *region* and Phrygia, making strong all the disciples.

24 ¶ But a certain Jew, Apollos by name, an Alexandrian by people, an eloquent man, came into Ephesus, being powerful in the Scriptures.

25 This *one* having been orally taught in the way of the Lord, and glowing in spirit, he spoke and taught accurately the things about the Lord, understanding only the baptism of John.

26 And this *one* began to speak boldly in the synagogue. And hearing him Priscilla and Aquila took him and more accurately expounded the way of God to him.

27 And he having intended to go through into Achaia, having been encouraged, the brothers wrote to the disciples to welcome him; who, arriving, helped much the *ones* who were believing through grace.

28 For he powerfully confuted the Jews publicly, proving through the Scriptures Jesus to be the Christ.

Acts 19

6 The Holy Spirit is given by Paul's hands. 11 His doctrine is confirmed by miracles. 24 Demetrius raises an uproar against him.

1 ¶ And it happened, in the *time* Apollos was in Corinth, Paul *was* passing through the higher parts to come to Ephesus. And finding some disciples,

2 he said to them, Having believed, if you received *the* Holy Spirit? And the *ones* said to him, We did not even hear whether *the* Holy Spirit is.

3 And he said to them, Then into what were you baptized? And the *ones* said, To the baptism of John.

4 And Paul said, John indeed baptized *with* a baptism of repentance, saying to the people that they should believe into the *One* coming after him, that is, into the Christ, Jesus.

5 And hearing, they were baptized into the name of the Lord Jesus.

6 And Paul laying hands on them, the Holy Spirit came on them, and they spoke in languages and prophesied.

7 And all the men were about twelve.

8 ¶ And going into the synagogue, he spoke boldly over three months, having reasoned with *them*, and persuading concerning the things of the kingdom of God.

9 But when some were hardened, and did not obey, speaking evil of the Way before the multitude, going away from them, he separated the disciples, conversing according to a day in the school of a certain Tyrannus.

10 And this happened over two years, so that all the *ones* living in Asia heard the Word of the Lord Jesus, both Jews and Greeks.

11 And God did uncommon works of power through the hands of Paul,

12 so that even handkerchiefs or aprons from his skin to be brought onto the *ones being* sick, and the diseases to be released from them, and the evil spirits to go out from them.

13 ¶ But certain from the going about Jewish exorcists undertook to name the name of the Lord Jesus over the *ones* having evil spirits, saying, We adjure you *by* Jesus whom Paul preaches.

14 And there were seven sons of Sceva, a Jewish chief priest, the *ones* doing this.

15 But answering the evil spirit said, I know Jesus, and I comprehend Paul, but who are you?

16 And the man in whom was the evil spirit leaped on them, and having subdued them, *he* was strong against them, and having been wounded and naked, *they* fled out of that house.

17 And this became known to all, both Jews and Greeks, the *ones* living in Ephesus. And fear fell on them all, and the name of the Lord Jesus was magnified.

18 And many of the *ones* having believed came confessing, and reporting their practices.

19 And a considerable *number* of the *ones* practicing the magical *arts*, bringing together the books, burned *them* before all. And they counted the prices of them, and found *it to be* fifty thousands of silver.

20 So with might, the Word of the Lord was growing and was strong.

21 ¶ And when these things were fulfilled, passing through Macedonia and Achaia, Paul purposed in the Spirit to go to Jerusalem, saying, After I have come there, I must also see Rome.

22 And having sent into Macedonia two of the *ones* who ministered to him, Timothy and Erastus, he stayed a time in Asia.

23 And at that time there came to be no small disturbance about the Way.

24 For a certain silversmith, Demetrius by name, *was* making silver shrines of Artemis, providing no little trade *for* the craftsmen,

25 whom assembling the workmen about such things, *he* said, Men, you understand that from this trade our wealth is.

26 And you see and hear that not only Ephesus, but this Paul has persuaded almost all of Asia, perverting a considerable crowd, saying that they are not gods, the *ones* being made by hands.

27 And not only this is in danger to us, *lest our* part come to *be in* contempt, but also the temple of the great goddess Artemis will be counted nothing, and her majesty is also about to be brought down, whom all Asia and the world worships.

28 And hearing, and becoming full of anger, they cried out, saying, Great *is* Artemis of *the* Ephesians!

29 And all the city was filled with confusion. And they rushed with one mind into the theater, having seized Gaius and Aristarchus, Macedonians, traveling companions of Paul.

30 And Paul purposing to go in to the assembled people, the disciples did not allow him.

31 And also some of the Asiarchs, being his friends, sending to him begged *him* not to give himself into the theater.

32 Then others indeed *were* crying out something different, for the assembly was confused, and the majority did not know on what account they came together.

33 But out of the crowd they put forward Alexander, the Jews thrust him forward. And signaling *with his* hand, Alexander desired to defend himself to the assembled people.

34 But recognizing that he is a Jew, one voice came to be from all, as *they were* crying out over two hours, Great *is* Artemis of *the* Ephesians!

35 And quieting the crowd, the town clerk said, Men, Ephesians, for what man is there who does not know the city of the Ephesians to be temple keepers of the great goddess Artemis, and of the *image* Fallen from Zeus?

36 Therefore, these things being undeniable, it is necessary for you, being calmed, to be *so*, and to do nothing rash.

37 For you brought these men, *being* neither temple-robbers nor blaspheming your goddess.

38 If then, indeed, Demetrius and the craftsmen with him have a matter against anyone, the courts lead, and there are proconsuls. Let them accuse one another.

39 But if you seek concerning other things, it will be settled in a lawful assembly.

40 For we are in danger to be accused of insurrection concerning today, there being no cause about which we will be able to give account of this crowding together.

41 And saying these things, he dismissed the assembly.

Acts 20

1 Paul goes to Macedonia. 10 Eutychus is raised to life. 17 At Miletus Paul calls the elders together, 36 prays with them, and goes his way.

1 ¶ And after the ceasing of the tumult, calling and greeting the disciples, Paul went away to go into Macedonia.

2 And passing through those parts, and exhorting them with much speech, he came into Greece.

3 And having acted three months *there*, a plot by the Jews having occurred *against* him, being about to sail into Syria, he was *of a* mind to return through Macedonia.

4 And was accompanying him as far as Asia Sopater, a Berean; and Aristarchus and

Secundus of the Thessalonians, and Gaius of Derbe, and Timothy, and Asians Tychicus and Trophimus.

5 These *men* having gone ahead awaited us in Troas.

6 But we sailed along after the days of Unleavened *Bread* from Philippi, and came to them at Troas within five days, where we stayed seven days.

7 ¶ And on the one of the sabbaths, the disciples being assembled to break bread, Paul was discoursing to them, being about to depart on the next day, and he continued his speech until midnight.

8 And many lamps were in the upper room where they were gathered.

9 And a certain young man. Eutychus by name, *was* sitting on the window *sill* being overborne by deep sleep, Paul discoursing *for* a longer *time*, having been overborne by the sleep, he fell down from the third floor and was taken up dead.

10 But going down Paul fell on him, and embracing *him*, he said, Do not be troubled, for his soul is in him.

11 And going up, and breaking bread, and eating, and conversing over a considerable *time*, until daybreak, he went out thus.

12 And they brought the boy alive and were comforted not a little.

13 ¶ But going before onto the ship, we set sail for Assos, being about to take up Paul in there; for so it was arranged, he being about to go on foot.

14 And when he met us in Assos, taking him up we came to Mitylene.

15 And sailing away from there, on the next *day* we arrived off Chios, and on the next we crossed to Samos. And staying in Trogyllium, the following *day* we came to Miletus.

16 For Paul had decided to sail by Ephesus, so as it might not happen to him to spend time in Asia; for he hastened if it were possible for him to be into Jerusalem *on* the day of Pentecost.

17 ¶ And having sent to Ephesus from Miletus, he called for the elders of the assembly.

18 And when they came to him, he said to them: You understand, from *the* first day on which I set foot in Asia, how I was with you all the time,

19 serving the Lord with all humility, and many tears and trials happening to me, the *ones* by the plots of the Jews;

20 as I drew nothing back of the *things* profiting you, *so as* not to declare and to teach you publicly, and according to houses,

21 earnestly testifying both to Jews and to Greeks repentance toward God and faith toward our Lord Jesus Christ.

22 And now, behold, being bound by the Spirit, I am going to Jerusalem, not knowing the things going to meet me in it,

23 but that the Holy Spirit according to *each* city solemnly testifies, saying that bonds and afflictions await me.

24 But I make account of nothing, nor do I hold my life precious to myself, so that I might finish my course with joy, and the ministry which I received from the Lord Jesus, to solemnly testify the gospel of the grace of God.

25 And now, behold, I know that you all will see my face no more, among whom I went about preaching the kingdom of God.

26 Therefore I testify to you in this very day that I *am* clean from the blood of all.

27 For I did not draw back from declaring to you all the counsel of God.

28 Therefore take heed to yourselves and to all the flock, in which the Holy Spirit placed you *as* overseers, to shepherd the assembly of God which He purchased through *His* own blood.

29 For I know this, that after my departure unsparing wolves will come in among you, not sparing the flock;

30 and out of you *your*selves will rise up men speaking perverting *things* in order to draw away the disciples after themselves.

31 Therefore, be alert, remembering that I did not cease admonishing each one with tears night and day *for* three years.

32 And now, brothers, I commend you to God and to the Word of His grace, the *One* being able to build up and to give you inheritance among all the *ones* having been sanctified.

33 I have desired *the* silver, or gold, or clothing of no one.

34 But you yourselves know that these hands ministered to my needs, and to the *ones* who were with me.

35 I showed you by all things that working hard in this way it is needful to help the *ones* being feeble, and to remember the words of the Lord Jesus, that He said, It is more blessed to give than to receive.

36 ¶ And having said these things, placing his knees, he prayed with them all.

37 And there was much weeping of all; and falling on the neck of Paul, they tenderly kissed him,

38 most of all grieving for the word which he said, that they were going to see his face no more. And they went with him to the ship.

Acts 21

1 Paul will not be dissuaded from going to Jerusalem. 27 He is rescued, and arrested, 31 is permitted to speak to the people.

1 ¶ And when it was *time* to sail, we tearing away *ourselves* from them, sailing a straight course we came to Cos, and on the next *day* to Rhodes, and from there to Patara.

2 And finding a ship crossing over to Phoenicia, going on board we set sail:

3 and sighting Cyprus, and leaving it on the left, we sailed to Syria, and came down to Tyre; for the ship was unloading the cargo there.

4 And having found disciples, we remained there seven days; who told Paul through the Spirit not to go up to Jerusalem.

5 But when it was *time for* us to finish out the days, having gone out, we traveled. *And they*, with all *the* women and children went with us as far as outside the city. And placing the knees on the shore, we prayed.

6 And having given parting greetings to one another, we went up into the ship, and those went back to their own *homes*.

7 And completing the voyage from Tyre, we arrived at Ptolemais. And having greeted the brothers, we remained one day with them.

8 ¶ And on the next day, the *ones* around Paul going out, *we* came to Caesarea. And going into Philip the evangelist's house, *he* being of the Seven, we remained with him.

9 And to this *one* there were four virgin daughters who prophesied.

10 And we remaining more days, a certain prophet from Judea, Agabus by name, came down.

11 And coming to us, and taking Paul's girdle-band, and binding his hands and feet, he said, The Holy Spirit says these *things*: In Jerusalem the Jews will bind in this way the man whose girdle-band this is, and will give *him* over into the hands of *the* nations.

12 And when we heard these things, both we and the resident *saints* begged him not to go up to Jerusalem.

13 But Paul answered, What are you doing, weeping and breaking my heart? For not only am I ready to be bound, but also to die at Jerusalem for the name of the Lord Jesus.

14 And he not being persuaded, we were silent, saying, The will of the Lord be *done*.

15 ¶ And after these days, having packed up, we went up to Jerusalem.

16 And also *some* of the disciples from Caesarea went with us, bringing Mnason, a certain Cypriot, an old disciple, with whom we might lodge.

17 And we being in Jerusalem, the brothers joyfully received us.

18 And on the next *day*, Paul went in with us to James. And all the elders arrived.

19 And having greeted them, he related according to each one what things God had worked among the nations through his ministry.

20 And hearing, they glorified the Lord, and said to him, You see, brother, how many myriads there are of Jews, the *ones* having believed, and all are zealots of the Law.

21 And they have been informed about you, that you are teaching falling away from Moses, telling all the Jews throughout the nations, saying not to circumcise *their* children, nor to walk in the customs.

22 What is it, then? Certainly a multitude must come together, for they will hear that you have come.

23 Therefore, do this, which we say to you: There are four men who have a vow on themselves;

24 taking these, be purified with them, and be at expense on them, that they may shave the head. And all shall know that all what they have been told about you is nothing, but you yourself walk by rule, and yourself keeping the Law.

25 And as to the believing nations, we wrote, having judged them to observe no such thing, except to keep themselves from both idol sacrifice, and *from* the blood, and *from* a strangled *thing*, and *from* fornication.

26 Then having taken the men on the following day, having been purified with them, Paul went into the temple, declaring the fulfillment of the days of the purification, until the offering should be offered for each one of them.

27 ¶ But when the seven days were about to be completed, having seen him in the temple, the Jews from Asia were stirring up all the crowd, and *they* laid hands on him,

28 crying out, Men, Israelites, help! This is the man, the *one* teaching all everywhere against the people and the Law and this place. And even more, *he* also brought Greeks into the temple and has defiled this holy place.

29 For they were seeing before Trophimus the Ephesian in the city with him, whom they supposed that Paul brought into the temple.

30 And the whole city was stirred up and there was a running together of people. And laying hands on Paul, they drew him outside of the temple, and at once the doors were shut.

31 But as they *were* seeking to kill him, a report came up to the chiliarch of the cohort, that all Jerusalem has been stirred up.

32 *He* at once ran down to them, taking soldiers and centurions. And seeing the chiliarch and the soldiers, they stopped beating Paul.

33 Then going near, the chiliarch laid hold of him, and commanded *him* to be bound with two chains. And *he* asked who he might be, and what he is doing.

34 But others cried the other *thing* in the crowd, and not being able to know the certain *thing* because of the uproar, he commanded him brought into the barracks.

35 But when he came on the stairs, it happened *for* him to be borne by the soldiers because of the violence of the crowd.

36 For the multitude of the people followed, crying out, Take him away!

37 But being about to be brought into the barracks, Paul said to the chiliarch, Is it lawful for me to say a thing to you? And he said, Do you know Greek?

38 Then are you not the Egyptian, the *one* before these days caused a riot, and led four thousand men of the assassins out into the desert?

39 But Paul said, Indeed I am a man, a Jew of Tarsus, of Cilicia, a citizen *of* a not insignificant city. And I beg you, allow me to speak to the people.

40 And he allowing him, standing on the stairs, Paul signaled with *his* hand to the people. And much silence taking place, he spoke in the Hebrew dialect, saying,

Acts 22

1 Paul declares how he was converted. 22 At the mention of the nations, the people seek his death.

1 ¶ Men, brothers, and fathers, hear my defense now to you.

2 And hearing that he spoke in the Hebrew dialect to them, they showed more quietness. And he said:

3 ¶ Indeed I am a man, a Jew having been born in Tarsus of Cilicia, but having been brought up in this city at the feet of Gamaliel, having been trained according to the exactness of the ancestral law, being a zealot of God, even as you all are today.

4 *I* persecuted this Way as far as death, binding and giving over both men and women to prisons,

5 as also the high priest, and all the elderhood witnesses to me. And receiving letters from *them* to the brothers, I was going into Damascus, also bringing to Jerusalem the *ones* being bound there, in order that they might be punished.

6 And it happened to me, going and drawing near to Damascus: suddenly, about midday, a considerable light out of the heaven shone around me.

7 And I fell to the ground, and heard a voice saying to me, Saul, Saul, why are you persecuting Me?

8 And I answered, Who are you, Sir? And He said to me, I am Jesus the Nazarene whom you persecute.

9 But the *ones* being with me indeed beheld the light, and were terrified, but did not hear the voice of the *One* speaking to me.

10 And I said, What shall I do, Lord? And the Lord said to me, Rising up, go into Damascus, and there you will be told about all things which has been appointed to you to do.

11 And as I was not seeing, from the glory of that light, being led by the hand by the *ones* being with me, I went into Damascus.

12 And a certain Ananias, a devout man according to the Law, being testified to by all the Jews living *there*,

13 coming to me and standing by, *he* said to me, Brother Saul, see again. And in the same hour I saw again to him.

14 And he said, The God of our fathers has beforehand chosen you to know His will, and to see the Righteous *One*, and to hear a voice out of His mouth;

15 for you shall be a witness for Him to all men of what you have seen and heard.

16 And now what are you going *to do*? Rising up, be baptized and wash away your sins, calling on the name of the Lord.

17 And it happened to me, having returned to Jerusalem and praying in the temple, for me coming to be in an ecstasy,

18 and I saw Him saying to me, Hurry and go out quickly from Jerusalem, because they will not receive your testimony concerning Me.

19 And I said, Lord, they understand that I was imprisoning and beating the *ones* believing on You throughout the synagogues.

20 And when the blood of Your witness Stephen was poured out, I myself also was standing by and consenting to the murder of him, and guarding the garments of the *ones* killing him.

21 And He said to me, Go, for I will send you to the nations afar off.

22 ¶ And they heard him as far as this word, and lifted up their voice, saying, Take away such a one from the earth, for it is not fitting that he should live!

23 And they *were* shouting, and casting off *their* garments, and throwing dust into the air,

24 the chiliarch gave command to bring him into the barracks, saying for him to be examined with scourges, that he may know for what crime they cried out so against him.

25 But as they stretched him with the thongs, Paul said to the centurion standing by, Is it lawful for you to scourge a man, a Roman not found guilty?

26 And hearing, coming near the centurion reported to the chiliarch, saying, Watch what you are about to do, for this man is a Roman.

27 And coming up, the chiliarch said to him, Tell me, are you a Roman? And he said, Yes.

28 And the chiliarch answered, I bought this citizenship with a *great* sum *of money*. And Paul said, But I even was born *free*.

29 Then at once the *ones* being about to examine him stood away from him. And the chiliarch also feared, fully knowing that he was a Roman, and that he had bound him.

30 And on the next day, purposing to know the certain *thing* as to why he was accused by the Jews, he freed him from the bonds. And *he* commanded the chief priests and all their sanhedrin to come. And having brought Paul down, *he* stood *him* among them.

Acts 23

1 As Paul pleads his cause, 2 Ananias commands them to smite him. 11 God encourages him. 14 The Jews' laying wait for Paul 20 is revealed to the chiliarch. 23 He sends him to Felix.

1 ¶ And looking intently at the sanhedrin, Paul said, Men, brothers, I in all good conscience have conducted myself toward God until this day.

2 But Ananias the high priest ordered those standing by him to strike his mouth.

3 Then Paul said to him, God is going to strike you, whitewashed wall! And do you sit judging me according to the Law, and breaking the Law command me to be stricken?

4 And the *ones* standing by said, Do you revile the high priest of God?

5 And Paul said, Brothers, I did not know that he is high priest; for it has been written, "You shall not speak badly" "of a ruler of your people." *Ex. 22:28*

6 ¶ But knowing that the one part consisted of Sadducees, and the other of Pharisees, Paul cried out in the sanhedrin, Men, brothers, I am a Pharisee, a son of Pharisees; I am being judged concerning hope and resurrection of *the* dead *ones*!

7 And *he* speaking this, there was a discord between the Pharisees and the Sadducees; and the multitude was divided.

8 For the Sadducees indeed say there is no resurrection, nor angel, nor spirit. But Pharisees confess both the things.

9 And there was a great cry. And the scribes of the part of the Pharisees rising up, they were contending, saying, We find nothing bad in this man. And, If a spirit spoke to him, or an angel, let us not fight against God.

10 And much discord taking place, fearing lest Paul should be torn apart by them, the chiliarch commanded the soldiers to go down to seize him out of their midst, and to bring *him* into the barracks.

11 And in the following night standing by him the Lord said, Be cheered, Paul, for as you fully testified the things concerning Me in Jerusalem, so you must also testify at Rome.

12 ¶ And *it* becoming day, some of the Jews making a conspiracy bound themselves by an oath, saying neither to eat nor to drink until they should kill Paul.

13 And the *ones* making this plot were more *than* forty;

14 who, having come near to the chief priests and to the elders, said, With a curse we have bound ourselves by an oath to taste of nothing until we shall kill Paul.

15 Now, therefore, you with the sanhedrin inform the chiliarch, so that tomorrow he may bring him down to you, as being about to more accurately determine the things about him. And before his drawing near, we are ready to kill him.

16 But the son of Paul's sister hearing of the ambush, coming, and entering into the barracks, reported to Paul.

17 And calling near one of the centurions, Paul said, Bring this young man to the chiliarch, for he has something to report to him.

18 Therefore, indeed, taking him, he brought *him* to the chiliarch and said, Paul the prisoner having called me near asked me to bring this young man to you, having a thing to tell you.

19 And taking hold of his hand, and drawing aside to his own *place*, the chiliarch asked, What is *it* that you have to report to me?

20 And he said, The Jews agreed to ask you that tomorrow you bring down Paul into the sanhedrin, as going to learn something more accurate about him.

21 Therefore, you do not be persuaded by them, for more than forty men of them lie in wait for him who bound themselves by an oath neither to eat nor to drink until they kill him. And now they are ready, awaiting the promise from you.

22 Then the chiliarch sent away the young man, charging *him*, Tell no one that you made known these things to me.

23 And having called near a certain two of the centurions, he said, Get two hundred soldiers ready, so that they may go to Caesarea, and seventy horsemen, and two hundred spearmen, from the third hour of the night;

24 and animals to stand by, so that setting Paul on, they may bring *him* safely to Felix the governor.

25 *and* writing a letter, having this form:

26 Claudius Lysias to the most excellent governor, Felix, greeting:

27 This man being seized by the Jews, and being about to be killed by them, coming on with the soldiers I rescued him, learning that he was a Roman.

28 And purposing to know the charge for which they were accusing him, I brought him down to their sanhedrin;

29 I found *him* to be accused concerning questions of their law, and having no accusation worthy of death or of bonds.

30 And it being made known to me that a plot against the man was about to be *executed* by the Jews, I at once sent *him* to you, also commanding the accusers to say the things against him before you. Farewell.

31 Then indeed taking up Paul according to that order given to them, the soldiers brought *him* through the night to Antipatris.

32 And on the next day, allowing the horsemen to go with him, they returned to the barracks.

33 Entering into Caesarea, and giving over the letter to the governor, *they* also presented Paul to him.

34 And having read *it*, the governor asked from what province he is. And having learned that *he was* from Cilicia,

35 he said, I will hear you fully when your accusers arrive. And *he* commanded him to be guarded in the praetorium of Herod.

Acts 24

1 Paul, being accused, 10 answers for his life and doctrine. 24 He preaches Christ to the governor and his wife.

1 ¶ And after five days Ananias the high priest came down with the elders, and a certain orator, Tertullus, who made a statement to the governor against Paul.

2 And him being called, Tertullus began to accuse, saying,

3 Obtaining much peace through you and successful achievements having come to this nation due to your forethought, both in every *thing* and everywhere we accept with all thankfulness, most excellent Felix.

4 But that I not hinder you more, I beseech you to hear us briefly in your fairness.

5 For having found this man a pestilence and moving insurrection among all the Jews throughout the world, and a leader of the Nazarene sect;

6 who also attempted to profane the temple, whom we also seized and wished to judge according to our law;

7 but Lysias the chiliarch coming up with much force took *him* away out of our hands,

8 commanding his accusers to come to you, from whom you will be able yourself to know, having examined as to all these things of which we are accusing him.

9 And the Jews also joined in, asserting these things to have *been so*.

10 ¶ But the governor having nodded to him to speak, Paul answered: Understanding you as being a judge to this nation many years, I cheerfully defend myself *as to the* things concerning myself.

11 You *are* able to know that not more than twelve days are to me since I went worshiping in Jerusalem;

12 and neither did they find me discussing with anyone in the temple, or making a gathering of a crowd, neither in the synagogues, nor throughout the city;

13 nor are they able to prove that about which they now accuse me.

14 But I confess this to you that according to the Way, which they call a sect, so I worship the paternal God, believing all things according to that having been written in the Law and the Prophets,

15 having hope toward God, which these themselves also are awaiting, *of* a resurrection being about to be of *the* dead *ones*, both of just *ones* and unjust ones.

16 And in this I exercise myself to have always a blameless conscience toward God and men.

17 And through many years I arrived doing merciful deeds and offerings to my nation,

18 among whom they found me purified in the temple, not with a crowd, nor with tumult, *but by* some Jews from Asia,

19 *for* whom it is right to be present before you and to accuse if they have anything against me.

20 Or these themselves say if they found anything unjust in me, I standing before the sanhedrin,

21 than about this one voice which I cried out standing among them, that I am being judged today before you about a resurrection of *the* dead *ones*.

22 ¶ And hearing these things, Felix put them off, knowing more accurately about the Way, saying, When Lysias the chiliarch comes down, I will examine the things as to you.

23 And ordering the centurion to keep Paul, and to have relaxation and to forbid no one of his own to minister or to come to him, *he dismissed them*.

24 And after some days, Felix having arrived with his wife Drusilla, who was a Jewess, he sent for Paul. And *he* heard him concerning the faith into Christ.

25 And *Paul* discoursing about righteousness and self control, and the Judgment, the *one* that is about to be, becoming terrified,

Felix answered, *For* now having *no time*, go; but taking a time later, I will call for you;

26 but at the same time also hoping that money would be given to him by Paul, that he might free him. Because of this *he* also more frequently sent for him *and* conversed with him.

27 But two years being completed, Felix received a successor, Porcius Festus. And wishing to lay up favors to the Jews, Felix left Paul being bound.

Acts 25

2 The Jews accuse Paul before Festus. 11 Paul appeals to Caesar. 25 Festus decides that He had done nothing worthy of death.

1 ¶ Then going into the province, after three days Festus went up to Jerusalem from Caesarea.

2 And the high priest and the first *ones* of the Jews informed to him against Paul, and they entreated him,

3 asking a favor against him, so as he might send for him to Jerusalem, making an ambush to kill him on the way.

4 Then indeed Festus answered *that* Paul *was* to be kept at Caesarea, and *he* himself being about to go shortly.

5 Therefore he said, the powerful *ones* among you going down with *me*. If there is a thing amiss in this man, let them accuse him.

6 And spending among them more than ten days, going down to Caesarea, on the next day sitting on the tribunal, he ordered Paul to be brought.

7 And he arriving, the Jews having come down from Jerusalem stood around, also bringing many and weighty charges against Paul, which they were not able to prove.

8 Defending himself, *Paul* said, Neither against the Law of the Jews, nor against the temple, nor against Caesar have I sinned in anything.

9 But desiring to lay up a favor to the Jews, answering Paul, Festus said, Going up, are you willing to *go to* Jerusalem to be judged before me there about these things?

10 But Paul said, I am standing before the tribunal of Caesar where I must be judged. I have wronged the Jews *in* nothing, as also you very well know.

11 For if I indeed do wrong and have done anything worthy of death, I do not refuse to die. But if there is nothing of which they accuse me, no one can give me up to them. I appeal to Caesar.

12 Then conferring with the sanhedrin, Festus answered, You have appealed to Caesar; you shall go before Caesar.

13 ¶ And some days having passed, Agrippa the king and Bernice arrived at Caesarea, greeting Festus.

14 And when they remained there more days, Festus set out to the king the things *as to* Paul, saying, A certain man is *here* having been left a prisoner by Felix,

15 about whom, I being in Jerusalem, the chief priests and the elders of the Jews informed, asking judgment against him;

16 to whom I answered, It is not a custom with Romans to give up any man to destruction before the *one* being accused may have the accusers face to face, and may receive place of defense concerning the charge.

17 Therefore, they coming together here, having made no delay, sitting on the tribunal on the next *day*, I commanded the man to be brought;

18 about whom, standing up, the accusers brought no charge of which I supposed,

19 but they had certain questions about *their* own demon worship, and about a certain Jesus dying, whom Paul claimed to be living.

20 And I being perplexed about this inquiry, I said, If he was willing to go to Jerusalem and to be judged there concerning these things?

21 But Paul appealing *for* him to be kept to the examination of Augustus, I commanded him to be held until I might send him to Caesar.

22 And Agrippa said to Festus, I myself also was purposing to hear the man. And he said, Tomorrow you shall hear him.

23 Therefore on the next day, Agrippa and Bernice coming with much pomp and entering into the auditorium, with both the chiliarchs and the men of eminence being of the city, also Festus commanding, Paul was brought out.

24 And Festus said, King Agrippa, and all the men present with us, you see this *one*

about whom all the multitude of the Jews pleaded with me, both here and in Jerusalem, crying out that he ought to live no longer.

25 But I having understood nothing he had done worthy of death, also this *one* himself having appealed to Augustus, I decided to send him;

26 about whom I have nothing certain to write to *my* lord. So I brought him out before you, and especially before you, King Agrippa, so as the examination taking place, I may have something I may write.

27 For it seems unreasonable to me to send a prisoner, and not also to signify the charges against him.

Acts 26

2 Paul, before Agrippa, declares his life, 12 and how he was converted. 24 Festus believes him to be mad. 28 Agrippa almost persuaded to be a Christian.

1 ¶ And Agrippa said to Paul, It is allowed for you yourself to speak. Then Paul made a defense, stretching out the hand:

2 Concerning all of which I am accused by Jews, King Agrippa, I consider myself blessed being about to make defense before you today,

3 you being especially expert, knowing of all the customs and questions also among the Jews. Therefore, I beg you patiently to hear me.

4 Truly, then, all the Jews know my way of life from youth, which from *the* beginning had been in my nation in Jerusalem,

5 who before knew me from the first, if they will testify, that according to the most exact sect of our religion, I lived a Pharisee.

6 And now for *the* hope of the promise having been made by God to the fathers, I stand being judged;

7 to which our twelve tribes hope to arrive, worshiping in earnestness night and day, concerning which hope I am accused by the Jews, King Agrippa.

8 Why is it judged unbelievable by you if God raises *the* dead?

9 Indeed, I then thought to myself that I ought to do many things hostile to the name of Jesus the Nazarene,

10 which I also did in Jerusalem I also shut up many of the saints in prisons, re-ceiving authority from the chief priests; and they being put to death, I cast a vote.

11 And often punishing them through all the synagogues, I compelled *them* to blaspheme. And *being* exceedingly furious against them, I even persecuted *them* as far as the outer cities.

12 ¶ In which also traveling to Damascus with authority and permission from the chief priests,

13 at midday along the highway, *O* king, I saw a light from Heaven shining around me above the brightness of the sun, also the *ones* traveling with me.

14 And all *of* us falling to the ground, I heard a voice speaking to me, and saying in the Hebrew dialect, Saul, Saul why are you persecuting Me? *It is* hard for you to kick against the goads.

15 And I said, Who are you, Sir? And He said, I am Jesus whom you are persecuting;

16 but rise up and stand on your feet, for *it is* for this *reason* I appeared to you, to appoint you a servant and a witness both of *the things* which you saw, and *the things* in which I shall appear to you,

17 delivering you from the people and the nations, to whom I now am sending you,

18 to open their eyes, and to turn *them* from darkness into light, and *from* the authority of Satan onto God, *in order for* them to receive remission of sins, and an inheritance among the *ones* being sanctified by faith into Me.

19 For which reason, King Agrippa, I was not disobedient to the heavenly vision,

20 but firstly to the *ones* in Damascus, and Jerusalem, and to all the region of Judea, and to the nations, I proclaimed *the command* to repent and to turn to God, practicing works worthy of repentance.

21 Because of these things, seizing *me* in the temple, the Jews tried to lay violent hands on *me*.

22 Then obtaining help from God, I stand until this day, witnessing both to small and to great, saying nothing except what the prophets and Moses also said was going to happen:

23 whether the Christ *was* liable to suffer, whether first by a resurrection from *the* dead *ones* He was going to proclaim a light to the people and to the nations.

24 ¶ And he defending himself *with* these things, Festus said with a loud voice, Paul, You rave! Your many letters turns *you* into madness.

25 But he said, Not to rave, most excellent Festus, but I declare words of truth and sanity.

26 For the king understands about these things, to whom I speak, also speaking openly. For I am persuaded not any of these things lie hidden *from* him, nothing. For *the* doing of this is not in a corner.

27 Do you believe the prophets, King Agrippa? I know that you believe.

28 And Agrippa said to Paul, In *but* a little do you persuade me to become a Christian!

29 And Paul said, I would pray to God, both in a little and in much, not only you, but also the *ones* hearing me today to become such as I also am, except *for* these bonds.

30 And he saying these things, the king and the governor and Bernice rose up, and the *ones* sitting with them.

31 And having withdrawn, they spoke to one another saying, This man does nothing worthy of death or of bonds.

32 And Agrippa said to Festus, This man was able to have been released, if he had not appealed to Caesar.

Acts 27

1 Paul sailing toward Rome, 10 foretells of the danger of the voyage. 14 They are tossed to and fro with a storm, 41 and suffer shipwreck, 22, 34, 44 yet all come safe to land.

1 ¶ And when it was decided for us to sail to Italy, they gave over both Paul and certain other prisoners to a centurion by name Julius, of a cohort of Augustus.

2 And boarding a ship of Adramyttium which was about to sail to the places alongside Asia, we set sail, Aristarchus a Macedonian of Thessalonica being with us.

3 And on the next *day* we brought to land at Sidon. And treating Paul kindly, Julius allowed *him,* going to *his* friends to obtain care.

4 And setting sail from there, we sailed close to Cyprus, because of the winds being contrary.

5 And sailing over the sea against Cilicia and Pamphylia, we came to Myra of Lycia.

6 And the centurion finding there an Alexandrian ship sailing to Italy, he put us into it.

7 And in many days, sailing slowly and with difficulty, hardly coming against Cnidus, the wind not allowing us, we sailed close to Crete against Salmone.

8 And sailing along it with difficulty, we came to a certain place being called Fair Havens, near to which was a city, Lasea.

9 And considerable time having passed, and the voyage already being dangerous, because the Fast already had gone by, Paul advised *them,*

10 saying to them, Men, I perceive that the voyage is about to be with hardship and much loss, not only of the cargo and of the ship, but also of our souls.

11 But the centurion was rather persuaded by the helmsman and the ship-owner, than by the things being said by Paul.

12 ¶ And the harbor not being fit for wintering, the majority gave counsel to set sail from there, if somehow they may be able to pass the winter, having arrived at Phoenix, a harbor of Crete looking toward *the* southwest, and *with winds* toward *the* northwest.

13 And a south wind blowing gently, thinking to have gained the purpose, raising *anchor* they sailed by nearer Crete.

14 But not much after, a typhonic wind, being called Euroclydon, smote down *on* it.

15 And the ship being seized, and not being able to face into the wind, giving over we were borne along.

16 But running under an islet being called Clauda, we hardly had strength to get mastery of the boat;

17 which taking, they used helps, undergirding the ship. And fearing lest into the Syrtis *shoals* they fall, lowering the tackle, so they were borne along.

18 But we being violently storm tossed, they made a jettisoning on the next *day.*

19 And on the third *day* we threw *out* the ship's tackle with *our* hands.

20 And neither sun nor stars having appeared over many days, and no small tempest pressing hard, finally all hope *for* us to be saved was taken away.

21 ¶ And there being much abstinence, then standing up in their midst, Paul said,

Truly, O men, obeying me *you* ought not to have set sail from Crete, and to spare *yourselves* and this hardship and loss.

22 And now I exhort you to be cheered, for there will be not one loss of life from you, except of the ship.

23 For this night an angel of God stood by me, whose I am, and whom I serve,

24 saying, Do not fear, Paul, You must stand before Caesar. And, behold, God has granted to you all the *ones* sailing with you.

25 Therefore, be cheered, men, for I believe God, that it will be so according to the way it was spoken to me.

26 But it is necessary *for* us to fall off onto a certain island.

27 And when *the* fourteenth night came, we being carried about in the Adriatic Sea, toward the middle of the night the sailors supposed *us* to be coming near to them some land.

28 And taking soundings, they found *it to be* twenty fathoms; and having gone a little farther, and taking soundings again, they found *it to be* fifteen fathoms.

29 And fearing lest they should fall off onto rough places, and casting four anchors out of *the* stern, they prayed day to come on.

30 But the sailors seeking to flee out of the ship, and lowering the boat into the sea, *as a* pretext to be about to cast out anchors from *the* prow,

31 Paul said to the centurion, and to the soldiers, If not these *men* remain in the ship, you cannot be saved.

32 Then the soldiers cut away the ropes of the boat, and let it fall.

33 And until day was about to come on, Paul begged all to receive *a* share of food, saying, Today *is the* fourteenth day you continued waiting *in* abstinence, not having taken anything.

34 Therefore I exhort you to take of food, for this is to your deliverance, for not one hair of your head will fall.

35 And having said these things, and having taken bread, he gave thanks to God before all; and having broken, he began to eat.

36 And all becoming cheered, they also took food.

37 And we were, all the souls in the ship, two hundred seventy-six.

38 And being satisfied *with* food, they lightened the ship, throwing the wheat out into the sea.

39 And when day came on, they did not recognize the land, but they noted a certain bay having a beach, into which they purposed, if they were able, to drive the ship.

40 And casting off the anchors, they left *them* in the sea, at the same time loosening the bands of the rudders, and raising the foresail to the blowing *wind*, they headed to the beach.

41 And having fallen on a place *with an inlet* between two seas, they drove the vessel. And indeed the prow having stuck firmly, *it* remained. But the stern was broken by the violence of the waves.

42 And the mind of *the* soldiers was that they should kill the prisoners, lest any swimming out should escape.

43 But purposing to save Paul, the centurion stopped them *from their* purpose and commanded the *ones* able to swim, first throwing *themselves* down, to go out on the land.

44 And the rest *went*, this *one* indeed on planks, and this *one* on some of the *things* from the ship. And so it happened all to be saved on the land.

Acts 28

1 Paul is kindly entertained by the foreigners.
8 He heals many diseases on the island.
30 He preaches in Rome two years.

1 ¶ And being saved, then they knew that the island is called Melita.

2 And the foreigners were showing not the common kindliness to us, for having kindled a fire because of the rain coming on, and because of the cold, they took us all to heart.

3 And Paul gathering a great number of sticks, and putting *them* on the fire, a snake coming out from the heat fastened on his hand.

4 And when the foreigners saw the beast hanging from his hand, they said to one another, No doubt this man is a murderer, whom being saved out of the sea, Justice did not permit to live.

5 Then he shaking the beast off into the fire, *he* suffered nothing bad.

6 But they were expecting him to be about to be swollen up, or suddenly to

fall down dead. But over much *time*, they expecting and observing nothing out of place happening to him, changing their minds, they said him to be a god.

7 And in the *parts* about that place were pieces of land to the first *man* of the island, Publius by name. Welcoming us, *he* hosted us three days in a friendly way.

8 And it happened the father of Publius was lying down, suffering from fevers and dysentery; to whom Paul, entering and praying, laying on his hands, healed him.

9 Then, this taking place, the *ones* in the island having infirmities also were coming up, and *they* were healed,

10 who also honored us with many honors. And on *our* setting sail, they laid on *us* such things for *our* need.

11 ¶ And after three months we sailed in a ship having wintered in the island, an Alexandrian marked with an ensign, Twin Brothers.

12 And landing at Syracuse, we remained three days.

13 From where having gone around, we arrived at Rhegium. And after one day, a south wind having come on, on the second we came to Puteoli,

14 where finding brothers, we were entreated by them to remain seven days. And so we went toward Rome.

15 And the brothers from there hearing the *things* about us, *they* came out for a meeting with us, as far as Forum of Appius, and Three Taverns; whom Paul seeing, thanking God, he took courage.

16 And when we went into Rome, the centurion gave over the prisoners to the camp commander. But Paul was allowed to remain by himself, with the soldier guarding him.

17 ¶ And after three days, it happened that Paul *decided* to call together the *ones* being first *ones* of the Jews. And they coming together, he said to them, Men, brothers, I having done nothing hostile to the people, or to the paternal customs, *yet* I was given over a prisoner from Jerusalem into the hands of the Romans,

18 who examining me were of a mind to let *me* go, because no cause of death was in me.

19 But the Jews speaking against *it*, I was compelled to appeal to Caesar, not as having anything to accuse my nation.

20 Therefore, because of this, I called for you, to see and to speak to *you*. For I have this chain around *me* for the sake of the hope of Israel.

21 But the *ones* said to him, We neither received letters about you from the Jews, nor arriving has any one of the brothers reported or spoken anything evil about you.

22 But we think *it* fit to hear from you *as to* what you think, for truly as concerning this sect, it is known to us that it is spoken against everywhere.

23 ¶ And having appointed him a day, more came to him in the lodging, to whom he expounded, earnestly testifying the kingdom of God and persuading them the things concerning Jesus, both from the Law of Moses and the Prophets, from morning until evening.

24 And some indeed were persuaded by that being said, but others disbelieved.

25 And disagreeing with one another, they were let go, Paul saying one word: Well did the Holy Spirit speak through the prophet Isaiah to our fathers,

26 saying, "Go to this people and say, In hearing you shall hear, and not at all understand; and seeing you will see, and not at all perceive;

27 for the heart of this people was fattened, and they have heard with the ears heavily; and they closed their eyes lest at any time they see with *their* eyes, and hear with *their* ears, and understand with *their* heart, and be converted, and I should heal them." *Isa. 6:9, 10*

28 Then let it be known to you that the salvation of God was sent to the nations, and they will hear. *LXX-Psa. 66:3; MT-Psa. 67:2*

29 And he saying these things, the Jews went away, having much discussion among themselves.

30 ¶ And Paul remained two whole years in *his* own rented place, and he welcomed all the *ones* coming in to him,

31 proclaiming the kingdom of God, and teaching the things concerning the Lord Jesus Christ with all freedom *and* without hindrance.

The Epistle of Paul the Apostle to the
Romans

Romans 1

1 Paul commends his calling to the Romans, 9 and his desire to come to them. 18 God is angry with all manner of sin.

1 ¶ Paul, a slave of Jesus Christ, a called apostle, having been separated to the gospel of God,

2 which He promised before through His prophets in *the* Holy Scriptures,

3 concerning His Son, the *One* coming of the seed of David according to flesh,

4 the *One* designated *the* Son of God in power, according to *the* Spirit of holiness, by *the* resurrection of dead *ones*, Jesus Christ our Lord;

5 by whom we received grace and apostleship to obedience of faith among all the nations, for His name's sake,

6 among whom are you also, called of Jesus Christ;

7 to all the *ones* being in Rome, beloved of God, called saints: Grace and peace to you from God our Father and *the* Lord Jesus Christ.

8 ¶ Firstly, truly, I thank my God through Jesus Christ for you all, that your faith is spoken of in all the world.

9 For God is my witness, whom I serve in my spirit in the gospel of His Son, how without ceasing I make mention of you

10 always at my prayers, if somehow now sometime I shall be successful by the will of God to come to you.

11 For I long to see you, that I may impart some spiritual gift to you, for the establishing of you;

12 and this is to be comforted together among you, through the faith in one another, both yours and mine.

13 But I do not wish you to be ignorant, brothers, that often I purposed to come to you, and was kept back until the present, that I might have some fruit among you also, even as among the other nations.

14 I am a debtor both to Greeks and to foreign *ones*, both to wise *ones*, and to foolish *ones*,

15 so as far as *lies* in me, I am eager to preach the gospel to you, the *ones* in Rome also.

16 ¶ For I am not ashamed of the gospel of Christ, for it is *the* power of God to salvation to every *one* believing, both to Jew first, and to Greek;

17 for in it the righteousness of God is revealed from faith to faith; even as it is written, "But the just *one* shall live by faith." *Hab. 2:4*

18 For God's wrath is revealed from Heaven on all ungodliness and unrighteousness of men, the *ones* holding back the truth in unrighteousness,

19 ¶ because the thing known of God is clearly known within them, for God revealed *it* to them.

20 For the unseen things of Him from *the* creation of the world are clearly seen, being understood by the things made, both His eternal power and divinity, for them to be without excuse.

21 Because knowing God, they did not glorify *Him* as God, nor were thankful. But *they* became vain in their reasonings, and their undiscerning heart was darkened.

22 Professing to be wise *ones*, they became foolish

23 and changed the glory of the incorruptible God into a likeness of an image of corruptible man, and of birds, and fourfooted animals, and creeping things.

24 Therefore, God gave them over to impurity in the lusts of *their* hearts, their bodies to be dishonored among themselves,

25 who exchanged the truth of God into the lie, and worshiped and served the created thing more than the Creator, who is blessed forever. Amen.

26 Because of this, God gave them over to dishonorable passions, for even their

females changed the natural use to the *use* contrary to nature.

27 And likewise, the males also forsaking the natural use of the female burned in their lust toward one another, males with males working out shamefulness, and receiving back within themselves the recompense which is right for their straying away.

28 And even as they did not think fit to have God in *their* knowledge, God gave them over to an unfit mind, to do the things not fitting

29 having been filled with all unrighteousness, fornication, iniquity, covetousness, malice, *being* full of envy, murder, quarrels, deceit, evil habits, *becoming* whisperers,

30 slanderers, God-haters, insolent men, arrogant *ones*, braggarts, devisers of evil things, disobedient to parents,

31 without understanding, untrustworthy *ones*, without affection, implacable *ones*, unmerciful *ones*,

32 who having known the ordinance of God, that the *ones* practicing such things are worthy of death, not only do them, but also approve the *ones* practicing *them*.

Romans 2

1 They that sin, though they condemn it in others, cannot excuse themselves, 6 and much less escape the judgment of God. 14 The nations cannot escape, 17 nor yet the Jews, 25 if they keep not the law.

1 ¶ Therefore, O man, you are without excuse, every *one* judging, for in that in which you judge the other, you condemn yourself; for you, the *one* judging, practice the same things.

2 But we know that the judgment of God is according to truth on the *ones* practicing such things.

3 And, O man, the *one* judging the *ones* practicing such things, and doing them, do you think that you will escape the judgment of God?

4 Or do you despise the riches of His kindness, and the forbearance and the long-suffering, not knowing that the kindness of God leads you to repentance?

5 But according to your hardness and your impenitent heart, you are treasuring up to yourself wrath in *the* day of wrath, and revelation of a righteous judgment of God.

6 who "will give to each *one* according to his works": *LXX-Psa. 61:13; MT-Psa. 62:12*

7 truly to the *ones* who with patience *in* good work seeking glory and honor and incorruptibility *and* everlasting life;

8 but to the *ones* truly disobeying the truth out of self-seeking, but obeying unrighteousness, *will be* anger and wrath,

9 trouble and distress on every soul of man fully working evil, both of Jew firstly, and of Greek.

10 But glory and honor and peace *will be* to every*one* working the good, both to *the* Jew firstly, and to *the* Greek.

11 For there is no partiality with God.

12 For as many as sinned without Law will also perish without Law. And as many as sinned within Law will be judged through Law.

13 For not the hearers of the Law are just with God, but the doers of the Law shall be justified.

14 For whenever nations not having law do the things of the law, these, not having law, are a law to themselves,

15 who demonstrate the work of the law written in their hearts, witnessing with their conscience and between one another the thoughts accusing or even defending

16 in a day when God judges the hidden things of men, according to my gospel, through Jesus Christ.

17 Behold, you are named a Jew and rest in the Law, and boast in God, and know the will and approve the things excelling, being instructed out of the Law,

18 and you have persuaded yourself to be a guide to blind *ones,* a light to the *ones* in darkness,

20 an instructor of foolish *ones,* a teacher of the child-like, having the form of knowledge and of the truth in the Law.

21 Therefore the *one* teaching another, do you not teach yourself? The *one* preaching not to steal, do you steal?

22 The the *one* saying not to commit adultery, do you commit adultery? The *one* detesting the idols, do you rob temples?

23 *You* who boast in Law, do you dishonor God through transgression of the Law?

24 For the name of God is blasphemed among the nations through you, even as it is written. *Isa. 52:5*

25 For indeed circumcision profits if you practice *the* Law, but if you are a transgressor of Law, your circumcision becomes uncircumcision.

26 Therefore if the uncircumcision keeps the ordinances of the Law, *will* not his uncircumcision be counted for circumcision?

27 And will the uncircumcision by nature, *by* fulfilling the Law, judge you through *your* letter and circumcision *as being* transgressor of Law?

28 For not in the *one* being evident, he is *the* Jew, nor *is* the circumcision in flesh the *one* being evident;

29 but in the secret *one* is *the* Jew, and circumcision *is* of heart, in spirit, not in letter; of whom the praise *is* not from men, but from God.

Romans 3

1 The Jews' prerogative. 20 No flesh is justified by the law, 28 but all, by faith only, not by works.

1 ¶ What then *is* the superiority of the Jew? Or what the advantage of circumcision?

2 Much according to every way. For firstly, indeed, that they were entrusted with the words of God.

3 For what if some did not believe? *Will* not their faithlessness nullify the faithfulness of God?

4 Let it not be! But let God be true, and every man a liar; even as it is written, "That You should be justified in Your words, and will overcome in Your being judged." *LXX-Psa. 50:6; MT-Psa. 51:4*

5 But if our unrighteousness demonstrates the righteousness of God, what shall we say? *Is* not God unrighteous inflicting wrath? I speak according to man.

6 Let it not be! Otherwise, how will God judge the world?

7 For if the truth of God abounded by my lie to His glory, why am I yet judged as a sinner?

8 And not (as we are spoken evil of, and as some report us to say), Let us do the bad things so that the good things may come, *the* judgment of whom is just.

9 What then? Do we excel? Not at all! For we before have charged both Jews and Greeks all to be under sin;

10 according as it is written, "*There* is not a righteous *one*, not even one!"

11 "*There* is not *one* understanding, *there* is not *one* seeking God."

12 All turned aside; together *they* became worthless, not *one is* doing goodness, not so much as one!" *LXX-Psa. 13:1-3*

13 "Their throat *is* a tomb being opened;" "they used deceit with their tongues; *the* poison of asps *is* under their lips;

14 whose mouth *is* full of cursing and bitterness.

15 Their feet *are* swift to shed blood;

16 ruin and misery *are* in their ways;

17 and they did not know a way of peace;

18 there is no fear of God before their eyes." *LXX-Psa. 5:10; 139:4; 9:28; Isa. 59:7, 8; Psa. 35:2; MT-Psa. 14:1-3; 5:9; 140:3; 10:7; Isa. 59:7, 8; Psa. 36:1*

19 ¶ But we know that as many *things* as the law says, it says to the *ones* within the law, so that every mouth may be stopped, and all the world be accountable to God.

20 Because by works of law not one of all flesh will be justified before Him, for through law *is* full knowledge of sin. *Psa. 143:2*

21 But now apart from law a righteousness of God has been revealed, being witnessed by the Law and the Prophets,

22 even the righteousness of God through the faith of Jesus Christ toward all and upon all the *ones* believing; for there is no difference,

23 for all sinned and fall short of the glory of God,

24 being justified undeservedly by His grace through the redemption in Christ Jesus,

25 whom God set forth *as* a propitiation through the faith in His blood, for a demonstration of His righteousness through the passing over of the sins that had taken place before, in the forbearance of God,

26 for a demonstration of His righteousness in the present time, for His being a just *One* and justifying the *one* that *is* of the faith of Jesus.

27 Then where *is* the boasting? It was shut out. Through what law? Of works? No, but through a Law of faith.

28 Therefore we count a man to be justified by faith without works of Law.

29 Or *is He* the God of Jews only, and not also of the nations? Yes, of the nations also,

30 since *it is* one God who will justify circumcision by faith, and uncircumcision through the faith.

31 Then *is* Law annulled through the faith? Let it not be! But we establish *the* Law.

Romans 4

1 Abraham justified by faith. 13 By faith only he and his seed received the promise.

1 ¶ What then shall we say our father Abraham to have found according to flesh?

2 For if Abraham was justified by works, he has a boast, but not with God.

3 For what does the Scripture say? "And Abraham believed God, and it was imputed to him for righteousness." *Gen. 15:6*

4 But *to one* working, the reward is not imputed according to grace, but according to debt.

5 But to the *one* not working, but believing on the *One* justifying the ungodly, his faith is imputed for righteousness.

6 Even as also David says of the blessing of the man to whom God imputes righteousness apart from works:

7 "Blessed *are they* whose lawlessnesses have been remitted, and whose sins are covered;

8 blessed *is the* man to whom *the* Lord will not impute sin." *LXX-Psa. 31:1, 2*

9 ¶ *Is* this blessing then on the circumcision, or also on the uncircumcision? For we say the faith "was imputed to Abraham for righteousness." *Gen. 15:6*

10 How then was it imputed? Being in circumcision, or in uncircumcision? Not in circumcision, but in uncircumcision!

11 And he received a sign of circumcision *as* a seal of the righteousness of the faith, the *one while* in uncircumcision, for him to be a father of all the *ones* believing through uncircumcision, for righteousness to be imputed to them also,

12 and a father of circumcision to the *ones* not of circumcision only, but also to the *ones* walking in the steps of the faith of our father Abraham, the *one he had* during uncircumcision.

13 For the promise *was* not through Law to Abraham, or to his seed, *for* him to be the heir of the world, but through a righteousness of faith.

14 For if the *ones* of Law *are* heirs, faith has been made void, and the promise has been annulled.

15 For the Law works out wrath; for where no law is, neither *is* transgression.

16 Because of this, *it is* of faith, that *it be* according to grace, for the promise to be confirmed to all the seed, not to the *seed* of the Law only, but also to the *one* of *the* faith of Abraham, who is the father of us all,

17 even as it is written, "I have appointed you a father of many nations"; before God, whom he believed, the *One* making the dead *ones* live, and calling the things not being as *if* being, *Gen. 17:5*

18 who beyond hope believed on hope, for him to become a father of many nations, according to what was said, "So shall your seed be." *Gen. 15:5*

19 And being about a hundred years *old*, not weakening in the faith, he did not consider his body already being *as good as* dead, nor yet the dead state of Sarah's womb,

20 and did not hesitate by unbelief at the promise of God, but was empowered by faith, giving glory to God,

21 and being fully persuaded that what He has promised, He is also able to do.

22 Therefore "it was also imputed to him for righteousness." *Gen. 15:6*

23 ¶ But it was not written on account of him only, that it was imputed to him,

24 but also because of us, to whom it is going to be imputed, to the *ones* believing on the *One* having raised our Lord Jesus from *the* dead *ones*,

25 who was given over on account of our deviations, and was raised on account of our justification.

Romans 5

1 Being justified by faith, we have peace with God. 12 As sin and death came by Adam, 17 so much more righteousness and life by Jesus Christ.

1 ¶ Therefore being justified by faith, we have peace with God through our Lord Jesus Christ,

2 through whom also we have had access by the faith into this grace in which we stand, and we glory on the hope of the glory of God.

3 And not only so, but we glory also in afflictions, knowing that affliction fully works patient endurance,

4 and patient endurance *fully works* proven character; and proven character, hope.

5 And the hope not puts to shame, because the love of God has been poured out in our hearts through *the* Holy Spirit, the *One* given to us;

6 ¶ for we yet being without strength, in due time Christ died for ungodly *ones*.

7 For hardly anyone will die on behalf of a righteous *one*, (for perhaps anyone even dares to die for the sake of the good *one*),

8 but God demonstrates His love to us in that we being yet sinners, Christ died for us.

9 Much more then, having been justified now by His blood, we shall be saved from the wrath through Him.

10 For if *while* being hostile *ones* we were reconciled to God through the death of His Son, much more, having been reconciled, we shall be saved by His life;

11 and not only *so*, but also glorying in God through our Lord Jesus Christ, through whom we now received the reconciliation.

12 Because of this, even as sin entered the world through one man, and death through sin, so also death passed to all men, inasmuch as all sinned.

13 For sin was in *the* world until Law, but sin is not imputed *there* not being law;

14 but death reigned from Adam until Moses, even over the *ones* not sinning on the likeness of Adam's transgression, who is a type of the *One* going to come.

15 But not as the deviation, so also is the free gift. For if by the deviation of the one the many died, much more the grace of God, and the gift in grace, which *is* of the one Man, Jesus Christ, abounded to the many.

16 And the gift *is* not as through one having sinned; for indeed the judgment *was* of one to condemnation, but the free gift *is* of many deviations to justification.

17 For if by the deviation of the one death reigned through the one, much more the

ones receiving the abundance of grace and the gift of righteousness shall reign in life through the One, Jesus Christ.

18 So therefore, as through one deviation *came* to all men unto condemnation, so also through one effected righteousness *came* to all men unto justification of life.

19 For as through the one man's disobedience the many were constituted sinners, so also through the obedience of the One the many shall be constituted righteous *ones*.

20 But Law came in besides, that the deviation might abound; but where sin abounded, grace much more abounded,

21 that as sin ruled in death, so also grace might rule through righteousness to everlasting life, through Jesus Christ our Lord.

Romans 6

1 We may not live in sin. 12 Let not sin reign any more, 23 for death is the wages of sin.

1 ¶ What then shall we say? Shall we continue in sin that grace may abound?

2 Let it not be! We who died to sin, how shall we still live in it?

3 Or are you ignorant that as many as were baptized into Christ Jesus were baptized into His death?

4 Therefore, we were buried with Him through baptism into death, that as Christ was raised up from *the* dead *ones* by the glory of the Father, so also we should walk in newness of life.

5 For if we have been united together in the likeness of His death, so also shall we be in the resurrection,

6 knowing this, that our old man was crucified with *Him*, that the body of sin might be done away with, so that we no longer serve sin.

7 For the *one* having died has been justified from sin.

8 But if we died with Christ, we believe that also we shall live with Him,

9 knowing that Christ being raised from *the* dead *ones* dies no more; death no longer rules Him.

10 For in that He died, He died to sin once for all; but in that He lives, He lives to God.

11 So also you count yourselves to be truly dead to sin, but alive to God in Christ Jesus our Lord.

12 Therefore do not let sin reign in your mortal body, to obey it in its lusts.

13 Neither present your members *as* instruments of unrighteousness to sin, but present yourselves to God as *one* living from *the* dead, and your members instruments of righteousness to God.

14 For your sin shall not rule over you, for you are not under Law, but under grace.

15 What then? Shall we sin because we are not under law, but under grace? Let it not be!

16 Do you not know that to whom you present yourselves *as* slaves for obedience, you are slaves to whom you obey, whether of sin to death, or obedience to righteousness?

17 But thanks *be* to God that you were slaves of sin, but you obeyed from *the* heart a form of doctrine to which you were given over.

18 But having been set free from sin, you were enslaved to righteousness.

19 I speak as a man on account of the weakness of your flesh. For as you presented your members *as* slaves to uncleanness and to lawlessness unto lawlessness, so now present your members as slaves to righteousness unto sanctification.

20 For when you were slaves of sin, you were free to righteousness.

21 Therefore what fruit did you have then over *the things* which you are now ashamed? For the end of those *things is* death.

22 But now having been set free from sin, and having been enslaved to God, you have your fruit unto sanctification, and the end everlasting life.

23 For the wages of sin *is* death, but the gift of God *is* everlasting life in Christ Jesus our Lord.

Romans 7

1 The law rules over a man as long as he lives.
7 Is the law sin? 12 No, but holy, just, good.

¶ Or are you ignorant, brothers, (for I speak to those knowing *the* law), that the law rules over the man for as long a time as he lives?

2 For the married woman was bound by law to the living husband; but if the husband dies, she is set free from the law of the husband.

3 So therefore, *if* the husband *is* living, she will be called an adulteress if she becomes another man's. But if the husband dies, she is free from the law, *so as for* her not to be an adulteress *by* becoming another man's.

4 So that, my brothers, you also were made dead to the law through the body of Christ, for you to become Another's, to *the One* having been raised from *the* dead *ones*, so that we may bear fruit to God.

5 For when we were in the flesh, the passions of sin were working in our members through the law for the bearing of fruit unto death.

6 But now we have been set free from the Law, having died *to that* in which we were held, so as *for* us to serve in newness of spirit, and not *in* oldness of letter.

7 ¶ What shall we say then? *Is* the law sin? Let it not be! But I did not know sin if not through law; for also I did not know lusting if not the law said, "You shall not lust." *Ex. 20:17*

8 But sin taking opportunity through the commandment worked every lust in me; for apart from law, sin *is* dead.

9 And I lived apart from Law once, but the commandment coming, and sin came alive again, and I died.

10 And the commandment which *was* to life, this was found *to be* death to me;

11 for sin taking opportunity through the commandment deceived me, and through it killed *me*.

12 So indeed the law *is* holy, and the commandment holy and just and good.

13 Then *has* the good become death to me? Let it not be! But sin, that it might appear *to be* sin, having worked out death to me through the good, in order that sin might become excessively sinful through the commandment.

14 ¶ For we know that the Law is spiritual, but I am fleshly, having been sold under sin.

15 For what I fully work I do not know. For what I do not will, this I do. But what I hate, this I do.

16 But if I do what I do not will, I agree with the Law, that *it is* good.

17 But now I no longer fully work it, but the sin dwelling in me.

18 For I know that in me, that is in my flesh, dwells no good. For to will is present to me, but to fully work the good *thing* I do not find.

19 For what good *thing* I will, I do not do. But the evil I do not will, this I do.

20 But if I do what I do not will, *it is* no longer I fully working it , but the sin dwelling in me.

21 I find then the law, to me the *one* willing to do the good, that evil is present with me.

22 For I delight in the Law of God according to the inward man;

23 but I see another law in my members warring against the law of my mind, and capturing me by the law of sin being in my members.

24 O wretched man *that* I *am*! Who shall deliver me from the body of this death?

25 I thank God through Jesus Christ our Lord! So then I myself with the mind truly serve *the* Law of God, but *with* the flesh *the* law of sin.

Romans 8

1 They that are in Christ are free from condemnation. 5, 13 What harm comes of the flesh, 6, 14 and what good of the Spirit.

1 ¶ *There is* therefore now no condemnation to the *ones* in Christ Jesus, not walking according to flesh, but according to Spirit.

2 For the law of the Spirit of life in Christ Jesus set me free from the law of sin and of death.

3 For the law *being* powerless, in that it was weak through the flesh, God sending His own Son in *the* likeness of sinful flesh, and concerning sin, condemned sin in the flesh,

4 so that the righteous demand of the Law might be fulfilled in us, the *ones* not walking according to flesh, but according to Spirit.

5 For the *ones* being according to flesh are mindful of the things of the flesh. And the *ones* according to Spirit the things of the Spirit.

6 For the mind of the flesh *is* death, but the mind of the Spirit *is* life and peace.

7 Therefore the mind of the flesh *is* enmity towards God; for it is not being subject to the law of God, for neither can it *be.*

8 And the *ones* being in the flesh are not able to please God.

9 But you are not in *the* flesh, but in *the* Spirit, if indeed *the* Spirit of God dwells in you. But if anyone has not *the* Spirit of Christ, this one is not His.

10 ¶ But if Christ *is* in you, the body indeed *is* dead because of sin, but the Spirit *is* life because of righteousness.

11 But if the Spirit of the *One* having raised Jesus from *the* dead *ones* dwells in you, the *One* having raised the Christ from *the* dead *ones* will also give life to your mortal bodies through the indwelling of His Spirit in you.

12 So, then, brothers, we are debtors, not to the flesh, to live according to flesh,

13 for if you live according to flesh, you are going to die. But if by *the* Spirit you put to death the practices of the body, you will live.

14 For as many as are led by *the* Spirit of God, these are sons of God.

15 For you received not a spirit of slavery again to fear, but you received a Spirit of adoption by which we cry, Abba! Father!

16 The Spirit Himself witnesses with our spirit that we are children of God.

17 ¶ And if children, also heirs; truly heirs of God, and joint-heirs of Christ, if indeed we suffer together, that we may also be glorified together.

18 For I consider that the sufferings of the time now *are* not worthy to *be compared to* the coming glory to be revealed in us.

19 For the earnest expectation of the creation eagerly awaits the revelation of the sons of God.

20 For the creation was not willingly subjected to vanity, but through the *One* subjecting *it*, on hope;

21 that also the creation will be freed from the slavery of corruption into the freedom of the glory of the children of God.

22 For we know that all the creation groans together and travails together until now.

23 And not only *so*, but also we ourselves having the firstfruit of the Spirit, even we ourselves groan within ourselves, eagerly awaiting adoption, the redemption of our body;

24 for we were saved by hope, but hope being seen is not hope; for what anyone sees, why does he also hope?

25 But if we hope for what we do not see, by patient endurance we eagerly await *it*.

26 ¶ And likewise the Spirit also joins in to help our weaknesses. For we do not know what we should pray as it is right, but the Spirit Himself intercedes on our behalf with groanings that cannot be uttered.

27 But the *One* searching the hearts knows what *is the* mind of the Spirit, because He petitions on behalf of *the* saints according to God.

28 But we know that *to* the *ones* loving God all things work together for good, *to* the *ones* being called out *ones* according to purpose;.

29 ¶ because whom He foreknew, He also predestinated *to be* conformed to the image of His Son, for Him to be *the* First-begotten among many brothers.

30 But whom He predestinated, these He also called; and whom He called, these He also justified; and whom He justified, these He also glorified.

31 ¶ What then shall we say to these things? If God *be* for us, who *can be* against us?

32 *He* who indeed did not spare His own Son, but gave Him over on behalf of us all, how will He not freely give all things to us with Him?

33 Who will bring any charge against *the* elect *ones* of God? God *is* the *One* justifying!

34 Who *is* the *one* condemning? Christ *is* the *One* having died, but rather also having been raised, who also is at *the* right *hand* of God, who also intercedes on our behalf.

35 Who shall separate us from the love of Christ? *Shall* tribulation, or distress, or persecution, or famine, or nakedness, or danger, or sword?

36 Even as it is written, "For Your sake we are killed all the day; we are counted as sheep of slaughter." *Psa. 44:22*

37 But in all these things we are more than a conquerer through Him loving us.

38 For I am persuaded that neither death, nor life, nor angels, nor rulers, nor powers, nor *things* present, nor *things* to come,

39 nor height, nor depth, nor any other creature will be able to separate us from the love of God in Christ Jesus, our Lord.

Romans 9

1 Paul is grieved for the Jews. 25 The calling of the nations and rejecting of the Jews were foretold.

1 ¶ I say *the* truth in Christ, I do not lie, my conscience bearing witness with me in *the* Holy Spirit,

2 that my sadness is great, and a never-ceasing grief *is* in my heart,

3 for I myself was wishing to be accursed from Christ for the sake of my brothers, my kinsmen according to flesh,

4 who are Israelites, of whom *are* the adoption and the glory, and the covenants, and the Law-giving, and the service, and the promises;

5 of whom *are* the fathers, and from whom *is* the Christ according to flesh, He being God over all, blessed to the ages. Amen.

6 ¶ *It is* not, however, that God's Word has failed. For not all the *ones* of Israel, these *are of* Israel,

7 nor because they are Abraham's seed *are* all children, but "In Isaac a Seed shall be called to you." *Gen. 21:12*

8 That is: not the children of flesh *are* children of God, but the children of the promise *are* reckoned for a seed.

9 For the Word of promise *is* this, "According to this time I will come, and a son will be to Sarah." *Gen. 18:10*

10 And not only so, but also Rebekah having conceived by a man, our father Isaac.

11 for *the children* not yet being born, nor having done any good or evil, that the purpose of God according to election might stand, not of works, but of the *One* calling,

12 it was said to her, "The greater shall serve the lesser"; *Gen. 25:23*

13 even as it has been written, "I loved Jacob, but I hated Esau." *Mal. 1:2, 3*

14 ¶ What then shall we say? *Is there* not unrighteousness with God? Let it not be!

15 For He said to Moses, "I will have mercy on whomever I will have mercy, and I will pity whomever I pity." *Ex. 33:19*

16 So, then, *it is* not of the *one* willing, nor of the *one* running, but of the *One* having mercy, of God.

17 For the Scripture says to Pharaoh, "For this very thing I raised you up, so that I might show forth My power in you, and so that My name might be publicized in all the earth." *Ex. 9:16*

18 So, then, to whom He wills, He shows mercy; but to whom He wills, He hardens.

19 You will then say to me, Why does He yet find fault? For who has resisted His will?

20 *Nay*, rather, O man, who are you, the *one* answering back to God? Shall the thing formed say to the *One* forming *it*, Why did You make me like this? *Isa. 29:16*

21 Or does not the potter have authority *over* the clay, out of the same lump to make one vessel to honor, and one to dishonor? *Jer. 18:6*

22 But if God, desiring to display wrath, and to make His power known, endured in much long-suffering vessels of wrath having been fitted out for destruction,

23 and that He make known the riches of His glory on vessels of mercy which He before prepared for glory,

24 whom He also called, not only us, of Jews, but also out of nations.

25 ¶ As also He says in Hosea, I will call the *ones* Not My People, My People! And the *ones* Not Being Loved, Being Loved! *Hosea 2:23*

26 "And it shall be, in the place where it was said to them, You are Not My people, there they will be called, "Sons of the Living God." *LXX-Hos. 2:1; MT-Hos. 2:23*

27 But Isaiah cries on behalf of Israel, "If the number of the sons of Israel be as the sand of the sea, the remnant will be saved."

28 For *He is* finishing and finishing quickly the matter "in righteousness," "because *the* Lord" "will do a thing having finished quickly" "on the earth." *Isa. 10:22, 23*

29 And as Isaiah predicted, "If not *the* Lord of hosts left a seed to us, we would have become as Sodom, and as Gomorrah we would have been compared." *Isa. 1:9*

30 ¶ What then shall we say? That *the* nations, the *ones* not pursuing righteousness, have taken over righteousness, but a righteousness of faith;

31 but Israel pursuing a law of righteousness did not arrive to a law of righteousness?

32 Why? Because *it was* not of faith, but as of works of Law. For they stumbled at the Stone-of-stumbling,

33 as it has been written, "Behold, I place in" "Zion a Stone-of-stumbling," "and a Rock-of-offense," "and everyone believing on Him will not be shamed." *LXX and MT-Isa. 28:16; MT-Isa. 8:14*

Romans 10

1 The scripture shows the difference between the righteousness of the law, and of faith, 11 and that all, both the Jew and anyone of the nations that believe, shall not be confounded.

1 ¶ Brothers, truly my heart's pleasure and supplication to God on behalf of Israel is unto salvation.

2 For I testify to them that they have zeal to God, but not according to knowledge.

3 For not knowing the righteousness of God, and seeking to establish their own righteousness, they did not submit to the righteousness of God.

4 For the end of the law *is* Christ for righteousness to everyone that believes.

5 For Moses writes *of* the righteousness *which is* of the Law: "The man doing these things shall live by them." *Lev. 18:5*

6 But the righteousness of faith says this: "Do not say in your heart, Who will go up into Heaven?" (that is, to bring down Christ);

7 or, "Who will go down into the abyss?" (that is, to bring Christ up from dead *ones*.)

8 But what does it say? "The Word is near you, in your mouth and in your heart" (that is, the Word of the faith which we proclaim) *Deuteronomy 30:12-14.*

9 Because if you confess *the* Lord Jesus with your mouth, and believe in your heart that God raised Him from *the* dead *ones*, you will be saved.

10 For with *the* heart *one* believes unto righteousness, and with *the* mouth *one* confesses unto salvation.

11 For the Scripture says, "Everyone believing on Him will not be put to shame." *Isa. 28:16*

12 ¶ For there is no difference both of Jew and of Greek, for the same Lord of

all is rich toward all the *ones* calling on Him.

13 For every *one*, "whoever may call on the name of *the* Lord will be saved." *Joel 2:32*

14 How then may they call on *One* into whom they have not believed? And how may they believe *One* of whom they have not heard? And how may they hear without preaching?

15 And how may they preach if they are not sent? Even as it is written, "How beautiful" "the feet of the *ones* preaching the gospel of peace, of the *ones* preaching the gospel of good things." *Isa. 52:7*

16 But not all obeyed the gospel, for Isaiah says, "Lord, who has believed our report?" *Isa. 53:1*

17 Then the faith *is* of hearing, and hearing through the Word of God.

18 But I say, Did they not hear? Nay, rather, "into all the earth their voice went out, and to the ends of the world their words." *LXX-Psa. 18:5; MT-Psa. 19:4*

19 But I say, Did not Israel know? First, Moses says, "I will provoke you to jealousy by a non-nation, by an undiscerning nation I will anger you." *Deut. 32:21*

20 But Isaiah *is* very bold and says, "I was found by the *ones* not seeking Me; I became manifest to the *ones* not inquiring after Me." *Isa. 65:1*

21 But to Israel He says, "All the day I stretched out My hands to a disobeying and contradicting people." *Isa. 65:2*

Romans 11

1 God has not cast off all Israel. 16 There is hope of their conversion. 33 God's judgments are unsearchable.

1 ¶ I say then, Did not God put away His people? Let it not be! For I also am an Israelite, out of Abraham's seed, of *the* tribe of Benjamin.

2 "God did not put away His people" whom He foreknew. *Psa. 94:14* Or do you not know what the Scripture said in Elijah, how he pleaded with God against Israel, saying,

3 Lord, "they killed Your prophets," "and they dug down Your altars," "and only I am left, and they seek my life." *1 Kg. 19:10*

4 But what does the Divine answer say to him, "I reserved to Myself seven thousand men who did not bow *the* knee to Baal." *1 Kg. 19:18*

5 So then, also in the present time a remnant according to election of grace has come to be.

6 But if by grace, no longer *is it* of works; else grace no longer becomes grace. But if of works, it is no longer grace; else work is no longer work.

7 What then? What Israel seeks, this it did not obtain, but the election obtained *it*, and the rest were hardened;

8 even as it is written, "God gave to them a spirit of slumber, eyes not seeing and ears not hearing" until today, *this* day. *Isa. 29:10; Deut. 29:4*

9 And David said, "Let their table become for a snare and a trap, and for a stumbling block," and a recompense to them;

10 "let their eyes be darkened, not to see, and their back through all bent." *LXX-Psa.68:23, 24; MT-Psa. 69:22, 23*

11 I say, then, Did not they stumble that they might fall? Let it not be! But by their deviation *came* salvation to the nations, to provoke them to jealousy.

12 But if their deviation *is the* riches of *the* world, and their default *the* riches of *the* nations, how much more their fulfilling?

13 For I speak to you, the nations, inasmuch as I am indeed an apostle of the nations (I glorify my ministry),

14 if *some*how I may provoke to jealousy my flesh, and may save some of them.

15 For if their casting away *is the* reconciliation of *the* world, what *is* the reception, except life from *the* dead *ones*?

16 Now if the firstfruit *is* holy, *so* also the lump. And if the root *is* holy, *so* also *are* the branches.

17 But if some of the branches were broken off, and you, being a wild olive tree were grafted in among them, and became a sharer of the root and the fatness of the olive tree,

18 do not boast against the branches. But if you do boast, *it is* not you *that* bears the root, but the root bears you.

19 You will say then, The branches were broken off that I might be grafted in.

20 Well! For unbelief they were broken off. And you stand by faith. Do not *be* highminded, but fear.

21 For if God did not spare the according to nature branches, *fear* lest neither He will spare you.

22 Behold, therefore, *the* kindness and severity of God: On the *ones* having fallen, severity. But on you, kindness, if you continue in the kindness. Otherwise, you will also be cut off.

23 And those also, if they do not continue in unbelief, will be grafted in. For God is able to graft them in again.

24 For if you were cut out of the according to nature wild olive *tree*, and against nature were grafted into a cultivated olive *tree*, how much more these, the *ones* according to nature, will be grafted into *their* own olive tree?

25 For I do not want you to be ignorant of this mystery, brothers, so that you may not be wise among yourselves, that hardness in part has happened to Israel until the fulfilling of the nations comes in;

26 and so all Israel will be saved, even as it has been written, "The *One* delivering will come out of Zion, and He will turn away ungodliness from Jacob.

27 And this *is* My covenant with them, when I take away their sins." *Isa. 59:20, 21*

28 Indeed, as regards the gospel, *ones* hostile toward you, but as regards the election, beloved on account of the fathers.

29 For the free gifts and the calling of God *are* not to be repented of.

30 For as you then also disobeyed God, but now have obtained mercy by the disobedience of these,

31 so also these now have disobeyed, so that they also may obtain mercy by your mercy.

32 For God shut up all into disobedience, that He may show mercy to all.

33 ¶ O *the* depth of *the* riches and of *the* wisdom and *the* knowledge of God! How unsearchable *are* His judgments and His ways past finding out!

34 "For who has known the mind of *the* Lord? Or who came to be His counselor?" *Isa. 40:13*

35 "Or who first gave to Him, and it will be repaid to him?" *Job 41:11*

36 Because of Him, and through Him, and to Him *are* all things. To Him be the glory forever! Amen.

Romans 12

1 God's mercies must move us to please God.
9 Love and many other duties are required of us.

1 ¶ Therefore, brothers, I call on you through the compassions of God to present your bodies a living sacrifice, holy, pleasing to God, *which is* your reasonable service.

2 And be not conformed to this age, but be transformed by the renewal of your mind, in order to prove by you what *is* the good and pleasing and perfect will of God.

3 For through the grace having been given to me, I say to every *one* being among you, not to think too highly beyond what is right to think. But think to be of sound mind, even as God divided a measure of faith to each *one*.

4 For even as we have many members in one body, but all members do not have the same function,

5 so we the many are one body in Christ, and members to one another,

6 but having differing gifts according to the grace given to us, whether prophecy, according to the proportion of the faith;

7 or ministry, in the ministry; or the *one* teaching, in the teaching;

8 or the *one* exhorting, in the encouragement; the *one* sharing, in simplicity; the *one* leading, in diligence; the *one* showing mercy, in cheerfulness.

9 *Let* love *be* without hypocrisy, shrinking from the evil, cleaving to the good,

10 in brotherly love toward one another, loving tenderly, going before one another in honor;

11 in diligence, not slothful, fervent in spirit, serving the Lord;

12 in hope, rejoicing; in distress, enduring; in prayer, steadfastly continuing;

13 imparting to the needs of the saints, pursuing hospitality.

14 Bless the *ones* persecuting you; bless, and do not curse.

15 Rejoice with rejoicing *ones*, and weep with weeping *ones*;

16 be mindful of the same thing toward one another, not being mindful of high things, but be accommodating to the lowly *ones*. Do not become wise *ones* among yourselves;

17 returning evil for evil to no one; considering beforehand good things before all men. *Prov. 3:4*

18 If possible, from you being in peace with all men;

19 not avenging yourselves, beloved, but giving place to wrath, for it has been written, "Vengeance *is* Mine," "I will repay," says *the* Lord. *Deut. 32:35*

20 Then "if a hostile *one to* you hungers, feed him; if he thirsts, give him drink; for doing this you will heap coals of fire on his head." *Prov. 25:21, 22*

21 Do not be overcome by evil, but overcome the evil with good.

Romans 13

Subjection, and other duties, we owe to magistrates.

1 ¶ Let every soul be subject to higher authorities having power, for there is no authority except from God, but the existing authorities have been ordained by God.

2 So that the *one* resisting authority has opposed the ordinance of God, and the *ones* opposing will receive judgment to themselves.

3 For the rulers are not a terror to good works, but to the bad *ones*. And do you desire not to fear the authority? Do the good *thing*, and you will have praise from it;

4 for it is a servant of God to you for the good. But if you do the bad *things*, be afraid; for it does not bear the sword in vain; for it is a servant of God, an avenger for wrath to the *one* practicing bad *things*.

5 Therefore *it is* necessary to be subject, not only on account of wrath, but also on account of conscience.

6 For on this account you also pay taxes, for *they* are ministers of God, attending continually to this very thing.

7 ¶ Therefore give over to all *their* dues: to the *one due* tax, the tax; to the *one due* tribute, the tribute; to the *one due* fear, the fear; to the *one due* honor, the honor.

8 Do not continue to owe, no one, nothing, if not to love one another. For the *one* loving the other has fulfilled the Law.

9 For, "Do not commit adultery," "do not murder," "do not steal," do not bear false witness, "do not covet," *Ex. 20:13-15, 17* and if *there is* any other commandment, in this Word it is summed up, in the *words*, "You shall love your neighbor as yourself." *Lev. 19:18*

10 Love does not work bad *things* to the neighbor. Then the fulfillment of Law *is* love.

11 ¶ Also this, knowing the time, that *it is* now the hour for you to be aroused from sleep, for now our salvation *is* nearer than when we *first* believed.

12 The night *is* advanced, and the day has drawn near; therefore let us cast off the works of darkness, and let us put on the weapons of the light.

13 Let us walk becomingly, as in *the* day, not in revelries and drunkenesses, not in co-habitations and lustful acts, not in strife and envy.

14 But put on the Lord Jesus Christ, and do not make forethought of the flesh, for *its* lusts.

Romans 14

3 Men may not despise nor condemn one the other, 13 but take heed that they give no offense.

1 ¶ And receive the *one* who is weak in the faith, not to judgments of thoughts.

2 One indeed believes to eat all things, but being weak, *another* one eats vegetables.

3 The *one* eating, do not despise the *one* not eating. And the *one* not eating, do not judge the *one* eating, for God received him.

4 Who are you judging another's servant? To his own master he stands or falls. But he will stand, for God is able to make him stand.

5 One indeed judges a day above *another* day; and *another* one judges every day *alike*. Let each *one* be fully assured in his own mind.

6 The *one* being mindful of the day, he is mindful of *it* to *the* Lord. And the *one* not being mindful of the day, he is not mindful of *it* to *the* Lord. The *one* eating, he eats to *the* Lord; for he gives thanks to God. And the *one* not eating, he does not eat to *the* Lord, and gives thanks to God.

7 For no one of us lives to himself and no one dies to himself.

8 For both if we live, we live to *the* Lord; and if we die, we die to *the* Lord. Therefore both if we live, and if we die, we are the Lord's.

9 For this Christ both died and rose and lived again, that He might be Lord over both *the* dead *ones* and the living.

10 But why do you judge your brother? Or why, also, do you despise your brother? For all shall stand before the judgment seat of Christ.

11 For it is written, *"As* I live, says the Lord, that every knee will bow to Me, and every tongue confess to God." *Isa. 45:23*

12 So then each *one* of us will give account concerning himself to God.

13 Therefore let us no longer judge one another, but rather judge this, not to put a stumbling block or a snare toward a brother.

14 I know and have been persuaded in *the* Lord Jesus that nothing by itself is common; except to the *one* deeming anything to be common, *it is* common.

15 But if your brother is grieved because of *your* food, you no longer walk according to love. Do not by your food destroy that one for whom Christ died.

16 Therefore do not let your good be spoken evil of.

17 For the kingdom of God is not eating and drinking, but righteousness and peace and joy in *the* Holy Spirit.

18 For the *one* serving Christ in these things *is* pleasing to God, and approved by men.

19 So therefore let us pursue the things of peace, and the things for building up one another.

20 Do not for the sake of your food tear down the work of God. Truly, all things *are* clean, but *it is* a bad *thing* to the man who eats through a stumbling block.

21 *It is* good not to eat flesh, nor to drink wine, nor *anything* by which your brother stumbles, or is caused to stumble, or is weak.

22 Do you have faith? Have *it* to yourself before God. Blessed *is* the *one* not judging himself in what he approves.

23 But the *one* doubting, if he eats, *he* has been condemned, because it is not of faith; and all which *is* not of faith is sin.

Romans 15

1 The strong must bear with the weak. 2 We may not please ourselves, 3 for Christ did not do so.

1 ¶ But we, the powerful *ones*, ought to bear the weaknesses of the *ones* not powerful, and not to please ourselves.

2 For let each *one* of us please *his* neighbor for good, to building up.

3 For also Christ did not please Himself, but even as it has been written, "The reproaches of the *ones* reproaching You fell on Me." *LXX-Psa. 68:10; MT-Psa. 69:9*

4 For as many *things* as were written before were written for our instruction, that through the patience and the encouragement of the Scriptures we might have hope.

5 ¶ And may the God of patience and encouragement give to you to be mindful of the same thing among one another according to Christ Jesus,

6 that with one accord *and* with one mouth you may glorify *the* God and Father of our Lord Jesus Christ.

7 ¶ Therefore receive one another as Christ also received us, to *the* glory of God.

8 And I say, Jesus Christ has become a minister of circumcision for the truth of God, to confirm the promises of the fathers,

9 and the nations on behalf of mercy to glorify God, even as it is written, "Because of this I will confess to You among *the* nations, and I will sing praise to Your name." *Psa. 18:49*

10 And again He says, "Rejoice, nations, with His people." *Deut. 32:43*

11 And again, "Praise the Lord, all the nations, and praise Him all the peoples." *Psa. 117:1*

12 And again Isaiah says, *"There* shall be the Root of Jesse, and the *One* rising up to rule the nations; on Him nations will hope." *Isa. 11:10*

13 ¶ And may the God of hope fill you with all joy and peace in believing, for you to abound in hope, in power of *the* Holy Spirit.

14 ¶ Now, my brothers, I myself also am persuaded concerning you, that you yourselves also are full of goodness, having been

filled with all knowledge, being able to admonish one another.

15 But I wrote to you more boldly, brothers, as reminding you in part, because of the grace given to me by God,

16 for me to be a minister of Jesus Christ to the nations, sacredly ministering the gospel of God, that the offering of the nations might be acceptable, sanctified by *the* Holy Spirit.

17 ¶ Therefore I have glorying in Christ Jesus *as to* the things with regard to God.

18 For I will not dare to speak of anything which Christ did not work out through me for *the* obedience of the nations in word and work,

19 in power of *miraculous* signs and wonders, in power of *the* Spirit of God, so as *for* me to have fulfilled *the preaching of* the gospel of Christ from Jerusalem and in a circle as far as Illyricum.

20 And so eagerly striving to preach the gospel where Christ was not named, so that I should not build on another's foundation,

21 but even as it is written, "They shall see, to whom nothing was announced concerning Him; and the *ones* that have not heard, *they* shall understand." *Isa. 52:15*

22 ¶ On this account I also was much hindered from coming to you,

23 but now having no more place in these regions, and having a longing to come to you for many years,

24 when ever I may go into Spain, I will come to you; for I hope *in* traveling through to see you and to be set forward there by you, if first I may be filled of you in part.

25 But now I am going to Jerusalem, doing service to the saints.

26 For Macedonia and Achaia thought it good to make certain contribution to the poor of the saints in Jerusalem.

27 For they thought it good, and their debtors *they* are; for if the nations shared in their spiritual things, they ought also to minister to them in the fleshly things.

28 Therefore being completed and having sealed this fruit to them, I will go through you into Spain.

29 And I know that I will come to you in the fullness of *the* blessing of the gospel of Christ *when* I come.

30 ¶ But I beseech you, brothers, by our Lord Jesus Christ, and by the love of the Spirit, to strive together with me in *your* prayers to God on my behalf,

31 that I be delivered from the *ones* disobeying in Judea, and that my ministry, which is to Jerusalem, may be acceptable to the saints,

32 that *I may* come to you in joy through *the* will of God, and that I may be refreshed with you.

33 And the God of peace *be* with all of you. Amen.

Romans 16

3 Paul wills the brethren to greet many, 17 and advises them to take heed of those which cause dissension and offenses.

1 ¶ But I commend our sister Phoebe to you, being a servant of the assembly in Cenchrea,

2 that you may receive her in *the* Lord, *as is* worthy of the saints, and may assist her in whatever thing she may need of you. For she also became a helper of many, and of me myself.

3 Greet Priscilla and Aquila, my fellow workers in Christ Jesus,

4 who laid down their neck for my soul, to whom not only I give thanks, but also all the assemblies of the nations.

5 And *greet* the assembly at their house, and my beloved Epenetus, who is a firstfruit of Achaia for Christ.

6 Greet Mary, who did much labor for us.

7 Greet Andronicus and Junias, my kinsmen and fellow prisoners, noted among the apostles, who also were in Christ before me.

8 Greet Amplias my beloved in *the* Lord.

9 Greet Urbanus, our helper in Christ, and my beloved Stachys.

10 Greet Apelles, the approved in Christ; Greet those of Aristobulus.

11 Greet Herodion, my kinsman. Greet the *ones* of Narcissus, the *ones* being in *the* Lord.

12 Greet Tryphena and Tryphosa, the *ones* laboring in *the* Lord. Greet Persis the beloved, who has labored in many things in *the* Lord.

13 Greet Rufus, the chosen in *the* Lord, and his mother and mine.

14 Greet Asyncritus, Phlegon, Hermas, Patrobas, Hermes, and the brothers with them.

15 Greet Philologus and Julias, Nereus and his sister, and Olympas, and all the saints with them.

16 Greet one another with a holy kiss. The assemblies of Christ greet you.

17 ¶ And brothers I exhort you to watch the *ones* making divisions and causes of stumbling contrary to the doctrine which you learned, and turn away from them.

18 For such *ones* do not serve our Lord Jesus Christ, but their own belly, and by smooth speech and fine speeches *they* deceive the hearts of the *ones* without guile.

19 For your obedience reached to all; therefore, I rejoice over you. But I desire you to be truly wise to the good, but simple toward the bad.

20 And the God of peace shall crush satan under your feet shortly. The grace of our Lord Jesus Christ *be* with you. Amen.

21 ¶ Timothy, my fellow-worker, and Lucius, and Jason, and Sosipater, my kinsmen, greet you.

22 I, Tertius, the *one* writing the epistle, greet you in *the* Lord.

23 Gaius, the host of all the assembly and me, greets you. Erastus, the steward of the city, and Quartus the brother, greet you.

24 The grace of our Lord Jesus Christ *be* with you all. Amen.

25 ¶ Now to the *One who is* able to establish you according to my gospel, and the proclaiming of Jesus Christ, according to the revelation of *the* mystery having been kept unvoiced during eternal times,

26 but now has been made plain, and by prophetic Scriptures, according to the commandment of the everlasting God, made known for obedience of faith to all the nations;

27 to *the* only wise God through Jesus Christ, to whom *be* the glory forever. Amen.

The First Epistle of Paul the Apostle to the
CORINTHIANS

1 Corinthians 1

10 He calls for unity. 18 God destroys the wisdom of the wise, 21 by the foolishness of preaching.

1 ¶ Paul, a called apostle of Jesus Christ, by *the* will of God, and Sosthenes the brother,

2 to the assembly of God being in Corinth, having been sanctified in Christ Jesus, called out saints, with all the *ones* calling on the name of our Lord Jesus Christ in every place, both theirs and ours:

3 Grace to you, and peace, from God our Father and *the* Lord Jesus Christ.

4 I give thanks to my God always concerning you *for* the grace of God given to you in Christ Jesus,

5 that in everything you were enriched in Him, *in* all discourse and all knowledge,

6 even as the testimony of Christ was confirmed in you,

7 so that you *are* not lacking in any gift, awaiting the revelation of our Lord Jesus Christ,

8 who also will confirm you until *the* end, blameless in the day of our Lord Jesus Christ.

9 God *is* faithful, through whom you were called into *the* fellowship of His Son, Jesus Christ, our Lord.

10 ¶ Now I exhort you, brothers, through the name of our Lord Jesus Christ that you all say the same, and there be no schisms among you, but you be restored to harmony, in the same mind and in the same judgment.

11 For about you, my brothers, it was shown to me by the *ones* of Chloe that there are contentions among you.

12 But I say this, that each of you says, I am of Paul, and I of Apollos, and I of Cephas, and I of Christ.

13 Has Christ been divided? Was Paul crucified for you? Or were you baptized into the name of Paul?

14 ¶ I thank God that I did not baptize one of you, except Crispus and Gaius,

15 that not anyone should say that you were baptized in my name.

16 And I also baptized the house of Stephanas. For the rest, I do not know if I baptized any other.

17 ¶ For Christ did not send me to baptize, but to preach the gospel, not in wisdom of words, lest the cross of Christ be nullified.

18 For the Word of the cross is foolishness to the *ones* perishing, but to us being saved it is *the* power of God.

19 For it is written, "I will destroy the wisdom of the wise *ones*, and I will set aside the understanding of the understanding *ones.*" *Isa. 29:14*

20 Where *is the* wise *one*? Where *is the* scribe? Where *is the* disputer of this world? Did God not make the wisdom of this world to be foolish?

21 For since in the wisdom of God the world *by* wisdom did not know God, God was pleased through the foolishness of preaching to save the *ones* believing.

22 And since Jews ask for a sign, and Greeks seek wisdom,

23 we, on the other hand, preach Christ crucified (truly a stumbling block to Jews, and a pitfall to Greeks),

24 but to them, the called *ones*, both to Jews and to Greeks, Christ *is* the power of God and the wisdom of God;

25 because the foolish *thing* of God is wiser *than* men, and the weak *thing* of God is stronger *than* men.

26 For you see your calling, brothers, that *there are* not many wise *ones* according to flesh, not many powerful *ones*, not many wellborn *ones*.

27 But God chose the foolish *things* of the world that the wise *ones* might be put to shame, and God chose the weak *things* of the world so that He might put to shame the strong *things*.

28 And God chose the low-born *ones* of the world, and the things beng despised,

and the things not being, so that He might nullify the things being,

29 so that no flesh might glory in His presence.

30 But of Him, you are in Christ Jesus, who was made to us wisdom from God, both righteousness and sanctification and redemption,

31 so that even as it is written, "He that glories, let him glory in" *the* "Lord." *Jer. 9:24*

1 Corinthians 2

Though his preaching bring not excellency of speech, or of human wisdom, yet it consists in the 4 power of God.

1 ¶ And when I came to you, brothers, I did not come with excellency of word or wisdom, declaring to you the testimony of God.

2 For I decided not to know anything among you except Jesus Christ, and Him being crucified.

3 And I was with you in weakness, and in fear, and in much trembling.

4 And my word and my preaching *was* not in persuasive words of human wisdom, but in proof of *the* Spirit and of power,

5 that your faith might not be in *the* wisdom of men, but in *the* power of God.

6 ¶ But we speak wisdom among the mature *ones*, but not the wisdom of this age, nor of the rulers of this age, the *ones* being caused to cease.

7 But we speak *the* wisdom of God having been hidden in a mystery, which God predetermined before the ages for our glory,

8 which none of the rulers of this age has known. For if they had known, they would not have crucified the Lord of glory;

9 but even as it is written, "The things *which* an eye did not see, and an ear did not hear," and did not come up on *the* heart of man, the *things* which God has prepared for the *ones* loving Him. *Isa. 64:4*

10 But God revealed *them* to us through His Spirit, for the Spirit searches all things, even the depths of God.

11 For who among men knows the things of a man, except the spirit of a man within him? So also no one has known the things of God if not the Spirit of God.

12 But we have not received the spirit of the world, but the Spirit from God, so that we might know the things freely given to us by God.

13 Which things we also speak, not in words taught in human wisdom, but in *words* taught of *the* Holy Spirit, comparing spiritual *things* with spiritual *things*.

14 But a natural man does not receive the things of *the* Spirit of God, for they are foolishness to him, and he is not able to know *them*, because they are spiritually discerned.

15 But the spiritual *one* discerns all things, but he is discerned by no one.

16 For "who has known *the* mind of *the* Lord?" "Who will instruct Him?" But we have *the* mind of Christ. *Isa. 40:13*

1 Corinthians 3

2 Milk is fit for children. 7 He that plants, and he that waters, is nothing. 9 The ministers are of God, fellow-workers; a field of God. 11 Christ the foundation.

1 ¶ And, brothers, I was not able to speak to you as to spiritual *ones*, but as to fleshly *ones*, as to babes in Christ.

2 I gave you milk to drink, and not *solid* food, for you were not then able, for neither are you yet able now.

3 For you are yet fleshly *ones*. For where among you *is* jealousy, and strife, and divisions, are you not fleshly *ones* and walking according to man?

4 For when one says, Truly I am of Paul, and another, I of Apollos; are you not fleshly *ones*?

5 ¶ Who then is Paul? And who *is* Apollos, but ministers through whom you believed, and to each *one* as the Lord gave?

6 I planted, Apollos watered, but God the *One* made to grow.

7 So as neither the *one* planting is anything, nor the *one* watering, but God the *One* making to grow.

8 So the *one* planting and the *one* watering are one, and each *one* will receive *his* own reward according to *his* own labor.

9 For of God we are fellow-workers, a field of God, *and* you are a building of God.

10 According to God's grace given to me, as a wise master builder, I laid a founda-

tion, but another builds on *it*. But let each *one* look how he builds on *it*.

11 ¶ For no one is able to lay another foundation beside the *one* having been laid, which is Jesus, the Christ.

12 And if anyone builds on this foundation gold, silver, precious stones, wood, grass, straw,

13 the work of each *one* will be revealed; for the Day will make *it* known, because it is revealed in fire; and the fire will prove the work of each *one*, what sort it is.

14 If the work of anyone which he built remains, he will receive a reward.

15 If the work of anyone shall be burned down, he shall suffer loss; but he will be saved, but so as through fire.

16 ¶ Do you not know that you are a temple of God, and the Spirit of God dwells in you?

17 If anyone corrupts the temple of God, God will corrupt this *one*; for the temple of God is holy, which you are.

18 ¶ Let no one deceive himself. If anyone thinks to be a wise *one* among you in this age, let him become a foolish *one*, that he may become a wise *one*.

19 For the wisdom of this world is foolishness with God; for it is written, "He is taking the wise *ones* in their *own* craftiness." *Job 5:13*

20 And again, "*The* Lord knows the reasonings of the wise *ones*, that they are useless." *LXX-Psa. 93:11; MT-Psa. 94:11*

21 ¶ So then let no one glory in men; for all things are yours,

22 whether Paul, or Apollos, or Cephas, or *the* world, or life, or death, or things present, or things to come; all are yours,

23 and you are Christ's, and Christ *is* God's.

1 Corinthians 4

1 In what account the ministers ought to be had.
9 The apostles spectacles to the world, angels, and men: 15 yet our fathers in Christ.

1 ¶ Let a man count us as under-servants of Christ and stewards of *the* mysteries of God.

2 For the rest, it is sought among stewards that one be found faithful.

3 But to me it is a small thing that I should be judged by you, or by a man's day. But I do not even judge myself.

4 For I know nothing of myself, but I have not been justified by this; but He judging me is *the* Lord.

5 So then do not judge anything before *the* time, until the Lord comes, who will both shed light on the hidden things of darkness and will reveal the purposes of the hearts. And then praise will be to each *one* from God.

6 And, brothers, I transferred these things to myself and Apollos because of you, that in us you may learn not to think above what is written, that you not *be* puffed up one against the other.

7 ¶ For who makes you to differ? And what do you have that you did not receive? And *if* you received *it*, why do you boast as not receiving *it*?

8 You are already being satiated; you already became rich; you reigned without us (and I would that you really did reign, so that we also might reign together with you!)

9 For I think that God pointed us out *as* last, the apostles, as condemned to death, because we became a spectacle to the world, even to angels and to men.

10 We *are* fools for the sake of Christ, but you *are* wise in Christ. We *are* weak, but you *are* strong. You *are* honored, but we *are* not honored.

11 Until the present hour we also hunger and thirst, and are poorly clothed, and are buffeted, and wander homeless,

12 and we labor, working with our own hands. Being cursed, we bless; persecuted, we bear;

13 being defamed, we entreat. We have become as offscouring of the world, dirt wiped off by all until now.

14 ¶ I do not write these things shaming you, but admonishing *you* as my beloved children.

15 For if you should have myriads of tutors in Christ, yet not many fathers; for I fathered you in Christ Jesus through the gospel.

16 Therefore I urge you, be imitators of me.

17 ¶ Because of this I sent Timothy to you, who is my beloved child, and faithful in *the* Lord, who will remind you *of* my ways in Christ, even as I teach everywhere in every assembly.

18 As to my not coming to you now, some were puffed up.

19 But if the Lord wills, I will come to you shortly. And I will know, not the word of the *ones* who being puffed up, but the power.

20 For the kingdom of God *is* not in word, but in power.

21 What do you desire? *Shall* I come to you with a rod, or *in* love and a spirit of meekness?

1 Corinthians 5

1 The incestuous person 6 is cause of shame.
7 The old leaven is to be purged out.

1 ¶ Everywhere *it is* heard that fornication *is* among you, and such fornication which is not named among the nations, so as *for* someone to have *his* father's wife.

2 And you are being puffed up, and have not rather mourned, that he that did this deed might be taken from your midst.

3 For as being absent in body, but being present in spirit, I have already judged the *one* who has perpetrated this deed, as being present:

4 In the name of our Lord Jesus Christ, you being assembled with my spirit also, with the power of our Lord Jesus Christ,

5 to give over such a one to Satan for destruction of the flesh, that the spirit may be saved in the day of the Lord Jesus.

6 Your boast *is* not good. Do you not know that a little leaven leavens all the lump?

7 ¶ Therefore clean out the old leaven so that you may be a new lump, even as you are unleavened. For also Christ our Passover was sacrificed for us.

8 So then let us keep *the* feast, not with old leaven, nor with leaven of malice and of wickedness, but with unleavened *bread* of sincerity and truth.

9 ¶ I wrote to you in the letter not to associate with fornicators;

10 and not altogether with the fornicators of this world, or with the covetous one, or with rapacious *ones*, or with idolaters, since then you must go out of the world.

11 But now I wrote to you not to associate intimately; if anyone being named a brother *and is* either a fornicator, or a cov-

etous one, or an idolater, or a reviler, or a drunkard, or a rapacious *one*, with such a one not to eat.

12 For what *is it* to me also to judge the *ones* outside? Do you not judge those inside?

13 But God will judge the *ones* outside. "And take away from yourselves the wicked *one*." *Deut. 17:7*

1 Corinthians 6

1 Against going to law. 18 Against sensuality.

1 ¶ Does anyone of you having a matter against another dare to be judged before the unjust, and not before the saints?

2 Do you not know that the saints will judge the world? And if the world is judged by you, are you unworthy of small judgments?

3 Do you not know that we shall judge angels, not to speak of this life?

4 If, then, you truly have judgments of this life, the *ones* being least esteemed in the assembly, you seat these.

5 For I say *this,* Shame to you. So, is there not a wise *one* among you, not even one in your midst who will be able to judge his brother?

6 But brother is judged with brother, and this before unbelievers!

7 Indeed, therefore, there is already actually a defeat with you, that you have lawsuits with yourselves. Why not instead be wronged? Why not instead be defrauded?

8 But you do wrong, and defraud, and these things to brothers!

9 ¶ Or do you not know that unjust *ones* will not inherit *the* kingdom of God? Do not be led astray, neither fornicators, nor idolaters, nor adulterers, nor boy-abusers, nor homosexuals,

10 nor thieves, nor covetous ones, nor drunkards, nor revilers, nor rapacious *ones* shall inherit *the* kingdom of God.

11 And some were these things, but you were washed, but you were sanctified, but you were justified in the name of the Lord Jesus, and in the Spirit of our God.

12 ¶ All things are lawful to me, but not all things are profitable. All things are lawful to me, but I will not be subjected by any.

13 Foods for the belly, and the belly for foods, but God will destroy both this and these. But the body *is* not for fornication, but for the Lord, and the Lord for the body.

14 And God both raised up the Lord, and *He* will raise us up through His power.

15 Do you not know that your bodies are members of Christ? Then taking the members of Christ, shall I make *them* members of a prostitute? Let it not be!

16 Or do you not know that he being joined to a prostitute is one body? For He says, "The two *shall be* into one flesh." *Gen. 2:24*

17 But the *one* being joined to the Lord is one spirit.

18 Flee fornication. Every sin which a man may do is outside the body, but he doing fornication sins against *his* own body.

19 Or do you not know that your body is a temple of *the* Holy Spirit in you, which you have from God, and you are not of yourselves?

20 You were bought with a price; then glorify God in your body, and in your spirit, which are of God.

1 Corinthians 7

2 He treats of marriage, 10 and shows that the bond should not lightly be dissolved.

1 ¶ But concerning what you wrote to me, *it is* good for a man not to touch a woman;

2 but because of fornication, let each *one* have his *own* wife, and let each *one* have her own husband.

3 Let the husband give due kindness to the wife, and likewise the wife also to the husband.

4 The wife does not have authority of *her* own body, but the husband. And likewise also the husband does not have authority *over his* own body, but the wife.

5 Do not deprive one another, if not by agreement for a time, that you may devote *yourselves* to fasting and to prayer. And come together again on the same *place*, that Satan may not tempt you through your lack of self-control.

6 But I say this by concession, not by command.

7 But I desire all men also to be as myself. But each *one* has his own gift from God, thus and thus.

8 But I say to the unmarried men, and to the widows, it is good for them if they also remain as I.

9 But if they do not have self control, let them marry; for it is better to marry than to be inflamed.

10 ¶ But I command the *ones* being married (not I, but the Lord), a woman not to be separated from her husband;

11 but if indeed she is separated, remain unmarried, or be reconciled to the husband; and a husband not to let *his* wife go.

12 But to the rest I say, not the Lord, if any brother has an unbelieving wife, and she consents to live with him, let him not let her go.

13 And a woman who has an unbelieving husband, and he consents to live with her, let her not let him go.

14 For the unbelieving husband has been sanctified by the wife, and the unbelieving wife has been sanctified by the husband; else, then, your children are unclean, but now they are holy.

15 But if the unbelieving *one* separates, let *them* be separated; the brother or the sister is not in bondage in such matters; but God has called us in peace.

16 For what do you know, wife, whether you will save the husband? Or what do you know, husband, whether you will save the wife?

17 ¶ If not as God has apportioned to each *one,* to each *one* as the Lord has called, so let him walk. So I command in the assemblies.

18 *Was* anyone called having been circumcised? Do not be uncircumcised. Was anyone called in uncircumcision? Do not be circumcised.

19 Circumcision is nothing, and uncircumcision is nothing, but the keeping of God's commands.

20 Each *one* in the calling in which he was called, in this remain.

21 Were you called as a slave? It does not matter to you. But if you are able to be free, rather use *it.*

22 For the *one* having been called as a slave in *the* Lord is a free man of *the* Lord. And likewise, the *one* being called a free man is a slave of Christ.

23 You were bought with a price; do not become slaves of men.

24 Each *one* in which *state* he was called, brothers, in this remain with God.

25 ¶ But about the virgins, I have no command of *the* Lord. But I give judgment, as having received mercy by *the* Lord to be faithful.

26 Therefore I think this to be good, because of the present necessity: that *it is* good for a man to be so.

27 Have you been bound to a wife? Do not seek to be released. Have you been released from a wife? Do not seek a wife.

28 But if you also marry, you do not sin. And if the virgin marries, she does not sin. But such will have trouble in the flesh; and I am sparing you.

29 But I say this, brothers, that the time having been cut short, the remaining *thing* is, that even the *ones* having wives should be as not having,

30 and the *ones* weeping as not weeping, and the *ones* rejoicing as not rejoicing, and the *ones* buying as not possessing,

31 and the *ones* using this world as not overusing *it*; for the fashion of this world is passing away.

32 But I desire you to be without care. The unmarried *one* cares *for* the things of *the* Lord, how to please the Lord;

33 but the *one* marrying cares *for* the things of the world, how to please the wife.

34 The wife and the virgin *are* different. The unmarried *one* cares *for* the things of *the* Lord, that she be holy in both body and spirit. But the married one cares *for* the things of the world, how to please the husband.

35 And I say this for your advantage, not that I put a noose *before* you, but for the fitting thing, and waiting on the Lord without distraction.

36 ¶ But if anyone thinks *he* acts unseemly toward his virgin (if she is beyond *her* prime, and so it ought to be), let him do what he desires; he does not sin; let them marry.

37 But *he* who stands firm in heart, not having necessity, but has authority as to *his* own will, and has judged this in his heart, to keep his virgin; he does well.

38 So that he giving in marriage does well, and he not giving in marriage does better.

39 ¶ A wife is bound by law for as long a time as her husband lives; but if her husband sleeps, she is free to be married to whomever she desires, only in *the* Lord.

40 But she is happier if she remains so, according to my judgment. And I think I also have *the* Spirit of God.

1 Corinthians 8

9 We must not abuse our Christian liberty, 11 but bridle our knowledge with charity.

1 ¶ But concerning the sacrifices to idols, we know that we all have knowledge. Knowledge puffs up, but love builds up.

2 But if anyone thinks to know anything, he still has known nothing as he ought to know.

3 But if anyone loves God, this *one* has been known by Him.

4 ¶ Therefore concerning the eating of idolatrous offerings, we know that an idol *is* nothing in *the* world, and that *there* is no other God except one.

5 For even if *some* are called gods, either in *the* heavens or on the earth; (just as there are many gods, and many lords);

6 but to us *is* one God, the Father, of whom *are* all things, and we to Him, and one Lord Jesus Christ, through whom are all things, and we through Him.

7 ¶ But the knowledge *is* not in all; but some being aware of the idol eat as an idolatrous offering until now; and their conscience, being weak, is defiled.

8 But food will not commend us to God. For neither if we eat do we excel, nor if we do not eat are we lacking.

9 But watch how this authority of yours may not become a cause of stumbling to the *ones* being weak.

10 For if anyone sees you, the *one* having knowledge, reclining in an idol's temple, will not the conscience of the *one* being weak be built up so as to eat the idolatrous offering?

11 And on your knowledge the weak brother shall perish, *he* for whom Christ died.

12 But sinning so against *your* brothers, and wounding their conscience, being weak, you sin against Christ.

13 On account of this, if food causes my brother to stumble, I will not eat flesh into the age, not *ever*, so that I do not cause my brother to stumble.

1 Corinthians 9

1 He shows his liberty, 7 and that the minister ought to live by the gospel. 24 Our life is like a race.

1 ¶ Am I not an apostle? Am I not free? Have I not seen our Lord Jesus Christ? Are you not my work in *the* Lord?

2 If I am not an apostle to others, yet I am indeed to you; for you are the seal of my apostleship in *the* Lord.

3 ¶ My defense to the *ones* examining me is this:

4 Have we not authority to eat and to drink?

5 Have we not authority to lead about a sister, a wife, as *do* the rest of the apostles also, and Cephas, and the Lord's brothers?

6 Or *is it* only Barnabas and I *who* have no authority not to work?

7 Who serves as a soldier at *his* own wages ever? Who plants a vineyard and does not eat of its fruit? Or who shepherds a flock and does not eat of the milk of the flock?

8 Do I speak these things according to man, or does not the Law say these things also?

9 For it has been written in the Law of Moses, "You shall not muzzle an ox threshing grain." *Deut. 25:4* Not *that* it matters to God for the oxen, *is it?*

10 Or does He certainly say *it* because of us? It is written because of us, so that the *one* plowing ought to plow *in* hope, and the *one* threshing *in* hope to partake of hope.

11 If we sowed spiritual things to you, *is it* a great thing if we shall reap of your fleshly things?

12 If others have a share of the authority *over* you, *should* not rather we? But we did not use this authority, but we endured all things, so that we might not give a hindrance to the gospel of Christ.

13 Do you not know that the *ones* laboring *about* the holy things of the temple eat? Those attending on the altar share together with the altar.

14 So also the Lord ordained the *ones* proclaiming the gospel to live from the gospel.

15 ¶ But I have not used one of these. And I do not write these things that it be so in me. For *it is* good to me rather to die than that anyone nullify my glorying.

16 For if I preach the gospel, no glory is to me; for necessity is laid on me, and *it* is woe to me if I do not preach the gospel.

17 For if I do this willingly, I have a reward; but if unwillingly, I am entrusted with a stewardship.

18 What then is my reward? That preaching the gospel I may make the gospel of Christ free, so as not to use fully my authority in the gospel.

19 ¶ For being free from all *men* I enslaved myself to all *men*, that I might gain the more.

20 And I became as a Jew to the Jews, that I might gain Jews; to the *ones* under Law as under Law, that I might gain the *ones* under Law;

21 to the *ones* without Law as without Law (not being without Law of God, but under *the* law of Christ), that I might gain *the ones* without Law.

22 I became to the weak *ones* as weak, that I might gain the weak *ones*. To all *people* I have become all things, that in any and every way I might save some.

23 And I do this for the gospel, that I might become a fellow partaker of it.

24 ¶ Do you not know that the *ones* running in a stadium indeed all run, but one receives the prize? So run that you may obtain.

25 But everyone striving controls himself *in* all things. Then the *ones* truly that they may receive a corruptible crown, but we an incorruptible.

26 Therefore, so I run, as not uncertainly; so I fight, as not beating air;

27 but I buffet my body and enslave *it*, lest having preached to others I myself might be disapproved.

1 Corinthians 10

1 The sacraments of the Jews 6 are types of ours, 7 and their punishments. 11 examples for us. 14 We must flee from idolatry.

1 ¶ And I do not want you to be ignorant, brothers, that our fathers were all under the cloud, and all passed through the Sea.

2 And all were baptized into Moses in the cloud, and in the Sea,

3 and all ate the same spiritual food.

4 And all drank the same spiritual drink; for they drank of the spiritual rock following, and that Rock was Christ.

5 But God was not well-pleased with most of them, "for they were scattered in the wilderness " *Num. 14:16*

6 ¶ But these things became examples for us, so that we may not be lusters after bad *things*, even as those indeed lusted.

7 Neither be idolaters, even as some of them, as it is written, "The people sat down to eat and drink, and stood up to play." *Ex. 32:6*

8 Nor should we commit fornication, as some of them fornicated, and twenty-three thousand fell in one day.

9 Neither over-tempt the Christ, as some of them tempted, and were destroyed by serpents.

10 Neither murmur, as also some of them murmured, and were destroyed by the destroyer.

11 And all these things happened to those *people as* examples, and *it* was written for our admonition, on whom the ends of the ages have come.

12 So then the *one* thinking to stand, let him watch *that* he not fall.

13 No temptation has taken you if not a human *one*; but God *is* faithful, who will not allow you to be tempted above what you are able. But with the temptation, *He* will also make the way out, *so as* for you to be able to bear *it*.

14 On account of this, my beloved, flee from idolatry.

15 ¶ I speak as to prudent *ones*; you judge what I say.

16 The cup of blessing that we bless, is *it* not a communion of the blood of Christ? The bread which we break, is *it* not a communion of the body of Christ?

17 Because we, the many, are one bread, one body, for we all partake of the one bread.

18 Look at Israel according to flesh; are not the *ones* eating the sacrifices sharers of the altar?

19 What then do I say, that an idol is anything, or that an idolatrous offering is anything?

20 But the things the nations sacrifice, "*they* sacrifice to demons, and not to God."

Deut. 32:17 But I do not want you to become sharers of demons;

21 Not you are able to drink *the* cup of *the* Lord and a cup of demons; not you are able to partake of *the* table of *the* Lord and a table of demons.

22 Or do we provoke the Lord to jealousy? Are we stronger than He?

23 ¶ All *things* are lawful to me, but not all things are profitable. All things are lawful to me, but not all *things* build up.

24 Let no one seek the *thing* of himself, but each *one* the *thing* of the other.

25 Eat everything being sold in a meat market, examining nothing because of conscience,

26 for "the earth *is* the Lord's, and the fullness of it." *Psa. 24:1*

27 And if any of the unbelieving *ones* invite you, and you desire to go, eat everything set before you, examining nothing because of conscience.

28 But if anyone tells you, This is an idolatrous offering, do not eat because of that one disclosing *it*, and the conscience; for "the earth *is* the Lord's, and the fullness of it." *Psa. 24:1*

29 But I say conscience, not the *one* of himself, but the *one* of the other. For why is my freedom judged by another's conscience?

30 But if I partake by grace, why am I evil spoken of because of that *for* which I give thanks?

31 Then whether you eat or drink, or anything you do, do all things to the glory of God.

32 Be not led into sin, both to Jews and Greeks, and to the assembly of God.

33 Even as I also please all *in* all *things*, not seeking *my* own advantage, but that of the many, that they may be saved.

1 Corinthians 11

1 He reproves them because in holy assemblies
4 their men prayed with their heads covered,
and 6 women with their heads uncovered,
21 and for profaning with their own feasts the
Lord's supper.

1 ¶ Be imitators of me, as I *am* also of Christ.

2 But I praise you, brothers, that in all *things* you have remembered me, and even

as I gave *them* over to you, you hold fast the traditions.

3 But I want you to know that Christ is *the* head of every man, and *the* man *is* the head of a woman, and God *is the* head of Christ.

4 Every man praying or prophesying, having *covering* down over his head shames his head.

5 And every woman praying or prophesying with *the* head uncovered dishonors her head, for it is one and the same *as* being shaved.

6 For if a woman is not covered, let her also be shorn. But *if it* is shameful for a woman to be shorn, or to be shaved, let her be covered.

7 For truly a man ought not to have *the* head covered, being *the* image and glory of God. But woman is *the* glory of man;

8 for man is not of the woman, but woman of man;

9 for also man was not created for the sake of the woman, but woman for the sake of the man;

10 because of this, the woman ought to have authority on the head, because of the angels.

11 But neither is the man apart from woman, nor woman apart from man, in *the* Lord.

12 For as the woman *is* out of the man, so also the man through the woman; but all *things* from God.

13 You judge among yourselves: is it fitting *for* a woman to pray to God uncovered?

14 Or does not nature herself teach you that if a man indeed wears long hair, it is a dishonor to him?

15 But if a woman wears *her* hair long, it is a glory to her; because the long hair has been given to her instead of a covering.

16 But if anyone thinks to be contentious, we do not have such a custom, nor the assemblies of God.

17 ¶ But enjoining this, I do not praise *you*, because you come together not for the better, but for the worse.

18 Indeed, first, I hear divisions to be among you *when* you come together in the assembly. And I believe *it in* some part.

19 For also factions need to be among you, so that the approved *ones* may become revealed among you.

20 Therefore you coming together into one place, it is not to eat *the* Lord's supper.

21 For each *one* takes his own supper first in *order* to eat; and one is hungry, and another drunken.

22 For do you not have houses *in which* to eat and to drink? Or do you despise the assembly of God, and shame the *ones* who have not? What should I say to you? Shall I praise you for this? I do not praise.

23 ¶ For I received from the Lord what I also gave over to you, that the Lord Jesus in the night in which He was given over took bread;

24 and having given thanks, He broke and said, Take, eat; this is My body, the *one* being broken on behalf of you; this do in remembrance of Me.

25 In the same way the cup also, after the *order* to *eat* supper, *He* said, This cup is the New Covenant in My blood; as often as you drink, do this in remembrance of Me.

26 For as often as you may eat this bread, and drink this cup, you solemnly proclaim the death of the Lord, until He shall come.

27 So then whoever should eat this bread, or drink the cup of the Lord unworthily, will be guilty of the body and of the blood of the Lord.

28 But let a man examine himself, and so let him eat from the bread, and let him drink from the cup;

29 for the *one* eating and drinking unworthily eats and drinks judgment to himself, not discerning the body of the Lord.

30 Because of this many among you *are* weak and infirm, and a considerable number sleep.

31 For if we judged ourselves, we would not be judged.

32 But being judged, we are chastened by *the* Lord, that we not be condemned with the world.

33 So that, my brothers, coming together to eat, wait for one another.

34 But if anyone is hungry, let him eat at home, that you may not come together for judgment. And the remaining things I will set in order whenever I come.

1 Corinthians 12

1 Spiritual gifts 4 are diverse, 7 yet all to profit.
   8 And for that end are diversely given.

1 ¶ But concerning the spiritual *gifts*, brothers, I do not wish you to be ignorant.

2 You know that *when* you were nations, how you were led, being carried away to voiceless idols.

3 Therefore I make known to you that no one speaking by *the* Spirit of God says, Jesus *is* a curse. And no one is able to say Jesus *is* Lord, if not by *the* Holy Spirit.

4 And there are varieties of gifts, but the same Spirit;

5 and there are varieties of ministries, yet the same Lord.

6 And there are varieties of workings, but the same is God, the *One* working all things in all.

7 And to each *one* is given the showing forth of the Spirit to the profiting *of* each *one*.

8 For through the Spirit is given to one a word of wisdom, and to another a word of knowledge, according to the same Spirit;

9 and to another, faith by the same Spirit; and to another, gifts of healing by the same Spirit,

10 and to another; workings of powers; and to another, prophecy; and to another, discerning of spirits; and to another, kinds of languages; and to another, interpretation of languages.

11 But the one and the same Spirit works all these things, distributing separately to each *one* as He purposes.

12 ¶ Even as the body is one, and has many members, but all the members of the one body, being many, *are* one body; so also *is* Christ.

13 For also we all were baptized into one Spirit into one body, whether Jews or Greeks, whether slaves or free, even all were given to drink into one Spirit.

14 For also the body is not one member, but many.

15 If the foot says, Because I am not a hand, I am not of the body; on account of this, is it not of the body?

16 And if the ear says, Because I am not an eye, I am not of the body, on account of this, is it not of the body?

17 If all the body *were* an eye, where *would be* the hearing? If all hearing, where the smelling?

18 But now God set the members, each *one* of them, in the body, even as He willed.

19 But if all was one member, where *would* the body *be*?

20 But now, indeed, many *are* the members, but one body.

21 And the eye is not able to say to the hand, I have no need of you; or again the head to the feet, I have no need of you.

22 But by much more the members of the body seeming to be weaker are necessary.

23 And *those* of the body we think to be less honorable, to these we put more abundant honor around *them*. And our unpresentable *members* have more abundant propriety.

24 But our presentable *members* have no need. But God tempered the body together, giving more abundant honor to the *member* lacking *it*,

25 that there not be division in the body, but *that* the members might have the same care for one another.

26 And if one member suffers, all the members suffer with *it*. If one member is glorified, all the members rejoice with *it*.

27 ¶ And you are Christ's body, and members in part.

28 And God placed some in the assembly, firstly, apostles; secondly, prophets; thirdly, teachers; then works of power; then gifts of healing, helps, governings, kinds of languages.

29 *Are* all apostles? All prophets? All teachers? All workers of power?

30 Do all have gifts of healings? Do all speak languages? Do all interpret?

31 But zealously strive after the better gifts. And yet I show you a way according to excellence:

1 Corinthians 13

1 All gifts, 2,3 however excellent, are worth nothing without love. 4 The praises of it.

1 ¶ If I speak with the tongues of men and of angels, but do not have love, I have become *as* sounding brass or a clanging cymbal.

2 And if I have prophecies, and know all mysteries and all knowledge, and if I have

all faith so as to move mountains, but do not have love, I am nothing.

3 And if I give out all my possesssions, and if I give over my body that I be burned, but I do not have love, I am profited nothing.

4 ¶ Love patiently endures, is kind; love is not envious; love boasts not itself, is not puffed up;

5 does not behave unbecomingly, does not seek the *things of* itself, is not *easily* provoked, does not impute evil;

6 does not rejoice over unrighteousness, but rejoices in the truth.

7 *Love* quietly covers all things, believes all things, hopes all things, endures all things.

8 ¶ Love never fails. But if *there are* prophecies, they will be caused to cease; if tongues, they shall cease; if knowledge, it will be caused to cease.

9 For we know in part, and we prophesy in part;

10 but when the perfect *thing* comes, then that *which is* in part will be caused to cease.

11 When I was a little child, I spoke as a little child, I thought as a little child, I reasoned as a little child. But when I have become a man, I have done away with the *things* of the little child.

12 For now we see through a mirror in dimness, but then face to face. Now I know by part, but then I will fully know even as I also was fully known.

13 And now faith, hope, and love, these three things remain; but the greatest of these *is* love.

1 Corinthians 14

1 Prophecy is commended 2, 3, 4 and preferred before speaking with tongues. 12 Both must be referred to building up 22 as to their true end. 34 Women are to be silent in the assembly.

1 ¶ Pursue love, and seek eagerly the spiritual *things*, but rather that you may prophesy.

2 For the *one* speaking in a language does not speak to men, but to God; for no one hears, but in spirit he speaks mysteries.

3 But the *one* prophesying to men speaks *for* building up, and encouragement, and comfort.

4 The *one* speaking in a langusge builds himself up, but he prophesying builds up an assembly.

5 And I wish all of you to speak in languages, but rather that you may prophesy. For the *one* prophesying *is* greater than the *one* speaking in languages, if not he interpret, that the assembly may receive building up.

6 ¶ But now, brothers, if I come to you speaking in languages, what will I profit you, if not I speak to you either in revelation, or in knowledge, or in prophecy, or in teaching?

7 Likewise lifeless *things* giving a sound, whether flute or harp, if they do not give a distinction in the sound, how will it be known what is being fluted or being harped?

8 For also if a trumpet gives an uncertain sound, who will get himself ready for war?

9 So also you, if you do not give a clear word through the language, how will the *thing* being said be known? For you will be speaking into air.

10 So it may be many kinds of sounds are in *the* world, and not one *is* without *distinct* sound.

11 If, then, I do not know the power of the sound, I will be a foreigner to the *one* speaking, and the *one* speaking in me a foreigner.

12 So also you, since you are zealots of spiritual *gifts*, seek to build up the assembly that you may abound.

13 Therefore, the *one* speaking in a language, let him pray that he may interpret.

14 For if I pray in a *foreign* language, my spirit prays, but my mind is unfruitful.

15 ¶ What then is it? I will pray with the spirit, and I will also pray with the mind; I will sing with the spirit, and I will also sing with the mind.

16 Else, if you bless in the spirit, the one occupying the place of the unlearned, how will he say the amen at your giving of thanks, since he does not know what you say?

17 For you truly give thanks well, but the other *person* is not built up.

18 I thank my God *that* I speak more languages than all of you.

19 But in an assembly I desire to speak five words with my mind, that I may also instruct others, than myriads of words in a *foreign* language.

20 Brothers, do not be children in your minds, but in malice be like children, and in your minds be mature.

21 ¶ It is written in the Law, "By other languages" and "by other lips" "I will speak to this people," "and even so they will not hear" Me, says *the* Lord. *Isa. 28:11, 12*

22 So that languages are not a sign to the *ones* believing, but to the faithless *ones*. But prophecy *is* not to the faithless *ones*, but to the *ones* believing.

23 Then if the whole assembly comes together, and all speak in *foreign* languages, and uninstructed *ones* or faithless *ones* come in, will they not say that you rave?

24 But if all prophesy, and some faithless *one* or an uninstructed *one* comes in, he is convicted by all, he is judged by all.

25 And so the secrets of his heart become revealed; and so, falling on *his* face, he will worship God, declaring that God is truly among you.

26 ¶ Then what is it, brothers? When you come together, each *one* of you has a psalm, he has a teaching, he has a language, he has a revelation, he has an interpretation. Let all things be for building up.

27 If one speaks in a language, *let it be* by two or three *at* the most, and in turn, also let one interpret.

28 And if there is no interpreter, let him be silent in *the* assembly, and let him speak to himself and to God.

29 And *if there are* two or three prophets, let them speak, and let the others judge.

30 But if *a revelation* is revealed to another sitting *by*, let the first *one* be silent.

31 For you can all prophesy one by one, that all may learn, and all may be encouraged.

32 And the spirits of prophets *are* subject to prophets.

33 For God is not *God* of confusion, but of peace, as in all the assemblies of the saints.

34 ¶ Let your women be silent in the assemblies, for it is not allowed to them to speak, but to be in subjection, as also the Law says.

35 But if they desire to learn anything, let them question their husbands at home; for it is a disgraceful *thing* for a woman to speak in an assembly.

36 ¶ Or did the Word of God go out from you? Or did it reach only to you?

37 If anyone thinks to be a prophet, or a spiritual *one*, let him recognize the things I write to you, that they are commandments of the Lord.

38 But if any be ignorant, let him be ignorant.

39 So then, brothers, seek eagerly to prophesy, and do not forbid to speak in languages.

40 And let all things come to be *done* decently and according to order.

1 Corinthians 15

3 By Christ's resurrection, 12 he proves the necessity of our resurrection.

1 ¶ Now, brothers, I make known to you the gospel which I preached to you, which you also received, in which you also stand,

2 through which you also are being saved, if you hold fast the Word which I preached to you, except if not you believed in vain.

3 For I gave over to you among the first *things* what I also received, that Christ died in behalf of our sins, according to the Scriptures,

4 and that He was buried, and that He has been raised the third day, according to the Scriptures,

5 and that He appeared to Cephas, and then to the Twelve.

6 Then He appeared to more than five hundred brothers at once, of whom the most remain until now, but some also fell asleep.

7 Then He appeared to James, then to all the apostles;

8 and last of all, even as if to an untimely birth He also appeared to me.

9 For I am the least of the apostles, who am not sufficient to be called an apostle, because I persecuted the Assembly of God.

10 But by the grace of God I am what I am, and His grace which *was* toward me has not been fruitless, but I labored more abundantly than all of them, yet not I, but the grace of God with me.

11 Whether therefore I or those, so we preach, and so you believed.

12 ¶ But if Christ is being preached, that He has been raised from *the* dead *ones*, how do some among you say *there* is not a resurrection of the dead *ones*?

13 But if there is not a resurrection of *the* dead *ones*, neither has Christ been raised.

14 But if Christ has not been raised, then our preaching *is* worthless, and your faith is also worthless.

15 And also we are found *to be* false witnesses of God, because we witnessed according to God that He raised Christ, whom He did not raise, if then dead *ones* are not raised.

16 For if dead *ones* are not raised, Christ has not been raised.

17 But if Christ has not been raised, your faith *is* vain; you are still in your sins.

18 And then the *ones* that fell asleep in Christ perished.

19 If we only have hope in Christ in this life, we are of all men most pitiable.

20 ¶ But now Christ has been raised from the dead *ones*; He became the firstfruit of the *ones* having fallen asleep.

21 For since death *is* through man, also through a Man *is* a resurrection of dead *ones*;

22 for as in Adam all die, so also in Christ all will be made alive.

23 But each *one* in *his* own order: Christ, the firstfruit; afterward the *ones* of Christ in His coming.

24 Then *is* the end, whenever He gives over the kingdom to God, even the Father, whenever He causes to cease all rule and all authority and power.

25 For it is right for Him to reign until He puts all the hostile *ones* under His feet; *Psa. 110:1*

26 *the* last hostile *thing* caused to cease *is* death.

27 For "He subjected all things under His feet;" but when He says that all things have been subjected, *it is* evident that *this is* except the *One* having subjected all things to Him. *Psa. 8:6*

28 But when all things are subjected to Him, then the Son Himself also will be put in subjection to the *One* who has subjected all things to Him, that God may be all things in all.

29 Otherwise, what will they do, the *ones* being baptized on behalf of the dead *ones*? If *the* dead *ones* are not at all raised, why indeed are they baptized on behalf of the dead *ones*?

30 Why are we also in danger every hour?

31 According to a day I die, by your boasting, which I have in Christ Jesus our Lord.

32 If according to man I fought with beasts in Ephesus, what *is* the profit to me if *the* dead *ones* are not raised? ("Let us eat and drink, for tomorrow we die"). *Isa. 22:13.)*

33 Do not be led astray; bad companionships corrupt good habits.

34 Be sober uprightly, and do not sin; for some have ignorance of God. I speak to your shame.

35 ¶ But someone will say, How are dead *ones* raised? And with what body do they come?

36 Foolish *ones*! What you sow is not made alive if not it dies.

37 And what you sow, you do not sow the body that *is* going to be, but a naked grain, (if it may be of wheat, or of some of the rest),

38 but God gives it a body according as He willed, and to each *one* of the seeds *its* own body.

39 Not every flesh *is* the same flesh, but, indeed, another flesh of men, and another flesh of beasts, and another of fish, and another of birds.

40 And *there are* heavenly bodies, and earthly bodies. But the glory of the heavenly *is* truly different, and the *ones* of the earthly *one* different;

41 another glory of *the* sun, and another glory of *the* moon, and another glory of *the* stars; for star differs from star in glory.

42 So also the resurrection of dead *ones*. It is sown in corruption, it is raised in incorruption.

43 It is sown in dishonor, it is raised in glory. It is sown in weakness, it is raised in power.

44 It is sown a natural body, it is raised a spiritual body; *there* is a natural body, and *there* is a spiritual body.

45 So also it has been written, "The" first "man", Adam, "became a living soul;" the last Adam a Spirit giving life. *Gen. 2:7*

46 But not the spiritual first, but the natural; afterward the spiritual.

47 The first man *was* out of earth, an earthy *one*. The second Man *was* the Lord out of Heaven. *Gen. 2:7*

48 Such *as is* the earthy *man*, such also *are* the earthy *ones*. And such as is the heavenly *Man*, such also *are* the heavenly *ones*.

49 And as we bore the image of the earthy *man*, we shall also bear the image of the heavenly *Man*.

50 And I say this, brothers, that flesh and blood are not able to inherit *the* kingdom of God, nor does corruption inherit incorruption.

51 ¶ Behold, I tell a mystery to you: we shall not all sleep, but we shall all be changed.

52 In a moment, in a glance of an eye, at the last trumpet; for a trumpet will sound, and the dead *ones* will be raised incorruptible, and we shall all be changed.

53 For this corruptible must put on incorruption, and this mortal *one must* put on immortality.

54 But when this corruptible shall put on incorruption, and this mortal *one* shall put on immortality, then will come to pass the Word, the *one* having been written, "Death was swallowed up in victory." *Isa. 25:8*

55 "O death, where *is your* sting? Hades, where *is your* victory?" *Hos. 13:14*

56 Now the sting of death *is* sin, and the power of sin *is* the Law;

57 but thanks *be* to God, the *One* giving us the victory through our Lord Jesus Christ!

58 So that, my beloved brothers, *you* be firm, immovable, abounding in the work of the Lord always, knowing that your your labor is not fruitless in *the* Lord.

1 Corinthians 16

1 He exhorts them to relieve the want of the brethren at Jerusalem. 10 He commends Timothy.

1 ¶ And about the collection, the *one* for the saints, as I charged the assemblies of Galatia, so also you do.

2 On *the* first of *the* sabbaths, let each *one* of you put by himself, storing up whatever he is prospered, that there not be collections then when I come.

3 And when I arrive, whomever you approve through these epistles, I will send to carry your gift of grace to Jerusalem.

4 And if it is suitable for me to go also, they shall go with me.

5 ¶ But I will come to you when I go through Macedonia. For I am going through Macedonia.

6 And it may be I will stay with you, or even spend the winter, that you may send me forward wherever I may go.

7 For I do not desire to see you now in passage, but I am hoping to remain some time with you, if the Lord permits.

8 But I will remain in Ephesus until Pentecost.

9 For a door opened to me, great and effective, and many *are* opposing.

10 ¶ But if Timothy comes, see that he is with you without fear; for he works the work of the Lord, even as I.

11 Therefore do not let anyone despise him, but send him forward in peace, that he may come to me; for I am awaiting him with the brothers.

12 And about the brother Apollos, I much urged him that he come to you with the brothers, but it was not at all *his* will that he come now. But he will come when he his opportunity.

13 ¶ Watch! Stand fast in the faith! Be men! Be strong!

14 Let all your things be in love.

15 But I exhort you, brothers. You know the house of Stephanas, that it is the firstfruit of Achaia, and they appointed themselves to ministry to the saints.

16 *See* that you also may submit to such *ones*, and to everyone working and laboring with *us*.

17 And I rejoice at the coming of Stephanas, and of Fortunatus and Achaicus, because these supplied your lack.

18 For they refreshed my spirit and yours. Then recognize such ones.

19 ¶ The assemblies of Asia greet you. Aquila and Priscilla greet you much in *the* Lord, with the assembly in their house.

20 The brothers all greet you. Greet one another with a holy kiss.

21 The greeting with my hand, Paul.

22 If anyone does not love the Lord Jesus Christ, let him be accursed. The Lord comes!

23 The grace of the Lord Jesus Christ *be* with you.

My love *be* with all of you in Christ Jesus. Amen.

The Second Epistle of Paul the Apostle to the
CORINTHIANS

2 Corinthians 1

3 The apostle encourages them against troubles,
by the comforts which God had given him.
15 He excuses his not coming to them.

1 ¶ Paul, an apostle of Jesus Christ, through the will of God, and Timothy the brother, to the assembly of God being in Corinth, with all the saints being in all Achaia,

2 Grace to you and peace from God our Father and *the* Lord Jesus Christ.

3 ¶ Blessed *be* the God and Father of our Lord Jesus Christ, the Father of compassions and God of all comfort,

4 the *One* comforting us on all our affliction, for us to be able to comfort the *ones* in every affliction, through the comfort by which we ourselves are comforted by God.

5 Because *even as* the sufferings of Christ abound in us, so also our comfort abounds through Christ.

6 But if we are troubled, *it is* for your comfort and salvation, being worked out in *the* endurance of the same sufferings which we also suffer. If we are comforted, *it is* for your comfort and salvation;

7 ¶ and our hope for you *is* firm, knowing that even as you are sharers of the sufferings, so also of the comfort.

8 For, brothers, we do not want you to be ignorant as to our affliction having happened to us in Asia, that we were beyond measure burdened beyond *our* power, so as for us even to despair of living.

9 But we ourselves have the sentence of death in ourselves, that we should not trust on ourselves, but on God, the *One* raising the dead *ones*,

10 who delivered us from so great a death, and does deliver; in whom we have hope that He will still deliver *us*,

11 you also laboring together for us in prayer, that the gracious gift by many per-sons be *the cause of* thanksgiving through many for us.

12 ¶ For our glorying is this, the testimony of our conscience, that we had our conduct in the world in simplicity and sincerity of God, not in fleshly wisdom, but in the grace of God, and especially toward you.

13 For we do not write other things to you than what you read or even recognize; and I hope that you will recognize even to *the* end,

14 even as you also *in* part recognized us, that we are your glorying, even as also you *are* ours in the day of the Lord Jesus.

15 ¶ And in this confidence, I purposed to come to you before now, that you might have a second grace,

16 and to go through you into Macedonia, and again from Macedonia to come to you and to be set forward by you to Judea.

17 Therefore purposing this, did I indeed use lightness? Or what I purposed, did I purpose according to flesh, that *it* may be with me yes, yes, and no, no?

18 But God *is* faithful, that our word to you did not become yes and no.

19 For Jesus Christ the Son of God, the *One* proclaimed among you by us, through me and Silvanus and Timothy, did not become Yes and No, but has been Yes in Him.

20 For as many promises as *are* of God, in Him *they are* Yes, and in Him *are* Amen, for glory to God through us.

21 But He confirming us and anointing us together with you in Christ *is* God,

22 even He having sealed us, and having given the earnest of the Spirit in our hearts.

23 And I call God *as* witness to my soul that to spare you I came no more to Corinth.

24 Not that we rule over your faith, but we are fellow-workers of your joy. For by the faith you stand.

2 Corinthians 2

1 He shows why he did not come to them, 6 he tells
them to forgive that excommunicated person,
10 even as he himself also had forgiven him.

1 ¶ But I decided this within myself, not to come to you again in grief.

2 For if I grieve you, who yet will be making me glad, if not the *one* being grieved by me?

3 And I wrote this same thing to you, lest coming I might have grief from *those* of whom I ought to rejoice, trusting in you all that my joy is *the joy* of all of you.

4 For out of much affliction and distress of heart I wrote to you, through many tears, not that you be grieved, but that you know the love which I have especially toward you.

5- ¶ But if anyone has grieved, he has not grieved me, but from *in* part, that I not burden all of you.

6 This punishment by the majority *is* enough for such a one.

7 So that on the contrary, you *ought* rather to forgive and comfort such a one, that *he* not be swallowed up *by* the excessive grief.

8 So I beseech you to confirm *your* love to him.

9 For to this end I also wrote, that I might know the proof of you, if you are obedient in all things.

10 But to whom you forgive anything, I also *forgive*. For also if I have forgiven anything, of whom I have forgiven *it, it is* for you, in Christ's person,

11 so that we should not be deceitfully coveted by Satan, for we are not ignorant of his designs.

12 ¶ And coming to Troas for the gospel of Christ, and a door having been opened to me in *the* Lord,

13 I had no rest in my spirit at my not finding my brother Titus, but taking leave of them, I went out to Macedonia.

14 But thanks *be* to God, the *One* always leading us in triumph in Christ, and *the One* revealing through us the fragrance of the knowledge of Him in every place.

15 For we are a sweet smell to God because of Christ in the *ones* being saved, and in the *ones* being lost;

16 to the *ones,* an odor of death unto death, and to the *ones*, an odor of life unto life. And who is sufficient for these things?

17 For we are not as the many, peddling the Word of God; but as of sincerity, but as of God. We speak in Christ before God.

2 Corinthians 3

Lest their false teachers should charge him with
vainglory, he shows the faith and graces of the
Corinthians to be a sufficient commendation of
his ministry.

1 ¶ Do we begin again to commend ourselves? Or do we, as some, need commendatory letters to you, or commendatory *ones* from you?

2 You are our letter, having been inscribed in our hearts, being known and being read by all men,

3 *it* being made known that you are Christ's letter, ministered by us, not having been inscribed by ink, but by *the* Spirit of *the* living God, not in tablets of stone, but in fleshly tablets of *the* heart.

4 And we have such confidence through Christ toward God;

5 not that we are sufficient of ourselves to reason out anything as *being* out of ourselves, but our sufficiency *is* of God,

6 ¶ who also made us able ministers of a new covenant, not of letter, but of Spirit. For the letter kills, but the Spirit makes alive.

7 But if the ministry of death having been engraved in letters in stone came to be in glory, so as *that* the sons of Israel could not gaze into "the face of Moses" because of the glory of his face, which was to be caused to cease,

8 how much rather the ministry of the Spirit will be in glory!

9 For if the ministry of condemnation *was in* glory, much rather the ministry of righteousness abounds in glory.

10 For even not has been made glorious the *thing* having been made glorious in this part, because of the surpassing glory.

11 For if the thing done away *was* through glory, much rather the *thing* remaining *is* in glory.

12 ¶ Therefore having such hope, we use much boldness.

13 And not as "Moses put a veil over his face," for the sons of Israel not to look intently at the end of the *thing* being done away. *Ex. 34:35*

14 But their thoughts were hardened, for until this very day the same veil remains on the reading of the Old Covenant, not being unveiled, that it is being done away in Christ.

15 But until this very day, when Moses is being read, a veil lies on their heart.

16 But whenever it shall have turned to *the* Lord, the veil is taken away. *Ex. 34:34*

17 And the Lord *is* the Spirit; and where the Spirit of *the* Lord *is*, there *is* freedom.

18 But we all with *our* face having been unveiled, having beheld the glory of *the* Lord in a mirror, are being transformed *into* the same image from glory to glory, as from *the* Lord Spirit.

2 Corinthians 4

He declares how he has used all sincerity and faithful diligence in preaching the gospel.

1 ¶ Because of this, having this ministry, even as we obtained mercy, we do not fail *in heart*.

2 But we have renounced the hidden things of shame, not walking in craftiness, nor corrupting the Word of God, but *by* the revelation of the truth commending ourselves to every conscience of men before God.

3 But if even our gospel is being hidden, it has been hidden in the *ones* perishing,

4 in whom the god of this age has blinded the thoughts of the faithless *ones, so that* the illumination of the gospel of the glory of Christ, who is the image of God, *should* not shine on them.

5 For we do not proclaim ourselves, but Christ Jesus as Lord, and ourselves your slaves for the sake of Jesus.

6 Because *it is* God who said, "Out of darkness Light shall shine," the *One* who shone in our hearts to *give the* illumination of the knowledge of the glory of God in the face of Jesus Christ. *Isa. 42:6, 7, 16*

7 But we have this treasure in earthen vessels, so that the excellence of the power may be of God, and not from us;

8 ¶ in every *way* being pressed, but not being constricted; being perplexed, but not utterly despairing;

9 being persecuted, but not being forsaken; being thrown down, but not perishing;

10 alway bearing about the dying of the Lord Jesus in the body, that also the life of Jesus may be revealed in our body.

11 For we, the *ones* living, are always being given over to death on account of Jesus, that also the life of Jesus may be revealed in our mortal flesh;

12 so that death indeed works in us, and life in you.

13 But having the same spirit of the faith, according to the *thing* having been written, "I believed, therefore I spoke," we also believe, therefore we also speak, *LXX-Psa. 115:1; MT-Psa. 116:10*

14 knowing that He who raised up the Lord Jesus will also raise us up through Jesus, and will present *us* with you.

15 For all things *are* for you, that the grace, superabounding through the greater number may cause the thanksgiving to abound to the glory of God.

16 Therefore we do not fail *in heart*, but if indeed our outward man is being consumed, yet the inward *man* is being renewed day by day.

17 For the lightness of our present affliction works out for us an eternal weight of glory, surpassing *moment* by surpassing *moment*;

18 we not looking at the things being seen, but the things not being seen; for the things being seen *are* not lasting, but the things not being seen *are* everlasting.

2 Corinthians 5

1 That in his assured hope of immortal glory 9 he labors to keep a good conscience 18 and by his ministry to reconcile others also in Christ to God.

1 ¶ For we know that if our earthly house of *this* tabernacle is taken down, we have a building from God, a house not made with hands, eternal in Heaven.

2 For also in this we groan, greatly desiring to be clothed with our dwelling place out of Heaven,

3 if indeed *in* being clothed, we shall not be found naked.

4 For also, being in the tabernacle, we groan, having been weighted down, inasmuch as

we do not wish to put off *the body*, but *the spiritual* to be put on, so that the mortal life may be swallowed up by the life.

5 And the *One* having worked in us for this same thing *is* God, who also *is* giving us the earnest of the Spirit.

6 Therefore always being fully confident, and knowing that being at home in the body we are away from home from the Lord

7 (for we walk by faith, not by sight),

8 even we are fully confident, and think it good rather to go away from home out of the body, and to come home to the Lord.

9 Therefore we also are striving to be pleasing to Him, whether being at home, or being away from home.

10 For we all must appear before the judgment seat of Christ, so that each *one* may receive the things *done* through the body, according to what he did, whether a good *thing* or a bad *thing*.

11 Therefore knowing the fear of the Lord, we persuade men, and we have been made known to God; and I also hope to have been known in your consciences.

12 ¶ For we do not again commend ourselves to you, but are giving you occasion of glorying on our behalf, that you may have *it* toward the *ones* boasting before the face and not in heart.

13 For if we were out of *our* mind, *it was* to God; if *we are* clear-minded, *it is* for you.

14 For the love of Christ constrains us, judging this, that if One died for all, then the all died;

15 and He died for all, that the *ones* living may live no more to themselves, but to the *One* dying *for* them and having been raised.

16 ¶ So as we now know no one according to flesh, but even if we have known Christ according to flesh, yet now we no longer know *Him so*.

17 So then if anyone *is* in Christ, *that one* is a new creation; the old things have passed away; behold, all things have come to be new!

18 And all things *are* from God, the *One* having reconciled us to Himself through Jesus Christ, and having given to us the ministry of reconciliation,

19 as, that God was in Christ reconciling *the* world to Himself, not charging their deviations to them, and putting the Word of reconciliation in us.

20 Then on behalf of Christ, we are ambassadors, as God *is* exhorting through us, we beseech on behalf of Christ, Be reconciled to God.

21 For He made the *One* who knew no sin *to be* sin for us, that we might become *the* righteousness of God in Him.

2 Corinthians 6

1 He has approved himself a faithful minister of Christ, by his exhortations, 3 and by integrity of life, 4 and by patiently enduring all kinds of affliction for the gospel.

1 ¶ But working together, we also call on you not to receive the grace of God in vain.

2 For He says, "In an acceptable time I heard you, and in a day of salvation I helped you." Behold, now *is* the acceptable time! Behold, now *is* the day of salvation! *Isa. 49:8*

3 *We* in nothing are giving a cause of stumbling, *to* no one, that the ministry may not be blamed,

4 but in everything commending ourselves as God's servants, in much patience, in afflictions, in necessities, in distresses,

5 in stripes, in imprisonments, in riots, in labors, in sleepinesses, in fastings,

6 in pureness, in knowledge, in long-suffering, in kindness, in the Holy Spirit, in unfeigned love,

7 in *the* Word of truth, in *the* power of God, through the weapons of righteousness on the right *hand* and on *the* left,

8 through glory and dishonor, through evil report and good report; as deceivers, and *yet* true;

9 as being unknown, and *yet* being well known, as dying, and *yet*, look, we live; as scourged, and *yet* not put to death;

10 as being grieved, yet always rejoicing; as a poor *one* , yet enriching many; as having nothing, yet possessing all things.

11 ¶ Our mouth is opened to you, Corinthians, our heart has been enlarged.

12 You are not constricted in us, but you are constricted in your *own* bowels.

13 But for the same reward, I speak as to children, you also be enlarged.

14 Do not be unequally yoked *with* unbelieving *ones; for* what partnership does righteousness *have* with lawlessness? And what fellowship light with darkness?

15 And what agreement does Christ *have* with Belial? Or what part does a believing *one have* with a unbelieving *one*?

16 And what agreement does a temple of God *have* with idols? For you are a temple of *the* living God, even as God said, "I will" dwell in them and "walk among *them*, and I will be their God, and they shall be My people." *Lev. 26:12; Ezek. 37:27*

17 Because of this, "come out from among them" "and be separated," says *the* Lord, "and do not touch *the* unclean *thing*," and I will receive you. *Isa. 52:11*

18 "And I will be a Father to you, and you will be sons" and daughters to Me, says *the* Lord Almighty. *2 Sam. 7:8, 14; Isa. 43:6*

2 Corinthians 7

1 He exhorts them to purity of life, 5 and declares what comfort he took in his afflictions.

1 ¶ Therefore having these promises, beloved, let us cleanse ourselves from all defilements of flesh and of spirit, perfecting holiness in *the* fear of God.

2 Make room for us. We wronged no one, we corrupted no one, we deceitfully coveted no one.

3 I do not speak to condemnation, for I have said before that you are in our hearts, for dying together and living together.

4 My boldness toward you *is* great. My boasting on your behalf *is* much. I have been filled with comfort; I am overflowing with joy on all our affliction.

5 ¶ For, indeed, we coming into Macedonia, our flesh had no rest, but being troubled in every way, *with* fightings *on the* outside and fears *on the* inside.

6 But the *One* comforting the lowly *ones* comforted us by the coming of Titus.

7 And not only by his coming, but also by the comfort with which he was encouraged over you, relating to us your longing, your mourning, your zeal on my behalf, so as for me to rejoice more.

8 For even if I grieved you in the letter, I do not regret, if indeed I did regret, for I see that letter grieved you for an hour.

9 Now I rejoice, not that you were grieved, but that you were grieved to repentance. For you were grieved according to God, that you might suffer loss in nothing by us.

10 For the grief according to God works repentance to salvation without regret, but the grief of the world works death.

11 For behold this very same thing, you being grieved according to God, how much it fully worked earnestness in you, but *also* defense, but *also* indignation, but *also* fear, but *also* desire, but *also* zeal, but *also* vengeance! In everything you commended yourselves to be clear in the matter.

12 ¶ Then even if I wrote to you, *it was* not for the sake of the *one* doing wrong, nor for the sake of the *one* being wronged, but for the sake of revealing our earnestness on your behalf, for you before God.

13 Because of this we have been comforted over your comfort, and we rather rejoice more abundantly over the joy of Titus, because his spirit has been refreshed by all of you.

14 Because if I have boasted anything to him about you, I was not ashamed. But as we spoke all things in truth to you, so also our boasting as to Titus became truth.

15 And his bowels are far greater toward you, remembering the obedience of all of you, as you received him with fear and trembling.

16 Therefore, I rejoice, that in everything I am fully assured in you.

2 Corinthians 8

He stirs them up to a liberal contribution for the poor saints at Jerusalem.

1 ¶ But, brothers, we make known to you the grace of God which has been given among the assemblies of Macedonia,

2 that in much testing of trouble, the overflowing of their joy and the depth of their poverty abounded to the riches of their generosity.

3 Because I testify *that* according to *their* ability and beyond *their* ability, of *their* own accord.

4 with much appeal begging us *to* receive of us the grace and the fellowship of the ministry to the saints.

5 And not as we hoped, but *they* gave themselves to the Lord firstly, and to us through *the* will of God,

6 for us to call on Titus, that even as he began before, so also he might complete this grace to you also.

7 ¶ But even as you abound in everything, in faith, and in word, and in knowledge, and in all earnestness, and in your love in us, that you also should abound in this grace.

8 I do not speak according to command, but through the diligence of others and testing the trueness of your love.

9 For you know the grace of our Lord Jesus Christ, that being rich, He became poor for your sake, so that you might become rich by the poverty of that One.

10 And I give judgment in this, for this is profitable for you, who began before not only to do, but also to be willing from last year.

11 But now also finish the doing *of it*, so that even as *there was* the readiness to will *it*, so also the finishing, *giving* out of *what you* have.

12 For if the readiness is present, *it is* acceptable according to *what* one has, not according to *what* one does not have.

13 For *it is* not that *there may be* ease to others, but affliction *to* you;

14 but by equality in the time now, your abundance for the need of those; but also that the abundance of those may be for your need, that there may be equality;

15 even as it is written, "He *gathering* much, he had nothing left over, and he *gathering* little did not lack." *Ex. 16:18*

16 ¶ But thanks *be* to God, who gives the same earnestness for you in the heart of Titus.

17 For truly he received the appeal, but being more earnest, he went out to you of his own accord.

18 But we sent with him the brother whose praise *is* in the gospel throughout all the assemblies,

19 and not only *so*, but also he having been chosen by the assemblies *as* a traveling companion to us with this gift being ministered by us to the glory of the Lord Himself, and your eagerness,

20 avoiding this, lest anyone should blame us in this bounty being ministered by us;

21 providing right things not only before *the* Lord, but also before men. *Prov. 3:4*

22 And we sent with them our brother whom we often proved in many things to be earnest, and now much more earnest by the great confidence which *I have* toward you.

23 If *any asks* about Titus, *he is* my partner and a fellow worker for you; or *about* our brothers, *they are* messengers of the assemblies, *the* glory of Christ.

24 Therefore show them a proof of your love and of our boastings on your behalf, even in the face of the assemblies.

2 *Corinthians* 9

1 He yields the reason why he sent Titus and his brethren beforehand, 6 and stirs them up to a bountiful alms.

1 ¶ For indeed concerning the ministry to the saints, it is beyond necessity for me to write to you.

2 For I know your eagerness, of which I boast to Macedonia on your behalf, that Achaia has made ready from last year, and your zeal arouses the greater number.

3 But I sent the brothers that our boasting which *is* on your behalf should not be made void in this respect, even as I said, you were being ready;

4 lest perhaps if Macedonians come with me and find you not ready, that we (we do not say you) should be ashamed in this assurance of boasting.

5 Therefore, I thought *it* necessary to exhort the brothers, that they go forward to you and arrange beforehand your promised blessing, this to be ready, thus as a blessing and not as by greediness.

6 ¶ And this: the *one* sowing sparingly will also reap sparingly, and the *one* sowing on *hope of* blessings will also reap *of* blessings.

7 Each *one* as he purposes in his heart, not out of grief or out of necessity, for God loves a cheerful giver. *Prov. 22:8*

8 And God *is* able to make all grace to abound toward you, that in every*thing*, always having all self sufficiency, you may abound to every good work;

9 even as it is written, "He scattered, he gave to the poor ones, his righteousness abides forever." *Psa. 112:9*

10 Now He that supplies seed to the sower and bread for eating, may He supply and multiply your seed and increase the fruits of your righteousness,

11 in everything *you* being enriched to all simplicity, which works out thanksgiving to God through us.

12 Because the ministry of this service is not only completely filling up the things lacking of the saints, but also multiplying through many thanksgivings to God,

13 through the proof of this ministry, *they* glorifying God by your subjection to the gospel of Christ, and the simplicity of the fellowship toward them and toward all;

14 and with their petition for you, a longing after you, because of the overflowing grace of God on you.

15 But thanks *be* to God for His unspeakable gift.

2 Corinthians 10

1 He sets out the spiritual might and authority, with which he is armed against all adversary powers, 7 assuring them that at his coming he will be found as mighty in word, as he is now in writing.

1 ¶ And I myself, Paul, call on you through the meekness and gentleness of Christ, I, who indeed according to face am lowly among you, but being absent am bold toward you;

2 but I ask, not being present, that I may be bold with the confidence which I think to be bold against some, the *ones* reckoning us as walking according to flesh.

3 For walking about in flesh, we do not war according to flesh;

4 for the weapons of our warfare *are* not fleshly *ones,* but powerful *ones* to God to the demolition of strongholds,

5 demolishing reasonings and every high thing lifting up *itself* against the knowledge of God, and bringing into captivity every thought into the obedience of Christ,

6 and having readiness to avenge all disobedience, whenever your obedience is fulfilled.

7 ¶ Do you look at things according to face? If anyone has persuaded himself to be of Christ, let him think this again as to himself, that as he *is* of Christ, so also we *are* of Christ.

8 For even if I also somewhat more abundantly may boast about our authority, which the Lord gave us for building up and not for your destruction, I will not be put to shame,

9 so that I may not seem to terrify you by letters.

10 Because, they say, the letters *are* weighty and strong, but the bodily presence *is* weak, and *his* speech being despised.

11 Let such a one think this, that such as we *are* in word through letters, being absent, such *we are* also being present in deed.

12 ¶ For we dare not rank or compare ourselves with some of those commending themselves, but they measuring themselves among themselves and comparing themselves to themselves, *are* not perceptive.

13 But we will not boast beyond measure, but according to measure of the rule which the God of measure distributed to us, to reach even as far as to you.

14 For we do not overstretch ourselves as *if* not reaching to you, for even as far as to you we came to you in the gospel of Christ,

15 not boasting beyond measure in the labors of others, but having hope that the growing faith among you will be made larger according to our rule, to overflowing,

16 in order to preach the gospel *to* the *regions* beyond you, not to glory in another's rule in things *made* ready.

17 "But the *one* glorying, let him glory in" *the* "Lord." *Jer. 9:24*

18 For not the *one* commending himself is the one approved, but *he* whom the Lord commends.

2 Corinthians 11

Out of his jealousy over the Corinthians, he enters into a forced commendation of himself.

1 ¶ I would that you endured me a little *in* foolishness, but, indeed, endure me.

2 For I am jealous *over* you with a jealousy of God. For I have betrothed you to one Man, to present *you* a pure virgin to Christ.

3 But I fear lest by any means, as the serpent deceived Eve in his craftiness, so your thoughts should be corrupted from the simplicity *which is due* to Christ.

4 For if, indeed, the *one* coming proclaims another Jesus, whom we have not proclaimed, or *if* you receive another spirit which you have not received, or another gospel which you never accepted, you might well endure *these*.

5 ¶ For I reckon *myself* to have been inferior to the exceedingly great apostles *in* nothing.

6 But even if *I am* unskilled in speech, yet not in knowledge. But in every way *I* have been made known to you in all things.

7 Or did I commit sin, humbling myself that you might be exalted, because I preached the gospel of God to you freely?

8 I stripped other assemblies, taking wages for the ministry of you.

9 And being present with you and lacking, I was not a burden to anyone. The brothers coming from Macedonia completely made up for my need. And in every way I kept myself without burden *to you*, and I will keep *myself*.

10 The truth of Christ is in me, that this boasting shall not be silenced in me in the regions of Achaia.

11 Why? Because I do not love you? God knows.

12 But what I do, I also will do, that I may cut off the occasion of the *ones* desiring an occasion, so that in that which they boast, they be found also as we.

13 For such *ones are* false apostles, deceitful workers, transforming themselves into apostles of Christ.

14 And *it is* not marvelous, for Satan transforms himself into an angel of light?

15 *It is* not a great thing, therefore, if also his ministers transform themselves as ministers of righteousness, whose end will be according to their works.

16 ¶ Again I say, let not anyone think me to be a foolish *one*. But if not, even if as a foolish *one*, receive me, that I also may boast a little.

17 What I speak, I speak not according to *the* Lord, but as in foolishness, in this boldness of boasting.

18 Since many boast according to the flesh, I also will boast.

19 For you gladly endure the foolish *ones*, *you* being wise *ones*.

20 For you endure if anyone enslaves you, if anyone devours *you*, if anyone takes away *from you*, if anyone exalts *self*, if anyone beats you in the face.

21 I speak according to dishonor, as if we have been weak. But in whatever anyone dares (I say it in foolishness), I also dare.

22 ¶ Are they Hebrews? I also. Are they Israelites? I also. Are they Abraham's seed? I also.

23 Are they ministers of Christ? (I speak as beside myself) I *being* beyond *them*: in labors, more abundantly; in stripes, beyond measure; in prisons, much more; in deaths, many times.

24 Five times I received forty *stripes* minus one from the Jews.

25 I was beaten with a rod three times; I was stoned once; I was shipwrecked three times; I have *spent* a night and a day in the deep.

26 in travels many times, in dangers of rivers, in dangers of robbers, in dangers from *my* race, in dangers from *the* nations, in dangers in *the* city, in dangers in a wild place, in dangers in *the* sea, in dangers among false brothers,

27 in hardship and toil, in sleepless *nights* many times, in hunger and thirst, in fastings many times, in cold and nakedness.

28 In addition to the *things* besides, the conspiratorial gathering against me according to a day, the care of all the assemblies.

29 Who is weak, and I am not weak? Who is caused to stumble, and I do not burn?

30 If it is right to boast, I will boast *of* the things of my infirmity.

31 The God and Father of our Lord Jesus Christ knows, the *One* being blessed to the ages, that I am not lying.

32 In Damascus the ethnarch *under* Aretas the king guarded the city of *the* Damascenes, desiring to seize me.

33 And I was let down through a window through the wall in a basket and escaped their hands.

2 Corinthians 12

1 For commending of his apostleship, though he might glory of his wonderful revelations, 9 yet he rather chooses to glory of his infirmities, 11 blaming them for forcing him to vain boasting.

1 ¶ Really, to boast *is* not profitable to me, for I will come to visions and revelations of *the* Lord.

2 I know a man in Christ fourteen years before—whether in *the* body, I do not know, or out of *the* body, I do not know, God knows—such a one *was* caught up to *the* third Heaven.

3 And I know such a man—whether in *the* body or out of the body, I do not know; God knows—

4 that he was caught up into Paradise and heard unspeakable words which a man is not permitted to speak.

5 On behalf of such a one I will boast. But I will not boast on my behalf, if not in my weaknesses.

6 For if I desire to boast, I will not be a foolish *one*, for I speak the truth. But I spare, lest anyone considers me *to be* beyond what he sees me or hears anything from me.

7 And *by* the pre-eminence of the revelations, that I not exalt myself, a thorn in the flesh was given to me, a messenger of Satan, that he might buffet me, that I not exalt myself.

8 Concerning this I entreated the Lord three times, that it depart from me.

9 And He said to me, My grace is sufficient for you, for My power is perfected in weakness. Therefore, I will rather gladly boast in my weaknesses, that the power of Christ might dwell on me.

10 Therefore I am pleased in weaknesses, in insults, in calamities, in persecutions, in distresses, for the sake of Christ. For whenever I may be weak, then I am powerful.

11 ¶ Boasting, I have become a foolish *one*. You compelled me. For I ought to be commended by you, for I lacked nothing of the exceedingly great apostles, even though I am nothing.

12 Truly the signs of the apostle were fully worked among you in all patience, in *miraculous* signs, and in wonders, and by works of power.

13 For what is it in which you were less than the rest of the assemblies, except that I myself did not burden you? Forgive me this wrong.

14 Behold, I am ready to come to you a third *time*. And I will not burden you, for I do not seek your things, but you. For the children ought not to lay up treasure for the parents, but the parents for the children.

15 But I will most gladly spend and be utterly spent for your souls, even if loving you more and more, I am loved *the* less.

16 But let it be so, I did not burden you; but being crafty, I took you with bait.

17 By any whom I have sent to you, did I take advantage of you by him?

18 I begged Titus and sent the brother with *him*. Did Titus deceitfully covet you? *Did we* not walk in the same spirit? *Did we* not *walk* in the same steps?

19 Again, do you think we are defending *ourselves* to you? We speak before God in Christ, but in all things for your building up, beloved.

20 For I fear lest somehow, coming, I not find you as I wish, and I be found by you such as you do not wish; lest somehow *there be* strifes, envyings, angers, intrigues, evil speakings, slanders, puffings up, disturbances;

21 that *it* not *be, in* my having come again, my God may humble me with you, and I shall mourn many of the *ones* sinning before and not having repented over the uncleanness and fornication and lustfulness which they have practiced.

2 Corinthians 13

He threatens severity, and the power of his apostleship against obstinate sinners.

1 ¶ I am coming to you this third *time*. "In the mouth of two or three witnesses every word shall be established." *Deut. 19:15*

2 I said before, and I say beforehand, as being present the second *time* and being absent now, I write to the *ones* having

sinned before, and all the rest, that if I come again I will not spare,

3 since you seek a proof of Christ speaking in me, who is not a weak *one* toward you, but is powerful in you,

4 (for even if He was crucified out of weakness, yet He lives by *the* power of God). For even also we are weak in Him, yet we shall live by *the* power of God toward you.

5 Test yourselves, whether you are in the faith; examine yourselves. Or do you not yourselves perceive that Jesus Christ is in you, unless you are disapproved?

6 And I hope you will know that we are not disapproved.

7 ¶ But I pray to God *for* you not to do the evil *thing,* none; not that we may appear *to be* approved, but that you may do the good *thing,* and we may be disapproved.

8 For we cannot have any power against the truth, but on behalf of the truth.

9 For we rejoice when we are a weak *one* and you are the powerful *ones.* But we pray for this also, your perfection.

10 Because of this, I write these things while absent, that being present I may not deal severely*with you* according to the authority which the Lord gave me for building up and not for destruction.

11 ¶ For the rest, brothers, rejoice! Perfect yourselves; encourage yourselves, think the same thing, be at peace; and the God of love and of peace will be with you.

12 Greet one another with a holy kiss.

13 All the saints greet you.

14 The grace of the Lord Jesus Christ and the love of God and the fellowship of the Holy Spirit *be* with you all. Amen.

The Epistle of Paul the Apostle to the
GALATIANS

Galatians 1

6 He wonders that they have so soon left him and the gospel. 11 He learned the gospel not of men, but of God.

1 ¶ Paul, an apostle, not from men nor through man, but through Jesus Christ and God *the* Father, the *One* raising Him from *the* dead *ones,*

2 and all the brothers with me, to the assemblies of Galatia.

3 Grace to you and peace from God *the* Father and our Lord Jesus Christ,

4 who gave Himself for our sins, so that He might deliver us out of the evil age being present, according to the will of our God and Father,

5 to whom *be* the glory unto the ages of the ages. Amen.

6 ¶ I wonder that you are so quickly turning away from the *One* having called you in *the* grace of Christ to another gospel,

7 which is not another; if not there are some troubling you, even determined to pervert the gospel of Christ.

8 But even if we, or an angel out of Heaven, should preach a gospel to you beside the gospel we preached to you, let him be accursed.

9 As we have said before, and now I say again, If anyone preaches a gospel beside what you received, let him be accursed.

10 ¶ For do I now persuade men or God? Or do I seek to please men? For if I yet pleased men, I would not be a slave of Christ.

11 And, brothers, I make known to you the gospel preached by me, that it is not according to man.

12 For I did not receive it from man, nor was I taught *it,* but by a revelation of Jesus Christ.

13 For you heard *of* my way of life when *I was* in Judaism, that with surpassing *zeal* I persecuted the Assembly of God and ravaged it.

14 And *I* advanced in Judaism beyond many of my own age; in my race being much more a zealot of the traditions of my paternal fathers.

15 But when God was pleased, He having separated me from my mother's womb, and having called *me* through His grace, *Isa. 49:1*

16 to reveal His Son in me, that I might preach Him among the nations, immediately I did not confer with flesh and blood,

17 nor did I go up to Jerusalem to the apostles before me, but I went away into Arabia and returned again to Damascus.

18 Then after three years, I went up to Jerusalem to know Peter and remained with him fifteen days.

19 But I saw *no* other of the apostles if not James, the brother of the Lord.

20 And what I write to you, behold, before God I do not lie.

21 Then I went into the regions of Syria and of Cilicia,

22 but I was being unknown by face to the assemblies of Judea in Christ.

23 But only they were hearing that the *one* who *was* persecuting us once, now preaches the gospel, the faith which he once ravaged;

24 and they glorified God in me.

Galatians 2

1 He shows when he went up again to Jerusalem, and for what purpose. 14 Of justification by faith, and not by works.

1 ¶ Then through fourteen years, I again went up to Jerusalem with Barnabas, also taking Titus with *me.*

2 And I went up according to revelation. And I put before them the gospel which I proclaim in the nations, but privately to the *ones* thought *to be pillars,* lest perhaps I run, or I ran, to no purpose.

3 But not even Titus, the *one* with me, a Greek, was compelled to be circumcised.

4 But *it was* because of the *ones* brought in stealthily, false brothers, who stole in to spy on our freedom which we have in Christ Jesus, they desiring to enslave us,

5 to whom not even for an hour did we yield in subjection, that the truth of the gospel might continue with you.

6 But from the *ones* thought to be something (of what kind they were then does not matter to me; God does not accept the face of man), for the *ones* thought *to be pillars* conferred nothing to me;

7 but on the contrary, seeing that I have been entrusted *with* the gospel of the uncircumcision, even as Peter to the circumcision,

8 (for the *One* working in Peter to an apostleship of the circumcision, also worked in me to the nations),

9 and knowing the grace being given to me, James and Cephas and John, the *ones* thought to be pillars, gave right *hands* of fellowship to Barnabas and to me, that we *go* to the nations, but they to the circumcision;

10 only that we might remember the poor *ones*, which same thing I was eager to do.

11 ¶ But when Peter came to Antioch, I opposed *him* to his face, because he was to be blamed.

12 For before some came from James, he ate with the nations. But when they came, he drew back and separated himself, being afraid of the *ones* of the circumcision.

13 And also the rest of the Jews joined in hypocrisy *with* him, so as even Barnabas was led away with their hypocrisy.

14 But when I saw that they did not walk uprightly with the truth of the gospel, I said to Peter before all, If you being a Jew, live heathen-like and not Jewishly, why do you compel *the* nations to Judaize?

15 We, Jews by nature, and not sinners of the nations,

16 knowing that a man is not justified by works of Law, if not through the faith of Jesus Christ (we also believed into Christ Jesus, that we may be justified by the faith of Christ and not by works of Law, because all flesh will not be justified by works of Law). *Psa. 123:2*

17 But if seeking to be justified in Christ, we ourselves also were found *to be* sinners, *is* Christ then a minister of sin? Let it not be!

18 For what if I build again these things which I destroyed, I myself stand out *as* a transgressor.

19 For through Law I died to Law, that I might live to God.

20 I have been crucified with Christ, and I live; *yet* no longer I, but Christ lives in me. And the *life* I now live in the flesh, I live in the faith of the Son of God, the *One* loving me and giving Himself over on my behalf.

21 I do not set aside the grace of God; for if righteousness *is* through Law, then Christ died for nothing.

Galatians 3

1 He asks what moved them to leave the faith, and hang on the law? 6 They that believe are justified, 9 and blessed with Abraham.

1 ¶ O foolish Galatians, who bewitched you not to obey the truth, to whom before *your* eyes Jesus Christ was portrayed afore among you being crucified?

2 This only I desire to learn from you: Did you receive the Spirit by works of Law or by hearing of faith?

3 Are you so foolish? Having begun in *the* Spirit, are you now being perfected in the flesh?

4 Did you suffer so much vainly, if indeed *it* also *was* vainly?

5 Therefore the *One* supplying the Spirit to you and working works of power in you, *is it* by works of Law or by hearing of faith?

6 ¶ Even "as Abraham believed God, and it was imputed to him for righteousness," *Gen. 15:6*

7 know, therefore, that the *ones* of faith, these are sons of Abraham.

8 And the Scripture foreseeing that God would justify the nations by faith, preached the gospel before to Abraham: "All the nations will be blessed" "in you." *Gen. 12:3*

9 So that the *ones* of faith are blessed with the faithful Abraham.

10 For as many as are out of works of Law, *these* are under a curse. For it is

written, "Accursed *is* everyone who does not continue in all the things having been written in the book of the Law, to do them." *Deut. 27:26*

11 And that no one is justified by Law before God *is* clear because, "The just *one* shall live by faith." *Hab. 2:4*

12 But the Law is not of faith, but, "The man doing these things shall live in them." *Lev. 18:5*

13 Christ redeemed us from the curse of the Law, having become a curse for us; for it is written, "Accursed *is* everyone having been hung on a tree;" *Deut. 21:23*

14 that the blessing of Abraham might be to the nations in Christ Jesus, that we might receive the promise of the Spirit through the faith.

15 Brothers, I speak according to man, a covenant having been ratified, even *among* mankind, no one annuls or adds to *it.*

16 But the promises were spoken to Abraham and to his Seed (it does not say, And to seeds, as of many, but as of one, "And to your Seed," which is Christ). *Gen. 3:15; 21:12; 22:18, Rom. 9:7; Heb. 11:18*

17 And I say this, A covenant having been ratified before to Christ by God, *the* Law coming into being four hundred and thirty years after, does not annul the promise, so as to abolish *it.*

18 For if the inheritance *is* of Law, *it is* no more of promise; but God has given *it* to Abraham through promise.

19 ¶ Why the Law then? It was added for the sake of transgressions, until the Seed should come, to whom it had been promised, being ordained through angels in a mediator's hand.

20 But the Mediator is not *mediator* of one, but God is one.

21 Therefore is the Law against the promises of God? Let it not be! For if a law had been given which had been able to make alive, indeed righteousness would have been out of Law.

22 But the Scripture shut up together all under sin, that the promise by faith of Jesus Christ might be given to the *ones* believing.

23 But before the coming of the faith, we were guarded under Law, being shut up to the faith being about to be revealed.

24 So that the Law has become a tutor of us *until* Christ, that we might be justified by faith.

25 But the faith coming, we are no longer under a tutor;

26 for you are all sons of God through the faith in Christ Jesus.

27 For as many as were baptized into Christ, you put on Christ.

28 There cannot be Jew nor Greek, there is no slave nor freeman, there is no male and female; for you are all one in Christ Jesus.

29 And if you *are* of Christ, then you are a seed of Abraham, and heirs according to promise.

Galatians 4

1 We were under the law till Christ came. 5 But Christ freed us from the law. 7 Therefore we are servants no longer to it.

1 ¶ But I say, Over so long as time the heir is a little child, he being lord of all, in nothing he differs from a slave,

2 but is under guardians and house-managers until the *term* set before by the father.

3 So we also, when we were little children, we were under the elements of the world, being enslaved.

4 But when the fullness of the time came, God sent forth His Son, becoming of a woman, becoming under Law,

5 that He might redeem the *ones* under Law, that we might receive the adoption of sons.

6 And because you are sons, God sent forth the Spirit of His Son into your hearts, crying, Abba! Father!

7 So that you no more are a slave, but a son, and if a son, also an heir of God through Christ.

8 ¶ But then, indeed, not knowing God, you served as slaves *to* the *ones* by nature not being gods.

9 But now, knowing God, but rather being known by God, how do you turn again to the weak and poor elements to which again you desire to be a slave anew?

10 You observe days and months and seasons and years.

11 I fear *for* you, lest somehow I have labored among you in vain.

12 ¶ Be as I *am*, I beg of you, b*rothers*, because I *am* as you. You wronged me *in* nothing.

13 But you know that because of weakness of the flesh, I announced the gospel to you before;

14 and you did not despise my affliction, the *one* in my flesh, nor disdained *it*, but you received me as an angel of God, as Christ Jesus.

15 What then was your blessedness? For I testify to you that if you were able, digging out your eyes, *you* would have given *them* to me.

16 So then have I become a hostile *one* to you speaking truth to you?

17 ¶ They are zealous for you, *but* not well; but they *only* desire to shut you out, that you be zealous to them.

18 But *it is* good to be zealous always in *a* good thing, and not only in my being present with you.

19 ¶ My children, *for* whom I again travail until Christ should be formed to you,

20 even now I desired to be present with you and to change my voice, for I am in doubt *as* to you.

21 ¶ Tell me, the *ones* desiring to be under Law, do you not hear the Law?

22 For it is written, Abraham had two sons, one out of the slave woman and one out of the free woman.

23 But, indeed, the *one* of the slave woman has been born according to flesh, and the *one* out of the free *woman* through the promise,

24 which things are being allegorized, for these are two covenants, one, indeed, from Mount Sinai bringing forth to slavery (which is Hagar,

25 for Hagar is Mount Sinai in Arabia and corresponds to the present Jerusalem, and she slaves with her children),

26 but the Jerusalem *from* above is free, who is the mother of us all;

27 for it is written, "Rejoice, barren *one* not bearing; break forth and shout, the *one* not travailing; for more *are* the children of the desolate rather than she having the husband." *Isa. 54:1*

28 But, brothers, we are children of promise according to Isaac.

29 But even as then, the *one* being generated according to flesh persecuted the *one* according to Spirit, so *it is* also now.

30 But what says the Scripture? "Cast out the slave woman and her son, for not shall the son of the slave *woman* inherit with the son of the free *woman*," not *ever*! *Gen. 21:10*

31 Then, brothers, we are not children of a slave woman but of the free *woman*.

Galatians 5

1 He moves them to stand in their liberty, 3 and not to observe circumcision: 13 but rather love, which is the sum of the law.

1 ¶ Therefore stand firm in the freedom with which Christ made us free and do not be held again with a yoke of slavery.

2 Behold, I, Paul, say to you that if you are circumcised, Christ will profit you nothing.

3 And I testify again to every man being circumcised, that he is a debtor to do all the Law,

4 *you*, whoever are justified by Law, you were severed from the Christ, you fell from grace.

5 For we through *the* Spirit eagerly wait for *the* hope of righteousness out of faith.

6 For in Christ Jesus, neither circumcision nor uncircumcision has any strength, but faith working through love.

7 You were running well; who beat you back *that* you do not obey the truth?

8 The persuasion *is* not from Him calling you.

9 A little leaven leavens all the lump.

10 I trust as to you in *the* Lord that you will think nothing else, but that the *one* troubling you shall bear the judgment, whoever he may be.

11 But I, brothers, if I proclaim circumcision, why am I still persecuted? Then the stumbling-block of the Cross has passed away.

12 O that also the *ones* unsettling you will cut themselves off.

13 ¶ For, brothers, you were called to freedom. Only do not *use* the freedom for *an* opening to the flesh. But through love be slaves to one another.

14 For the whole Law is fulfilled in one word, in *this*: "You shall love your neighbor as yourself." *Lev. 19:18*

15 But if you bite and devour one another, be careful that you are not consumed by one another.

16 But I say, Walk in *the* Spirit, and you will not fulfill *the* lust of *the* flesh.

17 For the flesh lusts against the Spirit, and the Spirit against the flesh; and these are contrary to one another; that not whatever you may will, *but* these things you do.

18 But if you are led by *the* Spirit, you are not under Law.

19 Now the works of the flesh are clearly revealed, which are: adultery, fornication, uncleanness, lustfulness,

20 idolatry, sorcery, enmities, fightings, jealousies, angers, intrigues, dissensions, heresies,

21 envyings, murders, drunkennesses, revelings, and things like these; of which I tell you beforehand, even as I also said before, that the *ones* practicing such things will not inherit *the* kingdom of God.

22 But the fruit of the Spirit is: love, joy, peace, long-suffering, kindness, goodness, faith,

23 meekness, self-control. Against such things there is not a law.

24 But the *ones* belonging to Christ crucified the flesh with *its* passions and lusts.

25 If we live in *the* Spirit, let us also walk in *the* Spirit.

26 Let us not become self-conceited, provoking one another, envying one another.

Galatians 6

2 He moves them to bear one another's burdens.
14 He glories in nothing, except in the cross of
Christ.

1 ¶ Brothers, if a man is taken in some deviation, you, the spiritual ones, restore such a one in the spirit of meekness, considering yourself, that you not also be tempted.

2 Bear one another's burdens, and so you will fulfill the law of Christ.

3 For if anyone thinks to be something, he deceives himself, being nothing.

4 But let each *one* prove his own work, and then he alone will have a boast in himself and not in the other.

5 For each *one* will bear *his* own load.

6 But let the *one* being taught in the Word share with the *one* teaching, in all good things.

7 Do not be deceived, God is not mocked. For whatever a man may sow, that he also will reap.

8 For the *one* sowing to his own flesh will reap corruption of the flesh. But the *one* sowing to the Spirit will reap everlasting life of the Spirit.

9 But let us not be wearied in doing a good *thing*; for in its own time we shall reap, not growing faint-hearted.

10 So, then, as we have time, let us work the good toward all, and especially toward the household of the faith.

11 ¶ See in what large letters I write to you with my *own* hand.

12 As many as desire to look well in *the* flesh, these compel you to be circumcised, only that they may not be persecuted for the cross of Christ.

13 For neither the *ones* being circumcised themselves do not even keep *the* Law, but they desire you to be circumcised so that they may boast in your flesh.

14 But may it never be for me to boast, except in the cross of our Lord Jesus Christ, through whom the world has been crucified to me, and I to the world.

15 For in Christ Jesus neither circumcision *has* any strength nor uncircumcision, but a new creation.

16 And as many as shall walk by this rule, peace and mercy *be* on them and on the Israel of God.

17 For the rest, let no one give troubles to me, for I bear in my body the brands of the Lord Jesus.

18 The grace of our Lord Jesus Christ *be* with your spirit, brothers. Amen.

The Epistle of Paul the Apostle to the
EPHESIANS

Ephesians 1

1 After salvation and thanksgiving for the
Ephesians, 4 our election, 6 and adoption.

1 ¶ Paul, *an* apostle of Jesus Christ through *the* will of God, to the saints being in Ephesus and faithful in Christ Jesus:

2 Grace to you and peace from God our Father and *the* Lord Jesus Christ.

3 ¶ Blessed *is* the God and Father of our Lord Jesus Christ, who blessed us with every spiritual blessing in the heavenly *realms* with Christ,

4 even as He elected us in Him before *the* foundation of *the* world, for us to be holy and without blemish before Him in love,

5 to Himself predestinating us to adoption through Jesus Christ according to the good pleasure of His will,

6 to *the* praise of *the* glory of His grace in which He has favored us in the *One* being loved,

7 in whom we have redemption through His blood, the remission of deviations, according to the riches of His grace

8 which He caused to abound toward us in all wisdom and understanding,

9 making known to us the mystery of His will, according to His good pleasure which He purposed in Himself,

10 for the administration of the fullness of the times to head up all things in Christ, both the things in the heavens, and the things on earth, in Him,

11 in whom we also were chosen to an inheritance, being predestinated according to *the* purpose of the *One* working all things according to the counsel of His *own* will,

12 for us to be to *the* praise of His glory, the *ones* who had before trusted in Christ;

13 in whom also you, hearing the Word of truth, the gospel of your salvation, in whom also believing you were sealed with the Holy Spirit of promise,

14 who is an earnest of our inheritance, unto *the* redemption of the purchased possession, to *the* praise of His glory.

15 ¶ Because of this, hearing of your faith in the Lord Jesus and love toward all the saints,

16 *I also* do not cease giving thanks on your behalf, making mention of you in my prayers,

17 that the God of our Lord Jesus Christ, the Father of glory, may give to you a spirit of wisdom and revelation in *the* full knowledge of Him,

18 the eyes of your mind having been enlightened, for you to know what is the hope of His calling, and what *are* the riches of the glory of His inheritance in the saints,

19 and what *is* the surpassing greatness of His power toward us, the *ones* believing according to the working of His mighty strength

20 which He worked in Christ *in* raising Him from *the* dead *ones*; yea, *He* seated *Him* at His right *hand* in the heavenly *realms*, *Psa. 110:1*

21 far above all rule, and authority, and power, and lordship, and every name being named, not only in this age, but also in the coming *age*;

22 and He "put all *things* under His feet" and gave Him *to be* Head over all *things* to the Assembly, *Psa. 8:6*

23 which is His body: the fullness of the *One* filling all things in all;

Ephesians 2

1 By comparing what we were by nature, 3 with
what we are 5 by grace: 8 faith is a gift of God
10 we are made for good works.

1 ¶ and you being a dead *one* in deviations and sins,

2 in which you formerly walked according to the course of this world, according to the ruler of the authority of the air, the spirit now working in the sons of disobedience,

3 among whom we also all conducted our-selves in times past in the lusts of our flesh, acting out the wills of the flesh and of the understandings, and were by nature the children of wrath, even as the rest.

4 ¶ But God, being rich in mercy, because of His great love *with* which He loved us,

5 even we being dead in deviations, *He* made us alive together with Christ; by grace you are having been saved,

6 and *He* raised *us* up together and seated *us* together in the heavenly *realms* in Christ Jesus,

7 that He might demonstrate in the ages coming on the exceeding great riches of His grace in kindness toward us in Christ Jesus,

8 for by grace you are having been saved, through faith, and this not of yourselves; *it is* the gift of God;

9 not of works, that not anyone should boast;

10 for we are *His* workmanship, created in Christ Jesus unto good works, which God before prepared that we should walk in them.

11 ¶ Therefore, remember that you, the nations, *were* then in *the* flesh (the *ones* being called Uncircumcision by the *ones* being called Circumcision in the flesh made by hand),

12 that at that time you were without Christ, alienated from the commonwealth of Israel and strangers of the covenants of promise, having no hope and without God in the world.

13 But now, in Christ Jesus you who then were afar off, came to be near by the blood of Christ.

14 ¶ For He is our peace, He making us both one, and breaking down the wall of partition,

15 in His flesh having made to cease the enmity, the Law of the commandments in decrees, that He might in Himself create the two into one new man, making peace,

16 and might reconcile both in one body to God through the cross, slaying the en-mity in Himself.

17 And coming, *He* proclaimed "peace to you, the ones afar off, and to the *ones* near." *Isa. 57:19*

18 For through Him we both have access by one Spirit to the Father.

19 So, then, you are no longer strangers and aliens, but *you are* fellow citizens of the saints and *of the* household of God,

20 being built up on the foundation of the apostles and prophets, Jesus Christ Him-self being *the* cornerstone,

21 in whom all the building being fitly joined together grows into a holy temple in *the* Lord,

22 in whom you also are being built to-gether into a dwelling place of God in *the* Spirit.

Ephesians 3

5 The hidden mystery, 6 that the Gentiles should be saved, 3 was made known to Paul by revela-tion.

1 ¶ Because of this, I, Paul, the prisoner of Christ Jesus on behalf of you, the na-tions,

2 if, indeed, you heard of the stewardship of the grace of God given to me for you,

3 that by revelation He made known to me the mystery, as I wrote before in brief,

4 by the reading of which you are able to realize my understanding in the mystery of Christ,

5 which was not made known to the sons of men in other generations, as now it was revealed to His holy apostles and prophets in *the* Spirit,

6 *for* the nations to be joint-heirs, and a joint-body and joint-partakers of His prom-ise in Christ through the gospel,

7 of which I was made a minister ac-cording to the gift of the grace of God given to me, according to the working of His power.

8 This grace was given to me, *I being* less than the least of all the saints, to preach the gospel of the incomprehensible riches of Christ among the nations,

9 and to enlighten all, what *is* the fellow-ship of the mystery having been hidden from eternity in God, the *One* creating all things through Jesus Christ,

10 so that now to the rulers and to the authorities in the heavenly *realms* might be made known through the Assembly the manifold wisdom of God,

11 according to the eternal purpose which He accomplished in Christ Jesus our Lord,

12 in whom we have boldness and access in confidence through His faith.

13 Therefore, I ask *you* not to weaken at my afflictions on your behalf, which is your glory.

14 ¶ For this reason I bow my knees to the Father of our Lord Jesus Christ,

15 of whom every family in Heaven and on earth is named,

16 that He may give you, according to the riches of His glory, by *His* power to be empowered in the inward man through His Spirit,

17 that through the faith Christ may dwell in your hearts, having been rooted and founded in love,

18 that you may have full strength to grasp, with all the saints, what *is* the breadth and length and depth and height,

19 and to know the surpassing knowledge and love of Christ, that you may be filled to all the fullness of God.

20 Now to the *One* being able to do beyond all things exceedingly above *all of* which we ask or think, according to the power *of* the *One* working in us,

21 to Him *be* the glory in the Assembly in Christ Jesus, to all the generations of the age of the ages. Amen.

Ephesians 4

1 He exhorts to unity, 24 and to put on the new man.

1 ¶ Then I, the prisoner in *the* Lord, exhort you to walk worthily of the calling in which you were called,

2 ¶ with all humility and meekness, with long-suffering, bearing with one another in love,

3 being eager to keep the unity of the Spirit in the bond of peace.

4 *There is* one body and one Spirit, even as you also were called in one hope of your calling;

5 one Lord, one faith, one baptism,

6 one God and Father of all, the *One* above all and through all and in you all.

7 But to each one of us was given grace according to the measure of the gift of Christ.

8 Therefore He says, "Ascending to *the* height, He led captivity captive," and gave "gifts to men." *Psa. 68:18*

9 But that He ascended, what is it except that He also first descended into the lower parts of the earth?

10 The *One* descending Himself is also the *one* ascending far above all the heavens, that He might fill all things.

11 And indeed He gave the *ones to be* apostles; and the *ones* prophets; and the *ones* evangelists; and the *ones* shepherds and teachers;

12 for the equipping of the saints for the work of the ministry, for the building up of the body of Christ,

13 until we all may come to the unity of the faith and of the full knowledge of the Son of God, to a full-grown man, to *the* measure of *the* stature of the fullness of Christ,

14 so that we may no longer be little children, being blown and carried about by every wind of doctrine, in the trickery of men, in craftiness to the deceit of error,

15 but speaking the truth in love, we may grow up into Him in all things, who is the head, the Christ,

16 from whom all the body, having been fitted and compacted together through every assisting bond, according to *the* effectual working of one measure *in* each part, produces the growth of the body to the building up of itself in love.

17 ¶ Therefore, I say this, and testify in *the* Lord, that you no longer walk even as also the rest *of the* nations walk, in *the* vanity of their mind,

18 having been darkened in the intellect, being alienated *from* the life of God through the ignorance which is in them because of the hardness of their heart,

19 who, having become callous, gave themselves up to unbridled lust, to *the* working of all uncleanness with greediness.

20 But you have not so learned Christ,

21 if indeed you heard Him and were taught in Him, as *the* truth is in Jesus,

22 *for* you to put off the old man, as regards the former behavior, the *one* being corrupted according to the deceitful lusts,

23 and to be renewed in the spirit of your mind,

24 and to put on the new man, the *one* being created according to God in righteousness and holiness of truth.

25 Therefore, putting off the lie, "speak truth each with his neighbor," because we are members of one another. *Zech. 8:16*

26 "Be angry, but do not sin;" do not let the sun go down on your wrath, *LXX-Psa. 4:4; MT-Psa. 4:5*

27 nor give place to the devil.

28 The one stealing, let him steal no more, but rather let him labor, working the good *thing* with the hands, that he may have *something* to give to the *one* that has need.

29 Let not any rotten word go out of your mouth, but if any *is* a good *word* to building up *in respect to* the need, that it may give grace to the ones hearing.

30 And do not grieve the Holy Spirit of God, in whom you were sealed to *the* day of redemption.

31 Let all bitterness, and anger, and wrath, and tumult, and evil speaking be put away from you, along with all malice.

32 And be kind to one another, tenderhearted, having forgiven one another, even as also God forgave you in Christ.

Ephesians 5

2 After general exhortations, 22 he shows how wives ought to obey their husbands, 25 and husbands ought to love their wives.

1 ¶ Therefore become imitators of God, as beloved children,

2 and walk in love, even as Christ also loved us and gave Himself for us, an offering and a sacrifice to God for a fragrance of a sweet smell.

3 ¶ But let not fornication, and all uncleanness, or greediness, be named among you, as is fitting for saints;

4 also baseness, and foolish talking, or joking (the things not becoming), but rather thanksgiving.

5 For be knowing this, that every fornicator, or unclean *one*, or covetous *one*, who is an idolater, has no inheritance in the kingdom of Christ and of God.

6 Let no one deceive you with empty words, for through these the wrath of God comes on the sons of disobedience.

7 Therefore do not become joint-partakers with them;

8 for you then were darkness, but *are* now light in *the* Lord; walk as children of light.

9 For the fruit of the Spirit *is* in all goodness and righteousness and truth,

10 proving what is pleasing to the Lord.

11 And have no fellowship with the unfruitful works of darkness, but rather even reprove *them*.

12 For it is shameful even to speak of the things being done by them in secret.

13 But all things being exposed by the light are clearly revealed, for everything being revealed *is* light.

14 Therefore He says, "Rise up, the *one* sleeping, and stand up out of the dead *ones*, and Christ will shine on you." *No O. T. passage*

15 Then watch how carefully you walk, not as unwise *ones*, but as wise *ones*,

16 redeeming the time, because the days are evil.

17 For this reason, do not become foolish, but understanding what the will of the Lord *is*.

18 And "do not be drunk with wine," in which is unsavednes, but be filled by the Spirit, *Prov. 23:31*

19 speaking to yourselves in psalms and hymns and spiritual songs, singing and psalming in your heart to the Lord,

20 giving thanks at all times for all things in the name of our Lord Jesus Christ, even to God *the* Father,

21 ¶ subjecting ourselves to one another in *the* fear of God.

22 Wives, subject yourselves to *your* own husbands, as to the Lord,

23 because a husband is head of the wife, as also Christ *is* Head of the Assembly, and He is Savior of the body.

24 But even as the Assembly is subject to Christ, so also the wives to their own husbands in everything.

25 Husbands, love your wives, even as Christ also loved the Assembly and gave Himself up on her behalf,

26 that He might sanctify her, cleansing *it* by the bathing of the water in *the* Word,

27 that He might present her to Himself *as* the glorious Assembly, not having spot or wrinkle, or any such things, but that she be holy and without blemish.

28 So, husbands ought to love their wives as their *own* bodies, the *one* oving his wife loves himself),

29 for then no one hated his *own* flesh, but nourishes and cherishes her, even as also the Lord the Assembly.

30 For we are members of His body, of His flesh, and of His bones.

31 "For this *reason*, a man shall leave his father and mother, and shall be joined to his wife, and the two shall be one flesh." *Gen. 2:24*

32 The mystery is great, but I speak as to Christ and as to the Assembly.

33 However, you also, everyone, let each *one* love his wife as himself, and the wife, that she give deference to the husband.

Ephesians 6

1 The duty of children towards their parents, 5 of servants towards their masters.

1 ¶ Children, obey your parents in *the* Lord, for this is right.

2 "Honor your father and mother," which is *the* first commandment with a promise, *Ex. 20:12*

3 "that it may be well with you, and you may be long-lived on the earth". *Deut. 5:16*

4 And fathers, do not provoke to anger your children, but nurture them in *the* discipline and admonition of *the* Lord.

5 Slaves, obey *your* lords according to flesh, with fear and trembling, in simplicity of your heart, as to Christ;

6 not with eye-service as men-pleasers, but as slaves of Christ doing the will of God from *the* soul,

7 serving as slaves with good will to the Lord, and not *as to* men,

8 each *one* knowing that whatever good thing he does, this he shall receive from the Lord, whether a slave or a freeman.

9 And lords, do the same things toward them, forbearing threatening, knowing that the Lord of you and of them is in Heaven, and there is no partiality with Him.

10 ¶ For the rest, my brothers, be made powerful in *the* Lord and in the might of His strength.

11 Put on the full armor of God, for you to be able to stand against the wiles of the devil,

12 because our wrestling is not against flesh and blood, but against the rulers, against the authorities, against the world-rulers of the darkness of this age, against the spiritual *powers* of evil in the heavenly *realms.*

13 Because of this, take up the full armor of God that you may be able to withstand in the evil day, and having worked out all things, to stand.

14 Therefore stand firm, "having girded your loins about with truth" and having put on the breastplate of righteousness," *Isa. 11:5; 59:17*

15 and having shod the feet with *the* preparation of the "gospel of peace." *Isa. 52:7*

16 Above all, taking up the shield of the faith, with which you will be able to quench all the darts of the evil *one* having been made fiery.

17 Also, take "the helmet of salvation," and the sword of the Spirit which is the Word of God; *Isa. 59:17 LXX-Isa. 11:4; MT-Isa. 49:2; LXX and MT-Hos. 6:5*

18 through all prayer and petition, praying at all seasons in *the* Spirit, and being alert to this same *end,* with all perseverance and petition concerning all the saints.

19 ¶ *Pray* also on my behalf, that to me may be given speech in *the* opening of my mouth with boldness to make known the mystery of the gospel,

20 for which I am an ambassador in a chain, that in it I may speak boldly as it is right for me to speak.

21 But that you also may know the things about me, what I am doing, Tychicus, the beloved brother and faithful minister in *the* Lord, will make known all things to you,

22 whom I sent to you for this same thing, that you might know the things about us, and *he* may comfort your hearts.

23 Peace to the brothers, and love with faith, from God *the* Father and *the* Lord Jesus Christ.

24 Grace *be* with all those that love our Lord Jesus Christ in incorruptibility.

The Epistle of Paul the Apostle to the
PHILIPPIANS

Philippians 1

1 ¶ Paul and Timothy, slaves of Jesus Christ, to all the saints in Christ Jesus who are in Philippi, with the overseers and deacons:

2 Grace to you and peace from God our Father and *the* Lord Jesus Christ.

3 ¶ I thank my God on all the remembrance of you,

4 always in my every prayer on your behalf making *my* prayer with joy

5 over your fellowship in the gospel, from *the* first day until now,

6 being persuaded of this very thing, that the *One* having begun a good work in you will complete *it* until *the* day of Jesus Christ;

7 ¶ as it is righteous for me to think this of you all because you have me in *your* heart, both in my bonds and in the defense and confirmation of the gospel, you are all sharers of the grace with me.

8 For God is my witness how I long after you all in *the* bowels of Jesus Christ.

9 ¶ And this I pray, that your love may yet abound more and more in full knowledge and all perception,

10 for your examining the things different, that you may be sincere and without blame unto *the* day of Christ,

11 being filled *with* fruits of righteousness, the *ones* through Jesus Christ, to *the* glory and praise of God.

12 ¶ Now I want you to know, brothers, that the things concerning me have more fully come to *the* advancement of the gospel,

13 so that in all the praetorium, and to all the rest, my bonds have become clearly revealed *to be* in Christ.

14 And the most of the brothers in *the* Lord, having been persuaded in my bonds, more exceedingly dare to speak the Word fearlessly.

15 Some, indeed, even proclaim Christ because of envy and strife, but some also because of good will.

16 These, indeed, proclaim Christ out of self-seeking, not sincerely, thinking to bring affliction to my bonds.

17 But the *others* out of love, knowing that I am appointed for defense of the gospel.

18 What then? Yet in every way, whether in pretense or in truth, Christ is proclaimed, and I rejoice in this; yet also I will rejoice.

19 For I know that this will turn out into deliverance to me through your petition and *the* supply of *the* Spirit of Jesus Christ, *Job 13:16*

20 according to my earnest expectation and hope, that in nothing I shall be ashamed, but as always in all boldness even now Christ will be magnified in my body, whether through life or through death.

21 ¶ For to me to live *is* Christ, and to die *is* gain.

22 But if *I* live in *the* flesh, this to me *is* fruit of *my* labor, and what I shall choose I do not know.

23 For I am pressed together by the two: having a desire to depart and to be with Christ, *which is* far better,

24 but to remain in the flesh *is* more necessary on account of you.

25 And being persuaded of this, I know that I will remain and will continue with you all for your advancement and joy of the faith,

26 so that your glorying may abound in Christ Jesus in me through my presence with you again.

27 ¶ Only conduct yourself worthily of the gospel of Christ, so that whether coming and seeing you or being absent, I hear the things concerning you, that you stand fast in one spirit and one soul, striving together in the faith of the gospel,

28 and not being terrified in no *thing* by the *ones* opposing, which to them truly is a proof of destruction, but to you of salvation, and this from God;

29 because it was granted to you on be-half of Christ not only to believe in Him, but also to suffer on His behalf,

30 having the same struggle which you saw in me and *even* now you hear *to be* in me.

Philippians 2

He persuades them to unity, and to all humble-ness of mind, by the example of Christ.

1 ¶ Therefore, if *there is* any comfort in Christ, if any consolation of love, if any fellowship of *the* Spirit, if any *tender* bow-els and mercies,

2 fulfill my joy, that you think the same, having the same love, one in soul, being mindful of the one thing,

3 *doing* nothing according to intrigue or self-glory, but in humility, esteeming one another, as being better than themselves;

4 each *one* not looking at the things of themselves, but each *one* also *the* things of others.

5 For think this within you, which *mind was* also in Christ Jesus,

6 who subsisting in the form of God thought *it* not robbery to be equal with God,

7 but emptied Himself, taking *the* form of a slave, coming to be in *the* likeness of men

8 and coming to be found in figure as a man, He humbled Himself, coming to be obedient until death, even *the* death of a cross.

9 Because of this also God highly exalted Him and gave Him a name above every name,

10 that at the name of Jesus "every knee should bow," of heavenly *beings*, and earthly *beings*, and under *the* earth *beings*,

11 and "every tongue should confess" that Jesus Christ *is* "Lord," to *the* glory of God *the* Father. *Isa. 45:23*

12 ¶ So, then, my beloved *ones*, even as you always obeyed, not as in my pres-ence only, but now much rather in my absence, cultivate your salvation with fear and trembling,

13 for it is God who is working in you both to will and to work for the sake of *His* good pleasure.

14 ¶ Do all things without murmurings and disputings,

15 that you may be blameless and guile-less, children of God, without fault in *the* midst of a crooked generation, even being perverted, among whom you shine as lu-minaries in *the* world,

16 holding forth *the* Word of life, for a boast to me in *the* day of Christ, that I ran not in vain, nor labored in vain.

17 But if indeed I am poured out on the sacrifice and service of your faith, I re-joice; yea, I rejoice with you all.

18 And you also rejoice *in* the same and rejoice with me.

19 But I hope in the Lord Jesus to send Timothy to you soon, that I may also be of good cheer, knowing the things about you.

20 For I have no one like-minded, who genuinely will care for the things about you.

21 For all seek their own things, not the things of Christ Jesus.

22 But you know the proof of him, that as a child to a father, he served with me for the gospel.

23 Therefore I hope to send this *one* at once, when ever I have seen the things about me.

24 But I am convinced in *the* Lord that I myself also will come soon.

25 But I thought it needful to send to you Epaphroditus, my brother and fellow-worker, and my fellow soldier, and your messenger and minister of my need,

26 since he was longing after you all and being distressed because you heard that he was sick.

27 For indeed he was sick, coming near to death; but God had mercy on him, and not only on him, but also me, lest I should have grief on grief.

28 Therefore, I sent him more eagerly, that seeing him again you may rejoice, and I may be less grieved.

29 Therefore receive him in *the* Lord with all joy and hold such in honor,

30 because through the work of Christ he drew near as far as *to* death, *his* life having been exposed, that he may fill up your lack of service toward me.

Philippians 3

1 He warns them to beware of false teachers.
18 He persuades them to reject the ways of carnal Christians.

1 ¶ For the rest, my brothers, rejoice in *the* Lord. To write the same things to you truly *is* not troublesome to me, but safe for you.

2 Watch *for* the dogs, watch *for* the evil workers, watch *for* the cutting off *party*.

3 For we are the circumcision, the *ones* who worship by the Spirit of God, and who glory in Christ Jesus, and who do not trust in flesh.

4 ¶ Even though I *might* have trust in flesh; if any other thinks to trust in flesh, I more;

5 in circumcision, *the* eighth day, of *the* race of Israel, *the* tribe of Benjamin, a Hebrew of the Hebrews; according to Law, a Pharisee;

6 according to zeal, persecuting the Assembly; according to righteousness in Law, being blameless.

7 But what things were gain to me, these I have counted loss because of Christ.

8 But, nay, rather I also count all things to be loss because of the excellency of the knowledge of Christ Jesus my Lord, for whose sake I have suffered the loss of all things and count *them to be* trash, that I might gain Christ

9 ¶ and be found in Him; not having my own righteousness of Law, but through the faith of Christ, *having* the righteousness of God by the faith,

10 to know Him and the power of His resurrection, and the fellowship of His sufferings, being conformed to His death,

11 if somehow I may arrive to the resurrection out of *the* dead *ones*.

12 Not that I already received or already have been perfected, but I pursue, if I also may lay hold, inasmuch as I also was laid hold of by Christ Jesus.

13 Brothers, I do not count myself to have laid hold, but one *thing I do*, forgetting the things behind, and stretching out for the *things* before,

14 I am pursuing a goal for the prize of the upward calling of God in Christ Jesus.

15 ¶ Therefore as many as *are* perfect, think this; and if you think any other thing, God will also reveal this to you.

16 Yet *as* to where we have arrived, walk by the same rule, *being* of the same mind.

17 ¶ Be fellow-imitators of me, brothers, and consider the *ones* walking this way, even as you have us *for* a pattern.

18 For many walk *as* the hostile *ones to* the cross of Christ, of whom I often told you, and now even weeping I say it,

19 whose end *is* destruction, whose god *is* the belly, and who glory in their shame, the *ones* thinking earthly *things*.

20 For our citizenship is in Heaven, from where we also wait for a Savior, *the* Lord Jesus Christ,

21 who will transform the body of our humiliation, for it to be conformed to His body of glory, according to the working *of* Him to be able even to subject all things to Himself.

Philippians 4

He proceeds to general persuasions.

1 ¶ So then, my brothers, beloved and longed for, my joy and crown, so stand firm in *the* Lord, beloved *ones*.

2 I entreat Euodias, and I entreat Syntyche, to mind the same thing in *the* Lord.

3 And I also ask you, true yoke-fellow, together help with them, *women* who struggled along with me and with Clement in the gospel, and the rest, fellow-workers with me, whose names *are* in the Book of Life.

4 Rejoice in *the* Lord always. Again I will say, Rejoice!

5 Let your kind *spirit* be known to all men. The Lord *is* near.

6 Be anxious about nothing, but in everything by prayer and by petition with thanksgivings, let your requests be made known to God;

7 and the peace of God which surpasses all understanding will guard your hearts and your minds in Christ Jesus.

8 For the rest, brothers, as many *things* as are true, as many as *are* honorable, as many as *are* right, as many as *are* pure, as many as *are* pleasing, as many as *are* of good report, if *of* any virtue, and if *of* any praise, meditate on these things.

9 And what *things* you learned and received and heard and saw in me, practice these things, and the God of peace will be with you.

10 ¶ But I rejoiced in *the* Lord greatly that now once again you revived *your* thinking on my behalf, on which you also were thinking, but lacked opportunity.

11 Not that I speak as to need, for I have learned to be content in whatever state I am.

12 And I know to be humbled, and I know to abound; in everything, and in all things, I am taught both to be full and to hunger, both to abound, and to be in need.

13 I have strength *to do* all things in Christ, the *One* strengthening me.

14 Yet you did well in sharing my affliction.

15 And you know, too, Philippians, that in *the* beginning of the gospel, when I went out from Macedonia, not one assembly shared with me in *the* matter of giving and receiving, if not you only.

16 Because truly in Thessalonica you sent to my need, both once and twice.

17 Not that I seek a gift, but I seek the fruit, the *one* multiplying to your account.

18 But I have all things and more than enough; I have been made full, receiving from Epaphroditus the things *from you*, a fragrance of sweet smell, an acceptable sacrifice, well-pleasing to God.

19 And my God will fill your every need according to His riches in glory in Christ Jesus.

20 ¶ Now may glory *be* to our God and Father to the ages of the ages. Amen.

21 Greet every saint in Christ Jesus. The brothers with me greet you.

22 All the saints greet you, most of all the *ones* of Caesar's house.

23 The grace of our Lord Jesus Christ *be* with all of you. Amen.

The Epistle of Paul the Apostle to the
COLOSSIANS

Colossians 1

1 He thanks God for their faith, 14 describes the true Christ, 21 and encourages them to receive their reconciliation through Christ.

1 ¶ Paul, *an* apostle of Jesus Christ through the will of God, and Timothy the brother,

2 to the saints and faithful brothers in Christ in Colosse: Grace and peace to you from God our Father and *the* Lord Jesus Christ.

3 ¶ We give thanks to God and *the* Father of our Lord Jesus Christ, praying continually about you,

4 hearing of your faith in Christ Jesus and the love toward all the saints,

5 because of the hope being laid up for you in Heaven, the *one* which you heard before in the Word of the truth of the gospel,

6 the *one* coming to you, as also in all the world, and it is bearing fruit even also among you, from the day in which you heard and knew the grace of God in truth;

7 even as you also learned from Epaphras our beloved fellow-slave, who is a faithful minister of Christ for you,

8 he also showing to us your love in *the* Spirit.

9 ¶ Because of this also, from the day in which we heard, we do not cease praying on your behalf, and asking that you may be filled *with* the full knowledge of His will in all wisdom and spiritual understanding,

10 *for* you to walk worthily of the Lord unto all pleasing, bearing fruit in every good work and growing into the full knowledge of God;

11 being empowered with all power according to the might of His glory, to all patience and long-suffering with joy;

12 ¶ giving thanks to the Father, who has made us fit for a share of the inheritance of the saints in light,

13 who delivered us out of the authority of darkness, and transferred *us* into the kingdom of the Son of His love,

14 in whom we have redemption through His blood, the remission of sins;

15 who is *the* image of the invisible God, *the* First-begotten of every creature.

16 For all things were created in Him, the things in the heavens, and the things on the earth, the visible and the invisible; whether thrones, or lordships, or rulers, or authorities, all things have been created through Him and for Him.

17 And He is before all things, and all things have subsisted in Him.

18 And He is the Head of the body, the Assembly, who is *the* Beginning, *the* First-born out of *the* dead *ones* that He may be having first place in all things;

19 because all the fullness was pleased to dwell in Him,

20 and through Him making peace by the blood of His cross, to reconcile all things to Himself; through Him, whether the things on the earth, or the things in the heavens.

21 And you then being alienated and a hostile *one* in *your* mind by evil works, but now He reconciled

22 in the body of His flesh, through death, to present you holy and without blemish and irreproachable before Him,

23 if indeed you continue in the faith having been founded and steadfast, and not being moved away from the hope of the gospel which you heard, the *one* being proclaimed in all the creation under the heaven, of which I, Paul, became a servant.

24 who now rejoice in my sufferings on your behalf and fill up in my flesh the things lacking of the afflictions of Christ on behalf of His body, which *is* the Assembly,

25 of which I became a servant, according to the stewardship of God given to me for you, to fulfill the Word of God,

26 the mystery having been hidden from the ages and from the generations, but now was revealed to His saints;

27 to whom God willed to make known what *are* the riches of the glory of this mystery among the nations, who is Christ in you, the hope of glory;

28 whom we proclaim, warning every man and teaching every man in all wisdom, that we may present every man full-grown in Christ Jesus,

29 for which also I labor, struggling according to the working of Him, the *One* working in me in power.

Colossians 2

He persuades them to be constant in Christ.

1 ¶ For I want you to know how great a struggle I have concerning you, and those in Laodicea, and as many as have not seen my face in *the* flesh,

2 that their hearts may be comforted, being joined together in love, and to all riches of the full assurance of the understanding, to *the* full knowledge of the mystery of God, even of *the* Father and of Christ,

3 in whom are hidden all the treasures of wisdom and of knowledge.

4 ¶ And I say this that no one may beguile you with persuasive speech.

5 For though I am indeed absent in the flesh, yet I am with you in spirit, rejoicing and seeing your order and the firmness of your faith into Christ.

6 Therefore, as you received Christ Jesus the Lord, walk in Him,

7 having been rooted and being built up in Him, and being confirmed in the faith, even as you were taught, abounding in it with thanksgiving.

8 Watch that there will not be one abducting you through philosophy and empty deceit, according to the tradition of men, according to the elements of the world, and not according to Christ.

9 For in Him dwells all the fullness of the Godhead bodily;

10 and having been filled, you are in Him, who is the Head of all rule and authority,

11 in whom also you were circumcised with a circumcision not made by hands, in the putting off of the body of the sins of the flesh, by the circumcision of Christ,

12 having been buried together with Him in baptism, in whom also you were raised through the faith of the working of God, the *One having* raised Him from among the dead *ones*.

13 ¶ And you, being a dead *one* in the deviations and the uncircumcision of your flesh, He made alive together with Him, having remitted all your deviations,

14 blotting out the handwriting in the ordinances against us, which was contrary to us, even *He* has taken it out of the midst, nailing it to the cross;

15 having stripped the rulers and the authorities, He made a show of them in freely speaking, triumphing *over* them in it.

16 ¶ Therefore do not let anyone judge you in eating, or in drinking, or in part, of a feast, or of a new moon, or of sabbaths,

17 which are a shadow of coming things, but the body *is* of Christ.

18 Let no one rule against you, willing in humility and worship of the angels, intruding into things which he has not seen, being puffed up by the mind of his flesh without cause,

19 and not holding fast the Head, from whom all the body being supplied *through* the joints and bands, and being joined together, will grow with the growth of God.

20 If, then, you died with Christ from the elements of the world, why are you under *its* decrees, as living in *the* world?

21 Touch not, taste not, handle not,

22 which things are all for corruption in the using, according to the "injunctions and teachings of men." *Isa. 29:13*

23 Which things indeed are a matter of having wisdom in self-imposed worship and humility, and severity *in abuse* of *the* body, *but are* not of any honor unto gratification of the flesh.

Colossians 3

1 He advises to charity, humility, and other duties.

1 ¶ Therefore if you were raised with Christ, seek the things above, where Christ is sitting at *the* right of God; *Psa. 110:1*

2 Be mindful of the things above, not the things on the earth.

3 For you died, and your life has been hidden with Christ in God.

4 Whenever Christ our life is revealed, then also you will be revealed with Him in glory.

5 ¶ Therefore put to death your members which *are* on the earth: fornication, uncleanness, passion; bad lust, and covetousness, which is idolatry;

6 on account of which things the wrath of God is coming on the sons of disobedience,

7 among whom you also walked once when you were living in these.

8 ¶ But now, you also, put off all *these* things: wrath, anger, malice, foul-speaking, shameful speech out of your mouth.

9 Do not lie to one another, having put off the old man with his practices,

10 and having put on the new, being renewed unto full knowledge according to *the* image of the *One* creating him,

11 where there is no Greek and Jew, circumcision and uncircumcision, foreigner, Scythian, slave *or* free *ma*n, but Christ *is* all things and in all.

12 ¶ Therefore, as elect *ones* of God, holy and beloved, put on bowels of compassion, kindness, humility, meekness, long-suffering,

13 bearing with one another and forgiving yourselves, if anyone has a complaint against any; even as Christ forgave you, so also you.

14 But above all these, *put on* love, which is *the* bond of perfection.

15 And let the peace of God rule in your hearts, to which you also were called in one body, and be thankful.

16 Let the Word of Christ dwell in you richly, in all wisdom teaching and admonishing yourselves in psalms and hymns and spiritual songs, singing with grace in your hearts to the Lord.

17 And every *thing,* whatever you do in word or in work, *do* all things in the name of *the* Lord Jesus, giving thanks to God and *the* Father through Him.

18 ¶ Wives, be subject to *your* own husbands, as is becoming in *the* Lord.

19 Husbands, love the wives and do not be bitter against them.

20 Children, obey the parents in all things, for this is well-pleasing to the Lord.

21 Fathers, do not provoke to anger your children, that they may not be disheartened.

22 Slaves, obey the masters according to flesh in all things, not with eye-service as men-pleasers, but in simplicity of heart, fearing God.

23 And every *thing,* whatever you may do, work from the soul as to the Lord and not to men,

24 knowing that from the Lord you shall receive the reward of the inheritance. For you serve *the* Lord Christ.

25 But the *one* doing wrong will receive back what he did wrong, and there is no partiality.

Colossians 4

He persuades them to be fervent in prayer.

1 ¶ Masters, give what *is* the just and the equality to the slaves, knowing that you have a Master in Heaven also.

2 ¶ Steadfastly continue in prayer, being vigilant in it with thanksgiving,

3 praying together about us also, that God may open to us a door of the Word, to speak the mystery of Christ, on account of which I also have been bound,

4 that I may make it clear, as I ought to speak.

5 ¶ Walk in wisdom toward the *ones* outside, redeeming the time.

6 Let your word *be* always with grace, having been seasoned with salt, to know how you ought to answer each one.

7 ¶ All the things about me, Tychicus the beloved brother and faithful minister and fellow-slave in *the* Lord, will make known to you,

8 whom I sent to you for this very thing, that he *might* know the things about you, and that he might comfort your hearts,

9 with Onesimus the faithful and beloved brother, who is of you. They will make known to you all the things here.

10 Aristarchus, my fellow prisoner, greets you, also Mark the nephew of Barnabas, about whom you received orders. If he comes to you, receive him.

11 And Jesus, the *one* being called Justus, the *ones* being of the circumcision, *greet*

you, these only fellow workers for the kingdom of God, who became a comfort to me.

12 Epaphras greets you, he of you, a slave of Christ, always striving for you in prayers, that you may stand full-grown and being complete in all *the* will of God.

13 For I bear witness to him, that he has much zeal on your behalf, and the *ones* in Laodicea, and the *ones* in Hierapolis.

14 Luke the beloved physician greets you, also Demas.

15 Greet the brothers in Laodicea, and Nymphas and the assembly in his house.

16 And when this letter is read before you, cause that it be read also in the Laodicean assembly, and that you also read the *one* of Laodicea.

17 And say to Archippus, Look to the ministry which you received in *the* Lord, that you may fulfill it.

18 The greeting by my hand, Paul. Remember my bonds. Grace *be* with you. Amen.

1 Thessalonians 1

The Thessalonians are given to understand how mindful of them Paul was at all times in thanksgiving and prayer.

1 ¶ Paul and Silvanus and Timothy to the assembly of *the* Thessalonians in God *the* Father and *the* Lord Jesus Christ: Grace and peace to you from God our Father and *the* Lord Jesus Christ.

2 ¶ We give thanks to God always concerning you all, making mention of you on our prayers,

3 remembering without ceasing your work of faith and labor of love, and the patient endurance of hope of our Lord Jesus Christ before our God and Father,

4 knowing, brothers, having been loved, your election by God.

5 For our gospel did not come to you in word only, but also in power, and in *the* Holy Spirit, and in much assurance, even as you know what kind we were among you for your sake.

6 ¶ And you became imitators of us and of the Lord, welcoming the Word in much affliction with joy of *the* Holy Spirit.

7 So that you became examples to all the *ones* believing in Macedonia and Achaia.

8 For the Word of the Lord sounded out from you not only in Macedonia and Achaia, but also in every place your faith toward God has gone out, so that there is no need for us to have to say anything.

9 For they themselves report about us what kind of entrance we have to you, and how you had turned to God from the idols, to be a slave to *the* true and living God,

10 and to await His Son from Heaven, whom He raised from *the* dead *ones*, Jesus, the *One* delivering us from the coming wrath.

1 Thessalonians 2

In what manner the gospel was preached to the Thessalonians, and in what sort they received it.

1 ¶ For brothers, you yourselves know our entrance to you, that it has not come to be in vain.

2 But also suffering before and being insolently mistreated, even as you know in Philippi, we were bold in our God to speak the gospel of God to you in much struggle.

3 For our exhortation *was* not of error, nor of uncleanness, nor in guile;

4 but even as we have been approved by God to be entrusted *with* the gospel, so we speak, not as pleasing men, but God, the *One* trying our hearts.

5 For neither were we then *found* with *a* word of flattery, even as you know, nor with pretense of covetousness (God *is* witness),

6 nor seeking glory from men, neither from you, nor from others, being able to be in authority, as apostles of Christ.

7 ¶ But we came to be gentle in your midst, even as a nurse should warmly cherish her children.

8 So yearning over you, we were well-pleased to impart to you not only the gospel of God, but also our own souls, because you had become beloved *ones* to us.

9 For, brothers, you remember our labor and toil, night and day, working in order not to put a burden on any one of you, we proclaimed to you the gospel of God.

10 You and God *are* witnesses how holily and righteously and blamelessly we were to you, the *ones* believing;

11 even as you know each one of you how, as a father *to* his children, exhorting and consoling you,

12 testifying for you to walk worthily of God, the *One* calling you to His kingdom and glory.

13 ¶ And because of this we give thanks to God without ceasing, that having received

the Word of hearing from us, you welcomed *it as* of God, not *as* a word of men, but as it is, truly *the* Word of God, which also works in you, the *ones* believing.

14 For, brothers, you became imitators of the assemblies of God, the *ones* being in Judea in Christ Jesus, because you also suffered these things by *your* own fellow countrymen, as they *did* also by the Jews,

15 both the *ones* killing the Lord Jesus and their own prophets, and persecuting us, and not pleasing God, and *being* contrary to all men,

16 forbidding us from speaking to the nations in order that they be saved, to the filling up *of* their sins always. But the wrath *of God* is come on them to *the* end.

17 ¶ But, brothers, we being bereaved from you for an hour's time, in presence, not in heart, we were much more eager with much desire to see your face.

18 Because of this, we desired to come to you, truly I, Paul, both once and twice; but Satan hindered us.

19 For what *is* our hope, or joy, or crown of glorying? *Are* you not even *to be* before our Lord Jesus Christ at His coming?

20 For you are our glory and joy.

1 Thessalonians 3

Paul testifies his great love to the Thessalonians by sending Timothy to them to strengthen and comfort them.

1 ¶ So no longer enduring, we were pleased to be left in Athens alone,

2 and sent Timothy, our brother and servant of God, and our fellow worker in the gospel of Christ to *be* the *one* to establish you and to encourage you concerning your faith,

3 that no one be moved by these afflictions. For you yourselves know that we are appointed to this.

4 For even when we were with you, we said to you before that we are about to be afflicted, as it also happened, even you know.

5 Because of this, no longer enduring, I also sent to know your faith, that the tempting *one* not somehow tempt you, and our labor should come to be in vain.

6 ¶ But now Timothy coming to us from you, and announcing good news to us *of* your love and faith, and that you have good remembrance of us always, longing to see us, even as also we you.

7 Because of this we were comforted over you, brothers, on all our affliction and distress through your faith,

8 because now we live, if you should stand fast in *the* Lord.

9 For what thanks are we able to return to God about you, over all the joy *with* which we rejoice because of you before our God,

10 night and day praying beyond all measure for *me* to see your face, and to complete the things lacking in your faith?

11 ¶ But may our God and Father Himself, and our Lord Jesus Christ, direct our way to you.

12 And may the Lord make you to increase and to abound in love toward one another and toward all, even as we *do* also toward you,

13 in order to establish your hearts blameless in holiness before our God and our Father at the coming of our Lord Jesus Christ with all His saints.

1 Thessalonians 4

1 He exhorts to godliness, 6 to live justly, 9 to love one another, 13 to sorrow moderately for the dead. 15 A description of the second coming.

1 ¶ For the rest then, brothers, we beg you and we exhort in *the* Lord Jesus, even as you received from us how you ought to walk and to please God, that you abound more.

2 For you know what commandments we gave you through the Lord Jesus.

3 For this is God's will, your sanctification, *for* you to abstain from fornication,

4 each *one* of you to know to possess his vessel in sanctification and honor,

5 not in passion of lust, even as also the nations *do*, the *ones* not knowing God;

6 not to go beyond and to take advantage of his brother in the matter, because the Lord *is the* avenger concerning all these, even as we told you before, and solemnly testified.

7 For God did not call us to impurity, but in sanctification.

8 Therefore, the *one* that despises does not despise man, but God, even the *One* giving His Holy Spirit to us.

9 ¶ Now as to brotherly love, you have no need *for me* to write to you, for you your-

selves are taught by God to love one another.

10 For you also do it toward the brothers in all Macedonia. But, brothers, we exhort you to abound more.

11 And eagerly aspiring to be quiet, and to do *your* own *things*, and to work with *your* own hands, as we enjoined you,

12 that you may walk becomingly toward the *ones* outside, and that you may have need of nothing.

13 ¶ But I do not want you to be ignorant, brothers, about the *ones* having fallen asleep, that you not grieve, as the rest also, the *ones* not having hope.

14 For if we believe that Jesus died and rose again, also God will also bring with Him all the *ones* having fallen asleep through Jesus.

15 For we say this to you in *the* Word of *the* Lord, that we the living who remain to the coming of the Lord will not at all go before the *ones* having fallen asleep.

16 Because the Lord Himself shall come down from Heaven with a commanding shout of an archangel's voice, and with God's trumpet. And the dead *ones* in Christ will rise again first.

17 Then we who remain alive will be caught up together with them in *the* clouds to a meeting with the Lord in *the* air. And so we will always be with *the* Lord.

18 So, then, comfort each other with these words.

1 Thessalonians 5

1 He proceeds in the former description of Christ's coming to judgment, 16 and gives diverse precepts, 23 and so concludes the epistle.

1 ¶ But about the times and the seasons, brothers, you have no need *for it* to be written.

2 For you yourselves know accurately that the day of *the* Lord, as a thief in *the* night, so it comes.

3 For when they say, Peace and safety! Then sudden destruction comes upon them, like the birth-pain to the *one* having *babe* in womb, and they shall not escape, not *one*.

4 But you, brothers, are not in darkness, that the Day should overtake you as a thief.

5 You are all sons of light and sons of day; we are not of night, nor of darkness.

6 ¶ So then, we should not sleep, as the rest also do, but we should be awake and be sober.

7 For the *ones* sleeping sleep by night, and the *ones* being drunk are drunk by night.

8 But we being of day should be sober, "having put on *the* breastplate" of faith and love, and *the* hope of "salvation *as* a helmet;" *Isa. 59:17*

9 because God has not appointed us to wrath, but for obtaining salvation through our Lord Jesus Christ,

10 the *One* dying on our behalf, so that whether we are awake or we are sleeping, we may live together with Him.

11 ¶ Therefore, encourage one another, and build up one another, as you indeed do.

12 But, brothers, we entreat you to know the *ones* laboring among you, and taking the lead of you in *the* Lord, and exhorting you,

13 even esteem them most exceedingly in love because of their work. Be at peace among yourselves.

14 And we exhort you, brothers, to admonish the disobedient ones, comfort the *ones being* faint-hearted, sustain the *ones* being weak, be long-suffering towards all.

15 See *that* not any one returns an evil *deed* for an evil *deed* to anyone, but always pursue the good, both towards one another and towards all.

16 ¶ Rejoice always.

17 Pray without ceasing.

18 In everything give thanks, for this *is the* will of God in Christ Jesus toward you.

19 Do not quench the Spirit.

20 Do not despise prophecies.

21 Test all things, hold fast the good.

22 Keep back from every form of evil *acts*.

23 ¶ And may the God of peace Himself fully sanctify you, and may your whole spirit and soul and body be kept blameless at the coming of our Lord Jesus Christ.

24 Faithful is the *One* calling you, who also will perform *it*.

25 Brothers, pray concerning us.

26 Greet all the brothers with a holy kiss.

27 I charge you by the Lord that this letter be read to all the holy brothers.

28 The grace of our Lord Jesus Christ *be* with you. Amen.

The Second Epistle of Paul the Apostle to the
THESSALONIANS

2 Thessalonians 1

Paul certifies them of the good opinion which he had of their faith, love, and patience.

1 ¶ Paul and Silvanus and Timothy to the assembly of *the* Thessalonians in God our Father and *the* Lord Jesus Christ:

2 Grace to you and peace from God our Father and *the* Lord Jesus Christ.

3 Brothers, we ought always to give thanks to God about you, even as it is right, because your faith grows exceedingly, and the love of each *one* of all of you multiplies toward one another,

4 so as for us to boast ourselves in you in the assemblies of God for your patient endurance and faith in all your persecutions, and the afflictions which you endure,

5 ¶ a clear token of the just judgment of God, for you to be counted worthy of the kingdom of God, for which you indeed suffer;

6 since *it is* a just thing with God to repay affliction to the *ones* afflicting you,

7 and to *give* you, the *ones* being afflicted, rest with us at the revelation of the Lord Jesus from Heaven with angels of His power,

8 in flaming fire giving full vengeance to the *ones* not knowing God, and to the *ones* not obeying the gospel of our Lord Jesus Christ, *Isa. 66:15; Jer. 10:25*

9 who will pay the penalty: everlasting destruction from the face of the Lord, "and from the glory of His strength," *Isa. 2:19*

10 when He comes to be glorified in His saints, and to be marveled at among all the *ones* having believed in that Day, because our testimony to you was believed.

11 ¶ For which we also continually pray concerning you, that our God would deem you worthy of the calling, and would fulfill all the good pleasure of *His* goodness, and work of the faith in power,

12 so that the name of our Lord Jesus Christ may be glorified in you, and you in Him, according to the grace of our God and of *the* Lord Jesus Christ.

2 Thessalonians 2

1 He wills them to be steadfast, 3 shows that there shall be a departure from the faith, 9 and a discovery of antichrist, before the Day of the Lord comes.

1 ¶ And, brothers, we entreat you, by the coming of our Lord Jesus Christ, and of our gathering together to Him,

2 for you not to be quickly shaken *in* the mind, nor to be disturbed, neither through a spirit, nor through speech, nor through letter, as through us, *that* the Day of Christ has come.

3 ¶ Do not let anyone deceive you, by no manner, because it, *that Day will not come* if not the apostasy comes first and the man of sin is revealed, the son of eternal destruction,

4 the *one* opposing and exalting himself over every *thing* being called God, or object of worship, so as for him "to sit in the temple of God" as God, setting forth himself, that he is God. *Dan. 11:36; Eze. 28:2*

5 Do you not remember that I told you these things, I yet being with you?

6 And now you know the *thing* holding back, for him to be revealed in his time.

7 For the mystery of lawlessness already is working, only The *One is* holding back now, until He comes out of the midst.

8 And then "the lawless *one*" will be revealed, "whom" "the Lord" "will consume" "by the spirit of His mouth," and will bring to nought by the appearance of His presence. *Isa. 11:4*

9 *His* coming is according to the working of Satan in all power and *miraculous* signs and lying wonders,

10 and in all deception of unrighteousness in the *ones* perishing, because they did not

receive the love of the truth in order for them to be saved.

11 And because of this, God will send to them a working of error, for them to believe the lie,

12 that all may be judged, the *ones* not believing the truth, but being well-pleased in unrighteousness.

13 ¶ But we ought to thank God always concerning you, brothers, having been loved by the Lord, because God chose you from the beginning to salvation in sanctification of *the* Spirit and belief of *the* truth,

14 to which He called you through our gospel, to obtain the glory of our Lord Jesus Christ.

15 So, then, brothers, stand firm and strongly hold the teachings you were taught, whether by word or by our letter.

16 ¶ But may our Lord Himself, Jesus Christ, and our God and Father, the *One* having loved us and having given everlasting comfort and good hope by grace,

17 encourage your hearts, and may He establish you in every good word and work.

2 Thessalonians 3

1 He craves their prayers, 5 makes request to God in their behalf, 6 and gives them diverse precepts.

1 ¶ For the rest, brothers, pray concerning us, that the Word of the Lord may run and be glorified, even as also *it has* with you,

2 and that we may be delivered from harmful and evil men. For the faith *is* not of all *men.*

3 But the Lord is faithful who will establish and will guard *you* from the evil *one.*

4 But we are persuaded in *the* Lord as to you, that whatever things we command to you, you both are doing and you will do.

5 And the Lord direct your hearts into the love of God and into the patience of Christ.

6 ¶ And we command you, brothers, in the name of our Lord Jesus Christ, to draw yourselves back from every brother walking in a disorderly way, and not according to the teaching which you received from us.

7 For you yourselves know how it is right to act like us, because we were not disorderly among you;

8 nor did we eat bread from anyone *as* a gift, but by labor and toil, working night and day in order not to burden any of you.

9 Not that we do not have authority, but that we give ourselves *as* an example to you, for you to act like us.

10 For even when we were with you, we commanded this to you: If anyone wills not to work, neither let him eat.

11 For we hear some are walking in a disorderly way among you, not working at all, but bustling about uselessly.

12 And we command to such *ones,* and exhort through our Lord Jesus Christ that, working with quietness, they may eat their own bread.

13 And you, brothers, do not lose heart in well doing.

14 But if anyone does not obey our word through the letter, mark this *one,* and do not associate with him, that he be shamed.

15 But do not count *him a* hostile *one,* but warn *him* as a brother.

16 ¶ And may the Lord of peace Himself continually give peace to you in every way. The Lord *be* with all of you.

17 The greeting of Paul by my hand is *the* sign in every letter; so I write.

18 The grace of our Lord Jesus Christ *be* with you all. Amen.

The First Epistle of Paul the Apostle to
TIMOTHY

1 Timothy 1

*Timothy is put in mind of the charge given to him
by Paul at his going to Macedonia. 5 Of the
right use and end of the law.*

1 ¶ Paul an apostle of Jesus Christ according to a command of God our Savior, even *the* Lord Jesus Christ, *our* Hope,

2 to Timothy, a true child in *the* faith: Grace, mercy, peace from God our Father and our Lord Jesus Christ.

3 Even as I encouraged you to remain *in* Ephesus (I going to Macedonia), that you might charge certain *ones* not to teach a different doctrine,

4 nor to pay attention to myths and to endless genealogies, which provide questionings, rather than a stewardship of God, the *one being* in faith,

5 ¶ but the end of the commandment is love out of a pure heart and a good conscience, and faith without hypocrisy,

6 from which certain *ones* missing the mark   turned aside to empty talking,

7 wishing to be teachers of law, not understanding, neither what things they say, nor about what things they confidently affirm.

8 And we know that the Law *is* a good *thing*, if anyone uses it lawfully,

9 knowing this, that Law *is* not laid down for a righteous *one*, but for lawless *ones* and insubordinate *ones*, for ungodly *ones* and sinful *ones*, for unholy *ones* and profane *ones,* for slayers of fathers and slayers of mothers, for murderers,

10 for fornicators, for homosexuals, for slave-traders, for liars, for perjurers, and if any other thing is opposed to sound doctrine,

11 according to the gospel of the glory of the blessed God *with* which I was entrusted.

12 ¶ And I have thanks to Him empowering me, our Lord Jesus Christ, because He counted me faithful, putting *me* into the ministry;

13 the *one* who before was a blasphemer, and a persecutor, and an insolent *man*; but I received mercy, because being ignorant I did *it* in unbelief.

14 *But* the grace of our Lord abounded exceedingly with faith and love in Christ Jesus.

15 Faithful *is* the Word and worthy of all acceptance, that Christ Jesus came into the world to save sinners, of whom I am chief.

16 But for this reason I received mercy, that in me first Jesus Christ might show forth all long-suffering, for an example to the *ones* being about to believe on Him unto everlasting life.

17 Now to the King eternal, incorruptible, invisible, *the* only wise God, *be* honor and glory forever and ever. Amen.

18 ¶ This charge I commit to you, *my* child Timothy, according to the prophecies going before concerning you, that you might war the good warfare by them,

19 having faith and a good conscience, which certain *ones* thrusting away, made shipwreck concerning the faith,

20 of whom are Hymenaeus and Alexander, whom I gave over to Satan, that they may be taught not to blaspheme.

1 Timothy 2

*1 It is meet to pray and give thanks for all men.
9 How women should be attired. 12 They are
not permitted to teach.*

1 ¶ First of all therefore, I exhort *that* petitions, prayers, supplications, *and* thanksgivings be made on behalf of all men,

2 for kings and all the *ones* being in preeminence, that we may lead a tranquil and quiet life in all godliness and dignity.

3 For this *is* good and acceptable before God our Savior,

4 who desires all men to be saved and to come to a full knowledge of truth.

5 For God *is* one, also *there is* one Mediator of God and of men, *the* Man Christ Jesus,

6 the *One* having given Himself a ransom on behalf of all, the testimony *to be given* in its own time,

7 to which I was appointed a herald and apostle (I speak the truth in Christ, I do not lie), a teacher of *the* nations, in faith and truth.

8 Therefore, I purpose the men to pray in every place, lifting up holy hands without wrath and doubting.

9 ¶ So also the women to adorn themselves in respectable clothing, with modesty and sensibleness, not with plaiting, or gold, or pearls, or expensive garments,

10 but what becomes women professing fear of God, through good works.

11 Let a woman learn in silence, in all subjection.

12 And I do not allow a woman to teach nor to exercise authority *over* a man, but to be in silence.

13 For Adam was formed first, then Eve.

14 And Adam was not deceived, but *the* woman being deceived has come to be in transgression;

15 but she will be kept safe through the childbearing, if they continue in faith and love and holiness, with sensibleness.

1 Timothy 3

2 How overseers, deacons, and their wives should be qualified. 15 Of the assembly, and the blessed truth therein taught.

1 ¶ Faithful *is* the Word: If anyone reaches out to overseership, he desires a good work.

2 Therefore it is right *for* the overseer to be blameless, husband of one wife, a temperate, sensible, well-ordered, *and* hospitable *one*, apt at teaching;

3 not given to wine, not a quarreler, not loving silver, but gentle, not contentious, not eager for ill gain;

4 ruling his own house well, having children in subjection with all honor.

5 But if anyone does not know *how* to rule *his* own house, how will he care for an assembly of God?

6 *He should* not *be* a novice, lest being puffed up he may fall into the devil's judgment.

7 And it is right *for* him to also have a good witness from the *ones* outside, that he not fall into reproach and *into* a snare of the devil.

8 ¶ Likewise, deacons *are to be* honorable, not double-tongued, not being given to much wine, not eager for ill gain,

9 having the mystery of the faith with a pure conscience.

10 And also let these be tested first, then let them serve, being without reproach.

11 Likewise, *their* wives *are to be* reverent, not slanderers, temperate, faithful in all things.

12 Let deacons be husbands of one wife, ruling *their* own houses and children well.

13 For the *ones* having served well as a deacon acquire a good standing for themselves and much boldness in faith, the *ones* in Christ Jesus.

14 ¶ I write these things to you, hoping to come to you shortly;

15 but if I delay, that you may know how to conduct oneself in the house of God, which is *the* assembly of the living God, *the* pillar and foundation of the truth.

16 And, confessedly, great is the mystery of godliness: God was manifested in flesh, was justified in Spirit, was seen by angels, was proclaimed among nations, *was* believed on in *the* world, was taken up in glory.

1 Timothy 4

He foretells that in the latter times there shall be a departure from the faith.

1 ¶ But the Spirit expressly says that in latter times some will depart from the faith, paying attention to deceiving spirits and teachings of demons,

2 in hypocrisy of liars, being seared in *their* own conscience,

3 forbidding to marry, *saying* to abstain from foods, which God created for partaking with thanksgiving by the believing *ones* and the *ones* fully knowing the truth.

4 Because every creature of God *is* good, and nothing to be thrust away, but being received with thanksgiving;

5 for through God's Word and supplication it is sanctified.

6 ¶ Having laid down these things to the brothers, you will be a good servant of Jesus Christ, having been nourished by the words of the faith, and by the good doctrine which you have followed.

7 But refuse the profane and old-womanish myths. And exercise yourself to godliness.

8 For bodily exercise is profitable for a little, but godliness is profitable for all things, having promise of the life now, and *of that* coming.

9 Faithful *is* the Word and worthy of all acceptance;

10 for to this we also labor and *are* reproached, because we hope on *the* living God, who is Savior of all men, especially of believing *ones*.

11 Enjoin and teach these things.

12 Let no one despise your youth, but become an example of the believing *ones* in word, in conduct, in love, in spirit, in faith, in purity.

13 Until I come, attend to reading, to exhortation, to the doctrine.

14 Do not neglect the gift in you, which was given to you through prophecy, with laying on of the hands of the elderhood.

15 Give care to these things; be in these things in order that your progress may be evident among all.

16 Give attention to yourself and to the doctrine; continue in them, for doing this, you will both deliver yourself and the *ones* hearing you.

1 Timothy 5

1 Rules to be observed in reproving. 3 Of widows.
17 Of elders. 23 A precept for Timothy's health.

1 ¶ Do not sharply chastise an older *man*, but exhort as a father; *and* younger *ones* as brothers,

2 older women as mothers, younger *ones* as sisters, in all purity.

3 ¶ Honor widows, the *ones* being really widows.

4 But if any widow has children or grandchildren, let them learn first to be godly to their own house and to make a return payment to *their* forefathers, for this is good and pleasing before God.

5 But *honor* the *one* being really a widow, even having been left alone, *who* has set her hope on God and continues in petitions and prayers night and day.

6 But the *one* living for self-pleasure has died *while* living.

7 And enjoin these things that they may be blameless.

8 But if anyone does not provide for *his* own, and especially *his* family, he has denied the faith and is worse than a faithless *one*.

9 Let a widow be enrolled having become not less than sixty years, *the* wife of one man,

10 being witnessed by good works, if she brought up children, if she was hospitable, if she washed the feet of the saints, if she relieved afflicted *ones*, if she followed after every good work.

11 But refuse younger widows; for whenever they grow lustful against Christ, they desire to marry,

12 having guilt because they set aside the first faith;

13 and with it all, they also learn *to be* idle, going around the houses, and not only idle, but also bubbling *gossip*, and trifling *ones*, speaking the things not proper.

14 Therefore, I purpose the younger women to marry, to bear children, to rule the house, giving no occasion to the *one* opposing, because of reproach.

15 For some already have turned aside behind Satan.

16 If any believing man or believing woman has widows, let them relieve *them*, and do not burden the assembly, that it may relieve the *ones* being really widows.

17 ¶ Let the elders who take the lead well be counted worthy of double honor, especially the *ones* laboring in Word and teaching.

18 For the Scripture says, "You shall not muzzle an ox treading out grain," and, the laborer is worthy of his pay. *Deut. 25:4*

19 Do not receive an accusation against an elder if not on *"the testimony of"* "two or three witnesses". *Deut. 19:15*

20 The *ones* sinning before all, rebuke, that the rest also may have fear.

21 I solemnly testify before God and *the* Lord Jesus Christ and the elect angels, that you should guard these things without

pre-judgment, doing nothing by way of partiality.

22 Lay hands quickly on no one, nor share in *the* sins of others. Keep yourself pure.

23 No longer drink water, but use a little wine on account of your stomach and your frequent infirmities.

24 The sins of certain men are plain before all, brought forth to judgment, but certain *ones* follow after also.

25 Likewise also the good works are plain before all, and the *ones* otherwise are not able to be hidden.

1 Timothy 6

1 Of the duty of servants. 6 Godliness is great gain, 10 and love of money the root of all evil.

1 ¶ Let as many as are slaves under a yoke count their own masters worthy of all honor, that the name and teaching of God may not be blasphemed.

2 And the *ones* having believing masters, let them not despise *them*, because they are brothers, but rather let them serve as slaves, because they are faithful and beloved *ones*, the *ones* receiving of the benefit in return. Teach and exhort these things.

3 If anyone teaches differently, and does not consent to sound words, the *ones* of our Lord Jesus Christ and the teaching according to godliness,

4 he has been puffed up, understanding nothing, but *is* sick concerning questions and disputes, out of which comes envy, strife, evil-speakings, evil suspicions,

5 idle uselessness of men whose mind has been corrupted and deprived of the truth, supposing gain to be godliness. Withdraw from such *persons*.

6 ¶ But godliness with contentment is great gain.

7 For we have brought nothing into the world, *and it is* evident that neither can we carry anything out.

8 But having food and coverings, we will be satisfied with these.

9 But the *ones* purposing to be rich fall into temptation, and a snare, and many foolish and hurtful lusts, which plunge men into ruin and destruction.

10 For the love of money is a root of all evils, *by means* of which some stretching toward *it* were led astray from the faith, and *they* themselves pierced through by many pains.

11 But you, O man of God, flee these things and pursue righteousness, godliness, faith, love, patience, and meekness.

12 Fight the good fight of faith. Lay hold on eternal life, to which you were also called and confessed the good confession before many witnesses.

13 ¶ I charge you before God, He making all things alive, and Christ Jesus, the *One* witnessing the good confession *to* Pontius Pilate,

14 that you keep the commandment spotless, beyond reproach, until the appearing of our Lord Jesus Christ;

15 who in His own time will reveal *who is* the blessed and only Potentate, the King of the *ones* reigning and Lord of the *ones* exercising lordship,

16 the only *One* having immortality, living in light that cannot be approached, whom no one of men saw, nor can see; to whom be honor and everlasting might. Amen.

17 Charge the *ones* in the age now, not to be high-minded, nor to set hope on the uncertainty of riches, but in the living God, the *One* offering to us richly all things for enjoyment;

18 to do good *things*, to be rich in good works, to be ready to impart, to be generous *ones*,

19 treasuring away for themselves a good foundation for the coming *age*, that they may lay hold on everlasting life.

20 O Timothy, guard the Deposit, having turned away from the profane empty babblings and opposing theories of the falsely named knowledge,

21 which some professing have missed the mark concerning the faith. Grace *be* with you. Amen.

The Second Epistle of Paul the Apostle to
TIMOTHY

2 Timothy 1

1 Paul's love to Timothy. 6 He is encouraged to stir up the gift of God which is in him.

1 ¶ Paul an apostle of Jesus Christ by *the* will of God according to the promise of life which *is* in Christ Jesus,

2 to *my* beloved child Timothy: Grace, mercy, peace from God *the* Father and Christ Jesus our Lord.

3 I have thanks to God, whom I worship from *my* forefathers in a pure conscience, how unceasingly I have remembrance concerning you in my petitions night and day,

4 longing to see you, being reminded of your tears, that I may be filled with joy,

5 taking recollection of the unfeigned faith in you, which first dwelt in your grandmother Lois and *in* your mother Eunice, and I am persuaded that *it is* also in you.

6 ¶ For which cause I remind you to fan into flame the gift of God which is in you through the laying on of my hands.

7 For God did not give a spirit of cowardice to us, but of power and of love and of self-control.

8 Therefore do not be ashamed of the testimony of our Lord, nor *of* me, His prisoner. But suffer hardship with the gospel, according to *the* power of God,

9 the *One* having saved us and having called *us* with a holy calling, not according to our works, but according to *His* own purpose and grace given to us in Christ Jesus before eternal times,

10 but now revealed through the appearance of our Savior, Jesus Christ, indeed making death of no effect, bringing life and incorruption to light through the gospel,

11 to which I was appointed a herald and apostle and a teacher of nations.

12 For which cause I also suffer these things. But I am not ashamed, for I know whom I have believed, and I am persuaded that He is able to guard my deposit until that Day.

13 Hold fast a pattern of sound words which you heard from me, in faith and love in Christ Jesus.

14 Guard the good Deposit *given* through *the* Holy Spirit indwelling in us.

15 ¶ You know this, that all the *ones* in Asia turned away from me, of whom are Phygellus and Hermogenes.

16 May the Lord give mercy to the house of Onesiphorus, because he often refreshed me, and he was not ashamed *of* my chain,

17 but coming to Rome, he more diligently sought and found me.

18 May the Lord give to him to find mercy from *the* Lord in that Day, and how much he served in Ephesus, you know very well.

2 Timothy 2

1 He is encouraged again to constancy and perseverance. 22 Whereof to beware, and what to follow after.

1 ¶ You, therefore, my child, be empowered by grace in the Christ Jesus.

2 And what things you heard from me through many witnesses, commit these things to faithful men, such as will be competent also to teach others.

3 You, therefore, suffer hardship as a good soldier of Jesus Christ.

4 No one serving as a soldier entangles *himself* with the affairs of *this* life, so that he might please the *One* having enlisted *him.*

5 And also if anyone competes, he is not crowned unless he competes lawfully.

6 *It is* right *for* the laboring farmer to partake first of the fruits.

7 Consider what I say, for the Lord will give you understanding in all *things.*

8 ¶ Remember Jesus Christ, having been raised from *the* dead *ones,* of *the* seed of David, according to my gospel,

9 in which I suffer hardship as an evil-doer, unto bonds; but the Word of God has not been bound.

10 Because of this, I endure all things on account of the elect, that they also may obtain salvation, the *one* in Christ Jesus, with everlasting glory.

11 Faithful *is* the Word: for if we died with *Him*, we also shall live with *Him*;

12 if we endure, we shall also reign with *Him*; if we deny *Him*, also that One will deny us;

13 if we are faithless, that One remains faithful; He is not able to deny Himself.

14 ¶ Remind *them of* these things, solemnly testifying before the Lord not to dispute about words for nothing useful, to *the* subversion *of* the *ones* hearing.

15 Be eager, *study* to present yourself approved to God, a workman unashamed, rightly dividing the Word of Truth.

16 But shun profane, empty babblings, for they will go on to more ungodliness,

17 and their word will have spreading like gangrene, of whom *are* Hymenaeus and Philetus,

18 who deviated concerning the truth, saying the resurrection already has come, and overturn the faith of some.

19 ¶ However, the foundation of God stands firm, having this seal, "*The* Lord knew the *ones* being His." Also, Let every *one* naming the name of Christ stand away from unrighteousness.

20 But in a great house not only are there vessels of gold and silver, but also of wood and of earth, and some to honor and some to dishonor.

21 Therefore if anyone purifies himself from these, he will be a vessel unto honor, having been sanctified and made useful unto the Master, having been prepared to every good work.

22 ¶ But flee youthful lust and pursue righteousness, faith, love, peace, with the *ones* calling on the Lord out of a pure heart.

23 But refuse the foolish and uninstructed questionings, knowing that they generate quarrels.

24 But a slave of *the* Lord ought not to quarrel, but to be gentle towards all, apt to teach, forbearing,

25 in meekness instructing the *ones* opposing, if perhaps God may give them repentance for a full knowledge of *the* truth,

26 and they regain their senses out of the snare of the devil, being captured by him to *do* the will of that one.

2 Timothy 3

6 He describes the enemies of the truth, 16 and commends the Holy Scriptures.

1 ¶ But know this, that in *the* last days grievous times will be *upon us*.

2 For men will be self loving *ones*, money-loving *ones*, boasters, arrogant *ones*, blasphemers, disobedient to parents, unthankful, unholy *ones*,

3 without natural affections, implacable *ones*, slanderous *ones*, without self-control, savage *ones*, haters of good,

4 betrayers, reckless *ones*, being puffed up, lovers of pleasure rather than lovers of God,

5 having a form of godliness, but denying the power of it; even turn away from these.

6 For of these are the *ones* creeping into houses and leading silly women captive, having been heaped with sins, being led away by various lusts,

7 always learning, but never being able to come to a full knowledge of *the* truth.

8 But in the way Jannes and Jambres withstood Moses, so also these withstand the truth, men having been corrupted *in* mind, found worthless concerning the faith.

9 But they will not go further, for their foolishness will be plain to all, as also that of the *one* of *theirs* became.

10 ¶ But you have closely followed my doctrine, conduct, purpose, faith, long-suffering, love, patient endurance,

11 persecutions, sufferings, such as happened to me in Antioch, in Iconium, in Lystra, what persecutions I bore. And the Lord delivered me out of all.

12 And, indeed, all the *ones* desiring to live godly in Christ Jesus will be persecuted.

13 But evil men and impostors will go forward to worse, leading astray and being led astray.

14 But you keep on in what you learned and were assured of, knowing from whom you learned,

15 and that from a babe you know the Holy Scriptures, the *ones* being able to make you wise to salvation through belief in Christ Jesus.

16 All Scripture *is* God-breathed and profitable for doctrine, for reproof, for correction, for instruction in righteousness,

17 so that the man of God may be complete, having been fully equipped for every good work.

2 Timothy 4

1 He encourages him to do his duty with all care and diligence, 14 and warns him to beware of Alexander the smith.

1 ¶ Therefore, I solemnly witness before God and the Lord Jesus Christ, The *One* being about to judge *the* living and dead *ones at* His appearance and His kingdom:

2 preach the Word, stand by seasonably, unseasonably, convict, warn, encourage with all long-suffering and teaching.

3 For a time will be when they will not endure sound doctrine, but according to their own lusts, they will heap up to themselves teachers tickling the ear;

4 and *they* will turn away the ear from the truth and will be turned aside to myths.

5 But you be clear-minded in all, suffer hardship, do *the* work of an evangelist, fully carry out your ministry.

6 For I am already being poured out, and the time of my release is present.

7 I have fought the good fight. I have finished the course. I have kept the faith.

8 For the rest, the crown of righteousness is laid up for me, which the Lord, the righteous Judge, will give to me in that Day, and not only to me, but also to all the *ones* loving His appearance.

9 ¶ Make haste to come to me quickly.

10 For Demas deserted me, loving the present age, and *he* went to Thessalonica. Crescens *went* to Galatia, Titus to Dalmatia.

11 Only Luke is with me. Taking Mark, bring *him* with you, for he is useful to me for ministry.

12 But I sent Tychicus to Ephesus.

13 When you come, bring the cloak which I left in Troas with Carpus, and the books, especially the parchments.

14 Alexander the coppersmith showed many evil things to me. The Lord "will give back to him according to his works." *LXX-Psa. 61:13; MT-Psa. 62:12 ; Prov. 24:12*

15 You also *be on* guard against *him*, for he greatly stood against our words.

16 ¶ In my first defense no one came to *my* aid, but all deserted me. May it not be reckoned to them.

17 But the Lord stood with me and gave me power, that through me the preaching might be fulfilled, and all the nations might hear. And I was delivered out of *the* mouth of the lion.

18 And the Lord will deliver me from every wicked work and will save *me* for His heavenly kingdom; to whom *be* the glory to the ages of the ages. Amen.

19 Greet Prisca and Aquila and the house of Onesiphorus.

20 Erastus remained in Corinth, but I left Trophimus sick in Miletus.

21 Make haste to come before winter. Eubulus greets you, and Pudens, and Linus, and Claudia, and all the brothers.

22 The Lord Jesus Christ *be* with your spirit. Grace *be* with you. Amen.

The Epistle of Paul the Apostle to
TITUS

Titus 1

1 For what end Titus was left in Crete. 6 How they that are to be chosen ministers ought to be qualified.

1 ¶ Paul, a slave of God and an apostle of Jesus Christ according to *the* faith of *the* elect of God and full knowledge of *the* truth according to godliness,

2 on hope of eternal life which the never-lying God promised before eternal times,

3 but revealed in its own times in a proclamation of His Word, with which I was entrusted by *the* command of our Savior God;

4 to Titus, a true child according to *our* common faith: Grace, mercy, peace from God *the* Father and *the* Lord Jesus Christ our Savior.

5 ¶ For this cause I left you in Crete, that you might set in order the things lacking and appoint elders in every city, as I prescribed to you:

6 ¶ If anyone is a blameless *one*, husband of one wife, having faithful children, not in accusation of unsavedness, or an unruly *one*,

7 (It is right for the overseer to be a blameless *one* as a steward of God) not a self-pleasing *one*, not prone to anger, not given to wine, not a quarreler, not greedy of ill gain;

8 but a hospitable *one*, a lover of good, a self-controlled *one*, a just *one*, holy, a disciplined *one*,

9 clinging to the faithful Word according to the teaching, that he may be able both to encourage by sound doctrine and to convict the *ones* contradicting.

10 For there are indeed many insubordinate men, empty talkers and mind-deluders, especially the *ones* of *the* circumcision,

11 whose mouth *you* must stop, who overturn whole houses, teaching things which *they* ought not for the sake of ill gain.

12 One of them, a prophet of their own, said: Cretans *are* always liars, evil beasts, lazy gluttons.

13 This testimony is true; for which cause convict them severely, that they may be sound in the faith,

14 not listening to Jewish myths and commandments of men, having turned away from the truth.

15 Truly, all things *are* pure to the pure, but to the *ones* being defiled and unbelieving, nothing *is* pure, but even their mind and conscience has been defiled.

16 They profess to know God, but by *their* works they deny *Him*, being abominable and disobedient, and to every good work disapproved.

Titus 2

1 Direction given to Titus both for his doctrine and life. 9 Of the duty of servants.

1 ¶ But you speak things which become sound doctrine:

2 aged men to be temperate, honorable, sensible, sound in faith, in love, in patience;

3 aged women likewise in reverent behavior, not slanderers, not having been enslaved by much wine, teachers of good,

4 that they might train the young women to be lovers of husbands, dhild-lovers,

5 sensible, chaste, home-keepers, good, subject to *their* own husbands, so that the Word of God may not be blasphemed,

6 the younger men in the same way exhort to be sensible;

7 holding forth yourself *as* a pattern of good works about all *things* in doctrine, in purity, dignity, incorruption,

8 sound speech, without condemnation, that the hostile *ones* may he shamed, having nothing bad to say about you.

9 Let slaves be subject to *their* own masters, well-pleasing in all *things*, not contradicting,

10 not embezzling, but showing all good faith, that they may adorn the doctrine of our Savior God in every *thing*.

11 ¶ For the saving grace of God has appeared to all men,

12 instructing us that having denied ungodliness and worldly lusts, we should live prudently and righteously and godly in the now age,

13 looking for the blessed hope and appearance of the glory of our great God and Savior Jesus Christ,

14 who gave Himself on our behalf, "that He might redeem us from all lawlessness" "and purify" "for Himself a people for Himself for possession," zealous of good works. *Psa. 130:8; Eze. 37:23; Deut. 14:2*

15 ¶ Speak these things and exhort and convict with all authority. Let no one despise you.

Titus 3

1 Titus is directed by Paul concerning the things he should and should not teach.

1 ¶ Remind them to be subject to rulers and authorities, to be obedient, to be ready in every good work,

2 to speak evil of no one, not quarrelsome, *but* gentle, having displayed all meekness to all men.

3 For we also once were foolish *ones*, uncompliant *ones*, being led astray, slaving for various lusts and pleasures, living in malice and envy, hateful, hating one another.

4 But when the kindness and love of God our Savior toward man appeared,

5 not out of works in righteousness which we had done, but according to His mercy, He saved us through *the* bathing of regeneration and renewal of *the* Holy Spirit,

6 whom He poured out on us richly through Jesus Christ, our Savior;

7 that being justified by the grace of that *One*, we should become heirs according to *the* hope of eternal life.

8 Faithful *is* the Word, and concerning these things I purpose you to strongly affirm that the *ones* believing God should take thought to maintain good works. These things are good and profitable to men.

9 ¶ But keep back from foolish questionings and genealogies and arguments and quarrels of law, for they are unprofitable and vain.

10 Reject a heretical man after a first and second admonition,

11 knowing that such a one has been perverted and sins, being self-condemned.

12 When I shall send Artemas to you or Tychicus, hasten to come to me at Nicopolis. For I have decided to winter there.

13 Diligently set forward Zenas the lawyer and Apollos, that nothing be lacking to them.

14 And let ours also learn to maintain good works for necessary uses, that they may not be without fruit.

15 All the *ones* with me greet you. Greet the *ones* who love us in *the* faith. Grace *be* with you all. Amen.

The Epistle of Paul the Apostle to
PHILEMON

Philemon 1

4 He rejoices to hear of the faith and love of Philemon, 8 whom he desires to forgive Onesimus.

1 ¶ Paul, a prisoner of Christ Jesus, and Timothy the brother, to Philemon the beloved and our fellow-worker,

2 and to Apphia the beloved, and to Archippus our fellow-soldier, and to the assembly in your house:

3 Grace to you and peace from God our Father and *the* Lord Jesus Christ.

4 I thank my God always making mention of you in my prayers,

5 hearing of your love and faith which you have toward the Lord Jesus, and toward all the saints,

6 so that the fellowship of your faith may be effective in a full knowledge of every good thing in you for Jesus Christ.

7 For we have much joy and encouragement over your love, in that the hearts of the saints have been refreshed through you, brother.

8 ¶ Because of this, having much boldness in Christ to enjoin you *to do* what *is* becoming,

9 rather because of love I entreat, being such a one as Paul *the* aged, and now also a prisoner of Jesus Christ;

10 I entreat you concerning my child Onesimus, whom I fathered in my bonds,

11 the *one* once worthless to you, but now useful to you and to me; whom I sent back to you.

12 Even receive him, that is, my heart;

13 whom I purposed to hold with myself, that for you he *might* serve me in the bonds of the gospel.

14 But I was willing to do nothing without your consent, that your good might not be by way of necessity, but by way of willingness.

15 For perhaps for this he was separated for an hour, that you might receive him eternally;

16 no longer as a slave, but beyond a slave, a beloved brother, especially to me, and how much more to you, both in *the* flesh and in the Lord.

17 Then if you have me as a partner, receive him as me.

18 And if he wronged you *in* anything, or owes, charge this to me.

19 I, Paul, wrote with my hand; I will repay (that I not say to you that you even owe yourself to me also).

20 Yes, brother, *that* I may have your help in *the* Lord, refresh my bowels in *the* Lord.

21 Trusting to your obedience, I wrote to you, knowing that you will do even beyond what I say.

22 But at once prepare lodging for me; for I hope that through your prayers I shall be given to you.

23 Epaphras, my fellow-captive in Christ Jesus, greets you,

24 *also* my fellow-workers Mark, Aristarchus, Demas, *and* Luke.

25 The grace of our Lord Jesus Christ *be* with your spirit. Amen.

The Epistle to the
HEBREWS

Hebrews 1

1 Christ in these last times coming to us from the Father, 4 is preferred above the angels.

1 ¶ In many ways and in various ways of old, God having spoken to the fathers in the prophets;

2 in these last days *He* spoke to us in *the* Son, whom He appointed heir of all *things*; through whom He indeed made the ages;

3 who being the shining splendor of *His* glory, and the express image of His essence, and bearing up all things by the Word of His power, having made purification of our sins through Himself, *He* sat down on *the* right of the Majesty on high, *Psa. 110:1*

4 having become so much better than the angels, as much as He has inherited a name more excellent beyond them.

5 ¶ For to which of the angels did He ever say, "You are My Son; today I have begotten You"? And again, "I will be a Father to Him, and He shall be a Son to Me." *Psalm 2:7*

6 And again, when He brought the First-begotten into the world, He said, "And let all *the* angels of God worship Him."

7 And as to the angels, He said, "Who makes His angels spirits, and His servants a flame of fire;"? *LXX-Psa. 103:4; MT-Psa. 104:4*

8 but as to the Son, "Your throne, *O* God, *is* forever and ever, A scepter of uprightness *is* the scepter of Your kingdom;

9 You have loved righteousness and hated lawlessness; because of this God, Your God, has anointed You *with* the oil of gladness above Your fellows." *Psa. 45:6, 7*

10 And, "You, Lord, at *the* beginning laid the foundation of the earth, and the heavens are works of Your hands.

11 They will vanish away, but You will continue; and all *things will* become old, like a garment,

12 and You shall fold them up like a covering, and *they* shall be changed. But You are the same, and Your years shall not fail." *LXX-Psa. 101:26-28; MT-Psa. 102:25-27*

13 But to which of the angels did He ever say, "Sit at My right *hand* until I place Your hostile *ones as* a footstool of Your feet"? *LXX-Psa. 109:1; MT-Psa. 110:1*

14 Are they not all ministering spirits for service, being sent out because of the *ones* being about to inherit salvation?

Hebrews 2

We ought to be obedient to Christ Jesus.

1 ¶ Because of this *it is* needful *for* us more abundantly to take heed to the things having been heard that we should not slip away at any time.

2 For if the word spoken by angels was confirmed, and every transgression and disobedience received a just repayment;

3 how shall we escape *while* neglecting so great a salvation? Which, having received a beginning to be spoken through the Lord, was confirmed to us by the ones having heard,

4 God bearing witness with *them,* both by *miraculous* signs and wonders, and by various works of power, even by distributions *of the* Holy Spirit, according to His will.

5 ¶ For He did not subject the world, the *one* coming, under angels, about which we speak,

6 but one fully testified somewhere, saying, "What is man, that You are mindful of him; or the son of man, that You look upon him?"

7 You made him a little less than *the* angels; You crowned him with glory and honor;" and, "You made him rule over the works of Your hands."

8 You subjected all things under his feet." *Psa. 8:4-6* For in order to subject all things under him, He left nothing not subjected to him. But now we do not yet see all things having been subjected to him;

9 but the *One* for a little *time,* we do see Jesus, having been made less than the angels because of the suffering of death, having been crowned with honor and glory so as by *the* grace of God He might taste of death for every *son.*

10 ¶ For it was fitting for Him, because of whom *are* all things, and through whom *are* all things, bringing many sons into glory, to make complete *Him* as the Author of their salvation through sufferings.

11 For both the *One* sanctifying and the *ones* being sanctified *are* all of One; for which cause He is not ashamed to call them brothers,

12 saying, "I will announce Your name to My brothers; I will hymn to You in *the* midst of the Assembly." *Psa. 22:22*

13 And again, "I will be trusting on Him." *Isa. 8:17* And again, "Behold, I and the children whom God gave to Me." *Isa. 8:18*

14 ¶ Therefore since the children have partaken of flesh and blood, in like manner He Himself also shared the same things, that through death He might do away with the *one* having the power of death, this is, the devil;

15 and might set these free, as many as by fear of death were subject to slavery through all the *time* to live.

16 For indeed He does not take hold of angels, "but He takes hold of" "*the* Seed of Abraham". *Isa. 41:8, 9*

17 For which reason He was obligated in all things to become like *His* brothers, that He might become a merciful and faithful High Priest in the things respecting God, in order to propitiate for the sins of *His* people. For in what He has suffered, being tried, He is able to help the *ones* being tried.

Hebrews 3

Christ is more worthy than Moses.

1 ¶ For which reason, holy brothers, partakers of a heavenly calling, fully consider the Apostle and High Priest of our confession, Christ Jesus,

2 "being faithful" to Him having made Him, as also "Moses" *was* "in all his house". *Num. 12:7*

3 For This *One* was counted worthy of more glory than Moses, by so much as the one having prepared it has more honor than the house.

4 For every house is built by someone; but the *One* who prepared all things *is* God.

5 And "Moses" truly "*was* faithful in all his house" as a servant for a testimony of all the *things* being spoken; *Num. 12:7*

6 but Christ as Son over His house, whose house we are, if truly we hold fast the boldness and rejoicing of the hope firm to the end.

7 ¶ Therefore, even as the Holy Spirit says, "Today, if you hear His voice,

8 do not harden your hearts, as in the provocation by rebelliousness, in the day of temptation in the wilderness,

9 there where your fathers tested Me, examining Me, and saw My works forty years.

10 Therefore, I was very angry with that generation and said, They always go astray in heart; and they did not know My ways;

11 so I swore in My wrath, They shall not enter into My rest." *LXX-Psalm 94:7-11; MT-Psalm 95:7-11*

12 Watch, brothers, lest perhaps *there* shall be in any one of you an evil heart of unbelief to depart from *the* living God.

13 But exhort yourselves each day, as long as it is being called today, that not any of you be hardened by *the* deceitfulness of sin.

14 For we have become partakers of Christ, if truly we hold the beginning of the assurance firm to *the* end;

15 as in the saying, "Today, if you hear His voice, do not harden your hearts, as in the provocation by rebelliousness," *Psa. 95:7,8 MT*

16 For having heard, some provoked *Him,* but not all the *ones* coming out of Egypt through Moses.

17 But with whom was He angry forty years? *Was it* not with the *ones* sinning, whose corpses fell in the wilderness?

18 And to whom did "He swear" "*they would* not enter into His rest," except to the *ones* having disobeyed? *LXX-Psa. 94:11; MT-Psa. 95:11*

19 And we see that they were not able to enter in because of unbelief.

Hebrews 4

The rest of Christians is attained by faith.

1 ¶ Therefore, let us fear lest perhaps a promise having been left to enter into His rest, *that* any of you may seem to have come short.

2 For, indeed, we are having the gospel preached *to us*, even as they also; but the Word did not profit those hearing *it*, not having been mixed with faith in the *ones* having heard *it*.

3 For we, the *ones* having believed, enter into the rest, even as He said, "As I swore in My wrath, they shall not enter into My rest," though the works had come into being from *the* foundation of the world. *LXX-Psa. 94:11; MT-Psa. 95:11*

4 For He has spoken somewhere about the seventh *day* this way, "And God rested from all His works in the seventh day." *Gen. 2:2*

5 And in this again, "They shall not enter into My rest." *MT-Psalm 95:11*

6 Therefore, since it remains *for* some to enter into it, and the *ones* who formerly had the gospel preached did not enter in on account of disobedience,

7 He again marks out a certain day, saying in David, Today (after so long a time, according as He has said), "Today, if you hear His voice, do not harden your hearts." *MT-Psalm 95:7, 8*

8 For if *Joshua* brought them rest, He was not speaking about another day after these things.

9 So, then, there remains a sabbath rest to the people of God.

10 For he entering into His rest, *he* himself also rested from his works, as God *had rested* from *His* own. *LXX-Psa. 95:11; Gen. 2:2*

11 ¶ Therefore, let us exert ourselves to enter into that rest, that not anyone fall in the same example of disobedience.

12 For the Word of God *is* living, and working effectively, and sharper than every two-mouthed sword, and piercing as far as *the* division of both soul and spirit, of both joints and marrows, and able to judge of the thoughts and intentions of *the* heart;

13 and there is no creature unrevealed before Him; but all things *are* naked and having been laid open to His eyes, with whom *is* our account.

14 Therefore having a great High Priest who has passed through the heavens, Jesus the Son of God, let us hold fast the confession.

15 For we do not have a high priest not being able to sympathize with our infirmities, but *One* having been tried according in all things according to *our* likeness, apart from sin.

16 Therefore, let us draw near with confidence to the throne of grace, that we may receive mercy, and we may find grace for timely help.

Hebrews 5

Authority and honor of our Savior's priesthood.

1 ¶ For every high priest being taken from men is appointed on behalf of men in the things as regards to God, that he may offer both gifts and sacrifices for sins;

2 being able to feel gently for the *ones* not knowing and being led astray, since he also is circled about *with* weakness.

3 And because of this he ought to offer on account of sins as concerning the people, so also concerning himself.

4 And no one takes the honor to himself, but the *one* being called by God, even as Aaron also.

5 So also the Christ *has* not glorified Himself to become a high priest, but He speaking to Him, "You are My Son; today I have begotten You." *Psa. 2:7*

6 As He also says in another *place*, "You *are* a priest unto the age according to the order of Melchizedek," *Psa. 110:4*

7 who in the days of His flesh *was* offering both petitions and entreaties to the *One* being able to save Him from death, with strong crying and tears, and being heard from *His* godly fear;

8 though being a Son, He learned obedience from *the things* which He suffered,

9 and having been made complete, He came to be *the responsible* Author of eternal salvation to all the *ones* obeying Him,

10 having been called out by God *to being* a High Priest according to the order of Melchizedek.

11 Concerning whom we *have* much discourse, and hard to interpret, *or* to speak, since you have come to be sluggish in the hearings.

12 ¶ For indeed because of the time being due to be teachers, *yet* you need *for* the *one* to teach you again what *are* the rudiments of the beginning of the words of God, and you have come to be *ones* having need of milk, and not of solid food;

13 for every *one* partaking of milk *is* without experience *in the* Word of righteousness, for he is an infant.

14 But solid food is for mature *ones*, of the *ones of whom* the faculties having been exercised through habit, for judgment of both good and bad.

Hebrews 6

He encourages not to fall back from faith.

1 ¶ Therefore, having left the word of the beginning of Christ, let us be borne on to maturity, not laying down again a foundation of repentance from dead works, and of faith toward God,

2 of baptisms, of doctrine, and of laying on of hands, and of resurrection of dead *ones*, and of eternal judgment.

3 And this we will do, if indeed God permits.

4 For *it is* impossible for the *ones* once having been enlightened, and having tasted of the heavenly gift, and becoming sharers of *the* Holy Spirit,

5 and tasting *the* good Word of God, and *the* works of power of a coming age,

6 and having fallen away, it is impossible *for them* again to renew to repentance, crucifying again for themselves the Son of God, and holding *Him* up to public shame.

7 (For the earth drinking in the rain often coming upon it, and producing vegetation suitable for those for whom it is also cultivated, receives blessing from God;

8 "but bearing thorns and thistles," *it is* deemed unfit and near a curse, of which the end *is* for burning.) *Gen. 3:17, 18*

9 ¶ But, beloved *ones*, even if we indeed speak so, we have been persuaded better things concerning you, even holding fast *to* salvation.

10 For God *is* not unjust, to forget your work and the labor of love which you showed to His name, serving to the saints, and *now are* serving.

11 But we desire each of you to show the same diligence, to the full assurance of the hope to *the* end;

12 that you not become dull, but imitators of the *ones* who through faith and long-suffering *are* inheriting the promises.

13 For God having made promise to Abraham, since He had no greater to swear by, "*He* swore by Himself,"

14 saying, "Surely blessing I will bless you, and multiplying I will multiply you." *Gen. 22:16, 17*

15 And so, having patiently endured, he obtained the promise.

16 For men indeed swear by the greater, and an oath for confirmation *is* to them the end of all speaking against *it*.

17 In which God purposing to more fully declare to the heirs of the promise the unchangeableness of His purpose, He interposed by an oath,

18 that through two unchangeable things, in which *it was* not possible *for* God to lie, we might have a strong consolation, the *ones* having fled to lay hold on the hope being set before *us*,

19 which we have as an anchor of the soul, both certain and sure, and entering into the inner *side* of the veil, *Lev. 16:12*

20 where Jesus entered as forerunner for us, having become a High Priest forever, according to the order of Melchizedek.

Hebrews 7

Christ Jesus is a priest after the order of Melchizedek.

1 ¶ For this "Melchizedek, king of Salem, priest of the Most High God," the *one* having met Abraham "returning from the slaughter" "of the kings," "and having blessed him";

2 to whom also Abraham "divided a tenth from all" (first being interpreted, king of righteousness; and then also king of Salem, which is, king of peace, *Gen. 14:17-20*

3 without father, without mother, without descent, nor beginning of days, nor having end of life, but having been made like

the Son of God, *he* remains a priest in perpetual *continuity*).

4 Now behold how great this *one was*, to whom even the patriarch Abraham gave a tenth of the spoils;

5 and indeed the *ones* of the sons of Levi receiving the priesthood have a command to tithe the people according to Law, (that is, from their brothers, though coming forth out of Abraham's loins),

6 but he not tracing *his* descent from them has tithed Abraham, and the *one* having the promises, *this one* blessed.

7 But without contradiction, the lesser is blessed by the better.

8 And here dying men indeed receive tithes, but there *it* being witnessed that he lives;

9 and as a word to say, through Abraham Levi also, the *one* receiving tithes, has paid tithes.

10 For he was yet in his father's loins when Melchizedek met him.

11 ¶ Therefore, indeed, if perfection was through the Levitical priestly office (for the people had been given Law under it), why yet *was there* need *for* another priest to arise according to the order of Melchizedek and not to be called according to the order of Aaron?)

12 For the priestly office having been changed, of necessity a change of law also occurs.

13 For the *One* of whom these things are said has partaken of another tribe, from which no one has given devotion at the altar.

14 For *it is* openly evident that our Lord has risen out of Judah, as to which tribe Moses spoke nothing concerning priesthood.

15 And it is still more abundantly clear that if another priest arises according to the likeness of Melchizedek,

16 who has not become *so* according to a law of a fleshly command, but according to *the* power of an indissoluble life,

17 for He testified, "You are a priest unto the age according to the order of Melchizedek." *Psa. 110:4*

18 For, indeed, an annulment of the preceding command comes about because of its *being a* weak *one* and an unprofitable *one*.

19 For the Law perfected nothing, but a bringing in of a better hope, through which we draw near to God.

20 And by how much *it was* not without oath-taking;

21 for the *ones* truly without oath-taking are become priests, but He with oath-taking, through the *One* saying to Him, *The* Lord swore, and will not care *to change*, "You *are* a priest unto the age according to the order of Melchizedek"; *Psalm 110:4*

22 by so much Jesus has become Surety of a better covenant.

23 And, indeed, the many are become priests, because of being prevented to continue by death;

24 but He, because of Him remain*ing* unto the age, has a non-transmissible priesthood.

25 And from this He is able to save to the *end* completely the *ones* coming near to God through Him *who is* always living to intercede on their behalf.

26 For such a High Priest was fitting for us: holy, guileless, undefiled, and having been separated from sinners, and having become higher than the heavens;

27 who has no need, as do the high priests, to offer sacrifices according to a day, firstly for His own sins, then for the *ones* of the people, for this He did once for all, having offered up Himself.

28 For the Law makes men high priests who have infirmity, but the word of the oath-taking after the Law *appoints the* Son having been perfected unto the age.

Hebrews 8

By the eternal priesthood of Christ the Levitical priesthood of Aaron is abolished.

1 ¶ Now *the* main point over the things being said: We have such a High Priest, who sat down on *the* right of the throne of the Majesty in Heaven, *Psa. 110:1*

2 Minister of the *Holy of* Holies, and of the true tabernacle which the Lord pitched, and not man.

3 For every high priest is set in place to offer both gifts and sacrifices; from which *it is* necessary *for* this *One* also to have something which He may offer.

4 For if indeed He were on earth, He would not *even* be a priest, there being priests, the *ones* offering gifts according to the Law,

5 who serve the pattern of and shadow of heavenly things, even as Moses was divinely warned, being about to complete the tabernacle: For "See," He says, *"that* you make all things according to the pattern, the *one* being shown to you in the mountain." *Ex. 25:40*

6 ¶ But now He has gotten a more excellent ministry, also by so much as He is a Mediator of a better covenant, which has been enacted on better promises.

7 For if that first *covenant* was faultless, place would not have been sought for a second.

8 For finding fault, He said to them, "Behold, days come, says *the* Lord, and I will bequeath on the house of Israel and on the house of Judah a new covenant,

9 not according to the covenant which I made with their fathers in *the* day of My taking hold of their hand to lead them out of the land of Egypt; because they did not continue in My covenant, and I cared not for them, says *the* Lord.

10 Because this *is* the covenant which I will bequeath to the house of Israel after those days, says *the* Lord, giving My laws into their mind, and I will write them on their hearts, and I will be for God to them, and they shall be for a people to Me.

11 And they shall no more teach each *one* their *fellow*-citizen, and each *one* his brother, saying, Know the Lord; because all shall know Me, from the little *one* of them *to the* great *one* of them.

12 For I will be merciful to their unrighteousnesses, and I will not at all remember their sins and their lawlessnesses." *LXX-Jer. 38:31-34; MT-Jer. 31:31-34*

13 In the saying, New, He has made the first old. And the thing being made old and growing aged *is* near disappearance.

Hebrews 9

1 The description of the rites and bloody sacrifices of the law, 11 far inferior to the dignity and perfection of the blood and sacrifice of Christ.

1 ¶ Truly, then, the first *covenant* also had ordinances of service, and the earthly holy place.

2 For the tabernacle was prepared, the first, in which *was* both the lampstand and the table, and the setting out of the loaves, which is called holy.

3 But behind the second veil *is* a tabernacle, being called Holy of Holies,

4 having a golden altar of incense, and the ark of the covenant covered around on all sides with gold, in which *was* the golden pot having the manna, and Aaron's rod that budded, and the tablets of the covenant;

5 and above it *the* cherubs of glory overshadowing the mercy seat (about which is not *enough time* now to speak according to a piece).

6 And these *things* having been prepared thus, the priests go into the first tabernacle through all, completely fulfilling the services.

7 But into the second the high priest *goes* alone once *in* the year, not without blood, which he offers on behalf of himself and the sins of ignorance of the people;

8 the Holy Spirit signifying *by* this *that* the way of the Holies has not yet been made manifest, the first tabernacle still having standing;

9 which *was* a parable for the present time, according to which both gifts and sacrifices are offered, *but* as regards conscience, not being able to perfect the *one* serving,

10 but only on foods and drinks, and various washings, and fleshly ordinances, until *the* time of reformation being imposed.

11 ¶ But Christ having appeared *as* a High Priest of the coming good things, through the greater and more perfect tabernacle not made by hands, that is, not of this creation,

12 nor through the blood of goats and of calves, but through *His* own blood, *He* entered once for all into the *Holy of* Holies, having procured everlasting redemption.

13 For if the blood of bulls and goats, and ashes of a heifer, sprinkling those having been defiled, sanctifies to the purity of the flesh,

14 by how much more the blood of Christ (who through *the* eternal Spirit offered Himself without blemish to God), will purify your conscience from dead works, to serve *the* living God!

15 ¶ And because of this He is Mediator of a new covenant, so that, death having occurred for redemption of transgressions under the first covenant, the *ones* being called might receive the promise of the everlasting inheritance.

16 For where a testament *is*, the death of the *one* testating must be offered.

17 For a testament *is* firm over dead *ones*, since it never has force when the *one* testating lives.

18 From which neither the first *covenant* was dedicated without blood.

19 For *when* every command had been spoken according to Law by Moses to all the people, having taken the blood of the calves and goats, with water and scarlet wool and hyssop it*self*, and he sprinkled both the scroll and all the people,

20 saying, "This *is* the blood of the covenant which God enjoined to you." *Ex. 24:8*

21 And he likewise sprinkled both the tabernacle and all the service vessels with the blood.

22 And almost all things are purified by blood according to the Law; and apart from shedding of blood not *any* remission occurs.

23 ¶ Therefore *it was* needful for the figures of the things in the heavens to be cleansed *with* these; but the heavenly things them*selves* by better sacrifices than these.

24 For Christ did not enter into *the Holy of* Holies made by hands, antitypes of the true things, but into Heaven itself, now to appear in the presence of God on our behalf,

25 not that He should often offer Himself, even as the high priest enters into the *Holy of* Holies, according to a year with blood of others;

26 since it was necessary *for* Him to suffer often from *the* foundation of the world. But now once, at the completion of the ages, He has been revealed for putting away of sin through the sacrifice of Himself.

27 And as much as it is reserved to men once to die, and after this, Judgment;

28 so also Christ having been once offered "to bear *the* sins of many," Christ shall appear a second *time* without sin to the *ones* eagerly awaiting Him unto salvation. *Isa. 53:12*

Hebrews 10

The law sacrifices weak 10 Christ's body offered once for all has taken away sins.

1 ¶ For the Law having a shadow of the coming good things, not the image it*self* of *the* things, *appearing* according to a year with the same sacrifices, which they offer to the carrying through, they never are able to perfect the *ones* drawing near.

2 Otherwise, would they not have ceased to be offered? Because the *ones* serving did not still have consciousness of sins, having once been cleansed.

3 But in these *there is* a remembrance of sins according to a year,

4 for *it is* not possible for the blood of bulls and goats to take away sins.

5 Therefore, coming into the world, He says, "Sacrifice and offering You did not will, but You prepared a body for Me.

6 You were not well-pleased in burnt offerings and *sacrifices* concerning sins."

7 ¶ "Then I said, Behold, I have come, *in the* roll of the Book it was written concerning Me, to do Your will, O God." *LXX-Psa. 39:7 -9; MT-Psa. 40:6 -8*

8 Above, saying that sacrifice and offering, and burnt offerings and *sacrifices* concerning sin," You willed not, nor were You well-pleased (which are offered according to the Law),

9 then He has said, "Behold, I have come to do Your will, O God." He takes away the first in order that He may establish the second;

10 by which will we are sanctified through the offering of the body, of Jesus Christ once for all.

11 And indeed every priest stands according to a day ministering, and often offering the same sacrifices, which can never take away sins.

12 But He, offering but one sacrifice for sins, to the carrying through of *all* "sat down *at the* right *hand*" of God,

13 from then on expecting "until the hostile *ones* of Him are placed *as* a footstool" of His feet. *Psa. 110:1*

14 For by one offering He has perfected the carrying through of the *ones* being sanctified.

15 And the Holy Spirit witnesses to us also. For after having said before,

16 "This *is* the covenant which I will covenant to them after those days, says *the* Lord: Giving My Laws on their hearts, and I will write them on their minds";

17 "and their sins and their lawlessnesses I will not remember no longer, not *ever.*" *MT-Jer. 31:33, 34*

18 But where remission of these *is*, there *is* no longer offering concerning sins.

19 ¶ Therefore, brothers, having confidence for the entering of the *Holy of* Holies by the blood of Jesus,

20 which He consecrated for us, a new and living way through the veil; that is, His flesh;

21 and *having* a Great Priest over the house of God,

22 let us draw near with a true heart in full assurance of faith, our hearts having been sprinkled from an evil conscience, and *our* body having been washed in pure water;

23 let us hold fast the confession of the hope unyielding, for the *One* having promised is faithful.

24 And let us consider one another, unto incitement of love and of good works,

25 not forsaking the assembling together of ourselves, as *is the* custom of some, but exhorting, and by so much more as you see the Day drawing near.

26 For *if* we *are* willfully sinning after receiving the full knowledge of the truth, there remains no more sacrifice concerning sins,

27 but a certain fearful expectation of judgment and "zealous fire being about to consume the adversaries." *Isa. 26:11*

28 *If* anyone did not regard *the* Law of Moses, without compassions on "*the word of* two or three witnesses" dies. *Deut. 17:6*

29 How much worse punishment do you think will be thought worthy *to receive*, the *one* having trampled the Son of God, and having counted common the blood of the covenant in which he was sanctified, and having insulted the Spirit of grace?

30 For we know Him who has said, "Vengeance *belongs* to Me; I will repay," says *the* Lord. And again, "The Lord will judge His people." *Deut. 32:35, 36*

31 *It is* a fearful thing to fall into *the* hands of *the* living God.

32 But call to mind the former days in which having been enlightened you endured much struggle of sufferings.

33 Indeed, this, being exposed both to reproaches and to afflictions; and this, having come to be sharer of the *ones* so living;

34 for indeed you suffered together in my bonds; and you accepted the plunder of your possessions with joy, knowing yourselves to have a better and abiding possession in Heaven.

35 Therefore do not throw away your confidence, which has great reward.

36 For you have need of enduring patience, that having done the will of God you may obtain the promise.

37 For, yet a little as long as the *One* coming will come, "and will not delay." *Hab. 2:3*

38 "But the just shall live by faith;" "and if he draws back," "My soul is not well-pleased in him." *Hab. 2:4; Zeph. 1:6; Mal. 1:10*

39 But we are not of a drawing back to destruction, but of faith, to *the* preservation of *the* soul.

Hebrews 11

1 What faith is. 6 Without faith we cannot please God.

1 ¶ Now faith is *the* essence of things being hoped, the evidence of things not being seen.

2 For by this the elders obtained witness.

3 By faith we understand the ages to have been framed by a Word of God, so that the things being visible *should* not come into being out of things being seen.

4 ¶ By faith Abel offered a greater sacrifice to God than Cain, by which he obtained witness to be righteous, God testifying over his gifts; and through it, having died, he yet speaks.

5 By faith "Enoch" was translated *so as* not to see death, and "was not found, because God translated him." For before his translation, he had obtained witness to have been well-pleasing to God. *Gen. 5:24*

6 But without faith *it is* impossible to be pleasing to *God*. For it is necessary for the *one* drawing near to God to believe that

He is, and *that* He becomes a rewarder to the *ones* seeking Him out.

7 By faith, Noah having been divinely warned *by God* about the *things* not yet being seen, being moved with fear, *he* prepared an ark for *the* salvation of his house; through which he condemned the world and became heir of the righteousness according to faith.

8 Being called out by faith, Abraham obeyed to go forth to a place which he was going to receive for an inheritance; and *he* went out not understanding where he goes.

9 By faith he temporarily resided as a foreigner into a land of promise, living in tents with Isaac and Jacob, the joint-heirs of the same promise;

10 for he waited for a city having foundations, of which the builder and maker is God.

11 Also by faith Sarah her*self* received power for laying down of seed even beyond *the* time of age, *and* gave birth; since she deemed the *One* having promised *to be* faithful.

12 Therefore, even from one were generated *seed*, and these *of one* being as good as dead, even "as the stars of the heaven" in *their* fullness, and countless as sand by the lip of the sea". *Gen. 15:5; 22:17*

13 These all died by way of faith, not having received the promises, but seeing them from afar, and being persuaded, and having welcomed *them* and confessed that they are strangers and aliens on the earth.

14 For the *ones* saying such things make clear that they seek a fatherland.

15 And truly if they were mindful *of the place* from which they came out, they might have had opportunity to return.

16 But now they stretch forth to a better, that is, a heavenly *land*. Therefore, God is not ashamed *of* them, *for Him* to be called their God; *for* He prepared a city for them.

17 By faith, being tested, Abraham offered up Isaac; and the *one* receiving the promises was offering up the only begotten,

18 as to whom it was said, "In Isaac your Seed shall be called" *Gen. 21:12*

19 considering that; God *was* able to raise even from dead *ones*; from where indeed he obtained him in a parable.

20 By faith concerning things to come Isaac blessed Jacob and Esau.

21 By faith dying Jacob blessed each *one* of the sons of Joseph, and "worshiped on the top of his staff". *LXX- Gen. 47:31*

22 Dying Joseph by faith made mention of the Exodus of the sons of Israel, and *he* gave orders about his bones.

23 Having been generated, Moses was by faith hidden by his parents three months, because they saw the child *was* fair; and they did not fear the king's edict.

24 Having become great, Moses by faith refused to be called *the* son of Pharaoh's daughter,

25 having chosen rather to suffer mistreatment with the people of God than to have *the* temporary enjoyment of sin;

26 having counted the reproach of Christ greater riches than the treasures *of* Egypt, for he was looking to the reward.

27 By faith he left Egypt, not fearing the anger of the king; for he endured as seeing the Unseen *One*.

28 By faith he has made the Passover, and the pouring forth of blood, that the *one* destroying the first-born might not touch them.

29 By faith they passed through the Red Sea, as through dry *land*; by which attempt the Egyptians taking, *they* were swallowed.

30 By faith the walls of Jericho fell down, having been circled during seven days.

31 By faith Rahab the harlot did not perish with the *ones having* disobeyed, having received the spies with peace.

32 ¶ And what more may I say? For the time will fail me telling about Gideon, Barak, and also Samson and Jephthah, and also David and Samuel, and the prophets,

33 who through faith overcame kingdoms, worked out righteousness, obtained promises, stopped *the* mouths of lions,

34 quenched *the* power of fire, escaped the mouths of *the* sword, acquired power from weakness, became strong in war, armies of foreigners *being* made to bow.

35 Women received their dead *ones* by resurrection; but others were beaten to death, not accepting deliverance, that they might obtain a better resurrection.

36 And others received trial of mockings and of scourgings; yea, more, of bonds and of prison:

37 they were stoned; they were tried; they were sawn in two; they died by murder of sword; they went about in sheep-skins and in goat-skins, being in need, being afflicted, being tormented;

38 of whom the world was not worthy, wandering in deserts, and mountains, and caves, and the holes of the earth.

39 And having obtained witness through the faith, these all did not obtain the promise,

40 God having foreseen something better concerning us, that they should not be perfected apart from us.

Hebrews 12

An exhortation to faith, patience, and godliness.

1 ¶ So therefore we also, having so great *a* cloud of witnesses lying around us, having laid aside every weight and the easily surrounding sin, through patience let us also run the race being set before us,

2 looking to the Author and Finisher of *our* faith, Jesus, who for the joy set before Him endured *the* cross, despising the shame, "and has sat down at *the* right *hand*" of the throne of God."

3 For consider Him who had endured such opposition of sinners against Himself, that you do not grow weary, being faint-hearted in your souls,

4 ¶ You did not resist unto blood, wrestling against sin.

5 And you have forgotten the exhortation which *He* speaks with you, as with sons, "My sons, do not despise the chastening of *the* Lord, nor faint *while* being corrected by Him.

6 For whom the Lord loves, He disciplines, and scourges every son whom He receives." *Proverbs 3:11, 12*

7 If you endure discipline, God is dealing with you as with sons; for who is *the* son whom a father does not discipline?

8 But if you are without discipline, of which all have become sharers, then you are illegitimate *children*, and not sons.

9 Furthermore, indeed we have had fathers of our flesh as correctors, and we respected *them*. Shall we not much more be subject to the Father of spirits, and we shall live?

10 For the *ones* truly disciplined *as* for a few days according to the thing seeming good to them, but He for *our* profit, *so as for us* to partake of His holiness.

11 And all discipline for the present in deed does not seem to be of joy, but of grief; but afterward it gives back peaceable fruit of righteousness to the *ones* having been exercised through it.

12 Therefore straighten up the having been weakened hands "and the having been enfeebled knees;"

13 "and make straight tracks for your feet," that the lame *one* not be turned aside, but rather healed. *Isa. 35:3; Prov. 4:26*

14 Eagerly pursue peace and holiness with all, without which no one will see the Lord,

15 watching diligently that not any lack from the grace of God, that "no root of bitterness growing up" may crowd "in *on you*," and through this many be defiled; *Deut. 29:18*

16 that not any fornicator, or profane *one*, as Esau, who for one eating gave up his birthright;

17 for you know also that afterwards desiring to inherit the blessing, he was rejected, for he found no place of repentance, although having sought it out with tears. *Gen. 27:36-39*

18 ¶ For you have not drawn near to *the* mountain being touched, and having been lit with fire, and to gloom, and darkness, and tempest,

19 and to a sound of trumpet, and to a voice of words, which the *ones* hearing begged that not a word be added to them;

20 for they could not bear the thing enjoined: "Even" "if a beast" "touches the mountain, it will be stoned, or shot through" with a dart. *Ex. 19:12, 13*

21 And so fearful was the thing appearing, Moses said, "I am terrified and trembling." *Deut. 9:19*

22 But you have drawn near Mount Zion, even *the* city of *the* living God, to a heavenly Jerusalem, and to myriads of angels,

23 and to a festal gathering and an assembly of the first-born *ones* having been enrolled in Heaven; and to God *the* Judge of

all, and to spirits of just *ones* who have been perfected;

24 and to Jesus the Mediator of a new covenant, and to blood of sprinkling speaking better things than *that* of Abel.

25 Watch *that* you do not refuse the *One* speaking; for if these refusing the *One* divinely warning *them* did not escape on the earth, much rather we, the *ones* turning away from Heaven;

26 whose voice shook the earth then, but now He has promised, saying, "Yet once" "I will shake not only the earth, but also the heavens." *Hag. 2:6*

27 Now the *words* "Yet once" make clear the removal of the *things* being shaken, as having been made, so that the things not being shaken may remain.

28 Therefore receiving an unshakable kingdom, let us have grace, by which we may serve God well-pleasingly, with reverence and godly fear;

29 for also, "Our God *is* a consuming fire." *Deut. 4:24*

Hebrews 13

1 Diverse admonitions, as to charity, 5 to avoid covetousness, 15 to confess Christ.

1 ¶ Let brotherly love abide.

2 Do not forget hospitality, for by this some unknowingly took in angels as guests.

3 Be mindful of the prisoners, as having been bound with *them*; of the *ones* ill-treated, as also being in the body yourselves.

4 Marriage *is* honorable in all, and the bed undefiled; but God will judge fornicators and adulterers.

5 *Set your* way of life without money-loving, being satisfied with present things; for He has said, "Not I will leave you, not *ever*! Nor I will not forsake you, not *ever*!" *Deut. 31:6*

6 So that we may boldly say, "*The* Lord *is* my helper, and I will not be afraid. What shall man do to me?" *Psa. 118:6*

7 Remember your leaders who spoke the Word of God to you, considering the issue of *their* conduct, imitate *their* faith:

8 Jesus Christ, the same yesterday and today and forever.

9 Do not be carried away by various and strange doctrine; for *it is* good *that* the heart be confirmed by grace, not by foods, in which the *ones* walking *in them* were not profited.

10 We have an altar of which the *ones* serving the tabernacle have no authority to eat.

11 For of the animals *whose* "blood is brought" by the high priest "into the *Holy of* Holies" concerning sin, of these the bodies "are burned outside the camp". *Lev. 16:2, 27*

12 Therefore, indeed, in order that He might sanctify the people by His own blood, Jesus suffered outside the gate.

13 Therefore let us go forth to Him outside the camp bearing His reproach.

14 For we do not have here a continuing city, but we seek the *one* coming.

15 Therefore through Him let us offer up a sacrifice of praise to God always, this is, *the* fruit of the lips, confessing to His name.

16 But do not be forgetful of doing good and sharing, for God is well pleased with such sacrifices.

17 Yield to the *ones* taking the lead of you, and submit, for they watch for your souls, giving an account, that they may do this with joy, and not *with* groaning; for this *would be* unprofitable to you.

18 ¶ Pray about us, for we are persuaded that we have a good conscience, in all things desiring to conduct *ourselves* well.

19 But I even more urge *you* to do this that I may sooner be restored to you.

20 Now the God of Peace, the *One* leading up out of *the* dead *ones*, the great Shepherd of the sheep, in *the* blood of *the* everlasting covenant, our Lord Jesus,

21 perfect you in every good work, in order to do His will, doing in you that *which* is pleasing in His sight, through Jesus Christ, to whom *be* the glory forever and ever. Amen.

22 And, brothers, I exhort you, bear with the word of exhortation, for I indeed wrote to you by *a* few *words*.

23 You know the brother, Timothy, having been freed, with whom if he comes quickly, I will see you.

24 Greet all the *ones* leading you, also all the saints. The *ones* from Italy greet you.

25 Grace *be* with you all. Amen.

The Epistle of the Apostle
JAMES

James 1

1 We are to rejoice under the cross, 5 to ask wisdom of God, 13 and in our trials not to impute our weakness, or sins, to Him.

1 ¶ James, a slave of God and of *the* Lord Jesus Christ, to the twelve tribes in the Dispersion, greeting:

2 ¶ My brothers count *it* all joy when you fall into various trials,

3 knowing that the testing of your faith works enduring patience.

4 But let enduring patience have its perfective work, that you may be mature and complete, lacking in nothing.

5 But if any of you lacks wisdom, let him ask from God, the *One* giving to all bountifully and not reproaching, and it will be given to him.

6 But let him ask in faith, doubting nothing. For the *one* doubting *is* like a wave of *the* sea, being driven by wind and being tossed;

7 for do not let that man suppose that he will receive anything from the Lord;

8 *he is* a double-souled man, and unstable *one* in all his ways.

9 But let *the* lowly brother rejoice in his exaltation;

10 and the rich *one* in his humiliation, because he will pass away like the flower of the grass.

11 For the sun rose with the burning heat and dried up the grass, and its flower fell out, and the beauty of its appearance perished; so also the rich *one* will fade away in his journeys. *Isa. 40:6, 7*

12 Blessed *is* the man who endures temptation, because, becoming approved, he will receive the crown of life which the Lord promised to the *ones* loving Him.

13 ¶ Let no one being tempted say, I am tempted from God. For God is not temptable by evils, and He tempts no one.

14 But each *one* is tempted by *his* own lusts, being drawn out and being enticed *by them.*

15 Then, having conceived, lust brings forth sin. And sin being fully formed brings forth death.

16 Do not go astray, my beloved brothers,

17 every good gift, and every perfect gift, is from above, coming down from the Father of lights, with whom is not *any* change or shadow of turning.

18 Having purposed, He brought us forth by *the* Word of truth, for us to be a certain firstfruit of His creatures.

19 ¶ So that, my beloved brothers, let every man be swift to hear, slow to speak, slow to wrath.

20 For *the* wrath of man does not fully work *the* righteousness of God.

21 Therefore, putting away all filthiness and overflowing of evil, in meekness receive the implanted Word, the *one* being able to save your souls.

22 But become doers of *the* Word, and not hearers only, deceiving yourselves.

23 Because if anyone *is* a hearer of *the* Word, and not a doer, this one is like a man observing the face of his birth in a mirror;

24 for he observed himself, and has gone away, and immediately *he* forgot what sort he was.

25 But the *one* having looked into the perfect law of liberty, and having continued *in it*, this one not having become a forgetful hearer, but a doer of *the* work, this one will be blessed in his doing.

26 If anyone thinks to be a God-fearer among you, *yet* not bridling his tongue, but deceiving his heart, this *one's* worship *is* vain.

27 Pure and undefiled worship before God and *the* Father *is* this: to visit orphans and widows in their afflictions, *and* to keep oneself without blemish from the world.

James 2

1 We are not to regard the rich man nor despise the poor, 13 but rather to be loving, and merciful.

1 ¶ My brothers, do not in partiality have the faith of our Lord Jesus Christ, the *Lord* of glory.

2 For if a gold-fingered man in splendid clothing comes into your synagogue, and a poor *one* in dirty clothing also comes in;

3 and you look on the *one* wearing the splendid clothing, and say to him, You sit here well; and to the poor *one* you say, You stand there, or, Sit down here under my footstool;

4 did you not also discriminate among yourselves and become judges of evil thoughts?

5 Hear, my beloved brothers, did not God choose the poor *ones* of this world to be rich *ones* in faith, and heirs of the kingdom which He promised to the *ones* loving Him?

6 But you dishonored the poor *one*. Do not the rich *ones* oppress you, and they drag you to judgment seats?

7 Do they not blaspheme the good Name, the *one* being called on you?

8 ¶ If you truly fulfill *the* royal Law according to the Scripture, "You shall love your neighbor as yourself," you do well. *Lev. 19:18*

9 But if you have partiality you work sin, being convicted by the Law as transgressors.

10 For whoever shall keep all the Law, but stumbles in one, he has become guilty of all.

11 For the *One* who said, "You shall not commit adultery," also said, "You shall not murder." *Ex. 20:14, 13; Deut. 5:18, 17* But if you do not commit adultery, but commit murder, you have become a transgressor of *the* Law.

12 So speak and so do as being about to be judged through a law of liberty.

13 For judgment *will be* without mercy to the *one* not doing mercy. And mercy rejoices over judgment.

14 ¶ My brothers, what *is* the profit if anyone says he has faith, but he does not have works? Is the faith able to save him?

15 But if a brother or a sister is naked and may be lacking in daily food,

16 and any one of you say to them, Go in peace, be warmed and filled, but does not give them the things the body needs, what *is* the profit?

17 So also the faith, if it does not have works, is dead being by itself.

18 But someone will say, You have faith, and I have works. Show me your faith apart from your works, and I will show you my faith out of my works.

19 You believe that God is One. You do well; even the demons believe and shudder.

20 But are you willing to know, O vain man, that the faith apart from works is dead *faith*?

21 Was not our father Abraham justified by works offering up his son Isaac on the altar? *Gen. 22:9*

22 You see that the faith worked with his works; and out of the works the faith was made complete.

23 And the Scripture was fulfilled, saying, "And Abraham believed God, and it was counted for righteousness to him;" and he was called Friend of God. *Gen. 15:6; Isa. 41:8*

24 You see then that a man is justified out of works and not out of faith only.

25 But in the same way Rahab the harlot was also justified out of works, receiving the messengers and sending *them* out by another way.

26 For as the body is dead apart from the spirit, so also the faith is dead apart from works.

James 3

1 We are not rashly or arrogantly to reprove others, 5 but rather to bridle the tongue. 13 They who be truly wise are mild and peaceable.

1 ¶ My brothers, do not become many teachers, knowing that we will receive greater judgment.

2 For we all stumble *in* many *ways*. If any one does not stumble in word, this *one is* a mature man, able also to bridle the whole body.

3 Behold, we put bits in the mouths of the horses, for them to obey us; and we turn about their whole body.

4 Behold, the ships also, being so great, and being driven by rough winds, *they are* directed by a very small rudder, where the impulse of the *one* steering purposes.

5 So also the tongue is a little member, and boasts great things. Behold, how little a fire kindles how large a forest!

6 And the tongue *is* a fire, the world of unrighteousness. So the tongue is set among our members, defiling the whole body, and inflaming the course of nature, and being inflamed by Hell.

7 For every species of beasts, both indeed of birds, of creeping things, and of sea animals, is tamed, and has been tamed by the human nature;

8 but no one of men is able to tame the tongue; *it is* an unrestrainable evil, full of death-bringing poison.

9 By this we bless God and *the* Father; and by this we curse men, the *ones* having come into being according to *the* image of God. *Gen. 1:26*

10 Out of the same mouth comes forth blessing and cursing. My brothers, it is not fitting *for* these things to be so.

11 The fountain does not send forth the sweet and the bitter out of the same hole, *does it?*

12 My brothers, a fig tree is not able to produce olives, or a vine figs. So neither *can* a fountain produce both salt and sweet water.

13 ¶ Who *is* a wise *one* and knowing among you? Let him show his works by *his* good behavior, in meekness of wisdom.

14 But if you have bitter jealousy and contention in your heart, do not boast and lie against the truth.

15 This is not the wisdom coming down from above, but *is* earthly, natural, demonic.

16 For where jealousy and contention *are*, there *is* confusion and every evil deed.

17 But the wisdom from above is firstly truly pure, then peaceable, gentle, yielding, full of mercy and of good fruits, not partial and not pretended.

18 And *the* fruit of righteousness is sown in peace for the *ones* making peace.

James 4

1 We are to strive against covetousness, 4 intemperance, and rash judgment of others, 13 to commit all our affairs to God's providence.

1 ¶ From where *are* wars and fightings among you? *Is it* not from this, from your lusts, the *ones* warring in your members?

2 You desire and do not have. You murder, and are jealous, and are not able to obtain. You fight and you war, and you do not have, because you do not ask.

3 You ask, and do not receive, because you ask badly, in order that you may spend on your pleasures.

4 Adulterers and adulteresses! Do you not know that the friendship of the world is hostility *toward* God? Therefore whoever purposes to be a friend of the world is put down *as* a hostile *one to* God.

5 Or do you think that vainly the Scripture says, The spirit which has dwelt in us yearns to envy?

6 But He gives greater grace. Because of this it says, "God sets *Himself* against proud *ones*, but He gives grace to humble *ones*." *Prov. 3:34*

7 Therefore be subject to God. Resist the devil, and he will flee from you.

8 Draw near to God, and He will draw near to you. Cleanse *your* hands, sinners! And purify *your* hearts, double-souled *ones*!

9 Be distressed, and mourn, and weep. Let your laughter be turned to mourning, and *your* joy into shame.

10 Be humbled before the Lord, and He will exalt you.

11 ¶ Do not speak against one another, brothers. The *one* speaking against a brother, and judging a brother, *he* speaks against Law, and judges Law. But if you judge Law, you are not a doer of Law, but a judge.

12 One is the Lawgiver, who is able to save and to destroy; who are you who judges the other?

13 Come now, the *ones* saying, Today or tomorrow we will go into this city, and we will spend one year there, and we will trade and will make a profit,

14 who do not know of the morrow. For what *is* your life? For it is a mist,

which for a little *is* appearing, and then disappearing. *Ps. 94:11*

15 Instead of you saying, If the Lord wills, even we will live, and we will do this or that;

16 but now you boast in your presumptions. All such boasting is evil.

17 Therefore, to *anyone* knowing to do good, and not doing *it*, it is sin to him.

James 5

1 Wicked rich men are to fear God's vengeance.

7 We ought to be patient in afflictions.

1 ¶ Come now, rich *ones*, weep, howling over your miseries, the *ones* coming upon you.

2 Your riches have rotted, and your garments have become moth-eaten.

3 Your gold and silver have become corroded, and their poison will be a testimony to you, and will eat your flesh as a fire. You heaped treasure in *the* last days.

4 Behold, the wages of the workmen having reaped your fields cry out, being kept back by you. And the cries of the *ones* having reaped have entered "into the ears of *the* Lord of Hosts." *Isa. 5:9*

5 You lived luxuriously on the earth, and lived for self-pleasure; you nourished your hearts as in a day of slaughter;

6 you condemned; you murdered the righteous *one*; he does not resist you.

7 Therefore, brothers, be patient until the coming of the Lord. Behold, the farmer awaits for the precious fruit, being patient over it until it may receive *the* early and the latter rain.

8 You also be patient. Set your hearts firmly, because the coming of the Lord has drawn near.

9 Do not murmur against one another, brothers, that you not be judged. Behold, *the* Judge stands before the door.

10 My brothers, *as* an example of suffering ill, and of long-suffering, take the prophets who spoke in the name of *the* Lord.

11 Behold, we call blessed the *ones* enduring. You have heard of the patience of Job, and you saw *the* end of the Lord, "that the Lord is full of compassion and merciful." *Psa. 103:8*

12 ¶ But before all t*hings*, my brothers, do not swear, neither by the heaven, nor by the earth, nor any other oath; but let *your* yes be yes, and the no, no; that you may not fall under judgment.

13 Does anyone suffer hardships among you? Let him pray. Is anyone cheerful? Let him praise in song.

14 Is any among you feeble? Let him call the elders of the assembly, and let them pray over him, anointing him with oil in the name of the Lord.

15 And the prayer of the faith will save the *one* being sick, and the Lord will raise him up. And if he may have committed sin, it will be forgiven him.

16 Confess to one another the deviations *from the Law*, and pray for one another, that you may be healed; being very strong, *the* prayer of *a* righteous *one* works effectually.

17 Elijah was a man of like feeling to us, and he prayed in prayer *for it* not to rain; and it did not rain on the earth three years and six months.

18 And he prayed again, and the heaven gave rain, and the earth caused its fruit to sprout.

19 If anyone among you goes astray from the truth, brothers, and anyone turns him back,

20 know that the *one* turning back a sinner from *the* error of his way will save *the* soul from death, and will cover a multitude of sins.

The First Epistle of the Apostle
PETER

1 Peter 1

*1 He blesses God for his manifold spiritual graces,
13 and exhorts them to a godly conduct foras-
much as they are born anew by the Word of
God.*

1 ¶ Peter, an apostle of Jesus Christ, to *the* elect sojourners of *the* dispersion of Pontus, of Galatia, of Cappadocia, of Asia, and of Bithynia,

2 according to the foreknowledge of God the Father, in sanctification of *the* Spirit to obedience and sprinkling of *the* blood of Jesus Christ: Grace and peace be multiplied to you.

3 ¶ Blessed *be* the God and Father of our Lord Jesus Christ, the *One* according to His great mercy having regenerated us to a living hope through *the* resurrection of Jesus Christ from *the* dead *ones,*

4 to an inheritance incorruptible and undefiled and unfading, having been kept in Heaven for you,

5 the *ones* in *the* power of God being guarded through faith to a salvation ready to be revealed in the last time;

6 ¶ in which you exult; yet a little *while,* if it is needful, having been grieved in many various kinds of trials,

7 so that the testing of your faith, much more precious than perishing gold, but being tested through fire, may be found to praise and honor and glory at the revelation of Jesus Christ;

8 whom having not known, you love; in whom not yet seeing, but believing, you exult with joy unspeakable and being glorified,

9 obtaining the end of your faith, *the* salvation of *your* souls.

10 ¶ About which salvation the prophets sought out and searched out, prophesying about the grace for you,

11 searching for what, or what sort of time the Spirit of Christ made clear within them; testifying beforehand of the sufferings *belonging* to Christ, and the glories after these.

12 To whom it was revealed that not to themselves, but to us they ministered the same things, which now were proclaimed to you through the *ones* having preached the gospel to you in *the* Holy Spirit having been sent from Heaven; into which things angels long to look into.

13 ¶ Therefore, having girded up the loins of your mind, being sober, completely hope on the grace being borne to you at *the* revelation of Jesus Christ,

14 as children of obedience, not being conformed yourselves to your former lusts in your ignorance,

15 but according to the Holy *One* having called you *is* holy, *your*selves also become holy in all conduct;

16 because it has been written, "Be holy," "because I am holy". *Lev. 19:2*

17 And if you call on *the* Father, the *One* judging according to the work of each *one* without respect of persons, in the time of your sojourning, conduct yourselves in fear,

18 knowing that not with corruptible things, silver or gold, were you redeemed from your worthless way of life handed down from *your* fathers,

19 but with precious blood of Christ, as a lamb without blemish and without spot,

20 indeed having been foreknown before *the* foundation of *the* world, but revealed in *the* last times because of you,

21 the *ones* believing into God through Him, The *One* raising Him from *the* dead *ones,* and giving glory to Him so that your faith and hope may be in God.

22 Having purified your souls in the obedience of the truth through the Spirit to unpretended brotherly love, love one another fervently out of a pure heart,

23 having been generated, not by corruptible seed, but incorruptible, through the living Word of God, and remaining unto the age.

24 ¶ Because "all flesh *is* as grass, and all *the* glory of men as *the* flower of grass; the grass was dried, and its flower fell off,

25 but *the* Word of *the* Lord remains unto the age." And this is the Word preached as gospel to you. *Isaiah 40:6-8*

1 Peter 2

He exhorts them to endure patiently.

1 ¶ Therefore putting aside all malice, and all guile, and hypocrisies, and envies, and all evil speakings,

2 as newborn babes desire the pure soul-nourishing milk, that you may grow by it;

3 if indeed you "tasted" "that the Lord is kind"; *LXX-Psa. 33:9; MT-Psa. 34:8*

4 ¶ to whom having drawn near, a living Stone, indeed having been rejected by men, but by God, an elect *One*, precious;

5 you also as living stones are being built a spiritual house, a holy priesthood, to offer spiritual sacrifices acceptable to God through Jesus Christ.

6 Therefore, it is also contained in the Scripture: "Behold, I lay in Zion" an elect, "precious Stone," "a Corner-foundation"; "and the *one* believing on Him shall not be put to shame, not *ever!*" *Isa. 28:16*

7 Therefore to you, the *ones* believing, *belongs* the preciousness. But to disobeying *ones, He is the* "Stone which the *ones* building rejected; this *One* became *the* Head of the Corner," *Psa. 118:22*

8 and "a Stone-of-stumbling, and a Rock-of-offense" to the *ones* stumbling, being disobedient to the Word, to which they were also appointed. *Isa. 8:14*

9 But you *are* "an elect race," "a royal priesthood," "a holy nation," "a people for possession," so that "you may proclaim the excellencies" of the *One* who has called you out of darkness into His marvelous light; *LXX-Ex. 23:22; MT-Ex. 19:5, 6*

10 who then were "not a people, but now *are* the people" of God; "who not having received mercy, but now receiving mercy". *Hos. 1:6, 9; 2:1, 23,*

11 Beloved *ones*, I exhort *you* as foreigners and aliens to abstain from fleshly lusts which war against the soul;

12 having your behavior good among the nations, in that which they speak against you as evildoers; having watched *your* good works, they may glorify God in *the* day of visitation.

13 ¶ Therefore be in obedience to every human creation because of the Lord; whether to a king, as being supreme;

14 or to governors, as through him having indeed being sent for vengeance *on* evildoers, but praise of being well-doers

15 because so is the will of God, doing good to silence the ignorance of foolish men;

16 as free *men*, and not having freedom as a cover of evil, but as slaves of God;

17 honor all, love the brotherhood, fear God, honor the king.

18 Servants, *be* obedient to *your* masters in all fear, not only to the good *ones* and gentle *ones*, but also to the perverse *ones*.

19 For this *is* a grace, if because of conscience *toward* God anyone bears grief, suffering unjustly.

20 For what credit *is it* if sinning and being hit by the fist, you patiently endure? But if you *are* suffering *while* doing good, and patiently endure, this *is* a grace from God.

21 For you were called to this, for even Christ suffered on our behalf, leaving behind an example for us, that you should follow His footsteps;

22 "who did not sin, nor was guile found in His mouth"; *Isa. 53:9*

23 who, being reviled, did not revile in return; suffering, He did not threaten, but gave *Himself* over to the *One* judging righteously;

24 who "Himself carried up in His body our sins" onto the tree; that having died to sins, we might live to righteousness; of whom "by His wound you were healed."

25 For you were "straying sheep," *Isa. 53:4-6* but now you *are* turned back to the Shepherd and Overseer of your souls.

1 Peter 3

1 He teaches the duty of wives and husbands to each other. 19 The benefits of Christ towards the old world.

1 ¶ Likewise, wives, submitting yourselves to *your* own husbands, that even if any disobey the Word, through the behavior of the wives, without a word they will be won,

2 observing your pure behavior in fear.

3 Of whom let it not be the outward *act* of braiding of hairs, and of putting gold around, or putting on garments of adornment,

4 but the hidden man of the heart, in the incorruptible *adornment* of the meek and quiet spirit, which is of great value before God.

5 For so formerly also the holy women, the *ones* hoping on God, adorned themselves, submitting themselves to their own husbands,

6 as Sarah obeyed Abraham, calling him lord; whose children you became, doing good, and fearing no terror. *Gen. 18:12*

7 Likewise, husbands, dwelling together according to knowledge, as with a weaker vessel, the feminine *one*, bestowing honor, as truly *being* co-heirs of *the* grace of life, not cutting off your prayers.

8 ¶ And, finally, *be* all like-minded, sympathetic, loving the brothers, tender-hearted *ones*, friendly *ones*,

9 not giving back evil for evil, or reviling against reviling; but, on the contrary, *give* blessing; knowing that you were called to this in order that you might inherit blessing.

10 "For the *one* desiring to love life, and to see good days, let him restrain his tongue from evil *speaking*, even his lips not to speak deceit.

11 Let him turn aside from evil *doing*, and let him do good *things*. Let him seek peace, and pursue it;

12 because the eyes of *the* Lord *are* on the righteous *ones*, and His ears *open* to their prayer. But *the* face of *the* Lord *is* on *all* doing evil things." *LXX-Psa. 33:13-17; MT-Psa. 34:12-16*

13 And who *is* the *one* harming you if you become imitators of the good?

14 But if you truly suffer because of righteousness, blessed *are you*. "But do not fear their fear, nor be disturbed,

15 but sanctify" the Lord God in your hearts, and always *be* ready to speak in defense to every *one* asking you a word about the hope in you, with meekness and fear, *Isa. 8:12, 13*

16 ¶ having a good conscience, that while they speak against you as evil-doers, they may be shamed, the *ones* falsely accusing your good behavior in Christ.

17 For *it is* better, if the will of God wills *it*, to suffer *for* doing good than *for* doing evil.

18 ¶ Because even Christ once suffered concerning sins, the Just *One* on behalf of the unjust *ones*, that He might bring us to God; indeed being put to death in *the* flesh, but being made alive in the Spirit;

19 in which also, going in to the spirits in prison, He then proclaimed

20 to the *ones* disobeying, when once the long-suffering of God waited in *the* days of Noah, an ark being prepared, into which a few, that is, eight souls, were saved through water.

21 ¶ Which Antitype now also saves us; baptism, not a putting away of *the* filth of *the* flesh, but a demand of a good conscience toward God through *the* resurrection of Jesus Christ;

22 who having gone into Heaven is at *the* right *hand* of God, *the* angels, and authorities, and powers being subjected to Him.

1 Peter 4

1 He exhorts them to cease from sin by the example of Christ, and the consideration of the general resurrection, and that it now approaches.

1 ¶ Therefore, Christ having suffered on behalf of us in *the* flesh, also you arm yourselves *with* the same thought, because He having rested in *the* flesh has rested from sin,

2 in order to *live* no longer in *the* lusts of men, but *to* live the remaining time in *the* flesh in *the* will of God.

3 For *the* time of life having passed is sufficient for us to have worked out the will of the nations, having gone on in wantonness, lusts, drunkennesses, revelries, carousings, and lawless idolatries;

4 ¶ in which they are surprised, you not running together with *them* into the same pouring out of unsavedness, blaspheming;

5 who will give account to the *One* having readily to judge *the* living and dead *ones*.

6 For to this *end* also the gospel was preached to *the* dead *ones*, that they might be judged according to men in *the* flesh, but might live according to God in *the* Spirit.

7 ¶ But the end of all *things* has drawn near. Therefore be of sound mind, and be self-controlled unto prayers;

8 but before all *things* having fervent love to yourselves, "because love will cover a multitude of sins". *Prov. 10:12*

9 Be hospitable *ones* to one another without murmurings,

10 each *one* as he received a gift, ministering it to yourselves as good stewards of the manifold grace of God.

11 If anyone speaks, *let it be* as *the* words of God; if anyone serves, as by strength which God supplies, that in all *things* God may be glorified through Jesus Christ; to whom is the glory and the might to the ages of the ages. Amen.

12 ¶ Beloved *ones*, do not be astonished *at the* fiery trial taking place among you for a test, as *if* a strange *thing were* happening to you;

13 but according as you share the sufferings of Christ, rejoice; so that you may rejoice exultingly at the revelation of His glory.

14 If you are reviled in *the* name of Christ, *you are* blessed, because "the Spirit of God and of glory rests on you." Truly, according to them, He is blasphemed; but according to you, He is glorified. *Isa. 11:2*

15 For do not let any of you suffer as a murderer, or a thief, or an evil-doer, or as a meddler in the affairs of others.

16 But if as a Christian, do not let him be shamed, but glorify God in this respect.

17 Because the time *has come* to begin the judgment from the house of God; and if firstly from us, what *will be* the end of the *ones* disobeying the gospel of God?

18 And "if the righteous *one* is scarcely saved, where will the ungodly and sinner appear?" *Proverbs 11:31*

19 So as indeed the *ones* suffering according to God's will, as to a faithful Creator, let them commit their souls in doing good.

1 Peter 5

1 He encourages the elders to feed their flocks, 5 the younger to obey, 8 and all to be sober, watchful, and constant in the faith.

1 ¶ I exhort the elders among you, *I being* a fellow-elder, and *a* witness of the sufferings of Christ, and *being* sharer of the glory about to be revealed:

2 shepherd the flock of God among you, exercising oversight, not by compulsion, but willingly, nor eagerly for base gain, but readily;

3 nor as exercising lordship over the allotment *given to you*, but becoming examples of the flock.

4 And *at* the appearing of the Chief Shepherd, you will receive the never-fading crown of glory.

5 ¶ Likewise, younger *ones* be subject to older *ones*; and all being subject to one another. gird on humility, because God sets *Himself* "against proud *ones*, but He gives grace to humble *ones*". *Prov. 3:34*

6 Therefore, be humbled under the mighty hand of God, that He may exalt you in time;

7 "casting all your anxiety onto Him," because it matters to Him concerning you. *LXX-Psa. 54:23; MT-Psa. 55:22*

8 ¶ Be self-controlled. Be watchful, because your adversary *the* devil walks about as a roaring lion seeking someone he may devour;

9 whom firmly resist in the faith, knowing the same sufferings are being completed in your brotherhood in *the* world.

10 ¶ Now the God of all grace, the *One* having called you to His eternal glory in Christ Jesus, *you* having suffered a little, Himself will perfect, confirm, strengthen, establish *you*.

11 To Him *be* the glory and the might to the ages of the ages. Amen.

12 I wrote to you by a few *words* by way of Silvanus the faithful brother, as I reckon, exhorting and witnessing this to be *the* true grace of God, in which you stand.

13 Greets you the fellow-elected in Babylon; also Mark my son.

14 Greet one another with a kiss of love. Peace *be* to you, all the *ones* in Christ Jesus. Amen.

The Second Epistle of the Apostle
PETER

2 Peter 1

1 Confirming them in hope of the increase of God's graces, 5 he encourages them, by faith and good works, to make their calling sure 16 and warns them to be constant in the faith of Christ.

1 ¶ Simon Peter, a slave and apostle of Jesus Christ, to the *ones* equally precious with us, having obtained faith in *the* righteousness of our God and our Savior, Jesus Christ:

2 Grace to you, and peace be multiplied by a full knowledge of God, and of Jesus our Lord.

3 As His divine power having given as a gift to us all things *pertaining* to life and godliness through the full knowledge of the *One* calling us through glory and virtue,

4 through which have been given as a gift to us the very great and precious promises, so that through these we might become partakers of *the* divine nature, having escaped from the corruption in *the* world by lust.

5 ¶ But also in this very thing having brought in all diligence, fully supply in your faith virtue, and with virtue knowledge,

6 and with the knowledge self-control, and with the self-control patience, and with the patience godliness,

7 and with the godliness brotherly love, and with brotherly love, love.

8 For these things being in you, and abounding, causes *you* not to be idle, not unfruitful into the full knowledge of our Lord Jesus Christ.

9 For the one in whom these things are not present is blind, being shortsighted, receiving forgetfulness of the cleansing of his sins in time past.

10 Therefore, brothers, rather be diligent to make sure of your calling and election; for doing these things, you will not stumble, not ever!

11 For so will be richly furnished to you the entrance into the eternal kingdom of our Lord and Savior, Jesus Christ.

12 ¶ Therefore I will not neglect to cause you to remember always concerning these *things*, though *you* know and have been confirmed in the present truth.

13 But I deem *it* right, so long as I am in this tabernacle, to arouse you by a reminder,

14 knowing that the putting off of my tabernacle is soon, as indeed our Lord Jesus Christ made clear to me.

15 And I will also be diligent to cause you always to have memory of these things after my departure.

16 ¶ For not following fables having been cleverly devised, but having become eyewitnesses of the majesty of that *One*, Jesus Christ, we made known to you the power and coming of our Lord.

17 For receiving honor and glory from God *the* Father such a voice being borne to Him from the Magnificent Glory, "This is My Son, the Beloved, in whom I was well-pleased," *Psa. 2:7; Gen. 22:2; Isa. 42:1; Matt. 17:5*

18 even we heard this voice being borne out of Heaven, being with Him in the holy mountain,

19 ¶ and we have the more established prophetic Word, in which you do well to pay attention, as to a lamp shining in a murky place, until day dawns and the Light-bearing *One* rises in your hearts;

20 knowing this first, that every prophecy of Scripture did not come into being of *its* own interpretation;

21 for prophecy was not at any time borne by *the* will of man, but being borne along by *the* Holy Spirit, holy men of God spoke.

2 Peter 2

He foretells of false teachers, showing the impiety and punishment both of them and their followers.

1 ¶ But *there* also came to be false prophets among the people, as also among you will be false teachers who will secretly bring in

destructive heresies, even denying the *One* having bought them, *the* Master, bringing swift destruction on themselves.

2 And many will follow their destructive ways, through whom the way of truth will be evil spoken of.

3 ¶ And by covetousness, with feigned words, they will use you for gain, for whom judgment of old does not linger, and their destruction does not slumber.

4 For if God did not spare sinning angels, but giving *them* over to chains of darkness, thrust down into Tartarus, having been kept to judgment;

5 and did not spare *the* ancient world, but protected Noah *the* eighth, a herald of righteousness, bringing a flood on a world of ungodly *ones*;

6 and covering the cities *of* Sodom and Gomorrah with ashes, *He* condemned *them* with an overthrow, setting an example to men intending to live ungodly.

7 ¶ And He delivered righteous Lot, who had been oppressed by the behavior of lawless *ones* in unbridled lusts.

8 For that righteous *one* living among them day after day, in seeing and in hearing, *his* righteous soul *was* tormented with *their* lawless works.

9 *But the* Lord knows to deliver the godly *ones* out of temptation, and to keep the unjust *ones* for a day of judgment, being punished,

10 ¶ and most of all the *ones* going after flesh in *the* lust of defilement, and despising rulership, darers, self-pleasing; they do not tremble *at* glories, blaspheming;

11 where angels, being greater in strength and power, do not bring against them a blasphemous charge before *the* Lord.

12 But these as unreasoning natural beasts, having been born for capture and corruption, blaspheming in that *of* which they are ignorant, they shall utterly perish in their corruption,

13 receiving *the* wages of unrighteousness, deeming luxuriousness in the day *to be* pleasure; *they are* spots and blemishes, reveling *in* their deceptions, feasting together with you,

14 having eyes full of an adulteress, and never ceasing from sin; alluring unstable souls; having a heart being busied *with* covetousness; cursed children;

15 forsaking the straight way, they went astray, following the way of Balaam the *son* of Beor, who loved *the* wages of unrighteousness,

16 but had reproof of *his* own lawlessness, the voiceless ass speaking in a man's voice restrained the madness of the prophet.

17 These are springs without water, clouds being driven by tempest, for whom the blackness of darkness has been kept to *the* ages.

18 For speaking great swollen-over *words* of vanity, by *the* lusts of the flesh, by unbridled lusts, they allure the *ones* indeed escaping, the *ones* walking in error,

19 promising to them freedom, *though* themselves being slaves of corruption; for by whom anyone has been overcome, even to this *one* he has been enslaved.

20 For if by a recognition of the Lord and Savior, Jesus Christ, having escaped the defilements of the world, and again being entangled *they* are overcome by these, *then* the last things of them have become worse *than* the first.

21 For it was better for them not to have fully known the way of righteousness than fully knowing *it* to turn from the holy commandment having been given over to them.

22 But *the* word of the true proverb has happened to them: "*The* dog turning back to *his* own vomit;" and, *the* sow being washed *returns* to a wallowing *in* mud. *Prov. 26:11*

2 Peter 3

1 He assures them of the certainty of Christ's coming for judgment, 8 warning the godly, for the long patience of God, to hasten their repentance.

1 ¶ Beloved *ones*, I now write to you this second epistle, in which I stir up your pure mind in a reminder

2 to remember the words having been spoken previously by the holy prophets, and the commandment of the Lord and Savior by us, the apostles;

3 ¶ first, knowing this, that during *the* last days scoffers will come, going on according to their own lusts,

4 and saying, Where is the promise of His coming? For from which *time the* fathers fell asleep, all things remain so from *the* beginning of creation.

5 For this escapes their notice *by their* willing *it so*, that heavens were of old, and earth by water, and through water, subsisting by the Word of God,

6 through which the world which then was, being flooded by water, perished.

7 But the heavens and the earth now, being stored up by the same Word, are being kept for fire to a day of judgment and destruction of ungodly men.

8 ¶ But let not this one *thing* escape you, beloved *ones*, that one day with *the* Lord *is* "as a thousand years, and a thousand years as one day." *Psa. 90:4*

9 ¶ The Lord of the promise is not slow, as some deem slowness, but is long-suffering toward us, not purposing any to perish, but all to turn one's self to repentance.

10 But the day of the Lord will come as a thief in *the* night, in which the heavens will pass away with a rushing sound, and being burning up *the* elements will be dissolved, and earth and the works in it will be burned up.

11 ¶ Therefore, all these *things* being *about* to be dissolved, *of* what sort ought you to be in holy behavior and godliness,

12 looking for and hastening the coming of the Day of God, through which *the* heavens being set on fire will be dissolved; and *the* elements will melt?

13 But according to His promise, we look for "new heavens and a new earth," in which righteousness dwells. *Isa. 65:17*

14 Therefore, beloved *ones*, looking for these things, be diligent, spotless, and without blemish, to be found in peace by Him.

15 And think of the long-suffering of our Lord *as* salvation, as also our beloved brother Paul wrote to you, according to the wisdom having been given to him;

16 as also in all his letters, speaking in them concerning these things, in which are some things hard to understand, which the unlearned and unstable *ones* pervert, as also *they do* the rest of the Scriptures, to *their* own destruction.

17 Therefore, beloved *ones*, you knowing beforehand, be on guard lest being led away by the error of the lawless *ones* you fall from *your* own firmness.

18 But grow in grace and knowledge of our Lord and Savior, Jesus Christ. To Him *be* the glory, both now and to *the* day of eternity. Amen.

The First Epistle of the Apostle
JOHN

1 John 1

He describes the person of Christ, in whom we have eternal life, by a communion with God.

1 ¶ That which was from the beginning, that which we have heard, that which we have seen with our eyes, that which we beheld, and our hands touched, as regards the Word of Life.

2 And the Life was revealed, and we have seen, and we bear witness, and we announce to you the everlasting Life which was with the Father, and was revealed to us.

3 That which we have seen and we have heard, we proclaim to you, that you also may have fellowship with us. And truly our fellowship *is* with the Father and with His Son, Jesus Christ.

4 And we write these things to you, that your joy may be full.

5 ¶ And this is the message which we have heard from Him, and we announce to you: God is light, and no darkness is in Him, none!

6 If we say that we have fellowship with Him, and we walk in darkness, we lie and are not practicing the truth.

7 But if we walk in the light, as He is in the light, we have fellowship with one another, and the blood of His Son Jesus Christ cleanses us from all sin.

8 ¶ If we say that we have no sin, we deceive ourselves, and the truth is not in us.

9 If we confess our sins, He is faithful and righteous that He may forgive us the sins, and may cleanse us from all unrighteousness.

10 If we say that we have not sinned, we make Him a liar, and His Word is not in us.

1 John 2

1 He comforts them against the sins of infirmity.
3 To know God is to keep his commandments.

1 ¶ My little children, I am writing these things to you so that you do not sin. And if anyone sins, we have an Advocate with the Father, Jesus Christ *the* Righteous *One*.

2 And *He* Himself is *the* propitiation concerning our sins, and not concerning ours only, but also concerning the whole world.

3 ¶ And by this we know that we have known Him, if we keep His commands.

4 The *one* saying, I have known Him, and not keeping His commands is a liar, and the truth is not in this *one*.

5 But whoever keeps His Word, truly in this *one* the love of God has been perfected. By this we know that we are in Him.

6 The *one* saying to abide in Him ought so to walk himself even as that *One* walked.

7 ¶ Brothers, I do not write a new commandment to you, but an old commandment which you had from *the* beginning. The old commandment is the Word which you heard from *the* beginning.

8 Again I write a new commandment to you which is true in Him and in you, because the darkness is passing away, and the true Light already shines.

9 The *one* claiming to be in the light, and hating his brother, is in the darkness until now.

10 The *one* loving his brother rests in the light, and a cause of stumbling is not in him.

11 But the *one* hating his brother is in the darkness, and walks in the darkness, and does not know where he is going, because the darkness blinded his eyes.

12 ¶ Little children, I am writing to you because you have been forgiven *your* sins through His name.

13 Fathers, I am writing to you because you have known Him from *the* beginning. I am writing to you, young men, because you have overcome the evil *one*. I am writing to you, little children, because you have known the Father.

14 Fathers, I wrote to you because you have known the *One* from *the* beginning.

I wrote to you, young men, because you are strong, and the Word of God abides in you, and you have overcome the evil *one*.

15 Do not love the world nor the things in the world. If anyone loves the world, the love of the Father is not in him,

16 because every*thing* in the world: the lust of the flesh, and the lust of the eyes, and the pride of life, is not from the Father, but is from the world.

17 And the world is passing away, and its lust. But the *one* doing the will of God abides unto the age.

18 ¶ Little children, it is a last hour, and as you heard that the antichrist is coming to be, even now many antichrists have come to be, from which you know that it is a last hour.

19 They went out from us, but they were not of us. For if they were of us, they would have remained with us; but *it was* so that it might be revealed that they all are not of us.

20 ¶ And you have an anointing from the Holy *One*, and you know all things.

21 I did not write to you because you do not know the truth, but because you know it, and because every lie is not of the truth.

22 Who is the liar, if not the *one* denying, *saying* that Jesus is not the Christ? This is the antichrist, the *one* denying the Father and the Son.

23 Everyone denying the Son does not have the Father. The *one* confessing the Son also has the Father.

24 Therefore, what you heard from *the* beginning, let it abide in you. If what you heard from *the* beginning abides in you, you will abide both in the Son and in the Father.

25 And this is the promise which He promised us: everlasting life.

26 I have written these things to you concerning the *ones* leading you astray.

27 And the anointing which you received from Him abides in you, and you have no need that anyone teach you, but the same anointing teaches you concerning all *things*, and is true, and is not a lie, and as He taught you, abide in Him.

28 ¶ And now, little children, abide in Him, that when He appears we may have confi-dence, and not be shamed from Him in His coming.

29 If you know that He is righteous, know that every *one* doing righteousness has been generated from Him.

1 John 3

He declares the singular love of God towards us.

1 ¶ See what manner of love the Father has given us, that we may be called children of God. Because of this the world does not know us, because it did not know Him.

2 Beloved *ones*, now we are the children of God, and it was not yet made known what we shall be. But we know that if He is made visible *to us*, we shall be like Him, because we shall see Him as He is.

3 And everyone having this hope upon Him purifies himself even as that One is pure.

4 ¶ Everyone practicing sin also practices lawlessness, and sin is lawlessness.

5 And you know that that One was revealed that He might take away our sins, and sin is not in Him.

6 Everyone remaining in Him does not sin. Everyone sinning has not seen Him, nor known Him.

7 Little children, let no one lead you astray; the *one* practicing righteousness is righteous, even as that One is righteous.

8 The *one* practicing sin is of the devil, because the devil sins from *the* beginning. For this the Son of God was made known, that He might undo the works of the devil.

9 Everyone having been generated of God does not sin, because His seed abides in him, and he is not able to sin, because he has been generated from God.

10 By this the children of God and the children of the devil are made known: Everyone not practicing righteousness is not of God; also the *one* not loving his brother.

11 ¶ Because this is the message which you heard from *the* beginning, that we should love one another,

12 not as Cain was, of the evil *one*, and slaughtered his brother. And for the sake of what did he slaughter him? Because his works were evil, but the things of his brother *were* righteous *works*.

13 Do not marvel, my brothers, if the world hates you.

14 ¶ We know that we have passed from death to life because we love the brothers. The *one* not loving the brother abides in death.

15 Everyone hating the brother is a murderer, and you know that every murderer does not have everlasting life abiding in him.

16 By this we have known the love *of* God, because that One laid down His life for us; and on behalf of the brothers we ought to lay down *our* lives.

17 Whoever has the means of life of the world, and sees his brother having need, and shuts up his bowels from him, how does the love of God abide in him?

18 My little children, let us not love in word, or in tongue, but in deed and in truth.

19 And in this we shall know that we are of the truth, and shall persuade our hearts before Him,

20 ¶ that if our heart condemns us, *we know* that God is greater than our heart and knows all things.

21 Beloved *ones*, if our heart does not condemn us, we have confidence with God.

22 And whatever we ask, we receive from Him, because we keep His commandments, and we do the things pleasing before Him.

23 ¶ And this is His commandment, that we should believe *into* the name of His Son, Jesus Christ, and love one another, even as He gave command to us.

24 And the *one* keeping His commandments abides in Him, and He in him. And by this we know that He abides in us, by the Spirit whom He gave to us.

1 John 4

He warns them not to believe all teachers, who boast of the Spirit, but to try them.

1 ¶ Beloved *ones*, do not believe every spirit, but test the spirits, whether they are from God; for many false prophets have gone forth into the world.

2 By this you know the Spirit of God: every spirit which confesses that Jesus Christ has come in *the* flesh is from God.

3 And every spirit which does not confess that Jesus Christ has come in *the* flesh is not from God; and this is the antichrist which you heard is coming, and now is already in the world.

4 ¶ Little children, you are of God and have overcome them, because the *One* in you is greater than the *one* in the world.

5 They are of the world; because of this, *as* from the world they speak, and the world hears them.

6 We are of God; the *one* knowing God hears us; *he* who is not of God does not hear us. From this we know the spirit of truth and the spirit of error.

7 ¶ Beloved *ones*, let us love one another, because love is from God, and every *one* who loves has been generated from God, and knows God.

8 The *one* not loving did not know God, because God is love.

9 By this the love of God was revealed in us, because His Son, the only begotten, God has sent into the world that we might live through Him.

10 In this is love, not that we loved God, but that He loved us, and sent His Son *to be* a propitiation concerning our sins.

11 Beloved *ones*, if God so loved us, we also ought to love one another.

12 No one ever has seen God at any time. If we love one another, God abides in us, and His love being perfected is in us.

13 By this we know that we abide in Him, and He in us, because of His Spirit He has given to us.

14 ¶ And we have beheld and bear witness that the Father has sent the Son *as* Savior of the world.

15 Whoever confesses that Jesus is the Son of God, God abides in him, and he in God.

16 And we have known and have believed the love which God has in us. God is love, and the *one* abiding in love abides in God, and God in him.

17 ¶ By this, love has been perfected with us, that we have confidence in the day of judgment, that as that *One* is, we are also in this world.

18 There is no fear in love, but perfect love casts out fear, because fear has punishment; and the *one* fearing has not been perfected in love.

19 We love Him because He first loved us.

20 If anyone says, I love God, and hates his brother, he is a liar. For the *one* not loving

his brother whom he has seen, how is he able to love God whom he has not seen?

21 And we have this commandment from Him, that the *one* who loves God also loves his brother.

1 John 5

He that loves God loves his children, and keeps his commandments.

1 ¶ Everyone believing that Jesus is the Christ has been generated from God. And everyone loving the *One* generating also loves the *one* having been generated of Him.

2 By this we know that we love the children of God: whenever we love God and keep His commandments.

3 For this is the love of God, that we keep His commandments; and His commandments are not heavy.

4 Because everything having been generated of God overcomes the world, and this is the victory overcoming the world, our faith.

5 Who is the *one* overcoming the world if not the *one* who believes that Jesus is the Son of God?

6 ¶ This is the *One* having come through water and blood, Jesus Christ; not by the water only, but by the water and the blood. And the Spirit is the *One* witnessing, because the Spirit is the truth.

7 For three are the *ones* bearing witness: *in Heaven: the Father, the Word, and the Holy Spirit; and these three are one.*

8 *And there are three who bear witness on the earth:* The Spirit, and the water, and the blood; and the three are into the one.

9 If we receive the witness of men, the witness of God is greater; because this is the witness of God which He has witnessed about His Son:

10 ¶ The *one* believing into the Son of God has the witness in himself. The *one* not believing God has made Him a liar, because he has not believed into the witness which God has witnessed concerning His Son.

11 And this is the witness:, that God has given us everlasting life, and this life is in His Son.

12 The *one* having the Son has life. The *one* not having the Son of God does not have life.

13 I wrote these things to you, the *ones* believing into the name of the Son of God, that you may know that you have everlasting life, and that you may believe into the name of the Son of God.

14 ¶ And this is the confidence we have toward Him, that if we ask anything according to His will, He hears us.

15 And if we know that He hears us, whatever we ask, we know that we have the requests which we have requested from Him.

16 If anyone sees his brother sinning a sin not unto death, he shall ask; and He shall give life to the *one* not sinning unto death. There is a sin unto death. I do not say that he should ask about that.

17 All unrighteousness is sin, and there is a sin not unto death.

18 ¶ We know that everyone having been generated from God does not sin, but the *one* being generated from God keeps himself, and the evil *one* does not touch him.

19 We know that we are of God, and the whole world lies in the evil *one*.

20 And we know that the Son of God has come, and *He* has given to us an understanding that we may know the True *One*, and we are in the True *One*, in His Son Jesus Christ. This is the true God and the life everlasting.

21 Little children, guard yourselves from idols. Amen.

The Second Epistle of the Apostle
JOHN

2 John 1

He encourages a certain honorable matron, with her children, to persevere in Christian love and belief.

1 ¶ The elder to *the* elect lady and her children, whom I love in truth; and not I only, but also all the *ones* who have known the truth,

2 because of the truth abiding among us, and will be with us to the age.

3 Grace, mercy, peace will be with you from God *the* Father and from *the* Lord Jesus Christ, the Son of the Father, in truth and love.

4 I rejoiced greatly because I found *some* of your children walking in truth, as we received commandment from the Father.

5 ¶ And I now request you, lady, not writing as a new commandment, but *one* which we had from *the* beginning, that we should love one another.

6 And this is love, that we should walk according to His commandments. This is the commandment, even as you heard from *the* beginning, that you should walk in it.

7 ¶ Because many deceivers entered into the world, those not confessing Jesus Christ to have come in *the* flesh, this is the deceiver and the antichrist.

8 Watch yourselves, that we may not lose the things we worked out, but that we may receive a full reward.

9 Everyone transgressing and not abiding in the doctrine of Christ does not have God. The *one* abiding in the doctrine of Christ, this one has the Father and the Son.

10 ¶ If anyone comes to you and does not bear this doctrine, do not receive him into the house, and do not speak a greeting to him.

11 For the *one* speaking a greeting shares in his evil works.

12 ¶ Having many things to write to you, I do not intend *to speak* by means of paper and ink, but I am hoping to come to you, and to speak mouth to mouth, that our joy may be full.

13 The children of your elect sister greet you. Amen.

The Third Epistle of the Apostle
JOHN

3 John 1

1 He commends Gaius for his piety, 5 and hospitality 7 to true preachers, 12 and gives special testimony to the good report of Demetrius.

1 ¶ The elder to Gaius the beloved, whom I love in truth.

2 Beloved *one*, in regard to all things, I pray *for* you to prosper and to be in health, even as your soul prospers.

3 ¶ For I rejoiced greatly *at the* coming of *the* brothers, also bearing witness of you in the truth, as you walk in truth.

4 I have no greater joy than these things, that I hear my children are walking in truth.

5 Beloved *one*, you do a faithful *thing* whatever you work for the brothers and for the strangers,

6 who in love bore witness of you before *the* assembly, whom you will do well to send forward worthily of God.

7 For on behalf of His name they went out, taking nothing from the nations.

8 Therefore, we ought to entertain such *men*, that we may become co-workers with the truth.

9 ¶ I wrote to the assembly, but the *one* loving to be first of them, Diotrephes, does not receive us.

10 Because of this, if I come, I will recall his works which he does, slandering us with evil words. And not being satisfied *with* these, neither does he receive the brothers; and the *ones* purposing *it* he stops, and thrusts *them* out from the assembly.

11 Beloved *one*, do not imitate the bad *things*, but the good *things*. The *one* doing good is of God; but the *one* doing evil has not seen God.

12 ¶ Witness has been borne to Demetrius by all, and by the truth itself. And we also bear witness, and you know that our witness is true.

13 I had many things to write, but I do not desire to write by means of pen and ink.

14 But I am hoping to see you at once, and we will speak mouth to mouth. Peace to you. The friends greet you. Greet the friends by name.

The Epistle of the Apostle
JUDE

Jude 1

He encourages them to be constant in the profession of the faith.

1 ¶ Jude, a slave of Jesus Christ, and brother of James, to the *ones* called in God the Father, having been sanctified, and having been kept to Jesus Christ:

2 Mercy and peace, and love be multiplied to you.

3 ¶ Beloved *ones*, making all diligence to write to you about the common salvation, I had need to write to you to exhort *you* to contend earnestly for the faith once given over to the saints.

4 For certain men slipped in stealthily, the *ones* having been of old written before to this judgment, ungodly *ones* perverting the grace of our God into unbridled lust, and denying the only Master, God, even our Lord Jesus Christ.

5 But I purpose to remind you, you once knowing these things, that the Lord, having saved a people out of the land of Egypt, in the second place destroyed the *ones* not believing.

6 And the *ones of the* angels not having kept their first place, but having left behind their dwelling place, He has kept in everlasting chains under darkness for the judgment of *the* great Day;

7 as Sodom and Gomorrah, and those cities around them, in like manner to these, committing fornication, and having gone after other flesh, are set forth an example, undergoing vengeance of everlasting fire.

8 ¶ Likewise, indeed, also these dreaming *ones* even defile flesh, and reject lordship, and blaspheme glories.

9 But Michael the archangel, when contending with the devil, he argued about the body of Moses; he dared not bring a judgment of blasphemy, but said, "Let the Lord rebuke you!" *Zech. 3:2*

10 But as many *things* as they do not know, they speak evil of these. And what things they understand naturally, like the animals without reason, they are corrupted by these.

11 Woe to them, because they went the way of Cain, and gave themselves up to the error of Balaam for reward, and perished in the rebellion of Korah!

12 These are sunken rocks in your love feasts, feasting together with you, feeding themselves without fear, waterless clouds being carried about by winds, fruitless autumn trees, having died twice, having been plucked up by the roots;

13 wild waves of the sea foaming up their shames, wandering stars for whom blackness of darkness has been kept to the age.

14 And "the seventh from Adam," Enoch, also prophesied to these men, saying, Behold, "the Lord came with" myriads "of His saints,"

15 ¶ "to do judgment against all, and to rebuke all" the ungodly *ones* of them concerning all their ungodly works which they ungodly did, "and concerning all the hard *things* ungodly sinners spoke against Him."

16 These are murmurers, complainers, walking according to their lusts, and their mouth speaks over-swollen *words*, admiring faces for the sake of gain.

17 But you, beloved *ones*, remember the words spoken before by the apostles of our Lord Jesus Christ,

18 because they told you that at *the* last time there will be mockers going after ungodlinesses according to their lusts.

19 These are the *ones* setting themselves apart, animal-like *ones*, not having the Spirit.

20 But you, beloved *ones*, building yourselves up by your most holy faith, praying in the Holy Spirit,

21 keep yourselves in the love of God, eagerly awaiting the mercy of our Lord Jesus Christ to everlasting life.

22 And have mercy on some, making a distinction.

23 But save others with fear, snatching *them* out of the fire, hating even the garment having been stained from the flesh.

24 Now to Him being able to guard you without stumbling, and to set you before His glory without blemish, with exultation;

25 to the only wise God, our Savior, *be* glory and majesty, might and authority, even now and to all the ages. Amen.

The REVELATION
of Jesus Christ

Revelation 1

4 John writes his revelation to the seven assemblies of Asia. 7 The coming of Christ.

1 ¶ A Revelation of Jesus Christ, which God gave to Him to show to His slaves things which must occur quickly. And He signified *by* sending through His angel to His slave, John,

2 who testified of the Word of God and the witness of Jesus Christ, even as many things as he saw.

3 ¶ Blessed *is* the *one* reading, and the *ones* hearing the words of this prophecy, and keeping the things having been written; for the time *is* near.

4 John to the seven assemblies in Asia: Grace to you, and peace, from the *One* being, and the *One who* was, and the *One* coming, and from the seven spirits which are before His throne;

5 even from Jesus Christ the faithful Witness, the First-born *One* out of the dead *ones*, and the Ruler of the kings of the earth. To the *One* loving us and having washed us from our sins by His blood,

6 and made us kings and priests to God, even His Father. To Him *is* the glory and the might to the ages of the ages. Amen.

7 "Behold, He comes with the clouds," and "every eye will see Him, and those pierced" with Him, and all the tribes of the earth "will wail on account of Him." Yes, Amen. *Dan. 7:13; Zech. 12:10*

8 I am the Alpha and the Omega, *the* Beginning and *the* End, says the Lord, the *One* being, and the *One who* was, and the *One* coming, the Almighty.

9 ¶ I, even your brother John, and co-sharer in the affliction, and in the kingdom and patience of Jesus Christ, came to be in the island being called Patmos on account of the Word of God, and on account of the witness of Jesus Christ.

10 I came to be in *the* Spirit on *the* day belonging to the Lord, and I heard behind me a great voice, as of a trumpet,

11 saying, I am the Alpha and the Omega, the First and the Last; also, What you see, write in a book, and send to the seven assemblies of Asia: to Ephesus, and to Smyrna, and to Pergamos, and to Thyatira, and to Sardis, and to Philadelphia, and to Laodicea.

12 And I turned to see the voice which spoke with me.

13 And having turned, I saw seven golden lampstands, and in *the* midst of the seven lampstands *One* like *the* Son of Man, having been clothed to *the* feet, and having been girded with a golden girdle at the breasts.

14 And the hairs of His head *were* white as white wool, as snow, and His eyes as a flame of fire;

15 and His feet like burnished brass having been fired in a furnace; and His voice as a sound of many waters;

16 and having in His right hand seven stars; and a sharp, two-edged sword proceeding out of His mouth, and His face shining as the sun in its power.

17 And when I saw Him, I fell at His feet, as a dead *one*. And He put His right hand on me, saying to me, Do not fear. I am the First and the Last,

18 and the *One* Living; and I became a dead *one*; and, behold, I am living to the ages of the ages. Amen. And I have the keys to hell, and of death.

19 Write the things which you saw, and the things which are, and the things which are about to occur after these things.

20 The mystery of the seven stars which you saw on My right, and the seven golden lampstands: the seven stars are angels of the seven assemblies, and the seven lampstands you saw are seven assemblies.

Revelation 2

What is commanded to be written to the angels,
that is, the ministers of the assemblies.

1 ¶ To the angel of the Ephesian assembly, write: These things says the *One* holding the seven stars in His right *hand*, the *One* walking in *the* midst of the seven golden lampstands:

2 I know your works, and your labor, and your patience, and that you cannot bear evil *ones*; and *you* tried the *ones* pretending to be apostles and are not, and found them *to be* liars.

3 And *I know you* bore up and have patience and on account of My name you have labored and have not wearied.

4 But I have against you that you left your first love.

5 Therefore, remember from where you have fallen, and repent, and do the first works. And if not, I am coming to you quickly, and will remove your lampstand from its place, unless you repent.

6 But you have this, that you hate the works of the Nicolaitans, which I also hate.

7 The *one* having an ear, hear what the Spirit says to the assemblies. To the *one* overcoming, I will give to him to eat of the Tree of Life which is in *the* midst of the Paradise of God.

8 ¶ And to the angel of the assembly *in* Smyrna, write: These things says the First and the Last, who became a dead *one*, and lived:

9 I know your works, and the affliction, and the poverty; but you are rich *ones*. And *I know* the blasphemy of the *ones* saying themselves to be Jews, and they are not, but *are* a synagogue of Satan.

10 Fear nothing *of* what you are about to suffer. Behold, the devil is about to throw *some* from you into prison, so that you may be tried; and you will have affliction ten days. Be faithful until death, and I will give you the crown of life.

11 The *one* having an ear, hear what the Spirit says to the assemblies. The *one* overcoming will not be hurt by the second death, not *ever!*

12 ¶ And to the angel of the assembly *in* Pergamos, write: These things says the *One* having the sharp, two-edged sword:

13 I know your works, and where you dwell, where the throne of Satan *is*. And you hold My name, and did not deny My faith even in the days in which Antipas *was* My faithful witness; who was killed alongside you, where Satan dwells.

14 But I have a few *things* against you, that you have there *some* holding the teachings of Balaam, who taught Balak to cast a stumbling block before the sons of Israel, to eat idol sacrifices, and to commit fornication.

15 So you also have *some* holding the teaching of the Nicolaitans, which thing I hate.

16 Repent! But if not, I will come to you quickly, and I will make war with them by the sword of My mouth.

17 The *one* having an ear, hear what the Spirit says to the assemblies. To the *one* overcoming, I will give him to eat from the hidden manna. And I will give to him a white pebble, and on the pebble a new name having been written, which no one knows if not the *one* receiving *it*.

18 ¶ And to the angel of the assembly in Thyatira, write: These things says the Son of God, the *One* having His eyes as a flame of fire, and His feet like burnished brass.

19 I know your works, and the love, and the ministry, and the faith, and your patience, and your works; and the last more than the first.

20 But I have a few things against you, that you allow the woman Jezebel to teach, the *one* saying herself *to be* a prophetess, and to cause My slaves to go astray, and to commit fornication, and to eat idol sacrifices.

21 And I gave time to her that she might repent of her fornication. And she did not repent.

22 Behold, I am throwing her into a bed, and into great affliction the *ones* committing adultery with her, unless they repent of their works.

23 And I will kill her children with death; and all the assemblies will know that I am the *One* searching the kidneys and hearts. And I will give to you, each *one*, according to your works.

24 But I say to you and to the rest in Thyatira, as many as do not have this teaching, and who did not know the deep

things of Satan, as they say; I am not casting another burden on you;

25 but what you have, hold until I shall come.

26 And the *one* overcoming, and the *one* keeping My works until *the* end, "I will give to him authority over the nations,"

27 and "he will shepherd them with an iron staff" (they are "broken to pieces like clay vessels"), as I also have received from My Father. *Psa. 2:8, 9*

28 And I will give to him the Morning Star.

29 The *one* having an ear, hear what the Spirit says to the assemblies.

Revelation 3

2 The angel of the assembly in Sardis is reproved, 3 and encouraged to repent. 8 The angel of the assembly in Philadelphia is approved.

1 ¶ And to the angel of the assembly in Sardis, write: These things says the *One* having the seven spirits of God, and the seven stars: I know your works, that you have the name that you live, and are a lifeless *assembly*.

2 Be watching, and establish the things remaining which are about to die. For I have not found your works being fulfilled before God.

3 Therefore, remember how you received and heard, and keep, and repent. If, therefore, you do not watch, I will come upon you like a thief and you will not know what hour I come upon you, not *at all*.

4 You also have a few names in Sardis which did not defile their garments, and they shall walk with Me in white because they are worthy.

5 The *one* overcoming, this *one* shall be clothed in white garments, and I will not blot his name out of the Book of Life, not *ever*! And I will acknowledge his name before My Father, and before His angels.

6 The *one* having an ear, hear what the Spirit says to the assemblies.

7 ¶ And to the angel of the assembly in Philadelphia, write: These things says the Holy *One,* the True *One,* the *One* having "the key of David", "the *One* opening, and no one shuts; and shuts, and no one opens": *Isa. 22:22*

8 I know your works. Behold, I have given a door being opened before you, and no one is able to shut it, for you have a little power and have kept My Word, and have not denied My name.

9 Behold, I give out of the synagogue of Satan the *ones* saying themselves to be Jews, and they are not, but they lie. Behold, I will make them come and prostrate themselves before your feet, and they shall know that I loved you.

10 Because you kept the Word of My patience, I also will keep you out of the hour of trial, the *one* being about to come on the whole inhabited earth in order to try the *ones* dwelling on the earth.

11 Behold, I am coming quickly. Hold what you have that no one take your crown.

12 The *one* overcoming, I will make him a pillar in the temple of My God, and he shall not go out any more, not *ever*! And I will write the name of My God on him, and the name of the city of My God, the new Jerusalem which comes down out of Heaven from My God, and My new name.

13 The *one* having an ear, hear what the Spirit says to the assemblies.

14 ¶ And to the angel of the Laodicean assembly, write: These things says the Amen, the faithful and true Witness, the Beginning of the creation of God:

15 I know your works, that you are neither cold nor hot. I would that you were cold or hot.

16 So, because you are lukewarm, and neither cold nor hot, I am about to vomit you out of My mouth.

17 Because you say, I am a rich *one*, and I am made wealthy, and I have need of nothing, and do not know that you are the wretched *one* and miserable *one* and poor *one* and blind *one* and naked *one*.

18 I advise you to buy from Me gold having been fired by fire, that you may be wealthy; and white garments, that you may be clothed, and your shame and nakedness may not appear. And anoint your eyes with eye salve, that you may see.

19 I, as many "as I love, I rebuke and I chasten." Be zealous, then, and repent. *Prov. 3:12*

20 Behold, I stand at the door and am knocking. If anyone hears My voice and opens the door, I will enter to him, and I will dine with him, and he with Me.

21 The *one* overcoming, I will give to him to sit with Me in My throne, as I also overcame and sat with My Father in His throne.

22 The *one* having an ear, hear what the Spirit says to the assemblies.

Revelation 4

John sees the throne of God in Heaven.

1 ¶ After these things I saw. And behold, a door being opened in Heaven! And I heard the first voice as a trumpet speaking with me, saying, Come up here, and I will show you what needs to happen after these things.

2 And at once I became in spirit. And, behold, a throne was set in Heaven, and *One* sitting on the throne.

3 And the *One* sitting was in appearance like a jasper stone, and a sardius; and a rainbow was around the throne, in appearance of emeralds.

4 And around the throne *I saw* twenty-four thrones, and on the thrones I saw twenty four elders sitting, having been clothed in white garments. And they had golden crowns on their heads.

5 And out of the throne come forth lightnings and thunders and voices. And seven lamps of fire *were* burning before the throne, which are the seven Spirits of God;

6 and a glassy sea before the throne, like crystal. And in *the* midst of the throne and around the throne *were* four living creatures, full of eyes before and behind.

7 And the first living creature *was* like a lion; and the second living creature like a calf; and the third living creature having a face like a man; and the fourth living creature like an eagle flying.

8 ¶ And the four living creatures one by one had six wings around, and within being full of eyes. And they have no rest day and night, saying, "Holy, holy, holy, Lord God Almighty," the *One who* was, and the *One* being, and the *One* coming! *Isa. 6:3*

9 And whenever the living creatures shall give glory and honor and thanks to the *One*

sitting on the throne, to the *One* living to the ages of the ages,

10 the twenty-four elders fall down before the *One* sitting on the throne; and they will worship the *One* living unto the ages of the ages, and will throw their crowns before the throne, saying,

11 Lord, You are worthy to receive the glory and the honor and the power, because You created all things, and through Your will they exist and were created.

Revelation 5

1 The book sealed with seven seals: 9 which only the Lamb that was slain is worthy to open.

1 ¶ And I saw on the right of the *One* sitting on the throne a scroll having been written within and on the back, having been sealed with seven seals.

2 And I saw a strong angel proclaiming with a great voice: Who is worthy to open the scroll, and to loosen its seals?

3 And no one in Heaven was able to open the scroll nor to look at it, neither on the earth, nor underneath the earth.

4 And I wept much, because no one worthy was found to open and to read the scroll, nor to look at it.

5 And one of the elders said to me, Do not weep. Behold, the Lion being of the tribe of Judah, the Root of David, overcame *so as* to open the scroll, and to loose its seven seals.

6 ¶ And I saw, and behold, in *the* midst of the throne, and of the four living creatures, and in *the* midst of the elders, *was* a Lamb standing, as having been slaughtered, having seven horns and seven eyes, which are the seven Spirits of God, having been sent out into all the earth.

7 And He came and has taken the scroll out of the right *hand* of the *One* sitting on the throne.

8 And when He took the scroll, the four living creatures and the twenty-four elders fell down before the Lamb, each *one* having harps, and golden bowls full of incenses, which are the prayers of the saints.

9 And they sing a new song, saying, Worthy are You to receive the scroll, and to open its seals, because You were slaughtered, and by Your

blood purchased us to God out of every tribe and tongue and people and nation,

10 and made us kings and priests to our God; and we shall reign over the earth.

11 And I saw, and I heard a sound of many angels around the throne, and the living creatures, and the elders, and their number was myriads of myriads, and thousands of thousands,

12 saying with a great voice, Worthy is the Lamb having been slaughtered to receive the power and riches and wisdom and strength and honor and glory and blessing.

13 And every creature which is in Heaven, and in the earth, and underneath the earth, and the things that are on the sea, and the things in all of them, I heard saying: To the *One* sitting on the throne, and to the Lamb be the blessing and the honor and the glory and the might unto the ages of the ages.

14 And the four living creatures said, Amen. And the twenty-four elders fell down and worshiped the *One* living to the ages of *the* ages.

Revelation 6

The opening of the seals in order.

1 ¶ And I saw that the Lamb opened one of the seals. And I heard one of the four living creatures, like a sound of thunder, saying, Come and see.

2 And I saw, and behold, a white horse! And the *One* sitting on it had a bow. And a crown was given to him, and He went out conquering, and that He might conquer.

3 ¶ And when He opened the second seal, I heard the second living creature saying, Come and see.

4 And another horse went out, fiery red. And it was given to the *one* sitting on *it* to take peace from the earth, and that they should slay one another. And a great sword was given to him.

5 And when He opened the third seal, I heard the third living creature saying, Come and see. And I saw, and behold, a black horse, and the *one* sitting on it having a balance in his hand.

6 And I heard a voice in *the* midst of the four living creatures saying, A choenix of wheat *for* a denarius, and three choenicies

of barley *for* a denarius; and do not harm the oil and the wine.

7 And when He opened the fourth seal, I heard a voice of the fourth living creature saying, Come and see.

8 And I saw, and behold, a pale green horse, and the name of the *one* sitting on it, the name to him *was* Death; and Hades followed after him. And authority was given to them to kill over the fourth of the earth with sword, and with famine, and with death, and by the wild beasts of the earth.

9 ¶ And when He opened the fifth seal, I saw under the altar the souls of the *ones* having been slaughtered for the Word of God, and for the witness which they had.

10 And they cried with a great voice, saying, Until when, holy and true Master, do You not judge and take vengeance *for* our blood, from the *ones* dwelling on the earth?

11 And there was given to each *one* a white robe. And it was said to them that they should rest yet a little time, until might be fulfilled also *the number* of their fellow-slaves and their brothers, the *ones* being about to be killed, even as they.

12 And I saw when He opened the sixth seal. And behold, a great earthquake occurred. And the sun became black as sackcloth made of hair; and the moon became as blood;

13 and the stars of the heaven fell to the earth, as a fig tree being shaken by a great wind casts its unripe figs.

14 And *the* heaven was torn away like a scroll being rolled up. And every mountain and island were torn away out of their places.

15 And the kings of the earth, and the great *ones*, and the rich *ones*, and the chiliarchs, and the powerful *ones*, and every slave, and every free *man* hid themselves in the caves and in the rocks of the mountains.

16 And "they said to the mountains" and to the rocks, "Fall on us," and hide us from *the* face of the *One* sitting on the throne, and from the wrath of the Lamb, *Hos. 10:8*

17 because the great day of His wrath has come; and who is able to stand?

Revelation 7

3 An angel seals the servants of God in their fore-
heads. 4 The number of them that were sealed.

1 ¶ And after these things I saw four angels standing on the four corners of the earth, holding the four winds of the earth, that wind should not blow on the earth, nor on the sea, nor on every tree.

2 And I saw another angel coming up from the rising of the sun, having a seal of the living God. And he cried with a great voice to the four angels to whom it was given to them to harm the earth and the sea,

3 saying, Do not harm the earth, nor the sea, nor the trees, until we seal the slaves of our God on their foreheads.

4 And I heard the number of the *ones* having been sealed: one hundred forty four thousands, having been sealed out of every tribe of the sons of Israel:

5 Out of the tribe of Judah, twelve thousand having been sealed. Out of the tribe of Reuben, twelve thousand having been sealed. Out of the tribe of Gad, twelve thousand having been sealed.

6 Out of the tribe of Asher, twelve thousand having been sealed. Out of the tribe of Naphtali, twelve thousand having been sealed. Out of the tribe of Manasseh, twelve thousand having been sealed.

7 Out of the tribe of Simeon, twelve thousand having been sealed. Out of the tribe of Levi, twelve thousand having been sealed. Out of the tribe of Issachar, twelve thousand having been sealed.

8 Out of the tribe of Zebulun, twelve thousand having been sealed. Out of the tribe of Joseph, twelve thousand having been sealed. Out of the tribe of Benjamin, twelve thousand having been sealed.

9 After these things I saw, and behold, a large multitude which no one was able to number them, out of every nation, even tribes and peoples and languages, standing in front of the throne, and before the Lamb, having been clothed with white robes, and in their hands palm branches.

10 And they cry with a great voice, saying, Salvation to our God, the *One* sitting on the throne, and to the Lamb.

11 And all the angels and of the elders and of the four living creatures stood around the throne. And they fell before the throne on their faces, and worshiped God,

12 saying, Amen. Blessing and glory and wisdom and thanksgiving and honor and power and strength to our God to the ages of the ages. Amen.

13 ¶ And one of the elders answered, saying to me, These, the *ones* having been clothed in the white robes, who are they, and from where did they come?

14 And I said to him, Sir, you know. And he said to me, These are the *ones* coming out of the great tribulation; and they washed their robes and whitened them in the blood of the Lamb.

15 Because of this they are before the throne of God, and serve Him day and night in His temple. And the *One* sitting on the throne tabernacled over them.

16 And they will not hunger still, nor will they thirst still, nor the sun shall not fall on them, nor any *kind of* heat.

17 Because the Lamb in the midst of the throne will shepherd them, and will lead them on *the* living springs of waters; and God will wipe off every tear from their eyes.

Revelation 8

1 At the opening of the seventh seal, 2 seven an-
gels seven trumpets are given them. 6 Four of
them sound their trumpets, and plagues follow.

1 ¶ And when He opened the seventh seal, a silence occurred in Heaven, about a half hour.

2 And I saw the seven angels who stood before God, and seven trumpets were given to them.

3 And another angel came and stood on the altar, having a golden censer. And many incenses were given to him, that he give them with the prayers of all the saints on the golden altar before the throne.

4 And the smoke of the incenses went up with the prayers of the saints out of the hand of the angel before God.

5 And the angel has taken the censer, and has filled it from the fire of the altar, and cast *it* into the earth; and voices and thunders and lightnings and earthquakes occurred.

6 And the seven angels, the *ones* having the seven trumpets, prepared themselves, that they might sound the trumpets.

7 ¶ And the first angel sounded *his* trumpet. And hail and fire mixed with blood occurred. And it was cast onto the earth; and the third *part* of the trees was burned down; and all green grass was burned down.

8 And the second angel sounded *his* trumpet. And as, *it were*, a great mountain burning with fire was thrown into the sea. And the third *part* of the sea became blood;

9 and the third *part* of the creatures, the *ones* having souls, died in the sea; and the third *part* of the ships was destroyed.

10 And the third angel trumpeted. And a great burning star, like a lamp, fell out of the heaven. And it fell onto the third *part* of the rivers, and onto the springs of waters.

11 And the name of the star is said to be Wormwood. And the third *part* of the waters became changed into wormwood. And many men died from the waters, because they were made bitter.

12 And the fourth angel sounded *his* trumpet. And the third *part* of the sun, and the third *part* of the moon, and the third *part* of the stars, was struck, that the third *part* of them might be darkened, and the third *part* of the day might not appear; and likewise the night.

13 And I saw, and I heard one angel flying in mid-heaven, saying with a great voice, Woe! Woe! Woe to the *ones* dwelling on the earth, from the remaining voices of the trumpet of the three angels being about to trumpet!

Revelation 9

The sounding of the fifth angel.

1 ¶ And the fifth angel sounded *his* trumpet. And I saw a star out of the heaven falling onto the earth. And the key to the pit of the abyss was given to it.

2 And he opened the pit of the abyss. And smoke went up out of the pit, like smoke of a great furnace. And the sun was darkened, and the air, by the smoke of the pit.

3 And out of the smoke locusts came forth to the earth. And authority was given to them, as the scorpions of the earth have authority.

4 And it was said to them that they should not harm the grass of the earth, nor every green thing, nor every tree, if not only the men who do not have the seal of God on their foreheads.

5 And it was given to them that they should not kill them, but that they be tormented five months. And their torment *is* as the torment of a scorpion when it strikes a man.

6 And in those days men will seek death, and they will not find it. And they will long to die, yet death will flee from them.

7 And the likenesses of the locusts *were* like horses having been prepared for war; and on their heads as crowns, like gold; and their faces like the faces of men.

8 And they had hairs like the hairs of women; and their teeth were like those of lions.

9 And they had breastplates like iron breastplates; and the sound of their wings *was* like the sound of chariots with many horses running into battle.

10 And they have tails like scorpions, and stings were in their tails; and their authority *is* to harm men five months.

11 And they have a king over them, the angel of the abyss. In Hebrew his name *was* Abaddon, and in Greek he *has* the name Apollyon.

12 The first woe has gone away; behold, after these things come two woes.

13 ¶ And the sixth angel sounded *his* trumpet. And I heard one voice out of the four horns of the golden altar before God,

14 saying to the sixth angel who had the trumpet, Loose the four angels, the *ones* having been bound at the great river Euphrates.

15 And the four angels were loosed, the *ones* having been prepared for the hour and day and month and year that they should kill the third *part* of men.

16 And the number of the armies of the horse *was* two myriads of myriads; and I heard their number.

17 And so I saw in the vision the horses, and the *ones* sitting on them, having fiery red breastplates, and hyacinth *blue* and sulfur-like *yellow*; and the heads of the horses as heads of lions; and out of their mouths come fire and smoke and brimstone.

18 By these three were killed the third *part* of men, by the fire, and by the smoke, and by the brimstone coming out of their mouths.

19 For their authority is in their mouth, and in their tails; for their tails *are* like snakes, having heads, and they do harm with them.

20 And the rest of men, the *ones who were* not killed by these plagues, did not repent of the works of their hands, that they will not worship demons, and "golden idols, and silver, and bronze, and stone, and wooden idols, which neither are able to see, nor to hear," nor to walk. *Dan. 5:23; Psa. 115:47 135:15-17*

21 And they did not repent of their murders, nor of their sorceries, nor of their fornications, nor of their thefts.

Revelation 10

1 A strong angel appears with a book in his hand.
9 John is commanded to take and eat the book.

1 ¶ And I saw another strong angel coming down out of the heaven, having been clothed with a cloud, and a rainbow on the head; and his face as the sun, and his feet as pillars of fire.

2 And he had in his hand a little scroll having been opened. And he placed his right foot on the sea, and *the* left *one* on the land,

3 and cried with a great voice, as a lion roars. And when he cried, the seven thunders spoke their sounds.

4 And when the seven thunders spoke their sounds, I was about to write. And I heard a voice out of Heaven saying to me, Seal the things which the seven thunders spoke, and do not write these things.

5 And the angel whom I saw standing on the sea and on the land lifted his hand to Heaven,

6 and swore by the *One* living to the ages of the ages, "who created the heaven" and the things in it, "and the earth" and the things in it, "and the sea and the things in it," that time shall no longer be; *Ex. 20:11*

7 but in the days of the voice of the seventh angel, whenever he is about to sound *his* trumpet, was even ended the mystery of God, as He preached to His slaves, the prophets.

8 ¶ And the voice which I heard out of the Heaven was again speaking to me, and say-ing, Go, take the little scroll having been opened in the hand of the angel standing on the sea and on the land.

9 And I went away toward the angel, saying to him, Give the little scroll to me. And he said to me, Take and eat it up, and it will make your belly bitter, but it will be sweet as honey in your mouth.

10 And I took the little scroll out of the angel's hand, and ate it up. And it was sweet as honey in my mouth; and when I ate it, my belly was made bitter.

11 And he said to me, You must again prophesy before peoples and nations and languages and many kings.

Revelation 11

3 The two witnesses prophesy. 15 The seventh trumpet sounds.

1 ¶ And a reed like a staff was given to me, and the angel stood, saying, Rise and measure the temple of God and the altar, and the *ones* worshiping in it.

2 And cast aside the outside court of the temple, and do not measure it. For it was given to the nations, and they will trample the holy city forty-two months.

3 ¶ And I will give to My two witnesses, and they will prophesy a thousand two hundred and sixty days, having been clothed *in* sackcloth.

4 These are the two olive trees, and the two lampstands, standing before the God of the earth.

5 And if anyone desires to harm them, fire comes out of their mouth and devours their enemies. And if anyone desires to harm them, thus it is necessary for him to be killed.

6 These have the authority to shut up the heaven, that no rain may rain in the days of the prophecy. And they have authority over the waters, to turn them into blood, and to strike the earth with every plague, as often as they will.

7 And when they complete their witness, the beast coming up out of the abyss will make war with them, and will overcome them, and will kill them.

8 And their bodies *will be* on the street of the great city, which spiritually is called

Sodom, and Egypt, where also our Lord was crucified.

9 And *some* from the peoples and tribes and languages and nations will see their corpses three days and a half; and they do not allow their corpses to be put in tombs.

10 And the *ones* living on the earth will rejoice over them, and will make merry. And they will send one another gifts, because these two prophets tormented the *ones* living on the earth.

11 And after three days and a half, a spirit of life from God entered into them, and they stood on their feet. And great fear fell on the *ones* beholding them.

12 And they heard a great voice out of Heaven saying to them, Come up here. And they went up into the heaven in the cloud. And their enemies saw them.

13 And in that hour a great earthquake occurred, and the tenth *part* of the city fell. And there were killed in the earthquake seven thousand names of men. And the rest became terrified, and gave glory to the God of Heaven.

14 ¶ The second woe passed away. And, behold, the third woe is coming quickly.

15 And the seventh angel sounded *his* trumpet. And there were great voices in Heaven, saying, The kingdoms of the world became our Lord's, even of His Christ; and He shall reign to the ages of the ages.

16 And the twenty-four elders, the *ones* before God sitting on their thrones, fell on their faces and worshiped God,

17 saying, We thank You, Lord God Almighty, the *One* being, and the *One who* was, and the *One* coming, because You have taken Your great power and reigned.

18 And the nations were full of wrath; and Your wrath came, and the time of the the dead *ones* to be judged, and to give the reward to Your slaves, to the prophets, and to the saints, and to the *ones* fearing Your name, to the small and to the great, and to consume the *ones* consuming the earth.

19 And the temple of God in Heaven was opened, and the ark of His covenant was seen in His temple, and lightnings, and voices, and thunders, and an earthquake, and a great hail occurred.

Revelation 12

Of the woman clothed with the sun.

1 ¶ And a great sign was seen in the heavens, a woman having been clothed with the sun, and the moon was underneath her feet; and on her head a crown of twelve stars;

2 and having *a babe* in womb. She cries out, being in travail, and being in great pain to give birth.

3 And another sign was seen in the heavens. And, behold, a great fiery red dragon having seven heads and ten horns! And on his heads were seven diadems,

4 and his tail drew the third *part* of the stars of the heaven, and he throws them to the earth. And the dragon stood before the woman being about to bear, so that when she bears he might devour her child.

5 And she bore a son, a male, who is going to shepherd all the nations with an iron staff. And her child was caught up to God, and *to* His throne.

6 And the woman fled into the wilderness, where she had a place, it having been prepared from God, that there they might nourish her a thousand two hundred and sixty days.

7 And war occurred in Heaven, Michael and His angels making war against the dragon. And the dragon and his angels made war,

8 but they did not have strength, nor was place found for them still in Heaven.

9 And the great dragon was cast out, the old serpent, the *one* being called the devil, even Satan; the *one* leading astray the whole inhabited earth, was cast into the earth, and his angels were cast *down* with him.

10 And I heard a great voice saying in Heaven, Now has come the salvation and power and the kingdom of our God, and the authority of His Christ, because the accuser of our brothers is thrown down, the *one* accusing them before our God day and night.

11 And they overcame him because of the blood of the Lamb, and because of the Word of their testimony. And they did not love their soul even unto death.

12 ¶ Because of this, be glad, the heavens and the *ones* tabernacling in them. Woe to the *ones* dwelling on the earth, and in the

sea, because the devil came down to you having great anger, knowing that he has a little time!

13 And when the dragon saw that he was cast out onto the earth, he pursued the woman who bore the male.

14 And two wings of the great eagle were given to the woman, that she might fly into the wilderness, to her place, where she is nourished there a time, and times, and half a time, away from the serpent's face.

15 And the serpent threw water out of his mouth like a river after the woman, that he might cause her *to be* swept away by the river.

16 And the earth helped the woman, and the earth opened its mouth and swallowed the river which the dragon threw out of his mouth.

17 And the dragon was enraged over the woman, and went away to make war with the rest of her seed, the *ones* keeping the commandments of God, and having the testimony of Jesus Christ.

Revelation 13

A beast rises out of the sea with seven heads and ten horns, to whom the dragon gives his power.

1 ¶ And I stood on the sand of the sea. And I saw a beast coming up out of the sea, having seven heads and ten horns, and on his horns ten diadems, and on its heads names of blasphemy.

2 And the beast which I saw was like a leopard, and its feet as of a bear, and its mouth as a lion's mouth. And the dragon gave its power to it, and its throne, and great authority.

3 And I saw one of its heads, as having been slaughtered to death, and its deadly wound was healed. And all the earth wondered after the beast.

4 And they worshiped the dragon who gave authority to the beast; and they worshiped the beast, saying, Who *is* like the beast; who is able to make war with it?

5 And a mouth speaking great things and blasphemies was given to it. And authority to act forty-two months was given to it.

6 And it opened its mouth in blasphemy toward God, to blaspheme His name and His tabernacle, and the *ones* tabernacling in Heaven.

7 And it was given to it "to war with the saints, and to overcome them." And authority was given to it over every tribe and tongue and nation. *Dan. 7:21*

8 And all the *ones* dwelling in the earth will worship it, of whom the names had not been written in the Book of Life of the Lamb having been slaughtered from the foundation of the world.

9 If anyone has an ear, let him hear.

10 If anyone gathers captivity, into captivity he goes away. If anyone will kill by a sword, by a sword he must be killed. Here is the patience and the faith of the saints.

11 ¶ And I saw another beast coming up out of the earth. And it had two horns like a lamb, but spoke like a dragon.

12 And it executes all the authority of the first beast before it. And it causes that the earth and the *ones* dwelling in it that they should worship the first beast, of which was healed its deadly wound.

13 And it does great signs, that it even causes fire to come down out of the heaven onto the earth before men.

14 And it leads astray the *ones* dwelling on the earth, because of the signs which were given to it to do before the beast, saying to the *ones* dwelling on the earth to make an image to the beast who has the wound of the sword, and lived.

15 And it was given to it to give a spirit to the image of the beast, so that the image of the beast might even speak, and might cause as many as would not worship the image of the beast to be killed.

16 And it makes all *people*, the small *ones* and the great *ones*, and the rich *ones* and the poor *ones*, and the free*men* and the slaves, that it may give to all of them a mark on their right hand, or on their foreheads,

17 even that not any could buy or sell, if not the *one* having the mark, or the name of the beast, or the number of its name.

18 Here is wisdom: Let the *one* having reason count the number of the beast, for it is the number of a man and its number *is* six hundred *and* sixty-six.

Revelation 14

1 The Lamb standing on mount Zion with his company. 8 The fall of Babylon.

1 ¶ And I saw, and behold, the Lamb standing on Mount Zion! And with Him were a hundred *and* forty-four thousands, with the name of His Father having been written on their foreheads.

2 And I heard a sound out of Heaven, as a sound of many waters, and as a sound of great thunder. Also I heard a sound of harpers harping on their harps.

3 And they sing as a new song before the throne, and before the four living creatures and the elders. And no one was able to learn the song if not the hundred *and* forty-four thousands, the *ones* being redeemed from the earth.

4 These are the *ones* who were not defiled with women, for they are virgins. These are the *ones* following the Lamb wherever He may go. These were redeemed from among men as *a* firstfruit to God and to the Lamb.

5 And no guile was found in their mouth, for they are without blemish before the throne of God.

6 ¶ And I saw another angel flying in midheaven, having an everlasting gospel to proclaim to the *ones* dwelling on the earth, even to every nation and tribe and language and people,

7 saying in a great voice, Fear God, and give glory to Him, because the hour of His judgment has come; also, Worship the *One* "who has made the heaven, and the earth, and the sea," and the springs of waters. *Ex. 20:11*

8 And another angel followed, saying, The great city, Babylon, has fallen, has fallen because of the wine of the anger of her fornication she made all nations to drink.

9 And a third angel followed them, saying in a great voice, If anyone worships the beast and its image, and receives a mark on his forehead, or in his hand,

10 he also shall drink of the wine of the anger of God having been mixed undiluted in the cup of His wrath. And he will be tormented by fire and brimstone before the holy angels and before the Lamb.

11 And the smoke of their torment goes up forever and ever. And the *ones* worshiping the beast and its image have no rest night and day, even if anyone receives the mark of its name.

12 Here is the patience of the saints; here *are* the *ones* keeping the commands of God, and the faith of Jesus.

13 ¶ And I heard a voice out of Heaven saying to me, Write: Blessed *are* the dead *ones*, the *ones* dying in the Lord from now. Yes, says the Spirit, they shall rest from their labors, and their works follow with them.

14 And I saw; and behold, a white cloud and on the cloud *One* sitting like the Son of Man, having on His head a golden crown, and in His hand a sharp sickle.

15 And another angel went forth out of the temple, crying in a great voice to the *One* sitting on the cloud, Send Your sickle and reap, because Your hour to reap came, because the harvest of the earth was dried.

16 And the *One* sitting on the cloud thrust His sickle onto the earth, and the earth was reaped.

17 And another angel went forth out of the temple in Heaven, he also having a sharp sickle.

18 And another angel went forth from the altar having authority over the fire. And he spoke with a great cry to the *one* having the sharp sickle, saying, Send your sharp sickle and gather the clusters of the vine of the earth, because its grapes are ripened.

19 And the angel thrust his sickle into the earth and gathered the vine of the earth, and threw into the winepress of the great anger of God.

20 And the winepress was trodden outside the city, and blood went out of the winepress as far as the bridles of the horses, from a thousand six hundred stadia.

Revelation 15

The seven angels with the seven last plagues.

1 ¶ And I saw another sign in Heaven, great and marvelous: seven angels having the last seven plagues, because the anger of God was completed in them.

2 And I saw, like a glassy sea having been mixed with fire. And the *ones* overcoming

from the beast, and from its image, and from its mark, *and* from the number of its name, were standing on the glassy sea, having harps of God.

3 And they sing the song of Moses the slave of God, and the song of the Lamb, saying, Great *and* marvelous *are* Your works, Lord God Almighty, righteous and true *are* Your ways, King of the saints.

4 Who will not fear You, Lord, and not glorify Your name, not *any*? For You only *are* holy. For all the nations will come and will worship before You, because Your righteous deeds were made known.

5 ¶ And after these things I saw; and behold, the temple of the tabernacle of the testimony in Heaven was opened!

6 And the seven angels having the seven plagues, came forth out of the temple, having been clothed in clean and bright linen, and girdles of gold having been girded around the breasts.

7 And one of the four living creatures gave to the seven angels seven golden bowls filled *with* the anger of God, the *One* living to the ages of the ages.

8 And the temple was filled with the smoke of the glory of God, and with His power. And no one was able to enter into the temple until the seven plagues of the seven angels should be completed.

Revelation 16

The angels pour out their vials full of wrath.

1 ¶ And I heard a great voice out of the temple saying to the seven angels: Go and pour out the bowls of the anger of God onto the earth.

2 And the first went away and poured out his bowl onto the earth. And it came to be a bad and evil sore on the men, the *ones* having the mark of the beast, and the *ones* worshiping his image.

3 And the second angel poured out his bowl onto the seas; and it became blood, as of a dead *one*, and every soul of life died in the sea.

4 And the third angel poured out his bowl onto the rivers, and onto the springs of the waters; and it became blood.

5 And I heard the angel of the waters saying, Lord, You are righteous, the *One* be-

ing, and the *One who* was, and the *One* who will be, because You judged these things,

6 since they poured out the blood of the saints and of the prophets; and You gave blood to them to drink, for they were deserving.

7 And I heard another out of the altar saying, Yes, Lord God Almighty, Your judgments *are* true and righteous.

8 ¶ And the fourth angel poured out his bowl onto the sun and it was given to him to burn men with fire.

9 And men were burned with great heat. And they blasphemed the name of God, the *One* having authority over these plagues, and they did not repent to give Him glory.

10 And the fifth angel poured out his bowl onto the throne of the beast; and its kingdom became darkened; and they gnawed their tongues from the pain.

11 And they blasphemed the God of Heaven, from their pains and from their sores. And they did not repent of their works.

12 ¶ And the sixth angel poured out his bowl onto the great river Euphrates, and its water was dried up so that might be prepared the way of the kings from *the* rising of *the* sun.

13 And I saw three unclean spirits like frogs *come* out of the mouth of the dragon, and out of the mouth of the beast, and out of the mouth of the false prophet.

14 For they are spirits of demons doing signs, *which* go forth to the kings of the earth, even of the whole inhabited earth to assemble them to the war of that day, the great day of God Almighty.

15 Behold, I am coming as a thief. Blessed *is* the *one* watching and guarding his garments, that he does not walk naked, and they may see his shame.

16 And He assembled them in the place having been called in Hebrew, Armageddon.

17 ¶ And the seventh angel poured out his bowl into the air; and a great voice came from the throne from the temple of Heaven, saying, It has been done!

18 And voices and thunders and lightnings occurred. And a great earthquake occurred,

such as did not occur since man came into being on the earth, so great an earthquake, so *very* great!

19 And the great city came to be into three parts, and the cities of the nations fell. And Babylon the great was remembered before God, to give to her the cup of the wine of the anger of His wrath.

20 And every island fled away, and mountains were not found.

21 And a great hail, as the size of a talent, came down out of the heaven upon men. And men blasphemed God from the plague of the hail, because its plague is exceedingly great.

Revelation 17

The woman arrayed in purple and scarlet.

1 ¶ And one of the seven angels having the seven bowls came and spoke with me, saying to me, Come, I will show you the judgment of the great harlot, the *one* sitting on the many waters,

2 with whom the kings of the earth committed fornication, and the *ones* inhabiting the earth became drunk from the wine of her fornication.

3 And he carried me away into a deserted *place*, by *the* Spirit. And I saw a woman sitting on a scarlet beast, filled with names of blasphemy, having seven heads and ten horns.

4 And the woman was clothed in purple and scarlet, and being adorned with gold and precious stone and pearls, having a golden cup in her hand, filled with abominations and uncleanness of her fornication.

5 And on her forehead was a name having been written: Mystery, Babylon the Great, the Mother of the Harlots and of the Abominations of the Earth.

6 And I saw the woman being drunk from the blood of the saints, and from the blood of the witnesses of Jesus. And seeing her, I wondered with a great wonder.

7 ¶ And the angel said to me, Why did you wonder? I will tell you the mystery of the woman, and of the beast sustaining her, the *one* having the seven heads and the ten horns.

8 The beast which you saw was, and is not, and is about to come up out of the abyss, and goes to eternal destruction. And the *ones* dwelling on the earth will wonder, *the ones* whose names have not been written on the Book of Life from the foundation of the world, seeing the beast, that it was a thing, and is not, yet it is.

9 Here *is* the mind having wisdom: the seven heads are seven mountains, where the woman sits on them.

10 And the kings are seven. The five fell, and the one is, *and* the other has not yet come. And when he does come, he must remain a little.

11 And the beast which was, and is not, even he is the eighth, and is of the seven, and goes to destruction.

12 And the ten horns you saw are ten kings who have not yet received a kingdom, but will receive authority as kings one hour with the beast.

13 These have one mind, and their power and authority they shall give up to the beast.

14 ¶ These will make war with the Lamb, and the Lamb will prevail over them, because He is Lord of lords and King of kings, and the *ones* with Him *are* the called out *ones* and elect *ones* and faithful *ones*.

15 And he says to me, The waters which you saw, where the harlot sits, are peoples and crowds and nations and languages.

16 And the ten horns which you saw on the beast, these will hate the harlot, and will make her desolated and naked. And they will eat her flesh, and will burn her up with fire.

17 For God gave into their hearts to do His mind, and to act in one mind, and to give their kingdom to the beast, until the words of God shall be fulfilled.

18 And the woman whom you saw is the great city, the *one* having a kingdom over the kings of the earth.

Revelation 18

2 Babylon is fallen. 20 The saints rejoice for the judgments of God upon her.

1 ¶ And after these things I saw another angel coming down out of Heaven having great authority, and the earth was lighted up from his glory.

2 And he cried in a strong, great voice, saying, Babylon the great has fallen! *It* has

fallen, and it has become a dwelling place of demons, and a prison of every unclean spirit, and a prison of every unclean bird, and hated,

3 because of the wine of the anger of her fornication which all the nations have drunk, even the kings of the earth have committed fornication with her; and the merchants of the earth became rich from the power of her luxury.

4 And I heard another voice out of Heaven saying, My people, come out of her, that you may not share in her sins, and that you may not receive of her plagues;

5 that *are* joined together with her sins, even up to Heaven, and God remembered her unjust deeds.

6 Give back to her as also she gave back to you, and double to her double, according to her works. In the cup which she mixed, mix to her double.

7 By as many things as she glorified herself, and luxuriated, by so much give to her torment and mourning, because she says in her heart, I sit as a queen, and I am not a widow; and I shall not see mourning, not *ever!*

8 Because of this, in one day her plagues shall come: death, and mourning, and famine; and she will be consumed with fire, for the Lord God, the *One* judging her, *is* strong.

9 ¶ And the kings of the earth will weep for her, and will wail over her, the *ones* having fornicated and having luxuriated with her, when they see the smoke of her burning;

10 standing from afar because of the fear of her torment, saying, Woe! Woe to the great city, Babylon, the strong city! For in one hour your judgment came.

11 And the merchants of the earth weep and mourn over her, because no one buys their cargo, no more,

12 cargo of gold, and silver, and of precious stone, and of pearls, and of fine linen, and of purple, and of silk, and of scarlet, and all thyine wood, and every ivory vessel, and every vessel of very precious wood, and of bronze, and of iron, and of marble,

13 and cinnamon, and incenses, and ointment, and frankincense, and wine, and oil, and fine wheat flour, and wheat, and beasts, and sheep, and horses, and chariots, and of bodies and souls of men.

14 And the ripe fruits of the lust of your soul went away from you, and all the fat things, and the bright things went away from you, and you will not find them, not *ever!*

15 The merchants of these things, the *ones* being enriched from her, will stand from afar because of the fear of her torment, weeping and mourning;

16 and saying, Woe! Woe to the great city having been clothed in fine linen and purple and scarlet, and having been adorned with gold and precious stone, and pearls!

17 For in one hour such great wealth was desolated. And every helmsman and all on the ships, and sailors, and as many as work the sea, stood from afar,

18 and cried out, seeing the smoke of her burning, saying, What *is* like the great city?

19 And they threw dust on their heads, and cried out, weeping and mourning, saying, Woe! Woe to the great city, by which all the *ones* having ships in the sea were enriched, from her costliness, because in one hour she was laid waste.

20 Be glad over her, Heaven, and the holy apostles, and the prophets, because God judged your judgment on her.

21 And one strong angel lifted a stone like a great millstone, and threw *it* into the sea, saying, Thus on a violent impulse, Babylon the great city will be thrown down, and it will not still be found, not *ever!*.

22 And the sound of harpers, and of musicians, and flutists, and of trumpeters will not still be heard in you, not *ever!* And every craftsman of every craft will not still be found in you, not *ever!* And the sound of a mill will not still be heard in you, not *ever!*

23 And the light of a lamp will not still shine in you, not *ever!* And the voice of the bridegroom and bride will not still be heard in you, not *ever!* For your merchants were the great *ones* of the earth, for by your sorcery all the nations were led astray.

24 And in her was found the blood of prophets, and of saints, and of all the *ones* having been slaughtered on the earth.

Revelation 19

God is praised in heaven for judging the great whore, and avenging the blood of his saints.

1 ¶ And after these things, I heard a great voice of a large multitude in Heaven, saying, Alleluia! The salvation and the glory and the honor and the power of the Lord our God!

2 For true and righteous *are* His judgments, because He judged the great harlot who defiled the earth with her fornication. And He avenged the blood of His slaves out of her hand.

3 And secondly they said, Alleluia! Also her smoke goes up to the ages of the ages.

4 And the twenty-four elders, and the four living creatures fell down and worshiped God sitting on the throne, saying, Amen! Alleluia!

5 ¶ And a voice came out from the throne, saying, Praise our God, all His slaves, and the *ones* fearing Him, the small *ones* and the great *ones*.

6 And I heard as a sound of a large crowd, and as a sound of many waters, and as a sound of strong thunders, saying, Alleluia! Because the Lord God reigned, the Almighty.

7 Let us rejoice and let us exult, and we will give glory to Him, because the marriage of the Lamb came, and His wife prepared herself.

8 And it was given to her that she be clothed in fine linen, pure and bright; for the fine linen is the righteous deeds of the saints.

9 And he says to me, Write: Blessed *are* the *ones* having been called to the supper of the marriage of the Lamb. And he says to me, These are the true words of God.

10 And I fell before his feet to worship him, but he said to me, See, do not *do it*! I am a fellow-slave of yours, and of your brothers, the *ones* having the testimony of Jesus. Worship God. For the testimony of Jesus is the spirit of prophecy.

11 ¶ And I saw Heaven having been opened. And, behold! A white horse, and the *One* sitting on it being called Faithful and True. And He judges and wars in righteousness.

12 And His eyes *were* as a flame of fire, and on His head many diadems, having a name written, which no one knows if not Himself;

13 and having been clothed in a garment having been dipped in blood. And His name is called The Word of God.

14 And the armies in Heaven followed Him on white horses, being dressed in fine linen, white and pure.

15 And out of His mouth goes forth a sharp sword, that with it He might smite the nations. And He will shepherd them with an iron rod. And He treads the winepress of the wine of the anger and of the wrath of God Almighty.

16 And He has on *His* garment and on His thigh a name having been written: KING OF KINGS AND LORD OF LORDS.

17 And I saw one angel standing in the sun. And he cried with a great voice, saying to all the birds flying in mid-heaven, Come and gather together to the supper of the great God,

18 that you may eat the flesh of kings, and *the* flesh of chiliarchs, and *the* flesh of strong *ones*, and *the* flesh of horses, and of the *ones* sitting on them, and *the* flesh of all, both free*men* and slaves, even of the small *ones* and great *ones*.

19 And I saw the beast and the kings of the earth, and their armies being assembled to make war with the *One* sitting on the horse, and with His army.

20 And the beast was seized, and with this *one* the false prophet, the *one* doing signs before it, by which he led astray the *ones* receiving the mark of the beast, and the *ones* worshiping its image. The two were thrown living into the Lake of Fire burning with brimstone.

21 And the rest were killed with the sword of the *One* sitting on the horse, the *sword* going forth from His mouth. And all the birds were filled from their flesh.

Revelation 20

2 Satan bound for a thousand years. 6 The first resurrection. 12 The last and general resurrection.

1 ¶ And I saw an angel coming down out of Heaven, having the key of the abyss, and a great chain on his hand.

2 And he laid hold of the dragon, the ancient serpent who is the devil, even Satan, and bound him a thousand years,

3 and threw him into the abyss, and shut him up, and sealed over him, that he should not mislead the nations any more, until the thousand years are fulfilled. And after these things, he must be set loose a little time.

4 And I saw thrones, and they sat on them. And judgment was given to them, and the souls of the *ones* having been beheaded because of the witness of Jesus, and because of the Word of God, and who had not worshiped the beast nor its image, and had not received the mark on their forehead and on their hand. And they lived and reigned with Christ a thousand years.

5 But the rest of the dead *ones* did not live again until the thousand years were ended. This *is* the first resurrection.

6 Blessed and holy *is* the *one* having part in the first resurrection. The second death has no authority over these, but they will be priests of God and of Christ, and will reign with Him a thousand years.

7 And whenever the thousand years are ended, Satan will be set loose out of his prison,

8 and he will go to lead astray the nations in the four corners of the earth, Gog and Magog, to assemble them into war, whose number *is* as the sand of the sea.

9 And they went up over the breadth of the land and encircled the camp of the saints, and the beloved city. And fire from God came down out of Heaven and devoured them.

10 And the devil leading them astray was thrown into the Lake of Fire and Brimstone, where the beast and the false prophet *were*. And they were tormented day and night to the ages of the ages.

11 ¶ And I saw a great white throne, and the *One* sitting on it, from whose face the earth and the heaven fled; and a place was not found for them.

12 And I saw the dead *ones*, the small *ones* and *the* great *ones*, standing before God. And books were opened. And another Book was opened, which is the *Book* of Life. And the dead *ones* were judged out of the

things written in the books, according to their works.

13 And the sea gave up the dead *ones* in it. And death and hell gave up the dead *ones* in them. And they were each *one* judged according to their works.

14 And death and hell were thrown into the Lake of Fire. This is the second death.

15 And if anyone was not found written in the Book of Life, he was thrown into the Lake of Fire.

Revelation 21

1 A new heaven and a new earth. 10 The heavenly
  Jerusalem, with a full description of it.

1 ¶ And I saw a new heaven and a new earth, for the first heaven and the first earth passed away, and the sea not still is.

2 And I, John, saw the holy city, New Jerusalem, coming down out of Heaven from God, having been prepared as a bride, having been adorned for her Husband.

3 And I heard a great voice out of Heaven, saying, Behold, the tabernacle of God with men! And He will tabernacle with them, and they will be His peoples, and God Himself will be with them as their God.

4 And God will wipe away every tear from their eyes. And death shall be no longer, nor mourning, nor outcry, nor will *there* be pain *still*; for the first things passed away.

5 And the *One* sitting on the throne said, Behold! I make all things new. And He says to me, Write, because these words are faithful and true.

6 And He said to me, It is done! I am the Alpha and the Omega, the Beginning and the End. To the *one* thirsting, I will freely give of the fountain of the water of life.

7 The *one* overcoming will inherit all things, and I will be God to him, and he will be the son to Me.

8 But for the cowardly *one* and faithless *ones*, and disgusting *ones*, and murderers, and fornicators, and users of magic, and idolaters, and all the lying *ones*, their part will be in the Lake burning with fire and brimstone, which is the second death.

9 ¶ And one of the seven angels came to me, the *ones* having the seven bowls being filled with the seven last plagues, and spoke

with me, saying, Come, I will show you the bride, the wife of the Lamb.

10 And he carried me in spirit on to a great and high mountain, and showed me the great city, holy Jerusalem, coming down out of Heaven from God,

11 having the glory of God; and its light *was* like a very precious stone, as a jasper stone, *being clear* as crystal,

12 also having a great and high wall, having twelve gates, and twelve angels at the gates and names having been inscribed, which are of the twelve tribes of the sons of Israel.

13 From the east, three gates; from the north, three gates; from the south, three gates; and from the west, three gates.

14 And the wall of the city had twelve foundations, and in them the names of the twelve apostles of the Lamb.

15 And the *one* speaking with me had a golden reed, that he may measure the city, and its gates, and its wall.

16 And the city lies four cornered, even its length as much as the width also. And he measured the city with the reed at twelve thousand stadia; its length and width and height are equal.

17 And he measured its wall, a hundred *and* forty four cubits, a measure of a man, which is of an angel.

18 And the structure of its wall was jasper; and the city *was* pure gold, pure like glass.

19 And the foundation of the wall of the city having been adorned with every precious stone: The first foundation, jasper; the second, sapphire; the third, chalcedony; the fourth, emerald;

20 the fifth, sardonyx; the sixth, sardius; the seventh, chrysolite; the eighth, beryl; the ninth, topaz; the tenth, chrysoprasus; the eleventh, hyacinth; the twelfth, amethyst.

21 And the twelve gates *were* twelve pearls; *respectively* each one of the gates was of one pearl. And the street of the city was pure gold, as transparent glass.

22 And I saw no temple in it, for the Lord God Almighty is its temple, even the Lamb.

23 And the city had no need of the sun, nor of the moon, that they might shine in it, for the glory of God illuminated it, and its lamp *is* the Lamb.

24 And the nations of the *ones* saved will walk in its light; and the kings of the earth bring their glory and honor into it.

25 And its gates may not be shut by day, for no night will be there, not *ever*!

26 And they will bring the glory and the honor of the nations into it.

27 And all profaning may not enter into it, or any making an abomination or a lie; not *ever*; if not the *ones* having been written in the Book of Life of the Lamb.

Revelation 22

1 The river of the water of life. 2 The tree of life. 5 The light of the city of God is himself.

1 ¶ And he showed me a pure river of water of life, bright as crystal, coming forth out of the throne of God and of the Lamb.

2 In the midst of its street and of the river, from here and from there, *was* a tree of life producing twelve fruits: according to one month each yielding its fruit. And the leaves of the tree were for healing of the nations.

3 And every curse will no longer be. And the throne of God and the Lamb will be in it; and His slaves will serve Him.

4 And they will see His face; and His name *will be* on their foreheads.

5 And night will not be there; and they have no need of a lamp or a light of the sun, because the Lord God will illumine them. And they shall reign to the ages of the ages.

6 ¶ And he said to me, These words *are* faithful and true. And the Lord God of the holy prophets sent His angel to show His slaves what must occur quickly.

7 Behold, I am coming quickly. Blessed *is* the *one* keeping the words of the prophecy of this Book.

8 And I, John, *was* the *one* seeing and hearing these things. And when I heard and saw, I fell down to worship before the feet of the angel showing me these things.

9 And he said to me, Behold! See, do not *do it*! For I am your fellow-slave, and of your brothers, the prophets, and of the *ones* guarding the words of this Book. Worship God.

10 And he said to me, Do not seal the words of the prophecy, of this Book, because the time is near.

11 The *one* acting unjustly, let him still act unjustly; and the *one* being filthy, let him still be filthy; and the righteous *one*, let him still do righteousness; and the holy *one*, let him still be holy.

12 And, behold, I am coming quickly, and My reward *is* with Me, to give to each *one* as his work is.

13 I am the Alpha and the Omega, *the* Beginning and the End, the First and the Last.

14 Blessed *are* the *ones* doing His commands, that will be their authority over the Tree of Life, and by the gates they may enter into the city.

15 But outside *are* the dogs and the sorcerers, and the fornicators, and the murderers, and the idolaters, and every *one* loving and making a lie.

16 I, Jesus, sent My angel to testify these things to you over the assemblies. I am the Root and the Offspring of David, the bright and morning Star.

17 And the Spirit and the bride say, Come! And the *one* hearing, let him say, Come! And the *one* thirsting, let *him* come; and the *one* willing, let him take of the water of life freely.

18 For I testify together with every *one* hearing the words of the prophecy of this Book, if anyone adds to these things, God will add upon him the plagues having been written in this Book.

19 And if anyone takes away from the words of the Book of this prophecy, God will take away his part from the Book of Life, and out of the holy city, and of the things having been written in this Book.

20 ¶ The *One* testifying these things says, Yes, I am coming quickly. Amen. Yes, come, Lord Jesus!

21 The grace of our Lord Jesus Christ *be* with all of you. Amen.

Made in the USA
Las Vegas, NV
23 December 2022

64012217R00167